THE DEATH PENALTY

The Death Penalty

A Worldwide Perspective

Fourth Edition—Revised and Expanded

ROGER HOOD and CAROLYN HOYLE

Centre for Criminology
University of Oxford

OXFORD
UNIVERSITY PRESS

OXFORD
UNIVERSITY PRESS

Great Clarendon Street, Oxford ox2 6dp

Oxford University Press is a department of the University of Oxford.
It furthers the University's objective of excellence in research, scholarship,
and education by publishing worldwide in

Oxford New York

Auckland Cape Town Dar es Salaam Hong Kong Karachi
Kuala Lumpur Madrid Melbourne Mexico City Nairobi
New Delhi Shanghai Taipei Toronto

With offices in

Argentina Austria Brazil Chile Czech Republic France Greece
Guatemala Hungary Italy Japan Poland Portugal Singapore
South Korea Switzerland Thailand Turkey Ukraine Vietnam

Oxford is a registered trade mark of Oxford University Press
in the UK and in certain other countries

Published in the United States
by Oxford University Press Inc., New York

British Library Cataloguing in Publication Data

Data available

Library of Congress Cataloging in Publication Data
Hood, Roger G.
The death penalty : a worldwide perspective / Roger Hood and Carolyn
Hoyle.—4th edition, rev. and expanded.
    p.cm.
Includes bibliographical references and index.
ISBN 978–0–19–922846–1 (hardback: alk. paper)—
ISBN 978–0–19–922847–8 (alk. paper)
1. Capital punishment. I. Hoyle, Carolyn. II. Title.
HV8694.H657 2008
364.66—dc22   2008008014

Typeset by Newgen Imaging Systems (P) Ltd., Chennai, India
Printed in Great Britain
on acid-free paper by
Anthony Rowe, Chippenham, Wiltshire

ISBN 978–0–19–922846–1
ISBN 978–0–19–922847–8 (Pbk)

1 3 5 7 9 10 8 6 4 2

We dedicate this book to our spouses,
Nancy Hood and David Rose,
with thanks for their constant support

Acknowledgements

Six years have elapsed since the third edition of this book was published and in that time there have been major developments in the progress towards world-wide abolition of the death penalty. A further 16 countries have completely abolished capital punishment and the number that have executed anyone within the past 10 years has fallen by a quarter (from 71 to 51 at the end of 2007). This fourth edition considers the dynamics of these developments. In addition, it incorporates a new chapter on 'The Challenge of a Suitable Replacement' for the death penalty and for the first time discusses the role and reactions of the relatives of victims of murder in affecting the death penalty debate.

In undertaking this work we have been made even more aware that the picture as regards the implementation of judicial executions is forever changing, and changing fast. Who, for instance, in 2001 would have predicted that lethal injection as a method of execution would have come under attack as a cruel and unusual punishment? Or that China would have opened up a serious debate about the scope of its use of the death penalty?

RH was fortunate to have the honour of being invited once again by the United Nations to act as its consultant on the death penalty and to draft for the Secretary-General his Seventh Report on *Capital Punishment and Implementation of the Safeguards Guaranteeing the Rights of those Facing the Death Penalty*, the final version of which (E/2005/3) brought the information, as far as possible, up to date until the end of the year 2004. This book, on which we have collaborated with pleasure, has both incorporated some of the findings of this report and taken the story considerably further—generally up to the end of July 2007, but in a few instances up to the end of December 2007—by drawing on a large number of reports (official and from non-governmental organizations), internet resources (particularly the enormously helpful, US-based, Death Penalty Information Center website), books, and articles that have appeared since the last edition of this book was published in 2002.

Thanks must go to Amnesty International for permission to quote widely from its reports and publications,[1] in particular thanks to Piers Bannister, Asunta Cavalle, and Virginia Wenzel from Amnesty International for being ever ready to provide assistance. We are grateful to Peter Hodgkinson, Director of the Centre for Capital Punishment Studies at Westminster University, for a constant stream of information; to Saul Lehfreund and Parvais Jabbar, Executive Directors of the Death Penalty Project, for keeping us well informed on Caribbean issues; to

---

[1] ©Amnesty International Publications, 1 Easton Street, London WC1X 0DW, United Kingdom.

Bikram Jeet Batra for valuable information on the situation in India; to Professor Zhao Binghzi of Beijing Normal University School of Criminal Law Science for permission to cite his conference paper; and to Ravinder Thukral, Florence Seemungal, Michael Radelet, Brandon Garrett, William Schabas, and Cory Way, among others, for providing information at various stages. We are particularly grateful to Lucy Tulloch (for help with the UN survey), William Berry III, and Sophie Palmer for research assistance and to Eric Prokosch for helpful comments on our manuscript.

Roger Hood and Carolyn Hoyle

Oxford
31 December 2007

Contents

Acknowledgements   vii

Introduction   1
   1. Sources of Information   1
   2. Plan of the Book   4
   3. The Approach Taken towards Capital Punishment   6

1. The Abolitionist Movement: Progress and Prospects   9
   1. The Pace of Abolition   9
   2. Generating the New Wave of Abolition   18
   3. What Prospects for International Acceptance or
      Rejection of Capital Punishment?   32

2. In the Vanguard of Abolition   40
   1. Western Europe and Australasia:
      Death Penalty Free Zones   40
   2. Eastern Europe: Embracing Abolition   50
   3. States of the Former Soviet Union: From Moratoria
      to Abolition *De Jure*   53
   4. South and Central America: Long-term Supporters
      of Abolition   61

3. Where Capital Punishment Remains Contested   66
   1. The Middle East and North Africa: Cracks
      in the Bastion?   66
   2. Africa South of the Sahara: Resistance to
      Abolition Crumbling?   73
   3. Asia and the Pacific: Opening up the Issue   84
   4. The Caribbean: Colonial Legacies   103
   5. North America: Faltering Support   111

4. The Scope of Capital Punishment in Law   129
   1. Offences Punishable By Death   129
   2. The Scale of Death Sentences and Executions   146

5. **The Death Penalty in Reality: The Process of Execution
   and the Death Row Experience**   155

   1. Executing those found to be Guilty   155
   2. Under Sentence of Death   172
   3. Conclusion   186

6. **Excluding the Vulnerable from Capital Punishment**   187

   1. Juvenile Defendants   187
   2. The Question of the Aged   194
   3. The Exemption of Pregnant Women   195
   4. The Status of the Mentally Retarded   196
   5. Protection of the Insane and Severely Mentally Ill   203
   6. Conclusion   214

7. **Protecting the Accused and Ensuring Due Process**   215

   1. International Standards   215
   2. Ensuring a Fair Trial   217
   3. The Right to Appeal   250
   4. The Right to Seek a Pardon, Clemency, or
      Commutation of Sentence   257
   5. Finality of Judgment: Awaiting the Outcome
      of Legal Proceedings   264
   6. Wrongful Convictions and Innocent Persons Exonerated   266
   7. Conclusions   276

8. **Deciding Who Should Die: Problems of Inequity,
   Arbitrariness, and Racial Discrimination**   278

   1. Mandatory or Discretionary?   278
   2. Legal Analyses: The American Experience   287
   3. Criminological Investigations   299
   4. Policy Implications   311

9. **The Question of Deterrence**   317

   1. Reliance on the Deterrent Justification   317
   2. Conceptual Issues: The Need for Clarification   321
   3. General Deterrence in Context   322
   4. Assessing Homicide Trends   325
   5. The Comparative Method   329
   6. Measuring the Immediate Impact   333

7. The Econometric Model — 337
8. Methodological Problems in Measuring the Deterrent Effect — 344
9. Implications for Policy — 347

10. A Question of Opinion or a Question of Principle? — 350
   1. Public Opinion and the Politics of Abolition — 350
   2. The Nature of Public Opinion — 358
   3. Changing Public Opinion — 366
   4. Abolition and its Effect on Public Opinion — 375
   5. The Impact of Victims' Advocates on Support for the Death Penalty — 378
   6. A Question of Principle — 381

11. The Challenge of a Suitable Replacement — 383
   1. The Nature of the Challenge — 383
   2. The Range of Alternative Penalties — 385
   3. The Ascendancy of Life Without Parole in America — 388
   4. Life Without Hope: The New Challenge to Human Dignity — 392
   5. Conditions of Confinement — 395
   6. The Challenge of Sentencing Juveniles Convicted of Murder — 398
   7. Implications for Policy — 402

Appendices — 404
   1. Lists of Retentionist and Abolitionist Countries — 404
   2. Ratification of International Treaties — 414
   3. International Instruments — 417

Bibliography — 422
Cases Cited — 455
Index — 461

Introduction

1. Sources of Information

This book, now in its fourth edition, began life as a report to the United Nations Committee on Crime Prevention and Control in 1988. That report was commissioned following a resolution of the Economic and Social Council of the United Nations (ECOSOC), which had called for 'a study of the question of the death penalty and new contributions of the criminal sciences in the matter'.[1] The main aim was to bring up to date the survey of world trends that had been provided, some years earlier, by two influential reports. Both of these reports, *Capital Punishment* (the Ancel Report, 1962) and *Capital Punishment: Developments 1961–1965* (the Morris Report, 1967), were based on replies to a questionnaire sent to member states of the United Nations (as well as to certain non-member states) by the UN Secretary-General, seeking information on the *de jure* and *de facto* status of capital punishment and the number of judicial executions carried out annually. These surveys were subsequently carried out every five years as a regular feature of UN activity in the area of capital punishment.

Since 1985 attempts have also been made to discover the extent to which countries that have yet to abolish capital punishment abide by nine 'Safeguards Guaranteeing Protection of the Rights of those Facing the Death Penalty' which were promulgated by resolution of ECOSOC in 1984 and endorsed by the General Assembly later that year, on the understanding that 'they would not be invoked to delay or prevent the abolition of the death penalty'.[2] These safeguards can be summarized as follows: to ensure that capital punishment is only implemented for the most serious, intentional crimes with lethal or other extremely grave consequences; to protect convicted persons from retrospective applications of the death penalty and to provide for the possibilities of lighter punishments; to exempt those under 18 years of age at the time of the commission of the crime, pregnant women, new mothers, and those who are or have become insane; to ensure that it is only applied when there is no possibility of wrongful conviction, and only after a fair trial with legal assistance; to provide for appeals and the possibility of a pardon or commutation of sentence and to ensure that no

---

[1] In pursuance of Economic and Social Council (ECOSOC) Resolution 1986/10, s. X, and Resolution 1989/64.
[2] Economic and Social Council Resolution 1984/50, Annex. General Assembly Resolution 29/118, 1984.

executions are carried out until all such procedures have been completed; and, where capital punishment does occur, to carry it out so as to inflict the minimum possible suffering.

After receiving a report (the first edition of this book), which reviewed the extent to which these safeguards were being implemented, ECOSOC recommended that they should be strengthened by adding four more injunctions.[3] These related to providing adequate time and facilities to prepare a defence against a capital charge; providing for a mandatory appeal or mandatory review with provision for clemency or pardon in all cases; establishing a maximum age beyond which no death sentences or executions may be imposed; and ensuring that no person suffering from mental retardation or extremely limited mental competence should be sentenced to death, let alone executed. The Seventh United Nations Congress on the Prevention of Crime and the Treatment of Offenders, held in 1989, requested the Secretary-General to publicize these safeguards widely, as well as the procedures necessary to implement them, and this was reiterated by ECOSOC in 1996. They are set out in Appendix 3, along with the text of Articles 6, 7, 10, 14, and 15 of the International Covenant on Civil and Political Rights, which incorporate nearly all these safeguards.

In 1996 the second edition of this book was published. It was based, in part, on replies to the Fifth Quinquennial Survey, covering the years 1989 to 1993, which Roger Hood had been commissioned to analyse for the United Nations. The third edition likewise drew on responses to the UN Sixth Quinquennial Survey, which covered the years 1994 to 1998. Similarly, this fourth edition has been able to make use of the responses to the Seventh Quinquennial Survey, covering the years 1999 to 2003.[4] But, as in the previous editions, a very much wider variety of literature and statistical evidence has been surveyed, as will be apparent from the references and Bibliography. Wherever possible we have tried to bring the information as up-to-date as possible and have included any changes in the status of the death penalty worldwide made up to the end of December 2007.

Earlier editions pointed to the paucity of information on the situation regarding the death penalty in many parts of the world. This was because many retentionist countries failed to respond to the Secretary-General's request, and even those that did could not be relied upon to provide accurate information on all aspects of the law and procedure governing the use of capital punishment, or statistics on the number of people sentenced to death and executed. As far as the Seventh Survey was concerned, the situation had not improved much. Two-thirds of the countries that replied had already abolished the death penalty but only 17 of the 70 replies came from the 78 countries that still retained the death penalty at the beginning of the survey period in 1999. These 17 accounted for only 22 per cent

---

[3] Economic and Social Council Resolution 1989/64, para. 1.

[4] United Nations, Economic and Social Council, *Capital Punishment and implementation of the safeguards guaranteeing protection of the rights of those facing the death penalty. Report of the Secretary-General*, March 2005, UN Doc. E/2005/3, 2005 (hereafter UN Seventh Survey).

of the 78 retentionist nations that were known to have executed someone within the previous 10 years. In fact only eight (10%) of them provided information on the number of persons sentenced to death or executed between 1999 and 2003.[5] These did not include several countries which, according to official announcements, press reports, and other sources, had most frequently executed offenders in the years covered by the survey: China, Democratic Republic of the Congo, Iran, Saudi Arabia, Singapore, Taiwan, Yemen, and Vietnam.[6]

It is difficult to obtain accurate data about retentionist countries from other sources, because several of them publish no regular official statistical returns of death sentences or executions, or even if they do they may be unobtainable outside the country in question. And although Amnesty International keeps a tally of reported death sentences and executions gathered by its representatives in countries around the world, and publishes the figures in its Annual Report, there is no way by which it can ensure that these data are always accurate and up-to-date. It will be impossible to present an accurate picture of capital punishment until all retentionist states take seriously their obligation to collect statistical data on this subject systematically and to report their practice, as requested, to the United Nations. Indeed, whether or not they report it to the UN, they have a duty to their citizens to publish such data so that the use of capital punishment is made transparent and those that administer it held accountable.

For this reason, it has been necessary to turn mainly to other sources of information obtained by the United Nations, other international bodies, and non-governmental organizations. Of particular value have been the reports of the UN Special Rapporteur on extra-judicial, summary, or arbitrary executions; the reports of and submissions to the UN Human Rights Committee; the reports of the Secretary-General to the UN Commission on Human Rights; the many valuable reports published by Amnesty International, other human rights organizations, and anti-capital punishment pressure groups, such as the Death Penalty Information Center in the United States and 'Hands Off Cain'; and the regular news service provided by the Centre for Capital Punishment Studies at the University of Westminster in London. In addition, of course, there is the large academic literature, including many excellent empirical studies, most of which emanate from the United States.

These sources reveal that frequently there is a disjunction between official replies on the formal state of the law and procedures, and what is discovered about the enforcement of law and the procedures adopted in practice. This means that we have been faced with the problem of veracity and objectivity where allegations

---

[5] UN Seventh Survey, Addendum, June 2005, UN Doc. E 2005/3 Add. 1, para. 4.

[6] The 17 retentionist countries that replied were: Bahrain, Egypt, Ghana, Jamaica, Japan, Morocco, Pakistan, Republic of Korea, Serbia and Montenegro, Thailand, Trinidad and Tobago, Tunisia, Ukraine, United Republic of Tanzania, the USA, Uzbekistan, and Zimbabwe. Only Bahrain, Jamaica, Japan, Trinidad and Tobago, and the USA provided information on death sentences and executions.

of failure to abide by the safeguards go unanswered or are flatly denied by the state. Who should one believe? The stance taken in this book is to try to make plain whenever the information has been unsubstantiated and to give, wherever possible, the source for any allegation of practices officially denied.

It has also to be recognized that information based on empirical studies of the use of the death penalty and its effects comes from only a few countries: those that have a strong tradition of such research and a body of scholars committed to challenging the legal and penological assumptions upon which support for a death penalty is often based. As West European countries have abandoned the death penalty, so have their scholars generally lost interest in it. Empirical inquiries are, with very few exceptions, concentrated on the situation in the United States, and even there, mainly, although not solely, on a few southern states. They are no less valuable for that. But they do, of course, provide a rather distorted and partial view of the death penalty looked at in its worldwide context. This is particularly so when it is recognized that the United States differs from other countries that retain the death penalty in many ways, such as: the definition of capital murder; prosecution and trial procedures; the number executed in relation to the number of homicides and per head of the population; and the complex state and federal appeal processes, let alone the racial, cultural, and political factors which shape criminal policies in those states of the United States that execute offenders.

2. Plan of the Book

Chapter 1 provides an overview of the extent to which the movement to bring about abolition of the death penalty worldwide had progressed by the end of December 2007. It shows that further progress has been made over the past five years since the third edition was published. Chapter 2 discusses the stance taken by those countries that have been in the vanguard of the abolitionist movement. Chapter 3 deals with those countries that have not yet abolished the death penalty, assessing across the main regions of the world the current state of the debate on capital punishment and the prospects for abolition or a reduction in the use of the death penalty. Chapter 4 provides information on the scope of capital punishment in those countries that retain it, especially with regard to their obligation to reserve it for only the most serious crimes. It discusses the range of crimes for which capital punishment may be imposed in various countries and then moves on to consider the frequency with which retentionist countries impose death sentences and carry out executions. The message is that capital punishment is more rarely enforced than it is threatened, and furthermore that the trend in most retentionist states has been to employ executions less and less frequently. Chapter 5 deals with the processes of implementing capital punishment; the modes of execution—paying particular attention to the current controversy over whether lethal injection can amount to 'cruel and unusual punishment'; public executions; whether physicians should play any part in the execution process; and, finally, the conditions and length of confinement for those sentenced to death but awaiting the outcome of appeals or clemency on 'death row'. Chapter 6 deals with the implementation of those safeguards that are meant to protect from execution those who commit capital crimes when juveniles (under the age of 18), who are aged, pregnant women and new mothers, are insane, are mentally retarded,[7] or are mentally ill. Chapter 7 reviews the evidence of the extent to which procedures are in place to guarantee a fair and impartial trial, adequate counsel for the defence of the accused, and the right to appeal and to seek pardon or clemency, so that no innocent persons (as well as others undeserving of such severe punishment) are sentenced to death and executed. It includes, for the first time, a discussion of the issues posed by allowing relatives of victims of murder to testify about the impact of the crime on them at the stage when the appropriate sentence—life or death—is under consideration. Chapter 8 begins with a review of the extent to which the death penalty in retentionist countries is the mandatory punishment for murder or other serious crimes. It shows that the mandatory use of capital punishment has come under increasing attack as an unacceptably inflexible penalty and so proceeds to a consideration of whether a discretionary use of capital punishment can ever be applied in an equitable and non-discriminatory manner. Legal scholarship and social science research on the American statutes that have sought to restrict and make more fair the imposition of the death penalty are examined to see whether they have in fact been successful in eliminating arbitrariness and discrimination in the infliction of the death penalty. Chapter 9 discusses the concept of general deterrence and analyses and weighs the research evidence on the subject, including recent econometric studies that have claimed to find a not insubstantial deterrent effect of executions. Chapter 10 analyses the role of opinion, particularly but not only public opinion, in relation to the politics of capital punishment. It includes a discussion of the possible impact that organisations of so-called 'survivors', the relatives of the victims of murder, may have on the politics of capital punishment and ends by raising the question of what should determine this issue: popular opinion or human rights principles? The final, and new, chapter considers what penalty or

---

[7] We recognize that the term 'mentally retarded' may be considered to be outdated. However, currently it is the accepted phrase within the USA, and as most of the literature and death penalty jurisprudence on mental disability comes from that jurisdiction we adopt this term throughout the book. Furthermore, the term 'mentally retarded or extremely limited mental competence' is used in the Additions to the UN Safeguards Guaranteeing Protection of the Rights of those Facing the Death Penalty, promulgated in 1989 (see Appendix 3). It should be noted, however, that the American Association on Intellectual and Development Disabilities, the group of experts responsible for defining the condition of intellectual disability, is now moving away from the term 'mental retardation' to the term 'intellectual disability', according to an article published in the April issue of the journal, *Intellectual and Developmental Disabilities*: Robert Schalock *et al.*, 'The Renaming of Mental Retardation: Understanding the Change to the Term Intellectual Disability' 45(2) (2007), pp. 116–124.

penalties might be available to replace capital punishment if the death penalty is to be abolished completely even for the 'worst of the worst' crimes. It considers, in particular, the moral, humane, and practical objections to the penalty of life-time imprisonment without the option of release on parole. Appendices chart the changing status of capital punishment and the extent of ratification of international treaties to prohibit its imposition.

A word must be said about a related issue which could not be covered by this book but which cannot be ignored by anyone concerned with the protection of human rights. We refer to the very regrettable fact that abolition of judicial capital punishment has not always guaranteed that state forces, whether military or police, have respected the rule of law and the right to life in enforcing the law. All too often governments—even abolitionist governments—have resorted to extra-judicial killing, and in recent times this has become a policy that is in danger of becoming legitimized as a means of dealing with those defined as 'terrorists'. However, it is our view that the abolition of capital punishment in all countries of the world will ensure that the killing of citizens by the state will no longer have any legitimacy and so even more marginalize and stigmatize extra-judicial executions.

3. The Approach Taken towards Capital Punishment

As already mentioned, this book began life as an official report, and was not intended to present an argument, as such, for the abolition of capital punishment. It was oriented instead towards assessing the extent to which the policy objectives of the United Nations are being achieved, and what impediments there appear to be in bringing them to fruition, namely 'progressively restricting the number of offences for which the death penalty may be imposed with a view to the desirability of abolishing the punishment'.[8]

Yet, one would be unlikely to embark on such a task without believing that this is a desirable goal. And, certainly, our involvement in researching this subject has convinced us of the strength of the case for abolishing judicial executions throughout the world.

The Introduction to the first edition in 1989 stated that 'no one can embark upon a study of the death penalty without making the commonplace observation that from a philosophical and policy standpoint there appears to be nothing new to be said'. This is still true: the arguments remain essentially the same. Yet the balance has changed, and the nature of the debate has moved on. There can be no doubt that the greater emphasis on the 'human rights' perspective on the

---

[8] General Assembly Resolution 32/61, 8 December 1977. See United Nations, 'United Nations Action in the Field of Capital Punishment', *United Nations Crime Prevention and Criminal Justice Newsletter* 12 and 13 (1986), pp. 2–4.

subject has added greatly to the moral force propelling the abolitionist movement. It has further 'internationalized' what was formerly considered an issue solely for national policy. And those who still favour capital punishment 'in principle' have been faced with yet more convincing evidence of the abuses, discrimination, mistakes, and inhumanity that appear inevitably to accompany it in practice. Some of them have set out on the quest to find the key to a 'perfect' system in which no mistakes or injustices will occur. In our view this quest is entirely chimerical.

Many protagonists of abolition believe that the death penalty is a fundamental violation of the human right to life: in essence, that it is an extreme form of cruel, inhuman, and degrading punishment. For such persons any discussion of its effectiveness as a deterrent is irrelevant. But it has to be recognized that not everyone regards this 'human rights' view as valid, especially outside Europe and the European hegemony. Indeed, many people appear to believe that (at least some) criminals who violate the right to life of others by murdering them deserve to lose their own right to life, and they parade horrifying and brutal cases in support of their contention. But usually this approach is supported by a belief that the death penalty, and execution in particular, is necessary to protect others from a similar fate. In some countries this argument is used to justify capital punishment for other crimes which can inflict grave personal or socially injurious harms such as the sale of narcotics, sexual offences against children, and even some very large scale cases of corruption and embezzlement. Sometimes capital punishment is said to be sanctioned by religious authority, as in Islamic countries, and sometimes by deeply embedded cultural norms or 'mindsets', as is claimed by some from Asian countries.

Thus, even where the human rights argument against capital punishment is not accepted, the case for capital punishment usually rests not only on retributive sentiments but also on assumptions about its unique deterrent effects as compared with alternative lesser punishments. If it were shown that it is unnecessary to retain the death penalty to control grave crimes perhaps many of those who favour it would not continue to do so merely on retributive grounds to exact revenge: they might well regard it as 'useless cruelty'. The same values that proclaim the 'rights of victims' not to be murdered, or of the relatives of victims to have their pain eased by seeing the prisoner put to death, can also be invoked to protect the rights of the accused, especially when innocent persons may be, whatever the safeguards, sentenced to death or it can be shown that the system as a whole inflicts capital punishment on persons who are 'undeserving' of it, such as the mentally retarded. Nor should the rights and feelings of the family members of the condemned be put simply to one side. One suspects that many of those who favour capital punishment 'in principle' would not continue to favour it if it were to be shown that it was accompanied by unnecessary cruelty, or that the system for administering it produced arbitrary judgments or class or racial bias on an unacceptable scale. In other words, there remains a large gap between believing that some persons 'deserve to die' for the crimes they commit, and believing that a state system for the administration of capital punishment can be devised which meets the high ideals of equal, effective, procedurally correct, and humane justice that civilized societies seek to implement.

It is necessary, therefore, to approach the question of capital punishment from both normative (moral) and utilitarian points of view, and always in relation to how it is applied in practice. In essence, therefore, the case for retaining the death penalty—and thus resisting the movement to make its abolition an international norm—cannot rest solely on moral, cultural, or religious arguments. It would also have to be shown that it is useful and that it can be applied fairly, without mistakes, and without any degree of arbitrariness or cruelty unacceptable to contemporary social and legal values. There is, as this book makes clear, sufficient evidence to indict capital punishment for failing the test of humanity on all these grounds.

1

The Abolitionist Movement: Progress and Prospects

1. The Pace of Abolition

(a) Setting the goal

It is not our purpose to provide a history of capital punishment, but the reader needs to be aware how entrenched capital punishment was until a movement for reform was generated by the liberal utilitarian and humanistic ideas spawned by the Enlightenment in Europe towards the end of the eighteenth century. From ancient times until the latter part of the eighteenth century, and in all parts of the world, the threat of punishment by death had been widely accepted as an effective penal weapon of social control, even though the extent to which it was enforced varied between countries and in different periods.[1] As the historian Stuart Banner has put it:[2]

The primary purpose of capital punishment was the emphatic display of power, a reminder of what the state could do to those who broke its laws... The link between cause and effect, between the commission of the crime and the imposition of the death sentence was made as conspicuous as it could be.

In many countries during the seventeenth and eighteenth centuries death became the appointed punishment for an ever-widening range of offences, varying enormously in their gravity. For example, in 1810 there were at least 223 capital offences in England. There was no proportionality between the crime committed and the punishment threatened. Every felony, with the exceptions of petty larceny and maiming, could be punished by death. This was 'the bloody code': maximum severity threatened but with no certainty of it being enforced.[3] Without effective

---

[1] For example, it was not enforced at all in Japan during the Heian Period of 794 to 1185 AD: D. T. Johnson, 'Where the State Kills in Secret: Capital Punishment in Japan' *Punishment and Society* 8 (2006) pp. 251–285 at 257.

[2] S. Banner, *The Death Penalty: An American History* (2002), pp. 13–16 at 14.

[3] L. Radzinowicz, *A History of English Criminal Law*, vol I (1948), p. 5.

police forces, many escaped prosecution. Even if they were prosecuted juries would often not convict those for whom the punishment of death was clearly too severe. And if convicted and sentenced to death, the sentence was frequently commuted or substituted by other punishments such as transportation overseas.

Methods of execution had been gruesome and calculated as a public spectacle both to create terror and to convey to the audience the consequences of living an immoral life.[4] In European countries in the seventeenth and eighteenth centuries criminals were 'broken on the wheel' or 'with the wheel';[5] pressed under weights; boiled to death in oil; burnt with red-hot pincers and then torn limb from limb by horses; hanged, drawn and quartered; or drowned. They were sometimes subject to additional torture in the process. Heads and whole bodies were put on display until they rotted. 'Hanging in chains' and 'gibbeting' did not, for example, cease in England until 1832.[6] In America during colonial times there were 'degrees of death' varying from hanging on the gallows to burning at the stake, dismemberment or dissection.[7] In China convicted offenders were sometimes sawn in half or flayed while alive, or suffered 'death by a thousand cuts'.[8]

Cesare Beccaria's famous treatise *On Crimes and Punishments,* published in 1764, advocated the replacement of this old regime of maximum terror, randomly inflicted, by a graded system of penalties proportionate to the crime committed and inflicted with greater certainty. Capital punishment, Beccaria declared, was both inhumane and ineffective: an unacceptable weapon for a modern enlightened state to employ, and less effective than the certainty of imprisonment. Furthermore, he argued that it was counterproductive if the purpose of law was to impart a moral conception of the duties of citizens to each other. For, if the state were to resort to killing in order to enforce its will, it would legitimize the very behaviour which the law sought to repress, namely the use of deadly force to settle disputes. It was recognized that death was a disproportionate punishment for crimes less serious than murder, for such a system drew no moral distinction between these crimes and murder and provided no incentive for an offender to choose not to murder but to commit instead a lesser crime which would not be visited by death. For instance, if robbers were to be deterred from murder the penalty for robbery should be less than that for murder. As mentioned above, juries had become reluctant to send people to their deaths for property offences. Thus, from a utilitarian standpoint, to threaten capital punishment that would only be rarely and haphazardly inflicted was bound to be a less effective deterrent than a more certain and proportionate punishment that was recognized as legitimate by citizens in general and therefore more likely to be enforced.

---

[4] Banner, n. 2 above, p. 43.
[5] R. J. Evans, *Rituals of Retribution: Capital Punishment in Germany 1600–1987* (1996), Ch. 5.
[6] V. Gatrell, *The Hanging Tree. Execution and the English People 1770–1868* (1994), pp. 268–269.
[7] Banner, n. 2 above, p. 54.
[8] G. R. Scott, *The History of Capital Punishment* (1950), reissued (1965), chs. 12–14.

In the 1780s Beccaria's ideas were taken up by the enlightened rulers of Tuscany and Austria, who put capital punishment into abeyance for several years. In Imperial Russia, under the Empresses Elizabeth and Catherine II, the death penalty was also suspended. Pressure to restrict the death penalty to only the gravest crimes began to mount in Britain, the USA, and several European countries. The reformers had their first successes in America, a fact that needs to be borne in mind when considering the position of the USA on the death penalty in modern times. Pennsylvania (in 1794) became the first state to abolish capital punishment for all crimes except 'first degree' murder and this policy of restricting it to all but the most serious crimes began to be widely accepted. For example, by the 1860s the death penalty had been restricted to murder throughout the northern states of the USA (where it became discretionary rather than mandatory), in most parts of Germany, and in England and Wales.[9] Even one of the most vigorous proponents of capital punishment, the English Victorian judge Sir James Stephen, declared: 'there is nothing that it is worthwhile to protect at the cost of human life, except human life itself, or the existence of government and society'.[10]

In 1846 the American state of Michigan became the first jurisdiction in modern times to abolish capital punishment for murder.[11] Rhode Island followed suit in 1852 (except for murder of a prison guard by a convict serving a life sentence) and one year later Wisconsin became the third abolitionist state. By the end of the first quarter of the twentieth century several European countries—Portugal, San Marino, the Netherlands, Norway, and Sweden, as well as Italy, Romania, Austria, and Switzerland (all four of which later reinstated it for a period)—had got rid of the death penalty for crimes committed in peacetime, and so had several South American states after gaining their independence: Brazil, Colombia, Costa Rica, Ecuador, Uruguay, and then Argentina in 1921. Venezuela in 1863 was the first country in the world to abolish permanently capital punishment for all crimes, whether committed in peacetime or wartime.

However, as mentioned above, the path to abolition in these countries was not always straight. Capital punishment was reinstated and expanded by various authoritarian regimes, or in response to the exigencies of warfare, during the twentieth century in both Europe and South America. It was reintroduced in Italy by Mussolini's Fascist regime in 1927 and in Germany was expanded beyond all recognition by the Nazis, where it was 'to be transformed from an instrument of penal policy into a tool of racial and political engineering... not merely a matter of retribution but also of eugenics policy'. Under the Third Reich 'some 16,500

---

[9] Save for treason, piracy with violence, and arson in the dockyards.

[10] Cited in L. Radzinowicz, *A History of English Criminal Law*, Vol. IV (1968), p. 339.

[11] Effective from 1 March 1847, although there had been no executions since it had become a state of the Union in 1837. The death penalty was retained for treason (but never used) until 1963; W. J. Bowers with G. Pierce and J. F. McDevitt, *Legal Homicide: Death as Punishment in America, 1864–1982* (2nd edn., 1984), pp. 6–15 at 9.

death sentences had been passed'.[12] The demise of both these regimes at the end of the Second World War was swiftly followed by abolition of the death penalty (see Chapter 2, page 41).

Writing in 1962, the French jurist, Marc Ancel, pointed out that abolition had usually been achieved over a considerable period of time; through a gradual 'testing of the waters' so to speak:[13]

The process of abolition has usually taken a long time and followed a distinctive pattern; first the reduction of the number of crimes legally punishable by death until only murder and (sometimes) treason are left, then systematic use of commutation, leading to *de facto* abolition, and eventual abolition *de jure*.

It is true that he was not arguing that such a slow step-by-step process was the only way in which abolition could be achieved. Nevertheless, his words were widely interpreted not simply as a description of the process as it had usually occurred up to that point, but by some countries as almost a normative prescription for how to achieve abolition. Furthermore, he did not take the absolutist position that capital punishment could never be justified. He stated, as if it were not to be doubted, just forty-six years ago, that: 'Even the most convinced abolitionists realise that there may be special circumstances, or particularly troublous times, which justify the introduction of the death penalty for a limited period'.[14] There was little in this analysis that would have led one to expect that within forty years only a minority of countries would be carrying out executions, or that a large number of countries would have abandoned the death penalty permanently for all crimes in all circumstances, in wartime as well as peacetime.

Progress towards the permanent abandonment of capital punishment on a worldwide scale had therefore not made enormous strides by the time that Professor Norval Morris reported to the United Nations on the situation up to 1965. There were, he discovered, still only 25 abolitionist countries. Eleven had completely abolished it, the only major European country among them being the Federal Republic of Germany (West Germany).[15] A further 14 countries,[16] 10 of them Western European nations, plus the Australian state of New South Wales, had abolished it for ordinary crimes in peacetime.[17]

---

[12] Evans, n. 5 above, pp. 613–637 at 630 and 795.

[13] M. Ancel, *The Death Penalty in European Countries* (1962), p. 3.

[14] *Ibid.*, p. 3.

[15] Colombia (1910), Costa Rica (1877), Ecuador (1906), Federal Republic of Germany (1949), Honduras (1956), Iceland (1928), Monaco (1962), Panama (1922), San Marino (1865), Uruguay (1907), and Venezuela (1863). In addition, one Australian state (Queensland), nine American states (Alaska, Hawaii, Iowa, Maine, Michigan, Minnesota, Oregon, West Virginia, and Wisconsin), and 24 of the 29 Mexican states had abolished the death penalty for all crimes.

[16] Austria (1950), Denmark (1933), Finland (1949), Israel (1954), Italy (1947), the Netherlands (1870), New Zealand (1961), Norway (1905), Portugal (1867), Sweden (1921), Switzerland (1942), and the United Kingdom of Great Britain and Northern Ireland (1965). Also Argentina (1921) and Brazil (1882), both of which reintroduced the death penalty under military decrees after 1965.

[17] That is, they retained the death penalty in exceptional circumstances only, notably in time of war for military crimes and for certain crimes against the state.

Over the next 20 years the pace of abolition was steady but hardly spectacular. Roughly one country a year abandoned capital punishment, so that by the end of 1998 there were 35 completely abolitionist countries and a further 17 that had abandoned it for all ordinary crimes in peacetime. They accounted for 28 per cent of the world nation communities (see Table 1.1). In contrast, there were still 101 countries (56%) that retained the death penalty for murder and quite often for other crimes as well (see Chapter 4) which had carried out executions within the past 10 years, plus a further 27 countries that retained the death penalty in law, but had not executed anyone for at least 10 years—a category which the United Nations referred to as *abolitionist de facto* but in reality were countries some of which could readily (as will be seen) resume executions. At this stage there were some well-informed observers who wondered whether many more countries could be persuaded to join the abolitionist movement. For instance, in 1986 the distinguished German professor of criminology Dr Günther Kaiser, after reviewing the provision of international efforts to achieve abolition, had come to the melancholy conclusion that 'there appears to be little hope that international bodies, whether private or official, will be able to achieve unanimity [among] the majority of countries concerning the restriction or abolition of capital punishment'.[18]

(b) A great leap forward

Kaiser was too pessimistic, for soon afterwards there was a striking increase in the number of countries that abandoned capital punishment. Over the 11 years from 1989 to 1999 inclusive, 40 countries became abolitionist: 39 of them for all crimes in all circumstances, in peacetime or wartime, in civil and military law: an average of over three a year. Only four of these 40 countries had, prior to 1989, first abolished capital punishment for ordinary crimes, and of the remaining 36, only 10 had preceded total abolition with a period of being abolitionist *de facto*. The remaining 26 (65 per cent of the total) had moved seamlessly from retention to abolition.[19]

Such a spurt led another distinguished commentator, the criminologist Sir Leon Radzinowicz, to the disheartening conclusion in 1999 that a plateau had been reached: meaning that almost all those countries that were likely to abolish the death penalty had already done so.[20] While the pace of abolition did somewhat decline, this prediction again proved to be too pessimistic. In the seven years from the end of 2000 to the end of December 2007 a further 15 countries abolished capital punishment completely and two more for all ordinary crimes. Only two of the 15 had abolished the death penalty for ordinary crimes prior to

---

[18] G. Kaiser, 'Capital Punishment in a Criminological Perspective' *United Nations Crime Prevention and Criminal Justice Newsletter* 12 and 13 (1986), pp. 10–18 at 16.

[19] The information from which this calculation was made can be found in App. 1 Table 5.

[20] L. Radzinowicz, *Adventures in Criminology* (1999), p. 293.

abolishing it for all crimes. But, in contrast to the period up to 1999, 14 of the 17 had first experienced a period of being abolitionist *de facto* when no executions had taken place for at least 10 years (see Appendix 1, Table 5).

Although the increase in the number of abolitionist countries since the end of December 1988 reflects to some extent the break-up of several states and the emergence from them of several newly independent nations, most notably in Africa and the former Soviet Union, the change has been nevertheless remarkable. As Table 1.1 shows, the proportion of countries that were 'actively retentionist' (i.e. those which had carried out at least one judicial execution within the past 10 years and which had not subsequently declared a permanent moratorium on executions) had fallen from 101 (56%) at the end of 1988 to 51 (26%) on 31 December 2007. The proportion of retentionist countries that were abolitionist de *facto* had increased from 15 to 23 per cent and the abolitionist states from 29 to 51 per cent, 91 per cent of them being completely abolitionist, a much higher proportion than at the end of 1988 (67%).

(c) The significance of these changes

Within a short period of time, and especially during the past twenty years, the view that the death penalty needs to be abolished for all crimes, in all circumstances has taken hold in an ever increasing number of countries. Furthermore, the recent spurt of abolition has had a different dynamic and been the result of different forces and ideas from those evident in the earlier phases of the abolitionist movement.

Ancel's opinion, some forty years ago, that it might need to be retained or reintroduced in emergencies is no longer valid in these jurisdictions. Although some countries still go through the process of first suspending the use of executions for a decade or longer, before moving to abolition, many have not done so. Similarly, whilst some have first abolished it solely for murder and any other crimes in peacetime, the vast majority (94%) have moved straight to complete

Table 1.1 Comparison of abolitionist and retentionist countries at the end of December 1988, December 1995, December 2001, and December 2007

Year	Complete abolitionist		Abolitionist for ordinary offences		Total retentionist		Retentionist with executions in the previous ten years		Abolitionist *de facto*		Total number of countries
	No.	%	No.	%	No.	%	No.	%	No.	%	
1988	35	19	17	9	128	71	101	56	27	15	180
1995	60	31	13	7	119	62	90	47	29	15	192
2001	75	39	14	7	105	54	71	37	34	18	194
2007	91*	46	10	5	94	48	51*	26	44	22	196

* This become 92 and 50 on 1 January 2008, when Uzbekistan abolished the death penalty.

abolition. Forty-nine of the 52 countries that *first* abolished the death penalty since the beginning of 1989 did so 'at one go', so to speak, only three (6%) of them (Chile, Kazakhstan, and Latvia) leaving it available for offences against the state, offences of terrorism, or for offences against the military code in time of war (see Table A1.5). Furthermore, as far as we have been able to ascertain, 18 of these 49 countries that have completely abolished capital punishment since the beginning of 1989 (having not abolished it for ordinary crimes prior to that date) have done so through constitutional reform, usually related to the article in the constitution that specifies the right to life and/or freedom from cruel and inhumane punishment and treatment. Yet others abolished the death penalty first by legislation and then embodied it in their constitutions. Certainly, over half of the 49 had taken this route by the end of December 2007.[21]

Whereas (as is shown in Chapter 2) the list of abolitionist countries in the Morris Report of 1965 included only two that were outside Western Europe and Central and South America, the movement has spread not only to every country but one (Belarus) in Europe—making it a 'death penalty free zone'—but to Central Asia and also into Africa. Fourteen African countries are now completely abolitionist,[22] and another 20 are abolitionist *de facto*.[23] While only four Asian states (Nepal, Bhutan, Cambodia, and Philippines) have so far completely abolished the death penalty, seven are now abolitionist *de facto* (according to the ten-year criterion). Among the islands of the Pacific, 11 have abolished the death penalty completely, and a further four are abolitionist *de facto*. Where abolition has not yet been achieved (see Chapter 3) there has been a movement to restrict the number of crimes for which the penalty is death, to make it discretionary

---

[21] Sometimes, as in Poland where the death penalty was abolished in the Penal Code of 1997, the change was reflected in a new constitution. Article 38 of Poland's 1997 Constitution stated that, 'The Republic of Poland shall ensure the legal protection of the life of every human being'. Also, abolition by the former government of Czechoslovakia in July 1990 was followed by embodiment of abolition in Article 6 of the Czech and Slovak Republic's Charter of Fundamental Rights and Freedoms, part of the new Constitution of 1991, and then applied to both Czech and Slovak Republics when they became independent in 1992. Moldova abolished the death penalty by legislation in 1995, and five years later the Constitutional Court agreed amendments to the Constitution to bring it into line with the legislation. Similarly, in Georgia, a constitutional reform in 2006 cleared up any ambiguity as to whether the death penalty had been completely abolished by the legislation of 1997. Sometimes constitutional reform preceded the legislation abolishing capital punishment in the criminal code, as in South Africa and recently in Kyrgyzstan. On other occasions the death penalty was first suspended by governmental action, such as occurred in Romania, where the provisional government, following the overthrow of President Ceausescu, issued a decree in January 1990 replacing the death penalty with life imprisonment. This was given legality by the new Constitution in November 1991. In Slovenia, where the last execution occurred in 1959, abolition of the death penalty was embodied in a constitutional amendment in 1989 and a year later a decree declared that the Yugoslavian Federal Code's provisions did not apply in Slovenia. One year later the death penalty was forbidden by the new Constitution of 1991.

[22] Angola, Cape Verde, Cote d'Ivoire, Djibouti, Guinea-Bissau, Liberia, Mauritius, Mozambique, Namibia, Rwanda, Senegal, Sao Tome and Principe, Seychelles, and South Africa.

[23] Benin, Burkina Faso, Cameroon, Central African Republic, Congo (Brazzaville), Eritrea, Gabon, Gambia, Ghana, Kenya, Lesotho, Madagascar, Malawi, Mali, Mauritania, Niger, Swaziland, Tanzania, Togo, and Zambia.

rather than mandatory (see Chapter 8), and even more so to restrict the number of people actually executed (see Chapter 5).

Although a very small number of abolitionist countries reported to the United Nations Seventh Quinquennial Survey in 2003–4 that there had been some proposals to reintroduce capital punishment emanating from individuals, members of Parliament or minority political parties, none of them had made any impact. Real setbacks have been rare, and in all but one instance have not led to a resumption of executions. Papua New Guinea, which had abolished the death penalty for ordinary crimes on obtaining independence in 1975, reinstated it for wilful murder in 1991, but in the 15 years that have since elapsed no executions have taken place. The period of abolition in Gambia was even shorter: 1993 to 1995, but again no executions have followed. Nepal reintroduced the death penalty for certain murders and terrorist offences in 1985, but no executions were carried out prior to it being abolished again for these offences in 1990. In effect, these countries moved from being abolitionist to abolitionist *de facto*. In the United States, New York State reinstated the death penalty in 1995 after thirty years without it and Kansas, which had not enacted a new law providing for the death penalty in accordance with the *Gregg* decision in 1967 (see Chapter 3, page 113 below), reinstated the death penalty in 1994, 29 years after the last execution had been carried out. But yet again no executions followed. Indeed, the death sentence was found unconstitutional by the Supreme Courts of both states. It appears unlikely that it will be reinstated in New York (see Chapter 3, page 122 below). And while the US Supreme Court upheld the constitutionality of the Kansas statute by a majority of 5 to 4 in 2006, no executions have as yet taken place. The only country to have abolished the death penalty and resumed executions is the Philippines. Abolished on the overthrow of President Marcos in 1987, it was brought back and greatly extended in scope six years later in 1993. Six people were executed in 1999 and another in 2000, but no more followed. After a period of uncertainty accompanied by a vigorous abolitionist campaign, capital punishment was again abolished completely in June 2006 (see Chapter 3, pages 85–87).

Another significant change from the past is the *speed* with which abolition has been achieved. Only a minority, 21 (40%), of the 52 countries that first abolished the death penalty since the beginning of 1989 (including the three that abolished it for ordinary crimes only) had been abolitionist *de facto*, having not executed anyone for at least 10 years, before achieving abolition *de jure* (see Appendix A1.5). The periods of time between the last execution and abolition varied enormously. Ten of them had been abolitionist *de facto* for over 30 years.[24] Thirty-one (60%) of the 52 countries (including two new states, Palau and Timor Leste) did so *without* first suspending executions for at least 10 years. For example, Turkmenistan abolished capital punishment in 1999, just two years

---

[24] Andorra (47 years), Belgium, (46), Bhutan, (40) Cote d'Ivoire (40), Ireland (36), Mexico, (68), Slovenia (32), Paraguay (64), Senegal (37), Samoa (42).

after the last execution; South Africa in 1995 just four years after; Latvia in 1999 after three years; Cambodia in 1989 two years after; both the Czech and Slovak republics only one year after; and Romania, immediately after the downfall and summary trial and execution of its President and his wife.[25] Thus, the pattern of a long drawn-out process leading to abolition was not observed in *over half* of those countries that have embraced abolition under the influence of the 'new dynamic'.

It needs to be recognized also that the status of abolitionist *de facto* has not been, as was once thought, a sure stepping-stone to abolition, building-up a sort of 'taboo' against executions that citizens and governments would not want to break. In several cases the 'ten-year gap' has occurred not because governments have wanted to curb executions, but because they were thwarted by success-ful legal interventions, as in countries of the Commonwealth Caribbean (see Chapter 3, pages 103–111). Some other countries have announced, from time to time, that they intend to resume executions, but they have not done so: Sri Lanka is a case in point. It is also true that, since 1994, 10 countries that appeared to be abolitionist *de facto* resumed executions—although none on a regular basis—and returned to the retentionist camp (Bahamas, Bahrain, Burundi, Chad, Comoros, Guinea, Guatemala, St Kitts and Nevis, Trinidad and Tobago, and Qatar). And in some American states executions have taken place after very long periods of abeyance. For example, as the new millennium got under way, both Tennessee and New Mexico resumed executions after 40 and 41 years respect-ively; in 2005 Connecticut executed a person just four days short of 45 years since the last execution; and, in 2007, South Dakota carried out its first execution for 60 years when Elija Page, aged 25, 'volunteered', having decided not to pursue any further appeals. Of even greater significance were the two federal executions in June 2001, the first for 38 years, of Timothy McVeigh and Juan Raoul Garza, sanctioned by the President of the United States, who decided not to exercise his power to grant clemency.

Because of these experiences, Amnesty International is cautious in classify-ing as 'abolitionist in practice' any country which keeps the death penalty on its statute books. Nevertheless, it accepts that at least 33 countries are genuinely abolitionist *in practice* in that they appear to have a settled policy not to resume executions, and that several of them have announced also that they are intent on moving to complete abolition.[26] When these are added to the number who have

---

[25] These 29 countries (i.e. excluding Palau and Timor Leste), with the number of years between the last execution and abolition in brackets is: Albania (5), Angola (date of last execution not known to us, but believed to be just a few years prior to abolition), Azerbaijan (5), Bosnia (6), Bulgaria (7), Cambodia (2), Croatia (4), Czech Republic (2), Estonia (7), Georgia (3), Guinea Bissau (7), Hungary (2), Kazakhstan (4), Kyrgystan (9), Latvia (3), Lithuania (3), Macedonia (former Yugoslavia) (4), Mauritius (8), Mozambique (4), Moldova (9), Namibia (2), Philippines (6), Poland (9), Romania (less than 1), Rwanda (9), Slovakia (2), South Africa (6), Turkmenistan (2), and Ukraine (2).

[26] e.g. Ghana, Malawi, Morocco, Myanmar, and Kenya.

become abolitionist in law, it becomes even clearer that the majority of states have embraced the goal of worldwide abolition: 134 (68%) of them compared with 62 who retain capital punishment,[27] although most of them carry out executions only occasionally and then a very small number (see Chapter 4).

Further momentum has been added to the abolitionist cause by the agreement reached at the United Nations that the International Criminal Tribunals for trying cases of genocide and crimes against humanity in the former Yugoslavia and Rwanda, and later in Sierra Leone and Lebanon, were not given the power to impose the death penalty. Similarly, the Statute of the International Criminal Court, adopted by the Rome Conference in July 1998, did not provide the death penalty for any of the exceptionally grave offences, encompassing genocide and other crimes against humanity, covered by the statute.[28] It could now be argued that if these, the most serious of all crimes, were not punishable by the death penalty, why should lesser offences be so punished?

The following section of this chapter examines the motivating ideals and political processes which have been at work to transform the issue of abolition into an international movement within such an historically short space of time.[29] We then discuss the resistance that has been encountered from those countries, including the USA, that have not yet accepted—or even have vigorously opposed—the claim that capital punishment should be banned by international agreement, just as slavery, torture, and genocide are.

2. Generating the New Wave of Abolition

(a) The emergence of the human rights perspective

The dynamo for the new wave of abolition was the development of international human rights law. Arising in the aftermath of the Second World War and sometimes linked to the emergence of countries from totalitarian imperialism and colonialism, the acceptance of international human rights principles created a climate that advocated, in the name of democracy and freedom, the protection of citizens from the power of the state and the tyranny of the opinions of the masses. Foremost among the factors that have promoted this new wave of abolition has

---

[27] See Table 1.1 above. 51 retentionist countries plus 11 (i.e. 44–33) retentionist countries that are classified under the '10-year rule' as abolitionist *de facto*, but which apparently still intend to carry out executions.

[28] Rome Statute of the International Criminal Court, UN Doc. A/CONF. 183/9 (17 July 1998), Art. 77. The Rome Statute of the International Criminal Court (ICC) entered into force on 1 July 2002 and the Court is now fully functional at its seat in The Hague. By 2006, 139 states had signed the Rome Statute of the International Criminal Court and 102 states had ratified or acceded to it. On 6 May 2002 the United States announced that it was withdrawing from the treaty.

[29] The dates of the last executions carried out by abolitionist countries can be found in App. 1, Tables 2 and 3.

been the political movement to transform consideration of capital punishment from an issue to be decided solely or mainly as an aspect of national criminal justice policy to the status of a fundamental violation of human rights: not only the right to life but the right to be free of excessive, repressive and tortuous punishments.[30] The human rights approach to abolition rejects the most persistent of the justifications for capital punishment, as described by Richard Evans in his monumental work *Rituals of Retribution*:[31]

Fundamentally the most powerful and persistent motive for execution has always been retribution, the belief that death can be the only adequate expiation for certain crimes, the feeling that lesser punishments are insufficient, the conviction that those who commit the most serious offences must pay for them by suffering the ultimate penalty, death.

It also rejects the utilitarian justification that nothing less severe can act as a sufficient general deterrent to those who contemplate committing capital crimes. This is not only because abolitionists believe that the social science evidence does not support the case for deterrence (see Chapter 9) but also because they would reject the deterrence argument even if it could be shown that there was some evidence in favour of it. They would argue that such deterrence could only be achieved by high rates of execution, mandatorily and speedily enforced, and that this would inevitably lead to the probability of a higher proportion of innocent or wrongfully convicted persons being executed as well as to the unjust execution of people who, because of the mitigating circumstances in which their crimes were committed, do not deserve to die. They also argue that it is precisely when there are strong reactions to serious crimes that the use of the death penalty as an instrument of crime control is most dangerous. Pressure on the police and prosecutors to bring offenders to justice, especially those suspected of committing outrages, is likely to lead to short cuts, breaches of procedural protections, and simple myopia in investigation once a suspect is identified. For instance, a Japanese abolitionist lawyer has reported that 'Almost half of death row inmates were indicted after interrogation without the presence of a lawyer at the police investigation stage'.[32] The Russian writer, Anatoly Pristavkin, former head of Russia's Pardons Commission, and an ardent abolitionist, has stated that prominent jurists in Russia estimated that wrongful convictions amounted to between 10 and 15 per cent of those sentenced to death.[33] In England, the wrongful

[30] F. E. Zimring, *The Contradictions of American Capital Punishment* (2003), pp. 16–41. See also the working paper by E. Neumayer, *Death penalty: the political foundations of the global trend towards abolition* (2005), available at SSRN: <http://ssrn.com/abstract=489628> or DOI: <10.2139/ssrn.489628>.
[31] Evans, n. 5 above, p. vii. Also, A. Kozinski 'Tinkering with Death' and L. P. Pojman, 'Why the Death Penalty is Morally Permissible', in H. Bedau and P. Cassell (eds.), *Debating the Death Penalty* (2004), pp. 1–14 and 51–75.
[32] Y. Yasuda, 'The death penalty in Japan' in *The Death Penalty—Beyond Abolition* (2004), p. 215 at 220.
[33] A. Pristavkin, 'A vast place of execution—the death penalty in Russia' in *The Death Penalty. Abolition in Europe* (1999), pp. 129–137 at 134.

convictions of Irishmen and women following terrorist outrages, in the 1970s and 80s, turned even strong supporters of a return to capital punishment against the idea. In the United States, investigative journalists uncovered cases of wrongful conviction which had passed through all the lengthy appeal processes without such errors being spotted, and in 14 of 123 instances where a person has, to date, been exonerated of a capital conviction, DNA has provided convincing evidence of innocence (see Chapter 7, pages 274–276 below). The problem appears to be endemic to the systematic use of the death penalty and not simply a reflection of human error or faults in the administration of criminal justice in a particular country. For many abolitionists even the smallest possibility that an innocent person could be executed is unacceptable. Thus, in a speech delivered in 2001, the then European Union Commissioner for External Relations, Chris Patten, spoke of:[34]

the inhumane, unnecessary and irreversible character of capital punishment, no matter how cruel the crime committed by the offender... That stance is rooted in our belief in the inherent dignity of all human beings and the inviolability of the human person... it is impossible to reduce the risk to zero of applying the penalty in error.

But, although the possibility of error is an important lever in the argument of the abolitionists, those committed to the cause contend that even if the system could be made 'foolproof' it could still not be supported. In particular, abolitionists who have embraced the view that all citizens have a 'right to life' argue that the issue cannot be left to public opinion, not only because such opinion may not be fully informed as to the consequences of employing capital punishment, but because the appeal to human rights centres on the protection of all citizens from cruel and inhumane punishment, whatever crimes they may have committed (see Chapter 10). Most abolitionists also contend that the means could never justify the ends: for them the control of serious crime is more appropriately and better achieved through tackling the factors that contribute to it, rather than relying on the inhumane punishment of putting people to death.

(b) The developments of international treaties committed to abolition

According to Leon Radzinowicz, because the crusade against capital punishment originated in Europe, 'then regarded as the centre of the world', it:[35]

was not conceived in strictly national or even regional terms. It should take root, so it was declared, in the world at large. It should suffer no territorial restrictions, indeed no restrictions of any kind. It became a universal question, an almost transcendental, absolute issue to be agitated for and put into effect, without regard for time, place, ethnicity or political system.

---

[34] Speech delivered in June 2001 to the First World Congress Against the Death Penalty in Strasbourg.

[35] L. Radzinowicz, *Adventures in Criminology* (1999), pp. 281–282.

This may have been the ideal, and indeed, when a heated campaign for abolition arose in England in the 1860s, proponents quickly compared the British position with those countries that had already done away with the death penalty.[36] But in political reality the way in which abolition was pursued remained almost entirely an issue of national criminal justice policy, until the development of political institutions and international covenants committed to making a worldwide movement a reality.

In the long process, lasting from the Universal Declaration of Human Rights in 1948 (which had made capital punishment an exception to Article 3's injunction that 'every human being has an inherent right to life'), until 1966, when the International Covenant on Civil and Political Rights (ICCPR) was adopted by the UN General Assembly (it did not come into force until 10 years later), the question of capital punishment in relation to the right to life was keenly debated. What emerged was a compromise allowing for 'limited retention', for, as mentioned above, only a minority of states at that time had embraced the abolitionist position. Article 6(1), the draft of which had been agreed in 1957, stated: 'Every human being has the inherent right to life. This right shall be protected by law. No one shall be arbitrarily deprived of his life'. And Article 6(2) stated: 'In countries that have not abolished the death penalty, sentence of death may be imposed only for the most serious crimes in accordance with the law in force at the time of the commission of the crime…'.

In the circumstances pertaining in 1957, it was hardly surprising that it was not possible to define more precisely those offences for which capital punishment could be retained. Certainly some countries would have preferred a clear and very narrow enumeration of the crimes for which it would remain permissible to impose the death penalty instead of relying on the concept of 'most serious'.[37] This is probably because they recognized that 'most serious' could be interpreted differently according to national culture, tradition and political complexion— the very antithesis of the notion of an attempt to create a *universal* declaration and definition of human rights.

In fact, the term 'most serious offences' in Article 6(2) was nothing more than a 'marker' for the policy of moving towards abolition through restriction. Far from indicating that those countries that had not abolished the death penalty could proceed under the protection of Article 6(2), as several countries have subsequently argued, the Chairman of the Working Party on the drafting of Article 6 stated: 'it is interesting to note that the expression: "in countries which have not abolished the death penalty" was intended to show *the direction* in which the drafters of the Covenant hoped that the situation would develop,' as was the addition of Article 6(6), namely that 'Nothing in this article shall be invoked to

---

[36] L. Radzinowicz and R. Hood, *A History of English Criminal Law and its Administration, Vol. V, The Emergence of Penal Policy* (1986), p. 672.

[37] William A. Schabas, *The Abolition of the Death Penalty in International Law* (3rd edn., 2002), p. 105.

delay or prevent the abolition of capital punishment by any State party to the present Covenant'.[38] The very notion of 'progressive restriction' made it clear that the degree of 'seriousness' that would justify the death penalty would need to be evaluated and re-evaluated always in a narrowing of definition until abolition was eventually achieved (see Chapter 4, pages 130–132).

It was in 1971 (resolution 28/57) and again in 1977 (resolution 32/61) that this message, this aspiration, was reinforced by the United Nations General Assembly, which stated that the main objective of the UN, 'in accordance with Article 3 of the Universal Declaration of Human Rights and Article 6 of the ICCPR' is to: 'progressively restrict the number of offences for which capital punishment might be imposed, *with a view to its eventual abolition*' (our emphasis). But this policy would have lacked political force had it not been taken up and insisted upon by two post-war political entities: first by the Council of Europe and a little later by the powerful European Union. It needed political leadership willing to accept the premise that the execution of citizens, whatever crimes they had committed, was a fundamental denial of their humanity and right to existence.[39] Towards the end of the 1970s, the Parliamentary Assembly of the Council of Europe, inspired by the advocacy of Dr Christian Broda, the Austrian Minister of Justice, invited the Committee of Ministers to consider capital punishment as 'inhuman'.[40] In 1980 the subject was also raised at the conference of Foreign Ministers of the European Community and subsequently the European Parliament adopted a resolution calling for complete abolition of the death penalty in the European Community.[41] Two years later, in December 1982, Protocol No 6 to the European Convention for the Protection of Human Rights and Fundamental Freedoms (ECHR) was adopted by the Parliamentary Assembly of the Council of Europe and opened for signature on 28 April 1983. Article 1 provided for the abolition of the death penalty in peacetime. Article 2, however, did allow a state to make provision in its law for the death penalty in time of war or of imminent threat of war.

Just over 18 years ago, in 1989, the European initiative was given a global dimension when the UN General Assembly adopted the Second Optional Protocol to the ICCPR, Article 1 of which stated that 'No one within the jurisdiction of a State Party . . . shall be executed'. Clause 2 of this Article established the important principle that 'The death penalty shall not be reestablished in States

---

[38] Schabas, *ibid.*, p. 68. See also N. Rodley, 'The United Nation's work in the field of the death penalty' in *The Death Penalty—Beyond Abolition* (2004), pp. 125–157 at 128–129.

[39] The EU Memorandum on the Death Penalty, dated 25 February 2000, states that 'Offenders are human beings who committed a crime but who also enjoy an inherent and inalienable dignity, the very same dignity claimed by rationalist philosophy, all relevant religions and by law, the death penalty being a denial of human dignity'.

[40] H. C. Krüger, 'Protocol No. 6 to the European Convention on Human Rights' in Council of Europe, *The Death Penalty: Abolition in Europe* (1999), pp. 69–78.

[41] See J. Yorke, 'The Evolving European Union Strategy Against the Death Penalty: from Internal Renunciation to Global Ideology—Part 1' *Amicus Journal* No. 16 (2006), pp. 23–28 at 23–24.

that have abolished it'. Although Article 2, like the Sixth Protocol to the ECHR, allows a reservation to be made which provides for the application of the death penalty in time of war pursuant to a conviction for a most serious crime of a military nature committed during wartime, the reservation can only be made at the time of ratification or accession. According to William Schabas 'only a handful [of such reservations] have been formulated'.[42] A year later, in 1990, the General Assembly of the Organization of American States adopted the Protocol to the American Convention on Human Rights to Abolish the Death Penalty. Article 1 calls upon states to abstain from the use of the death penalty, but does not impose an obligation on them to erase it from the statute book. Thus *de facto* abolitionist countries may also ratify the Protocol.[43] Furthermore, any country that has abolished the death penalty and ratified the American Convention on Human Rights is forbidden by Article 4(3) of the Convention from reintroducing it, even if they have not ratified the Protocol.

Of particular significance, given the limitation of all these prior protocols to offences committed in peacetime, was the adoption, in Vilnius, Lithuania, on 3 May 2002 by the Committee of Ministers of Protocol No 13 to the ECHR in order to send 'a strong political signal'. 'Convinced that everyone's right to life is a basic value in a democratic society and that the abolition of the death penalty is essential for the protection of this right and for the full recognition of the inherent dignity of all human beings', the member states resolved 'to take the final step to abolish the death penalty in all circumstances, including acts committed in time of war or the imminent threat of war'. Protocol No 13 came into force on 1 July 2003.

By the end of December 2007, Protocol No 6 to the ECHR had been ratified by 46 countries and signed by one country (Russia); Protocol No 13 had been ratified by 40 countries and signed by five (only Azerbaijan and Russia not having acceded). Further, the Second Optional Protocol to the ICCPR had been ratified by 64 countries and signed by a further eight; and the Protocol to the American Convention on Human Rights had been ratified by nine countries and signed by two. A further eight countries have not ratified any of the above treaties but have already abolished the death penalty and, having ratified the American Convention on Human Rights, cannot reintroduce it.[44] Thus, by the end of December 2007, a total of 76 countries had undertaken a commitment, through their ratification of one or other of these treaties or conventions, not to reintroduce the death penalty and a further six had signed but not yet ratified one of

[42] William A. Schabas, 'International Law and the Death Penalty: reflecting or promoting change?' in P. Hodgkinson and W. A. Schabas (eds.), *Capital Punishment: Strategies for Abolition* (2004), pp. 36–63 at 43.

[43] On the provisions of these Protocols and questions of interpretation, see William A. Schabas, *The Abolition of the Death Penalty in International Law* (1997), pp. 147–191, 222–260, 273–294.

[44] C. M. Cerna, 'The Death Penalty and the Jurisprudence of the Inter-American System for the Protection of Human Rights', paper presented to the Conference on the Death Penalty, University of Galway, September 2001.

these treaties (see Appendix 2 for the full list). Thus only 19 of the 101 countries which had abolished the death penalty, either completely or for ordinary crimes, at this time were not party to one or other of these treaties.

In other parts of the world, regional human rights movements are seeking to follow this example. Thus, in November 1999, the African Commission on Human and People's Rights, meeting in Kigali, Rwanda urged states 'to envisage a moratorium on the death penalty'[45] and the Asian Human Rights Charter adopted in 1998 (under Article 3.7 'Right to Life') declares 'all states must abolish the death penalty'. On the other hand, the Arab Charter on Human Rights—a revised version of which was adopted by the League of Arab States in 2004— allows the imposition of the death penalty and executions of minors if allowed under national laws. The Charter makes no mention of 'cruel, inhuman or degrading punishment', although it does prohibit torture.[46]

(c) Mounting political pressure

The Parliamentary Assembly of the Council of Europe has been particularly trenchant in its opposition to capital punishment. In a series of resolutions, beginning in 1994 and reaffirmed in resolution 1187 (1999) on *Europe: A Death Penalty Free Continent*, the Assembly called upon 'all the Parliaments in the world which have not yet abolished the death penalty, to do so promptly, following the example of the majority of Council of Europe member states'.[47] In accordance with this, in 1994 the Assembly made it a precondition that any country that wished to become a member of the Council of Europe should agree to implement an immediate moratorium on executions and then sign and ratify, within a set number of years, the Sixth Protocol to the ECHR.[48] Four years later, in 1998, a year after the Amsterdam Treaty of the European Union had included a 'Declaration on the Abolition of the Death Penalty',[49] the European Union followed suit, making it a precondition for membership. This policy had an enormous impact on the countries of the former Soviet bloc in Eastern Europe as well as on several states of the former Soviet Union, including the Ukraine and the Russian Federation, all of which wished to gain the political and economic benefits associated with membership of the Council of Europe or, at a later date, of the European Union. Every one of these countries has abolished the death penalty, with the exception of Russia (which has signed but not yet ratified the 6th Optional Protocol to the ECHR, and has enforced a moratorium on executions since 1996) and Belarus,

---

[45] UN Doc. E/CN.4/2004/86/ p. 8.

[46] Amnesty International, *Report 2005*, p. 33.

[47] R. Wohlwend, 'The Efforts of the Parliamentary Assembly of the Council of Europe' in Council of Europe, *The Death Penalty: Abolition in Europe* (1999), pp. 55–67 and App. II, 'Europe a Death Penalty Free Continent', pp. 171–184.

[48] *Ibid.*, p. 57. See also Parliamentary Assembly Resolution 1097, 1996, para. 6.

[49] See Yorke, n. 41 above, p. 25.

which, as it is now seeking membership of the Council of Europe, will have in due course to comply by instituting a moratorium as a prelude to abolition within three years of acceding if it is to be successful.

Yet, important as the formal requirement of abolition for membership of these European bodies has been, it should be noted that the movement towards abolition in Eastern Europe had started well before 1994, beginning with the German Democratic Republic (East Germany) in 1987. In Slovenia in 1989, in the Czech and Slovak Republic in 1990, in Romania after the fall of Ceausescu at the end of 1989, and in Hungary in 1990, capital punishment was eliminated when independence was obtained from communist rule. Even in Lithuania, where abolition took somewhat longer to achieve, it was not simply that parliamentarians in 1998 chose 'national interests in strategically important international policy' (meaning the possibility of enjoying the benefits of joining the Council of Europe and the EU) over their constituents' preference for capital punishment. Rather, they came to recognize the inhumanity of capital punishment (see Chapter 2, page 56).[50]

Fundamentally important was the message that had been conveyed: a *principled* opposition to the death penalty as a violation of fundamental human rights. Both the Council of Europe and the European Union have declared that 'The death penalty has no legitimate place in the penal systems of modern civilized societies, and its application may well be compared with torture and be seen as inhuman and degrading punishment'.[51] The language is uncompromising. The Europeans will not accept the argument that capital punishment can be defended on relativistic grounds of religion or culture, or as a matter which sovereign powers ought to be left to decide simply for themselves. Thus, in 1998 the European Union embarked on a diplomatic offensive through the adoption of *Guidelines to European Union Policy towards Third Countries on the Death Penalty*. This document stated that the objectives of the European Union are to 'work towards the abolition of the death penalty [in those countries that still retained it] as a strongly held policy view agreed by all EU member states'. And the Guidelines stressed that 'abolition of the death penalty contributes to the enhancement of human dignity and the progressive development of human rights'.[52] Meeting in Nice in December 2000, the European Council, in conjunction with the European Parliament and Commission, welcomed the draft Charter of Fundamental Rights, Article 2 (2) of which states that 'No one shall be condemned to the death penalty or executed'.

---

[50] A. Dobryninas, 'The experience of Lithuania's journey to abolition' in P. Hodgkinson and William A. Schabas (eds.), *Capital Punishment: Strategies for Abolition* (2004), pp. 233–252 at 234.

[51] Parliamentary Assembly of the Council of Europe Resolution 1044 (1994), 4 October 1994.

[52] Council of the European Union, *Guidelines to EU Policy towards Third Countries on the Death Penalty*, Brussels, 3 June 1998; and *Death is not Justice: The Council of Europe and the Death Penalty* (updated March 2004). Also E. Girling, 'European Identity and the Mission against the Death Penalty in the United States' in A. Sarat and C. Boulanger (eds.), *The Cultural Lives of Capital Punishment: Comparative Perspectives* (2005), pp. 112–128.

The diplomatic offensive has been pursued through regular EU Human Rights Dialogues and Seminars with China and Vietnam. European Union and Council of Europe delegations have gone to or held seminars in many countries.[53] The EU has also been active in lobbying through diplomatic *démarches*. According to the UN Seventh Quinquennial Survey, the EU Presidency during the years 1999 to 2003 regularly sent letters to Governors and Boards of Pardons in the USA to plead for the reprieve of persons under imminent threat of execution, although none proved to be successful.[54] In addition, the EU has regularly provided an *Amicus Curiae* (Friend of the Court) brief to the United States Supreme Court when it has considered death penalty cases which raise constitutional issues, such as those relating to juveniles and the mentally retarded.[55] Furthermore, the EU has supported projects in other countries, especially by providing training for lawyers, parliamentarians and opinion-makers in states that still retain the death penalty,[56] as well as promoting research in China and Trinidad.

The EU made a veiled threat of more direct pressure when issuing, in July 2001, a resolution on 'The Death Penalty in the World', which called for a worldwide moratorium on executions. It stated that this was 'an essential element in relations between the European Union and third countries and one that should be taken into account, in concluding agreements with third countries'.[57] As a mark of its distaste for the continuation of capital punishment in the USA and Japan, the Parliamentary Assembly of the Council of Europe passed a resolution in June 2001 to remove the observer status of both these countries unless they made 'significant progress' on abolishing executions by 1 January 2003.[58] In October 2003 the Parliamentary Assembly found these countries 'in violation of their fundamental obligation to respect human rights due to their continued application of the death penalty'. They were given until the end of 2006 to comply, but have not done so. In October 2003 the European Presidency made a further declaration in support of a universal moratorium on capital punishment to mark the first 'World Day against the Death Penalty' and the European Parliament backed this up by adopting a resolution in favour of a universal moratorium on the death penalty to be promoted by the United Nations.[59] October 10 has been declared

[53] Such as Belarus, Botswana, Guinea, Japan, Lebanon, Malaysia, Palestine Authority, Philippines, Russia, South Korea, Sri Lanka, Taiwan, Uzbekistan, and Vietnam.

[54] Such letters have been sent to Alabama, Arkansas, Arizona, Georgia, Kentucky, Illinois, Mississippi, Missouri, Nevada, New Mexico, North Carolina, Ohio, Oklahoma, Tennessee, Texas, Virginia, and the US government.

[55] Jon Yorke, 'The Evolving European Union Strategy Against the Death Penalty: From Internal Renunciation to a Global Ideology—Part 2' *Amicus Journal* 17 (2007), pp. 26–33 at 29–30.

[56] *EU Policy and Action on the Death Penalty* at: <www.eurunion.org/legislat/DeathPenalty/deathpenhome.htm>.

[57] *Death Penalty in the World*, adopted by the European Parliament on 5 July 2001, para. 10.

[58] Resolution 1253 (2001) adopted on 25 June 2001.

[59] Minutes of 23/10/2003—final edn. The European Parliament had also passed resolutions applauding developments or discussions relating to the possible abolition of the death penalty in other countries, such as South Korea and Taiwan as well as in Japan: P5_TA (2002) 0332.

'European Day against the Death Penalty' from 2007 onwards.[60] In an attempt to keep up the pressure, the European Parliament, in January 2007, expressed its deep concern at 'the execution of thousands of people each year' when resolving to strongly support a further initiative at the United Nations General Assembly in 2007 to secure a universal moratorium (see below, pages 33–34).[61]

Some European scholars have suggested that, notwithstanding Article 6 of the ICCPR, the time has come to recognize that article 7, which states categorically that 'no one shall be subject to torture or cruel, inhuman or degrading punishment' should be interpreted to ban capital punishment.[62] Indeed, in the Grand Chamber judgment of 12 May 2005 in *Öçalan v Turkey*, the European Court of Human Rights noted that capital punishment in peacetime had come to be regarded as an unacceptable form of punishment which was no longer permissible under Article 2 of the ECHR, guaranteeing the right to life, thus endorsing the view that capital punishment amounts to a form of inhuman treatment which can 'no longer be seen as having any legitimate place in a democratic society'.[63]

Both European political entities have been strongly supported by Amnesty International, founded in 1961, which has made the abolition of capital punishment one of its major goals. It now has supporters and subscribers in over 150 countries and territories, enabling it to publish authoritative reports on the status of capital punishment worldwide. There is also the European organization Hands Off Cain, founded in Brussels in 1993 but now operating from Rome, which also regularly publishes reports and has as its main goal 'a UN moratorium on executions'.[64] The French-led organization, the International Federation for Human Rights (FIDH), whose headquarters is in Paris, has sent missions to many countries not only to proclaim its opposition to capital punishment but to investigate thoroughly how it is employed, resulting in many critical reports. *Ensemble Contre la Peine de Mort* (Together Against the Death Penalty) also campaigns for moratoria across the world and on behalf of particular individuals facing execution and has organized three international congresses.[65] In May 2002, at a meeting in Rome, the World Coalition Against the Death Penalty was founded to bring together non-governmental organizations, bar associations,

---

[60] In December 2006, at the UN General Assembly, 85 countries delivered a statement during the Report of the 3rd Committee reiterating the position of the European Union.

[61] <http://www.europarl.europa.eu/news/public/story_page/015-2573-029-01-05-902-20070130STO02572-2007-29-01-2007/default_en.htm>.

[62] M. Nowak, 'Is the Death Penalty an Inhuman Punishment?' in T. S. Orlin, A. Rosas, and M. Scheinin (eds.), *The Jurisprudence of Human Rights Law: A Comparative Interpretive Approach* (2000), pp. 27–45 at 44.

[63] *Öçalan v Turkey* (Application No. 46221/99) [2003] ECHR Judgment 12 March 2003 125. The Grand Chamber on 12 May 2005 held that the imposition of the death sentence on the applicant following an unfair trial by a court whose independence and impartiality were open to doubt amounted to inhuman treatment in violation of Art. 3 of the European Convention on Human Rights; UN Doc. E/CN.4/2006/83 p. 7.

[64] Both organizations provide up-to-date information and commentary on capital punishment across the world and we draw on these resources in this and following chapters.

[65] In Strasbourg in 2001, Montreal, 2004 and Paris, 2007.

unions, local governments, and other organizations in a campaign for the universal abolition of the death penalty. It represents over 38 human rights organizations and has declared 10 October as the annual 'World Day Against the Death Penalty', on which events, rallies and demonstrations are held in many countries. On 30 November each year there is now a 'Cities for Life' event, organized by the Rome-based Community of San Edigio. This is marked by the illumination of public buildings or spaces around the world to symbolize the value of life. In 2007 buildings were illuminated in 752 cities including 33 capital cities. In addition, the European media, broadly speaking, reflects and reinforces the message against the death penalty. For example, editorials in Western European newspapers expressed almost unanimous objection to the recent executions of Saddam Hussein and his associates, despite his abhorrent regime and well-documented human rights abuses. The press in Italy and France in particular regularly report on imminent executions and unfair trials, mostly, although not exclusively, in the United States.

(d) The strategy of non-cooperation

Another way in which abolitionist countries have put pressure on those who retain the death penalty is by refusing to cooperate with them whenever they request extradition of an offender wanted for trial on a capital charge in their country. In this regard, the judgment of the European Court of Human Rights in 1989 in the case of *Soering v United Kingdom and Germany* was of cardinal significance. The Court prohibited the extradition of Soering to the State of Virginia, where he had been charged with a capital offence, on the grounds that in facing the death penalty he would suffer from 'the death row phenomenon',[66] which would amount to 'inhuman or degrading treatment or punishment', contrary to Article 3 of the ECHR, especially in light of the fact that the United Kingdom itself had abolished capital punishment for murder.[67] Since then, this has developed into a firm policy, not just concerned with the possibility of suffering on death row, but with any possibility that the person for whom extradition had been requested could be sentenced to death. Article 19 (2) of The Charter of Fundamental Rights, adopted by the European Union in Nice in December 2000, states categorically that:[68]

No one may be removed, expelled or extradited to a State where there is a serious risk that he or she would be subjected to the death penalty, torture or other inhuman or degrading treatment or punishment.

---

[66] For a full discussion of the so-called 'death row phenomenon' see Ch. 5, pp. 180–183 below.
[67] *Soering v United Kingdom*, Federal Republic of Germany intervening, 161 Eur.Ct. H.R. (Ser. A) 34 (1989).
[68] Charter of Fundamental Rights of the European Union, OJ EC 18 December 2000, 2000/C 364/1, Art. 19 (2). Also AI, *United States of America. No Return to Execution: The US Death Penalty as a Barrier to Extradition* (2001).

In July 2002 the Committee of Ministers of the Council of Europe adopted *Guidelines on Human Rights and the Fight against Terrorism*. Guideline No XIII, paragraph 2, provides that extradition of a person to a country where they risk being sentenced to death may not be granted, unless the guarantees mentioned above are given by relevant authorities in the requesting state. A similar provision was included in the Amending Protocol to the 1977 European Convention on the Suppression of Terrorism, which opened for signature on 15 May 2003. The UN Sub-Commission on the Promotion and Protection of Human Rights has urged all states to endorse this policy[69] and it has also been affirmed by the UN Commission on Human Rights.[70]

A striking illustration of how views on this issue have changed is the decision of the Canadian Supreme Court in the case of *United States v Burns* (2001).[71] Ten years earlier the majority of the Court had ruled that it was not unconstitutional for the Canadian government to extradite a person accused of capital murder to the state of Pennsylvania, which had not entered an assurance that the death penalty would not be imposed. In reaching its judgment in *Kindler v Canada (Minister of Justice)* in 1991 the majority of the Court had stated:[72]

Extraditing an individual accused of the worst form of murder to face capital prosecution does not shock the conscience of the Canadian people, nor is it in violation of international standards... In determining what is fundamentally just, the global context must be considered. Although there is a growing trend towards the abolition of capital punishment, the vast majority of the nations in the world retain the death penalty. There is no international norm.

Furthermore, when the case came before the UN Human Rights Committee in 1993, it decided by a majority of 13 to 5 that there had been no breach of Article 6 (protecting the right to life) or Article 7 of the ICCPR (cruel and unusual punishment) by the Canadian government.[73] And yet, in February 2001, the Canadian Supreme Court in *Burns* decided that his unconditional extradition to the state of Washington for the crime of murder, without assurance that the death penalty

---

[69] UN Doc. E/CN.4/Sub.2/2003/6, para. 3(a).

[70] Commission on Human Rights Resolution 2004/67.

[71] [2001] 1 S.C.R. 283, 2001 SCC 7; W.A. Schabas, 'From *Kindler* to *Burns*: International Law is Nourishing the Constitutional Living Tree', paper presented at a conference on Capital Punishment and International Human Rights Law, Galway, 20 September 2001.

[72] Criminal Reports 8 C.R. (4th) (1991), at p. 4. The minority (two justices) held that the death penalty did constitute cruel and unusual punishment, and that extradition to a state with the death penalty would therefore be a breach of the Canadian Charter. See W. A. Schabas, 'Note on *Kindler v Canada (Minister of Justice)*' *American Journal of International Law* 87 (1993), pp. 128–133; also, A. Manson, '*Kindler* and the Courage to Deal with American Convictions' *Criminal Reports* 8 C.R. (4th) (1991), pp. 68–81.

[73] W A. Schabas, 'Soering's Legacy: The Human Rights Committee and the Judicial Committee of the Privy Council Take a Walk down Death Row' *International and Comparative Law Quarterly* 43 (1994), pp. 913–923 at 916–917. However, the Human Rights Committee did hold Canada's extradition of Charles Ng to California to face execution by lethal gas to be a breach of the Convention.

would not be imposed, would violate section 7 of the Canadian Charter of Rights and Freedom (right to life, liberty, and security of the person, and the right not to be deprived thereof except in accordance with 'the principles of fundamental justice'). There is no doubt that the Court was influenced by the controversy that surrounds the use of the death penalty in the United States, particularly as regards the danger of wrongful conviction. But it further made the following telling observation:[74]

While the evidence does not establish an international law norm against the death penalty, or against extradition to face the death penalty, it does show significant movement towards acceptance internationally of a principle of fundamental justice Canada has adopted internally, namely the abolition of capital punishment...It also shows that the rule requiring that assurances be obtained prior to extradition in death penalty cases not only accords with Canada's principled advocacy on the international level, but also is consistent with the practice of other countries with which Canada generally invites comparison, apart from retentionist jurisdictions in the United States.

In South Africa, too, the Constitutional Court made it plain that the authorities had acted wrongly in deporting to the United States illegal immigrants suspected of bombing the US Embassy in Dar es Salaam in 1998, without first obtaining an assurance from the US government that the suspects would not be executed if convicted of a capital offence.[75] According to the UN Secretary General's Seventh Quinquennial Report in 2004, all but one (Cambodia) of 32 abolitionist countries that replied stated that they had adopted a policy to refuse to extradite a person charged with a capital offence to a requesting state that had not abolished capital punishment unless that state would give assurances that he/she would not be sentenced to death or executed.[76]

Significantly, at the international level, the UN Human Rights Committee, in conformity with the *Burns* decision in Canada, also reversed the views it had held in 1993 in *Kindler v Canada*,[77] when it held in August 2003, in *Judge v Canada*, that abolitionist countries had an obligation not to expose a person to the real risks of its application, as this would constitute a violation of the defendant's right to life under Article 6 of the ICCPR.[78] The Committee reversed itself on the grounds that 'since that time [1993] there has been a broadening international

---

[74] 2001 SCC7. File No.: 26129. Once the state of Washington, which had sought the extradition, had given these assurances, the prisoner and his associate were surrendered to face trial in the United States.

[75] See *Mohamed v President of the Republic of South Africa and Others* 2001 (3) SA 893. The extradition or deportation of a Tanzanian national to the United States by South Africa to stand trial on federal capital charges was judged to be an infringement of the right to life, to dignity, and not to be subjected to cruel, inhuman, or degrading punishment embodied in the South African constitution. In due course this defendant was convicted of a capital offence, but the jury in New York did not impose the death penalty.

[76] Canada said 'in all but exceptional cases' and Azerbaijan that under its law 'an extradition request may be refused where the law of the requesting State provides for the death penalty for the offence'.

[77] No. 470/1991, views adopted 30 July 1993.

[78] Case No. 829/1998 (views adopted 5 August 2003), UN Doc. A58/40 (Vol. 1) pp. 85–87.

consensus in favour of abolition of the death penalty, and in states which have retained the death penalty, a broadening consensus not to carry it out'.[79]

This policy has proved to be effective. The UN Seventh Survey found that Morocco, Trinidad and Tobago, and the Philippines had all agreed to guarantee that persons for whom they had sought extradition would not be sentenced to death. Also China has signed extradition treaties with Spain, France, and Australia in which it has agreed not to execute criminals who are repatriated to it. This development is having a profound effect on the death penalty debate in China, especially as it concerns the abolition of the death penalty for major economic crimes. Furthermore, the principal reason why the death penalty was abolished in Rwanda in August 2006 was that European countries as well as the International Criminal Tribunal for Rwanda (sitting in Tanzania) would not extradite 'masterminds' of the genocide to Rwanda for fear that they would be sentenced to death and executed. And as far as the USA is concerned, the guarantees that it has been willing to give to Mexico as regards non-imposition of death sentences on 'drug lords' has led to a considerable increase in the number recently extradited from that country.[80] There is evidence that extraditions are also rising from abolitionist countries elsewhere in the Americas, such as Colombia, whenever guarantees are given.[81]

Thus, the recognition of the death penalty as a human rights issue, combined with the development of international human rights law and the political weight that has been given to the campaign led by European institutions to get rid of capital punishment completely, is the main explanation for the surge in abolition over the past quarter of a century. Yet, how it has been achieved in particular countries, as we shall see in Chapter 2, has varied. As William Schabas has pointed out, even though international human rights law has been the most significant factor: 'There are many paths to abolition... There appears to be no formula to follow as each country finds its own path to a civilized and humane system of criminal law'.[82] Certainly, there are no instances where it was initially achieved by popular consensus or the demand of the masses, although a consensus might emerge post-abolition, as was the case in Ireland where a firm majority

---

[79] UN Doc. CCPR/L/78//D/829/1998, 2003, para. 10.3.

[80] Since 1978 Mexico had denied extradition to any country which retained the death penalty.

[81] Up from 40 in 2002 to 134 in 2005. A note of caution is necessary. In the wake of the terrorist attacks of 11 September 2001, the EU and the USA drew up a new Agreement on Extradition. Jon Yorke has pointed out that Article 13 appears to allow extradition where for procedural reasons the state cannot guarantee that the death penalty will not be imposed as long as it guarantees that it will not be carried out by execution. It is unclear whether this means that the person could remain on death row indefinitely, which would be contrary to the European Convention on Human Rights. See Jon Yorke, n. 55 above, pp. 28–29.

[82] William A. Schabas, 'International Law, Politics, Diplomacy and the Abolition of the Death Penalty' *William and Mary Bill of Rights Journal* 13 (2004), pp. 417–444 at 444. Also William A. Schabas, 'International law and the death penalty: reflecting or promoting change?' in P. Hodgkinson and W.A. Schabas (eds.), *Capital Punishment: Strategies for Abolition* (2004), pp. 36–62 at 43.

voted in 2001 to have capital punishment barred by constitutional amendment. Abolition came about everywhere through political and/or judicial leadership, sometimes aided by local pressure groups. It should be noted that among the 52 countries that first abolished capital punishment for murder since 1988, 23 enshrined it in their constitutions, and in a further five countries the Supreme or Constitutional courts have interpreted the right to life provision in their constitutions as barring capital punishment. Thus 28 of these 52 countries have made it impossible for the death penalty to be reinstated.

3. What Prospects for International Acceptance or Rejection of Capital Punishment?

(a) Disputed norms

Despite the remarkable advances made in gaining commitment from so many countries to abolish capital punishment through diplomatic initiatives, democratic developments, and international treaties, there is obviously still a considerable way to go before it is fully accepted worldwide as an 'international human rights norm'. So to what extent is resistance to abolition likely to be overcome within, say, the next few decades? Until recently, it appeared to be embedded in Asia and, with the exception of Israel (where it remains for genocide and treason during wartime), throughout the Middle East. There are now signs of change in Asia and even in the Middle East and North Africa (for details see Chapter 3).

On the other hand, it cannot be denied that there has been some strong resistance to the political movement to force change ever since the Second Optional Protocol to the ICCPR was adopted by the UN General Assembly in 1989. While 59 countries voted in favour and 48 abstained, 26 voted against the Protocol. Most of the countries who opposed its adoption had a predominantly Muslim population, but also included Japan and the United States.[83] Attempts by the abolitionist nations at United Nations Congresses,[84] in the General Assembly, beginning in 1994[85] and at the Commission on Human Rights, annually since

---

[83] For an excellent account, see William A. Schabas, *The Abolition of the Death Penalty in International Law* (3rd edn., 2002), p. 175, fn. 231. The countries which voted against its adoption were: Afghanistan, Bahrain, Bangladesh, Cameroon, China, Djibouti, Egypt, Indonesia, Iran, Iraq, Japan, Jordan, Kuwait, Maldives, Morocco, Nigeria, Oman, Pakistan, Qatar, Saudi Arabia, Sierra Leone, Somalia, Syrian Arab Republic, Tanzania, United States, and Yemen. Malaysia and Sudan apparently advised the Secretariat that they had also intended to vote against.

[84] *Report of the Eighth United Nations Congress on the Prevention of Crime and the Treatment of Offenders, Havana, Cuba, 27th August to 7 September 1990*, A/CONF. 144/28, 5 October 1990, p. 277.

[85] General Assembly, A/C.3/49/L.32, 29 December 1994.

1997,[86] to press for a resolution calling for a moratorium of death sentences and executions so that the effects can be studied, has been met with hostility from many of the retentionist nations.

In October 1999 a draft resolution (A/C.3/54/L.8) was introduced at the fifty-fourth session of the UN General Assembly by Finland on behalf of the European Union with 73 co-sponsors. This urged all states that still maintained the death penalty to comply fully with their international obligations, to observe the safeguards, to restrict progressively the number of capital offences, to establish a moratorium with a view to abolishing the death penalty completely, and to make information available to the public with regard to the imposition of the death penalty. A series of amendments was tabled, led by Egypt and Singapore (which had made a similar objection in 1994),[87] referring to the right of states to choose their own political, economic, and social systems without interference from the United Nations or other states. These amendments also attracted over 70 co-sponsors. In view of such an irresolvable difference of opinion, the co-sponsors of both the resolution and the amendments decided not to press for action on the draft resolution or the amendments when they were considered at the fiftieth meeting of the Third Committee of the General Assembly in December 1999.[88] In speaking to the European Parliament about the withdrawal, Commissioner Chris Patten stated that it was necessary 'to freeze our resolution on the death penalty or risk the passing of a resolution that would have incorporated wholly unacceptable arguments that asserted that human rights are not universally applicable and valid'.[89]

However, when a resolution calling for a moratorium was debated in the third committee in November 2007 there were sufficient abolitionist countries to overcome objections from Singapore and other states who continued to proclaim that 'there is no international consensus on whether the death penalty is a violation of

---

[86] In 1997 a resolution was adopted (27 countries in favour, 11 against, and 14 abstentions). Also, in 1999 the UN Sub-Commission on the Promotion and Protection of Human Rights (previously the Sub-Commission on Prevention of Discrimination and Protection of Minorities) called upon retentionist states to apply a moratorium on executions throughout the year 2000 in order to mark the millennium and to commute the sentences of those under sentence of death on 31 December 1999. Resolution, UN Doc. E/CN.4/SUB.2/RES/1999/4, 24 August 1999.

[87] Singapore argued that the resolution went 'some way towards dictating a particular set of values from countries which have abolished capital punishment on those which have not' (Statement by Singapore proposing no action to L.32). Seventy-one states voted in favour of this amendment, 65 against, and 21 abstained. Many of those states which had originally sponsored the resolution for a moratorium were unwilling to accept the Singaporean amendment because it failed to uphold the universal principles of human rights and made no mention of international law. As a result, 74 countries abstained and the resolution was lost. See also similar statements by representatives of Libya, Algeria, Thailand, and the United States at the 57th Session of the UN Commission on Human Rights on 25 April 2001, Press Release 25/04/01, 'Commission of Human Rights Adopts Ten Resolutions, Measures on the Death Penalty, Impunity, and Other Issues Concerning the Promotion and Protection of Human Rights'.

[88] I. Bantekas and P. Hodgkinson, 'Capital Punishment at the United Nations: Recent Developments' *Criminal Law Forum* 11(1) (2000), pp. 23–34.

[89] Quoted by Yorke, n. 41 above, at p. 23.

human rights'.[90] The resolution was passed by 99 votes to 52, with 33 countries abstaining, and endorsed by the General Assembly by 104 to 55, with 25 abstentions. The fact that only 55 countries (including China and the USA) eventually voted against a world-wide moratorium suggests that the hard opposition is weakening. For at the UN Commission on Human Rights[91] in 2005, 66 countries had dissociated themselves from the moratorium resolution on the grounds that there was, in their view, no international consensus that capital punishment should be abolished.[92]

Thus it is clear that the number of countries that refuse to accept that capital punishment is a violation of human rights and therefore should be subject to a ban under international law is declining. Yet some continue to assert that it is a matter for national criminal justice policy, to be determined by the political, social and cultural circumstances of each country. Indeed, several of them at different times have characterized such resolutions as a form of cultural imperialism, dictating a particular set of values. Amongst them are those Muslim states that base their criminal justice system on Islamic law. However, a scholar with a deep knowledge of the Muslim faith, the human rights criminal lawyer M. Cherif Bassiouni, has recently argued that there is nothing in the *Qu'rān* or the *Sunna* that requires the death penalty, save perhaps for the crime of brigandage[93] when a death occurs: for all other crimes it is optional, not mandatory. There is much debate among the different schools of jurisprudence as to whether the *Qu'rān* and the *Sunna* are to be interpreted literally, or on the basis of the intent and purpose of the text, or both. Bassiouni's view is that the interpretation of the *Qu'rān* has been dominated by traditionalists and fundamentalists, who are in the main intransigent and literal, whereas the few secular reformists and 'forward-thinking traditionalists' would emphasize the need to interpret scripture in the light of scientific knowledge and the Islamic emphasis on mercy in order to create a just and humane society.[94] In this regard it is interesting to note that several secular states with large Muslim majorities have joined the abolitionist movement—Azerbaijan, Bosnia-Herzegovina, Turkey, Turkmenistan, and Senegal—or are abolitionist

---

[90] *Inter Press Service*, 4 January 2007. This follows the reasoning of the Singapore Court of Appeal in *Nguyen Tuong Van v Public Prosecutor* [2004] SGCA 47 which held that 'While the prohibition against cruel and inhuman treatment or punishment was a widely-accepted rule in customary international law, there was neither a general customary international law prohibition against the death penalty nor a specific customary international law prohibition against hanging as a mode of execution' [2005] SLR, 103 at 106.

[91] In 2005 the Commission became the UN Human Rights Council, with 47 member states, set up to conduct regular reviews of the human rights records of all countries.

[92] Amnesty International, *Death Penalty Developments in 2005*, p. 12: <http://web.amnesty.org/library/Index/ENGACT500052006?open&of=ENG-LBR>.

[93] In this context, 'brigandage', or 'Haraba', is the offence of waging war against Allah and the Prophet or against the rulers of Islamic societies.

[94] M.C. Bassiouni, 'Death as a Penalty in the Shari'a', in P. Hodgkinson and W. A. Schabas (eds.), *Capital Punishment: Strategies for Abolition* (2004), pp. 169–185 (see further Ch. 3, pp. 72–73).

de facto—Tunisia and Morocco. Despite the attempts of some countries to block or at least delay the advancement of the international movement towards final abolition of the death penalty, there can be no doubt that they are now the voices of a minority.

(b) The significance of the USA

The United States has not embraced the aspiration embodied in Article 6 of the ICCPR and UN Resolutions to abolish the death penalty in due course. The persistence of capital punishment in the United States has become, in our opinion, one of the greatest obstacles to the acceptance of the view that this ultimate penalty inherently and inevitably violates human rights. In China, the Caribbean, and no doubt elsewhere, proponents of capital punishment point to the United States to support their view that it is not inconsistent with democratic values and political freedom. So what prospects are there that the USA might join those nations with which it shares a cultural and political heritage in abandoning capital punishment? (See further, Chapter 3).

The United States government has made its position clear in its response to the Seventh UN Survey in 2005:[95]

When administered in accordance with all the aforementioned safeguards, the death penalty does not violate international law. Capital punishment is not prohibited by customary international law or by any treaty provisions under which the United States is currently obligated... We believe that in democratic societies the criminal justice system—including the punishment prescribed for the most serious and aggravated crimes—should reflect the will of the people freely expressed and appropriately implemented through their elected representatives.

Similarly, an article by two senior lawyers from the US Department of Justice (Margaret Griffey and Laurence Rothenberg), written for the OSCE publication *The Death Penalty in the OSCE Area, 2006*, not only made claims for the deterrent value of the death penalty but brushed aside criticisms relating to 'alleged racial disparities', innocence, adequate representation, and the 'death row phenomenon'. It concluded:[96]

Despite criticism of its justness and accuracy, public support for the death penalty in the United States remains high. Proponents and supporters cite its retributive and deterrent values as both morally required and practically necessary to ensure a safe society. Its application is subject to constitutional constraints and has been tested many times in court, leading to a complex jurisprudence that serves to protect defendants' rights while also enforcing the desire of the American public for just criminal punishment.

---

[95] UN Doc. E/2005/3/Add.1, para. 17.
[96] OSCE, *The Death Penalty in the OSCE Area: Background Paper 2006*, pp. 35–44 at 44.

The negative attitude of the United States government towards international treaties, the refusal to embrace abolition even as an ideal or distant goal—as China has done—and the hesitant approach of the Supreme Court towards claims based on international human rights norms have been the main barriers to change. The USA voted against the Second Optional Protocol, and when it ratified the ICCPR in 1992 it entered reservations with regard to Article 6, which prohibits the imposition of capital punishment on a person who is under the age of 18 at the time of the commission of the offence. The USA stuck to this position even though the UN Human Rights Committee stated that the US reservation was invalid because Article 4 of the ICCPR forbids derogation from Article 6, even in time of emergency. The USA also made a reservation to Article 7, concerning cruel or unusual treatment or punishment, which it declared it would only be bound by to the extent that '"cruel, inhuman or degrading treatment or punishment" means the cruel and unusual treatment or punishment prohibited by the Fifth, Eighth or Fourteenth Amendments to the Constitution of the United States, as interpreted by the US Supreme Court'. The Human Rights Committee ruled that this reservation was also 'incompatible with the object and purpose of the Covenant' and therefore invalid. A similar situation arose with regard to the US government's ratification of the Convention against Torture and other Forms of Cruel, Inhuman or Degrading Treatment or Punishment. In its report to the UN Committee against Torture, the government claimed that it was not obliged to report on the use of the death penalty because the USA had made a condition of its ratification the proposition that the USA was only bound to Article 16 of the Convention to the extent that the definition of 'cruel, inhuman or degrading treatment or punishment' matches the 'cruel and unusual punishment' prohibited by the US Constitution as interpreted by the US Supreme Court. The USA also registered an 'understanding' that the Convention did not 'restrict or prohibit the United States from applying the death penalty consistent [with the Constitution], *including any constitutional period of confinement prior to the imposition of the death penalty*' (our emphasis).[97]

It should be noted also that the USA has signed but not ratified the American Convention on Human Rights and is thus not subject to the Inter-American Court of Human Rights. However, as Richard Wilson, has pointed out, under the American Declaration on the Rights and Duties of Man, the Inter-American Commission on Human Rights can hear individual complaints against the USA. Yet the American government has refused categorically to accept that the findings and recommendations of the Commission have any legal force. For example, in 2001, it refused to comply with a call from the Commission to commute the death sentence on Raul Garza, on the grounds that he had been denied a fair trial.

---

[97] The United States' Response to the Questions Asked by the Committee Against Torture, Geneva, Switzerland, 8 May 2006.

Garza was executed on 19 June 2001.[98] Furthermore, the USA ignored an order from the International Court of Justice in 1999 calling upon it not to proceed with the execution of a Paraguayan citizen, Angel Breard, and later a German citizen, Walter La Grand, while the Court still had their cases under consideration because of breaches of their right to consular assistance under Article 36 of the Vienna Convention on Consular relations to which the USA was a party (see further Chapter 7, pages 233–235).

However, attitudes appear to be changing, partly, it appears, in response to international pressure, or at least a growing recognition that what is happening in the world at large should be taken into account in assessing the standards to be applied where human rights are concerned. For example, the former US Ambassador to France, Felix Rohatyn, publicly declared that hostility to the death penalty in Europe had opened his eyes to the issue because it was a direct challenge to the 'moral leadership' of the United States in world affairs, and turned him from a supporter of capital punishment to a sceptic who now supported a moratorium on executions so that the whole issue could be reviewed.[99] Professor Harold Koh, US Secretary of State for Democracy, Human Rights and Labor between 1998 and 2001, recalled that capital punishment had been America's 'Achilles heel' 'in almost every multilateral human rights forum'[100] and then, with the 'war on terror' following the attacks on the United States on 11 September 2001, America became even more isolated as regards gaining extradition of those apprehended by other countries unless it would guarantee that they would not face the death penalty.

It is of great significance that in two recent landmark cases, a majority on the US Supreme Court took cognizance of the international trends and development in international customary law in interpreting what it calls 'evolving standards of decency'.[101] First, in 2002 in *Atkins v Virginia*, the court cited the worldwide condemnation of the practice of executing the mentally retarded (to use the American phrase), as laid down in the UN safeguards for those facing the death penalty, among its reasons for deciding that it should now be regarded as 'cruel and unusual punishment'.[102] In 2003, Supreme Court Justice Ruth Bader Ginsburg told the American Constitutional Society that her colleagues were looking beyond America's borders for guidance in handling cases on issues

---

[98] Richard J. Wilson, 'The Influence of International Law and Practice on the Death Penalty in the United States' in James R. Acker, Robert M. Bohm and Charles S. Lanier, *America's Experiment with Capital Punishment* (2nd edn., 2003), pp. 147–165 at 154–155.

[99] F. G. Rohatyn, 'America's Deadly Image' *Washington Post*, 20 February 2001, p. 23.

[100] H. H. Koh, 'Paying "Decent Respect" to World Opinion on the Death Penalty' *UC Davis Law Review* 35 (2002), p. 1085 at 1105. Also, M. Warren, 'Death, Dissent and Diplomacy: the U.S. Death Penalty as an Obstacle to Foreign Relations' *William and Mary Bill of Rights Journal* 13 (2004), pp. 309–337.

[101] One of the criteria by which criminal sentences are judged to be unconstitutional by the Supreme Court is that they have become contrary to 'the evolving standards of decency that mark the progress of a maturing society' (*Trop v Dulles*, 356 U.S. 86, 78 S. Ct. 590, 2 L. Ed. 2d 630 [1958]).

[102] 536 U.S. 304 (2002).

like the death penalty and homosexual rights. And then, in March 2005, by a 5–4 majority the Supreme Court decided in *Roper v Simmons* that the execution of those who had committed offences as juveniles was unconstitutional, and declared that international norms and practice—it had been shown that the USA stood alone among nations in formally approving of the practice—had 'provided respected and significant confirmation of the Court's determination that the penalty is disproportionate punishment for offenders under 18'.[103] In both these cases, the Court had received *Amici Curiae* briefs from the EU and other organizations representing the international community, as well as from former United States diplomats, in support of the petitioners (see further Chapter 6, sections 4 and 5). To what extent the Supreme Court will build on these judgments, as capital punishment comes under more and more critical scrutiny in the USA, remains to be seen. It will depend on what the balance is between those who believe that international norms are relevant to US law in assessing 'evolving standards of decency', and those who side with Justices Scalia and Thomas who believe that it is not at all relevant. In this regard, a note of caution needs to be expressed, given the testimony of new Supreme Court Justice Alito before the Senate Judiciary Committee on his nomination. He declared 'I don't think it appropriate or useful to look at foreign law in interpreting the provisions of the Constitution. I think the framers would be stunned by the idea that the Bill of Rights is to be interpreted by taking a poll of countries of the world'.[104]

International criticism has continued unabated. Thus, in July 2006, the UN Human Rights Committee, when considering the report by the USA under Article 40 of the ICCPR, included, in its observations, a statement calling for a moratorium to be placed on capital sentences 'bearing in mind the desirability of abolishing the death penalty'. It criticized the USA for expanding the scope of capital punishment and urged a review of federal and state legislation so as to restrict the number of crimes carrying the death penalty. It also expressed concern that studies had shown that 'the death penalty may be imposed disproportionately on ethnic minorities as well as on low income groups, a problem which does not appear to be fully acknowledged'.[105] The International Committee of the National Association of Defense Lawyers (in a paper prepared by the co-chair Sandra Babcock) was 'troubled by its [the USA's] failure to adequately address human rights violations relating to the administration of the death penalty nationwide'. While applauding 'the important measures to prohibit

---

[103] 543 U.S. 551 (2005).

[104] See the strong criticism of this statement by former ambassador F. G. Rohatyn, 'Dead to the World' *The New York Times*, 26 January 2006. Justice Alito replaced Justice Sandra Day O'Connor, who in *Roper v Simmons* had sided with those who believed that the international experience was relevant, although she had not voted with the majority on other grounds.

[105] UN Human Rights Committee, 87th session, 10–28 July 2006, CCPR/c/USA/co/3/Rev.1 para. 29, p. 9.

the application of the death penalty to juvenile offenders and the mentally retarded...andwelcom[ing] the Supreme Court's newfound willingness to consider international law in assessing whether certain aspects of the death penalty violate the Eighth Amendment to the United States Constitution' it attacked the USA for failing to deal with five issues: arbitrary and discriminatory imposition of death sentences; failure to restrict it to the most serious crimes by retaining the felony murder rule; the execution of the severely mentally ill; for allowing severely painful lethal injection as the method of execution; and for death row conditions and the effects on the mental health of prisoners awaiting execution.[106]

When these criticisms are added to the growing unease about the administration of capital punishment throughout the USA, to the falling number of death sentences imposed[107] and executions carried out during this century, and the small number of states that regularly put offenders to death (see Chapter 3), it is not inconceivable that before many years have passed the Supreme Court will decide, in line with the practice of those countries with which it shares a common intellectual and legal culture, that capital punishment is truly beyond the standard of decency expected of a liberal democratic nation.

[106] *Report on the Death Penalty*, Executive Summary, p. 1: <http://ohchr.org/english/bodies/ hrc/docs/ngos/death%20penalty%20shadow%20rpt%20final.pdf>. It should be noted that in September 2007 the US Supreme Court agreed to consider the constitutionality of the drug protocol used in lethal injections in the state of Kentucky (*Base v Rees* No. 07–5439). The Court has since then upheld applications from prisoners in other states to stay executions by lethal injection until the Kentucky case is decided in the spring of 2008, raising the likelihood of a moratorium until this issue is settled. For further discussion see Ch. 5, p. 165.

[107] Information from the Death Penalty Information Center website: <http://www. deathpenaltyinfo.org/article.php?&did=2026.#sentence>.

2

In the Vanguard of Abolition

The objective of this and the following chapter is to chart the extent to which, and the processes through which (as far as can be ascertained), the abolition of capital punishment has been achieved in different parts of the world. Chapter 2 discusses those areas where abolition has almost everywhere been achieved: namely, Western Europe and Australasia, Eastern Europe, countries of the former Soviet Union, and South and Central America. Chapter 3 will deal with those areas of the world where the question of abolition, although making progress under the influence of the forces described in Chapter 1, is still contested: Africa, the Middle East, Asia, the Anglophone Caribbean, and the United States of America.

1. Western Europe and Australasia: Death Penalty Free Zones

As explained at the beginning of Chapter 1, the roots of the movement to abolish capital punishment are to be found in the liberal utilitarian and humanistic ideas that swept through Europe at the end of the eighteenth century. Portugal[1] was the first major European country permanently to abolish capital punishment for murder in 1867, and indeed no one had been executed there since 1849. It was followed before the end of the nineteenth century by the Netherlands, Romania, Italy, the Republic of San Marino, and the Federal Council of Switzerland (although two cantons quickly reverted to it). Norway, after the turn of the century, was the first of the Scandinavian countries to become abolitionist and was followed after the First World War by Sweden, Iceland, and Denmark. Most of these countries had followed the path described by Ancel (see Chapter 1, page 12) of abolition by stages, beginning with the restriction of offences to which it could be applied, followed by a lengthy period of non-enforcement (abolition *de facto*), leading to the final stage of abolition *de jure*.

However, taking Western Europe as a whole, the paths taken to reach abolition were nationally idiosyncratic. For example, abolition of the death penalty in Italy took a contorted route. First abolished *de facto* in 1876, then *de jure*

---

[1] Although executions for military crimes took place between 1916 and 1918.

in the New Code of 1889, it was restored by Mussolini in 1926 and expanded in the Penal Code of 1930. However, with the end of the Second World War and the fascist tyranny, capital punishment for all ordinary offences in the penal code was abandoned in 1944. After a short period of reintroduction in response to an outbreak of banditry, it was again abolished in 1947 for all but military offences during wartime. It was not until 47 years later, in 1994, that this country, which is now in the vanguard of the abolitionist movement, finally abolished capital punishment for all crimes. In Germany, where there had been substantial progress towards abolition prior to the rise of fascism, the experiences of the holocaust and other barbarities ensured that Article 102 of the Federal Republic's new Constitution of 1949 abolished the death penalty for all crimes in all circumstances, despite the fact that there were strong pressures domestically to retain it for murder.[2] Finland, where no one had been executed for murder since 1826, carried out executions for wartime offences during the Second World War, but abolished capital punishment for all ordinary crimes in 1949. So did Monaco in 1962, although no executions had been carried out there since 1847.

Yet, when Marc Ancel carried out his survey for the Council of Europe in 1962, executions for murder in non-Communist Europe were still being carried out, although by that time quite rarely, in the United Kingdom, France, Cyprus (the last being carried out in that year), Greece, Spain, and Turkey. It was on the statute books for murder in the Irish Republic, but the last hanging had taken place in 1954. Luxembourg and Belgium also retained it for murder, but the last time they had carried out executions was in 1949 and 1950 respectively, and only for collaboration with the enemy and other wartime offences. In addition, apart from West Germany, every Western European government that had by that time abolished the death penalty for murder had nevertheless retained it for possible use in relation to offences against the state, such as treason and for military offences in time of war. And indeed it had been used quite extensively after the Second World War to punish 'Quislings' (named after the Norwegian collaborator) and other war criminals by Norway, Denmark, and the Netherlands. It seemed that Marc Ancel's view, that 'even the most convinced abolitionists realize that there may be special circumstances, or particularly troublous times, which justify the introduction of the death penalty for a limited period' still had considerable support.[3]

Belgium finally abolished the death penalty for all offences in 1996 by an amendment to its Constitution, although only one execution for murder had taken

---

[2] Richard J. Evans, *Rituals of Retribution: Capital Punishment in Germany 1600–1987* (1996), pp. 613–737 at 630 and 795.

[3] Marc Ancel, *The Death Penalty in European Countries: Report, Council of Europe* (1962), p. 3. Also Amnesty International, *The Death Penalty in Wartime: Arguments for Abolition* (1994), AI Index: ACT 50/01/94.

place since 1863—in 1918—and none for any offences since 1950.[4] In Cyprus there were no executions for 21 years before capital punishment was abolished for premeditated murder in 1983, but another 19 years passed before it was extinguished for treason and military offences in 2002. An even more extreme example is the principality of Liechtenstein, which formally abolished capital punishment for all crimes in 1987 although no one had been executed since 1785.

The United Kingdom provides a good example of how long and tortuous the road to abolition could be. In 1810 there had been at least 223 offences punishable by death, but the number of persons executed was not so large. For instance, between 1800 and 1810, 939 persons were capitally convicted but only 123 executed. Furthermore, the 67 people who had been executed in 1810 had, between them, been convicted of only 14 of the very much larger number of capital crimes on the statute books: 18 of them for burglary, 18 for forgery, and only 9 for murder.[5] Those who wished to see the capital statutes reformed, led initially by Sir Samuel Romilly,[6] wished to see a wholesale amelioration of the severity of the criminal law. To sentence so many people to death, yet execute so few, was bound to lead to arbitrariness in the infliction of death. The threat that a death sentence might be imposed for a minor offence inhibited prosecutors from bringing cases to court and, when they did, juries often refused to convict the defendants. The old 'bloody code' of criminal justice, based on haphazard and random enforcement backed up by the terror of capital punishment, was to be replaced by a system of policing to try to ensure more certainty of punishment, and penalties that were proportionate to the crime committed. It was to this Benthamite utilitarian philosophy that the Criminal Law Commissioners appointed in 1833 were devoted. They held that punishments should be proportionate to the crime, both to reflect public values of the graded seriousness of offences and to discourage people from committing a worse rather than a lesser crime. If all crimes were to be punished, even if only occasionally, by the same penalty, why would one refrain from committing the greater crime? If robbers were to be deterred from murder the penalty for robbery should be less than that for murder.

So successful was the campaign that by the early 1840s murder had become in practice the only crime for which people in England and Wales were executed and in 1861 capital punishment was abolished in law for all crimes save murder and crimes against the state—treason, piracy, and arson in Her Majesty's dockyards—which were only in practice enforced (and then very rarely) in wartime.

[4] Philippe Toussaint, 'The Death Penalty and the "Fairy Ring"', in Council of Europe, *The Death Penalty: Abolition in Europe* (1999), pp. 29–34.

[5] See the authoritative account of the movement to abolish the death penalty for a large number of crimes in Leon Radzinowicz, *A History of English Criminal Law, Vol. 1, The Movement for Reform* (1948), at pp. 5 and 155.

[6] Romilly was a barrister and writer who had been greatly influenced in his thinking about capital punishment by Beccaria's *On Crimes and Punishments*.

But murder (for which the death penalty was mandatory) could, of course, take many forms and soon efforts were being made to define more precisely which types of murder, in what circumstances and by what types of perpetrators, merited capital punishment. Attempts made in the 1860s and 1870s to redefine in a more restricted way the common law of murder or to divide murders into those that were 'capital' and those that were not proved to be futile. No agreement could be reached on how this could be done.[7] Nor did the judges wish to be given the power to exercise discretion for, as the Lord Chancellor put it, the sentence of death would 'become the sentence of the Judge and not of the law ... [this] would place the judges in a position of very considerable embarrassment, and perhaps impair the respect in which they are held'. It was thus clear that the judiciary recognized that public opinion did not always favour capital punishment.[8] So, in order to restrict the death penalty to 'real murder', the system of clemency known as the Royal Prerogative of Mercy, exercised in practice by the Home Secretary [the nearest English equivalent to a Minister of Justice], was widely employed. Between 1900 and 1949, 1,080 men and 130 women were sentenced to death of whom 435 men (40%) and 118 women (90%) were reprieved and their sentences commuted to life imprisonment.[9]

Late Victorian society, with its emphasis on individual responsibility and the need for harsh deterrents, seen notably in the dreaded prison system and in the workhouses of the Poor Law, had become unsympathetic to the abolitionist movement. Even that great liberal thinker John Stuart Mill spoke out against abolition and the philanthropists who supported it for the gravest of cases. He declared that abolition would bring 'an enervation, an effeminacy, in the general mind of the country'. By taking the life of a man who has taken another's life 'we show most emphatically our regard for it, by the adoption of a rule that he who violates that right in another forfeits it for himself', he declared. In 1868 public executions were abolished and the whole apparatus was hidden from public view.[10]

No major moves to bring about abolition took place for another 50 years until the second Labour administration in 1929 set up a Select Committee of the House of Commons 'to consider the question of capital punishment ... and to report whether any penalty, and if so, of what nature, should be substituted for the sentence of death in such cases where that sentence is prescribed by law'. A bare majority of the Committee (six Labour members and two Liberals) recommended that the death penalty should be abolished for an experimental period of five years, and life imprisonment substituted for it of the kind that reprieved

---

[7] See Leon Radzinowicz and Roger Hood, *A History of English Criminal Law, Vol. 5, The Emergence of Penal Policy* (1986), pp. 661–671.

[8] *Ibid.*, p. 677.

[9] *Report of the Royal Commission on Capital Punishment 1949–1953* (Cmd. 8932, 1953), p. 13.

[10] Victor Gatrell, *The Hanging Tree. Execution and the English People 1770–1868* (1994), pp. 589–590.

murderers underwent. However the seven Conservative members resigned from the committee and refused to sign the report. Leon Radzinowicz regarded this as 'the seeds of a fundamental [political] discord which had a paralysing effect' for the next 35 years.[11]

When a Labour Government was returned to Parliament in 1945 after the Second World War, with a large majority, the abolitionists expected immediate success and with good reason. They had, before a 1938 Bill had to be withdrawn on account of impending hostilities, managed to secure support for a motion to the effect that the House of Commons would welcome legislation which would suspend capital punishment for a five-year period in time of peace. But the post-war Labour Cabinet, after considering the issue on six occasions, decided not to include the abolition of the death penalty in its flagship Criminal Justice Bill, introduced in 1947, despite the fact that it would have had a majority in the House of Commons to pass the Bill. The Cabinet had come collectively to the view that it would prove too controversial and assessed, quite rightly, that even if it were to be approved by the House of Commons it would be fiercely resisted in the Conservative-dominated House of Lords. A long constitutional battle would then ensue. A fight over abolition of the death penalty was not to be allowed to impede its other social legislation that was creating the Welfare State. In other words, abolition of capital punishment was not the top priority of this reforming government. It was simply 'not an opportune time for abolishing capital punishment'.[12]

In an attempt to find a solution the post-war Labour government established a Royal Commission in 1949 to review not whether capital punishment should be abolished completely, but whether 'liability to suffer capital punishment for murder...should be limited or modified, and if so, to what extent and by what means'.[13] After lengthy consideration of a great deal of evidence the Commission, when it reported in 1953, rejected the idea that it was possible to define in statute those murders that were 'death worthy' and those that were not. In telling passages the Commission stated:[14]

It is impracticable to frame a statutory definition of murder which would effectively limit the scope of capital punishment and would not have over-riding disadvantages in other respects...We conclude with regret that the object of our quest is chimerical and that it must be abandoned.

[11] Leon Radzinowicz, *Adventures in Criminology* (1998), p. 247.

[12] Andrew Rutherford, 'Abolitionism: A Tale of Two Struggles' in Peter Hodgkinson and Andrew Rutherford (eds.), *Capital Punishment. Global Issues and Prospects* (1996), pp. 261–277 at 263. For a detailed study of the attitude of the Labour Party see Victor Bailey, 'The Shadow of the Gallows: the Death Penalty and the British Labour Government, 1945–1951' *Law and History Review* 18 (2000), pp. 305–350.

[13] For an excellent account of the issues faced by the Royal Commission by an insider member, see Sir Leon Radzinowicz, *Adventures in Criminology* (1998), p. 252.

[14] See *Report of the Royal Commission on Capital Punishment 1949–1953* (Cmd. 8932, 1953), para. 483, p. 167, para. 534, p.189 and Conclusion 39, p. 278.

The Commission concluded that the only workable solution would be to leave the decision to the discretion of the jury. But recognizing that many would find this 'unBritish' solution unpalatable and unworkable, it stated boldly:[15]

If this view were to prevail, the conclusion to our mind would be inescapable that in this country a stage has been reached where little more can be done effectively to limit the liability to suffer the death penalty and that the real issue is now whether capital punishment should be retained or abolished.

The Conservatives were again in power when the report was published and, being generally in favour of no change whatsoever, they took their time. It was two years before the report was debated in the House of Commons, when a motion to suspend the death penalty for five years was defeated by 245 votes to 214.

However, the climate had changed, and it was not politically feasible for the government to ignore the issue. Public debate had been inflamed by three executions. First there was the case of Timothy Evans, a man of very limited mental ability, put to death in 1950 after confessing to the murder of his wife and baby daughter, only for the public to be shocked when it transpired three years later that the real murderer of his wife, and probably his baby daughter, had been John Christie, a mass murderer of women who had been living in the same house. Evans was granted a posthumous free pardon in 1966. Then there was the case of 19-year-old Derek Bentley, a man with the mental age of 11, executed in 1953 for his part in a burglary at a warehouse in which his 16-year-old companion, Christopher Craig, shot a policeman dead. Bentley had been in police custody for 15 minutes when the fatal shot was fired and the only case against him was that he was said to have shouted 'let him have it Chris'. It was disputed whether he had ever said such thing, and even if he had it was 15 minutes before the shot was fired, and it was persuasively argued that he really meant 'let him have the gun', not 'shoot the unarmed policeman'. Not surprisingly, the case created a swell of public sympathy for Bentley (he was eventually posthumously exonerated in 1998). Craig, being a juvenile, was sentenced to detention 'during Her Majesty's Pleasure'. He served 10 years and afterwards lived a blameless life. Public sympathy was probably even greater for a young woman, Ruth Ellis, executed in 1955 for what the French would call a *crime passionnel*: shooting dead her abusive lover (and at the same time slightly injuring a passer-by). All this public disquiet led to the founding of the National Campaign for the Abolition of Capital Punishment, which had amassed 30,000 members by January 1956.

A Conservative government was then in power. Ignoring the Commission's warnings, it went ahead with legislation—the Homicide Act of 1957—which aimed to define a narrow group of mandatory 'capital murders'. This 'most serious' group consisted of murders committed in the course or furtherance of theft or robbery, by using firearms or explosives, of police or prison officers, or multiple

---

[15] *Ibid.*, at para. 611, p. 214.

murders. These were the types of murder which it was believed would be likely to be committed by 'professional criminals'—not as a result of emotional turmoil or sudden loss of control but as a result of premeditated intent. Under this formula, most killers of young children for sexual purposes were spared, as were most who committed violent crimes, unless they committed theft before or afterwards; those who shot their lovers committed capital murder but not those who strangled, bludgeoned or poisoned them to death. So many anomalies occurred that considerable public sympathy welled up for some of those who had committed crimes that were subject to capital punishment yet were less heinous than those committed by others whose offences did not fall under the definition of 'capital murder'.

Labour was back in power in 1964. Harold Wilson, the new Prime Minister, had promised, if elected, to give time for a Private Member's Bill to abolish capital punishment. On a free vote, Silverman's Bill was passed by the Commons by 355 to 170 and in the Lords by a majority of 100. This time, the Lord Chief Justice, Lord Parker, told the House of Lords that he and the Queen's Bench Judges were unanimous on the question of abolition, for the Homicide Act had produced so many absurdities and injustices that they were 'completely disgusted as a result'.[16]

While the formula agreed in 1965 was the old one of suspension for a period of five years, to expire on 31 July 1970, unless both Houses of Parliament determined by affirmative resolutions that it should not expire, this was in reality the end of capital punishment for murder. In 1969 the House of Commons endorsed the 1965 Act by 343 to 185; in the Lords an attempt was made to extend the 'trial period' by three years, but after that was defeated the Lords accepted without division the 1965 legislation. Thus there had been, as the criminologist Andrew Rutherford has pointed out, a 'huge shift of opinion among Conservative parliamentarians... From the mid-1950s a solid abolitionist view was shared widely by much of Britain's elite'.[17]

Even so, successive governments, Labour as well as Conservative, regarded the question of the death penalty as one that ought to remain subject to the 'conscience' of individual Members of Parliament. Although the United Kingdom was a member of the Council of Europe, there was no enthusiasm for embracing international treaties to ban the death penalty. Between 1969 and 1993 there were repeated attempts—13 in all—made by Conservative Members of Parliament to persuade the House of Commons to reintroduce the death penalty for certain categories of murder, such as causing death through terrorist acts, in 1982 and 1983, or the murder of a child, in 1987. They were defeated for the same reasons that the Homicide Act of 1957 was scrapped; namely, that to pick out one or two classes of murder as deserving of death, when there might be equally heinous

---

[16] *House of Lords Debates*, Vol. 268, cols. 479–483.
[17] Rutherford, n. 12 above, at p. 264.

offences committed in categories of murder not subject to capital punishment, would inevitably produce anomalies and a sense of injustice.

But what put an end to these debates was a shocking spate of wrongful and unsafe convictions for just such offences. The most notable were the cases of the 'Birmingham Six', the 'Guildford Four', and the Price Sisters, all wrongfully convicted of murder through 'terrorist bombings', and Stefan Kisko, a man of limited intelligence, wrongfully convicted of a child sex murder. All would certainly have attracted the death penalty had it been available. This persuaded many who had previously supported the reintroduction of capital punishment to change their minds: most prominent among them was the then Conservative Home Secretary, Michael Howard. On the last occasion that the question of the reintroduction of capital punishment was debated in the British Parliament—14 years ago, in 1994—the motion was defeated by a very large majority.[18] Subsequently, in 1998, an amendment to criminal justice legislation, introduced not by the government which still insisted that it should be a matter for a free—non-party—vote,[19] but by a member of the House of Lords, abolished capital punishment for piracy, for which it had remained unused for very many years, as well as for treason.[20] This was followed in the same year by abolition for all offences under military law. It should be stressed, however, that *de facto* abolition had been achieved in 1965, the last execution in the United Kingdom having been carried out 44 years ago in 1964. Nevertheless, it was not until 1999 that the United Kingdom ratified Protocol No. 6 to the ECHR and Protocol No. 2 to the ICCPR, marking the final rejection of capital punishment by international treaty.

Executions for murder continued to be carried out in France until 1977. But there was no long hiatus before complete abolition was achieved in 1981.[21] This can be attributed to the strong political leadership from the head of state. Francois Mitterrand had, in 1981, when campaigning in the presidential election, declared his opposition to capital punishment even though opinion polls showed that 63 per cent of the public favoured retention. On his election he appointed as his Minister of Justice the distinguished lawyer Robert Badinter, a long-time opponent of the death penalty, who resolutely pushed the law to abolish capital punishment through the French National Assembly, with some support from the political right as well as solid support from the left.[22]

[18] Gavin Drewry, 'The Politics of Capital Punishment' in G. Drewry, G. and C. Blake (eds.), *Law and the Spirit of Inquiry* (1999), pp. 137–159 at 151 and 154. Also, Lord Windlesham, *Responses to Crime*, Vol. 3 (1996), pp. 60–61.

[19] The Home Office Minister, Alan Michael, had announced in the House of Commons on 23 June 1997 that the government had no plans to abolish the death penalty for treason and piracy and that it remained a matter for a free vote.

[20] The last person executed for treason was the wartime propagandist for Germany, 'Lord Haw Haw', who was hanged in 1946.

[21] UK: Human Rights Act 1998, s 21 (5); France: *Textes nationaux, Abolition de la peine de mort* (1981).

[22] By a majority of 368 to 113 and in the Senate by 160 votes to 126. For a full account see Robert Badinter, *L'Abolition* (2000), pp. 255–315.

In its reply to the fifth United Nations survey, in 1995, Switzerland stated that it had abolished the death penalty for military offences in 1992 because it constituted 'a flagrant violation of the right to life and dignity...the arguments in favour of the abolition of the death penalty in peacetime are just as valid concerning its abolition in wartime because there cannot be two ways to guarantee human rights'.[23] Spain, which had immediately abolished capital punishment for murder after the fall of General Franco's regime in 1978, did not abolish it for all crimes until 1995, having taken the view 'that the death penalty has no place in the general penal system of advanced, civilized societies...What more degrading or afflictive punishment can be imagined than to deprive a person of his life'.[24] And Greece, which had expressed similar sentiments when it abolished capital punishment for ordinary offences in 1993[25]—'human life is of supreme value...[and] efficiency of the death penalty has been proven non-existent'— nevertheless retained remnants of capital punishment in its military code until November 2004, when ratification of Protocol No. 13 to the ECHR was approved by the Greek Parliament, thus abolishing the death penalty for all crimes.

Turkey remains on the edge of Europe, although it has been a member of the Council of Europe since 1949. After a lengthy moratorium on executions between 1973 and 1980, the Turkish military junta, in power from 1980 to 1983, judicially executed 48 people, 25 for politically related offences and 23 for common crimes. Since the return to civilian government only two executions were carried out, the last in 1984 and both for politically motivated homicides. Nevertheless, death sentences continued to be imposed. In 1999 the Kurdish rebel leader Abdullah Öcalan was sentenced to death for treason and separatism, sparking international protests. His appeal to the European Court of Human Rights on the grounds that his treatment infringed twelve articles of the European Convention was accepted. It was widely recognized that Turkey's hopes of membership of the EU would be gravely prejudiced were Öcalan to be executed. The death penalty was rescinded for all ordinary crimes by a constitutional amendment passed in October 2001, so that it was retained solely for crimes committed 'in times of war, imminent threat of war and for terrorism'.[26] Less than a year later, in August 2002, the Parliament of Turkey abolished the death penalty for all crimes in peacetime. Protocol No. 6 to the ECHR was ratified in 2003, and Protocol No. 13 in 2006, thus ensuring that no Turkish government would be able to return to capital punishment without breaching its international treaty obligations.

---

[23] *Capital punishment and implementation of the safeguards guaranteeing the rights of those facing the death penalty*, UN Doc. E/1995/78, para. 15.

[24] *Ibid.*, para. 17.

[25] Art. 33 of 2172/1993 (16 December 1993); see Ilias G. Anagnostopoulos and Konstaninos D. Magliveras, *Criminal Law in Greece* (2000), p. 104.

[26] Amnesty International, *Death Penalty News*, September 2001, AI Index: ACT 53/004/2001, p. 3; Mehmet Semih Gemalmaz, 'The Death Penalty in Turkey (1920–21): Facts, Truths and Illusions' *Criminal Law Forum* 13 (2002), pp. 91–122.

At first sight it may appear rather strange to group Australia and New Zealand with the Western European nations, rather than with those of Asia and the Pacific, their present-day main sphere of influence. But with regard to the death penalty they belong with the former because the history of abolition in these two countries was linked so solidly to the European values we have discussed and their progress to abolition followed so closely the European experiences. Indeed, in earlier United Nations reports it was common to group Australia and New Zealand with Western Europe.

Executions had been relatively few in New Zealand—only 20 people had been put to death between 1900 and the commutation of all death sentences by the first Labour government in 1935. By 1941 capital punishment had been abolished for murder, leaving it available solely for treason and piracy (as in the United Kingdom). It was reinstated by the government of the National Party following an election pledge in 1951, but of the 22 people sentenced to death over the following six years only eight were executed, the last in 1957. In 1961, on a free vote, a sufficient number of National Party MPs, apparently influenced by the report of the British Royal Commission on Capital Punishment, joined with Labour members to abolish capital punishment for murder.[27] Twenty-eight years later, in 1989, it was finally abolished for all crimes and New Zealand ratified the Second Optional Protocol to the ICCPR a year later.

Queensland was the first Australian state to abolish capital punishment—for all crimes—in 1922, the last execution having taken place in 1913. New South Wales abolished it for murder in 1955 after 15 years without an execution and finally for all crimes in 1985. The last execution (a most contentious one) occurred in the state of Victoria in 1967. The Federal government abolished capital punishment for all crimes in 1973 and was followed by the remaining Australian states, Western Australia being the last to abolish it for murder (and at the same time other crimes) in 1984, 20 years after the last execution.[28] Australia ratified the Second Optional Protocol to the ICCPR in 1990. However, considerable concern was expressed in 2003 in abolitionist circles in Australia about the firmness of the government's commitment to oppose the use of the death penalty for terrorists in other countries. This arose from a statement made on a television programme by the Prime Minister, John Howard, in relation to the Bali bombers in Indonesia. He said: 'they should be dealt with in accordance with Indonesian law . . . and if [the death penalty] is what Indonesia provides, well that is how things should proceed. There won't be any protest from Australia'.[29] However, his successor, Prime Minister Kevin Rudd, has now sought clemency for the Bali Nine and there is no

---

[27] Pauline Engel, *The Abolition of Capital Punishment in New Zealand* (1977).

[28] NSW Council for Civil Liberties, *The Death Penalty in Australia and Oversees*, Background Paper 2005/3 (2005), p. 2. Also, Ivan Potas and John Walker, *Capital Punishment, Trends and Issues in Criminal Justice No. 3* (1987).

[29] See NSWCCL, *Australia's policy on the death penalty*: <http://www.nswccl.org.au/issues/death_penalty/aust_policy.php>.

likelihood of change in Australia's solidarity with Western Europe in opposing capital punishment worldwide.

Thus, although there had been no single pattern by which the Western European states had finally achieved the goal of abolishing capital punishment for all crimes, they were united by the end of the twentieth century in their resolute stance against capital punishment.

2. Eastern Europe: Embracing Abolition

While Communist governments held sway in Eastern Europe under Soviet dominance, the official attitude towards capital punishment was that whilst in principle it was incompatible with socialist ideals it was nevertheless necessary as:[30]

a temporary and exceptional measure of punishment...applied pending its complete abolition, and only for specific and extremely dangerous offences which threaten the foundations of the structure of the state and society and which are committed under especially aggravated circumstances.

This was a position not unlike that taken by the People's Republic of China today (see Chapter 3).

The first country in Eastern Europe to cast this doctrine aside was the former German Democratic Republic (East Germany) which, in 1987, as part of its attempt to shore up the regime by demonstrating its concern for human rights, declared that capital punishment was no longer essential to defend socialism from violent crimes or even the legacy of Nazi war crimes.[31] Soon afterwards, the advent of democracy in nearly all the states formerly under Soviet influence created the springboard for abolishing, or substantially reducing the scope of, the death penalty.[32] And this movement was given further impetus by the desire of most of these newly free states to become members of the Council of Europe. Romania led the way by abolishing capital punishment in January 1990 immediately after the fall, summary trial by a military tribunal, and execution on 25 December 1989 of President Ceausescu and his wife on charges of genocide and undermining the national economy.[33] In Hungary the Constitutional Court, after hearing

---

[30] Reply from the USSR to the 'Questionnaire on the Implementation of Safeguards Guaranteeing Protection of Rights of those Facing the Death Penalty', United Nations, Crime Prevention and Criminal Justice Branch (United Nations, *Safeguards Survey*, 1987).

[31] Resolution of the Council of the State of the German Democratic Republic on Abolishing the Death Penalty in the GDR of 17 July 1987. The last execution had taken place in 1981. See Evans, n. 2 above, pp. 859–864.

[32] As far as the countries of Eastern Europe are concerned we have been greatly helped by the excellent Master's thesis of Eva Puhar, prepared for the National University of Ireland, Galway in 2003, *The Abolition of the Death Penalty in Central and Eastern Europe*: <http://www.wmin.ac.uk/law/pdf/Eva.pdf>.

[33] Romania became a member of the Council of Europe in 1993 and ratified Protocol No. 6 in 1994.

the proposal from the League Against Capital Punishment, declared the death penalty unconstitutional in October 1990 on the main ground that it violated the fundamental right to life and human dignity.[34] After 'the elimination of the totalitarian regime' (as the new government described it), the Parliament of the Federal Czech and Slovak Republic voted in May 1990 to abolish capital punishment. Two months later this was embodied in the constitutions of the now separate Czech Republic and Slovakia, both of which became members of the Council of Europe in that year and ratified Protocol No. 6 in 1992.

The situation in Yugoslavia has been complicated, as in so many other ways, by the break-up of the former Federal Republic in 1991. Slovenia, where there had been a strong abolitionist movement, had already abolished the death penalty under its state law in 1989 and, on becoming independent in 1991, enshrined this in its new Constitution, Article 17 of which states, 'Human life is inviolable. There shall be no capital punishment in the Republic of Slovenia'. Similarly, Macedonia and Croatia marked their independence from Yugoslavia by making capital punishment unconstitutional. The newly independent state of Bosnia-Herzegovina initially retained the death penalty, but in 1997 it was abolished when the Human Rights Chamber of the Human Rights Commission (established under the General Framework Agreement for Peace in Bosnia-Herzegovina) ruled that the death penalty could not be imposed for crimes committed in peacetime.[35] The remaining parts of the Federal Republic of Yugoslavia (comprising Serbia and Montenegro) abolished the death penalty under the Federal Criminal Code in 1993, but it was not until the end of 2001 that both states took action to abolish it for aggravated murder under state law. The Republic of Serbia amended its criminal code in November 2001 and in June 2002 the newly independent Republic of Montenegro followed suit, abolishing the death penalty for all crimes, just 13 years after the last execution had taken place in 1989.[36]

The last execution in Bulgaria was also in 1989. The following year the President commuted all death sentences to thirty years' imprisonment and established a moratorium on executions in anticipation of Bulgaria's accession to membership of the Council of Europe in 1992. It took another six years, during which the moratorium was maintained, before capital punishment was abolished completely in 1998. Also in the Balkan area, Albania moved rapidly towards formal abolition of the death penalty as the country prepared for membership of the Council of Europe. The last execution took place in 1995 and a year later the

---

[34] Constitutional Court Decision No. 23/1990 (X.31) AB on the constitutionality of capital punishment. See Tibor Horvath, 'L'Abolition de la peine de mort en Hongrie', *Revue Internationale de Criminologie et de Police Technique* 2 (1992), pp. 167–179. In 1990 Hungary became a member of the Council of Europe and ratified Protocol No. 6 in 1992.

[35] The new Criminal Code of the Bosnia-Herzegovina entity of Republika Srpska, adopted in June 2000, has no provision for the death penalty.

[36] In October 2006 the Republic of Montenegro ratified the Second Optional Protocol to the ICCPR which prohibits the use of the death penalty (it was recognized as a United Nations member state on 28 June 2006).

President of the Parliament declared a moratorium on executions.[37] In December 1999 the Albanian Constitutional Court ruled that the death penalty was unconstitutional, and in September 2000 it was removed from the Criminal Code for ordinary crimes and Protocol No. 6 to the ECHR was then ratified. Seven years later, in 2007, Albania ratified Protocol No. 13, thus abolishing the death penalty completely.

After the Second World War, the death penalty had been used in Poland—as in other communist regimes—primarily for economic and property crimes, and potential political opponents were targeted.[38] In the 1950s it was imposed with few procedural rights for defendants and largely outside the criminal law apparatus:[39]

Quasi-legal judicial bodies were created at various levels of military and common courts to hear cases that were fabricated and at which evidence was presented that was procured by use of torture . . . thousands of people were charged and executed for crimes they had not committed.

Its arbitrary application and use as a political tool eroded its legitimacy amongst the citizenry. Thus support for abolition of the death penalty, which had gathered force by the late 1970s,[40] gained momentum with the birth of the Solidarity movement.[41] Articles appeared in the influential journal *Polityka,* and the Ministerial Commission for the Reform of the Penal Law, the Centre for Civil Legislative Incentives (an organ of Solidarity), and the Congress of the Polish Bar Association all called for abolition. But it was a relatively slow process compared with some other Eastern European countries.[42] It was not until 1988 that a moratorium on executions was announced, nor until 1990, the year prior to Poland becoming a member of the Council of Europe, that capital punishment was eliminated for the offence of organizing and directing a major economic crime. Early in 1998 capital punishment was removed entirely when the new Polish Penal Code of 1996 came into effect. In its response to the Sixth UN Survey on Capital Punishment in 1999, Poland stated that the motivation for abolition was a combination of 'political will, official inquiry, and the influence of United Nations policy'. In an explanatory report on the Penal Code, the legislator stated that 'the death penalty cannot be reconciled with the principle of human dignity

---

[37] *Status of the International Covenants on Human Rights, Question of the Death Penalty,* Report of the Secretary-General submitted pursuant to Commission Resolution 1997/12, Commission on Human Rights, 54th Session, E/CN.4/1998/82.

[38] A. Fijalkowski, 'Capital Punishment in Poland: An aspect of the "cultural life" of death penalty discourse', in A. Sarat and C. Boulanger (eds.), *The Cultural Lives of Capital Punishment: Comparative Perspectives* (2005), pp. 147–168.

[39] *Ibid.,* p. 151.

[40] See Alicja Grzeskowiak, 'Capital Punishment in Polish Penal Law', *United Nations Crime Prevention and Criminal Justice Newsletter* 12 and 13 (1986), pp. 43–46 at 44.

[41] Fijalkowski, n. 38 above, at p. 153.

[42] The process is discussed in detail by Fijalkowski, *ibid.*

and contemporary values, and it also does not deter [people] from committing a crime'.[43]

However, unlike her neighbours in the West, Poland's abolitionist stance appears to be vulnerable. Poland's Law and Justice Party, which won parliamentary elections in 2005, had made the reintroduction of the death penalty for genocide and murder 'committed with extreme cruelty and motives deserving special condemnation' one of the main elements of its election platform.[44] In October 2004, the lower house of the Polish Parliament had only narrowly rejected the proposal by a vote of 198–195, with 14 abstentions. Heartened by this, conservative lawmakers announced plans to take further steps to get the death penalty restored, including notifying the Council of Europe that Poland would withdraw from the European Convention on Human Rights. In early August 2006 the President of Poland was reported to have stated that the abolition of capital punishment had been a mistake. But after condemnation by the EU, the Prime Minister made it clear that no action that would jeopardize Poland's membership of the EU and the Council of Europe was envisaged.[45] Nevertheless, until capital punishment is declared unconstitutional by Poland's Constitutional Tribunal, the political and public pressure to re-instate it may take some time to dissipate.[46]

3. States of the Former Soviet Union: From Moratoria to Abolition *De Jure*

The history of capital punishment in the former Soviet Union was turbulent. It was abolished three times, in 1917–18, in 1920–1, and for peacetime offences between 1947 and 1950,[47] but each time was soon reinstated. On each occasion the rationale for its reintroduction was based on Lenin's assertion that the death penalty was necessary to defend the revolution from its class enemies— those involved in counter-revolutionary actions, terrorist acts, or deemed to be

[43] Aleksandra Gliszczyńska, Katarzyna Sękowska, and Roman Wieruszewski, 'The Abolition of the Death Penalty in Poland' in OSCE, *The Death Penalty in the OSCE Area*, *Background Paper* (2006), pp. 9–26.

[44] According to the proposal, capital punishment would not be imposed on pregnant women or persons below the age of 18 at the time of the commission of the crime.

[45] *The Guardian*, 31 August 2006.

[46] See A. Gliszczynska, K. Sekowska, And R. Wieruszewski, 'The Abolition of the Death Penalty in Poland' in *The Death Penalty in the OSCE Area* (2006), OSCE Background Paper, pp. 19–26. Research conducted by CBOS (Public Opinion Research Centre) shows that, in the last two decades, the majority of Polish society has supported the death penalty and that this number is growing. In 2004, 77% of people polled declared that they were in favour of capital punishment, perhaps a surprisingly high proportion given that 95% of Polish citizens identify themselves as Roman Catholic.

[47] A useful short history of capital punishment in Russia and the former Soviet Union can be found in Alexander S. Mikhlin, *The Death Penalty in Russia* (1999), pp. 8–22.

members of organizations set on rebellion. Such a formula, of course, lent itself to elastic definition, and during the Stalinist period and the heyday of the Security Police thieves as well as dissidents were classed as 'enemies of the people' and therefore political offenders liable to the death penalty. The number of executions at the height of the purges of 1937–38 probably reached one million: indeed, 'taking the [twentieth] century as a whole, few countries have used capital punishment so extensively, either judicially or extra-judicially'.[48] In the 1960s the death penalty in the Soviet Union was applied not only to premeditated murder but also to certain economic crimes, aggravated rape, and hijacking.[49] However, in 1980 it was abolished for rape of an adult as part of the movement to restrict its use 'pending its complete abolition'. This was further fuelled during the period of *perestroika*, and by 1991 the USSR in its new 'Fundamentals of Criminal Legislation' restricted the scope of the death penalty from eighteen offences to five, most notably dropping economic crimes and exempting women.

With the break-up of the Soviet Union in December 1991 and the abolition of the communist system, the Russian Federation adopted a new Constitution, Article 20 of which stated: 'Everyone has the right to life' and 'Until such time as it is repealed, the death penalty may be imposed under Federal Law as an extreme measure of punishment for particularly serious crimes against life, the accused possessing the right to have his case considered by a court with the participation of sworn assessors [meaning jurors]'. Then, in 1996, President Yeltsin issued a decree declaring a moratorium on all executions in the Russian Federation.[50] The catalyst for change was Russia's desire to ally itself with Europe and to become, eventually, part of the European Union. Upon accession to the Council of Europe in 1996, Russia undertook, as a condition of membership, to abolish the death penalty and ratify Protocol No. 6 to the ECHR within three years. But so far the Russian Criminal Code and Constitution have not been amended, leaving Russia as the only country among the Council's 46 members not to have abolished capital punishment *de jure* nor to have ratified the protocols to the European Convention on Human Rights enshrining the abolition of the death penalty. Thus, in practice the Russian Federation is an abolitionist *de facto* state but one in which strong sentiments stand in the way of formal abolition. Indeed, early in 2002 a large majority of the members of the State Duma, supported by a petition signed by 100 prominent citizens, appealed to President Putin to reinstate capital punishment because of the country's high murder rate.[51] But the President has resisted this pressure, stigmatizing the calls

---

[48] Introduction by W. E. Butler to Mikhlin, *ibid.*, p. 4.

[49] Ger P. van den Berg, 'The Soviet Union and the Death Penalty' *Soviet Studies* 35 (1983), pp. 154–174.

[50] However, executions continued in the breakaway republic of Chechnya under Islamic law in 1997, 1998, and 1999. See Amnesty International, *Report 2000*, p. 202.

[51] Van den Berg, n. 49 above, p. 90, above, described the frequency of murder in Russia, about 20 homicides per 100,000 inhabitants in 1993–5, as 'appalling'. Since then it has remained at this very high level, considerably more than twice as high as the United States: William Alex Pridemore,

for restoration 'foolish', and committed himself to uphold the moratorium on the death penalty.

In any case, capital punishment was in effect made redundant by a ruling of the Constitutional Court in February 1999, which laid down (in conformity with Article 20 (2) of the Constitution) that it could only be imposed when all citizens in all the Federation's 89 republics, regions, and territories had been granted the right to jury trial. In June 1999, according to information provided by the Organization for Security and Cooperation in Europe (OSCE), the President signed a decree commuting the sentences of all convicts on death row to either life sentences or terms of 25 years' imprisonment. And, in December 2006, the Russian Parliament extended the moratorium to 2010, by delaying the introduction of juries in court cases in the republic of Chechnya. This delaying tactic is not regarded as satisfactory by the Committee of Ministers of the Council of Europe, which has called on the Russian Federation to take, without delay, all the necessary steps to transform the existing moratorium on executions into *de jure* abolition of the death penalty, to ratify Protocol No. 6 to the ECHR, and to accede to the Second Optional Protocol.[52]

By 2003 eight of the other fourteen independent states that had emerged out of Russia's former empire had abolished capital punishment for all crimes,[53] and Latvia for ordinary crimes in 1999. In the European parts of the former empire the main impetus, once again, appears to have been the desire to join the Council of Europe and eventually the European Union, as well as a need to distance new governments from the past totalitarian regime. In the new secular states of Central Asia, countries with majority Muslim populations were similarly keen to embrace human rights and follow the path to abolition.

Moldova led the way in 1995 on accession to membership of the Council of Europe, with abolition formally written into the Moldovan constitution in 2005. However, several other countries found it difficult to achieve abolition so soon after accession. Thus Estonia, which had ceased executions in 1991, took five years from its accession in 1993 to abolish capital punishment finally in 1998, and Latvia, which acceded in 1994, carried out executions until 1996 before abolishing the death penalty for all ordinary crimes in 1999.

Lithuania, which had acceded in 1993, abolished the death penalty in 1998. Parliamentarians had referred the matter to the Constitutional Court, which declared that the provisions of the criminal code were unconstitutional. Hence, abolition was achieved despite a rise in the number of murders from 224 to 442 between 1990 and 1996 and a decline in support for abolition

'Change and Stability in the Characteristics of Homicide Victims, Offenders and Incidents During Rapid Social Change' *British Journal of Criminology* 47 (2007) pp. 331–345.

[52] UN Doc. HRC 2003/4 a/59/60 (Vol. 1), p. 22; E/CN.4/2006/83, p. 7.

[53] Moldova (1995); Georgia (1997); Azerbaijan, Lithuania, Estonia (1998); Turkmenistan, Ukraine (1999); Armenia (2003).

at the same time, from 27 to 18 per cent. It seems that parliamentarians, in choosing between their constituents' support for capital punishment and the state's desire to join the Council of Europe and the EU, gave priority to the latter. The groundwork was prepared by the dissemination of findings from public opinion polls which showed that support for the death penalty was, on the whole, contingent: that the majority of both the general public and members of the legal and political élite regarded retention as only a temporary measure until the security situation could be improved. A campaign to further inform the élites of the arguments against capital punishment made it clear to many that the state should not have the right to execute its citizens, that the death penalty could be abolished if offenders were securely imprisoned, and, importantly, that the death penalty contradicted Lithuanian aspirations to enter the EU. As Dobryninas puts it:[54]

The attitude towards the death penalty in Lithuanian society became a test of the maturity of its democratic outlook and of citizens' willingness to rid themselves of its former totalitarian and inhumane system.

Ukraine agreed to an immediate moratorium on executions and to ratify Protocol No. 6 to the ECHR within three years from the date of its accession to the Council of Europe in November 1995.[55] But executions continued on a considerable scale—a total of 180 from the beginning of 1996 until the moratorium was eventually put into effect in March 1997. The then Minister of Justice, Serhiy Holovatiy, a committed abolitionist, accused the President of Ukraine of failing in political leadership by not signing the decree to implement the moratorium, but it is also true to say that there was very strong public and press opposition to abolition.[56] However, in December 1999 the Supreme Court of Ukraine ruled that all provisions of the Criminal Code relating to the death penalty were incompatible with Articles 27 and 28 of the Ukrainian Constitution.[57] Finally, in February 2000 the Ukrainian Supreme Council (Parliament) removed provisions on the death penalty from the Ukrainian Criminal Code, the Code of Prosecutions Procedure, and the Penitentiary Code.

In Georgia capital punishment was abolished on the initiative of its President, Eduard Shevardnadze, in 1997, with the support of NGOs, political parties, the Georgian Orthodox Church, and newspapers, all of whom recognized that

---

[54] Alexandras Dobryninas, 'The experience of Lithuania's journey to abolition' in Peter Hodgkinson and William A. Schabas (eds.), *Capital Punishment, Strategies for Abolition* (2004), pp. 233–252 at 234.

[55] See Amnesty International, *News Release*, AI Index: EUR 50/16/95.

[56] Serhiy Holovatiy, 'Abolishing the Death Penalty in Ukraine: Difficulties Real or Imagined?' in Council of Europe, *The Death Penalty: Abolition in Europe* (1999), pp. 139–151 at 145 and 147.

[57] Organization for Security and Cooperation in Europe (OSCE), *The Death Penalty in the OSCE Area: A Survey*, January 1998–June 1999, Review Conference, September 1999, *Background Paper* 1999/1 (1999), pp. 23–24; Council of Europe, *Compliance with Member States Commitments* AS/Inf. (1999) 2, pp. 124–125; and Holovatiy, n. 56 above, pp. 139–151.

Georgia's place in Europe was dependent on it abolishing the death penalty.[58] Following its independence from the former Soviet Union in 1990, the number of capital offences was reduced and a moratorium on executions established. This broke down in 1994 in the face of a spate of murders—which rose from 270 in 1990 to 878 in 1993—and other acts of lawlessness. Executions were resumed in 1995, but, with stability restored, in 1997 President Shevardnadze commuted all death sentences and capital punishment was abolished. However, the Constitution still stated that:

until its complete abolition the death penalty can be envisaged by organic law for especially serious crimes against life. Only the Supreme Court has the right to impose this punishment.

In December 2006 President Mikheil Saakashvili signed a constitutional amendment regarding the complete abolition of the death penalty, deleting the reservation and replacing it with 'The death sentence has been abolished'.

Furthermore, abolition was followed by a remarkable decline in murders—only 243 in 1998 and 239 in 2000—suggesting that the rate of murder had increased not because of the moratorium but because of the security situation in general. There was no popular reaction to abolition, with the governing party being re-elected after a campaign in which 'reinstatement was not an election issue'.[59]

Similarly, the complete abolition of the death penalty by the Parliament of Azerbaijan in February 1998, following a moratorium on executions since June 1993, came about as the result of a bill introduced by the President of the Republic in support of human rights, despite the strong Islamic influences in that country.[60]

The change in policy and practice in Turkmenistan (where 89% of the people are Muslim) was also remarkable. Although no official figures were published, it was thought that well over 100 people were executed in each of the years 1994, 1995, and 1996—one of the highest ratios in the world, in relation to population. The new Criminal Code adopted in 1997 provided the death penalty for as many as 17 offences, yet on 1 January 1999 the President announced a moratorium on executions and by December of that year had abolished the death penalty completely by Presidential Decree.[61]

---

[58] Death sentences do, however, continue to be imposed in the Georgian disputed region of Abkhazia (an internationally unrecognized entity). However, no executions have been carried out there since Georgia abolished capital punishment. There have been no reports of death sentences being imposed in the other Georgian disputed area of South Osetia, which uses the criminal code of Russia. See Amnesty International, *Report 2001*, p. 107.

[59] Eric Svanidze, 'Georgia, former republic of the USSR: managing abolition' in Peter Hodgkinson and William A. Schabas (eds.), *Capital Punishment, Strategies for Abolition* (2004), pp. 273–308.

[60] Amnesty International, *Concerns in Europe, January–June 2001*. AI Index: EUR 01/003/2001. In May 2001 Azerbaijan also followed the policy of the EU in forbidding extradition to countries where the death penalty would be carried out.

[61] See OSCE, n. 57 above, pp. 22–23.

Other countries formerly in the Soviet bloc responded more gradually. Armenia reduced the number of capital offences and executed no one from 1991, although death sentences continued to be imposed.[62] Ten years later, in early 2001, Armenia signed Protocol No. 6 to the ECHR, as an indication of its intentions not to revert to executions, and then abolished the death penalty completely in 2003.

Three countries—Kyrgyzstan, Tajikistan, and Kazakhstan—imposed moratoria on the death penalty. Kyrgyzstan abolished capital punishment for economic crimes as well as for several other offences when a bill was introduced in 1997 supported by the President. A year later he established a moratorium on executions and in 2002 issued a policy decree stating that 'one of the objectives for Kyrgyzstan in the field of human rights is the gradual reduction of the application of the death penalty and its eventual abolition'.[63] A new Criminal Code reduced the number of capital offences from six to three (aggravated murder, rape of under-age children, and genocide).[64] The Ministry of Justice and the Constitutional Council of Kyrgystan then developed draft laws and amendments to the constitution that envisaged abolition of the death penalty and accession to the Second Optional Protocol of the ICCPR but they were rejected by the Kyrgyz Parliament in 2005 and again in 2006.[65] However, in November 2006, President Kurmanbek Bakiyev signed a new constitution, Article 1 of which declared 'every person in the Kyrgyz Republic has an inalienable right to life. No one can be deprived of life.' In June 2007 all provisions for the death penalty were removed from the criminal code and all existing death sentences were commuted to life imprisonment, to be reviewed after 20–25 years. It now remains for Kyrgyzstan to make an international commitment not to use the death penalty by ratifying the Second Optional Protocol to the ICCPR.

The scope of the death penalty has also been considerably reduced in law in several other countries with predominant or large Muslim populations. Tajikistan, where 85 per cent of the people are Muslim, reduced its list of capital crimes in 1998 from 44 to 15; further reducing it in 2003 to five crimes.[66] Subsequently, in April 2004, the President of Tajikistan introduced a moratorium on executions without limit of time, taking it into the camp of *abolitionist de facto* states.[67] President Rahmonov based his political decision on

---

[62] Amnesty International, n. 60 above.

[63] Reported in *Agence France Presse*, 5 January 2002.

[64] FIDH, 'EU-Kyrgyzstan Republic cooperation: Human Rights violations must not be under-evaluated', 16 July 2004.

[65] Amnesty International, *Death Penalty Developments 2005*, AI Index: ACT 50/005/2006, p. 2; OSCE, *The Death Penalty in the OSCE Area: Background Paper 2005*, p. 23; *2006*, p. 60).

[66] Murder with aggravating circumstances, rape with aggravating circumstances, terrorism, biocide, and genocide. See *The Death Penalty in the OSCE Area, Background Paper 2005*, p. 30.

[67] According to OSCE, but not Amnesty International.

natural law, affirming that 'the right to life is of supreme value and no one should deprive anyone else of this right'.[68] For almost a year, following the start of the moratorium, prison terms were set at 25 years. However, in March 2005 an additional form of punishment was introduced: life imprisonment,[69] which is to be used only as an alternative to the death penalty for 'the commission of especially grave crimes' and, when, on the basis of an appeal, it is decided that the death penalty could be replaced by life imprisonment (Article 59).[70]

According to an OSCE survey in 1998–1999, the scope of capital punishment in Kazakhstan (where about half the people are of the Muslim faith) had been reduced by a new Criminal Code in 1998 to three peacetime offences: premeditated murder, aggravated murder, and genocide, plus treason in time of war and eight military crimes.[71] Twenty-two people had been executed in 2002 and another three in the first quarter of 2003. Yet in December 2003 the President introduced a moratorium on executions without limit of time, to be in place until 'the full abolition of the death penalty is resolved'. This policy was embodied in the Criminal Code. The mandatory nature of the death penalty was abolished when in January 2004 life imprisonment was introduced as an alternative. In May 2007 President Nursalan Nazarbeyev proposed that in the Constitution the death penalty should only be permitted for terrorist offences involving loss of life and for especially grave crimes committed in wartime. This, in effect, meant that Kazakhstan had become abolitionist for ordinary crimes.

Belarus and Uzbekistan are the last executioners in the new countries of the former Soviet Union. Although the number of capital offences in Uzbekistan (where 88% of the population are Muslims) has been substantially reduced—first from thirteen to eight, then in October 2001 to four and finally in 2003 to two (murder with aggravating circumstances and terrorism)—as evidence of its policy 'to abolish the death penalty by stages', there have been continuing reports to Amnesty International of large numbers of death sentences and executions. According to the Uzbek law-enforcement agencies, 62 convicts were put to death in the country in 2004. Yet, in January 2005, President Islam Karimov announced to Parliament that he was considering complete abolition and then, on 1 August 2005, signed a decree to the effect that abolition would commence

---

[68] Reported by Khalifaboro Khamidov, 'International Experience and Legal Regulation of the Application of the Death Penalty in Tajikistan' in *The Death Penalty in the OSCE Area, Background Paper 2006*, pp. 27–34 at 33.

[69] Law No. 86 of the Republic of Tajikistan, 'On Amendments and Additions to the Criminal Code' (Art. 58(1)). See K. Khamidov, n, 68 above, at p. 33.

[70] This law stipulates that life imprisonment will not be prescribed for women, persons who committed a crime while under the age of 18, and men who had turned 63 by the time of sentencing (Art. 58(1)).

[71] *The Death Penalty in the OSCE Area. A Survey, January 1998–June 1999*, s. 4.7.

from 1 January 2008. But at least one execution has taken place (on 1 March 2005) since the President's announcement.[72] However, in June 2007 Uzbekistan's upper chamber of Parliament voted to amend the Constitution so as to abolish the death penalty completely. Uzbekistan announced on 1 January 2008 that the death penalty had been abolished completely.

Belarus, arguably the last 'Stalinist' country, also reduced the number of capital offences in 1995, most notably by abolishing the death penalty for economic crimes. It is still available for 14 offences including, in addition to premeditated murder, for some political offences (crimes against the security of humanity and conspiracy to seize power). In 2004 the Constitutional Court, after reviewing the extent to which the provisions of the Criminal Code complied with the Constitution, found a number of the provisions to be inconsistent with constitutional requirements, opening up the possibility of either abolition or a moratorium on executions.

Furthermore, in June 2005 the President of Belarus emphasized the 'temporary character of the death penalty' and stated that it must be applied 'only as an exceptional measure in cases of premeditated murder with aggravating circumstances'. Thus, although there has been no moratorium on executions, the movement towards abolition and the emphasis on it being an 'exceptional measure' has resulted in a sharp decline in the number of executions carried out. In 2005 439 people were convicted of murder with aggravating circumstances and yet only two were executed, illustrating, according to some 'a *de facto* moratorium on the death penalty' and a move towards full abolition.[73] But, according to the chairperson of the Clemency Commission and a parliamentary spokesman, public opinion in favour of capital punishment is still regarded as a barrier to immediate abolition.[74]

Twenty-one states in Eastern Europe and the former Soviet Union had by the end of December 2007 ratified Protocol No. 6 of the ECHR and one (Russia) had signed it.[75] Seventeen countries had ratified the Second Optional Protocol to the ICCPR, and one (Poland) had signed it.[76]

---

[72] OSCE, *The Death Penalty in the OSCE Area, Background Paper 2005*, pp. 41–43.

[73] Gregory A. Vasilevich and Elissa A. Sarkisova, 'Prospects for Abolition of the Death Penalty in the Republic of Belarus' in *The Death Penalty in the OSCE Area, Background Paper 2006*, pp. 9–17.

[74] *Ibid.*

[75] Albania, Armenia, Azerbaijan, Bosnia-Herzegovina, Bulgaria, Croatia, the Czech Republic, Estonia, Georgia, Hungary, Latvia, Lithuania, Poland, the Republic of Moldova, Romania, Serbia-Montenegro, Slovakia, Slovenia, Macedonia, and Ukraine ratified Protocol No. 6 to the ECHR, and the Russian Federation (1997) signed it.

[76] Azerbaijan, Bosnia-Herzegovina, Bulgaria, Croatia, the Czech Republic, Estonia, Georgia, Hungary, Lithuania, Macedonia (FYROM), the Republic of Moldova, Montenegro, Romania, Serbia, Slovakia, Slovenia, Turkmenistan, and Ukraine have ratified the Second Optional Protocol to the ICCPR, and Poland has signed it.

4. South and Central America: Long-term Supporters of Abolition

South and Central America have been in the vanguard of the abolitionist movement. Venezuela, Costa Rica, and Brazil, which had already abolished capital punishment by the end of the nineteenth century, were followed soon afterwards by Ecuador, Uruguay, Colombia, Argentina, Panama, and most of the Mexican states.[77] In 1956 these nine countries were joined by Honduras, where no executions had taken place since 1940. When the revolutionary government of Nicaragua came to power in 1979, it immediately abolished capital punishment for all crimes. Four years later, in 1983, El Salvador abolished it for ordinary crimes (Article 28 of the Constitution of the Republic states that the death penalty may only be imposed when the country is at war). All attempts to reintroduce it for common crimes have been resisted by the government.

Paraguay, which had been abolitionist *de facto* for decades, finally abolished the death penalty for all offences in 1992. The Bolivian Constitution of 1967 prohibited the use of the death penalty but the Penal Code of 1973 still provided for it. This discrepancy ended in 1997 when Bolivia formally abolished the death penalty by removing all remaining capital offences from the statute book.[78] Although it has yet to be formally abolished for all offences under the military code, the Bolivian Constitution provides the overriding legal authority and the Bolivian government has confirmed, in a response to the United Nations, that capital punishment is banned entirely from civil and military law.[79]

The last execution in Chile took place in 1985 and the death penalty was abolished for a number of crimes in 1989 and finally abolished for ordinary crimes in 2001, leaving it available only in the Code of Military Justice for possible use in time of war.[80] Suriname and Belize are *de facto* abolitionist states; the last executions took place in Suriname in 1982 and in Belize in 1985. In the early 1990s, and again in 2002, concern was expressed that Belize might resume executions,[81] and although this has not materialized eight people were still on death row at the end of 2005.[82] Death by hanging had been mandatory for murder in Belize, but the 1994 Criminal Justice Act introduced the option to pass a sentence of life imprisonment in special extenuating circumstances.[83]

---

[77] For dates of abolition see Table 4, App. 1.

[78] See Amnesty International, *The Death Penalty Worldwide: Developments in 1997*, AI Index: ACT 50/04/98, p. 2.

[79] *Capital Punishment and Implementation of the Safeguards Guaranteeing the Protection of the Rights of those Facing the Death Penalty*, E/CN.15/1996/19, para. 24.

[80] Amnesty International, *Death Penalty News*, June 2001, AI Index: ACT 53/003/2001, p. 2.

[81] See Amnesty International, *Belize, Update: Death by Hanging: The Death Penalty in Belize*, AI Index: AMR 16/01/94.

[82] Amnesty International, *Report 2006*, p. 70.

[83] *Ibid.*

Despite the early advance of the abolitionist movement in South America, there have been several setbacks during periods of political instability and military rule. Both Argentina and Brazil reintroduced and then again abolished the death penalty. Brazil, which had abolished capital punishment for ordinary offences as long ago as 1882, twice re-imposed the death penalty: for politically motivated crimes of violence between 1937 and 1945 and, under a military government, for political crimes against national security between 1969 and 1979. This turned out to be of little significance because no death sentences were handed down during either of these periods. Since 1979 such offences have only been punishable by death in time of war. Attempts to reintroduce capital punishment for robbery, rape, and kidnapping leading to murder were overwhelmingly defeated in the Constituent Assembly in Brazil in 1988 and 1991, in part because the Constitution provides that there shall be no capital punishment except in time of war.[84] Brazil informed the UN that a bill to abolish capital punishment completely had been introduced in 2003 but so far no final action has been taken by the Chamber of Deputies of the National Congress.

Military governments of Argentina have reintroduced the death penalty at various times: for political offences in 1971 (but abolished just a year later in 1972, except in the Military Penal Code) and, following a military coup, for a variety of violent crimes in 1976. The civilian government again abolished it when the military junta fell. In the 1990s there were several political initiatives aimed at reintroducing the death penalty, but they all failed to get parliamentary approval after the Roman Catholic Church and several other influential organizations had expressed strong opposition. In its reply to the UN Quinquennial Survey in 2004, Argentina stated that it 'should be considered a State that has effectively abolished capital punishment'.[85]

Mexico provides a good example of a country which for a long time retained capital punishment under its Constitution but which nevertheless appeared to have no intention of using it.[86] Although the Political Constitution of the United Mexican States of 1917 provided for the death penalty for several categories of murder, in fact it was abolished by the Federal Penal Code in 1930 and eventually by all Mexican States. The last execution took place in the state of Puebla in 1937.[87] And while the Code of Military Justice provided for capital punishment for specific offences, in practice death sentences had always been commuted to long-term imprisonment. The death penalty was abolished in military criminal

---

[84] UN Doc. E/2005/3 Add. 1, para. 7.

[85] *Ibid.*

[86] For a discussion of the cultural factors behind this, see P. Timmons, 'Seed of Abolition: Experience and Culture in the Desire to End Capital Punishment in Mexico 1841–1857' in A. Sarat and C. Boulanger (eds.), *The Cultural Lives of Capital Punishment: Comparative Perspectives* (2005), pp. 69–91.

[87] By 1965, 24 of the 29 Mexican states had abolished the death penalty, and by 1975 all of them had done so.

law in April 2005 and in June 2005 the Mexican House of Representatives approved a constitutional amendment to abolish the use of the death penalty for all crimes, by 412 votes to 2. It came into force on 9 December 2005.[88]

It is not clear why it took Mexico 150 years to abolish capital punishment. The country underwent regime change after the breakdown of the authoritarian and repressive dictatorship of Santa Anna in 1855 and the liberal government prepared a new constitution which outlawed torture, illegal imprisonment, and the death penalty. However, the death penalty was only abolished for political crimes, with full abolition for ordinary crimes being contingent on the construction of a national penitentiary regime. Abolition for political crimes, in line with European liberal ideals,[89] clearly represented a shift away from the practice of various previous governments who, in the first 30 years following independence from Spain, had used death to eradicate their political opponents. In Timmons's opinion, this partial abolition was driven by symbolic gestures, as well as by pragmatic concern for their own safety from political rivals.[90] Mexican liberals, largely of European descent, believed that the civilizing process would inevitably produce the conditions when full abolition would become possible. At the start of the twentieth century Diaz's government finally constructed Mexico's first modern penitentiary but the death penalty still remained on the statute book for a century, having nothing more than symbolic significance.

Peru abolished the death penalty for all ordinary crimes in 1979, the year of the last execution, but a Bill to completely abolish capital punishment submitted to the Peruvian Congress in 1994 was unsuccessful. A resurgence of support for capital punishment came in August 2006 when the President of Peru announced that he planned to introduce a Bill or conduct a referendum in order to amend the Constitution so as to be able to reintroduce the death penalty for those guilty of the rape of children; three months later he added terrorism to this list, although this was contrary to Peru's obligations under international law.[91] In January 2007 about 3,000 Peruvians marched in the capital Lima in support of the death penalty. The President, addressing this large crowd, said 'I cannot silence the clamor of the people of Peru. I promised to introduce capital punishment... during my election campaign and I want to be honest and loyal with the people'. Claiming that 85 per cent of Peruvian households supported the death penalty for those convicted of terrorism and child rape, he proposed changing the Constitution to allow a referendum on the issue.[92] Despite this popular support, the Peruvian

---

[88] This earned President Vicente Fox the 'Abolitionist of the Year 2006 Award' by Hands Off Cain.

[89] See Leon Radzinowicz and Roger Hood, n. 7 above, at pp. 401–402.

[90] Timmons, n. 86 above.

[91] In particular, Art. 4(3) of the Inter-American Convention on Human Rights, which forbids countries that have abolished the death penalty from re-establishing it.

[92] *BBC*, 20 January 2007.

Congress rejected the draft law on the introduction into legislation of the death penalty for crimes of terrorism.

Although it extended the death penalty in 1992 to drug-trafficking activities resulting in the death of others, and in 1995 to kidnapping (contrary to its obligations under Article 4 (2) of the American Convention of Human Rights),[93] Guatemala had also appeared to be abolitionist *de facto*. Nobody had been executed since 1983 and the Chief Judge of the Supreme Court of Justice had stated that the death penalty should be abolished.[94] Despite this, Guatemala executed the first persons for thirteen years in 1996—two men convicted of the rape and murder of a child. A further execution was carried out in 1998 and two more in June 2000, when two men were put to death by lethal injection for the kidnapping and murder of a woman—executions that were televised.[95] However, there have been no more executions since then, and in November 2000 the Constitutional Court of Guatemala revoked the death sentences of five men sentenced to death under the law extending capital punishment to kidnapping, declaring that in matters of human rights international law prevails over national legislation.[96] This was reinforced in September 2005 when the Inter-American Court of Human Rights held that the introduction of the death penalty for kidnapping was a violation of the American Convention on Human Rights that prohibits the extension of the death penalty after a country has ratified the treaty.[97] In 2004 the Supreme Court proposed a new penal code without capital punishment and President Burger made a public commitment to abolish the death penalty when in Rome for the funeral of Pope John Paul II in March 2005. So did Sergio Morales, his Secretary of State in charge of Human Rights, in spite of the very high level of violence.[98] In May 2005 a draft bill to completely abolish the death penalty for all crimes was placed before Parliament and the Congressional Commission on Legislation and Constitutional Issues, but this was rejected in 2006 after the Commission returned an unfavourable verdict. At the end of 2006, 21 prisoners remained under sentence of death but no death sentences were passed and no executions had taken place up to 31 December 2007.[99]

The more than one hundred-year tradition of abolition in South and Central America now holds sway, save for Guatemala, which is clearly considering

---

[93] Christina M. Cerna, 'The Death Penalty and the Jurisprudence of the Inter-American System for the Protection of Human Rights', paper presented to the Conference on the Death Penalty, University of Galway, September 2001.

[94] Reply to UN Fifth Quinquennial Survey (1995) in 1994.

[95] Amnesty International, *Report 2001*, p. 114.

[96] Amnesty International, *Death Penalty News*, December 2000, AI Index: ACT 53/001/2001.

[97] Currently, out of the 37 persons condemned to death, 11 were found guilty of kidnapping without loss of life.

[98] FIDH, *The Death Penalty in Guatemala: On the road towards abolition*, No. 422/2 July 2005.

[99] Amnesty International, *Report 2007*. But it should be noted that in October 2007 the two presidential candidates for the November election both stated that they will remove the current de facto moratorium on capital punishment; *IPS*, 1 October 2007, cited at Hands Off Cain website: <http://www.handsoffcain.info/news/index.php?iddocumento=9327637>.

abolition, and Guyana, which can properly be considered as part of the Anglophone Caribbean (see Chapter 3, page 111). Ten South American countries have either ratified or signed the Second Optional Protocol to the ICCPR[100] and six of them plus Brazil have ratified the Protocol to the American Convention on Human Rights to Abolish the Death Penalty.[101] Eighteen South American countries which have abolished the death penalty completely, or for ordinary crimes, have also ratified the American Convention on Human Rights and are thus banned from reintroducing capital punishment.

Most countries appear to support abolition because in this respect they see themselves as heirs of the European Enlightenment and share many of the human rights values of Western Europe. Furthermore, the positive influence of Catholicism is felt across the region in the sense of a respect for the sanctity of human life.[102] Nonetheless, abolition has not proved in the past to be permanent in all parts of this region due largely to political instability. Revolutionary struggles and military coups have both brought with them for a time extreme punitive responses, but the long-term commitment to the ideal of abolition has survived.

[100] Chile, Colombia, Costa Rica, Ecuador, Panama, Uruguay, and Venezuela have ratified, and Honduras and Nicaragua have signed the Protocol.

[101] Brazil, Costa Rica, Ecuador, Nicaragua, Panama, Uruguay, and Venezuela have ratified, and Chile and Paraguay have signed the Protocol to the American Convention.

[102] The Vatican delivered a strong abolitionist message to an international conference on the death penalty in Paris, in February 2007, which referred to the 'inviolability of all human life' and stated that 'the death penalty is not just a negation of the right to life, but also an affront to human dignity'. *Catholic World News* 7 February 2007: <http://www.cathnews.com/news/702/43.php>.

3

Where Capital Punishment
Remains Contested

This chapter deals with those parts of the world where there are still countries which have yet to abolish the death penalty or even to seriously question the moral or utilitarian case for executing criminals. Yet in every one of these areas the abolitionist cause continues to make progress, if not resulting in outright abolition or a state of abolition *de facto*, at least in the reduction of executions (see Chapter 4). Those countries that support the regular use of capital punishment are becoming, even within their own regional sphere, ever more marginalized.

1. The Middle East and North Africa: Cracks in the Bastion?

Israel remains the only country in the Middle East and North Africa to have abolished the death penalty. But even Israel, which abolished it for ordinary crimes in 1954, still retains it for crimes connected with the Holocaust, although there has been only one person executed, the notorious Adolf Eichmann in 1962.[1] However, the solid support for the death penalty in the other countries of this area, so evident and readily declared during the 1980s and 1990s, is showing signs of weakening. Elected representatives, lawyers, members of the public and the clergy are beginning to question the practice or even to call for it to end forthwith. Their voices are becoming louder all the time. In 1994 the League of Arab States adopted the Arab Charter for Human Rights, but it is not yet in force 13 years later. This allows for the death penalty for 'serious crimes', but not for political crimes. If this did come into force it could well significantly reduce the rate of executions in a number of middle Eastern countries.

Three states in North Africa—Tunisia, Morocco, and Algeria—are abolitionist *de facto*, having not carried out an execution for over a decade. Tunisia, where no executions have taken place since 1991, reaffirmed its 'general moratorium on the execution of capital punishment' in its response to the seventh UN survey in 2004. No executions have taken place in Morocco since 1993.

---

[1] For an informative discussion of this case see Hannah Arendt, *Eichmann in Jerusalem: A Report on the Banality of Evil* (new edn., 1994).

Indeed, Morocco has recently affirmed a settled policy never to execute persons sentenced to death, despite no official moratorium being in force. Furthermore, it had agreed to guarantee that two persons for which it successfully sought extradition from Spain in 2002 and 2003 would not be executed. Meanwhile, according to a report in January 2007 from the Italian-based organization *Adnkronos International*, a commission of jurists set up to review the Moroccan criminal code has been considering favourably the abolition of the death penalty.[2] In January 2007 Morocco hosted a press conference in preparation for the *3rd World Congress Against the Death Penalty* in Paris, at which the head of Morocco's state-appointed consultative committee on human rights confirmed that there is a consensus within Parliament to abolish the death penalty when conditions are right.[3] A bill has been drawn up, with the support of the King, but has yet to be presented to Parliament, probably due to a spate of suicide bombings.[4] However, in February 2007, immediately after the King's wife gave birth to the ruling couple's first daughter, Morocco's Minister of Justice, Mohamed Bouzouba, appeared on nation-wide television announcing a royal pardon for almost 9,000 prisoners, including 14 people sentenced to death.

A state of emergency has existed in Algeria since February 1992. The internal conflict over the past fifteen years has affected not only the crime rate—with torture, disappearances, abductions and extra-judicial killings being especially common during the 1990s—but also led to more crimes being made punishable by death.[5] However, the last executions, which were carried out under anti-terrorist legislation, took place in August 1993. Since December of that year a moratorium has prevailed—despite the fact that extra-judicial killings and massacres by rebel groups and security forces have continued, and several hundred persons remain under sentence of death.[6] In March 2006 the chairman of the National Advisory Commission for the Protection and Promotion of Human Rights announced that Algeria intended to abolish capital punishment. However, just a month later, Algeria's new criminal code, approved by the council of ministers and currently under parliamentary scrutiny, still included references to the death penalty.[7]

Four other countries in this region rarely carry out executions. Indeed, some of them have desisted at times for over 10 years, giving the impression that they have become abolitionist *de facto*. Yet executions have suddenly resumed. An example is Bahrain, which carried out an execution in 1977 after a lapse of 20 years, and followed this by 19 years of *de facto* abolition before carrying out

[2] Hands Off Cain, 5 January 2007.
[3] *Maghreb Arab Press*, 23 January 2007.
[4] Inter Press Service, May 2007.
[5] Report of the Human Rights Committee, General Assembly, Official Records, 53rd session, Vol. 1, Suppl. No. 40, 1998 (A/53/40), p. 81.
[6] Hands Off Cain, *Algeria Report*, 1 January 2007.
[7] Hands Off Cain, 3 April 2006.

another execution in March 1996 for the premeditated murder of a police officer. Just over 10 years later, in December 2006, two men and a woman, who had
been convicted of murder were executed by firing squad, thus bringing to an end
a third, though shorter, period of abolitionist *de facto* status. Likewise, Qatar
executed two men and a woman for murder in 2000, 11 years after its last execution, but none since then—although at least 19 people remain under sentence of
death in relation to a failed coup in 1996. It also appears that people are executed
only occasionally in Oman. Although there were at least 15 executions in 2001,
since then none have been reported and only one person remained under sentence
of death at the end of 2006.[8]

Libya too was a *de facto* abolitionist country between 1954 and 1977, when executions resumed, eight years after the republican revolution that brought Colonel
Gaddafi to power. Despite Gaddafi's public announcement in 1988 that he
favoured total abolition, reiterated to Amnesty International in February 2004,[9]
executions have been carried out, including at least six foreigners in 2005.[10]
Furthermore, the Libyan representative at the fifty-seventh session of the UN
Commission on Human Rights in April 2001 declared that 'The death penalty
concerned the justice system and was not a question of human rights'.[11] It seemed
that there might be further executions of foreigners when, in December 2006,
five Bulgarian nurses and one Palestinian physician were sentenced to death by a
firing squad after a trial in Arabic which they could not understand, for allegedly
deliberately causing an AIDS epidemic in a children's hospital. Their conviction
excited disbelief and international condemnation. Their appeal was dismissed by
the Libyan Supreme Court, but in July 2007 the families of the children accepted
one million US dollars as compensation. Their sentences were then commuted
and they were granted a pardon and repatriated.

Lebanon had also been classified as abolitionist *de facto* until a man was hanged
in 1994, eleven years after the previous execution. Between 1994 and 1998, 14
executions took place. However, at the start of the twenty-first century there were
signs of hope for the abolitionist cause. In July 2001 the Lebanese Parliament
unanimously abolished the mandatory death penalty for premeditated murder
and gave judges discretion to impose it only in extreme cases. Although Prime
Minister Emile Lahoud had made a commitment to impose a moratorium on
executions during his term of office, three executions were carried out in January
2004, the first since 1998.[12] However, after years of struggle by human-rights

---

[8] Amnesty International, *Report 2007*, p. 202.
[9] Amnesty International, *Report 2005*, p. 165.
[10] Amnesty International, *Report 2006*, p. 173. According to the Hands Off Cain *Report 2006*,
eight foreign nationals were executed in 2005.
[11] UN Commission on Human Rights resolution 2001/68, *The question of the death penalty*,
E/CN.4/RES/2001/68 and Press Release, 25 April 2001, *Commission on Human Rights Adopts Ten
Resolutions, Measures on the Death Penalty, Impunity, and Other Issues Concerning the Promotion and
Protection of Human Rights*, Commission on Human Rights 57th Session, 25 April 2001.
[12] Amnesty International, *Report 2005*, p. 161.

activists, abolition has been brought back on to the Lebanese political agenda as the result of discussions about how to respond to the assassination of the former Premier Rafik Hariri. In 2006 Lebanon and the UN established an International Independent Investigation Commission (UNIIIC) and a special court to try suspects in the murder but without the power to impose the death sentence. Human rights and abolitionist groups in Lebanon hope that this will lead to a renewed interest in total abolition.[13]

In November 2005 the King of Jordan stated that 'In co-ordination with the European Union we would like to modify our penal code. Jordan could soon become the first country in the Middle East without capital punishment'.[14] Following a mission to Jordan in July 2006 by the International Federation for Human Rights (FIDH), the Jordanian Government announced its intention to refer to Parliament a bill that would replace the death penalty with life imprisonment for some crimes, including the possession of weapons and explosives and drug-related offences, while retaining the death penalty for 'the most dangerous crimes'.[15] The effect of this remains to be seen, although FIDH remains concerned that the impact of the government's decision on the number of executions will remain 'symbolic at best'.[16]

In several other countries of the Middle East the scope of the death penalty and the use of executions is also becoming a contested issue. The Palestinian Authority has judicially executed 14 prisoners since 1994, two of them for 'collaboration' with Israel. However, over 100 Palestinians suspected of collaboration have been lynched or shot on the streets. According to the Palestinian Human Rights Monitoring Group, 11 Palestinians were brought to 'justice' this way in 2005 alone.[17] The five 'official' executions for murder in 2005 were the first since 2002, but none were recorded in 2006.[18]

Egypt has maintained the use of the death penalty, not only for premeditated murder and rape associated with kidnapping, but also for serious drug offences. In response to the violent protests of militant fundamentalists, the government extended the death penalty through an amendment to the Penal Code in 1992 to cover 'terrorist offences', broadly defined, and this led to a substantial rise in the number of death sentences—from 21 in 1992 to at least 108 in 1999, with the majority being handed out following conviction for murder.[19] Currently

---

[13] Amnesty International, *Death Penalty blog*, September 2006: <http://blogs.amnestyusa.org/death-penalty>.

[14] Amnesty International, *DP News*, January 2006, p. 7.

[15] Currently 16 crimes are punishable by death (including acts of treason and terrorism and the rape of females under the age of 15).

[16] International Federation for Human Rights (FIDH), *Abolition of the Death Penalty for Some Crimes Symbolic at Best*, 16 August 2006.

[17] Hands Off Cain, *2006 Report*.

[18] Amnesty International, *Report 2006*, p. 204; *Report 2007*, pp. 204–206.

[19] See Amnesty International, *Report 2000*, p. 96, and Amnesty International, *Report 2001*, p. 92. Also Amnesty International, *Egypt. Increasing Use of the Death Penalty* (2002), AI Index: MDE 12/017/2002.

there are no reliable figures on the death penalty in Egypt but government reports suggest that between 25 and 50 executions were carried out each year between 1999 and 2003. Yet since then there has been a marked decline, such that none were recorded by Amnesty International in 2005, although four were executed in 2006.[20]

Post-Taliban Afghanistan executed its first prisoner in 2004, although no official executions followed until October 2007, when 15 men were brutally executed by firing squad for crimes such as rape and robbery.[21] The situation in Iraq, following the invasion and overthrow of Saddam Hussein's regime, which had made very extensive use of the death penalty, both judicial and extra-judicial, is complex. In March 2003 the death penalty was suspended by the Coalition Provisional Authority, but in August 2004 the Interim Government of Iraq announced that it was being reinstated for murder, drug trafficking, kidnapping, and threats to national security. Although personally opposed to capital punishment, the Iraqi Minister for Human Rights announced in December 2004 that the Government 'had decided to apply the death penalty in Iraq as a temporary measure to have a dissuasive impact and to improve the security situation' but 'once the security situation had improved the intention was to abolish the practice altogether'.[22] The death penalty was reinstated by the newly elected Iraqi Parliament in October 2005 for anyone committing 'acts of terror' or 'financing, planning or provoking acts of terrorism'. The first executions were in September 2005 and continued through 2006 (many for insurgency). According to Amnesty International at least 270 persons, male and female, including former President Saddam Hussein, were executed in the period up to April 2007.[23] If this rate continues, Iraq will have one of the highest *per capita* execution rates in the world.[24] Saddam's execution, in particular the undisciplined and outrageous way in which it was celebrated by his executioners, drew international condemnation.[25]

Support for capital punishment remains strong in Syria, Kuwait, Yemen, and especially in Iran and Saudi Arabia under the influence of *Shari'a* law. At least seven people were executed in the small state of Kuwait in 2005 and 10 in 2006, making it one of the highest executioners *per capita* in the world (an average of 1.8 per million).[26] Yemen continues to be blighted by conflict between security forces

[20] Amnesty International, *Report 2006*, p. 108; Amnesty International, *Report 2007*, p. 106.
[21] *The Times*, 6 November 2007.
[22] Amnesty International, *Report 2005*, p. 137.
[23] *BBC News*, quoting Amnesty International, 20 April 2007.
[24] Amnesty International, *Iraq: Unjust and unfair: The death penalty in Iraq*, AI Index: MDE/14/014/2007.
[25] *BBC News*, 3 January 2007. It should be noted, however, that in June 2007 three of Hussein's senior military officers were found guilty of war crimes, including the notorious henchman, 'Chemical' Ali, and whilst Iraqi law requires that executions occur no more than thirty days after final appeals, as of the end of December 2007 none have been executed. Some advisers to President Talabani have suggested that Iraqis are losing their appetite for the retributive killing of members of the former government: *The New York Times*, 27 October 2007.
[26] Amnesty International, *Report 2006*, p. 162; *Report 2007*, p. 162 (compare with Table 4.2).

and political opponents of the government and hundreds have been arrested in the 'war on terror'. According to Amnesty International, at least 30 people were executed in 2006.[27] In Syria executions were frequently carried out in the 1980s during the suppression of the Muslim Brotherhood. The former Defence Minister Mustafa Tlas claimed that he had authorized the hanging of 150 political opponents a week and signed execution orders for thousands of detainees whose families were not notified.[28] The government informed the UN Human Rights Committee that 27 executions were carried out during 2002 and 2003, although it was unclear whether this was the total or if it excluded executions carried out after trials before the military courts. No reliable information is available for 2004–2006.[29]

After a decline in executions in Iran in recent years, the number known to Amnesty International started to rise again in 2006 (when 177 were executed), a trend which appears to have continued unabated in 2007 (when 297 were executed). There are regular protests by human rights groups in Iran and elsewhere about the profligate use of capital punishment for a wide range of offences, including for juveniles, and the continuation of public executions (see Chapters 4 and 5).

Likewise, Saudi Arabia appeared to be reducing its rate of executions, rather than as Amnesty put it in 2001 'defying world trends'.[30] In 2005, when at least 86 people were executed, almost half of them foreign nationals, this was the lowest number in recent years, followed by reports of an even lower number, at least 39, in 2006. However, this trend appears to have been reversed, for during 2007 there have been reports of at least 140 executions, the majority for violent crimes.

Saudi Arabia and Yemen are the only countries in this region to apply Islamic law in its entirety, although it has a pervasive influence in several other countries, most notably Iran. Apparently, to oppose the death penalty openly in Saudi Arabia would put the advocate in danger of being classified as apostate or 'corrupt on earth': crimes that are themselves subject to the threat of capital punishment.[31] Punishments in Islamic law are intended to be 'preventative before the event, and intimidating and salutary after the event', but free from any hint of vengeance or torture.[32] Thus, the justification for capital punishment is based on both just retribution and utilitarianism.

M. Cherif Bassiouni, a leading scholar of Muslim criminal law, has provided one of the most incisive and clearest accounts of the place of the death penalty within Islamic criminal law (see Chapter 1). Of the seven *Hudud* crimes

[27] Amnesty International, *Report 2007*, p. 283.
[28] Amnesty International, *Report 2006*, p. 250.
[29] Amnesty International, *Report 2006*, p. 251; *Report 2007*, p. 252.
[30] Amnesty International, *Saudi Arabia: Defying World Trends: Saudi Arabia's Extensive Use of Capital Punishment*, AI Index: MDE 23/105/2001.
[31] *Ibid.*, p. 11.
[32] N. Hosni, 'La Peine de Mort en Droit Egyptien et en Droit Islamique' *Revue Internationale de Droit Penal* 58 (1987), pp. 407–420 at 415–420.

established in the *Qu'rān,* supplemented by the *Sunna,* it appears that only *one* of them, *haraba* (brigandage, when a death occurs), *requires* the death penalty. It is an optional, not mandatory, punishment for *ridda* (apostasy), *zena* (adultery), and *baghi* (rebellion). *Qesas* crimes involving the physical integrity of persons, such as murder, also do not require the death penalty to be imposed, offering as they do the possibility that the victim's family will pardon the murderer or accept 'blood money'—compensation or forfeited rights of inheritance (*diyya*). The *Qu'rān* appeals for such forgiveness, promising absolution of sins for those who extend a pardon. According to a Saudi Arabian source, the government 'does its utmost, before the execution of *Qesas* to convince the relatives of the victim to commute the *Qesas* into . . . *Diyya,* in some cases these efforts have succeeded while in other cases they have failed'.[33] Yet it has been pointed out that this procedure much better protects Saudi nationals than it does foreign workers sentenced to death, many of whom do not have these familial resources to save them from execution (see Chapter 7, page 243).[34]

The death penalty can also be imposed as *Ta'azir'* punishment (one adopted by the state to fulfil 'the needs of society') and under the *Shari'ā* for espionage and for sodomy, although, as with adultery, there are very stringent evidential restrictions required in order to obtain a conviction.[35]

Professor Bassiouni argues that the use of capital punishment in many Muslim countries goes far beyond what is strictly required by Islamic religious sources and that it could be curtailed by legislation without rejecting the *Shari'ā*. He believes that this has not been done because traditionalists and fundamentalists have been in the ascendancy rather than 'secular reformists and forward-thinking traditionalists [the *ilmani*] . . . who seek to achieve the legislative goals of the *Shari'ā* by recognized jurisprudential techniques, including *ijtihad,* in light of scientific knowledge'. Nevertheless, he notes that 'No Muslim country has so far dared to open officially the door to *ijtihad,* even though the need to resort to it in light of so many scientific and technological developments is obvious'. In conclusion, he argues that:[36]

The *Qu'rān* offers ample guidance to enlightened legal policy for the purposes of establishing a just and humane society . . . It is mercy that is Islam's hallmark because it is Allah's foremost characteristic. The just, *el-Adel,* is also one of Allah's divine

---

[33] Sheik Mohammed Ibn Ibrahim Al-Hewesh, 'Shari'a Penalties and Ways of their Implementation in the Kingdom of Saudi Arabia' in *The Effects of Islamic Legislation on Crime Prevention in Saudi Arabia* (1980), pp. 349–400 at 377. Also, William A. Schabas, 'Symposium. Religion's Role in the Administration of the Death Penalty: Islam and the Death Penalty' *William and Mary Bill of Rights Journal* 9 (2000), pp. 223–236.

[34] Amnesty International, *Saudi Arabia: Defying World Trends: Saudi Arabia's Extensive Use of Capital Punishment,* AI Index: MDE 23/105/2001, p. 8.

[35] For details of these evidential requirements, see M. Cherif Bassouini, 'Death as a penalty in the Shari'ā' in Peter Hodgkinson and William A. Schabas (eds.), *Capital Punishment, Strategies for Abolition* (2004), pp. 169–185 at 180.

[36] *Ibid.,* at 174, 176 and 185.

characteristics. How Muslim societies have managed to stray so far from these and other noble characteristics of Islam can only be explained by reasons extraneous to Islam.

2. Africa South of the Sahara: Resistance to Abolition Crumbling?

When the Morris Report (covering the years up to 1965) was published, no country in the African region south of the Sahara had abolished the death penalty. Twenty-two years later, in 1987, the then Chief Justice of Zimbabwe told an international conference on the death penalty: 'Looking at Africa the depressing fact is...all African countries retain the death penalty'.[37] In fact, two small countries in the region (as defined by the United Nations)—Seychelles and Cape Verde—had by that time done away with capital punishment and five others could be classed as abolitionist *de facto*, having not executed anyone for at least 10 years, but for abolitionists the overall picture looked bleak.[38]

Since then there has been a remarkable transformation towards the abolitionist position; another 12 countries have abolished the death penalty completely: Mozambique, Namibia, and São Tomé and Principe in 1990, when it was prohibited by their new constitutions; Angola in 1992; Guinea Bissau by constitutional reform in 1993; Mauritius[39] and Djibouti[40] in 1995; South Africa (by a decision of the Constitutional Court in 1995 and the Criminal Law Amendment Act of 1997); Cote d'Ivoire in its new Constitution in July 2000; Senegal, a predominantly Muslim state, on the initiative of President Wade, in 2004; Liberia, after Charles Taylor had been driven from power in 2005; and Rwanda in 2007. In addition, Madagascar reported to the UN Seventh survey in 2004 that a draft law on abolition was being prepared by the Ministry of Justice. This has yet to be implemented but is an indicator of the direction is which the wind is blowing.

Several of these abolitionist countries—Cape Verde, Liberia, Mozambique, Namibia, and the Seychelles—have ratified the Second Optional Protocol to the ICCPR and Guinea Bissau and São Tomé and Principe have declared their intention to do so by signing it.

The change in South Africa, a country that had been renowned for its extensive use of the death penalty, was particularly remarkable. The Society for the

---

[37] E. Dumbutshena, 'The Death Penalty in Zimbabwe' *Revue Internationale de Droit Pénal* 58 (1987), pp. 521–532 at 524.

[38] There had been no executions in Madagascar for twenty years, the President always exercising his right to grant clemency and none for over ten years in Côte d'Ivoire, Niger, and Senegal. São Tomé and Principe had become independent in 1975 and retained the death penalty for mercenarism and military crimes, but no death sentences had been imposed.

[39] A moratorium had been in place since 1987.

[40] Only one person had received a—later commuted—death sentence in Djibouti since the country became independent in 1977.

Abolition of Capital Punishment in South Africa had been established in 1971, but while apartheid persisted the government had rejected all calls for inquiries into the system. However, with the release of Nelson Mandela in February 1990 and the beginning of negotiations for constitutional change, the death penalty became one of the touchstones of commitment to a new social order. President F. W. de Klerk announced an immediate moratorium on executions, the last one having taken place on 2 February 1989, and in July 1990 the Criminal Law Amendment Act abolished capital punishment for housebreaking with intent to commit a crime or with aggravating circumstances, and made the death penalty for murder discretionary rather than mandatory. A tribunal was set up to review death sentences imposed before July 1990 and, as a result, the Minister of Justice announced in 1992 that all executions would continue to be suspended, pending the introduction of a Bill of Rights for the new South Africa. Despite the fact that the South African Transitional Constitution of 1993 was silent on the matter of whether or not the death penalty was permissible, the Attorney-General, in line with President Mandela's long-held belief that the death penalty was barbaric, brought a case before the Constitutional Court, arguing that the death penalty should be declared unconstitutional. The Court, in the landmark judgment of *The State v T. Makwanyane and M. Mchunu* in 1995 decided that capital punishment was incompatible with the prohibition against 'cruel, inhuman or degrading' punishment and with a 'human rights culture' which made the rights to life and dignity the cornerstone of the Constitution.[41] A further influential argument was that it would be inconsistent with the spirit of reconciliation, post-apartheid. Thus, despite widespread concern about a tide of violent crime, and strong political pressures to reinstate the death penalty,[42] the South African Parliament endorsed the opinion of Judge Chaskalson, the President of the Constitutional Court, that the way to reduce violence was to create a 'human rights culture' which respects human life. In 1997 the Criminal Law Amendment Act removed all references to capital punishment from the statute book.

Despite the fact that political parties such as the Freedom Front Plus, the Christian Democratic Party, and the Pro-Death Penalty Party have argued for reinstatement of capital punishment in South Africa,[43] on the grounds that it is necessary to reduce the country's very high homicide rate, it is very unlikely that there would be a parliamentary majority for the constitutional amendment that would be necessary.[44]

---

[41] Case No. CCT/3/94, *State v T Makwanyane and M Mchunu*: judgment was delivered on 6 June 1995.

[42] Amnesty International, 'Backlash Follows South African Ruling', *Death Penalty News* (September 1995), AI Index: ACT 53/03/95.

[43] Moyiga Nduru, 'Death Penalty: Calls for the Return of Capital Punishment in South Africa', Inter Press Service, 7 June 2006.

[44] South Africa has one of the highest murder rates and lowest conviction rates in the world (official data show over 20,000 murders a year, 49.6 per 100,000 people), although murder rates

In 1998, 22 people found guilty of masterminding the genocide in Rwanda in 1994 were sentenced to death and executed, but after that no one was put to death. In January 2007 Rwanda's cabinet approved plans to scrap the death penalty, with the Justice Minister, Tharcisse Karugarama, claiming that a lengthy period of public consultation had shown that the majority of Rwandans favoured its abolition. But there can be little doubt that the proposed legislation was brought forward because the government desired to bring to justice more of those responsible for genocide who had fled to other countries. While Rwanda retained the death penalty the International Criminal Tribunal for Rwanda (ICTR) and many Western countries refused to extradite persons accused of leading roles in the genocide to Rwanda for trial.[45] In June 2007 the Rwandan Parliament voted by 45 to nil to abolish the death penalty in all circumstances and Rwanda's 600 or so death-row convicts (most of them guilty of crimes which took place during the genocide) had their sentences commuted to life imprisonment.

In addition to those countries that have rejected capital punishment, many others have ceased regularly to carry out executions. By the end of December 2007, 20 countries could be regarded as abolitionist *de facto*, having not executed anyone for at least 10 years: Benin, Burkina Faso, Cameroon, the Central African Republic, the Republic of Congo (Brazzaville), Eritrea, Gabon (where the cabinet announced in September 2007 that it would abolish capital punishment), Gambia, Ghana, Kenya, Lesotho, Madagascar, Malawi, Mali, Mauritania, Niger, Swaziland, Tanzania, Togo, and Zambia.

All of these countries, with the exception of Cameroon and Lesotho, are regarded by Amnesty International as truly abolitionist *de facto*, meaning that they appear to be committed not to resume executions. There have been no executions in Tanzania since 1994, although capital punishment remains the mandatory penalty for murder. In practice most prosecutions for murder result in a verdict of manslaughter.[46] In 2006 the President commuted all those sentenced to death to life imprisonment, entirely clearing a 'death row' of about 400 prisoners.[47] Cameroon is still listed by Amnesty International as a retentionist state, but according to the '10 year rule' it is now abolitionist *de facto,* the last recorded execution being in January 1997. In July 2004 a Justice Department Official said death sentences were no longer carried out, and in December of that year a Presidential Decree commuted death sentences to life imprisonment, 'except for some specific cases, including the killing of a child'.[48]

---

have decreased a little in recent years. A UN survey suggested it had the third highest murder rate, after Colombia and Swaziland; *The Guardian*, 21 June 2006.

[45] The ICTR, a UN-mandated court which sits in neighbouring Tanzania, only has powers to impose life imprisonment.

[46] FIDH, *Tanzania: The death sentence institutionalised?* (April 2005), p. 23.

[47] Amnesty International, *Report 2007*, p. 254.

[48] Amnesty International, *Report 2006*, p. 84.

Even though many African countries have become abolitionist *de facto*, persons nevertheless continue to be sentenced to death and often languish for many years on death row. Thus the UN Human Rights Committee, in response to Benin's report in 2004, expressed concern that while no one had been executed there in almost 18 years, the death penalty was still not limited to the most serious crimes and some individuals had been on death row for many years. The Committee called on Benin to limit the death penalty to the most serious crimes, or consider abolishing it and acceding to the Second Optional Protocol to the Covenant.[49] The Kenyan Minister of Justice and Constitutional Affairs announced during the meeting of the UN Commission on Human Rights in March 2005 that his country was 'committed to abolishing the death penalty' and that all death sentences would be commuted to life imprisonment.[50] There had been no executions since 1986.[51] Although the abolitionist cause was supported in 2006 and 2007 by reports from Kenya's National Commission on Human Rights,[52] a constitutional conference did not favour abolition and a motion to abolish the death penalty was heavily defeated in the Kenyan parliament in July 2007. Clearly, the issue of abolition remains highly contentious in Kenya and a large number of prisoners sentenced mandatorily to death remain on death row in appalling conditions.

Since gaining independence in 1960, only three executions have taken place in Swaziland, the last one in 1984. Nevertheless, three prisoners remain under sentence of death and the Justice Minister announced in 2005 that capital punishment must remain a part of the Penal Code, for purposes of deterrence, but could not be mandatory. A new Bill (the Sexual Offences and Domestic Violence Bill) proposed in 2005 to make 14 new offences subject to mandatory capital punishment but it had not been carried into law by the end of 2006.[53]

The last executions were carried out in Ghana in 1993 and in 2003 the President used his prerogative of mercy to commute all death sentences to life imprisonment. However, the judiciary continues to pass death sentences and at the end of May 2007 there were still 113 people on death row. The National Constitutional Conference had decided in March 2004 to retain the death penalty for murder and the rape of minors, but to abolish it for treason and robbery with violence. In October 2005, the Attorney General of Ghana, the Minister of Justice, and the Ghanaian Commission on Human Rights all called for the abolition of the death penalty.[54] This ambition is yet to be realized.

---

[49] UN, *Report of the Human Rights Committee* A/60/40, Vol. 1 (2005), p. 32.

[50] Amnesty International, *Report 2006*, p. 159.

[51] Amnesty International, *Report 2007*, p. 159.

[52] *The Nation*, 18 April 2007, reported at Hands Off Cain website: <http://www.handsoffcain. info/>.

[53] Amnesty International, *Report 2006*, p. 246; Amnesty International, *Report 2007*, p. 247.

[54] *Daily Graphic*, 26 October 2005, cited at the Hands Off Cain website: <http://www. handsoffcain.info/>.

Although Gambia abolished the death penalty completely in 1993, having ceased executions in 1981, the Armed Forces Provisional Ruling Council issued a decree in August 1995 which reintroduced capital punishment.[55] Even so, no judicial executions have been carried out since then.

There have been no executions in Malawi since 1992, the President having commuted all death sentences. In addition, the Malawi High Court on 27 April 2007 declared the death sentences of all persons currently on death row unconstitutional on the grounds that the mandatory death penalty for murder and other crimes in Malawi violated the right to life and amounted to inhuman punishment. As a result the applicant Francis Kafanteyeni and several dozen other prisoners will have to be re-sentenced with the death penalty as only one of the possible options.

Zambia reduced the scope of capital punishment in 1990 by making it discretionary for murder rather than mandatory. Consideration was given to abolition in the mid-1990s by the Constitutional Review Commission, but it reported in favour of retaining capital punishment.[56] At a conference held in September 2000 the Minister of Justice stated that he would like to see the death penalty abolished as soon as 'the public would accept it'. Yet, although no executions have taken place since 1997, concern has been raised by the number of death sentences that continue to be handed down by the courts, such that there were 200 people under sentence of death at the end of 2006.[57] In 2004, in commuting death sentences of 15 prisoners convicted in separate cases of murder and armed robbery and of 44 soldiers convicted of involvement in a failed coup in 1997, President Mwanawasa 'repeated assurances that there would be no executions during his presidency'.[58] This has made Zambia a new abolitionist *de facto* country. However, full abolition appears to be still some way off. In November 2006 the Zambian Supreme Court rejected a petition from two convicted persons on the grounds that Article 12(1) of the Constitution made capital punishment an exception to the right to life. The Court stated that the only way to abolish the death penalty was through the legislature.[59] Moreover, in February 2007 Justice Minister George Kunda told Parliament that because the death penalty is 'very contentious' it will be maintained on the statute books of Zambia despite President Levy Mwanawasa not signing any death warrants. This, he claimed, was because the majority of the people who

---

[55] The Constitution of Gambia (s. 18(3)) states that 'The National Assembly shall within ten years from the date of the coming into force of this constitution review the desirability or otherwise of the total abolition of the death penalty in the Gambia'. However, this has yet to happen: Editorial, *Foroyaa* newspaper, 26 March 2007.

[56] John Hatchard and Simon Coldham, 'Commonwealth Africa', in P. Hodgkinson and A. Rutherford (eds.), *Capital Punishment: Global Issues and Prospects* (1996), pp. 155–191 at 160.

[57] Amnesty International, *Zambia: Time to Abolish the Death Penalty*, AI Index: AFR 63/004/2001 (July 2001), pp. 1–4 and Amnesty International, *Report 2007*, p. 286.

[58] Amnesty International, *Report 2005*, p. 281.

[59] *Zambian National Broadcasting Corporation*, 13 November 2006.

submitted evidence before the recent Wila Mung'omba Constitution Review Commission were in favour of retention.

Four formerly abolitionist *de facto* countries in sub-Saharan Africa resumed executions after lengthy periods of abstention—Burundi, Chad, Comoros, and Guinea. In Burundi there were no executions between 1981 and 1997, when six civilians were executed for participation in the massacres of Tutsi civilians in 1993. Although a few soldiers were executed during the civil conflict that engulfed the country, no further executions of civilians have been reported. Burundi voted for the resolution for a moratorium at the UN in December 2007. Chad had briefly become *de facto* abolitionist in 2001 on the basis that the last execution had been carried out there in 1991. However, nine prisoners were executed in November 2003, although they had not exhausted the limited appeals procedure open to them.[60] During the 'National Consultations on Justice' held in N'Djamena in June 2003, the question of abolishing capital punishment was discussed at length. Committee No. 4, on 'Justice and its actors', after considering the *de facto* moratorium, recommended that the Chadian government abolish the death penalty. Yet in 2005 Chad, along with Guinea, signed for the first time the statement by a group of countries dissociating themselves from the UN resolution calling for a worldwide moratorium on executions but abstained in the resolution at the UN in December 2007.[61]

On his election in 1996, the then president of Comoros announced that people found guilty of murder could be condemned to death according to Islamic law. The first execution since the country became independent in 1975 was carried out in September 1996, with another reported in 1997, but while a few persons have been sentenced to death, none has been executed since 1999. In Guinea, 22 people were executed in 2001, 17 years after the previous execution.[62] Although no more have been reported since 2001, Amnesty International noted that in August 2005 the Minister of Security reiterated a tougher approach to crime when he announced 'whoever kills deliberately will also be killed'.[63]

The last executions in Sierra Leone—of 24 soldiers for treason—took place in public in October 1998.[64] The Sierra Leone Truth and Reconciliation Commission stated, in its Report published in October 2004, that it was imperative for the government to revoke all laws that authorized the death penalty (for murder, aggravated robbery, and treason). It also recommended the introduction of a moratorium on all judicial executions already sanctioned. However the government's response to the report made no commitment to abolish the death penalty. Indeed, in December 2004 the High Court sentenced 10 people to death

---

[60] FIDH, *Chad, Death penalty: ending a moratorium, between security opportunism and settling of scores*, report of the International Mission of Investigation, No. 404/2, September 2004.

[61] Amnesty International, *Death Penalty News*, AI Index: ACT 53/002/2005.

[62] Amnesty International, *Death Penalty News*, March 2001, AI Index: ACT 53/002/2001, p. 2.

[63] Amnesty International, *Report 2006*, p. 129.

[64] Amnesty International, AFR 51/009/2004.

for treason and the Government resisted appeals for the sentences to be set aside, arguing that the United States, Japan, and other African countries still support the use of capital punishment.[65] Then, in January, 2005, President Ahmad Tejan Kabbah declared he did not have the power to change laws and was duty bound to respect them while they were in force. Furthermore, in April 2005 Sierra Leone voted against the resolution for a moratorium on executions approved by the UN Commission on Human Rights. However, in April 2007 the Chairman of the Constitutional Review Commission announced amendments to the 1991 Constitution which would commit Parliament to review the death penalty every five years, and also to abolish it for treason. Sierra Seone abstained in the moratorium resolution at the UN in December 2007.

Although executions in Botswana are only occasionally carried out—in 1987, 1995, 2001, and 2006—when they have occurred they have been carried out in secret. In April 2006 Modisane Ping was executed after his death sentence for murder had been upheld by the Court of Appeal. There had been no public notification of the impending execution nor had his family been granted access to him prior to his execution: they had heard about it over the radio.[66] The circumstances were the same when Marriette Bosch was executed in 2001.[67]

The last execution of a civilian took place in Uganda in 1999. Since then 26 soldiers have been executed between 2002 and 2006 for crimes against military discipline.[68] The Ugandan Human Rights Commission (in its Sixth Annual Report, 2003) recommended to the Constitutional Review Commission the amendment of the legislation to remove politically related offences from the list of crimes punishable by death.[69] But the Constitutional Review Commission recommended that it be retained and should remain mandatory for murder, aggravated robbery, kidnapping with intent to murder, and rape of minors below the age of 15.[70] In June 2005 the Constitutional Court, in a 'class action' brought by Ugandan lawyers assisted by the British Death Penalty Project,[71] ruled that a mandatory death sentence, rather than death as the maximum sentence, was unconstitutional because it interfered with a judge's discretion in dispensing justice to take all circumstances into account. As a result, the mandatory death sentences of all 417 prisoners were set aside, with the expectation that all these prisoners would be re-sentenced to an appropriate period of imprisonment. However, the Attorney General appealed against the ruling and by the middle of 2007 the parties were still waiting for the appeal to be heard by the Ugandan Supreme

---

[65] Amnesty International, *Report 2005*, p. 222.
[66] Amnesty International, *Death Penalty News*, AI Index: ACT 53/002/2006.
[67] Amnesty International, *Botswana: Amnesty International appalled by secret execution*, AI Index AFR 15/002/2001.
[68] Amnesty International, *Report 2007*, p. 267.
[69] FIDH, *Uganda: Challenging the Death Penalty*, Report 425/2, October 2005, p. 12.
[70] Amnesty International, *Report 2005*, p. 262.
[71] *Susan Kigula and 416 others v The Attorney General*.

Court. The prisoners still remained on death row. Meanwhile mandatory death sentences have continued to be imposed in various parts of the country.[72]

For many years, and especially under military rule, Nigeria had one of the highest rates of execution in the world. The death sentence was mandatory for armed robbery, and public mass executions took place by firing squad. But since the country's return to civilian rule in 1999 only a few executions have taken place and President Obasanjo, who was personally opposed to capital punishment, granted an amnesty, early in 2000, to all those under sentence of death.[73] Yet the introduction of an Islamic penal code (*Shari'ā*) in 12 Northern provinces of Nigeria in 1999, where several death sentences have been imposed, suggests that abolition, even *de facto* abolition, throughout Nigeria will be difficult to achieve. Indeed, there has been strong opposition to the Nigerian Federal Government's attitude towards abolition in the Muslim states. The national President for the Supreme Council for Shari'ā was reported to have called it 'an attack on the fundamental beliefs of the Islamic faith'.[74] Although the Nigerian Penal Code prescribes the death penalty for murder, culpable homicide, armed robbery, and treason, the new *Shari'ā* penal codes have extended it to *zina* (sexual intercourse between a married and an unmarried person) and to homosexuality.[75] Amnesty International continues to express concern about unfair trials, women sentenced to death by stoning for having children out of wedlock, and execution of prisoners under 18 (see Chapter 7, page 218).

At the thirty-fourth meeting of the Third Committee at the United Nations General Assembly in November 2004, the Nigerian delegate, Mr Wali, stated that the National Assembly had been debating the issue of capital punishment and would be considering a report by the National Study group set up in November 2003, adding: 'Should the National Assembly decide to adopt a law abolishing the death penalty, the Government would take the necessary action'.[76] In August 2004 the National Study Group on the Death Penalty, in a telling phrase, concluded: 'A system that would take a life must first give justice'.[77] It therefore recommended a moratorium on executions, for at least five years, 'until the Nigerian Criminal Justice System can ensure fundamental fairness and due processin capital cases and minimize the risk that innocent people will be executed'.[78] In 2006 the Nigeria authorities commuted the

---

[72] Personal communication from The Death Penalty Project, London.

[73] Amnesty International, *The Death Penalty Worldwide: Developments in 2000*, AI Index: ACT 50/001/2001, p. 9.

[74] *Daily Trust*, August 2003.

[75] Amnesty International, *Nigeria. The Death Penalty and Women under the Nigerian Penal Systems*, 2004.

[76] UN Doc. A/C.3/59/SR.34, para. 37.

[77] Nigeria, *The Report of the National Study Group on the Death Penalty*, 2004, p. 81.

[78] *Ibid.*, pp. 63 and 81.

sentences of 107 condemned men, but in December 2007 Amnesty reported that it had uncovered evidence of at least seven executions in the last two years, despite denials by the Nigerian authorities. Furthermore, at the end of 2006 there were still 500 people under sentence of death in Nigeria (see Chapter 5).[79]

In Ethiopia there has only been one judicial execution since 1998, when an Army major was put to death in August 2007 for shooting the former head of the country's Security and Immigration Department.[80] In fact, the scope of capital punishment was extended in May 2005 when Ethiopia introduced an Amended Penal Code under which a person who deliberately infected someone with HIV/AIDS by rape would face a maximum penalty of death. Ethiopia also voted against the resolution at the UN General Assembly in December 2007 calling for a worldwide moratorium on executions.

In Zimbabwe, attempts to reduce the scope of capital punishment in the 1980s and 1990s met with no success. Indeed, hopes that executions were becoming a thing of the past were shattered when they resumed in 1995 after a seven-year gap. According to Hands Off Cain, 'the Human Rights activist John Dzvinamurungu, citing Zimbabwe Prisons Service figures, claims that of the total 244 people sentenced to death between 1980 and 2001, 76 were executed'. According to Hands Off Cain, the last executions were of four prisoners hanged for murder in 2003. Although Zimbabwe is another African country which voted in December 2007 at the UN against the resolution for a moratorium on capital punishment,[81] a meeting of traditional chiefs, anti-death-penalty activists, and governmental officials met in Harare in July 2007 to discuss the possibility of abolishing the death penalty.[82]

The Democratic Republic of Congo (formerly Zaire) seemed to be taking the path towards abolition until the outbreak of civil war in 1996. Between 1998 and 2000 serious concerns were expressed about the high number of executions being carried out[83] despite repeated assurances given to Amnesty International and the UN High Commissioner for Human Rights that the government would impose a moratorium on executions.[84] Many death sentences continued to be imposed, nearly all of them after unfair trials by military courts, and 200 people were executed in 2002, 15 in 2003, but none that we know of since then. In March 2005 argument over abolition of the death penalty resurfaced during parliamentary debates on the new national Constitution. An early draft of the Constitution

---

[79] Amnesty International, *Report 2007*, p. 199.

[80] *BBC News*, 7 August 2007.

[81] Hands Off Cain, *2006 Report*, p. 204.

[82] It was led by ZACRO (Zambia Association for Crime Prevention and Rehabilitation of Offenders).

[83] Amnesty International, *Report 2000*, p. 79, and *Democratic Republic of Congo: 61 People Face Imminent Execution*, AI Index: AFR 62/006/2000.

[84] Amnesty International, *Report 2001*, p. 78.

proposed abolition, but a majority in the Senate and National Assembly rejected the change.[85]

In the High Court of Tanzania, Justice James L. Mwalusanya ruled in a murder case in 1991 that the death penalty violated the Constitution because it was 'a cruel, inhuman and degrading punishment and or treatment and also that it offends the right to dignity of man in the process of execution of the sentence'.[86] It is interesting to note that the Tanzanian Court of Appeal agreed that capital punishment was 'cruel, inhuman and degrading' but nevertheless held that 'there was no conclusive proof regarding its effectiveness and it was for society to decide what was reasonably necessary': it was thus saved by Article 30 (2) of the Constitution of Tanzania, which provides for derogation from fundamental rights in the public interest.[87] The crux of its argument was that capital punishment could not be abolished while there was still such strong support for it.

The African Charter on Human and Peoples' Rights stipulates that 'torture, cruel, inhuman or degrading punishment and treatment shall be prohibited' (Article 5). It also deals with the right to a fair trial (Article 7) and guarantees the right to life (Article 4), but there is no specific provision on the death penalty. In 1999 the African Commission on Human and Peoples' Rights (ACHPR) adopted a resolution urging states to consider a moratorium on capital punishment, to limit the application of capital punishment to the most serious crimes, and to consider abolishing it. The Guidelines and Measures for the Prohibition and Prevention of Torture, Cruel, Inhuman or Degrading Treatment or Punishment in Africa adopted by the Commission in 2002 provide important guarantees for prisoners. In March 2003 the African Commission adopted the Directives and Principles on the right to a fair trial and legal aid in Africa and yet again called on: 'States that apply death penalty . . . to decree a moratorium on its application and to consider abolishing it'.[88]

Despite the substantial success of the abolitionist movement in Africa over the past two decades, several countries continue to support capital punishment, even if only sporadically. Yet there are only three countries that have executed prisoners in the last two years, 2005–2006 (Somalia, Sudan, and Botswana).

The death penalty is mandatory for murder in Equatorial Guinea, and although executions appear to be quite rarely carried out, Fernando Esono

---

[85] Amnesty International, *Report 2006*, p. 97.

[86] *Republic v Mbushuu alias Dominic Mnyaroje and Kalai Sangula*, Criminal Sessions Case No. 44 of 1991 [1994] Tanzania Law Reports 146–173 at 173.

[87] *Mbushuu v Republic* [1995] 1 LRC (Law Reports of the Commonwealth), 216 at 216–217 and 232.

[88] FIDH, *Chad: Death Penalty: Ending a moratorium, between security opportunism and settling of scores*, Report 404/2 2004, p. 12; also, Lilian Chenwi, *Towards the Abolition of the Death Penalty in Africa, A Human Rights Perspective*, 2007.

Ndjeng was publicly executed by a firing squad on 20 April 2006.[89] In Somalia, during the period of Islamist ascendancy that seemed to have ended—perhaps only temporarily—in January 2007, executions were carried out just hours after being imposed by *Shari'ā* courts, the defendants having had no rights of legal representation or defence. Since gaining independence in 1956, Sudan has witnessed a cycle of democratic governance alternating with military and authoritarian rule, together with an almost permanent state of civil war that appears to meet the legal definition of genocide.[90] In 1983 *Shari'ā* law was introduced into the Sudanese Penal Code by President Numeiri and remained in force under the rule of both the National Islamic Front and the Islamist junta which succeeded it in 1989. The death penalty can be imposed for a wide range of crimes, including sexual and political offences. Some indication of the extent of its use was given by the Sudanese Minister of Justice in 1998 when he stated that 112 of the 894 sentenced to death since 1989 for murder and armed robbery had been executed.[91] The return to normal political activity in 2000 (outside Darfur) and the conclusion of a peace treaty with the south-ern rebels have so far not had any effect on the issue of capital punishment. The Darfur conflict, besides being marked by large-scale extra-judicial killing, also continues to bring people into the criminal justice system. As recently as 2004 more than 100 death sentences were imposed and many executions were believed to have been carried out.[92] And in November 2006 seven men were sentenced to death for the murder of thirteen police officers who were killed during riots which took place in May 2005 at a camp for internally displaced people.[93]

It used to be claimed that support for the death penalty in many African countries is rooted in 'customs and culture' that assume that 'for particularly reprehensible crimes such as murder, death is the only fitting punishment'.[94] However, such opinions are just as prevalent in many abolitionist states, no doubt including South Africa and Mozambique. Perhaps it is more significant that countries which suffer from high rates of crime, weak policing, and fears of political instability often regard the threat of capital punishment as an essen-tial instrument of security, the abandonment of which would be interpreted as a sign of weakness in the apparatus of state control.[95] In states such as Sudan,

[89] *France Press*, 28 April 2006.

[90] First this was between the Muslim north and Christian south, but since 2003 it has been between rebels and Janjaweed pro-government militias in the province of Darfur.

[91] Amnesty International, *Report 1998*, p. 314.

[92] Amnesty International, *Report 2005*, p. 235.

[93] Amnesty International, *Sudan: Death Penalty*, AI Index: AFR 54/001/2007.

[94] D. D. N. Nsereko, *The Death Penalty in Botswana* (1987). Also, D. D. N. Nsereko and M. J. A. Glickman, 'Capital Punishment in Botswana' *United Nations Crime Prevention and Criminal Justice Newsletter* 12 and 13 (1986), pp. 51–53.

[95] A. A. Adeyemi, 'Death Penalty: Criminological Perspectives. The Nigerian Situation' *Revue Internationale de Droit Pénal* 58 (1987), pp. 485–502.

civil conflict further militates against abolition. Yet the fact that South Africa has abandoned the death penalty, despite having one of the highest crime rates in the world, on the grounds that it infringes fundamental principles of human rights, gives grounds for optimism.

3. Asia and the Pacific: Opening up the Issue

In recent years there has been an upsurge in anti-death penalty activism in this region. The Asia Pacific Forum on National Human Rights Institutions, in December 2000, published a reference report which urged all states to move to *de facto* and then to *de jure* abolition. And the Asian Human Rights Charter, adopted by a range of NGOs in 1998, declared in Article 3.7: 'All States must abolish the death penalty. Where it exists it may be imposed only rarely for the most serious crimes.' More recently, activists and organizations across the Asia-Pacific region joined up to launch an Anti-Death Penalty Asia Network (ADPAN) on the fourth World Day against the Death Penalty on 10 October 2006.

While nearly all the small, sparsely populated island states of the Pacific have abolished the death penalty for all crimes, abolition has yet to make many inroads into the larger states of the region, especially China, Japan, Vietnam, Pakistan, and Indonesia as well as the small island state of Singapore.

(a) Where abolition has been achieved

In neither of the Special Administrative Areas of the People's Republic of China that were former European colonies (Macao and Hong Kong) in which the death penalty had been abolished has the Chinese government sought to reinstate it.[96] However, residents of Hong Kong and Macao who have been tried in China are not exempt from execution, and there continue to be issues concerned with the rendition to the Chinese mainland of those who have fled from China to these non-death penalty areas to avoid execution.

The Pacific island states, when they became independent (Kiribati, 1979; Marshall Islands, 1986; Micronesia, 1986; Solomon Islands, 1978; and Tuvalu, 1976; followed by Palau and Vanuatu in 1994)[97] continued their pre-independence practice and did not introduce capital punishment. Fiji had become abolitionist for ordinary crimes in 1979, but only after a good deal of hesitation. Yet, following the sentencing to death of the former Prime Minister, George Speight, for treason

---

[96] Mark Gaylord and John F. Galliher, 'Death Penalty Politics and Symbolic Law in Hong Kong' *Howard Journal of Criminal Justice* 33 (1994), pp. 19–37.

[97] With the exception of the tiny island state of Nauru in 1968, but no executions have taken place since then.

in March 2002 and the setting aside of that penalty for life imprisonment, the Fijian Parliament unanimously voted to abolish capital punishment for all ordinary offences, save for crimes committed under military law in wartime. The Cook Islands (which are not a member of the UN) have also retained the death penalty for such exceptional crimes. The abolition of capital punishment by the new government of East Timor immediately after this former Indonesian territory had gained its independence in December 2001 is yet a further example, as is so often the case, of the association of this supreme punishment with tyranny. No executions had taken place in Western Samoa since it attained independence in 1962 and in 2004 it abolished the death penalty.

Only four other countries in this region have so far permanently abolished capital punishment: Cambodia, Bhutan, Nepal and, most recently, the Philippines. Following the end of its civil war, with its accompanying genocide, Cambodia abolished the death penalty in 1989, so as to mark with a powerful symbol the end of the Pol Pot regime. In 1993 Article 32(2) of a new Constitution, which had been prepared under the United Nations mandate, explicitly stated that 'there shall be no capital punishment'.[98]

The Kingdom of Nepal had been abolitionist for ordinary offences since 1945, but the death penalty was reintroduced for certain murders and terrorist offences in 1985. Nevertheless, by 1990 capital punishment was again abolished, both for offences against the state and for murder, although it was retained for 'exceptional crimes'. In 1997 the Supreme Court of Nepal ruled that these exceptions were inoperative, and two years later the death penalty was formally abolished when royal assent was given to amend the laws that still provided for it. No executions had taken place in the independent isolated Tibetan-Buddhist mountain kingdom of Bhutan since 1964 and in 2004 the King of Bhutan issued a Royal Decree abolishing capital punishment for all crimes, including treason.

The Philippines was the first Asian country to abolish capital punishment. Following the overthrow of President Marcos in 1987, the new Constitution of the Philippines, promulgated by the government of President Aquino, abolished the death penalty for all offences on the grounds that it infringed human rights, but with an important proviso. It was still possible under the new Constitution of 1987 for Congress to provide for capital punishment should there be an 'alarming upsurge of heinous crimes' that 'undermine the people's faith in the government and its ability to maintain peace and order in the country'.

By 1994 proponents of the death penalty had convinced the National Assembly that lawlessness in the country was such that it met these conditions, passing Republic Act 7659 (otherwise known as the Law Reimposing the Death Penalty for Heinous Crimes). Anti-death penalty campaigners—in particular the Free

---

[98] LICADHO (Cambodian League for the Promotion and Defence of Human Rights), *Abolition of Death Penalty: Ratification of 2nd Optional Protocol to the ICCPR and Cambodia,* Briefing Paper, January 2007.

Legal Assistance Group (FLAG), the Coalition Against the Death Penalty (CADP), and the Catholic Bishops' Conference—argued, however, that there were certainly no 'compelling reasons' at the time to justify the reintroduction of the death penalty.[99] In any case, the spirit of the proviso was severely breached, for capital punishment was reintroduced for a very wide variety of offences, covering 10 categories of crime in 46 defined circumstances. In 21 of these circumstances the death sentence was made mandatory. In 1997, FLAG, CADP, and Amnesty International consolidated their efforts by forming a Task Force, to campaign against the reintroduced death penalty.

Many death sentences were then imposed and executions resumed, after a period of 23 years, in February 1999, when a man was put to death for the rape of his step-child. Six more executions followed (three of them for rape) before President Estrada announced in March 2000 that there would be a moratorium on executions for the remainder of the year and that he would commute 107 death sentences that had been confirmed by the Supreme Court. Thirteen had been signed before his fall from power in March 2001. It appeared that his successor, President Arroyo, a former opponent of capital punishment, had also decided to suspend executions during her period of office. But in October 2001, in response to an increase in cases of kidnapping involving foreigners, including Chinese businessmen and holidaymakers, she announced that she would permit the execution of persons convicted of murder and kidnapping.[100] A series of Bills were introduced in 2001 by supporters of the death penalty to even further extend its scope and by opponents who wanted to abolish it completely, but none was successful. The President remained ambivalent, expressing support for 16 Senators who introduced a Bill early in 2002 to repeal the death penalty and put in its place the penalty of thirty years' imprisonment, to be served in its entirety. In May 2002 the House of Representatives Commission on Revision of Laws and Civil, Political, and Human Rights also passed Bills to repeal the death penalty and forwarded them to the House of Representatives for debate.[101] Meanwhile there were over a thousand prisoners under sentence of death (the majority still awaiting the outcome of the Supreme Court's review of their cases), more than half of them convicted of rape—the majority being incest-rape or statutory rape (unlawful sex with a person too young to be able to give legal consent).

---

[99] Free Legal Assistance Group (FLAG), *Position Paper on the Death Penalty Bills. Given in evidence before the Joint Meeting of the Committee on Revision of Laws and the Committee on Human Rights*, Congress of the Philippines, House of Representatives (10 December 2001). See FLAG, *Newsletter* (December 2001).

[100] Amnesty International, *Philippines: Alarm Bells Ring for Human Rights as President Announces About-Turn on the Death Penalty*, AI Index: ASA 35/005/2001; and Amnesty International, *Philippines: Executions Put on Hold*, AI Index: ASA 35/03/00, and *Death Penalty News*, March 2001, AI Index: ACT/53/002/2001, p. 1.

[101] FLAG, *Newsletter*, January–March 2002 and May 2002.

The official reply to the Seventh UN Survey from the Philippines makes it clear that the question of capital punishment was widely and passionately debated during the early years of the twenty-first century. This was reflected in the ambivalent announcements of President Arroyo. In January 2004 she said again that she would lift the moratorium on executions yet, with over a thousand prisoners on death row, no executions followed. Abolition was again called for by the Catholic Bishops' Conference of the Philippines and in April 2006 President Arroyo announced that she had decided to commute the death sentences of 1,200 persons on death row to life imprisonment and stated that she would block executions, whatever the crime, during the remainder of her term of office. Following this, in June 2006 both the House of Representatives by a vote of 119 for and 20 against, and the Senate, by a vote of 16 to 0, with one abstention, passed a Bill, which the President had certified as 'urgent' to abolish the death penalty completely. In a statement posted on her website she said:[102]

We celebrate the victory of life and I thank Congress for its immediate action in abolishing the death penalty law. But make no mistake about it; the abolition of the death penalty will be complemented by a stricter and sterner enforcement of the law on all fronts. This is not a victory for criminals as some would claim, but rather a clear proof that Filipinos respect and value the sanctity of human life and uphold the virtue and religious doctrines that are expected of us as a dominant Christian nation.

In her letter to the President of the Senate, copied to the House Speaker, she amplified her reasons for supporting abolition on the grounds that 'its imposition was shown not to have served its principal purpose of effectively deterring the commission of heinous crimes', that it was also 'anti-poor because poor people who cannot afford the services of good lawyers are the ones sentenced to death most of the time', and that 'it ... constitutes retributive not rehabilitative justice' and denies the convict the opportunity to reform.[103] Foreign Secretary Romulo signed on 20 September 2006 the Second Optional Protocol to the Convention on Civil and Political Rights at the UN headquarters in New York. But while abolition of judicial executions has been achieved, extra-judicial killings continue. The Asian Human Rights Commission, in its 2006 Report, stated[104]:

Although the abolition of the death penalty ... indicates the respect for 'right to life', the government's failure to stop the ongoing unabated targeted killings has put the country's sincerity in serious question. The abolition of the death penalty will have no meaning to the victims of extra-judicial killings and their families.

---

[102] Office of the President of the Philippines, 6 July 2006: <http://www.op.gov.ph/speeches.asp?iid=839&iyear=2006&imonth=6>.

[103] Amnesty International, *Asia Death Penalty Blog*, 7 June 2006.

[104] The Asian Human Rights Commission, *Human Rights Report 2006, The State of Human Rights in Eleven Asian Nations*, p. 253.

(b) No abolition but also no executions

Nine Asia-Pacific countries can be considered to be abolitionist *de facto* according to the 'ten-year no executions rule'. Papua New Guinea, where the last execution occurred in 1950, had experienced a period of abolition *de jure* between 1974 and 1991. In that year the Prime Minister, Rabbie Namaliu, justified its reintroduction for wilful murder as a response to 'the endless succession of vicious and mindless murders that are becoming a part of our daily lives'.[105] However, the first prisoner to be sentenced to death, in 1995, was exonerated on appeal just a year later and by the end of December 2006 no one had been executed. Furthermore, the new Minister of Justice has been outspoken in his opposition to the death penalty.[106]

No judicial executions have taken place in the Maldives since 1952, in Brunei Darussalam since 1957, in Tonga since 1982, in Nauru since 1968, in Laos or Myanmar (formerly Burma) since 1989, or in South Korea since 1997. However, there have been continuing reports of extra-judicial killings of ethnic minority civilians in Myanmar, and more recently of other protesters against the repressive military regime, providing further evidence that a cessation of judicial executions does not necessarily mean an end to state killing.

An official Commission on Capital Punishment in Sri Lanka recommended the experimental suspension of the death penalty for murder as long ago as 1959, but it was not until 1976 that executions ceased. A year later the death penalty was officially suspended. However, when serious crime began to rise, there were demands for a tough response, and from 1995 there were regular calls in the Sri Lankan parliament for the death penalty to be implemented for 'extreme cases of murder which shock the public conscience'. However, in May 2002 the President commuted the sentences of all the 196 prisoners who were then on 'death row' to life imprisonment, which in practice means 20 years with further reductions granted on religious anniversaries for good behaviour. It looked like the abolitionist *de facto* status of Sri Lanka was no longer under a serious threat of reversal but in November 2004, after High Court Judge Sarath Ambepity and his bodyguard were shot, President Kumaratunga announced that the 27-year moratorium on executions would be lifted for those convicted of rape, murder, and narcotics dealings. At that time there were 49 prisoners whose appeals had been concluded and whose clemency petitions had been denied. However, by the end of 2007 no executions had been carried out, although death sentences continue to be imposed. For example, in December, 2006 two Sri Lankans accused of grabbing a gold chain from a woman caught in the 2004 tsunami before letting her be swept to her death were sentenced to death for her murder.[107]

---

[105] Amnesty International, *Papua New Guinea: Possible Reintroduction of the Death Penalty*, AI Index: ASA 34/03/90.

[106] Amnesty International, *Death Penalty News*, May 2006.

[107] *Reuters*, 14 December 2006, reported on the Hands Off Cain website: <http://www.handsoffcain.info/>.

The question of abolition has been raised in the Republic of Korea (South Korea) a number of times and may soon become a reality. Since independence in 1948 at least 900 people had been executed in South Korea, but the last executions took place in December 1997 when 23 people were hanged. Then the new President of the Republic, Kim Dae Jung, who had been a political prisoner of a former regime, announced his opposition to the death penalty, and since then that policy has persisted. So, in December 2007, South Korea joined the abolitionist *de facto* nations. In 2000 a Bill, backed by 92 parliamentarians, had for the first time been brought before the National Assembly with the object of replacing capital punishment with life imprisonment.[108]

The Legislation and Judiciary Committee of the South Korean National Assembly has been considering a Special Bill on Abolishing the Death Penalty, which was initially passed by the South Korean National Assembly in December 2004. By February 2005, 175 members were in favour, and the Ministry of Justice announced that it was considering replacing the death penalty with a 'non-commutable' life sentence 'to better protect the human rights of the convicted'.[109] The agitation for abolition has come primarily from Catholics, Protestants, and Buddhists who have conducted a 'pan-religious anti-death penalty campaign'.[110] During this period of agitation, South Korea has strengthened its human rights work in the Ministry of Justice, has introduced the language of human rights into public discussion, and has also provided the new Secretary-General of the United Nations. As yet, the death penalty has not been abolished.

(c) Evidence of ambivalence

At the end of 1994 it looked as if Thailand might soon also join the *de facto* abolitionist countries, the last execution having taken place in 1986. During this eight-year period all those sentenced to death in this Buddhist country had been pardoned by the King. Yet despite the fact that the Deputy Interior Minister was reported to have said in 1993 that capital punishment should be banned in Thailand,[111] prisoners have continued to be executed. The government held public hearings on the issue during 1999 and claimed that these showed that 'the majority of the Thai people were still convinced that it is necessary to retain the death penalty as a crime deterrent measure as well as to ensure protection of the rights of the victims and their families'.[112] As the International Federation for Human Rights makes clear, 'Although the death penalty appears contrary

---

[108] Amnesty International, *The Death Penalty Worldwide: Developments in 2000*, AI Index: ACT 50/001/2001, p. 5.

[109] Amnesty International, *Asia Death Penalty blog*, April 2006.

[110] Byung-Sun Cho, 'The death penalty in South Korea and Japan' in Peter Hodgkinson and William A. Schabas (eds.), *Capital Punishment, Strategies for Abolition* (2004), pp. 253–272.

[111] *The Nation*, 16 January 1993.

[112] UN Commission on Human Rights, 57th Session, April 2001, *Press Release*, 25 April 2001.

to Buddhism, the Buddhist authorities in Thailand have no official position on the death penalty'.[113] Early in 2001 the recently elected government of Prime Minister Thaksin embarked on a new wave of executions, when five drug traffickers were shot on the same day,[114] leading to protests against the executions,[115] but no executions were carried out between 2004 and the end of 2007, although about 900 people remain under sentence of death.[116] Thus, although the death penalty is still available for more than 50 separately defined offences in Thailand, and is mandatory for murder and for crimes classified as felonies including certain narcotics offences, there is a now a long history of comparative restraint in using judicial executions. Indeed, Thailand claims that it abides by Article 6(2) of the ICCPR by only applying the death penalty to 'the most serious crimes'.[117] In June 2007 the new Constitutional Drafting Assembly removed all references to the death penalty from its draft charter, thus removing a possible obstacle to abolition in the future.[118] Regrettably, however, reports of widespread extra-judicial executions by the police and army during the 'war' on drugs and in confronting Muslim separatists in the south of the country create an entirely different impression of the Thai government's concern for protecting human life.

Several countries in this area have reduced the number of capital offences but have gone no further in the abolitionist direction. Amendments to the Mongolian Criminal Code in 1993, similar to those in other former Soviet territories, reduced the number of capital offences to five. Yet, under Mongolian law, human rights workers are denied access to those on death row, where conditions are said to be exceptionally poor. Furthermore, an execution is a secretive affair: Amnesty reports that:[119]

the state does not make public when or where it will take place; the press does not report that the execution has occurred; the family of the executed prisoner does not even receive the body for burial. As a consequence, the application of the death penalty in Mongolia exists under a shroud of state-imposed silence.

The question of abolishing the death penalty in Taiwan was aired by the Vice-Minister for Justice in 1990[120] and again by the Minister of Justice in 2006.[121]

---

[113] FIDH, *The death penalty in Thailand*, report 411/2, March 2005, p. 14.

[114] Seven of the 10 people executed in 2001 had been convicted of drugs offences.

[115] See the speech by the Chairman of Thailand's Foreign Affairs Committee: 'I disagree with the executions. I suggest that the government conduct a referendum...to see if such highly-publicized executions, which treat human beings like animals, is the right thing to do': *The Nation*, 20 April 2001.

[116] Amnesty International, *Report 2007*, p. 254.

[117] Department of Corrections, Ministry of Justice, Thailand website: <http://www.correct.go.th/eng/deathpenalty.htm>.

[118] *The Nation*, 13 June 2007.

[119] Kelly Jaske, *AI Mongolia*, Amnesty International Asia Office, May 2005.

[120] Amnesty International, Taiwan: *'Hsinchu Crime Ring' Death Sentences Upheld*, AI Index: ASA 38/01/91.

[121] Amnesty International, *Report 2007*, p. 252.

It had, in 2002, been abolished for certain crimes, such as corruption, and made discretionary rather than mandatory for others. In 2003 the Draft Human Rights Basic Law included provisions calling for the gradual abolition of capital punishment. Amendments to the Criminal Code passed by the Legislative Yuan in January 2005, which took effect in 2006, further reduced the number of offences carrying the death penalty and formally abolished it for those who committed capital crimes when under the age of 18 or over the age of 80.[122] The number of persons executed fell from 38 in 1997 to 10 in 2001 and to none in 2006. The Taiwanese Ministry of Justice announced in January 2007 a programme of research seminars and public hearings to encourage a national debate on the abolition of the death penalty.[123] Taiwan now appears well on the road to abolition.

Between 1983 and 2002 more than 200 people were hanged in Malaysia for drug offences.[124] In contrast, only three persons were executed in 2002 and only one since then—in 2006. An abolitionist movement is developing. In 2006, when the Malaysian Bar Association called for the abolition of the death penalty,[125] the Malaysian cabinet minister in charge of law was reported as saying 'I welcome this proposal. For me, a life is a life. No one has the right to take someone else's life, even if that person has taken another life'.[126] Nevertheless, the death penalty remains the mandatory punishment for certain drug-related offences (see Chapter 4) and has even been extended to cover serious cases of water pollution.[127]

Over the last forty years there has been pressure in India to restrict the use of the death penalty, following a period between 1953 and 1963 when there had been at least 1,422 executions. A challenge to its constitutionality in the case of *Bachan Singh v State of Punjab* (1980) failed to convince the Supreme Court of India, which declared: 'it cannot be said that the provision of the death penalty as an alternative punishment for murder, in Section 302, Penal Code, is unreasonable and not in the public interest'. Nevertheless, Sarkaria J giving judgment emphasized that:[128]

The extreme penalty can be inflicted *only in* gravest cases of extreme culpability...life imprisonment is the rule and the death sentence an exception...A real and abiding concern for the dignity of human life postulates resistance to taking life through law's

---

[122] FIDH, *The Death Penalty in Taiwan: Towards Abolition?* No. 450/2, June 2006.
[123] *The China Post*, 11 January 2007.
[124] Details from Hands Off Cain website: <http://www.handsoffcain.info/>.
[125] Amnesty International, *Asia Death Penalty blog*, March 2006.
[126] *Ibid.*
[127] Amnesty International, *Report 2007*, p. 177.
[128] *Bachan Singh v State of Punjab* [1980] 2 SCJ 474 at 522 and 524. See also the full judgment of the court which includes the dissent of Bhagwati J, who found the death penalty to be unconstitutional, *Bachan Singh v State of Punjab* [1983] 1 SCR (Supreme Court Review) 145 at 250, 252, and 256.

instrumentality. That ought not to be done save in *the rarest of rare cases* when the alternative option is unquestionably foreclosed. [Our emphasis].

The Court had in mind offences where 'the murder has been committed after previous planning and involves extreme brutality' or grave danger to the society at large. Subsequently, the Court has continued to uphold the constitutionality of the death penalty as applied on the 'rarest of rare cases' principle. Since this is not further defined and no clear guidelines have been developed, it is largely up to individual judges to interpret this phrase in deciding whether to impose a death sentence, subject of course always to correction on appeal.[129]

In recent years the 'rarest of rare' concept seems to have been applied to cases which have involved the murder of a child or children. For example, in February 2005 a man was sentenced to death for murdering six members of his family, including two children, by 'chopping them one by one'.[130] Similarly, premeditated multiple murders tend to attract the death penalty. For example, in March 2007 the prosecution sought the death penalty for three men found guilty of lynching three members of a Sikh family during the 1984 anti-Sikh riots. Describing the murder as a 'rarest of rare' case, the Chief Public Prosecutor said, 'This is a triple murder which was committed with a proper planning and in a gruesome manner'.[131]

The number of death sentences in relation to the size of the population of the country has remained very small in recent years. Although 77 defendants were sentenced to death in 2005, and according to *Prison Statistics India* 273 convicts, including six females, were under sentence of death at the end of 2005, there have been very few executions in India in recent years. One person was executed in 2004, the first since 1997, but none in 2005 or 2006.[132]

However, in recent years there has been an extension of the death penalty in India—a development criticized by the South Asia Human Rights Documentation Centre (SAHRDC) as an infringement of international standards and as a violation of the 'rarest of rare' doctrine, which SAHRDC regards as the final step before abolition.[133] However, although it may now be imposed for 11 types of offence, including various 'terrorist offences', for causing death through the use of illegal arms or ammunition, and for a second conviction of drug trafficking, no executions for these offences have yet taken place.[134]

---

[129] *Machhi Singh v State of Punjab* (1983) 3 SCC 470, AIR 1983 SC 957.
[130] *Times of India*, 3 February 2005.
[131] *Daily India*, 29 March 2007.
[132] Since 1995 the National Crime Records Bureau of the Ministry of Home Affairs has published figures of the number of persons executed or under sentence of death in its annual Prison Statistics.
[133] SAHRDC, *Use of the Death Penalty in India*, SAHRDC Submission to the United Nations Office on Drugs and Crime, 7 December 2004.
[134] *Ibid.*, at p. 13.

The SAHDR report is especially critical of the 187th Report of the Law Commission of India for choosing:[135]

> to overlook the fundamental question of the applicability of the death penalty in favour of assessing modes of execution on the spurious grounds that 'terrorism and the rate of crime in India has rendered redundant the question of abolition'.

In its report of 1967, on *The Mode of Executions of Death Sentences,* the Law Commission of India had insisted that:[136]

> having regard to the conditions in India, to the variety of social upbringing of its inhabitants, to the disparity in the level of morality and education in the country, to the vastness of the area, to the diversity of its population and to the paramount need for maintaining law and order in the country at the present juncture, India cannot risk the experiment of the abolition of capital punishment.

This argument, that 'India is different' from the West, has been used by others in India, including the Supreme Court.[137] Political assassinations, such as those of Indira and Rajiv Ghandi, and other upheavals have also played a part in India's reluctance to abolish the death penalty. As Subhash C. Gupta has pointed out, political leaders have remained in two minds on the issue. While being inclined towards abolition in theory, they have nevertheless recognized the existence of extremely heinous cases which, in their view, 'shock the conscience of society' and deserve death.[138]

Perhaps a major impediment to abolition in India has been, until very recently, the absence of a coherent voice to campaign on the issue. Indeed, it was only in July 2000 that the first national conference of about 100 representatives was held in New Delhi under the auspices of a new umbrella organization, the Campaign Against the Death Penalty. It is significant that it called not for immediate abolition, but for abolition only after a ten-year moratorium on executions.[139] However, Bikram Jeet Batra informs us that 'the campaign did not survive long and is now reduced to a mere "letterhead" authority'.[140] There might now be room for more optimism since President Kalam of India called (in 2005) for the death penalty to be discussed in the Indian Parliament

---

[135] *Ibid.,* at p. 28.

[136] *Report of the 35th Law Commission of India*, pp. 354–355, quoted in Mahendra P. Singh, 'Capital Punishment: Perspective and the Indian Context' in R. S. Agarwal and S. Kumar (eds.), *Crimes and Punishment in New Perspective* (1986), pp. 28–39 at 33.

[137] A. R. Blackshield, 'Capital Punishment in India' *Journal of the Indian Law Institute* 21 (1979), pp. 137–226 at 143–144.

[138] Subhash C. Gupta, *Capital Punishment in India* (1986), p. 107.

[139] Amnesty International, *The Death Penalty Worldwide: Developments in 2000*, AI Index: ACT 50/001/2001, p. 5.

[140] B. J. Batra, 'The Death Penalty in India—Issues and Aspects', paper given to the launch seminar of the China-EU project, *Moving the Debate Forward—China's Use of the Death Penalty*, 20–21 June, 2007, College for Criminal Law Science of Beijing Normal University and Great Britain-China Centre.

and the newly appointed Chief Justice Y. K. Suberwal has openly stated that as a citizen he is in favour of abolition, and as Chief Justice would only apply it in the 'rarest of rare cases'.[141] The fact of the matter is that while death sentences continue to be imposed, the executive branch of the Indian government is making sure that very few executions are carried out. Executions in India, the second most populous country in the world, are symbolic, rather than a major part of its crime control policy.

The situation in Japan appears to be changing as the question of capital punishment and the way in which it has been enforced has become more publicly contested. The official position of the Japanese government is that the death penalty must be retained because a very large majority of the public favours it (as made clear in Japan's reply to the UN Seventh Survey). In contrast, the response to the UN from the Japan Federation of Bar Associations (JFBA) stated that 'One of the main reasons' why capital punishment had not been abolished, 'is the extraordinary secrecy about the death penalty system and the consequent lack of proper information to discuss about the matter of abolition'. In October 2004 the JFBA adopted a resolution to implement former recommendations, passed in 2002, that a Moratorium Act should be passed and an all-over review of the death penalty undertaken. It further reported that The Diet Members' League for the Abolition of the Death Penalty had a plan to submit a bill the purpose of which would be to reduce the use of the death penalty by filling the gap between life imprisonment with the possibility of parole and the death penalty by a new penalty of life imprisonment without parole.[142] The abolitionist movement, in which the former Supreme Court judge Dr. Shigemitsu Dando played a prominent part, has grown considerably. In addition to the JFBA, an organization named 'Forum 90', which includes Amnesty International, and more than 50 lawyers and parliamentarians, has been founded. Professor David Johnson has estimated the overall membership to be about 5,000 with a core of about 50.[143]

The practice of carrying out executions has been erratic. For over three years between November 1989 and March 1993 there was a *de facto* moratorium, three consecutive Ministers of Justice having refused to sign execution orders. There was only one execution in 2003, two in 2004, and only one in 2005. On his appointment as Justice Minister in 2005 Seiken Sigiura also announced that he would not sign any execution orders because of his personal philosophy. Whilst he then retracted this reservation, he did not in fact sign any orders. No-one was executed until he was replaced in 2006; then four men were hanged on Christmas Day. Yet, while a 'get tough' policy has produced an increase in

---

[141] Amnesty International, *DP Developments 2005*, p. 4.

[142] Amnesty International, *The Death Penalty in Japan* (2006).

[143] David T. Johnson, 'Where the state kills in secret. Capital punishment in Japan' *Punishment and Society* 8 (2006), pp. 251–285 at 263.

the number of death sentences handed down in recent years,[144] the number executed has not increased. It is indicative of the unease that surrounds the use of the death penalty in Japan that all have been carried out in secret while the Diet was in recess, so ensuring that there could be no vigils or protest demonstrations. But in December 2007, the Justice Ministry for the first time disclosed the names of three men who had been executed with details of their crimes— primarily in consideration of the relatives of the victims.

The situation in Indonesia as regards the frequency of executions has fluctuated a great deal. When Indonesia became independent from the Netherlands in 1950 there were no provisions in the Penal Code for the death penalty. However, it was introduced during the 1950s for hoarding and market-fixing and in 1963, by Presidential Decree, for subversion. Premeditated murder was also made a capital offence and in 1975 so was drug trafficking. According to Amnesty International, few executions took place before President Suharto came to power following the failure of the coup attempt in 1965,[145] but in the 11 years between 1985 and 1995, 33 prisoners were executed, including members of the banned Communist Party and Muslim activists convicted of killings in the course of rebellion, as well as common murderers.[146] There was then a pause until May 2001, when the first executions in five years took place (in West Timor). Then there were none in 2002 or 2003, but three in 2004, two in 2005, and at least three in 2006.

In July 2006 the Indonesian Supreme Court upheld the death sentences of three Australian members of the so-called 'Bali 9', heroin smugglers, stating that the death penalty for drugs offences was not unconstitutional and excessive.[147] Pressure to institute a moratorium and then to end executions came from the European Union and the Catholic Church. A further appeal, directed to the recently established Indonesian Constitutional Court, was rejected at the end of October 2007. The court, by a majority of 6 to 3, held that a constitutional amendment introduced in 2000 guaranteeing the right to life was not absolute and did not apply to capital punishment, even for drug offences. Furthermore, the Chief Justice was reported by Reuters as saying that 'For the sake of legal certainty and justice, the constitutional court recommends that all death sentences that have permanent legal force be carried out'. All that stands between these defendants and the firing squad is a judicial review by the Supreme Court and, if that fails, the exercise of clemency.[148]

---

[144] Amnesty International, *Japan: the limbo of death row*, 28 February 2007; *Death Penalty blog* and *Japan Times*, 27 February 2007.

[145] Amnesty International, *When the State Kills* (1989), p. 148.

[146] Amnesty International, *The Death Penalty* (1979), AI Index: ACT 05/03/79.

[147] The Indonesian Supreme Court had increased the 20 years-to-life sentences imposed on the Australians in a lower court to death sentences without any request from the prosecutors to do so.

[148] *Reuters*, 1 November 2007. See also the NAPNT, *Bali Nine blog*, 28 March 2007: <http://www.napnt.org/balinineblog.html>.

(d) Where support is strong and opposition weak

The authorities in North Korea maintain that the last execution took place in 1992, but Amnesty International in February 2005 noted unconfirmed reports that about 70 North Korean defectors were executed in public in January after being forcibly repatriated from China.[149] In 2006 and 2007 there were reports of executions for economic crimes, such as stealing food.[150] In October 2007 a corrupt factory boss was shot before a crowd of 150,000. And reports of executions for political offences have emerged from Hands Off Cain.[151]

The Singaporean government, as pointed out in Chapter 1, is one of the most vociferous supporters of the death penalty. With a population of just over four million, Singapore at one time had the highest *per capita* execution rate in the world (see Chapter 5). More than 420 people have been executed since 1991, the majority for drug trafficking often on the basis of the possession of quite small amounts of illegal substances,[152] but more recent data suggest a significant decline in executions: there were 28 in 2002 and 19 in 2003, but only about five in 2006.[153] Early in 2007 two Africans were executed on drug charges, despite international appeals for clemency and an appeal by Nigerian President Olesegun Obasanjo, who asked Singapore Prime Minister Lee Hsien Loong to commute the death sentence.[154] Capital punishment on the island has long been shrouded in secrecy, news of an execution is only released after it has taken place, and there is little information about the whole issue to fuel public debate.[155]

In Pakistan, where there is strong support for capital punishment, due largely to a high crime rate, combined with Islamic law, the death penalty is available for a wide variety of offences and the number of death sentences imposed is high, reaching nearly 446 in 2006.[156] In that year 82 executions were reported. This appears to be an increase on earlier years: for example, according to the

[149] Amnesty International, *Report 2006*, p. 160.

[150] Amnesty International, *Report 2007*, p. 160.

[151] Hands Off Cain Secretary Sergio D'Elia, at Hands Off Cain website: <http://www.handsoffcain.info/news/index.php?iddocumento=8325839>.

[152] Singapore's Misuse of Drugs Act carries a mandatory death sentence for anyone found guilty of trafficking more than 15 grams of heroin and the Singaporean government rarely grants clemency for drug traffickers.

[153] Amnesty International, *Report 2007*, p. 231.

[154] Amnesty International, *Death Penalty blog*, 27 January 2007.

[155] Amnesty International was a victim of this government control in April 2005, when Singapore denied an Amnesty International member permission to speak at a conference on the death penalty organized by political opposition leaders and human rights activists: *Death Penalty blog*, 31 July 2006.

[156] FIDH, *Slow March to the Gallows: Death Penalty in Pakistan*, Report No. 464/2, January 2007, p. 19. When the late Benazir Bhutto (whose father, President Bhutto, had been hanged) was elected President in 1988, she declared a moratorium on executions and commuted 2,000 death sentences, but after the Islamic Democratic Alliance had come to power in 1990 executions were resumed in 1992: Amnesty International, *Death Penalty News*, February 1993.

figures published by FIDH, the number was around 28 in 2004 and at least 66 in 2005.[157] Given the disparity between the number of death sentences and the number of executions annually, the number remaining on death row is very high at approximately 7,400 (see Chapter 5, page 173).

Whether a person sentenced to death in Pakistan lives or dies may depend on the wealth and influence of his family. The system of 'blood money' (the provisions of the Qisas and Diya Ordinance that allow heirs of murder victims to accept compensation and pardon the offender) means that some rich defendants escape death whilst the poor are executed.[158] In August 2006 the Pakistan Human Rights Commission was reported by the BBC to have condemned a recent wave of executions as 'brutal' and Amnesty International reported an unlawful execution under tribal law.[159]

Bangladesh also imposes the death penalty for a wide range of offences, although the majority of those sentenced to death are murderers. As in Pakistan, there is a great disparity between the number of death sentences imposed (many under the Speedy Trial Tribunals: see Chapter 7, page 249) and the number carried out. Thus, in the four years 2003–2006 at least 597 people received a death sentence, while 20 people were hanged in the same period. As a result, the number of prisoners reported to be on death row increased enormously: from 160 at the end of 2000,[160] to 655 in 2005.[161]

In Vietnam, until very recently, death sentences could be imposed for 29 offences (cut from 44 in 1999), including crimes against national security, murder, rape, drug trafficking, and economic crimes.[162] An EU-Vietnam seminar in 2004 opened up discussion on abolition, and the Justice Ministry announced plans to abolish capital punishment for economic crimes (fraud, embezzlement, smuggling, counterfeiting, and bribery) and some other offences, further reducing the number of capital crimes to 20 'in accordance with the trend of humanization and democracy . . . and the general tendency around the world, which the Vietnamese should follow'.[163] Bearing in mind that the figures cannot be verified as they remain a state secret, it appears that a change is gradually taking place: the number of death sentences imposed and executions carried out appear to have been declining. Amnesty International reported 103 death sentences and at least 64 executions in 2003, but around 36 death sentences and 14 executions in 2006.

---

[157] FIDH, *ibid.*, p. 26.
[158] Amnesty International, *Report 2006*, p. 203. In January 2005 the Supreme Court ruled that the person convicted of murder could have the sentence reduced only if *all* the legal heirs agreed to forgive the offender.
[159] Amnesty International, *Death Penalty News*, May 2006.
[160] Amnesty International, *Report 2001*, p. 43.
[161] *Arab News*, 3 July 2005.
[162] Amnesty International, *Newsletter*, September 2000, AI Index: NWS 21/005/2000, p. 4.
[163] *Agence France Press*, 10 February 2006.

(e) China: on the verge of reform?

The precise number of executions carried out in China is one of the country's most closely guarded state secrets. Estimates of the number executed have varied from under a thousand a year to eight to ten thousand. Whatever the number, China accounts for at least 80 per cent and perhaps even 95 per cent of all recorded judicial executions worldwide (see Chapter 4, page 146). At present there is no way of assessing whether the proportion of serious offenders who are executed is high or low, declining or increasing. Nor is it known how many death sentences are suspended for a period of two years (as the law allows) to give the convicted person an opportunity, subject to hard labour, to show that they have repented—and of these how many fail and are eventually executed. A system which is not transparent and openly accountable is, of course, difficult to assess and to change.[164]

The official and academic view in the People's Republic of China has for many years been that the death penalty will be abolished when conditions are appropriate some time in the future, but in fact its use was fully endorsed for a substantial range of crimes, even at a time when Chinese scholars claimed that the crime rate in China was among the lowest in the world.[165] It was justified even more strongly at a time when political, economic, and social changes brought about by the 'opening up' policy brought with them a rising tide of crime.[166] The need to control this upsurge of crime associated with the development of a market economy, which was seen to threaten not only the social but also the political order, has been regarded as the main justification for retaining capital punishment for a wide range of offences in China. Furthermore, the speed with which the market economy has developed in China has caused a renaissance of behaviour which the revolution had supposedly eradicated, such as gambling, drug trafficking, organized prostitution, dissemination of pornography, and economic corruption. The latter has invaded the Communist Party and various other organs of the state and created concern for the reputation and legitimacy of government and the communist system as a whole. Thus, capital punishment is viewed as a necessary preventive measure in order to stave off anti-socialistic corrupting influences, as a necessary tool to ensure stability and security, and as a symbol of the state's determination to ensure its legitimacy with the masses

---

[164] Roger Hood, 'The Value of Statistical Returns and Empirical Research in Discussions on the Death Penalty', paper presented to the EU-China Human Rights Seminar, Beijing, 11–12 May 2001.

[165] Yu Shutong, 'Le Système de la peine capitale dans le droit pénal chinois', *Revue Internationale de Droit Pénal* 58 (1987), pp. 689–695; Jerome Cohen, *The Criminal Process in the People's Republic of China 1949–1963* (1968). For a helpful summary of the history of the death penalty in China, see Michael Palmer, 'The People's Republic of China', in P. Hodgkinson and A. Rutherford (eds.), *Capital Punishment: Global Issues and Prospects* (1996), pp. 105–141 at 105–112.

[166] Jianhong Liu, 'Crime Patterns During the Market Transition in China' *British Journal of Criminology* 45 (2005), pp. 613–633.

(studies of popular opinion have apparently shown overwhelming support for the death penalty: see Chapter 10, page 352).[167]

The official policy has been that executions should be confined to 'criminals who have committed particularly serious crimes of extremely profound subjective evil, when social order could not be maintained if they were not killed', a policy characterized as one of 'killing only a few' as 'negative examples'.[168] However, despite the fact that the Chinese authorities have stated that the 'standard of death penalty applicable to some crimes' has been raised, indicating that capital punishment would only apply to the most serious cases, they have nevertheless interpreted the injunction in Article 6 (2) of the ICCPR to restrict the death penalty to 'intentional crimes with lethal or extremely grave consequences' in a very wide manner. They have not restricted it to a few types of crime, but to what they regard as 'the most serious forms' of *many* types of crime. For example, recently the death penalty was imposed in the 'war' on white-collar crime. The public security ministry warned that the number of economic crimes rose by nearly 10 per cent in the first 11 months of 2006 as fraudsters sought to take advantage of the booming economy. Hence, the chairman of a trading company was sentenced to death for conning investors out of three billion yuan (approximately £200m) in an ant-breeding scam.[169] In December 2006 a high court upheld the death penalty for an accountant who had been found guilty of defrauding bank customers of $61m by offering them fake accounts with high interest rates.[170] And in 2007 the former Head of the Chinese Drug Regulation Authority was sentenced to death and swiftly executed for approving drugs without proper testing.[171]

The authorities have continued to employ the death penalty as an exemplary punishment through 'strike hard' campaigns (known as *Yanda*[172]), when large

---

[167] For example, Hu Yunteng, 'On the Death Penalty at the Turning of the Century', in M. Nowak and Xin Chunying (eds.), *EU-China Human Rights Dialogue: Proceedings of the Second EU-China Legal Experts Seminar*, held in Beijing on 19 and 20 October 1998 (2000), pp. 88–94 at 91–92.

[168] A popular slogan is 'execute one as a warning to a hundred'. 'China's Legislative Guarantees for Human Rights in the Judicial Field' *Guangming Daily*, 6 October 1998, quoted in Amnesty International, *People's Republic of China: The Death Penalty in 1998*, AI Index: ASA 17/57/99, p. 2.

[169] Justin McCurry, 'Chinese man sentenced to death for overpriced ants' *The Guardian*, 16 February 2007.

[170] Amnesty International, *Death Penalty blog*, 18 December 2006.

[171] *BBC Report*, 10 July 2007.

[172] *Yanda* refers to the policy and practice of meting out justice 'severely and swiftly'. The main *Yanda* ('Strike Hard') anti-crime campaign of 2001–3, officially termed the 'Strike Hard and Rectification Struggle' (*Yanda zhengzhi douzheng*) resulted in thousands of deaths. There have been numerous smaller 'specialized offensives' using *Yanda* policy and rhetoric since the end of *Yanda* in 2003, including a 'Summer *Yanda*' in Beijing for crimes in July 2003, a national 'People's War on Drugs' in 2005 and a province-wide *Yanda* campaign in Liaoning that began in September 2005. See Susan Trevaskes, 'Severe and Swift Justice in China' *British Journal of Criminology* 47 (2007), pp. 23–41.

numbers of persons are convicted and many are executed during a crackdown on criminals (see Chapter 4, pages 146–147).[173]

Until recently experts on Chinese law thought that 'China is unlikely to cast off easily its traditions of, and ideological commitment to, capital punishment'.[174] Indeed, when in 1998 Chinese lawyers began a discussion on 'The Way Towards the Abolishment of the Death Penalty in China', they pointed to the fact that it took almost 200 years to abolish the death penalty in Britain and France. In their view, China had made great strides by significantly reducing the number of capital crimes from more than 940 at the beginning of the twentieth century to 68 in 1997,[175] but that it would take at least 50 years and probably considerably longer to reach complete abolition of capital punishment.

However, the last few years have witnessed a distinct change in the discourse, evidenced by the willingness of the Chinese authorities to discuss the death penalty in human rights seminars and dialogues with European countries and the gradual opening up of the subject to research. Abolition of the death penalty for all economic crimes is now being openly discussed and a book of essays entitled *The Road to Abolition*, as a signifier of the final goal, was published by the People's Security University Press in 2004.[176]

While Chinese political leaders still strongly defend capital punishment as an essential tool to fight crime and preserve social order in a country of 1.3 billion that is undergoing wrenching economic and social changes, it appears that they are becoming increasingly uncomfortable that it is too readily applied, and apparently in an arbitrary way. Cases of innocent persons being sentenced to death have been uncovered and widely discussed. Reform of the death penalty would be in step with President Hu Jintao's commitment to 'build a harmonious society'.[177] As Professor Zhao Bingzhi of Beijing Normal University, has put it:

In a word, with the development of economy and society, and the better conditions of public security, the Chinese People show a more reasonable attitude towards the death penalty. They claim more eagerly that the judicial authority [should] apply the death penalty correctly.

Indeed, he claims that the former policy of 'severe striking' had not reduced crime but had had the effect of reducing 'the standards of the death penalty'. In line with

---

[173] Daniel C. Turack, 'The New Chinese Criminal Justice System' *Cardozo Journal of International and Comparative Law* 7 (1999), pp. 49–70 at 50–52. Also, John T. Boxer, 'China's Death Penalty: Undermining Legal Reform and Threatening National Economic Interest' *Suffolk Transnational Law Review* 22 (1999), pp. 593–618 at 604.

[174] Palmer, n. 165 above, p. 131.

[175] Hu Yunteng, n. 167 above, pp. 89–90. Under the Kuomintang Government in 1936 the Criminal Law of the Republic of China had stipulated 20 capital crimes.

[176] Zhao Bingzhi (ed.), *The Road of the Abolition of the Death Penalty in China. Regarding the Abolition of the Non-Violent Crime at the Present Stage* (2004), Renmin University of China, Series of Criminal Jurisprudence (44).

[177] Amnesty International, *Death Penalty blog*, 2 November 2006.

the 'Decision on the Construction of a Socialist Harmonious Society' in 2006 by the Sixteenth Central Committee of the Chinese Communist Party, criminal policy aims to 'Combine Punishment with Leniency'.[178] Now that China has signed the ICCPR (1998), and is preparing to ratify it, Zhao Binghzi and other scholars are pressing for China to make provisions in its domestic law so that it comes into line with international human rights standards, especially as regards greatly improving pre-trial and trial procedures and limiting the scope of capital punishment, pending complete abolition, as required by Article 6(2).

In order to ensure more uniformity in the imposition of the ultimate sanction, and to reduce its infliction only for the most serious crimes, the Supreme People's Court decided in 2004 that it would in future review all death penalty cases itself (thus returning the legal position to where it had been prior to 1983, when the power was devolved to the provincial High Courts). The new review system came into effect on 1 January 2007, with an order that execution should be reserved for 'an extremely small number of serious offenders' and that the death penalty should not be imposed in certain cases of crimes of passion, associated with family disputes, and economic crimes.[179] Chief Justice Xiao Yang, President of the Supreme People's Court, stated that as few executions as possible should be carried out and as cautiously as possible, in order to avoid wrongful executions. One cannot judge objectively how this policy is affecting the number of death sentences imposed and executions carried out because no data have yet been published, but already by June 2007 it was claimed that the number of executions ordered by two courts in Beijing had been reduced by 10 per cent,[180] and by August 2007 the authorities were claiming that the number of death sentences upheld by the Supreme People's Court had already been reduced by some 20 per cent.

The most definitive recent statement on China's position on the death penalty was made (as a right of reply) at the UN Human Rights Council, at the fourth session in March 2007. Mr. La Yifan stated that:[181]

China was a country with a rule of law, where the death penalty only applied to the worst crimes, and this was in agreement with the ICCPR. The death penalty's scope of application was to be reviewed shortly, and it was expected that this scope would be reduced, with the final aim of abolishment.

If one contrasts the rhetoric of China today with that reported in the three previous editions of this book, it will be seen that a great deal of progress, at

---

[178] Zhao Bingzhi, 'Existing State and Prospect of Death Penalty Reform in China at Present Time', *Working Papers, Launch Seminar of the China-EU project: Moving the Debate Forward: China's Use of the Death Penalty,* June 2007, Beijing: College for Criminal Law Science of Beijing Normal University and Great Britain-China Centre, pp. 162–168.

[179] *BBC News,* 'China to reduce death penalty use', 14 September 2007.

[180] Jim Yardley, 'With new law, China reports drop in executions' *New York Times,* 9 June 2007.

[181] Human Rights Committee, 'Human Rights Council Opens Fourth Session' HRC/07/3, 12 March 2007, p. 9.

least in dismantling the completely negative attitude towards abolition formerly prevailing, has been made in the last five years.

(f) Asian values?

There is no obvious explanation why so few countries in this region have abolished the death penalty. As David Johnson and Franklin Zimring have pointed out, it may merely be due to a 'temporal lag... Asia is merely a decade or two behind places of parallel economic and political development such as Central and Eastern Europe'. On the other hand, an alternative perspective posits an 'Asian difference'.[182] The latter explanation has certainly been advanced by advocates for capital punishment in Asian countries. It posits that Asian societies have a different conception of the right to life, in particular that the right of potential victims to life trumps the right to life of persons who have deprived victims of their right to life. Leaving aside the fact that this argument would not apply to a wide range of offences punishable by death, such as economic offences, in some Asian countries, they still maintain that there are culturally different traditions or religious beliefs that justify the use of the death penalty. For example, speaking at a press conference on 2 August 2007, Gau Yisheng, spokesman for the Central Commission for Disciplinary Inspection of the Communist Party of China Central Committee stated: 'The fact that China keeps the death penalty is due to its national conditions and cultural background. There is nothing to be criticized'.[183]

The South Korean scholar, Byung-Sun Cho, suggests that in rejecting western individualism and western concepts of universal human rights, some Asian states—despite the obvious differences between their own political systems—prefer to emphasize the importance of local cultures, claiming that appropriate laws and policies emerge to suit different countries at different stages of development.[184] States, they suggest, will differ in their understanding and practice of human rights according to their history, social system, cultural traditions, and economic development. These supposed Asian values are said to place a greater value on social harmony and the good of the community. Furthermore, it is argued that only when a country has attained a certain level of economic development can it afford the luxury of civil and political freedoms.[185]

According to Byung-Sun Cho, a major component of the 'Asian values' argument in China is Confucianism, which prioritizes justice and retribution.

---

[182] David T. Johnson and Franklin E. Zimring, 'Taking Capital Punishment Seriously' *Asian Criminology* 1, 2006, pp. 89–95 at 93.

[183] 'Official: China "prudent" in using death penalty to punish economic crimes', *China View News* (Xinhua News Agency), 2 August 2007.

[184] Cho, n. 110 above, at p. 253.

[185] Amnesty International, Asia Office; for a discussion of this thesis see <http://asiapacific. amnesty.org/apro/aproweb.nsf/pages/asian_values>.

Hence, execution, when deserved, in a true retributivist sense, is thought to be necessary for the offender's dignity (an argument based on individual responsibility and desert, which finds support in the writings of Confucius, but also Kant and Hegel). Accordingly, Asian values would favour the death penalty as retribution even if it did not further any utilitarian purpose, such as deterrence, and even if its administration occasionally resulted in the death of an innocent person. However, as Amnesty International has so strongly argued, the sacredness of life and human dignity and the importance of justice and fair treatment are consistent and recurring themes in all philosophical and religious traditions.[186] The Asian 'values' that political leaders speak of may merely reflect the past Asian experience of authoritarian rule, often cruelly enforced. Thus, when in 1998 the Asian Human Rights Commission established an 'Asian Charter of Human Rights', it rejected the 'Asian values' defence of their own governments as a poor justification for authoritarianism and a disregard for basic human rights. As the Charter makes clear:[187]

Authoritarianism has in many states been raised to the level of national ideology, with the deprivation of the rights and freedoms of their citizens, which are denounced as foreign ideas inappropriate to the religious and cultural traditions of Asia. Instead there is the exhortation of spurious theories of 'Asian Values' which are a thin disguise for their authoritarianism.

On the matter of the death penalty the Charter has this to say:[188]

All states must abolish the death penalty. Where it exists, it may be imposed only rarely for the most serious crimes. Before a person can be deprived of life by the imposition of the death penalty, he or she must be ensured a fair trial before an independent and impartial tribunal with full opportunity of legal representation of his or her choice, adequate time for preparation of defence, presumption of innocence and the right to review by a higher tribunal. Execution should never be carried out in public or otherwise exhibited in public.

This Charter shows that there are many within these Asian countries agitating for change and this suggests that the hope that countries such as South Korea, Taiwan, Malaysia and Thailand, and perhaps India and Sri Lanka and even Japan, will become abolitionist in the not too distant future are not far-fetched.

4. The Caribbean: Colonial Legacies

Whilst the death penalty remains on the statute books and is occasionally enforced across this region, there has been considerable progress for the

---

[186] Cho, n. 110 above, provides an interesting discussion of the differences between Confucianism and Buddhism in this context.

[187] Asian Human Rights Commission, *Asian Charter on Human Rights*, 1998 'Background to the Charter', para. 1.5.

[188] *Ibid.*, 'The Right to Life', para. 3.7.

abolitionist movement. During the past forty years the death penalty has been abolished in the Dominican Republic (1966) and Haiti (1987), in the French territories of Martinique, St. Martin and Guadeloupe (in 1981, as they are part of metropolitan France), and in those islands that have remained British dependencies.[189] There has been no death penalty for any crime in the islands that make up the Netherlands Antilles since the Netherlands itself abolished capital punishment for ordinary crimes in 1870.

It appeared that Cuba could be heading in the abolitionist direction when it reduced the scope of capital punishment in 1988 but this was not so, for in 1999 the death penalty was extended to include serious involvement in drug trafficking, corruption of minors, and armed robbery. In December 2001 Cuban lawmakers unanimously approved an expanded and toughened anti-terrorism law that affirmed capital punishment as the penalty for the most extreme acts of terror. Cuba's opposition leader, Sánchez, has claimed that between 5,000 and 6,000 people were executed in Cuba between 1959 and 2003, 'mostly for so-called crimes against the state or offences with political connotations'.[190] Yet according to Amnesty International, only three men have been executed (in April 2003 for hijacking a passenger ferry with the intent of sailing it to Florida) in the eight years 1999 to 2006.

In the English-speaking Caribbean, Trinidad and Tobago, the Bahamas, St. Kitts and St. Nevis, and St. Vincent and the Grenadines have all carried out executions in the last decade. Jamaica, Antigua, Grenada, St. Lucia, Dominica, Belize, and Barbados all currently have condemned prisoners and continue to impose sentences of death, but they have been frustrated in carrying out executions by the successful appeals made to the Judicial Committee of the Privy Council in London (JCPC). According to the '10-year rule' they would be counted as abolitionist *de facto*, but there is no doubt that they remain retentionist in intent. These former British colonies inherited, at the time of independence, both the death penalty as the mandatory penalty for murder, and many features of the death penalty system that had existed in the United Kingdom during the early part of the twentieth century. Indeed these laws were enshrined in the constitutions of all the Commonwealth Caribbean countries, with the exception of Belize, as so-called 'savings clauses' which either rule out altogether any constitutional attack on the laws in existence at the time of independence, or, at the least, prohibit any attack on the specific colonial penalties or punishments in existence at the time of independence based on the alleged cruelty or inhumanity of those punishments.[191] It appears ironic that these independent nations, not

---

[189] In 1999 it was abolished in all of the small British dependencies: Anguilla, Bermuda, Cayman Islands, Montserrat, the Turks and Caicos, and the British Virgin Islands.

[190] Patricia Grogg, 'Death Penalty—Cuba. No abolition in sight', Inter Press Service, 11 April 2006.

[191] Edward Fitzgerald, 'Savings Clauses and the Colonial Death Penalty Regime' in Penal Reform International, Simons Muirhead and Burton, Foreign and Commonwealth Office,

wishing to abolish capital punishment, have fallen back on these 'colonial' clauses as their defence. When urged to abolish it by the United Kingdom they accuse their former colonial power of acting in a 'neo-colonialist' fashion. Furthermore, their politicians often point to executions in the USA as justification for their own use of the death penalty.

Yet most of these countries have only occasionally carried out executions, with long periods in between. Thus Grenada executed five men in 1977 and 1978 after a lapse of fifteen years, but nobody has been judicially executed since then—although Maurice Bishop and his cabinet were summarily executed in 1983 after their *coup d'état* had failed.[192]

After eleven years without executions St. Christopher and St. Nevis hanged a man in 1985, but then the next hanging did not take place until 1998 and none have followed. The last execution in St. Vincent was in 1995, the same year that St. Lucia resumed executions after a lapse of nine years. None have been carried out since then, although in 2006 the Prime Minister of St. Lucia issued a statement to say that his government would seek constitutional reform 'To ensure that the death penalty is enforced'.[193] The execution of a man for murder in the Bahamas in 1996 was the first since 1984. Then further executions were carried out in 1998 and 2000, although none since. Following the fatal stabbing of a prison guard during a prison escape in January 2007, there have been public calls for the resumption of executions, supported by the Prime Minister. In both Dominica and Antigua-Barbuda, where the last executions were in 1996 and 1991 respectively, there is no indication that either island state is intending to abolish the death penalty. Indeed, since the last execution several men have had death warrants read to them in preparation for execution and have only been saved by decisions of the JCPC.

In April 1976 a four-year moratorium on executions commenced in Jamaica, and although the Jamaican House of Representatives decided in 1979 to retain capital punishment, it was agreed that all outstanding death sentences should be reviewed. The Fraser Committee of Inquiry, reporting in 1981, recommended that, in principle, the death penalty for murder should be abolished. Nevertheless, it bowed to public concern by suggesting that this should be done in stages and that at first the penalty should be restricted to murder committed by the principal party in offences committed with firearms or explosives.[194] Executions resumed

Attorney General's Ministry (Belize), *Commonwealth Caribbean Human Rights Seminar, 12–14 September 2000* (2001), pp. 113–126 at 113.

[192] Those accused of this crime were sentenced to death. Twenty-four years later their mandatory death sentences were overturned as unconstitutional, and they were referred back to the courts for resentencing; Peter Ischyrion, 'Grenada: Bishop's killers in emotional resentencing', *Inter Press Service*, 28 June 2007.

[193] 2006 New Year's Address to the Nation by the Prime Minister of St. Lucia, 16 January 2006, reported at <http://www.stlucia.gov.lc/primeminister/former_prime_ministers/kenny_d_anthony/statements/2006/2006_new_years_address.htm>.

[194] Amnesty International, *Report 2001*, p. 140.

in 1980 and were carried out on a considerable scale in relation to Jamaica's population until 1988. The cessation of executions meant that prisoners were kept on
death row for even longer periods of time. In a decision that would have major
consequences for the ability of the governments of Jamaica and elsewhere in the
Anglophone Caribbean to carry out executions, the Judicial Committee of the
Privy Council, in the case of *Pratt and Morgan v The Attorney General for Jamaica*,
decided in 1993 that it would amount to inhuman and degrading punishment to
execute a person who had been under sentence of death for longer than five years
(see Chapter 5, page 180).[195]

The Offences against the Person Amendment Act of 1992 created a distinction between capital and non-capital murder (modelled on the defunct and
discredited UK Homicide Act of 1957), with the death penalty being mandatory for the former. As this law was applied retroactively, all those under sentence of death were administratively reclassified. Over 60 per cent, defined as
having committed non-capital murders, had their death sentences commuted
to life imprisonment, in a process criticized for procedural unfairness.[196] The
decision of the JCPC in the case of Lambert Watson in 2004 abolished the
mandatory death penalty, even for the restricted category of capital murder,
and 45 cases were identified for re-sentencing under a discretionary system.
In its response to the UN Seventh Quinquennial Survey, Jamaica stated
that the main reasons why capital punishment had not been abolished were
'(a) perceptions that some aggravated murders deserved the death penalty,
(b) the majority of the public were in favour of capital punishment, (c) "religious
perspectives" and (d) social anxiety about crime' (Jamaica has the third highest
murder rate per capita in the world—32.4 per 100,000 people[197]). It further
explained that there had been no executions since 1988 because the JCPC had
'placed additional restrictions on the circumstances in which the death penalty
may be carried out'.[198] More recently, both the government and the opposition (the Jamaica Labour Party) have declared themselves in favour of resuming executions, with the support of the press.[199] Furthermore, in 2006 a new
Charter of Rights Bill, under consideration in the House of Representatives,
made no recommendations as to whether the death penalty should be made
an exception to the 'right to life'. In May 2006 the Justice Minister, Senator
A. J. Nicholson, was reported to have said, referring to the *Pratt and Morgan*
decision (see above):[200]

---

[195] *Pratt and Morgan v Attorney General for Jamaica* [1993] 4 All ER 769 (PC).

[196] Amnesty International, *Jamaica: Moves to Resume Hangings*, January 1993, AI Index: AMR
38/01/93. See generally Edward Fitzgerald, 'The Commonwealth Caribbean' in P. Hodgkinson
and A. Rutherford (eds.), *Capital Punishment: Global Issues and Prospects* (1996), pp. 143–153.

[197] <http://www.nationmaster.com>.

[198] UN Doc. E2005/3/Add. 1, paras. 11–12.

[199] See various articles in *The Jamaica Gleaner*, e.g. 'Tired Death Penalty Debate', 12 June 2007.

[200] Reported at *BN Village*, 'Death penalty "stalemate" remains, as inmate approaches five-year
limit', 14 May 2006.

As long as the law remains as it is, nobody is going to be hanged in Jamaica. Nobody. You have five years from conviction and sentence until the person is hanged. If the five years pass, the person cannot hang . . . the processes cannot be completed in five years.

The scope of capital punishment was also restricted in the Eastern Caribbean (the jurisdictions of Antigua and Barbuda, Dominica, Grenada, Montserrat, St. Christopher and St. Nevis, St. Lucia, and St. Vincent and the Grenadines[201]) when, in April 2001, the Eastern Caribbean Court of Appeal held the mandatory death penalty for murder to be unconstitutional because it deprived defendants of any opportunity to have the court consider mitigating circumstances.[202] In March 2002 this judgment, along with similar cases challenging the mandatory death penalty from Belize, was confirmed on appeal by the JCPC (see Chapter 8, page 282).[203] In addition, the UN Human Rights Committee[204] and the Inter-American Commission and Court had also held that the mandatory death penalty is a violation of the respective conventions.[205] All death row cases in these countries have had to be reviewed so as to ensure that the death penalty is only imposed on the 'worst of the worse' defendants. In 2006 the JCPC also ruled that the mandatory death sentence is in violation of the Bahamian Constitution.[206] And in December 2007 the Inter-American Court found the mandatory death sencence in Barbados to be a violation of the right to life.

However, the mandatory death penalty remains in Trinidad and Tobago. In June 1988 the Trinidadian Senate established the Prescott Commission of Inquiry into Capital Punishment, which recommended the replacement of the mandatory death penalty by a distinction between capital and non-capital murder,[207] but this was never put into effect. A fifteen-year moratorium on executions was broken when Glen Ashby was executed for murder in July 1994, even though legal proceedings aimed at obtaining a further stay of execution were under way (see Chapter 7, page 265). Five years later, ten men were executed, nine of them con-

---

[201] Anguilla and the British Virgin Islands are associate members of the Organisation of Eastern Caribbean States (OECS).

[202] *Spence and Hughes v The Queen*, Criminal Appeal No. 20 of 1998, Eastern Caribbean Court of Appeal Judgment (2 April 2001). See Saul Lehrfreund, 'International Legal Trends and the "Mandatory" Death Penalty in the Commonwealth Caribbean' *Oxford University Commonwealth Law Journal* 1 (2001), pp. 71–194.

[203] The *Queen v Peter Hughes* [2002] 2 AC 259; and in relation to Belize, *Reyes v The Queen* [2002] 2 AC 235.

[204] See *Kennedy v Trinidad and Tobago*, 28 March 2002, CCPR/C/74/D/845/1998 and *Thompson v St. Vincent and the Grenadines* (2000), CCPR/C/70/D906/1998, which held that the mandatory death penalty breached Article 6 (1)—the right to life—of the ICCPR.

[205] *Hilaire v Trinidad and Tobago*, Inter-American Commission Report 66/99 (1999). See also William A. Schabas, *The Abolition of the Death Penalty in International Law* (3rd edn., 2002), at p. 111.

[206] *Forrester Bowe Jr. and Trono Davis v The Queen* [2006] UKPC 10.

[207] *The Death Penalty in Trinidad and Tobago*, Report of the Commission of Inquiries into the Death Penalty, 27 September 1990.

victed of the same crime. While there have been no executions since 1999, this has only been because lawyers have been successful in keeping cases under review.

The attitude of the government of Trinidad and Tobago towards 'outside interference' in its capital punishment legislation was evident in its reaction to the *Pratt and Morgan* decision (see above). It decided to try to speed-up the process by eliminating the possibilities of appeal to international tribunals. In 1998 it took the unprecedented step of withdrawing its accession to the First Optional Protocol to the International Covenant on Civil and Political Rights (ICCPR), which allows the UN Human Rights Committee to receive claims from persons who believe that their treatment has been in violation of the Covenant. On re-acceding to the ICCPR Trinidad entered a reservation that the Human Rights Committee 'shall not be competent to receive and consider communications relating to any prisoner who is under sentence of death'. The Human Rights Committee held this reservation to be invalid,[208] but in 2000 the government again withdrew from the Optional Protocol, although still remaining a party to the Covenant. As a member of the Organization of American States (OAS) since 1967, having gained independence in 1962, Trinidad and Tobago was bound by the American Charter and the American Declaration on the Rights and Duties of Man which protects accused persons from 'cruel, infamous and unusual punishments'. It was also bound not to subject persons to cruel, inhuman or degrading punishment or treatment by the American Convention on Human Rights, which it ratified in 1991, and it recognized the jurisdiction of the Inter-American Court of Human Rights. In May 1998 (with effect from May 1999), the government withdrew from the Convention and the jurisdiction of the Court in a further attempt to shorten the period between conviction for murder and the ability to deal with all appeals within five years so as to be able to carry out executions. However, because it remains a member of the OAS its citizens can still petition the Inter-American Commission on Human Rights under the American Declaration.

Given the decisions made with regard to the unconstitutionality of a mandatory death sentence for murder in other parts of the Caribbean, it was not surprising that the Privy Council in 2003, in the case of *Balkissoon Roodal v The State of Trinidad and Tobago*, also found that the mandatory death penalty was an infringement of the right not to be subject to cruel and unusual treatment or punishment. The majority of the Board held that the 'savings clause' (Clause 6) of the 1976 Constitution of Trinidad and Tobago, which protected pre-constitution legislation from judicial change, could not override the duty of the courts 'to construe and apply' the Constitution and statutes so as to protect the guaranteed fundamental rights, including protection against the imposition of cruel and unusual punishment and treatment, laid down in Sections 1 and 2 of the Constitution. The Board noted that in Trinidad and Tobago 'the crime of murder

---

[208] Communication 31 December 1999, *Kennedy v Trinidad and Tobago*, decision on admissibility.

is based on the English common law [and thus] covers an extraordinarily wide spectrum of cases of homicide, most of which would not be regarded as murder in ordinary parlance'.[209] It therefore declared that the legislation should be interpreted to mean that death should be the maximum, not the only, penalty for murder, the sentence being left to the discretion of the trial judge.

A year later, on appeal from the State, a full nine-member Board of the Judicial Committee held, by 5 to 4, in the case of *Charles Matthew* and in the companion case of *Lennox Boyce and Jeffrey Joseph v the Queen* from Barbados, that, notwithstanding that the state of Trinidad and Tobago did not challenge the fact that a mandatory death penalty was cruel and unusual punishment, it was indeed protected by the savings clause, as was Barbados:[210]

[S]ection 6(1) provides that 'nothing in sections 4 [protecting "the right of the individual to life"] and 5 [5(2)(b) which states that Parliament may not impose or authorize the imposition of cruel and unusual treatment or punishment] shall invalidate... an existing law'. The law decreeing the mandatory death penalty was an existing law at the time when the constitution came into force and therefore, whether or not it is an infringement of the right to life or a cruel and unusual punishment, it cannot be invalidated for inconsistency with sections 4 and 5. It follows that... it remains valid.

Thus, the decision in *Matthew* and in *Boyce and Joseph* meant that the only way by which the mandatory death penalty could be repealed in Trinidad and Tobago and in Barbados is by Act of Parliament.[211]

This decision in *Matthew* was stigmatized by the minority, including Lord Bingham the Senior Law Lord:[212]

as a legalistic and over-literal approach to interpretation... unsound in law and productive of grave injustice to a small but important class of people in Trinidad and Tobago... The result of reversing *Roodal* is to replace a regime which is just, in accordance with internationally-accepted human rights standards and (as experience in the Eastern Caribbean has shown) workable by one that is unjust, arbitrary and contrary to human rights standards as accepted by the State.

---

[209] *Roodal v State of Trinidad and Tobago* [2005] 1 AC 328 at 338–9.

[210] *Matthew v State of Trinidad and Tobago* [2005] 1 AC 433 at 447. For a discussion of this and the preceding cases see Margaret A. Burnham, 'Saving Constitutional Rights from Judicial Scrutiny: the Savings Clause in the Law of the Commonwealth Caribbean' *The University of Miami Inter-American Law Review* 36 (2&3) (2005), pp. 249–269. And Julian Knowles, 'Capital Punishment in the Commonwealth Caribbean: Colonial Inheritance or Colonial Remedy?' in William A. Schabas and Peter Hodgkinson (eds.), *Capital Punishment. Strategies for Abolition* (2004), pp. 282–308. In 2006 The Privy Council held that the mandatory death penalty in the Bahamas was in violation of that country's Constitution: *Forrester Bowe Jr. and Trono Davis v The Queen* [2006] UKPC 10.

[211] In the related appeal of *Lennox Boyce and Jeffrey Joseph v The Queen*, from Barbados, [2004] UKPC 34, the panel came to the same decision by the same majority, in respect of the savings clause contained in the Barbados constitution. However, the same panel decided unanimously that the mandatory death penalty in Jamaica did violate the constitution of that country, as it was not subject to a savings clause. See *Lambert Watson v The Queen* [2005] 1 AC 400.

[212] *Ibid.*, [2005] 1 AC 453 and 469.

Matthew's death sentence was set aside and a sentence of life imprisonment substituted, on the grounds that it would be a cruel punishment to execute him when he had been previously told that his sentence could be reviewed. The Privy Council recommended that the same considerations should apply to all prisoners on death row at the time of its judgment.[213] Instead, in mid-2005, the Attorney General, John Jeremie, announced the intention of the state to hang everyone on death row who was eligible, as part of its overall strategy to deal with the escalating murder rate.[214] Although no executions have yet taken place, it is clear that the government has put its utilitarian justification for the death penalty— namely, the belief that it is necessary to deter citizens from murder—above the recognized human rights principle that such a punishment should not be applied to all cases of murder whatever the circumstances may have been.

One reason, perhaps it is fair to say a major reason, why there has been such resistance to change is that Trinidad has experienced an enormous increase in killings recorded as murder by the police. Although the annual number of deaths recorded by the police as murder had fallen from 143 in 1994 (when one person was executed) to 93 in 1999 (when 10 men were executed), it then began to rise sharply to 171 in 2002 and then to 387 in 2005. This was an increase from an already high rate of 7.6 recorded murders per 100,000 of the population of approximately 1.26 million in 1998 to 30.7 per 100,000 in 2005, one of the highest incidences of culpable homicide in relation to population in the world, and 19 times that of the 1.55 recorded homicides per 100,000 in England and Wales in 2004. This has, as one might expect, created enormous concern, made all the more significant by an apparent decline in the proportion of suspects brought to justice.[215] An opinion poll carried out by the Trinidad *Sunday Guardian* in November 2003 found that 62 per cent of respondents said they were fearful of being murdered and two years later a further poll revealed that 55 per cent of respondents put crime as the major problem facing the country, citing the murder rate as their main concern.

The Caribbean Court of Justice (CCJ), established in February 2001 and inaugurated in April 2005, will replace the JCPC as a final court of appeal in the region. At present it is the final court of appeal only for Barbados and Guyana. Grenada and Trinidad and Tobago have to pass constitutional amendments before being able to switch to its jurisdiction. It remains to be seen whether the CCJ, when it eventually comes into existence, will take a different stance to that taken by British judges sitting on the JCPC but human rights groups have warned that the court could be used to resume executions. Furthermore, the decision of Jamaica, Guyana, and Trinidad and Tobago to try to avoid their international commitments to abide by rulings of the UN Human Rights Committee under the ICCPR, and by Trinidad's

---

[213] *Ibid.*, p. 453.

[214] Douglas Mendes and Gregory Delzin, 'Using the Bill of Rights to halt executions: a reply to Peter Hodgkinson' *Amicus Journal* Issue 15 (2005), pp. 18–21.

[215] The number of persons committed for trial charged with murder fell from a high of 88 in 1999 to only 38 in 2002, a decline of over 50%.

withdrawal from the American Convention on Human Rights (see above), is a clear indicator of their determination to resist abolition of capital punishment.

Guyana, although on the continent of South America, is politically regarded as Caribbean.[216] Prior to 1985 there had been a fifteen-year moratorium on executions but Guyana's abolitionist *de facto* status was undermined when a newly elected government resumed executions for a period of six years. However, when they ceased in 1991 this did not, as abolitionists hoped, mark a return to a long moratorium, for in 1996 a prisoner named Rockliffe Ross was executed despite having an application for a review of his case pending before the UN Human Rights Committee. In 1999 the government of Guyana withdrew from the Second Optional Protocol to the ICCPR only to rejoin it the same day with a reservation preventing the Human Rights Committee from considering petitions from individuals that their human rights have been violated by capital proceedings brought against them. With this move Guyana followed Jamaica and Trinidad and Tobago—the only countries to withdraw from the ICCPR to date (see page 108 above). In 2002 a new law expanded the scope of the death penalty and whilst there have been no judicial executions since June 1996, making Guyana abolitionist *de facto* according to the '10-year rule', 23 people remain on death row and there are reports of killings by police 'death squads'.[217]

Despite this seemingly entrenched antipathy to the abolitionist cause in the Anglophone Caribbean, the European Union continues to be critical of those countries that carry out executions and now has a policy of blanket opposition to the death penalty. UK Member of Parliament, Chris Mullin, speaking in a debate addressing the use of the death penalty in Jamaica and Trinidad and Tobago in 1999, stated:[218]

When the High Commissioner of Jamaica tells me that his country has a sovereign right to do what it wants, I accept that is so. However, we have a sovereign right not to provide Jamaica with aid, trade preferences and debt relief. The Government has rightly committed to an ethical policy, seeking to forge a clear connection between the countries that we choose to help and the degree of democracy and civilized behaviour in them. That principle should be applied forcefully in the Caribbean.

5. North America: Faltering Support

(a) Canada

The process of abolition in Canada, as in Britain, went through various stages. In 1954 rape was removed as a capital offence and by 1956 a parliamentary

---

[216] Guyana is culturally part of the Caribbean world—in 2005 it formally adopted the Caribbean Court of Justice as its highest appellate court.

[217] Amnesty International, *Annual Report 2006*, p. 130; *Annual Report 2007*, p. 129.

[218] Amnesty International, *State killing in the English-speaking Caribbean: a legacy of colonial times*, AI Index: AMR 05/003/2002.

committee had recommended that juveniles should not be eligible for execution. In 1961 the death penalty was limited to a separate class of 'capital' murder, and in 1966 it was limited still further to the killing only of on-duty police officers and prison guards. Ten years later capital punishment was finally abolished for all ordinary crimes. No one had been executed since 1962.

An attempt was made to reintroduce the death penalty in June 1987, but this was defeated by a substantial majority of Members of Parliament. It was finally expunged from Canadian law in 1998 when all references to the death penalty for military offences and treason were removed from the National Defence Act. Canada ratified the Second Optional protocol to the ICCPR in November 2005.

(b) The United States of America

(i) *The changing pattern of support for capital punishment*

Before exploring some of the reasons that may explain why 37 states of the United States of America and US Federal and military jurisdictions currently retain the death penalty, and what the likelihood is that they will continue to do so, it is instructive to examine the recent history of its use in America. It is common for people, when discussing the attitude of America and Americans towards capital punishment, to speak as if the death penalty is on the statute books of all states and is used relatively frequently. This is not so. Indeed, 14 jurisdictions in the USA do not have capital punishment.[219] Furthermore, there are a majority of retentionist states may be regarded as 'symbolic executioners', given their very occasional resort to executions (see below).[220]

Broadly speaking, there was an initial movement toward abolition that culminated in the Supreme Court's decision in *Furman* in 1972 that it was administered in an unconstitutional form; a subsequent movement to restore the death penalty and to carry out an increasing number of executions, culminating around 1999; followed by the recognition in many states of serious flaws in the system which

[219] They are (with the date of abolition): Alaska (1957), District of Columbia (1973), Hawaii (1957), Iowa (1872, reinstated in 1878 and abolished in 1965), Maine (1887), Massachusetts (1984), Michigan (1846 for all crimes except for treason, total abolition in 1963), Minnesota (1911), New Jersey (2007), North Dakota (1915, except for murder by a prisoner serving a life term for murder, total abolition in 1973), Rhode Island (1852, restored the death penalty in 1882 for any murder by a prisoner serving a life sentence, total abolition in 1984), Vermont (1965, total abolition in 1987), West Virginia (1965), and Wisconsin (1853). These dates have been compiled from W. J. Bowers, *Legal Homicide: Death as Punishment in America, 1864–1982* (1984), pp. 25–26 and 53–55, and the Death Penalty Information Center, <http://www.deathpenaltyinfo.org>. See also, for a thorough discussion of the factors and circumstances associated with abolition in these states, John F. Galliher, Larry W. Koch, David Patrick Keys, and Teresa J. Guess, *America without the Death Penalty: States Leading the Way* (2002).

[220] Carol. S. Steiker and Jordan M. Steiker, 'A Tale of Two Nations: Implementation of the Death Penalty in "Executing" Versus "Symbolic" States in the United States' *Texas Law Review* (84) 2006, pp. 1869–1927.

has led to a marked decline in death sentences imposed and executions carried out, as well as to commissions of inquiry and moratoria on executions in many states. We highlight the most significant of these developments below.

After the end of World War II the number of executions carried out in America began to decline sharply. During the 1930s an annual average of 167 persons had been executed whereas by 1963 the number had fallen to 21, then to 15 in the following year, and finally to two in 1967. Shortly afterwards the Supreme Court, faced with the pressure of many challenges to the death penalty orchestrated by the Legal Defence Fund of the National Association for the Advancement of Colored People, ordered a moratorium until the question of the constitutionality of capital punishment could be settled.[221] When all death penalty statutes then in force were ruled unconstitutional by the US Supreme Court in 1972 in *Furman v Georgia*, many abolitionists heralded it as the final elimination of capital punishment in the USA.[222] The Court, however, did not hold that the death penalty was cruel and unusual punishment per se and therefore unconstitutional, but rather that it was unconstitutional because it was being applied in an arbitrary, capricious, and discriminatory manner contrary to the Eighth and Fourteenth Amendments of the US Constitution. But the states were not ready to accept abolition, so all but two (Kansas and New York) of the 38 previously retentionist states decided to redraft their statutes to restrict and more carefully define the class of murder subject to capital punishment so as to comply with the Court's decision in *Furman*. These new capital statutes, which provided the additional procedural safeguard of proportionality review in an attempt to eliminate arbitrariness in the infliction of the death penalty, were, for the most part, subsequently ruled to be constitutional by the Supreme Court in *Gregg v Georgia* and several other cases in 1976. The application of the death penalty was effectively restricted to murder when the Supreme Court ruled it unconstitutional for rape in 1977 (*Coker v Georgia*). Also, it was not to be a mandatory penalty: guided discretion, aimed at restricting the death penalty to the most egregious of murders only, was the essence of the new statutes (see Chapter 8, pages 278–279).

Executions recommenced in 1977, after a ten-year moratorium, with the dramatic execution of Gary Gilmore by firing squad in Utah, after he had determined to abandon all appeals.[223] That same year, Oklahoma became the first state to adopt lethal injection as a method of execution. During the decade after *Gregg*, states initially moved slowly to execute capital defendants. When material for the first edition of this book was gathered ten years after *Gregg*, in 1988, 25 of the 36 states which had retained capital punishment had not yet executed a prisoner. By the end of 2007, however, all but two of these states (New Hampshire

---

[221] Michael Meltsner, *Cruel and Unusual: The Supreme Court and Capital Punishment* (1973), pp. 106–148.

[222] F. E. Zimring and G. Hawkins, *Capital Punishment and the American Agenda* (1986), p. 26.

[223] A story dramatically told by Normal Mailer in *The Executioner's Song* (1979).

and New Jersey) had carried out an execution. In addition, neither Kansas nor New York, which reintroduced the death penalty in 1994 and 1995 respectively, has subsequently carried out an execution.

The 1980s and particularly the 1990s saw an increase in the number of persons sentenced to death and executed, reaching a height of 317 capital sentences in 1996, and 98 executions in 1999. Public opinion was in step with this trend. Whereas in 1965, pre-*Furman*, only four out of ten adults had supported the death penalty, by 1994 as much as 80 per cent of the population was in favour (see Chapter 10, page 365).

The scope of the death penalty was also expanded in Federal law: first in 1988, when the Anti-Drug Abuse Act amended earlier legislation aimed at controlling the involvement of 'continuing criminal enterprises' in drug trafficking, so as to enable the Federal government to seek the death penalty for murder committed while engaged in illegal drug activity and for killing a law enforcement officer in order to avoid apprehension for a drug violation.[224] The Violent Crime Control Act of 1994 not only made capital punishment a discretionary penalty for more than 50 offences in which death had ensued as a consequence, but also introduced it for several crimes in which death was not a consequence: the attempted assassination of the President, for large-scale drugs offences as part of 'a continuing criminal enterprise', and for a leader of such an enterprise who 'in order to obstruct the investigation or prosecution of the enterprise or an offence involved in the enterprise, attempts to kill or knowingly directs, advises, authorizes, or assists another to attempt to kill any public officer, juror, witness, or members of the family or household of such a person'. The Act also laid down the 'constitutional procedures for the imposition of the sentence of death' and prohibited it for those under the age of 18.[225] The 1996 Anti-Terrorism and Effective Death Penalty Act expanded the scope of capital punishment still further by providing the death penalty for crimes where death is caused, even if only proximately, by the use of explosives or arson.[226]

Until June 2001, no prisoner had been executed for a federal offence since 1963. But in that month federal executions began when Timothy McVeigh's life was ended by lethal injection for the infamous Oklahoma City bombing of a federal building with the loss of 168 lives. His execution aroused enormous interest and widespread support throughout the USA, although condemnation from many countries. For example, the Council of Europe called it 'sad, pathetic and wrong'.[227] Later in the same month a second prisoner, Juan Raoul Garza, was

---

[224] Charles W. Williams, 'The Federal Death Penalty for Drug-Related Killings' *Criminal Law Bulletin* 27 (1991), pp. 387–415 at 393–398. This involved any violation under the Continuing Criminal Enterprise Act (21 U.S.C.) ss. 841 (b) (1) (A), 960 (b) (1). The Anti–Drug Abuse Act was codified at 21 U.S.C., s. 848 (e) 1998.

[225] *Violent Crime Control Act*, P.L. 103–322, Title VI—Death Penalty, ch. 228, s. 3591 (b) (1 and 2), s. 3593.

[226] Anti-Terrorism and Effective Death Penalty Act of 1996, Public Law 104–132, Title VII.

[227] *New York Times*, 12 June 2001.

executed for drug-related murders, although this time with much less publicity, and in 2003 Louis Jones, Jr., a Gulf War veteran, was executed for the rape and murder of a 19-year-old woman Army private in Texas. A moratorium lasting 38 years had been broken.

Yet, during this period of expansion, the Supreme Court remained deeply divided on the legitimacy of capital punishment, rejecting systemic challenges to the constitutionality of death penalty statutes by only a narrow majority of 5 to 4 in two landmark cases: *McCleskey v Kemp* (1987) and *Blystone v Pennsylvania* (1990). In addition, the Court prohibited the execution of individuals who were 15 and under at the time of the crime (*Thompson v Oklahoma*, 1989) and insane individuals (*Ford v Wainwright*, 1986). The Court did, however, vote to allow the execution of those 16 and older at the time of the crime (*Stanford v Kentucky*, 1989) and mentally retarded individuals (*Penry v Lynaugh*, 1989), decisions which have only been recently been reversed in *Atkins v Virginia* in 2002 (for mental retardation, to use the American term) and in *Roper v Simmons* in 2005 (for defendants who were under 18 at the time of the commission of the crime) (see Chapter 6).

With the dawn of a new century, the strong public support for capital punishment began to wane (see Chapter 10) as it became clear that the legislation approved by the Supreme Court in 1976, even as developed by later decisions, had not created a system that was free from arbitrariness, discrimination and, most important of all, of mistakes. The confidence of prosecutors, juries, and government officials also began to wane, and when combined with several other factors, such as improvements in the quality of defence counsel, the exclusion of juveniles and the mentally retarded, and the spread of life without the prospect of parole, brought about a decline in death sentences imposed and executions carried out in all death penalty states, particularly those that 'historically have added the most inmates to their death rows—California, Texas, Florida, North Carolina, Pennsylvania, Oklahoma and Alabama'.[228] Death sentences fell from 317 in 1996 to 114 in 2006, and executions from 98 in 1999 to 53 in 2006. Executions became confined to relatively few states. Over the six years 2001 to 2006 just 21 of the 38 states with the death penalty carried out an execution (four of them only one execution, and a further 10 no more than four executions over the six years). The 53 executions in 2006 occurred in just 14 states: Texas (24), Ohio (5), Florida (4), North Carolina (4), Virginia (4), Oklahoma (4), Montana (1), Nevada (1), California (1), Indiana (1), Mississippi (1), Alabama (1), South Carolina (1), and Tennessee (1).[229] So, during this year, 22 states with the death penalty on their statute books did not execute anybody, and when the 12 wholly abolitionist states and the District of Columbia are

---

[228] Scott E. Sunby, 'The Death Penalty's Future: Charting the Crosscurrents of Declining Death Sentences and the McVeigh Factor' *Texas Law Review* 84 (2006), pp. 1929–1972 at 1955.
[229] Death Penalty Information Center website: <http://www.deathpenaltyinfo.org>.

added to them, 69 per cent (35 out of 51) of US state jurisdictions had no executions in 2006. Furthermore, Texas accounted for 45 per cent of the executions. Another way of looking at this is to note that 14 of the 38 retentionist states have executed no more than six people since 1976—at the most one every four to five years and for most of these states there has been much longer between executions. Indeed, since 1977, 83 per cent of all executions have been carried out in just nine states (Texas, Virginia, Oklahoma, Missouri, North Carolina, South Carolina, Georgia, Alabama, and Florida), and over one-third in Texas alone. Steiker and Steiker have accurately described the use of the death penalty in America as 'A tale of two nations'.[230]

(ii) Factors influencing the debate

Particularly dramatic in bringing about the reassessment of the death penalty in America was the action taken by the Governor of Illinois in January 2000, when he was informed that a study by student investigative journalists had uncovered convincing evidence that Anthony Porter, who had earlier come within two days of execution, had been wrongfully convicted of a crime for which another man had confessed; that a further innocent man was awaiting execution on Illinois's death row; and that a further 12 had been released because they were deemed to have been wrongfully convicted. In announcing an immediate moratorium on executions, pending the outcome of the review by a 14-member Commission on the administration of the death penalty, which had been ordered in May 1999 by the Illinois House of Representatives, Governor Ryan declared:[231]

I have grave concerns about our state's shameful record of convicting innocent people and putting them on death row. And, I believe, many Illinois residents now feel that deep reservation. I cannot support a system which, in its administration, has proven to be so fraught with error, and has come so close to the ultimate nightmare, the state's taking of innocent life.

This had an immediate impact. There were widespread calls for reform,[232] which some saw as the stepping stone to final abolition.[233] Public support for the death

---

[230] Steiker and Steiker, n. 220 above.

[231] Amnesty International (2000) *United States of America: Failing the Future*, AI Index: AMR 51/003/2000.

[232] James Liebman has argued: 'For me, the question of abolition does not arise. The capital punishment machine continues to kill…the machine's appetite for that outcome may be at the root of most of its existing problems, so reform almost inevitably must run in the direction of fewer death sentences'. He suggests 'a trade': 'In return for a genuine assurance of the trial and direct appeal protections…capital defendants would agree to give up state post-conviction review and a significant amount of federal habeas review': 'Opting for Real Death Penalty Reform' *Ohio State Law Journal* 63 (2002), pp. 315–342 at 320 and 334.

[233] In the same vein, Austin Sarat advocates a practical (as opposed to purely moral) approach to abolition, describing this approach as the 'new abolitionism': 'The new abolitionism provides an important contemporary avenue for engagement in the political struggle against capital punishment, allowing opponents to change the subject from the legitimacy of execution to the

penalty was shaken: a poll conducted by the Chicago Tribune in February 2000 found that 58 per cent of registered voters were in favour of it, compared to 76 per cent in 1994. An ABC News poll in April 2001 found that 51 per cent of Americans favoured a moratorium on executions until a commission could report on whether the death penalty was being applied fairly, and in some states as many as 70 per cent of citizens supported a moratorium[234] (see Chapter 10). Similar concerns about the fairness of the system were voiced in Maryland, Massachusetts, Nebraska, Washington, and many other states.[235] In April 2000 and again in January 2001 Bills (the National Death Penalty Moratorium Act of 2000) were introduced in the US Senate to establish a National Commission to review the administration of the death penalty and to suspend executions under state and federal law until it had reported. In both New Hampshire[236] and New Mexico[237] Bills to abolish the death penalty were narrowly defeated. Ten jurisdictions had set up such Commissions by the end of 2001 to study the way in which the death penalty was administered, with a view to ascertaining whether improvements could be made to eliminate the possibility of arbitrary or wrongful conviction. Furthermore, in five states Bills were passed to ensure that capitally convicted persons would have access to DNA testing and in a further nine states and the Federal system Bills were introduced to that effect.

In June 2000 the publication of a study carried out at Columbia University showed that about two-thirds of death sentences imposed between 1973 and 1995 had been reversed during the processes of state and federal reviews and appeals (see Chapter 7, pages 270–271). The patent flaws in police, prosecutorial, and judicial practice, brought out so vividly in Professor Liebman and his colleagues' analysis of why such a large proportion of death sentences have been overturned,

---

imperatives of due process, from the philosophical merits of killing the killers to the sociological question of the impact of state killing on our politics, law and culture': 'The "New Abolitionism" and the Possibilities of Legislative Action: the New Hampshire Experience' *Ohio State Law Journal* 63 (2002), pp. 343–369 at 368. See also Carol S. Steiker and Jordan M. Steiker, 'Should Abolitionists Support Legislative Reform?' *Ohio State Law Journal* 63 (2002), pp. 417–432.

[234] Death Penalty Information Center website, *Summaries of Recent Poll Findings*: <http://www.deathpenaltyinfo.org>. See also *San Francisco Chronicle*, 21 July 2000, reporting that 73% of citizens polled supported a moratorium in order to study the fairness of the state's capital punishment system.

[235] In the years 1999–2001 Bills to restrict the use of the death penalty, and some to abolish it (although with little hope of success), were introduced in at least 30 retentionist states, and attempts to introduce a moratorium to halt executions were under consideration in at least 15 states and the Federal system: Michael L. Radelet, 'More Trends toward Moratoria on Executions' *Connecticut Law Review* 33 (2001), pp. 845–860.

[236] In May 2000 the New Hampshire Senate endorsed the State House of Representatives' earlier decision to abolish the death penalty (which had not been imposed for many years) and to replace it with life imprisonment without parole. However, the Governor of the State, Jeanne Shaheen, vetoed the Bill, and when it was reintroduced in April 2000 it was narrowly (by a 188–180 vote) defeated.

[237] A Senate Bill to abolish capital punishment was lost by only one vote in February 2001. However, an execution took place later that year (at the defendant's own request), the first execution in New Mexico since 1960.

fully justified his assertion that capital punishment in the USA is a 'broken system'.[238] Far from convincing abolitionists that all errors were ultimately discovered, the opposite conclusion was drawn. Namely, that it was likely that some innocent persons had probably been executed. Undoubtedly, the concern about wrongful executions, an issue never previously at the fore of the American abolitionist debate,[239] has become of much greater significance, perhaps indicating a greater appreciation that the system of capital punishment in the USA (although largely a matter for state law) bears on the nation's reputation as a whole. The Death Penalty Information Center and the Innocence Project, led by Professor Barry Scheck of Cardozo Law School, have played an important role in bringing to public attention the fact that as many as 124 persons have been freed from death row between 1973 and July 2006 on the grounds that they were innocent, and that the annual rate has been increasing. Of particular note is the high standard of proof provided in 12 of these cases through the use of DNA evidence.[240]

Former Justice Sandra Day O'Connor, a staunch supporter of capital punishment, acknowledged the inadequacy of many defence lawyers in capital cases and expressed concern that 'the system may well be allowing some innocent defendants to be executed'.[241] Similarly, Judge Gerald Kogan, formerly Chief Justice of the State of Florida, announced his opposition to capital punishment after

---

[238] J. S. Liebman, *et al.*, 'A broken system: Error rates in capital cases, 1973–1995' *Columbia University School of Law*, 12 June 2000: <http://www2.law.columbia.edu/instructionalservices/liebman/liebman2.pdf>. It should be noted that in other countries as well the number of death sentences affirmed after appeal is usually very low. See, for example, Roger Hood and Florence Seemungal, *A Rare and Arbitrary Fate. Conviction for Murder, the Mandatory Death Penalty and the Reality of Homicide in Trinidad and Tobago* (2006), p. 31, available at <www.penalreform.org/resources/rep-2006-rare-and-arbitrary-en.pdf>.

[239] Samuel Gross, 'Lost Lives: Miscarriages of Justice in Capital Cases', *Law and Contemporary Problems* 61 (1988), pp. 125–217 at 125. Also, writing in 1998, Michael Radelet and Hugo Adam Bedau noted that, up to that time, 'The fact that innocent persons (in one or another sense of "innocence") are executed seems to have had little if any real impact on opinion towards the death penalty'. See 'The Execution of the Innocent' *Law and Contemporary Problems* 61 (1998), pp. 105–217 at 118. Note that when Herbert Haines published his book in 1996 he suggested that the question of miscarriages of justice had not up till then had an impact on the abolitionist debate because there had not been sufficient incontrovertible evidence that innocent people had been executed: Haines, *Against Capital Punishment. The Anti–Death Penalty Movement in America, 1972–1994* (1996), pp. 87–92. In part this may have been due to the impression that possibility of execution of the innocent was ruled out by the lengthy appeals process, in part because problems that arose in one state may have had little impact on the views of citizens in other states; but partly also because of a failure to mount an effective media campaign in relation to worrying cases of wrongful conviction. See Roger Hood, 'Capital Punishment' in Michael Tonry (ed.), *The Handbook of Crime and Punishment* (1998), pp. 739–776 at 764.

[240] See Barry Scheck, Peter Neufeld, and Jim Dwyer, *Actual Innocence: Five Days to Execution and other Dispatches from the Wrongfully Convicted* (2000). The website of the Innocence Project stated in September 2007 that there have been 207 post-conviction DNA exonerations in US history: <http://www.innocenceproject.org/>. Note that the different figures for this project and the Death Penalty Information Center are accounted for by a stricter definition of 'innocent' adopted by the latter (at the Death Penalty Information Center website: <http://www.deathpenaltyinfo.org>).

[241] Speech in Minneapolis to women lawyers on 2 July 2001, reported in Amnesty International, *Death Penalty News*, September 2001, AI Index: ACT 53/004/2001.

serving for twelve years as a Justice of Florida's Supreme Court, on the grounds that the court had 'certainly...executed those people who either didn't fit the criteria for execution in the state of Florida or who, in fact, were factually not guilty of the crime for which they were executed'.[242] The decision of Judge Rakoff in the Federal District court in Manhattan in June 2002, although overturned, may prove to be more than a straw in the wind. He held that the Federal Death Penalty Act is unconstitutional because it:[243]

not only deprives innocent people of a significant opportunity to prove their innocence, and thereby violates procedural due process, but also creates an undue risk of executing innocent people, and thereby violates substantive due process.

As one scholar has suggested, a wrongful execution during a time of 'soft' support for capital punishment may tip the balance toward abolition.[244]

In 2002, after two years of deliberation, the Illinois Commission issued its report on capital punishment, hailed as a blueprint for the way in which other states and the federal government should review the operation of capital punishment in their jurisdictions to ensure that it is administered fairly, equitably, and with sufficient due process.[245] A slight majority of the members declared itself in favour of abolition of the death penalty in Illinois, but all agreed that if it were to continue as a legally sanctioned punishment ('because it appears to have the support of the majority of Illinois citizens'), there would have to be sweeping reforms of legal, administrative, and criminal justice procedures.[246] Of particular significance, given that the Commission believed that such reforms

---

[242] See report in *The Spectator*, March 2001. In addition Justice Blackmun of the US Supreme Court, a former supporter of the death penalty, had in 1994 announced his opposition to it, and so had former Justice Powell, who had also while on the court favoured capital punishment (John C. Jeffries Jr., *Justice Lewis F. Powell, Jr.: A Biography* (1994)), both of them on the grounds that it could not be administered fairly. Other examples include former Chief Justice James Exum Jr. of the North Carolina Supreme Court, who in July 2000 castigated the death sentence which 'cheapens the rest of us; it brutalizes the rest of us; and we become a more violent society' (quoted in Jeffrey L. Kirchmeier, 'Another Place Beyond Here: The Death Penalty Moratorium Movement in the United States' *University of Colorado Law Review* 73 (2002), pp. 2–116 at 32).

[243] *New York Times*, 1 July 2002.

[244] Sunby, n. 228 above, at 1964–1968.

[245] Statement of Robert E. Hirshon, President of the American Bar Association, on the report of the Illinois Commission on Capital Punishment, 15 April 2002.

[246] Eighty-five recommendations were made including: that its scope should be substantially reduced from the 20 factual circumstances which made a defendant eligible for a death sentence in Illinois to only five circumstances, regarded as the most egregious types of murder; that procedural protections for suspects under interrogation should be greatly enhanced; that certain types of evidence could not be used to support a capital conviction, such as that from a jailhouse informant or accomplice, or from a single eyewitness; that a state-wide panel would have to review prosecutors' decisions to seek the death penalty to avoid the great disparities that were found to exist; that there should be enhanced training for trial lawyers and judges in capital cases; that judges must concur with the jury before a death sentence is imposed; and that the state Supreme Court should conduct in every case a proportionality review. The fact that such protections had not been in place for those currently on death row (about 160) was regarded as a potent reason for considering whether

were essential if the system were to be made 'fair, just and accurate', was its state-ment that:[247]

the death penalty itself is incredibly complex...there are few easy answers. The Commission was unanimous in the belief that no system, given human nature and frailties, could ever be devised or constructed that would work perfectly and guarantee absolutely that no innocent person is ever again sentenced to death.

On 11 January 2003, shortly before leaving office, Governor Ryan announced that he was granting clemency to all 167 prisoners on Illinois' death row, stating dramatically:[248]

Our systemic case-by-case review has found more cases of innocent men wrong-fully sentenced to death row. Because our three-year study has found only more ques-tions about the fairness of the sentencing; because of the spectacular failure to reform the system; because we have seen justice delayed for countless death row inmates with potentially meritorious claims; because the Illinois death penalty system is arbitrary and capricious—and therefore immoral—I no longer shall tinker with the machinery of death...Our capital system is haunted by the demon of error—error in determining guilt, and error in determining who among the guilty deserves to die. Because of all of these reasons today I am commuting the sentences of all death row inmates.

Similarly, the *Report of the Nevada Assembly Subcommittee to Study the Death Penalty and DNA Testing* called, in June 2002, for a host of reforms, includ-ing restricting the number of aggravating factors making defendants liable to the death penalty and the provision in all cases of proper legal representation. In the same year, the Governor of Maryland also announced a moratorium on executions until a study of racial bias in the administration of the death pen-alty had been completed. Five years later, in February 2007, Governor Martin O'Malley urged Maryland lawmakers to repeal the state's death penalty, saying the punishment is 'inherently unjust, does not serve as a deterrent to murder and saps resources that could be better spent on law enforcement'.[249] And in April 2007 Governor Timothy Kaine of Virginia, personally opposed to the death pen-alty, vetoed Bills aimed to expand its scope.[250]

In 2003 the American Bar Association (ABA), while taking 'no position on the death penalty per se', launched a series of inquiries (as part of its Death Penalty Moratorium Implementation project, established in 2001), 'to examine a

---

many of these persons should be granted clemency. Illinois, *Report of the Governor's Commission on Capital Punishment. George H. Ryan Governor* (April 2002), pp. i–iii.

[247] *Ibid.*, p. 207. In May 2002 Governor Ryan announced legislation to put into effect the Commission's recommendations. The reform package suggested by the Commission was overwhelmingly approved by the General Assembly in November of 2003.

[248] Rob Warden, 'Illinois Death Penalty Reform: How it happened, what it promises' *Journal of Criminal Law and Criminology* 95 (2005), pp. 381–426.

[249] *Washington Post*, 22 February 2007.

[250] *Washington Post*, 5 April 2007.

number of US jurisdictions' death penalty systems and preliminarily determine the extent to which they arrive at fairness and due process'. Each state was to be judged by a high-level state-based Assessment Team against protocols established by the ABA in its publication *Death without Justice: A Guide for Examining the Administration of the Death Penalty in the United States*. So far (July 2007) reports have been issued on the situation in Georgia, Arizona, Alabama, Indiana, and Tennessee. The Assessment teams have found flaws in the systems in all of these states—especially poor legal representation for those facing the death penalty; inadequate proportionality review of death sentences; flaws in the statutory definitions of capital murder; imprecise definitions of mental retardation; and a lack of means to ensure the absence of racial discrimination. In other words these states 'at this point in time...cannot ensure that fairness and accuracy are the hallmark of every case in which the death penalty is sought and imposed'.[251]

The Assessment Panel for Georgia, with one abstention, recommended that the State Georgia 'should impose a moratorium on both capital prosecutions and on executions until such time as the State is able to appropriately address the problem areas identified throughout this Report'. As regards Arizona, it did not recommend a moratorium, but called on the state to address the issues identified. The Alabama Assessment Panel, with one dissention, joined with over 450 other organizations—religious institutions, newspapers, and city/town/county councils—in calling on the State of Alabama 'to impose a temporary moratorium on executions until such time as the state is able to appropriately address the problem areas identified throughout this Report'.[252] In February 2007, the Indiana Assessment Team issued a similar recommendation that all executions be halted, based on its finding that the application of the death penalty in Indiana was arbitrary. The report stated that 'The seemingly random process of charging decisions, plea agreements, and jury recommendations is just part of a death penalty system that has aptly been called Indiana's "other lottery"'.[253] For similar reasons, the report on Tennessee also recommended that the state should impose a temporary moratorium on executions until it could ensure that 'fairness and accuracy are the hallmark of every case in which the death penalty is sought or imposed'.[254]

In 2003, Governor Mitt Romney of Massachusetts, a supporter of capital punishment in principle, appointed a Council on Capital Punishment. Its purpose was to consider 'any idea that might constitute "best practice" for a possible death penalty statute' in that State and 'the legal and forensic safeguards that would be necessary before a fair death penalty statute could be considered in

---

[251] American Bar Association (ABA), *Evaluating Fairness and Accuracy in State Death Penalty Systems: the Georgia Death Penalty Assessment Report*, 2006, Executive Summary p. v.

[252] ABA, *Evaluating Fairness and Accuracy in State Death Penalty Systems: The Alabama Death Penalty Assessment Report*, June 2006, p. vi.

[253] ABA, *Evaluating Fairness and Accuracy in State Death Penalty Systems: The Indiana Death Penalty Assessment Report*, February 2007.

[254] ABA, *Evaluating Fairness and Accuracy in State Death Penalty Systems: The Tennessee Death Penalty Assessment Report*, March 2007, executive summary, p. ix.

Massachusetts'. The Council recommended that any statute should include only a 'narrowly defined list of death-eligible murders...so that only "the worst of the worst" murders, and murderers, will be eligible for the ultimate punishment', plus a series of safeguards 'which will ensure—as much as is humanly possible—that no innocent person will ever be wrongly condemned to death'.[255] The five categories of murder chosen on the basis that 'the overwhelming majority of such murders are among the most heinous of all crimes' were:

(1) murder as an act of political terrorism,
(2) murder to obstruct justice,
(3) narrowly defined torture-murder,
(4) multiple murder in a single episode,
(5) multiple murder in more than one episode, and
(6) murder by a defendant who is already subject to a sentence of life imprisonment without possibility of parole for a prior murder.[256]

It has been disputed whether the crimes included in this list do include only those type of cases in which the overwhelming majority of defendants deserve death—take, for example, murders of multiple intra-family members—and whether there would not 'inevitably be' 'legislative' or 'aggravator creep' as categories were added in response to particularly heinous cases of other types of murder. As Professor Franklin Zimring tellingly put it:

If we ever do get an American state legislature that passes a death penalty statute without the killing of a law enforcement official as a normal aggravating circumstance, I will come back to the Indiana University campus and push a nickel with my nose from the Student Union to the Law School!

Zimring described the Commission's solution as 'all hat and no cattle' as it prescribed a death penalty that would never in all likelihood produce a single execution (see further, Chapter 8).[257] In fact, in 2005, the Massachusetts House of Representatives threw out a Bill based on Governor Romney's so-called 'gold standard' formula by 100 to 53 votes.[258]

  On 26 June 2004 the New York Court of Appeals held that a provision of the state's death penalty law was unconstitutional, and subsequently, in April 2005, the Codes Committee of the New York Assembly voted 11 to 7 against considering legislation to reinstate the death penalty.[259] One important factor in the

---

[255] 'Report of the Governor's Council on Capital Punishment—Introduction' *Indiana Law Journal* 80 (2005), pp. 1–27 at 2–3.
  [256] *Ibid.*, at p. 11.
  [257] Franklin E. Zimring, 'Symbol and Substance in the Massachusetts Commission Report' *Indiana Law Journal* 80 (2005) pp. 115–129 at 119–120 and 122.
  [258] Sunby, n. 228 above, at 1930–1931.
  [259] In 1995, following the defeat of Mario Cuomo, who, as Governor of New York, had continually resisted attempts by the legislature to reintroduce capital punishment, the new Governor, George E. Pataki, had reinstated capital punishment—32 years after New York's last execution.

decision not to reinstate the death penalty was the very high costs involved in capital trials with relatively little success for the state. Codes Committee Chair Joseph Lentol explained: 'We have spent more than $170 million administering the death penalty since 1995 but not a single person has been executed'.[260] Kansas, which had brought back the death penalty, despite the Governor's opposition in 1994, also had the constitutionality of its death penalty statute attacked. In December 2004 the Kansas Supreme Court held that the state's death penalty law was invalid under the Federal Constitution, because it gave the prosecution an unfair advantage over defendants during the sentencing process. This was overturned by the US Supreme Court in 2006 in *Kansas v Marsh*, holding that Kansas's death penalty law, which allowed for the imposition of the death penalty when a jury finds that the aggravating and mitigating circumstances in a case have equal weight, is in fact constitutional, thereby reinstating the death penalty in Kansas. However, a strong dissenting opinion from Justice Souter, joined by Justices Stevens, Ginsberg and Breyer, held that in such a case, by definition:[261]

the jury does not see the evidence as showing the worst sort of crime committed by the worst sort of criminal, in a combination heinous enough to demand death. It operates, that is, when a jury has applied the state's chosen standards of culpability and mitigation and reached nothing more than what the Supreme Court of Kansas calls a 'tie'.

Further Bills to create commissions to study the death penalty, to implement a moratorium, or to abolish it were introduced in a number of states in 2004, 2005, and 2006, but although they generally received strong support none passed the legislative process.[262] However, there was success in New Jersey in January 2006 when legislation (passed by the assembly by 55 to 21 and the senate by 30 to 6) was approved by the Governor of New Jersey, to impose a moratorium on executions until a study of the death penalty system had been completed. The Hon. John J. Gibbons, former Chief Justice of the United States Court of Appeals for the Third Circuit, summarized the situation of the death penalty in New Jersey for the Commission:[263]

Twenty-four years after the enactment of the New Jersey death penalty statute, no one has been executed in the State of New Jersey [the last execution was in 1963], and there

---

New York had previously abolished capital punishment in 1965, except for the murder of a police officer on duty or for murder committed by a prisoner serving a life sentence. In October 2007 the New York Court of Appeals ruled that the death sentence of the last remaining inmate on the state's death row was unconstitutional under state law: *New York Times*, 23 October 2007.

[260] *Assembly Release Death Penalty Report*, 4 April 2005, Assembly Speaker Sheldon Silver. The prosecution had sought the death penalty in 55 cases, with seven persons having been sentenced to death. In five of these cases the death sentence had been reversed on appeal, with two still awaiting the outcome of appeal at the time that the death penalty was declared unconstitutional.

[261] *Kansas v Marsh* 548 U.S. 548 (2006) at 5.

[262] Bills introduced in 2005 were unsuccessful in Connecticut, Mississippi, New Mexico, and Virginia: OSCE, *The Death Penalty in the OSCE Area, Background Paper* 2006, pp. 73–74.

[263] *The New Jersey Death Penalty Study Commission Report*, 2 January 2007, at p. 60.

are only nine people on death row. The result in this state is that a sentence of death is in reality a sentence to incarceration in death row for decades, with the threat of execution overhanging the prisoner at all times, and the prolongation of painful uncertainty for the families of victims.

In January 2007 the Commission submitted its report, and recommended that the death penalty in New Jersey be abolished and replaced with life imprisonment without the possibility of parole.[264] The Commission also recommended that any cost savings be used to benefit survivors of victims of homicide. On 17 December 2007 the Governor signed the Bill abolishing capital punishment.

A further, and to many an unexpected, challenge has arisen from claims that what was thought to be a 'humane' method of execution, namely lethal injection, may instead create a risk that the prisoner will suffer excruciating pain during the process. Beginning with a Federal Court decision in California in 2006, executions were temporarily suspended in eleven states while the efficacy of the protocols for administering the drugs—to ensure that the prisoner was completely unconscious before the fatal drugs that paralysed the body and stopped the heart were injected—were fully investigated.[265] The issue was not whether capital punishment was per se cruel and unusual but whether the method of achieving death by lethal injection carries with it too great a risk of unnecessary pain and suffering. The matter is now coming to a head, for the US Supreme Court in September 2007 agreed to consider the constitutionality of the drug protocol used in lethal injections in the state of Kentucky (*Base v Rees* No. 07–5439). The Court has since then upheld applications from prisoners in Arkansas, Mississippi, Texas, and Virginia to stay executions by lethal injection until the Kentucky case is decided in the spring of 2008, thus creating until then a de facto moratorium on executions. Whatever the outcome, it is clear that opponents of the death penalty will argue that no method of execution can be devised that avoids all risk of unnecessary pain, while proponents will seek to persuade the court that a different cocktail of drugs can 'do the trick' in an acceptably humane manner (for a more detailed discussion of this issue see Chapter 5, pages 160–165).

---

[264] There was one objection from the Public Defender to life without the possibility of parole (discussed in Ch 11). The Commission determined that '(1) There is no compelling evidence that the New Jersey death penalty rationally serves a legitimate penological intent; (2) The costs of the death penalty are greater than the costs of life in prison without parole, but it is not possible to measure these costs with any degree of precision; (3) There is increasing evidence that the death penalty is inconsistent with evolving standards of decency; (4) The available data do not support a finding of invidious racial bias in the application of the death penalty in New Jersey; (5) Abolition of the death penalty will eliminate the risk of disproportionality in capital sentencing; (6) The penological interest in executing a small number of persons guilty of murder is not sufficiently compelling to justify the risk of making an irreversible mistake; (7) The alternative of life imprisonment in a maximum security institution without the possibility of parole would sufficiently ensure public safety and address other legitimate social and penological interests, including the interests of the families of murder victims; and (8) Sufficient funds should be dedicated to ensure adequate services and advocacy for the families of murder victims'. *Ibid.*, Executive Summary, p. 1.

[265] Kavan Peterson, 'Death penalty: lethal injection on trial', 17 January 2007: <http://www.stateline.org/live/details/story?contentId=171776>.

In any event, the abolitionist movement in the USA, which as late as the 1990s appeared to have very little political weight behind it, has shown a remarkable revival in the last few years, as evidenced by the developments recounted in this chapter.[266] In light of these developments two related questions still remain: why do the majority of US jurisdictions continue to retain the death penalty, especially when most of them enforce it by executions only very rarely? And what is the likelihood that the USA will abolish the death penalty in the future?

(ii) Explaining the Continuance of Executions in America and Prospects for Abolition

David Garland has persuasively argued that the reason why the USA, 'the last nation in its peer group', has not abandoned capital punishment is not because of 'long standing cultural differences' between it and other democratic Western nations which have rejected capital punishment, but rather because of a series of 'proximate causes' which have acted on the USA during the time when the divergence between it and European nations over the last twenty to thirty years occurred. He was here referring to 'America's distinctive institutions of federalism, popular democracy and constitutional review' in the context of a conservative backlash against the *Furman* decision combined with punitive attitudes fuelled by fears of rising crime and violence. He concluded therefore that:[267]

America is the last Western nation to complete the abolition process not because of any peculiarly punitive attitudes or any deep-seated cultural commitment but because the political mechanisms for nation-wide abolition do not exist there in the form that they exist in other nations.

As a result, the death penalty has more of a symbolic meaning than any utilitarian justification. In a recent article, Garland described this as a form of political discourse:[268]

For the most part, American capital punishment is not about executions (which are relatively rare—more people are killed each year by lightning). It is about campaigns, taking polls, passing laws, bringing charges, bargaining pleas, imposing sentences, and

[266] For a first-class analysis of the reasons why the anti-death penalty movement was so weak, see Herbert H. Haines, *Against Capital Punishment. The Anti-Death Penalty Movement in America, 1972–1994* (1996), p. 167: 'In a nation where policy advocacy has become a capital-intensive enterprise, death penalty opponents have little money. On an issue that is fought mostly at the state level, abolitionism consists primarily of eastern-based national organizations with weak state affiliates and few local ones. These two disadvantages are linked intimately to a third. In the cynical and angry climate that exists in America, abolitionists have trusted mostly in their ability to bring about not just a national change of *mind* but a change of *heart*. What has remained undeveloped in the movement is a more pragmatic vocabulary, capable of doing more than just preaching to the choir'.

[267] D. Garland, 'Capital punishment and American culture: some critical reflections' *Punishment and Society* 7 (2005), pp. 347–376 at 347.

[268] David Garland, 'Death, denial, discourse: on the forms and functions of American capital punishment' in David Dwownes, Paul Rock, Christine Chinkin, and Conor Gearty (eds.), *Crime, Social Control and Human Rights: From moral panics to states of denial, Essays in Honour of Stanley Cohen* (2007), pp. 136–144.

rehearing cases. It is about talk rather than deeds, anticipated executions rather than actual executions. What gets performed, for the most part, is discourse and debate.

Another approach taken in recent years by academic commentators is to attribute the USA's retention of the death penalty to aspects of culture unique to the USA, particularly as compared to Western Europe. These authors term this cultural distinctiveness 'American exceptionalism'.[269] Franklin Zimring defines American exceptionalism in terms of vigilante values, primarily from the American South, that outweigh due process values.[270] The cultural tradition of lynching is expressed in the use of the death penalty in the contemporary world. James Q. Whitman highlights a different form of American exceptionalism, namely the cultural tendency towards 'harsh' punishment in America that does not exist in Western Europe. Specifically, Whitman argues that the American cultural characteristics of egalitarianism and distrust of state power result in an absence of mercy and respect towards defendants and hence have increased the willingness to use the death penalty.[271] However, David Garland regards the resort to notions of 'American Exceptionalism' as unhelpful because '[b]ut for specific events and decisions, above all the *Furman*, *Gregg* and *McCleskey* decisions, which could have unfolded differently, the United States could well have been in the abolitionists camp today'. Furthermore, although he agrees that 'many of the same forces that previously prompted lynchings nowadays prompt capital punishment', he insists that capital punishment today in the USA is 'the inverse of lynching' being 'heavily proceduralized, regulated by Federal law and administered by state officials ... The defendant's constitutional rights of due process are fastidiously upheld'.[272] The explanation of why some states of America cling to the death penalty remains a contentious issue.

Some commentators have suggested that the nature of American Federalism, under which capital punishment in practice (at least until McVeigh's execution) was a matter mainly for state law and for state politics, has meant that the issue

---

[269] See, e.g. James Q. Whitman, *Harsh Justice: Criminal Punishment and the Widening Divide Between America and Europe* (2003); Franklin E. Zimring, *The Contradiction of American Capital Punishment* (2003); Carol S. Steiker, 'Capital Punishment and American Exceptionalism' *Oregon Law Review* 81 (2002), pp. 97–130.

[270] See review by Paul J. Kaplan, 'American Exceptionalism and Racialized Inequality in American Capital Punishment' *Law and Social Inquiry* 31 (2006), pp. 149–175. Another aspect of Zimring's argument relates to the 'privatization' of post-*Furman* death penalty jurisprudence in using the death penalty as a means to provide 'closure' for secondary victims. For empirical support of Zimring's position, see David Jacobs, Jason T. Carmichael, and Stephanie L. Kent, 'Vigilantism, Current Racial Threat and Death Sentences' *American Sociological Review* 70 (2005), pp. 656–677.

[271] Kaplan, n. 270 above, at 149–175.

[272] David Garland, 'The Peculiar Forms of American Capital Punishment' *Social Research* 74 (2007), pp. 435–464 at 437, 439, and 459. Garland has also argued that both Zimring and Whitman are relying on eighteenth and nineteenth century notions which are incapable of explaining the late twentieth century divergence between the USA and Europe concerning death penalty abolition: 'Capital Punishment and American Culture' *Punishment and Society* 7(4) (2005), pp 347–376.

was isolated from the kind of international pressures described in Chapter 1.[273] Indeed, in a mission to the USA in 1996, the International Commission of Jurists was dismayed to find 'a general lack of awareness among state officials, and even amongst judges, lawyers, and teachers, of the obligations under the international instruments that the country had ratified'.[274] As Stuart Banner put it, in his history of the death penalty: 'The state judges and prosecutors responsible for administering capital punishment were scarcely concerned that citizens of Paraguay and Germany might consider them a bloodthirsty lot'. He was referring to the cases of Angel Breard and Walter La Grand, executed while their cases were still under consideration by the International Court of Justice in relation to the denial of their right to consular assistance under Article 36 of the Vienna Convention on Consular Relations (see Chapter 7, pages 234–235).[275]

This 'localization' of the debate is made potent by the embrace of 'populist democracy' through which populist sentiment and the views of powerful interest groups are much more keenly felt by elected representatives, including key players in the justice system such as public prosecutors and judges who are often elected and subject to re-election by popular vote, than they are in Europe. In the 1990s it was said that the populist nature of American politics had made it impossible for a candidate for high office 'to run for president, governor, or other high elective office if he or she can be selectively targeted as "soft on crime": the candidate's position of the death penalty is the litmus test'.[276] And it also appeared that 'the politics surrounding the election and retention of state judges has made it more difficult for judges to overturn or refuse to impose death sentences without losing their judgeship'.[277] The experience of Justice Penny White, ousted from the Tennessee Supreme Court after overturning the death sentence of a man convicted of raping and murdering an elderly woman, proves that this did not affect only trial judges.[278]

What, then, is the likelihood of death penalty abolition in the USA? There appears (as mentioned in Chapter 1, pages 37–38) to be some evidence that the US Supreme Court and governmental apparatus have begun to review the country's practices as regards the death penalty so as to bring them more in line with the development of international norms. It was of great significance that the majority of the Supreme Court in *Atkins v Virginia*, decided in June 2002,

---

[273] L. J. Hoffmann, 'Justice Dando and the "Conservative" Argument for Abolition' *Indiana Law Review* 72 (1996), pp. 21–24.

[274] International Commission of Jurists, *Administration of the Death Penalty in the United States* (1996).

[275] Stuart Banner, *The Death Penalty: An American History* (2002), p. 303.

[276] H. A. Bedau, 'The United States' in P. Hodgkinson and A. Rutherford (eds.), *Capital Punishment: Global Issues and Prospects* (1996), pp. 45–76 at 50.

[277] *Ibid.*, at 50; S. Bright, 'Political Attacks on the Judiciary: Can justice be done amid efforts to intimidate and remove judges from office for unpopular decisions?' *New York University Law Review* 72 (1997), p. 308.

[278] Verna Wyatt, 'Given them Death' *The Nashville Tennessean*, 22 July 1996.

cited worldwide condemnation of the execution of mentally retarded defendants among its reasons for deciding that it could now be declared 'cruel and unusual punishment', and in 2005 referred to the international opinion against the execution of minors in *Roper v Simmons* in holding that the execution of individuals who were under age eighteen at the time of the commission of the crime was cruel and unusual punishment (see Chapter 6, page 192).

Those who continue to support the death penalty obviously hope that the reforms emanating from the various State Commissions set up to examine the administration of capital punishment will tighten up the system sufficiently, so that citizens will come once again to believe that only the most egregious and clearly guilty cases are executed—especially if DNA evidence becomes statutorily available to inmates to help at least some of them to establish their innocence. Yet, given the evidence of the low incidence of its use in all but a handful of Republican-dominated southern states, where as Carol and Jordan Steiker put it, 'the legal process that follows the return of a death sentence is far more likely to be nasty, brutish and short',[279] the concerns about the possibility of error and the probability of unfairness in other 'symbolic' death penalty states, make it seem more likely that it will wither away in most jurisdictions, leaving a few 'outliers' and maybe in the end only Texas as an executing state.

As Frankin Zimring has opined: 'the endgame in the effort to purge the United States of the death penalty has already been launched'.[280] It may not be many years before the Supreme Court will be able to find that the majority of states do not support the death penalty, and that like other nations with which it shares common values, 'the emerging standards of decency' that mark the progress of a nation will no longer tolerate the use of capital punishment.[281]

---

[279] Carol S. Steiker and Jordan Steiker, 'A Tale of Two Nations...', n. 220 above, at 1915.
[280] Zimring, n. 269 above, at 205. See also Sunby, n. 228 above.
[281] See *Weems v United States* 217 U.S. 349, 378 (1910) and *Trop v Dulles*, 356 U.S. 86, 101 (1958).

4

The Scope of Capital Punishment in Law

This chapter reviews what is known about the range of offences that may be subject to capital punishment in various countries and the extent to which death sentences are imposed and carried out by execution.

1. Offences Punishable By Death

Unfortunately it is impossible to provide, for all countries, accurate and up-to-date information on the range of crimes for which offenders may be sentenced to death. This is because so few of them have provided such information to the United Nations and it is beyond the scope of this work to obtain information directly from every retentionist and abolitionist *de facto* country and to have statutes translated into English. We do know, however, that in line with the aspiration of United Nations policy 'to progressively restrict the number of offences for which capital punishment might be imposed' and with Article 6(2) of the ICCPR, which states that 'In countries which have not abolished the death penalty, sentence of death may only be imposed for the most serious crimes' (see Chapter 1, page 21), many retentionist countries have restricted the scope of capital punishment. Some have done this as a prelude to, or in conjunction with, a moratorium on executions, with a view to moving towards complete abolition, as was the case in Kazakhstan, Kyrgyzstan, and Tajikistan. And while Belarus has yet to announce a moratorium, it has also greatly reduced the number of capital crimes (see Chapter 2, page 60).

In 2001 the Human Rights Committee, on receiving a report from the Democratic People's Republic of Korea, welcomed the reduction of capital offences from 33 to 5 as well as the readiness, confirmed by the delegation, further to review the issue of capital punishment with a view to its abolition.[1] Vietnam has also signalled its intentions by reducing the number of capital crimes from 44 to 29—still, of course, a very high number. China too, has indicated that it will reduce the number of offences for which capital punishment can be inflicted (see Chapter 3, pages 98–101).

---

[1] UN Doc. A/56/40 Vol. 1, 2000–2001, pp. 99–100.

Nevertheless, as this chapter will show, the range of crimes for which the death penalty may be imposed in some countries is still very wide and the UN Human Rights Committee, established under the ICCPR, has criticized a number of them in recent years, including Vietnam,[2] Yemen,[3] and Syria,[4] for failing to restrict the scope of capital punishment in accordance with Article 6(2).[5] In addition, the Special Rapporteur on Extrajudicial, Summary, or Arbitrary Executions has expressed concern on various occasions and directed appeals to Nigeria, Pakistan, Saudi Arabia, and Somalia, all relating to persons sentenced to death for religious offences or offences against morals.[6]

There has been even greater concern when countries have expanded rather than contracted the number of offences that may be punished by death. Thus, the Committee were alarmed by the recent increase in the number of capital offences in Morocco, even though no persons had been executed for any crimes since 1994 and abolition appears to be under consideration (see Chapter 3, page 66).[7] However, this example illustrates an important point. The fact that various offences *can* be punished by death does not necessarily mean that those convicted of such offences *are* or *will be* executed. The threat of capital punishment may be intended to have a denunciatory force rather than a utilitarian one. A country that still executes some of its citizens convicted of murder may be abolitionist *de facto* as regards other capital offences that have yet to be abolished *de jure*. And a country already abolitionist *de facto* may remain so, however many new offences are added to the list of 'capital' crimes. If the measure is the trend in the actual enforcement of capital punishment, then the picture becomes much more optimistic.

(a) What are 'the most serious crimes'?

As pointed out in Chapter 1 (pages 21–22), the concept 'most serious crimes' was not, at the time the ICCPR was being drafted, given a precise meaning. It was a product of its time, for in 1957 when Article 6 was drafted only a minority of countries had abolished capital punishment. It was, in reality, a 'marker' for the policy of moving towards abolition through restriction, nothing more specific than that. In reaching judgments about what would be an acceptable use of the death penalty, reference would need to be made not only to changes in the

---

[2] UN Doc. A/57/40 Vol. 1, 2002, 82(7), p. 60.
[3] UN Doc. A/60/40 Vol. 1, 2005, p. 68.
[4] *Ibid.*, p. 79.
[5] And in previous years at least 15 other countries: Algeria, Belarus, Cameroon, Egypt, Guatemala, India, Iraq, Japan, Kuwait, Libya, Morocco, Peru, Sri Lanka, Sudan, and Zambia. See Martin Scheinin, 'Capital Punishment and the International Covenant on Civil and Political Rights: Some Issues of Interpretation in the Practice of the Human Rights Committee', paper presented to the EU-China Human Rights Seminar, Beijing, 10–12 May 2001.
[6] UN Doc. E/CN.4/2002/74, para. 114.
[7] UN Doc. A/60/40 (Vol. 1) 2005, pp. 36–37.

practices of nations as they affected the development of norms that define acceptable forms and levels of state punishments, but also to the development of the concept of human rights itself. Thus, the meaning of 'most serious' would need to be dynamically interpreted in an ever more restricted way.

The first attempt to do this came in 1984 when the Economic and Social Council of the United Nations adopted by resolution the Safeguards Guaranteeing Protection of the Rights of those Facing the Death Penalty.[8] The first of these safeguards specified that 'capital punishment may be imposed only for the most serious crimes, it being understood that their scope should not go beyond intentional crimes with lethal or other extremely grave consequences'. Although the definition of 'most serious crimes' could, of course, vary in different social, cultural, religious, and political contexts, the emphasis on *intention,* and on *lethal* or *other extremely grave consequences,* was intended to imply that the offences should lead to loss of life or be life-threatening, in the sense that death is a very likely consequence of the action. Indeed, the Human Rights Committee has laid it down that the concept of 'most serious crimes' employed in the Covenant (Article 6, paragraph 2) 'must be read restrictively to mean that the death penalty should be a *quite exceptional measure*'.

Several other attempts have been made to define more precisely what does constitute 'most serious crimes', usually by stating what should be excluded. Thus, Article 4(4) of the American Convention on Human Rights stipulates that 'in no case shall capital punishment be inflicted for political offences or related common crimes'. The Commission on Human Rights, in its resolutions 1991/61 and 2004/67, urged all states that still maintain the death penalty to ensure that it is not imposed for non-violent financial crimes or for non-violent religious practices or expressions of conscience. In a series of judgments[9] the UN Human Rights Committee has extended this list to include offences such as 'evading military service several times', abetting suicide, drug-related offences, apostasy, committing a third homosexual act, 'illicit sex', 'vague categories of offence relating to internal and external security', 'a person whose life endangers or corrupts society', and aggravated robbery where the use of firearms did not produce death or wounding of any person.[10] And at its fifty-eighth session in 2002 the Commission added to this list 'sexual relations between consenting adults'.[11] With respect to

---

[8]   On these safeguards more generally, see Chs. 5, 6, and 7.
[9]   William A. Schabas, 'International Law and the Death Penalty: Reflecting or Promoting Change', in P. Hodgkinson and William A. Schabas (eds.), *Capital Punishment: Strategies for Abolition* (2004), pp. 36–62 at 48–50.
[10]   See Official Records of the General Assembly, 37th Session (1982), Suppl. No. 40 (A/37/40), Annex V, para. 7.
[11]   UN Doc. E/CN.4/2002/L.104, para. 4c, 'Promotion and Protection of Human Rights'. Resolution 2005/59, para. f, of the UN Commission on Human Rights, declared 'that the death penalty is not [to be] imposed for non-violent acts such as financial crimes, religious practice or expression of conscience and sexual relations between consenting adults nor as a mandatory sentence'.

Vietnam, it noted that capital punishment could in that country be imposed for 'opposition to order and national security violations', both of which 'are excessively vague and inconsistent with Article 6(2) of the Covenant'.[12] However, no opinion has yet been expressed on whether rape or serious sexual offences against children fall into the prohibited category.

These attempts to define more clearly what does *not* constitute a 'serious crime' for the purpose of capital punishment, more specifically for which offences it is a *disproportionate* penalty whatever other justifications for capital punishment may be employed—is undoubtedly a step in the right direction. But it cannot be denied that the very wording of Article 6 and that of Safeguard No. 1, by retaining the amorphous phrases 'other extremely grave consequences' and 'most serious crimes' has left this issue open to wide interpretation by different jurisdictions. The policy objective of this safeguard has been to lead retentionist countries along the path taken by many (but not all) abolitionist states: namely, to the last stage where capital punishment is available solely for the most serious offences of murder. Our view is that countries that retain the death penalty should move to restrict it to the most serious offences of murder and thus we recommend that Safeguard No. 1 should now read: 'In countries which have not abolished the death penalty, capital punishment may be imposed only for the most serious offences of culpable homicide (murder), but it may not be mandatory for such crimes'.[13] It is encouraging to note that the UN Special Rapporteur, Philip Alston, has also adopted a similar definition.[14] But, of course, neither of us would employ it as a justification for retaining capital punishment for murder.

(b) The principle of non-retroactive enforcement

Article 6 (2) of the ICCPR (see n. 1, page 129 above) allows for the death penalty to be imposed only for crimes that were capital offences in law at the time that the offence was committed. The United Nations Safeguard No. 2 for the protection of the rights of those facing the death penalty added a further condition, namely of 'it being understood that if, subsequent to the commission of the crime, provision is made by law for the imposition of a lighter penalty, the offender shall benefit thereby'.

However, a few countries have introduced the death penalty and made provision for it to be applied retroactively for certain offences, mostly relating to crimes against the state or acts of terrorism. After the Second World War, Israel

---

[12] UN Docs. A/57/40 Vol. 1, 2002, 82(7), p. 68 and A/54/40/, para. 128.

[13] Roger Hood, *The Death Penalty: A Worldwide Perspective* (2002), p. 77.

[14] 'The death penalty can only be imposed where it can be shown that there was an intention to kill which resulted in the loss of life'. *Report of the Special Rapporteur on Extrajudicial, Summary, or Arbitrary Executions* A/HRC/4/20, 29 January 2007, para. 65.

passed legislation so as to make it possible for it to punish severely Nazis found guilty of perpetrating atrocities during the Holocaust. Adolf Eichmann was the first and so far only person to have been executed under this provision in 1962.[15] Iraq, when under Saddam Hussein's regime, also invoked the death penalty retroactively in 1980 for membership of outlawed political parties, and by Decree No. 115 of 1994 the death penalty could be applied retroactively to persons who had evaded military service for the third time. The Decree promulgated by the Algerian government in September 1992, which broadened the definition of 'terrorist and subversive acts', provided for the application of penalties which did not exist at the time of the offence,[16] as did the Acts of Terrorism Act introduced in the Maldives in 1990, although no one has yet been sentenced under that legislation.

There have also been some instances where the death penalty has been made retroactive for other crimes. In 1984 Nigeria extended the death penalty by decree retroactively to cover 19 offences: and two men are known to have been executed for drug offences committed before the decree was promulgated. But since then no other such executions have been reported. When Islamic law was introduced in Sudan in 1983 the death penalty was retroactively applied to adultery between married persons, and concern was expressed when the new Penal Code of 1991, also based on Islamic law, appeared to make it possible to sentence to death persons who had committed apostasy by renouncing Islam prior to 1991. Thus it is clear that not all countries have adhered to the safeguard against non-retroactive enforcement of capital punishment, although it is true to say that there have not been many examples of its breach in more recent years.

Some countries (Burundi, Chad, Chile, Guinea, Guyana, Lebanon, and South Korea) have informed the United Nations that if a crime became punishable by a lesser penalty than death, an offender under sentence would not be eligible to receive that lesser punishment, and thus not be protected under the safeguard. However, to our knowledge no persons have been executed in these circumstances.[17]

---

[15] Israel's official reply to the UN Fifth Survey stated: 'According to the Nazi and Nazi Collaborators (Punishment) Law 1950, crimes against the Jewish people and crimes against humanity are punishable if committed during the Nazi regime (30 Jan 1933–8 May 1945) and war crimes are punishable if committed during World War II (1 September 1939–14 August 1945)'. See Report of the Secretary-General, *Capital Punishment and Implementation of the Safeguards Guaranteeing the Protection of the Rights of those Facing the Death Penalty*, E/1995/78, 8 June 1995, para. 62.

[16] Amnesty International, *Report 1993*, p. 50.

[17] In the USA four states which raised the minimum age limit for the sentence of death to 18 in 1987 did not apply this benefit retroactively to those already under sentence of death, contrary not only to Safeguard No. 2, but also to Art. 15 (1) of the ICCPR, and Art. 9 of the American Convention on Human Rights. This is no longer a threat because the Supreme Court ruled in 2006 that no persons who had committed a capital offence when under the age of 18 could be sentenced to death or executed (see ch. 6, p. 192). The same situation occurred in Pakistan, although this also now appears to have been rectified (see ch. 6, p. 189).

(c) Offences against the state and public order

At present, most countries that retain capital punishment for murder also retain it for certain offences against the state or for offences against the military code in time of war. In some of them the death penalty is limited to offences of waging or attempting to wage war against the state, but in many others it can be imposed for a range of actions that can best be described as 'political offences'. These encompass: treason,[18] espionage, attempting to seize power by unconstitutional means; heading or organizing an insurrectionist movement; acts of terrorism and sabotage, including destruction or damage to buildings, railways, and other state property; and attempts on the life of the head of state, other government officials, or members of foreign embassies. Some of these offences may, in some circumstances, involve loss of life, and thus could be construed as a particular form of murder. For example, in July 2006, 10 men were sentenced to be publicly hanged for bomb attacks in Ahvaz in Iran which killed at least six people and wounded more than a hundred others and on 24 January 2007 four of them were executed at the city's jail in front of the victims' families.[19]

In Pakistan 11 persons were sentenced to death for an assassination attempt on a Pakistani general in 2004 in which 11 people were killed.[20] But many of these 'political offences' are so broadly defined that they can be subject to varying interpretations. Indeed, they may not actually involve death or even injury to any one. In Zambia, for example, 59 men were sentenced to death following the attempted coup of October 1997—despite the fact that no one was harmed—although their sentences were later commuted by President Mwanawasa.[21] In November 2003 nine men were sentenced to death in Myanmar for high treason (under Article 122 (1) of the Penal Code, which makes the death penalty mandatory for high treason), accused of plotting to plant bombs and also planning to assassinate members of the State Peace and Development Council.[22] In Sudan,

---

[18] In some countries, such as Singapore, the death penalty is mandatory for treason.

[19] According to Amnesty International, the four men were denied access to their lawyers in the two weeks prior to their execution. The bodies of the executed men were reportedly not handed to their families for burial, and there were fears that they would be buried in an unmarked, mass grave site *La'natabad* ('place of the damned'). Furthermore, the security forces reportedly prevented people from visiting the families to offer condolences: Amnesty International, *Public Statement: Iran: Four Iranian Arabs executed after unfair trials*, AI Index: MDE 13/005/2007.

[20] *BBC News*, 21 February 2006.

[21] Amnesty International, *Zambia: Time to Abolish the Death Penalty*, AI Index: AFR 63/004/2001, p. 14. On 18 December 2003 the Supreme Court upheld the treason convictions and death sentences of 44 of the 59 soldiers, ruling that the government had failed to prove the substantive involvement in the coup of 10 prisoners, who were immediately freed (5 soldiers died awaiting their appeal). Source: Bureau of Democracy, Human Rights, and Labor, US Dept. of State, 25 February 2004. In February 2004 President Levy Mwanawasa commuted the death sentences of the 44 coup plotters, saying he will never carry out an execution while in office: *BBC News*, 27 February 2004.

[22] According to an Amnesty International report, following a visit to Myanmar in December 2003 the Minister of Home Affairs reported that the government is considering commuting these

in 2004, a woman was sentenced to death 'for singing songs inciting men to go to war', although she was later released on appeal.[23] Although in these instances no persons have (as yet) been executed, the fact is that they all faced the uncertainty of whether they would be put to death.

In the last thirty years at least 24 countries[24] (including 13 since 1988[25]) have extended capital punishment variously to one or more of the following crimes: espionage, treason, terrorism or subversive acts, organized murders by a terrorist group, seriously endangering public security, attempting to assassinate the president, sabotage, counter-revolutionary activities, membership of revolutionary groups, threatening the geographical boundaries of the state (in Jordan the sale of occupied land to Israel and by the Palestine Authority for selling property to a Jew), organizing or promoting the secession of any parts of the country, evading military service several times, meeting to seek territorial or administrative dismemberment of the state, or even more broadly framed 'crimes against the state'.

To take some examples, in Saudi Arabia the law provides the death penalty for 'sabotage and corruption on earth' to a potentially very wide range of actions:[26]

Anyone proved to have carried out acts of sabotage and corruption on earth which undermines security by aggression against persons and private or public property such as the destruction of homes, mosques, schools, factories, bridges, ammunition dumps, water storage tanks, resources of the treasury such as oil pipelines, the hijacking and blowing up of airplanes, and so on...

In November 2000 legislation on the establishment of a Human Rights Court in Indonesia was passed, which ironically included the death penalty as the maximum penalty for a number of serious human rights violations.[27]

The Egyptian Penal Code was criticized by the United Nations Human Rights Committee in 1993 for similarly defining too widely the range of acts covered by

death sentences—as well as those of the other 200 people then on death row—and stated that the government would not carry out any executions: *Myanmar: The Administration of Justice—Grave and Abiding Concerns*, AI Index: ASA 16/001/2004.

[23] *Report of the Special Rapporteur on Extrajudicial, Summary, or Arbitrary Executions*, E/CN.4/2005/7/Add.2, August 2004, para. 56.

[24] Algeria, Bahrain, Bangladesh, Belarus, China, Dominica, Egypt, Ghana, Guatemala, Indonesia, Iraq, Japan, Jordan, Kenya, Malaysia, the Maldives, Morocco, Nigeria, Pakistan, Saudi Arabia, Sri Lanka, the USA under federal law, Uzbekistan, and Vietnam.

[25] Algeria (1992); Bahrain (2006); Bangladesh (1992); China (1982–1992); Egypt (1992); Iraq (1994); Japan (2000); the Maldives (1990); Morocco (2003); Nigeria (1994); Saudi Arabia (1988); Sri Lanka (1988) and the USA (1994).

[26] Amnesty International, *Saudi Arabia: Defying World Trends: Saudi Arabia's Extensive Use of Capital Punishment*, AI Index: MDE 23/105/2001.

[27] Amnesty International, *Indonesia: First Executions in Five Years—a Step Back*, AI Index ASA 21/016/2001.

Article 86 on terrorism, which can be punished by the death penalty. This states that:[28]

> terrorism means any use of force, violence, *threat or intimidation* perpetrated as part of an individual or collective plan aimed at *breaching public order*, or endangering *public safety* or security, if this leads to *harming* or terrorizing individuals or endangering their lives, *freedom or security, or causing damage to* the environment, means of transport or communications, public or private property or buildings, *or occupying or appropriating* any of these, *or preventing or obstructing the authorities, places of worship or educational establishments in the performance of their duties, or preventing the implementation of the Constitution, laws or regulations* [our emphasis].

Clearly there are many acts so encompassed which would not appear to fall within the meaning of Safeguard No.1 or Article 6 (2) of the International Covenant. The United Nations Human Rights Committee called on the Egyptian authorities 'to bring legislation in conformity with the provisions of Article 6 of the Covenant [the right to life] and, in particular, limit the number of crimes punishable by the death penalty'. However, Egypt has chosen to ignore these recommendations.[29]

In respect of the maintenance of *public order,* at least 14 countries have made it a capital offence to use firearms or explosives, especially but not necessarily when their use results in death.[30] Singapore, for example, has extended capital punishment to the use of firearms to commit or attempt to commit any crime. Furthermore, in Russia, where a moratorium is in force pending abolition, it remains a capital offence to make an attempt on the life of a person administering justice or making preliminary investigations, or of a police officer. And in China, Sri Lanka, and Uganda it is a capital offence to trade illegally in, or smuggle, arms.

Aircraft hijackings are often associated with *terrorist activities*. In the 1970s this seemed to be a growing problem, in the same way that terrorist bombings are considered in the first decade of the twenty-first century, and several countries responded by introducing the death penalty, especially, but not solely, in circumstances where there was loss of life. It remains a capital offence in China (sabotage), Indonesia, Egypt, Japan (for causing an air crash and for killing a hostage), Kuwait, Thailand, and the United States of America (under federal law). The last country to add aircraft hijacking or sabotage to its list of capital offences was Bangladesh, in 1997.

---

[28] This concern was reiterated by the International Federation for Human Rights in 2005: 'Of major concern is that acts of terrorism, which carry the death penalty and may be tried in Emergency State Security or military courts, are broadly and vaguely defined under article 86 of the Penal Code. As a result individuals are judged for loosely defined crimes in tribunals which lack the basic guarantees of a fair trial on charges for which they may pay with their life': <http://www.fidh.org/article.php3?id_article=2264>.

[29] Amnesty International, *Egypt: Increasing use of the death penalty*, AI Index: MDE 12/017/2002.

[30] Bangladesh, Cuba, Democratic Republic of Congo, Ghana, Grenada, India, Kuwait, Malaysia, Mali, Nigeria (including attacks on customs officers), Pakistan, Singapore, Sri Lanka, and the USA under the Anti-Terrorism Act 1996.

In retentionist countries the range of *military offences* for which capital punishment can be imposed on a serving soldier is very wide, including: mutiny, desertion, insubordination, refusal to execute an order, abandoning a post (especially by a sentry), and cowardice in the face of an enemy.[31] But in many retentionist countries military law can also be enforced on civilians for such offences as: leading an insurrection, inducement of foreign aggression, assisting an enemy, arson of an inhabited structure, destruction by explosives, damage to an inhabited structure by means of flooding, and use of explosives. However, in nearly all retentionist countries these crimes would only be subject to the death penalty in time of war or in a combat situation.

As pointed out in Chapter 1, most of the countries that have abolished capital punishment for crimes committed in peacetime have also abolished it for military offences, even those committed in time of war. This is because they do not find it necessary or desirable to enforce military discipline through threats of execution. Thus, of 101 abolitionist countries at the end of December 2007, only 10 had retained capital punishment for military or wartime offences.

(d) Trading in illicit drugs

Many countries in Asia, the Middle East, and North Africa, and in a few other parts of the world, have responded to international concern about the growth of illicit trafficking in 'dangerous' drugs by introducing the death penalty for both importation and 'possession for sale' of certain amounts of such drugs, or by making the death penalty mandatory for such offences where it was previously optional. According to a survey in 1979, the death penalty could be imposed for drug trafficking in 10 countries. Just six years later, in 1985, a United Nations survey revealed that such offences could, in certain circumstances, be punished by death in 22 countries.[32] By the end of 2006 the number was at least 31.[33] With the exceptions of Cuba (introduced in 1999 for the most serious cases),[34] the Democratic Republic of Congo, Guyana, and the United States of America (in restricted circumstances under federal law), these countries are in the Middle East, North Africa, Asia, and the Pacific region. Notable has been the introduction of the death penalty into the federal law of the United States for those involved in large-scale drugs offences as part of

---

[31] More than 300 British soldiers who were shot during World War I for alleged military offences, including cowardice in the face of the enemy and desertion, received posthumous pardons in 2006.

[32] Slawomir M. Redo, *United Nations Position on Drugs Crimes*, UNAFEI Resource Material No. 27 (1985).

[33] Bahrain, Bangladesh, Brunei Darussalam, China, Cuba, Democratic Republic of the Congo, Egypt, India, Indonesia, Iran, Iraq (drug trafficking with the aim of financing or abetting the overthrow of the government by force, Decree No. 3 of 2004), Jordan, Kuwait, Laos, Libya, Malaysia, Myanmar, Oman, Pakistan, Qatar, Saudi Arabia, Singapore, South Korea, Sri Lanka, Sudan, Syria, Taiwan, Thailand, United Arab Emirates, the USA (federal law), and Vietnam.

[34] UN Doc. E/CN.4/2000/3/Add.1, para. 163.

'a continuing criminal enterprise', even though no proof of ensuing death is called for.

In a few other countries the statute specifies that the death penalty will only apply if the trafficking or supplying of drugs results in the death of others. Sometimes, as in Kuwait, it also applies to the murder or attempted murder of law enforcement officials concerned with drug offences, and in some American states (Pennsylvania, New Hampshire, Illinois, and South Carolina), drug trafficking—'a calculated criminal drug conspiracy'—is a statutorily defined aggravating circumstance in murder. In Guatemala and Guyana the death penalty has been extended to embrace cases in which death results from either supplying or administering drugs. Yet, as mentioned above, in most countries the death penalty can be applied simply for the importation and supplying of drugs (and sometimes, as in Bangladesh, cultivation, possession, storage, and even purchase).[35] A number of these countries have made the death penalty mandatory, especially for recidivist drug offenders and trading on a large scale.[36] Others, such as Iran (1969), Thailand (1979), Singapore (1975 and 1989),[37] and Malaysia (1983) have made capital punishment mandatory for possession of even relatively small amounts. The Dangerous Drug Act of Malaysia 1952 (as amended in 1983) states that 'any person found, without authorization, in possession of 15 grams or more of heroin or morphine, 1,000 grams or more of opium or 200 grams or more of cannabis shall be presumed, until the contrary is proved, to be trafficking in the said drug' and thus sentenced to death. The amounts specified in the statutes of some countries, such as Iran (where many more drug offences were made subject to the death penalty under the Anti-Narcotic Drug Law of 1988), are even lower. For example, in Brunei Darussalam the death penalty is mandatory (although no executions have taken place since 1957) for: the unauthorized trafficking, import, or export of over 15 grams of morphine or heroin; possession of over 30 grams of morphine or heroin for the purpose of unauthorized trafficking; and unauthorized manufacture of morphine or heroin.[38] In Vietnam trading, possessing, or trafficking in more than 3½ ounces of heroin and 11 pounds of opium can be punishable by death.[39]

---

[35] For example, the Bangladesh Narcotics Control Act of 1990 gave discretion to the courts to impose a death sentence for offences regarding cultivation, production, possession, carrying, sale, purchase, or storage of heroin and cocaine (if the amount exceeds 25 grams) and other dangerous drugs (if the amount exceeds 10 grams) and for cannabis and opium if the amount exceeds 2 kilograms.

[36] In Saudi Arabia the death penalty is mandatory for recidivist drug distributors and drug smugglers; Amnesty International, *Defying World Trends: Saudi-Arabia's Extensive Use of the Death Penalty*, AI Index: MDE 23/015/2001.

[37] And in 1998 for trafficking in more than 250 grams of crystal methamphetamine; *Amnesty International, Death Penalty News*, June 1998, AI Index: ACT 53/03/98, pp. 4–5.

[38] Amnesty International, *Against the Tide: The Death Penalty in Southeast Asia*, AI Index: ASA 03/01/97.

[39] Vietnamese law states that the death penalty can be imposed on those found guilty of possessing, trading or trafficking in 100 grams or more of heroin, five kilograms or more of opium, or other narcotic substances such as pills weighing 300 grams or more. For this, and further information on the death penalty for drug offences in other Asian countries, see Amnesty International: *UN Anti-Drugs Day: Death Sentences for Drugs Crimes Rise in the Asia Pacific*, AI Index ASA/01/02/2007.

In all of these countries it has been argued that the death penalty is an indisputable deterrent to drug trafficking, but no evidence of a statistical kind has been forthcoming to support this contention. Nor is it likely that any such evidence could be gathered. The low rates of effectiveness of law enforcement, the relative immunity from the law of those who profit most from the trade in drugs, and the higher risks of violence and death they most probably run from others engaged in the drug racket, all make it seem implausible that the death penalty in itself will have a marginally stronger deterrent effect than long terms of imprisonment.

(e) Economic and property offences

The death penalty is provided for various kinds of economic crime in at least 24 countries.[40] For example, bribery or corruption of public officials is a capital offence in at least five countries;[41] embezzlement of public funds or theft of public property in at least nine countries;[42] manufacturing and distributing counterfeit money or securities in at least two;[43] and currency speculation in two.[44] Fraud and forgery, habitual theft, or aggravated forms of theft are also capital offences in at least seven countries,[45] and smuggling in two.[46] Sometimes what might seem like an economic crime is categorized as treason or some other political offence. For example, in February 2007 an officer and a sergeant from the border guard patrol in North Korea were sentenced to death for receiving money to assist defectors,[47] presumably under one of North Korea's five capital offences (conspiracy against the state power, high treason, terrorism, anti-national treachery, and intentional murder). As already mentioned, the question of abolishing the death penalty for economic crimes is now being publicly discussed in both China and Vietnam, where in February 2006 the Ministry of Public Security proposed a reduction in the number of offences punishable by the death penalty 'in tune with the general tendency around the world, which Vietnam should follow'. It was proposed, in particular,

---

[40] Algeria, Bangladesh, Burkina Faso, Cameroon, Cuba, China, Democratic Republic of Congo, Ethiopia, Iran, Libya, Malawi, Malaysia, Mali, Niger, Nigeria, North Korea, Singapore, Somalia, South Korea, Sudan, Thailand, Togo, Uganda, and Vietnam.

[41] Bangladesh, China, Iran (corruption on earth), Thailand, and Vietnam (including private firms).

[42] China, Democratic Republic of Congo, Mali, Niger, Somalia, South Korea, Sudan, Uganda, and Vietnam.

[43] Algeria and China.

[44] Democratic Republic of Congo (sabotage of the Congolese franc) and Libya (speculation in foreign currency). Under Saddam Hussein's regime it was imposed in the wake of the Gulf War for profiteering. However, when capital punishment was reinstated by the new government of Iraq in 2005, it was not made available for economic crimes.

[45] Burkina Faso (aggravated theft causing bodily harm or death), Cameroon, China (theft of cultural relics or large sums), Niger, South Korea (habitual theft), Thailand (aggravated theft causing bodily harm), and Vietnam (embezzling 500 million dong—$33,108—or more of state property).

[46] China (including smuggling giant pandas) and Iraq.

[47] Hands Off Cain: <http://www.handsoffcain.info/news/index.php?iddocumento=9307284>.

that economic crimes, such as fraud and embezzlement, smuggling, counterfeiting, and bribery should no longer be capital offences.[48]

The death penalty is also available for offences against property with violence, in particular robbery with violence in 21 countries,[49] but is now mandatory for this offence in only four countries.[50] At the beginning of January 2004 a delegation from FIDH found that prisoners convicted of aggravated robbery (140 of them) comprised 31 per cent of all prisoners on death row in Uganda.[51] However, mandatory death sentences have been declared unconstitutional by the Ugandan Constitutional Court and by the Supreme Court of Malawi (see Chapter 8, page 283). A challenge to the mandatory death penalty is now under way in Kenya, where over 90 per cent of those on Kenya's death row have been sentenced for 'capital robbery'. Under Section 297 of the Kenyan Penal Code it is sufficient to be convicted of capital robbery for the person to be apprehended in the company of one or more persons at the time the offence occurs and the person does not have to be in possession of a firearm or other dangerous weapon. For example, in June 2004, four men were sentenced to death in Kisumu for robbing a man of Ksh. 20/- (about 2 pence sterling). The sentence was passed by a magistrate without the accused having the benefit of a lawyer.[52] Such crimes, the Human Rights Committee, declared in 2005 'do not qualify as "most serious crimes" within the meaning of Article 6, paragraph 2, of the Covenant'.[53] In his report on his mission to Nigeria, the UN Special Rapporteur, Philip Alston commented on the effect of including armed robbery in the category of 'most serious crimes' subject to the death penalty:[54]

The problem lies in part in the elevation of armed robbery to a capital offence. This seems to have at least two perverse consequences: (1) criminals interrupted in an armed robbery have no disincentive to use arms (either way it will be a capital offence); (2) the police are given a justification to shoot to kill any person who has committed a capital offence and is seeking to flee.

(f) Sexual offences

At least 28 countries retain the death penalty for sexual offences, mostly for rape, especially aggravated rapes such as the kidnapping and rape of a child. For example,

---

[48] Amnesty International, *Socialist Republic of Vietnam Duong Quang Tri: Sentenced to Death for Fraud*, Index: ASA 41/004/2006.

[49] Benin, China, Cuba, Democratic Republic of the Congo, Ghana, Guinea, India, Iran, Malawi, Mali, Morocco, Nigeria, Saudi Arabia, Sierra Leone, South Korea, Sudan, Uganda, United Arab Emirates, Vietnam, Zambia, and Zimbabwe.

[50] Kenya, Saudi Arabia (where death results), Zambia, and Zimbabwe.

[51] FIDH, *Uganda: Challenging the Death Penalty*, Report 425, 2 October 2005, p. 21.

[52] The Death Penalty Project, information supplied to the Fourth Death Penalty Conference, Barbados 3–5 June 2005.

[53] UN Doc. A/60/40 (Vol. 1), 2005, p. 13.

[54] UN Doc. E/CN.4/2006/53/Add., 4 January 2006, para. 43.

rape is among the list of capital crimes in China (in special circumstances, including unlawful sexual intercourse with girls under the age of 14) and Cuba amended its Criminal Code in 1999 to make corruption of minors a capital offence but apparently only to be enforced in respect of the 'most serious crimes'. Rape is punishable by death also in Egypt (abduction combined with rape), Iraq (by a decree of the Revolutionary Command Council in 2001),[55] Kuwait, Lesotho, Malawi, Mongolia (aggravated rape or rape of a minor), Pakistan (gang rape), Saudi Arabia, South Korea, Syria (aggravated rape), Tajikistan (rape with aggravating circumstances), Thailand (other than rape resulting in death: 'rape of a girl resulting in serious injury or death; procuring, recruiting, luring, enticing or coercing a woman or minor for any act of indecency'), Tunisia, Uganda (defilement of a female under the age of 18, rape, and unlawful sexual intercourse with a prisoner), the United Arab Emirates, and Vietnam. The death penalty is mandatory in Jordan where the victim raped is under 15 years of age and in Guatemala when the victim is under the age of 10 and dies.[56]

Under the influence of Islamic law, several countries in the Middle East and North Africa have made adultery and sodomy capital offences: for example, Iran, Mauritania, Pakistan, Saudi Arabia, Sudan,[57] Yemen and Nigeria, where, since 1999, a number of northern states have introduced new penal legislation for Muslims based on the principles of the *Shari'a*, which makes adultery and sodomy capital offences, punishable by stoning to death.[58] According to Amnesty International 'The new *Sharia* penal legislation...criminalize[s] behaviour termed as *zina* (sexually related offences)' and increased the penalty 'from flogging to a mandatory death sentence, applicable to people who are or have been married' who have intercourse with another person.[59] In September 2004 an Islamic court in northern Nigeria sentenced a woman to death by stoning for having sex out of wedlock, although she was later reprieved.[60]

Homosexual acts with violence may be subject to capital punishment in Cuba,[61] and in February 2001 it was reported that a court in the self-declared autonomous region of Puntland in northern Somalia had sentenced to death two women who had had a lesbian relationship, for being guilty of 'exercising unnatural behaviour'.[62] Three men convicted by a Saudi criminal court of homosexual acts were publicly beheaded in Abha, Asir province, on 1 January 2002. As is customary

---

[55] Amnesty International, Iraq: *Unjust and unfair: The death penalty in Iraq*, AI Index: MDE 14/014/2007, 20 April 2007. On 11 February 2007 the Iraqi authorities announced that 14 people had been executed 'in recent weeks' for murder, rape and kidnapping (Hands Off Cain).

[56] Amnesty International, *Guatemala: In the Wake of the Pope's Visit*; AMR 34/054/2002, September 2002.

[57] In Sudan, under the new Penal Code of 1991, based upon an interpretation of the *Shari'a*, a third offence of sodomy is a capital offence.

[58] Amnesty International, *Death Penalty News*, September 2001, AI Index: ACT 53/004/2001.

[59] Amnesty International, *Report 2005*, p. 191.

[60] Hands Off Cain, *Report 2004*.

[61] See UN Report of the Secretary-General, Status of the International Covenants on Human Rights: *Question of the Death Penalty*, E/CN.4/1998/82, App.

[62] Reported by *BBC News*, 23 February 2001.

in Saudi Arabia, the trial proceedings were shrouded in secrecy.[63] The UN Special Rapporteur, Philip Alston, following his visit to Nigeria in 2005, stated: 'characterizing adultery and sodomy as capital offences leading to death by stoning is contrary to applicable Nigerian and International law. Neither can be considered to be one of the most serious crimes for which the death penalty may be prescribed.'[64]

Iranian law casts the shadow of the death penalty over a wide range of sexual offences: incest; sex between a non-Muslim male and a Muslim female; adultery; sodomy; and other homosexual acts after a fourth conviction. The death penalty can also be imposed in Sudan for recidivist prostitution, 'illicit sex', and on conviction for the third time of a homosexual act.[65] When the Taliban ruled Afghanistan, it was a capital offence not solely to commit adultery but for a woman to associate with unrelated males. Prostitution—becoming 'a cause of moral corruption'—is a capital offence in Saudi Arabia. Pimping or procurement for prostitution is also subject to the death penalty in China.

In 1977, in *Coker v Georgia*, the Supreme Court of the United States held that capital punishment was an excessive, disproportionate, penalty for the offence of rape. This was a decision of great importance given that prior to the *Furman* decision in 1972 a considerable number of men (almost all of them black) had been executed after being convicted of rape in southern states. Nevertheless, in 1995 the state of Louisiana passed a law making it a capital offence to rape a female under the age of 12, and the following year, in the case of *Louisiana v Wilson,* the Louisiana Supreme Court ruled that the death penalty for this crime was not unconstitutional. It held that the *Coker* decision applied only to the rape of an adult woman and left open the question whether capital punishment for a non-homicidal rape of a child was excessive. However, Louisiana inmate Patrick Kennedy is the only person on death row nationally for a non-fatal child molestation.[66] In addition to Louisiana, the states of South Carolina, Florida, Montana, and Oklahoma allow the death penalty in some cases of non-fatal child molestation and Texas and Utah are currently considering similar laws.[67] There can be little doubt, however, that these laws will be found to be unconstitutional when a test case reaches the United States Supreme Court.

(g) Religious dissent

Religious dissent in the form of blasphemy or apostasy can be punished with death in at least seven Muslim countries: notably, Egypt, Iran, Libya, Pakistan,

---

[63] Amnesty International, *The Death Penalty Worldwide: Developments in 2002*, Index: ACT 50/002/2003.

[64] UN Doc. E/CN.4/2006/53/Add. 4, p. 12, para. 35, January 2006.

[65] See Special Rapporteur's Report, UN Doc. E/CN.4/1999/39/Add. 1, para. 230. Also Report of the Human Rights Committee, A 53/40, Vol. 1 (1998), p. 33.

[66] Death Penalty Information Center; Kennedy is appealing his conviction to the US Supreme Court in 2007. He was convicted of raping his 13 year old step-daughter (the Louisiana legislature having increased the age below which rape of a child is a capital offence from 12 to 13).

[67] <http://standdown.typepad.com/weblog/2007/04/alabama_conside.html>.

Saudi Arabia, Sudan,[68] and Afghanistan, where, even after the overthrow of the Taliban government, a man was sentenced to death in 2006 for converting to Christianity.[69] In Pakistan capital punishment was made the mandatory penalty for 'defiling the sacred name of the prophet Mohammed' in 1986.[70] Although the Ministry of the Interior acknowledged that the blasphemy laws were in need of amendment,[71] a High Court in July 2001 upheld the death sentence of a Christian sentenced for blasphemy. The Supreme Court of Pakistan acquitted him in August 2002 and even though several more people have since been sentenced to death for blasphemy[72] no one has in fact been executed.

(h) Other crimes

Whilst there will always be regional and jurisdictional variations in what is considered to be a 'serious crime' (for example, there is disagreement over the seriousness of kidnapping),[73] some countries pass laws which make specific behaviours, considered to be a particular problem, or particularly offensive in that jurisdiction, capital offences. Hence, in response to a number of notorious instances, India made assisting to commit *sati* (the burning of widows) a capital crime in 1987. And in 1999 the United Arab Emirates announced that it would now be a capital crime to import banned materials or nuclear waste and to dump or store them in the country.[74] India and Sri Lanka provide the death penalty for giving false or fabricated evidence where the alleged offence is punishable by death and an innocent person is convicted and executed.

---

[68] However, the Sudanese Code gives the convicted apostate time to renounce his heresy and return to Islam and no persons have been charged with this offence since 1985.

[69] Attempting to convert Muslims to Christianity and for an Afghan Muslim to convert to Christianity were made a capital offence. Until freed during the war in Afghanistan in November 2001, eight foreign aid workers had been awaiting trial for 'preaching Christianity' and senior Taliban officials had warned that they might be executed if found guilty; *BBC News*, 5 September 2001. In post-Taliban Afghanistan Abdul Rahman, was charged with apostasy for converting to Christianity, and threatened with the death sentence. He was released from Kabul prison after international condemnation—on the grounds that he was mentally unstable.

[70] Amnesty International, *Pakistan: Insufficient protection of ethnic minorities*, ASA 33/008/2001, 15 May 2001.

[71] Amnesty International, *Pakistan: Blasphemy Laws should be Abolished*, AI Index: ASA 33/023/2001; see also Amnesty International, *Death Penalty News*, September 2001, AI Index: ACT 53/004/2001; also 'Amnesty International Welcomes Releases in Pakistan' *The Wire*, March 2002.

[72] <http://web.amnesty.org/report2003/pak-summary-eng>.

[73] No fewer than 14 countries provide the death penalty for kidnapping: Algeria, Bangladesh (kidnapping and trafficking in women and children in 1996: see Amnesty International, *Report 1996*, p. 90), China, Grenada, Guatemala (1995 for those who threaten to kill victims of kidnapping: see Special Rapporteur's *Report*, UN Doc. E/CN.4/1996/4/Corr.1, para. 210), Guinea, India (kidnapping for ransom), Iran, Pakistan, Singapore, Taiwan, Uganda, the United Arab Emirates, and Yemen. It is also a statutory aggravating circumstance to murder in several other countries, such as Morocco, Thailand, and the American state of Montana.

[74] Amnesty International, *Death Penalty News*, December 1999, AI Index: ACT 53/005/1999.

Perhaps the most extreme recent example of the application of the death penalty to activity that the state seeks to suppress is its introduction in Iran (1993) for dealing in 'obscene products' and producing and distributing pornographic audio or video material. These offences are not, even on the broadest of interpretations, life-threatening in the sense laid down by Article 6(2) of the ICCPR and the first United Nations Safeguard. It is notable that China removed similar offences from the list of capital crimes in the Penal Code of 1997.

(i) The position in China

The scope of the death penalty in China has been so wide that it deserves separate discussion. When the People's Republic of China enacted, in 1979, a new Penal Code and Code of Penal Practice, the death penalty was provided as the maximum sentence in 15 articles, encompassing 28 criminal offences.[75] Nine of the articles were concerned with military crimes and offences relating to national security or of a counter-revolutionary nature, such as sabotage. Six of them dealt with common offences: setting fires, breaking dykes, etc., when leading to serious injuries or death; intentionally killing others; rape; robbery; theft, fraud, or forcible seizure; using violence to resist arrest at the scene of a crime; and corruption.

However, in 1982 and 1983, in response to 'the constant increase of the crimes that seriously endanger social security and economic order',[76] the Standing Committee of the Chinese National People's Congress promulgated two decrees, 'Decision of the Standing Committee of the National People's Congress Regarding the Severe Punishment of Criminals who Seriously Undermine the Economy' and 'Decision of the Standing Committee of the National People's Congress Regarding the Severe Punishment of Criminal Elements who Seriously Endanger Public Security'. Under these two decrees there were 14 new criminal laws for which the death penalty was the maximum sentence. Although Chinese legal scholars criticized these provisions,[77] the tentacles of the death penalty spread to embrace even more offences, including theft, sale of narcotics, being the ringleader of a criminal hooligan group, intentionally injuring others, causing a person serious injury or death, organizing reactionary superstitious sects and secret societies to carry out counter-revolutionary activities, forcing or luring women into prostitution, and 'imparting criminal methods' (a new crime). By the time the New Criminal Law was promulgated in 1997, 'there were more than 50 articles of death penalty in Chinese laws, and more than 70 capital crimes'.[78]

---

[75] See Hu Yunteng, 'On the Death Penalty at the Turning of the Century' in M. Nowak and Xin Chunying (eds.), *EU-China Human Rights Dialogue* (2000), pp. 88–94 at 89.

[76] *Ibid.*

[77] See Amnesty International, *People's Republic of China: The Continuing Repression. The Death Penalty and Anti-Crime Campaigns* (September 1990), AI Index: ASA 17/56/90, pp. 9–12.

[78] Hu, n. 75 above, p. 89.

The New Criminal Law of 1997 abolished capital punishment for a few crimes, such as 'being a ringleader of hooliganism' and also for common theft, but despite the fact that Article 48 provided that the death penalty should be reserved 'for those criminal offenders who have committed extremely serious crimes' (the 1979 Code had used the words 'most vicious' rather than 'most serious'),[79] it still contained 51 articles stipulating the death penalty for 68 crimes, at the discretion of the court in all but two articles of the Criminal Law.[80] It is important to bear in mind that most articles of the Code providing for the death penalty do so with the limitation that it should only be applied in certain, listed, circumstances or more vaguely in 'especially serious circumstances'.[81] The offences include, besides murder: offences against state and public security; grave offences against the economic order including embezzlement, receiving bribes, corruption, racketeering, smuggling (from smuggling firearms and drugs to smuggling cultural relics and rare species of wildlife), tax and VAT evasion, counterfeiting, theft from a banking institution, and stealing precious cultural relics; violent offences including rape, robbery, and illegally manufacturing and trading in firearms; dereliction of duties; manufacturing and trading of drugs, but also providing drug manufacturers with the substances needed to manufacture drugs; kidnapping and abducting women and children, usually for sale; as well as many military offences codified in 11 articles. A judicial officer can receive the death penalty if he 'extorts confession from a criminal suspect or defendant by torture or extorts testimony from a witness by violence...if he causes injury, disability or death to the victim'.

On 6 October 1998 the semi-official *Guangming Daily* outlined China's 'Legislative Guarantees for Human Rights in the Judicial Field'. It stated:

China's principle in applying the death penalty has consistently been to kill only a few, not to kill when this is not absolutely necessary, and only to apply such a sentence for criminals who have committed particularly serious crimes of extremely profound subjective evil, when social order could not be maintained if they were not killed.

Nevertheless, Chinese practice reveals that the death penalty is imposed for some offences which by international standards do not fall under the scope of the most serious or heinous crimes. Offenders found guilty of corruption, embezzlement, VAT fraud, and other economic crimes continue to be sentenced to death and some of them executed. And even where crimes of violence are concerned, it is apparent that not only those who commit the most atrocious acts are sentenced to death.

---

[79] See Hans-Jörg Albrecht, 'The Death Penalty in China from a European Perspective', in M. Nowak and Xin Chunying (eds.), *EU-China Human Rights Dialogue: Proceedings of the Second EU-China Legal Experts Seminar* held in Beijing on 19 and 20 October 1998 (2000), pp. 95–118 at 96. And, Qi Shengui, 'Strike hard', *China Review*, Issue 33, 2005, p. 7.

[80] The death penalty is mandatory in Art. 121 for 'any hijacker who causes serious injury to or death of any other person or serious damage to an aircraft' and in Art. 239 for kidnapping 'if he causes death to the kidnapped person or kills the kidnapped person'.

[81] *The Death Penalty in the United Nations Standards and China's Legal System of Criminal Justice* (1998), p. 536.

However, as mentioned above, the question of abolishing the death penalty for all economic crimes is now being openly debated and a book of essays entitled *The Road to Abolition*, as a signifier of the final goal, was published in 2004. It seems likely that when China ratifies the ICCPR—perhaps in 2008—the death penalty, for these offences at least, will be abolished in order to come some way towards conforming to Article 6(2).

2. The Scale of Death Sentences and Executions

It is one thing for the law to mandate or allow discretion to impose the death penalty. It is another to put it into practice and carry out executions. As we shall see, retentionist countries vary greatly in the number of persons they judicially put to death each year. As the following facts reveal, the law generally and consistently appears to be more threatening than is the enforcement of it.

Table 4.1 shows the trends in the number of death sentences imposed, executions carried out, and the number of countries involved each year, as far as Amnesty International has been able to ascertain, for the twelve years 1995 to 2006.

The main trends revealed by Table 4.1 are:

(1) The number of countries that imposed at least one death sentence in a year was as high as 79 as recently as 1995. But by 2006, in line with the increase in the number of abolitionist countries, it had fallen to 55. Similarly, the number of countries carrying out an execution fell from 41 in 1995 to only 25 in 2006.

(2) The number of *recorded death sentences* has fluctuated a great deal over these twenty years, ranging between 2,756 in 2003 and 7,395 in the following year.

(3) Similarly, there have been large fluctuations in the annual number of *recorded executions*, the lowest being 1,146 in 2003 and the highest 4,272 in 1996.

These figures appear anomalous when seen in the light of the previously described successful movement to abolish capital punishment in so many countries and to reduce its legal scope in others. The explanation seems to lie mainly in the extent to which capital punishment is enforced by the People's Republic of China and the amount and reliability of information about death sentences and executions in that country that are available to Western observers, for the true figures remain a state secret. Indeed, the annual number of executions recorded by Amnesty International in China has fluctuated so much from year to year that they have accounted for between 55 and 90 per cent of all executions recorded worldwide. Thus, any changes in the estimated number in that country greatly affect the international picture. It is clear that in some years there has been a large real increase in the number sentenced to death and executed as a result of China's periodic adoption of *Yanda* or 'strike hard against crime' campaigns. Thus, owing

Table 4.1 Number of death sentences and executions worldwide, 1995–2006

Year	Numbers reported and recorded		Number of countries concerned	
	Death sentences	Executions	Death sentences	Executions
1995	4,165	3,276	79	41
1996	7,107	4,272	76	39
1997	3,707	2,607	69	40
1998	3,899	2,258	78	37
1999	3,857	1,813	63	31
2000	3,058	1,457	65	27
2001	5,265	3,048	68	31
2002	3,428	1,526	61	31
2003	2,756	1,146	63	28
2004	7,395	3,797	64	25
2005	5,186	2,148	53	22
2006	3,861	1,591	55	25

Source: Amnesty International

to the 'strike hard' campaign of 1996, the number of known executions soared to over 4,000. By 1998 the number recorded by Amnesty had more than halved, reflecting, according to the Supreme People's Court of China, the revisions to the Criminal Law, which came into force in October 1997.[82] Yet, in April 2001 another 'strike hard' campaign was set in train, and with such zeal that at least 1,781 people had been executed by the end of July 2001. Eighty-nine people were reported to have been executed in one day.[83] This was reflected in the total number of death sentences (5,265) and executions (3,048) for the whole year: the second largest number of death sentences and third largest number of executions since 1985. Again, in 2004, when the annual number of executions reached 3,797 (2.3 times the number recorded in the previous year), 3,400 (90%) were recorded by Amnesty in China. This may have been partly due to the fact that Amnesty had been able to improve its sources of information but it seems likely that it was a real fluctuation because in the following year, 2005, the number executed worldwide had fallen to 2,148.

Whatever the reason, Amnesty believes that the true numbers of executions, both in China and worldwide, are considerably higher than those it manages to record. For instance, it quoted a delegate to the National People's Congress, Chen Zhonglin, who said in 2004 that 'nearly 10,000' people are executed a year in China and Professor Liu Renwen of the Institute of Law, Chinese Academy of

[82] Amnesty International, *People's Republic of China in 1998* (Summary), AI Index: ASA 17/66/99.corr.
[83] *Agence France Presse*, 12 April 2001. See also Amnesty International, 'China's Execution Frenzy', *The Wire*, September 2001.

Social Sciences, who 'estimated that around 8,000 people are executed per year based on information obtained from local officials and judges'.[84] Also, it should be noted, other organizations provide different and higher estimates. Whereas Amnesty recorded 2,148 executions in 2005, Hands Off Cain reported 5,494 and 24 rather than 22 executing countries.

Nevertheless, there is no doubt that the number of countries that carry out executions has fallen. It appears that no more than 42 countries executed anyone within the five years 2002–2006. In other words, in 14 of the 56 retentionist states in this period there were no reports of anyone being executed. Furthermore, as far as can be ascertained—and one must read these data with a severe 'health warning' as many are merely estimates—only 13 of these 42 countries carried out an execution in every one of these five years. Also, only 15 countries that were *still* retentionist at the end of 2006 (i.e. excluding those that had established a moratorium, such as Kazakhstan and Tajikistan) were known to have executed 20 or more people during the years 2002–2006. Eighteen executed 10 or fewer people—on average, fewer than two a year. By this measure the number of actively retentionist countries, regularly carrying out executions, is now a distinct minority. Furthermore, as can be seen from Table 4.2, only eight nations are known to have executed at least 100 people over the five years 2002 to 2006, an average of 20 or more persons a year: China (by far the largest number), Democratic Republic of the Congo, Iran, Pakistan, Saudi Arabia, the USA, Vietnam, and Yemen.

In making comparisons between countries it is necessary, of course, to bear in mind the relative size of their populations. And it would be better still if it were possible also to relate executions to the number of recorded offences liable to capital punishment, and the number of persons convicted of those offences. But regrettably such data exist only for a few countries, and even for them they are hard to interpret.[85] Table 4.2 shows the estimated rate of executions per million of the population. These execution figures come with a serious 'health warning'. First, they mask quite large annual fluctuations, often associated with political upheavals or perceived threats to the stability of states associated with outbreaks of serious crime. For example, 200 of the 215 executions in the Democratic Republic of the Congo were carried out in one year, 2002, after trials in military courts, but no people were executed in 2004, 2005, or 2006. Secondly, as has already been illustrated in the case of China, many of the figures are acknowledged to be likely underestimates. Amnesty International believes this to be the

---

[84] Amnesty International, *Facts and figures on the death penalty*, AI Index ACT 50/006/2005; Amnesty International, *The People's Republic of China. The Olympics Countdown—failing to keep human rights promises*, AI Index ASA17/046/2006.

[85] David Johnson makes the point that although a relatively small number of executions are carried out in Japan, if they are related to the very low homicide rate 'when it comes to the probability of imposing a death sentence, Japan looks a lot like a US state': David T. Johnson, 'Where the State Kills in Secret. Capital Punishment in Japan' *Punishment and Society* 8 (2005), pp. 251–285 at 267.

Table 4.2 Judicial executions recorded by Amnesty International during the five years 2002–2006 for countries that were still retentionist on 31 December 2006

Country	Total known executions 2002–2006	Annual average number per million population (2004 estimates)
China (est. av. 1,473 p.a.)	7,366	1.12
Democratic Republic of Congo	215	0.68
Iran	651	1.74
Pakistan*	144	0.17
Saudi Arabia	256	1.91
USA	321	0.21
Texas	*123*	*1.17*
Oklahoma	*34*	*1.94*
Vietnam	197	0.46
Yemen	100	1.20

* Note: FIDH recorded at least 229 executions in this period (Report No 464/2 January 2007, page 26).

case in Iran, Egypt, Jordan, North Korea, Pakistan, Syria, Yemen, and Vietnam, because no reliable statistics of death sentences and executions are published by these countries and in some, such as Vietnam, they are regarded as a state secret.

Raw numbers can be misleading when countries vary so greatly in the size of their populations. Thus, China had an annual average of known executions per million inhabitants in the years 2002 to 2006 of 1.12 compared with 1.91 in Saudi Arabia, 1.74 in Iran, and 1.94 in the state of Oklahoma in the USA.

Despite the fluctuating number of executions reported in recent years, there is evidence to suggest that the abolitionist movement may have persuaded many retentionist countries to moderate the frequency with which they have had recourse to executions. Comparing the five years 1996–2000[86] with 2002–2006, it appears that there were substantial falls in the number of known executions in several countries, most notably: Nigeria from 56 to 1; Belarus from 130 to around 12; and in Singapore (which had previously executed the highest annual number of people per head in the five years 1994–1998, 13.85 per million) the number fell from approximately 112 in 1996–2000 to around 45 (2.04 per million annually) during 2002–2006.

Numbers continued to fall in several countries during the quinquennium 2002–2006. Thus, there were 29 reported executions in Egypt in 1999, 49 in 2002 but none reported in 2005 and only 4 in 2006. Forty-one executions were carried out in the province of Taiwan in 1999 and 2000, but only 3 in 2005 and none in 2006. In 1999, 98 people were executed in the USA, but the number fell to 66 in 2001 and to 53 in 2006.

[86] See 3rd edn. of this book (2002), Table 3.2, p. 92.

Only two retentionist countries (China and Iran) executed more people than the United States between 2002 and 2006, yet the United States had one of the lowest rates of execution (an annual average over these years of 0.22 per million population) during this period. However, the figure for the United States as a whole is misleading because executions are much more frequent in some states than others. Indeed, executions are now confined to a relatively few states. Over the five years 2002–2006 just 20 of the 38 states with the death penalty carried out an execution and only 14 of them did so in 2006. Thus 24 of the 38 states with the death penalty on their statute books did not execute anybody, and when the 12 wholly abolitionist states and the District of Columbia (Washington DC) are added to them, 37 of the 50 US state jurisdictions had no executions in 2006. Texas alone was responsible for 45 per cent of the executions in that year. Another way of looking at this is to note that 14 of the 38 retentionist states have executed no more than six people since 1976—at the most one every four to five years and for most of these states there has been much longer between executions.

(a) Executions for crimes other than murder

Although there are still a considerable number of countries that provide for the death penalty in law for crimes other than murder, it is obviously of crucial importance to examine the extent to which persons convicted of such crimes have, in fact, been sentenced to death and executed. Unfortunately, no accurate figures on the extent to which persons convicted of non-homicidal offences are executed are available and those that have been obtained must be regarded as only approximate. Furthermore, executions for 'other' offences may take place only sporadically and therefore a report of such an execution in a particular country cannot be taken to indicate that it is a common event or even that it will be repeated. Nevertheless, the evidence suggests that many fewer countries have carried out executions for crimes other than murder in the last five years than have the power to do so. Indeed, most countries have not executed anyone for such crimes during the past five years. In what follows, we refer only to those countries that still retained the death penalty for non-homicide crimes at the end of 2006.

In the period 2002–2006 reports have been received of executions for sex-related offences from only three of the 26 countries that provided for it. Prisoners have been executed for rape and adultery in Iran (for example, in 2004, Atefeh Rajabi, a 16-year-old girl, was hanged on a street in the city centre of Neka, in Iran, for 'acts incompatible with chastity', even though she was reported to have been mentally ill both at the time of her 'crime' and during her trial proceedings[87]), for homosexuality in Saudi Arabia, for 'pimping' and probably for rape, especially of a minor, in China. In February 2001, when Afghanistan was under

---

[87] Amnesty International, *The Death Penalty*, AI Index: ACT 50/010/2006.

Taliban rule, two women convicted of prostitution were hanged publicly in a sports stadium.[88]

There have been reports of executions since 2002 for armed robbery from only three of the 22 countries that allow for capital punishment for this crime: China, Democratic Republic of Congo, and Sudan. According to Amnesty International, people have been executed for other 'economic crimes', such as corruption, embezzlement, and fraud, in four countries: China, Iran, North Korea, and Vietnam.[89]

Persons convicted of trading in illicit drugs have, since 2002 been executed in eight of the 31 countries with capital punishment for this offence: China, Indonesia, Iran, Kuwait, Saudi Arabia, Singapore (accounting for about three-quarters of all those executed there), Thailand, and Vietnam. A recent survey of 100 death row inmates in Thailand found that 65 per cent of the 54 prisoners who replied had been sentenced for a drugs related offence. Furthermore, three of the four people who were the first to be executed by lethal injection in December 2003 had been convicted of the production of amphetamine tablets.[90]

A few politically motivated offenders have apparently been executed, sometimes for preparing explosives or for armed resistance, in China, Iran, Malaysia (armed treason), Syria, Vietnam, and, more recently, in Iraq. And, according to Amnesty International, in 2005 North Korea (Democratic Republic) executed in public about 70 defectors who had been 'forcibly repatriated' from China.[91]

Not only does China have the widest range of capital offences, it also appears to have executed persons for a wider variety of crimes than any other country. Although the last *Death Penalty Log* produced by Amnesty International for the year 2000 suggested that the majority of executions reported were for murder, often associated with robbery, the use of firearms, and rape,[92] nevertheless, a substantial number were executed for armed robbery, robbery, intentional injury, and the manufacture of, or trading in, large quantities of illicit drugs, the latter largely taking place to mark International Drugs Day in June each year. Indeed, of the 123 executions for drug offences recorded in 2000, 84 per cent also took place in June, 94 of them in the last week of that month.

In 2000 (according to the *Death Penalty Log*) there were quite a few executions of sex offenders for sexual assaults on children, rape, and for kidnapping and selling women into prostitution. A smaller number of white-collar offenders were executed for involvement in large-scale tax evasion, fraud, corruption, counterfeiting

[88] Amnesty International, *Death Penalty News*, March 2001, AI Index: ACT 53/002/2001.

[89] Amnesty International, 'Public Opinion and its Place in the Debate about Abolition of the Death Penalty', paper presented to the EU-China Seminar on Human Rights, Beijing, 10–12 May 2001. See also, Amnesty International, *Socialist Republic of Vietnam: The death penalty—inhumane and ineffective*, AI Index ASA41/023/2003.

[90] FIDH, *The Death Penalty in Thailand*, Report 411/2, March 2005, p. 9.

[91] Amnesty International, *Report 2006*, p. 160.

[92] Amnesty International, *People's Republic of China: The Death Penalty Log 2000*, ASA 17/031/02.

large amounts of money, accepting bribes, and smuggling large amounts of goods. Prominent among those executed for taking bribes and corruption amounting to over 41 million Yuan (about US$5 million) in 2000 was a top-ranking official, Cheng Kejie, a former Vice-Chairman of the Standing Committee of the National People's Congress and a former provincial governor.[93]

According to newspaper reports, executions of officials and traders involved in corruption, embezzlement, tax and VAT fraud, and other economic offences have continued to receive publicity in China. Not only have some high-ranking members of the Communist Party been executed (see Chapter 3, page 99), but so too have senior police officers, and customs and bank officials. In December 2006 two ex-employees of China's third-largest bank were put to death by lethal injection for defrauding customers of millions of dollars[94] and earlier that year, in April, a trade official convicted of corruption in northern China's Hebei province was executed.[95] The former head of China's State Food and Drug Administration, Zheng Xiaoyu, was sentenced to death on 29 May 2007 after pleading guilty to corruption and accepting bribes to the value of US$850,000, and dereliction of duty. He was swiftly executed just six weeks later on 10 July.

Executions have also taken place in recent years for political crimes, such as separatist activities or armed activities aimed at overthrowing the state, and there were some executions also for the theft of cultural relics from tombs and museums.

Some light has been shed on the use of capital punishment in China by a series of studies carried out by a team from the Law Institute of the Chinese Academy of Social Sciences and by Professor Hans Jörg Albrecht of the Max Plank Institute for Foreign and International Criminal Law, *Strengthening the Defence in Death Penalty Cases in the People's Republic of China*.[96] In one metropolitan area 61 per cent of the 119 files studied of persons sentenced to death at the trial of first instance (i.e. before appeal) had been convicted of a violent crime, including robbery with violence, 28 per cent for a property crime, and 8 per cent for 'disrupting social order'. Of 118 who were found guilty, 94 were sentenced to death with immediate effect, 22 had their death sentences suspended, and two were sentenced to imprisonment. An analysis of the sentences imposed on a total of 219 people at this metropolitan court and an Intermediate People's Court in a 'rural area' found that 127 (58%) had been sentenced to an unsuspended (immediate) death penalty, 111 of whom (51% of the total) were eventually executed. In another rural area 85 of the 99 death sentences imposed were immediate: 44 of them were for murder, but of the 44 who had received an immediate death sentence for murder, 18 had their sentence suspended and one had imprisonment

[93] *Ibid.*, at p. 137.
[94] AFP, 15 December 2006, reported at Hands Off Cain.
[95] *Agence France Presse*, 26 April 2006.
[96] Hans-Jörg Albrecht and Research Unit of the Death Penalty Cases Survey, Institute of Law, *Strengthening the Defence in Death Penalty Cases in the People's Republic of China* (2006), pp. 96–117.

substituted at appeal. Thus, 59 per cent had their immediate death sentences confirmed and 41 per cent had them reduced to a lesser sentence.

In a fourth area studied the sample was randomly drawn from cases appearing at the intermediate people's court, in all of which the persons charged were *eligible* for the death penalty. Of the 60 case files studied, 15 (25%) had been charged with murder and 14 with 'assault resulting in death' (manslaughter): 46% in total. At the trial of first instance 14 (23%) of these 60 were sentenced to death with immediate effect and 8 (13%) were given a suspended death penalty (36% in all). However, after the trial of second instance 8 (13%) remained sentenced to immediate execution. In all these areas, it appeared that the defendants most likely to be executed for a death-eligible crime were those who had committed 'stranger-stranger' murders.

(b) Non-enforcement of the death penalty

The findings of the analyses above show that as far as countries regarded as *actively* retentionist (i.e. at least one execution in the 10 years 1997–2006) are concerned, the death penalty in many of them is only rarely enforced by executions, especially for non-homicide offences. When the abolitionist *de facto* countries are also taken into account, it becomes clear that capital punishment, where it remains on the statute books, often has a far greater symbolic than practical significance. In maintaining the *status quo*, the perceived weight of public opinion; the enduring belief that the threat of death, even if not enforced, still has a deterrent power; the belief that it should remain available for the truly 'exceptional case'; and the political fear that abolition may be perceived as a 'sign of weakness', all play their part. For all these reasons, abolitionists cannot be satisfied with non-enforcement of capital punishment, even when it has lasted 10 years or so. This is because its dormant existence in law can readily be translated into a practical reality in response to a heightened fear of crime or to political instability, such that the practice of executing offenders can be revived after decades without use, as has been shown in Chapter 3.

(c) The need for accurate information

It cannot be regarded as satisfactory that the United Nations quinquennial surveys of member states produce such inconsistent and incomplete information on the death penalty and executions that it is impossible accurately to portray international trends. Nor can it be regarded as satisfactory that reliance has to be placed on incomplete reports gathered by the media, or by specialists, or even by non-governmental organizations, which often do not have access to official figures. It is even more regrettable that several retentionist countries publish no data at all on the number of persons sentenced to death or executed. In this respect China, Iran, and Vietnam stand out.

The question of whether the death penalty should be abolished is bound to be affected by citizens' and politicians' appreciation of the facts about its implementation. There is evidence to suggest that the better citizens were informed about the nature, use, and consequences of capital punishment the more they were likely to prefer alternatives to it (see Chapter 10, pages 366–370). Governments therefore have a duty to make sure that all their citizens have the opportunity to base their views about the death penalty on a rational appreciation of the facts. This cannot be done unless there is a commitment to publish all official data on capital crimes and the death penalty and also a commitment to encourage properly funded independent research on the operation of the system at all levels and upon its effects on capital crimes. For example, Article 212 of China's Criminal Procedure Law of 1997 provides for the publication of every execution of a death sentence, and all courts have to prepare written records of the execution, yet no statistics on capital punishment have been published.

Systems of criminal justice need to be accountable to the citizens on whose behalf they enforce the law. They therefore need to be patently transparent: the more so where the death penalty is concerned and the lives of human beings are at risk from misapplication of the law by criminal justice agencies and from judicial error. The UN Special Rapporteur, Philip Alston, has called such secrecy a violation of human rights standards.[97]

Without such transparency and accountability, capital punishment is likely to be regarded as a secretly administered system of social and political repression. Moreover, the lack of accurate and detailed information makes it impossible for anyone, official supporters or opponents of capital punishment, to debate the issue in relation to the realities of how capital punishment is administered and enforced.

In Resolution 1989/64 the Economic and Social Council of the United Nations urged member states 'to publish, for each category of offence for which the death penalty was authorized, and if possible on an annual basis, information on the use of the death penalty'. That information was to include the number of persons sentenced to death, the number of executions actually carried out, the number of persons under sentence of death, the number of death sentences reversed or commuted on appeal, and the number of instances in which clemency had been granted. The poor response from retentionist countries to the Secretary-General's Sixth and Seventh Surveys, as well as the continuing absence of officially published statistics on the use of the death penalty and on the number of executions in many of these countries, has shown, once again, how important it is for member states to respond positively to this request.

---

[97]   UN Doc. E/CN.4/2005/7, 2004.

5

The Death Penalty in Reality: The Process of Execution and the Death Row Experience

1. Executing those found to be Guilty

As mentioned at the beginning of Chapter 1, capital punishment in the past was intended to inflict pain and suffering and at the same time to be a public spectacle delivering a moral message through a dreadful example of the cost of sin and crime.[1] To take but one example: David Johnson tells us that in Japan in the period up to 1867, when most crimes were punished by death, 'execution methods ranged from boiling, burning and crucifixion to several levels of beheading... Prior to execution, condemned criminals were paraded through the streets on horseback. Afterwards, bodies and heads were displayed on platforms or carried through the streets...'.[2] This is not the place to review the history of how, in most countries, executions were removed from the public gaze, and made as swift and painless as appeared possible, but to note that by 1984 there was sufficient international consensus for the UN Economic and Social Council to promulgate Safeguard No. 9 for the protection of the rights of those facing the death penalty in countries that have yet to abolish capital punishment. This declared that: 'Where capital punishment occurs it shall be carried out so as to inflict the minimum possible suffering.' In 1996 the Economic and Social Council made it explicit that this also applied to those under sentence of death awaiting their fate. It urged those member states in which the death penalty may still be carried out 'to effectively apply the Standard Minimum Rules for the Treatment of Prisoners, in order to keep to a minimum the suffering of prisoners under sentence of death and to avoid any exacerbation of such suffering'. This was further strengthened by the Commission on Human Rights when, in Resolution 2004/67, it urged states to ensure that 'where capital punishment occurs it shall not be carried out in public or in any other degrading manner, and to ensure that any application of particularly cruel or inhuman means of execution, such as stoning, is stopped immediately'.

---

[1] Stuart Banner, The Death Penalty: An American History (2002).
[2] David T. Johnson, 'Where the state kills in secret. Capital punishment in Japan' *Punishment and Society* 8 (2006), pp. 251–285 at 257–258.

These safeguards raise questions about the extent to which countries now abide by these standards for treating and executing the condemned. By which method are judicial executions carried out? Are they ever carried out in public? Who carries them out, and, in particular, can and should physicians, who have a duty to preserve life, be involved in enforcing capital punishment? For how long and under what conditions are prisoners kept under sentence of death prior to execution or until their fate is otherwise determined?

(a) The method of execution

It must first be recognized that there is no guarantee that any method of execution will ensure that no physical pain is experienced by the person executed. Human beings can and do make mistakes on occasions when carrying out any activity, and therefore some 'botched' executions are, as Michael Radelet and Marian Borg have demonstrated, 'indisputably an inherent component of the modern practice of capital punishment'.[3]

Replies to the UN surveys and other sources reveal a variety of forms of execution.

At present, the methods used in most of the countries that retain the death penalty are either hanging (for example in Bangladesh,[4] Egypt, Iran, Japan, Jordan, Pakistan, Singapore, and the countries of the Commonwealth Caribbean) or shooting (Belarus, Somalia, and Taiwan, amongst others)—usually by firing squad, as in Guinea, Vietnam, and Yemen but in China by a bullet from a pistol in the back of the head and in Taiwan by a bullet through the back into the heart. Some employ hanging for civilians and shooting for military offences. In Sudan and Iran death can be inflicted by hanging, stoning, or shooting, according to the type of offence. In several other countries in the Middle East, as well as in Northern Nigeria under *Shari'a* law, adultery can still be punished by stoning to death (the person being executed being buried waist deep, or to above the breast if a woman). There have been reports of stoning to death in public in the Islamic Republic of Iran. Even though the head of the judiciary was reported to have sent a directive to judges in 2002 ordering a moratorium on executions by this method,[5] two people were reportedly stoned to death in 2006, whilst others remained under sentence of death by stoning.[6] The common method of execution in Saudi Arabia is beheading with a sword.[7]

---

[3] Marian J. Borg and Michael Radelet, 'On botched executions' in Peter Hodgkinson and William A. Schabas, *Capital Punishment: Strategies for Abolition*, (2004), pp. 143–168.

[4] In 2005, lacking an official hangman, prison authorities in Bangladesh resorted to using 'reliable' inmates. For example, on 6 May 2005 the hanging of Kamal Hossain Hawlader was carried out by four 'suitably prepared' inmates from another prison. See Hands Off Cain, *Annual Report 2006*. Since 1995 Zimbabwe has also found it hard to find a person willing to be the public hangman: *Financial Gazette*, 19 July 2007.

[5] Amnesty International, *Iran. Lives in the balance: An open appeal to Iran's judicial authorities*, AI Index: MDE 13/055/2004, p. 132.

[6] Amnesty International, *Report 2007*, p. 141.

[7] An extreme example of the methods that may still be ordered for executing an offender was the verdict of a Pakistan special court in March 2000, which ordered a man '[convicted of] serial

The American state of Oklahoma became the first jurisdiction to introduce lethal injection in 1977, in place of the electric chair, as the method of execution. Only one state (Nebraska, which still uses the electric chair) has not yet embraced this method.[8] Lethal injection is the sole method authorized in 20 states: in the others there are provisions for electrocution to be used in certain circumstances, the gas chamber, hanging, or a firing squad.[9] But only four states (Alabama, Florida, South Carolina, and Virginia) allow all prisoners to choose between death by lethal injection or electrocution. Almost all executions in recent years have, in fact, been carried out by lethal injection. In July 2006 a prisoner in Virginia chose to die in the electric chair, the first execution by this method for over two years, and another prisoner in Tennessee chose this method in September 2007.

It appears that there remain differing views on what method is least painful or least likely to cause a lingering death. Japan's reply to the UN Seventh Quinquennial Survey in 2004, for example, expressed the view that 'hanging as a way of execution is not particularly cruel in light of humanitarianism compared to other ways such as beheading, shooting, electrocution and lethal gas'. The reality of what may go wrong when hanging is employed is vividly illustrated in the testimony gathered by the organization FIDH in Uganda:[10]

Several death row inmates gave atrocious details about botched executions at Luzira prison. Mr. Godfrey Mugaanyi, now free and one of the founders of Friends of Hope for Condemned Prisoners gave a terrible account of the executions performed in 1991 and 1999… 'In 1999, the late James Kiyingi was hanged. He was the very last person executed that year. However, because of his weight, he did not die and merely fell down on the table in the basement. This prompted the prison warders and the executioners to bundle him up and take him back to the gallows and hang him again. Once again, the same thing happened. This time the prison warders stabbed him and hit him on the head with a hammer until he died.' … 'In 1999, it took Haji Musa Sebirumbi over one hour to die, and he supposedly died in excruciating pain. His execution was video-taped.' These events are not extraordinary exceptions.

It has been known since the nineteenth century that to kill a person by hanging as speedily as possible the length of the 'drop' has to be calculated according to the

---

killing and mutilation of dozens of runaway children … to be publicly strangled, cut … into pieces and thrown into acid'. This was, however, declared 'un-Islamic' by the Council of Islamic Ideology and an appeal was launched. Amnesty International, *Report 2001*, p. 186.

  [8] The last states to do so were Georgia and Florida. See American Bar Association, *A Gathering Momentum: Continuing Impacts of the American Bar Association Call for a Moratorium on Executions* (2000), p. 14. There was a moratorium on executions in Georgia from 1998 to 2001. The Georgia legislature in 2000 had made lethal injection the method of execution for all convicted after 1 May 2000, but left those sentenced prior to this under threat of execution by electrocution. But in September and October 2001, in the cases of *Dawson v the State* (274 Ga. 327) and *Moore v the State* (274 Ga. 229 and 552 S.E.2d. 832), the Georgia Supreme Court held that use of the electric chair violated the state's constitution because it 'inflicts purposeless physical violence and needless mutilation that makes no measurable contribution to accepted goals of punishment'.

  [9] See Death Penalty Information Centre, *Authorized Methods of Execution*.

  [10] International Federation of Human Rights (FIDH), *Uganda: Challenging the Death Penalty*, Report 425/2 October 2005, p. 39.

weight of the person to be executed. If the drop is too short, the neck is not broken and the person hanged dies by strangulation. If it is too long, the head may be torn from the body.[11] This was the fate of Saddam Hussein's former intelligence chief, Barzan Ibrahim al-Tikriti, when he was executed in Iraq in January 2007.

In 2003 a report from the Law Commission of India argued, in contrast to the official Japanese view, that hanging is a particularly painful method of execution and suggested that lethal injection is 'being accepted as the most civilized mode of execution of the death sentence', the pain it induces being 'only as the result of nee-dle prick'.[12] This view has become more widespread. Lethal injection is employed in Guatemala and was the method chosen by the Philippines, prior to abolition. It is now being used, as an alternative to shooting, on an increasing scale in China, where mobile vans equipped for the purpose have been employed to go from area to area. Recently a Chinese scholar, Liu Renwen, estimated that at least 40 per cent of executions are by lethal injection. It is also set to become the standard method in Taiwan, although shooting will still be employed where the condemned has donated organs.[13] On the initiative of the Ministry of Justice of Thailand, lethal injection replaced the firing squad in 2005[14] and this was recommended also by the Vietnamese Police Ministry in 2006. But in this case the reason given was not the pain caused to the prisoner but the adverse psychological effect on the marks-men, particularly when the person executed was a female.[15]

The electric chair—'old sparky' as it was sometimes referred to—was for a long time in America regarded as a modern, more efficient, and humane alternative to the hangman's rope: a view not shared by the British Royal Commission of 1949–53.[16] As recently as 1991, the majority of the Canadian Supreme Court in the *Kindler* extradition case had stated that 'As far as the method of execu-tion, electrocution, is concerned, there is a certain horror involved in any exe-cution and it is far from clear that there are more humane methods'.[17] And the

---

[11] As was made clear by the autobiographical account of the British executioner: see Albert Pierrepoint, *Executioner Pierrepoint: An Autobiography* (1974, new edn 2005). For a damning critique of the practice of hanging, see the minority judgment in *Campbell v Wood* No. 89–35210 US Court of Appeals, Ninth Circuit (1994, 18 F. 3d 662–729).

[12] See *Use of the Death Penalty in India*, New Delhi: South Asia Human Rights Documentation Centre (2004), pp. 21–26 citing the Law Commission of India.

[13] FIDH, *The Death Penalty in Taiwan: Towards Abolition?* 450/2 (June 2006), p. 35.

[14] Amnesty International, *Report 2006*, p. 281.

[15] *Agence France Presse*, 10 February 2006.

[16] See United Kingdom, *Royal Commission on Capital Punishment 1949–1953, Report* (Cmd. 8932, 1953), pp. 253–265 at para. 734: 'we cannot recommend that either electrocution or the gas-chamber should replace hanging as the method of judicial execution in this country. In the attributes we have called "humanity" and "certainty" the advantage lies on balance with hanging; and though in one aspect of what we have called "decency" the other methods are preferable we cannot regard that as enough to turn the scale'. In 1992 the Supreme Court of India held that hanging by the neck is the least painful and the most scientific method of execution: *Shashi Nayar v UOI* [1992] 1SCC 96. Howard Hillman has argued that 'with the certain exception of intravenous injection and the possible exception of shooting, all the procedures are likely to cause severe pain': Dr. Howard Hillman, 'The Possible Pain Experienced during Executions by Different Methods' *Perception* 22 (1993), pp. 745–753 at 750.

[17] *Criminal Reports* 8 CR (4th) (1991), p. 5.

UN Human Rights Committee, in reviewing the *Kindler* case in 1993, had nothing to say about the legality of electrocution. Nor did the US Supreme Court ever give an opinion on the matter.[18] Yet reports had circulated about dramatic instances of 'botched executions' where flames had shot from the prisoner's body. The American scholar Deborah Denno summarized the effects as follows:[19]

charring of the skin and severe external burning, such as the burning away of the ear; exploding of the penis; defecation and micturition, which necessitate the condemned person wearing a diaper; drooling and vomiting; blood flowing from facial orifices; intense muscle spasms and contractions; odors resulting from the burning of the skin and the body; and extensive sweating and swelling of skin tissue.

Considerable controversy also surrounded the use of the gas chamber in the United States. Although only four states still have laws which offer to the condemned this method of execution as an alternative to lethal injection,[20] it is very unlikely that a prisoner would choose it.[21] In any case, in *Fierro v Gomez* (1994) a Federal judge ruled that California's use of the gas chamber is unconstitutional on the grounds of the time that it took to render the prisoner unconscious: it had 'no place in a civilized society'.[22] Furthermore, the UN Human Rights Committee, in reviewing the *Kindler* case in 1993, held Canada to be in breach of the Convention for its extradition of another prisoner, Charles Ng, to California, because he would

[18] The US Supreme Court had granted *certiorari*, for the first time in a case concerning the means of execution, in *Bryan v Moore* in order to consider Florida's use of the electric chair: 528 U.S. 960 (1999). But, in January 2000, the Court dismissed the case as moot, citing Florida's recent legislation which changed its primary method of execution from electrocution to lethal injection: 528 U.S. 1133; 145 L.Ed.2d 927 (2000).

[19] Most notably at the execution of Jesse Joseph Tafero in Florida in 1990, Pedro Medina in 1997, Allen Lee Davis in 1999—and, where death has not been instantaneous, for example, Horace Dunkins in Alabama in 1989 and Derick Lynn Peterson in Virginia in 1990: Deborah W. Denno, 'Is Electrocution an Unconstitutional Method of Execution? The Engineering of Death over a Century' *William and Mary Law Review* 35 (1994), pp. 551–692 at 554–557, 668–670, and 672; and the list of 19 botched electrocution and 31 lethal injection executions in Deborah W. Denno, 'Lethally Humane? The Evolution of Executions in the United States', in Acker, Bohm and Lanier (eds.) (2nd edn., 2003), pp. 693–762 at 740–743. For a description of an execution see Robert J. Lifton and Greg Mitchell, *Who Owns Death? Capital Punishment, the American Conscience, and the End of Executions* (2000), pp. 42–69.

[20] Arizona (if sentenced before November 1992), California, Maryland (if the capital offence occurred before March 1994), Missouri, and Wyoming would allow it if lethal injection should prove to be unconstitutional.

[21] In 1992 lawyers for Robert Alton Harris and other prisoners on California's death row brought a class action claiming that death by lethal gas in California was unconstitutional, being cruel and unusual punishment. The Supreme Court held that Harris had brought this action too late and he was therefore executed on 21 April 1992. For the controversy surrounding the Supreme Court's decision, see Judge Stephen Reinhardt, 'The Supreme Court, the Death Penalty, and the *Harris* Case' *Yale Law Journal* 102 (1992), pp. 205–223; E. Caminker and E. Chemerinsky, 'The Lawless Execution of Robert Alton Harris', *ibid.*, pp. 225–254. For an alternative view, supporting the Supreme Court's decision, S. G. Calabresi and G. Lawson, 'Equity and Hierarchy: Reflections on the *Harris* Execution', *ibid.*, pp. 255–279.

[22] *Fierro v Gomez* (1994) 865 F.Supp 1387 (N.D.Cal.). This was subsequently upheld by a Federal Court of Appeal: *Fierro v Gomez* (1996), 77 F.3d 301 (9th Cir. 1996).

be exposed to execution in the gas chamber: 'a technique which the Committee considered to be torture or inhumane treatment'.[23]

Yet the assumption that lethal injection would be a painless 'clinical' and humane way to put a prisoner to death—merely 'a prick of the needle' as the Indian Law Commission had put it—has come under fierce and relentless scrutiny.[24] Problems soon arose, caused by the failure of those tasked with injecting the drugs to find immediately a suitable vein. This inevitably prolonged the execution process and probably caused the prisoner considerable distress— again, something that the British Royal Commission Report of 1953 had foreseen.[25] Newspaper reports of the execution of Raymond Landry in Texas in 1988 revealed the following scene:[26]

While Landry was strapped to a gurney, executioners in Texas 'repeatedly probed' his veins with syringes for forty minutes attempting to inject potassium chloride. Then two minutes after the execution began, the syringe came out of Landry's vein, 'spewing deadly chemicals towards startled witnesses'. What officials termed a 'blowout' resulted in the squirting of lethal injection liquid about two feet across the room…A plastic curtain was pulled so that witnesses could not see the execution team reinsert the catheter into Landry's vein. After 14 minutes, and after witnesses heard the sound of doors opening and closing, murmurs and at least one groan, the curtain was opened and Landry appeared motionless and unconscious. Landry was pronounced dead 24 minutes after the drugs were initially injected.

This was not a 'one-off' event. A detailed study of all 'botched executions' (those that involved 'unanticipated problems or delays that caused, at least arguably, unnecessary agony for the prisoner or that reflect gross incompetence of the execu- tioner') that had occurred between 1977 and 2001, showed that some lethal injections had 'gone wrong' (3.8%), mainly because 'unanticipated disruption of the flow of drugs to the inmate caused a prolongation of death'. Lawyers began to argue that since freedom from pain could not be guaranteed, lethal injection, like the gas chamber, is cruel and unusual punishment and therefore unconstitutional.[27] But what threw a

[23] William A. Schabas, '*Soering's* Legacy: The Human Rights Committee and the Judicial Committee of the Privy Council Take a Walk Down Death Row' *International and Comparative Law Quarterly* 43 (1994), pp. 913–923 at 916–917.

[24] Deborah Denno pointed out that 'some proponents [of capital punishment] feel that [lethal] injection can save the death penalty from abolition while some opponents believe injection can save inmates from torture': 'When Legislatures Delegate Death: The Troubling Paradox behind State Uses of Electrocution and Lethal Injection and what it Says about Us' *Ohio State Law Journal* 63 (2002), pp. 63–260 at 65–66.

[25] Deborah Denno reminds us that the British Royal Commission Report of 1953 had 'questioned both the humaneness and practicality of lethal injection because of the problems that could result from the peculiar physical attributes of many inmates (for example, abnormal veins) or the medical ignor- ance of the executioners'. Deborah W. Denno, 'Lethally Humane? The Evolution of Executions in the United States', in J. R. Acker, R. M. Bohm and C. S. Lanier (eds.), *America's Experiment with Capital Punishment* (2nd edn., 2003), pp. 693–762 at 711. Professor Denno provides details of the execution protocols for 36 states at pp. 749–762 and the chemical combinations used in 37 states at 745–747.

[26] Quoted by Deborah Denno, 'Execution and the Forgotten Eighth Amendment' in Acker, Bohm, and Lanier, *ibid.*, pp. 547–577 at 564.

[27] Denno, n. 24 above, pp. 100–116.

much larger spanner in the works was mounting evidence that the 'protocol' of drugs used, first, sodium pentothal (thiopental) to induce unconsciousness, then pancuronium bromide to paralyse the body, and, finally, potassium chloride to induce cardiac arrest, was not always administered so as to achieve a painless end. Indeed, death, it was claimed, might be excruciatingly painful if the person had not been rendered unconscious before the second and third drugs were injected.

In November 2004, Theo van Boven, the UN Special Rapporteur on Civil and Political Rights including the Question of Torture and Detention, drew the attention of the US government to toxicology reports of executions in North Carolina.[28] These had:

indicate[d] a great variation in the post-mortem barbiturate levels in persons following executions...a 140-fold variation in doses, from 2.6mg/L (i.e. October 1999 execution of Arthur Boyd) to only 'trace' levels (i.e. December 2002 execution of Desmond Carter)...If the sedative is not properly administered in a dose sufficient to cause death or at least the loss of consciousness for the duration of the execution procedure, the use of the pancuronium bromide places the person at risk for consciously experiencing paralysis, suffocation and the pain of the injection of potassium chloride; it essentially masks the suffering of the person during the execution and gives the appearance of tranquility. Therefore it is reported that this drug has no effect on the efficacy of the lethal injection nor does it render the execution more humane. Moreover, it is alleged that in North Carolina the drugs are administered successively without delay (i.e. without a saline flush between the administration of each drug), which may cause the sodium pentothal to crystallize upon contact with the pancuronium bromide, and result in extreme pain during the procedure.

The argument was further fuelled by the revelation that pancuronium bromide would not be acceptable to a 'veterinarian', more than 30 death penalty states having banned the use of it in the euthanasia of animals.[29]

The publication of an article entitled 'Inadequate anesthesia in lethal injection for execution' together with a leading article under the damning banner 'Medical collusion in the death penalty: An American atrocity' in the renowned medical journal *The Lancet* on 16 April 2005 could not be ignored. The article concluded that:[30]

Toxicology reports from Arizona, Georgia, North Carolina, and South Carolina showed that post-mortem concentrations of thiopental in the blood were lower than required for surgery in 43 of 49 executed inmates (88%); 21 (43%) inmates had concentrations consistent with awareness.

This implied that a painful death was not perhaps the result of an occasional mishap due to a failure of the system for administering the drugs or some physical

---

[28] By letter dated 30 November 2004. See *Torture and other Cruel Inhuman or Degrading Treatment or Punishment: Report of the Special Rapporteur*, Theo van Boven. Addendum. E/CN. 4/2005/62/Add.1, para. 1858, p. 420, 30 March 2005.

[29] John Gibeaut, 'A Painful Way to Die?' *ABA Journal* (April 2006).

[30] Leonidas G. Koniaris, Teresa A Zimmers, David A Lubarsky, and Jonathan P. Sheldon, 'Inadequate anaesthesia in lethal injection for execution' *The Lancet* 365 (9468) (16 April 2005–22 April 2005), pp. 1412–1414.

peculiarities of the person to be executed, but a characteristic failure of the drug sequence protocol itself.

The most graphic evidence to date of the problems involved with lethal injection have been revealed in the case of *Morales v Hickman* which was heard in the US District Court for the Northern District of California in February 2006 before Judge Fogel. The plaintiff sought an injunction to stay his execution so that the Court could conduct a full evidentiary hearing on his claim that lethal injection put him at risk of suffering excruciating pain. The plaintiff presented evidence from execution logs in California to argue that even though five grams of thiopental sodium would render a person unconscious and cause them to cease breathing within one minute of administration, in actual practice, 'for whatever reason', it had not had its intended effect in six of 13 executions carried out between 1999 and 2006, when respirations apparently continued well beyond one minute after the administration of thiopental and the later administration of the following drugs. The judge found that this raised 'at least some doubt as to whether the protocol actually is functioning as intended'. However, he denied the plaintiff's request for a delay in execution and instead ordered the state either to use only a sufficient amount of sodium thiopental or another barbiturate in order to kill the prisoner, or to provide independent verification by a person with formal training and experience in the field of general anaesthesia to verify that the plaintiff is 'in fact unconscious before either pancuronium bromide or potassium chloride is injected'.[31] Subsequently two anaesthesiologists agreed to undertake this task, only to withdraw their consent on ethical grounds the following day after a federal appeals court added the requirement that they should intervene to add medication if Morales appeared to be waking up.[32]

On 15 December 2006 Judge Fogel issued his judgment in *Michael Angelo Morales v James E. Tilton*.[33] The issue, said the judge, was purely about whether the execution 'protocols' were acceptable, not about the morality of capital punishment or the constitutionality of lethal injection *per se*. In other words, it was solely concerned with *the way* in which it was carried out. Nor, he ruled, was the case about whether the execution would be 'painless', for 'binding precedent holds that the Eighth Amendment prohibits only "the unnecessary and wanton infliction of pain"'.[34]

In fact, Judge Fogel uncovered an astonishing catalogue of 'critical deficiencies' in the way that executions had been carried out in California. There was 'inconsistent and unreliable screening of execution team members'; 'a lack of meaningful

---

[31] *Morales v Hickman*, 415 F. Supp. 2d 1037 (N.D. Cal. 2006).

[32] This is because of the Hippocratic Oath, which has, as one of its main tenets, that doctors should never cause intentional harm; see the statement by the American Medical Association and the National Association of Emergency Medical Technicians on Physician Participation in Lethal Injection <http://www.deathpenaltyinfo.org/article.php?did=1849&scid=64>.

[33] Case No. C 06 219 JF RS; C 06 926 JF RS.

[34] Citing *Gregg v Georgia*, 428 U.S. 153, at 173 (1976) (plurality opinion), and procedures that create an 'unnecessary risk' that such pain will be inflicted: *Cooper v Rimmer* 379 F.3d 1029, 1033 (9th Circuit 2004).

training, supervision, and oversight of the execution team' who, extraordinary as it may seem, 'almost uniformly have no knowledge of the nature or properties of the drugs that are used or the risks or potential problems associated with the procedure'. In addition there was unreliable record keeping: 'For example, there are no contemporaneous records showing that all the sodium thiopental in the syringes used for injections actually was injected, and, in fact, testimony revealed that in at least several executions it was not.' Indeed there was 'Improper mixing, preparation and administration of sodium thiopental by the execution team', who worked with inadequate lighting in overcrowded conditions and poorly designed facilities. This was because 'San Quentin officials simply made slight modifications to the existing gas chamber...execution members were too far away to permit effective observation of any unusual or unexpected movements by the condemned inmate, much less to determine whether the inmate is conscious'.

Judge Fogel ruled that:

Given that the State is taking a human life, the pervasive lack of professionalism in the implementation of OP 770 [the drug protocol] at the very least is deeply disturbing. Coupled with the fact that the use of pancuronium bromide masks any outward signs of consciousness, the systemic flaws in the implementation of the protocol make it impossible to determine with any degree of certainty whether one or more inmates may have been conscious during previous executions or whether there is any reasonable assurance going forward that a given inmate will be adequately anesthetized.[35]

However, he stated that, if properly administered, the sequence of drugs would provide for 'a constitutionally adequate level of anesthesia' and that 'the deficiencies in the implementation of the protocol appear to be correctable'. In other words, he concluded 'Defendants' [i.e. the state's] implementation of lethal injection is broken, but it can be fixed'. Consequently, the state was ordered to respond within 30 days as to how it would review and correct the procedures so that a favourable judgment could be given.[36]

For similar reasons a death row prisoner in Tennessee (*Abu-Ali Abdur'Rahman v Phil Bredesen*, on a petition to the Supreme Court, for a writ of *certiorari* to the Tennessee Supreme Court) argued in May 2006 that the execution of Joseph Clark in Ohio earlier that month had been badly flawed. Technicians had, for 22 minutes, searched for a vein in which to insert an intravenous line in each arm, as required by prison procedures, but were able to insert a line in only one arm. It was reported in the press that 'approximately three to four minutes after

[35] Note 33 above, p. 12.

[36] Ellen Kreizberg and David Richter, 'But can it be fixed? A look at constitutional challenges to lethal injection executions' *Santa Clara Law Review* 47 (2007), pp. 101–158, noting at 156 that 'the governors office and the CDCR [California Department of Corruptions] have continually failed to demonstrate any commitment to seriously review or evaluate the lethal injection process'. Seema Shah argues that recent attempts at lethal injection reform constitute unethical and illegal research on prisoners: S. Shah, 'How Lethal Injection Reform Constitutes Impermissible Research on Prisoners' *American Criminal Law Review* 45(3) (2008), available at SSRN: <http://ssrn.com/abstract=1028127>.

the administration of the drug cocktail began, Clark was able to lift his head off the gurney and say, "it's not working".[37] Prison officials then determined that Clark's vein had collapsed, and technicians spent more than a half-hour working behind the curtain to locate another vein in which to insert the IV line. Although the curtain separating the witnesses from the execution was drawn while the technicians attempted to place the new line, Clark 'could be heard moaning and groaning from behind the curtain'. The execution then continued, and Clark was pronounced dead nearly ninety minutes after the execution commenced.

However, the US Supreme Court declined to hear litigation on the constitutionality of lethal injection and let stand a ruling of the Tennessee Supreme Court that the state's use of lethal injection comports with contemporary standards of decency as required under the Eighth Amendment.[38] In November 2006 the Kentucky Supreme Court 'while conceding that the chemicals used to execute death row inmates in Kentucky might cause needless pain', nevertheless ruled that 'using them did not violate the Constitution's prohibition on cruel and unusual punishment'. It recognized that 'Conflicting medical testimony prevents us from stating categorically that a prisoner feels no pain. The prohibition is against cruel and unusual punishment and does not require a complete absence of pain.'[39]

Action has been taken in yet more states. In October 2006 US District Judge Fernando Gaitan Jr. halted all executions in Missouri by confirming an earlier ruling that the death penalty protocol, which uses a three-drug lethal injection, could subject Missouri inmates to an unreasonable risk of cruel and unusual punishment. Judge Gaitan ordered the state to improve the monitoring of inmates to be sure they get enough anesthesia during the execution process. He also ordered that a doctor trained in administering anesthesia either mix the chemicals or oversee the mixing of chemicals for executions.[40]

On 15 December 2006 Governor Jeb Bush of Florida issued an executive order setting up a Commission on Administration of Lethal Injection, 'charged with (and limited to) reviewing the method in which the lethal injection protocols are administered by the Department of Corrections'. This followed the execution of Angel Diaz on 13 December, an execution in which the prisoner was observed to have remained conscious for a protracted period of time before finally dying:[41]

Diaz's execution took more than twice as long as normal—it took 34 minutes—and required two rounds of the lethal chemicals (because the first injection punctured the

---

[37] *The Columbus Dispatch*, 2 May 2006.

[38] *Abu-Ali Abdur'rahman v Phil Bredesen, et al.* No. M2003–01767-SC-R11-CV, Supreme Court of Tennessee, 2005.

[39] Adam Liptak, 'Court rules on Kentucky executions' New York Times, 23 November 2006.

[40] Associated Press, 17 October 2006, reported on the Hands Off Cain website: <http://www.handsoffcain.info/bancadati/schedastato.php?idstato=9000451&idcontinente=26>.

[41] The Death Penalty Information Centre has up-to-date information on these developments: <http://www.deathpenaltyinfo.org>.

veins but entered soft tissue rather than the veins). Witnesses stated that Diaz appeared to be moving, grimacing, and trying to mouth words after the first injection.

The Commission's report laid the blame on the execution team for various failures to follow the execution protocol, rather than on the protocol itself, and their main recommendations therefore were that more oversight and close monitoring of executions was necessary to ensure that inmates were properly sedated and that 'less problematic' alternative chemicals be found. Although Governor Charlie Crist of Florida announced the end of the temporary suspension of executions in his state in July 2007, the issue became one for federal constitutional consideration when the Supreme Court announced in September 2007 that it would review a case from Kentucky. *Baze v Rees* raises yet again the issue of whether the protocol for administering lethal drugs during execution that is used in almost all states carries an unacceptable risk of causing such pain that it amounts to a violation of the Eighth Amendment prohibiting cruel and unusual punishment. As a result, it appears that executions by lethal injection are unlikely to be carried out pending the courts' decision, expected in the summer of 2008. In any case, it appears doubtful that a foolproof system can be devised without the cooperation of the medical profession in executions that employ a 'medicalized' method. This is discussed below (see pages 168–172).

(b) Public executions

Public executions have been condemned by the United Nations Human Rights Committee as 'incompatible with human dignity'.[42] And in Resolution 2004/67 the Commission on Human Rights urged states to ensure that where capital punishment occurs it shall not be carried out in public or in any other degrading manner. Yet executions have taken place in public, or been broadcast on television, in at least 19 countries or territories since 1995.[43] To take a few recent examples: In Uganda military executions took place in 2002 in the presence of about 1,000 people and again in 2003 before 200 people.[44] In Kuwait, in January and May 2004, the bodies of prisoners executed by hanging were afterwards publicly displayed and four men were hanged in public in Kuwait City in

---

[42] UN Doc. No. CCPR/C/79/Add.65, 24 July 1996, para. 16, referring to public executions in Nigeria.

[43] Afghanistan, Chechnya in the Russian Federation, Democratic Republic of Congo, Equatorial Guinea, Guatemala (televised), Guinea, Iran, Libya (televised), Nigeria (for robbery, but none since 1999), North Korea (2004 and 2005) Pakistan, Rwanda, Saudi Arabia, Sierra Leone, Somalia (by Islamic courts, by firing squad before several thousand people), Syria, Uganda, Vietnam, and Yemen. Under Argentinean military law the condemned can be shot in public, but there have been no such executions in recent years. The last substantiated report of public executions in China was in June 1986, when the *South China Morning Post* (Hong Kong) reported on 26 June that 31 criminals had been shot in public. In July 1986 the Supreme People's Court issued a directive to Provincial High Courts outlawing public executions.

[44] FIDH, *Uganda: Challenging the Death Penalty*, Report 425/2 October 2005, p. 35.

October 2005 for trafficking in drugs. A public execution for murder took place
by firing squad in Equatorial Guinea in April 2006, and in Vietnam, in April
2004, a woman was executed by firing squad 'in front of hundreds of spectators'
for smuggling heroin.[45] In Saudi Arabia, where public executions by beheading
persist, four Sri Lankans were executed in February 2007 and subsequently their
bodies were publicly displayed.[46] In March 2003 the North Korean government
announced that it would refrain from executing criminals in public. However,
there were reports of public executions in March 2005 in the northeastern cities
of Hwanyong and Yuson,[47] and again in July 2007, when a trade official was
publicly executed for smuggling timber to China.[48]

Each year there have been reports of death by stoning in Iran, which is a public
form of execution. For example, in 2006 a man and a woman were stoned to death
in the middle of the night in a cemetery in the north-eastern city of Mashad. Both
were accused of murdering the woman's husband. During the height of the Iranian
revolution bodies were left hanging in public view, sometimes at the site of the
crime. This practice has continued: in December 2006 an Iranian man convicted
of murdering 12 family members was publicly hanged in the southern town of
Jahrom, and just a month earlier another man, convicted of sodomy, was publicly
hanged in the western town of Kermanshah.[49] In July 2005 and December 2006
three young men, including two juveniles aged under 18, were publicly hanged,
two for sexual assault on a 13-year-old boy and one for murder, and in November
2007 two men were publicly hanged for raping a Dutch woman.[50] The Taliban
in Afghanistan have recently carried out executions in public after trials under
Islamic law. For example, Hands Off Cain reported that in September 2006 a
man was publicly executed for his alleged involvement in a murder in southern
Afghanistan's Helmand province. Dozens of people were said to have been present
to witness this extra-judicial execution. It was reported to be the eleventh case of
its nature in Helmand since the overthrow of the Taliban regime in 2001.

It has been rare in recent years for executions to be televised;[51] the last occasion
appears to have been in Guatemala in 2000, although in Thailand in April 2001
the Corrections Department for the first time allowed reporters and cameramen
to witness the execution of five prisoners by firing squad. It was reported that
dozens turned up and that it was partly shown on public television.[52]

---

[45] Amnesty International, *Report 2005*, p. 277.

[46] *Human Rights Watch*, Saudi Arabia: Four Sri Lankans Executed Without Warning,
*21 February 2007 at <http://hrw.org/english/docs/2007/02/21/saudia15377.htm>.

[47] Amnesty International, *North Korea: Briefing on present situation*, AI Index: ASA
24/002/2005, 28 July 2005.

[48] *Gulf Times*, 6 August 2007, reported by Hands Off Cain.

[49] Cases from Hands Off Cain, <http://www.handsoffcain.info>.

[50] Amnesty International, *Death Penalty News*, January 2006; *Reuters*, 7 November 2007, cited
at Hands Off Cain, <http://www.handsoffcain.info/news/index.php?iddocumento=9331025>.

[51] See 3rd edn. of this book for information on earlier periods, at pp. 101–104.

[52] *Bangkok Post*, 'Civilized Society in the Firing Line', 20 April 2001.

Representatives of the public and the press witness executions in the United States, and access is given to the media to interview prisoners awaiting death. A large number of witnesses, including the families of victims and the press, watched the execution of the Oklahoma bomber Timothy McVeigh in June 2001, some of them through a television relay. The question of right of access, including televising of executions, has provoked considerable controversy.[53] Indeed, some advocates of abolition believe, just as abolitionists in Britain believed when the Capital Punishment within Prisons Act was passed in 1868, that it would speed the cause of abolition if the general public were to be allowed to witness what was being done in their name: the cold and deliberate judicial execution of an offender.[54] This view received the imprimatur of a leading campaigner for abolition in the United States, Professor Austin Sarat. In his book *When the State Kills* (2001), he argued:[55]

I suggest that the survival of capital punishment in America depends, in part, on its relative invisibility... The exclusion of the public means the exclusion of the court of last resort; no longer can the people rise up to save the condemned; no longer is the people's judgment truly the last word in state killing... Making this shame and this zeal visible to a mass audience would be likely to reveal the sadism that is at the heart of the state's tenacious attachment to capital punishment and reveal and invite the 'bad taste' of its viewers. For me the possibility of the former is well worth the risk of the latter.

But, as David Garland has pointed out, one cannot think of anywhere in the world where such shock tactics have worked. Indeed, the process of abolition has, in most countries, been marked by its removal from the public gaze into a secretive and eventually marginalized activity of the criminal justice system, one that has generally brought shame, or at least no plaudits, for those who take part in it. It is possible that by making 'theatre' out of executions the public would be brutalized too.[56] Of course, wherever an execution is carried out in public there is scope, with modern mobile communications, to both film it and circulate those images effectively on the World Wide Web, as was evidence by the uploading of film showing Saddam Hussein's execution in December 2006. The spectre of 'liveblogging executions' is real.

In several countries members of the public have been involved in carrying out the executions, mostly by stoning. In Saudi Arabia and Iran the guardian of the murdered victim has the right to perform the execution himself, or hire another person to do it, but there is no information about how often this occurs, if at all.

---

[53] Note, 'The Executioner's Song: Is there a Right to Listen?' *Virginia Law Review* 69 (1983), pp. 373–401. In *KQED v Vasquez* 1991 US Dist. LEXIS 21163 a Californian court denied a public television station's request to televise the execution of Robert Alton Harris.

[54] Joe Keating, 'Out of Sight, Out of Mind' *Amicus Journal* 3 (2001), pp. 15–19.

[55] Austin Sarat, *When the State Kills: Capital Punishment and the American Condition* (2001), pp. 189–208.

[56] For a review essay of Sarat's book see David Garland, 'The Cultural Conditions of Capital Punishment' *Punishment and Society* 4 (2002) pp. 459–487.

However, in Somalia in May 2006 Omar Hussein was publicly executed by the 16-year-old son of his victim who stabbed him in the neck and the head under the order of a *Shari'a* court.

While the 1997 Law of Criminal Procedure outlaws public executions in China, reports of public rallies, some of them televised, where persons convicted of capital offences are paraded and humiliated, sometimes in full view of the public, prior to being taken to an execution ground, continue to be forthcoming. Thus, on 28 December 2006, *The Guardian* newspaper published a photograph taken two days earlier. The headline was: 'Hundreds of Chinese watch as seven men convicted of murder and robbery in Hunan province are paraded with details of their crimes around their necks before being taken away and executed'. Clearly, the imposition of the death sentence in China is still sometimes used to create a public spectacle. It is, and is meant to be, humiliating to the condemned and their families, and presumably a deterrent to onlookers, even if the public are not allowed to see the 'final moments'.

(c) The role of physicians

There remains much dispute about the proper role of doctors in the administration of the death penalty. In India the Supreme Court ruled in January 1995 that doctors employed in prisons had an obligation to participate in hangings by examining the body every few minutes after the drop to ensure that death had occurred.[57] In strong contrast, the World Medical Association at its fifty-second meeting, held in Edinburgh in 2000, 'Resolved, that it is unethical for physicians to participate in capital punishment, in any way, or during any step of the execution process'.[58]

The issue has become particularly contentious since states turned in increasing numbers to execution by lethal injection, which, to be effectively carried out without error, appears to necessitate medical assistance, or at the very least supervision, in establishing the intravenous portal through which the lethal preparation will pass, to monitor consciousness and life signs during the execution procedure, and to pronounce on death. The Council of the American College of Physicians in 1993 stated that participation contrary to medical ethics would include (but not be limited to):

[P]rescribing or administering tranquillizers and other psychotropic agents and medications that are part of the execution procedure; monitoring vital signs on site

---

[57] Amnesty International, 'India: Supreme Court Judgement Violates Medical Ethics' *Medical Death Penalty Newsletter* 7(3) (1995), p. 1.

[58] This was amended from the original position adopted by the 34th World Medical Assembly in Lisbon, Portugal in 1981. See the WMA's policy, at <http://www.wma.net/e/policy/c1.htm>. See also British Medical Association, *Medicine Betrayed* (1992), pp. 100–102.

or remotely (including monitoring electrocardiograms); attending or observing an execution as a physician; and rendering of technical advice regarding execution.

And in the case where the execution was to be by lethal injection, the following would be unethical conduct: selecting injection sites; 'starting intravenous lines as a port for a lethal injection device; prescribing, preparing, administering, or supervising injection drugs or their doses or types; inspecting, testing, or maintaining lethal injection devices; consulting with or supervising lethal injection personnel'. But it would not be counted as participation to certify death, provided that the person had been declared dead by another person (otherwise the physician might have to decide whether or not the execution should continue), nor to relieve acute suffering of condemned persons, provided that they voluntarily request it.[59] In 1996 the American Medical Association was joined by the American Nurses Association and the American Public Health Association in issuing a statement which, while taking no stand on the morality of capital punishment *per se*, specifically proscribes participation in state executions by its members, even if they are employed by the state government:[60]

Participation in executions contradicts the fundamental role of the health care professional as healer and comforter... Participation in executions by lethal injection is particularly troublesome. This process of ending life employs the same medical knowledge, devices, and methods used by health professionals to comfort, to heal, and to preserve life... For these reasons, participation in state executions by members of our professions is specifically proscribed by the ethical codes of the American Medical Association, the American College of Physicians, and the American Nurses Association. Since these ethical codes are also integral parts of state medical, nursing and other health professional practice and licensing acts, participation in execution violates state law. We, therefore, call on state professional licensure and discipline boards to treat participation in executions as grounds for active disciplinary proceedings, including license revocation. Furthermore, professional societies should impose disciplinary action on those members who participate in executions... Government agencies should not expect or require their employees of contractors to participate in executions or to perform any other unethical acts.

This stand was supported in 2001 by the House of Delegates of the American Society of Anesthesiologists (ASA), and in a statement issued on 30 June 2006, in response to Judge Fogel's decision in the *Morales* case to request two

[59] For the position of the American Medical Association, see Council on Ethical and Judicial Affairs, American Medical Association, 'Physician Participation in Capital Punishment' *Journal of the American Medical Association* 270 (1993), pp. 365–368; and American Medical Association's *Code of ethics* E-2.06; C. P. Ewing, ' "Above All Do No Harm": The Role of Health and Mental Health Professionals in the Capital Punishment Process' in J. R. Acker, R.M. Bohm, and C.S. Lanier (eds.), *America's Experiment with Capital Punishment* (2nd edn, 2003), pp. 597–612; M. Davis, 'What is Unethical About Physicians Helping at Executions?' in *Justice in the Shadow of Death: Rethinking Capital and Lesser Punishments* (1996), pp. 65–94.

[60] 'Professional Societies Oppose Health Care Professionals Participation in Capital Punishment', Joint statement, 13 September 1996, by The American Medical Association, The American Nurses Association, and The American Public Health Association.

anesthesiologists to monitor the execution process, the President of the American Society of Anesthesiologists, Orin F. Gundry MD concluded:[61]

Lethal injection was not anesthesiology's idea. American society decided to have capital punishment as part of our legal system and to carry it out with lethal injection. The fact that problems are surfacing is not our dilemma. The legal system has painted itself into this corner and it is not our obligation to get it out...This is a complex subject and anesthesiology is being reluctantly thrust into the middle of it. My advice would be to be well informed on the subject and steer clear.

Increasingly, para-medical personnel have been employed, albeit reluctantly. But the National Association of Emergency Medical Technicians (NAEMT) issued a statement in 2006 expressing its strong opposition to 'participation in capital punishment by an EMT, a Paramedic or other emergency medical professional. Participation in executions is viewed as contrary to the fundamental goals and ethical obligations of emergency medical services'.[62]

Illinois and Missouri in 1995 became the only American states that have so far abolished the statutory requirement that a qualified doctor should assist at executions. Despite this, the US District Court, Western District of Missouri ruled in 2006 that:[63]

A board certified anesthesiologist shall be responsible for the mixing of all drugs which are used in the legal injection process...or observe those who do...pancuronium bromide and potassium chloride shall not be administered until the anesthesiologist has certified that the inmate has achieved sufficient anesthetic depth from the dose of not less than 5 grams of thiopental; that the State shall ensure that the anesthesiologist has all the necessary equipment to adequately monitor anesthetic depth, and consider repositioning the gurney so that the inmate's face will be visible to the anesthesiologist, using a mirror or even allowing the anesthesiologist to be present in the room with the inmate when the drugs are injected.

The judge was also of the opinion that Missouri physicians who agreed to be involved in administering lethal injections were not 'violating their ethical obligations'. Similarly, in North Carolina in May 2006 Willie Brown Jr. was executed when a federal judge agreed to the state using a brain-wave monitoring machine, with a doctor present, to check his awareness level and a doctor agreed to participate. It appears, therefore, that the federal judiciary is willing to support the use of medical personnel to ensure that executions by lethal injection can be

---

[61] See 'Resources regarding Challenges to Lethal Injection' at <http://www.law.berkeley.edu/clinics/dpclinic/resources.html>. See also the statement attributable to Priscilla Ray, MD Chair, AMA Council on Ethical and Judicial Affairs, 17 February 2006, <http://www.ama-assn.org/ama/pub/category/16007.html>: 'The American Medical Association (AMA) is alarmed that Judge Jeremy Fogel has disregarded physicians' ethical obligations when he ordered procedures for physician participation in executions of California inmates by lethal injection.'

[62] NAEMT, 'Position Statement on EMT and Paramedic Participation in Capital Punishment', adopted 9 June 2006. Available at: <http://www.naemt.org/aboutNAEMT/capitalpunishment.htm>.

[63] As reported in a newsletter from the American Society of Anesthesiologists, <http://www.asahq.org/news/asanews063006.htm>.

carried out without fear that the constitutional requirement to avoid cruel and unusual punishment will be contravened, for without the aid of doctors it appears that this dispute might end capital punishment by technological default.

Members of the medical profession appear also to be divided in their opinion on whether they should participate, some arguing that it is better that a person die under proper medical supervision than suffer undue pain at death.[64] A postal survey in 2001 of 1,000 medical practitioners in the United States, asking about their willingness to be involved in and attitudes towards capital punishment, found that 41 per cent of the 413 who responded 'indicated that they would perform at least one action disallowed by the AMA'. Nineteen per cent said they 'would be willing to actually give the lethal injection, and 36 per cent said they would be willing to pronounce the prisoner dead'. Only three per cent of respondents were aware that there were such guidelines![65]

There have been many reports of court-appointed physicians in China administering lethal injections and particular concern has been expressed about the role of doctors in removing (often at the site of death) organs for transplantation from an estimated 2,000–3,000 executed persons a year. The Chinese authorities have claimed that this has only occurred for medical use with the full consent of the condemned or their families and have denied that organs are sold for profit.[66] Nevertheless, there are widespread allegations that they have been removed frequently without such consent, or at least without unforced consent, and sold.[67] Indeed, senior transplant surgeons in Israel claim that 90 per cent of available organs have been taken from death row prisoners in China and that most were taken without consent. One Chinese doctor, who escaped China and sought political refuge in the United States, described before a committee of the House of Representatives how he removed skin and corneas from the bodies of over 100 prisoners who were executed in Chinese prisons. He explained that the 'donors' receive a special injection which prevents their blood from clotting and aids in preserving their organs. The execution team would shoot the prisoners in the head while medical staff stood by in order to remove the organs meant

[64] Dr. Atul Gawande, 'When Law and Ethics Collide—Why Physicians Participate in Executions' *New England Journal of Medicine* 354 (12) 2006, pp. 1221–1229—based on interviews with four physicians and a nurse who had agreed to participate in executions.

[65] Neil J. Farber, B. M. Aboff, J. Weiner, E. B. Davis, E. G. Boyer, and P. A. Ubel, 'Physicians' Willingness to Participate in the Process of Lethal Injection for Capital Punishment' *Annals of Internal Medicine* 135(10) (2001), pp. 884–888. A real example was the action of a Chief Medical Officer who was alleged to have authorized, in November 2001, the acquisition and provision of the drugs to be used for the execution by lethal injection of the first death row prisoner in New Mexico for 41 years, contrary to both the stance of the American Medical Association and the provisions of the New Mexico Practice Act.

[66] The harvesting of organs was legally permitted in Taiwan but this practice ended in recent years and now Taiwan is a fierce critic of its neighbour's practices: 'Taiwan condemns China's organ harvesting', *The China Post*, Taiwan, 14 October 2006.

[67] *New York Times*, 'Execution in China, through a Brother's Eyes', 11 March 2001. Also *International Herald Tribune*, 'China's Bitter Harvest Shakes a Doctor', 28 June 2001. *Reuters* reported on 28 June 2001 the response to this 'vicious slander' by a Chinese Foreign Ministry spokeswoman.

for transplants. He recounted a particularly shocking case where kidneys were removed from a prisoner while he was still alive due to a faulty execution. Other testimonies brought before Congress confirmed other such cases.[68] This practice is regarded as not only counter to international standards of medical ethics, but also likely to stimulate the use of the death penalty.[69] The Chinese government has been very sensitive about this issue, asserting that all the organs are donated voluntarily by repentant prisoners prior to execution and thus denying these allegations of a connection between the desire to use capital punishment and the trade in organs. However, in December 2005 the Chinese Vice-Minister for Health told *Caijing Magazine* that new regulations were being drafted to end the lucrative trade in organ transplants.[70] Yet, according to the BBC, the British Transplantation Society reported in April 2006 that an accumulating weight of incontrovertible evidence suggests the organs of thousands of executed prisoners in China are being removed, and continue to be removed, for transplants without consent.[71]

2. Under Sentence of Death

(a) The 'death row' population

While the number of executions appears in many countries to have been declining, persons have still been sentenced to death in both retentionist and abolitionist *de facto* countries. In these circumstances, many people remain under sentence of death for very long periods of time, until either they are executed or have their sentences reduced by a Court of Appeal, or are released through the exercise of clemency or a more general amnesty.

In the United States, the number of prisoners on 'death row', which was about 1,000 in 1983, rose to over 3,700 at the end of December 2001.[72] Even following the recent fall in death sentences imposed, there were still 3,316 prisoners under sentence of death at the end of December 2006. The largest numbers are in California (660), Texas (393), Florida (397), and Pennsylvania (226). According to research published by Amnesty International in 2006, it has been estimated that the total number remaining under sentence of death in countries that have

---

[68] Amnesty International, *Death Penalty blog*, 30 October 2006.
[69] Human Rights Watch/Asia, *Organ Procurement and Judicial Execution in China* 6(9) (1994), <http://www.hrw.org/reports/1994/china1/china_948.htm>. For further discussion, see Michael Radelet, 'Physician Participation' in P. Hodgkinson and A. Rutherford (eds.), *Capital Punishment: Global Issues and Prospects* (1996), pp. 243–260 at 244–248.
[70] Amnesty International, *Death Penalty Developments 2005*, p. 11.
[71] *BBC News*, 19 April 2006.
[72] NAACP, *Death Row, U.S.A.—A Quarterly Report by the Capital Punishment Project of the NAACP Legal Defence and Education Fund, Inc.*, <http://www.naacpldf.org/content.aspx?article=297>.

not completely abolished the death penalty is probably somewhere between 19,500 and 25,500.[73]

(b) Time spent on death row

In the United States the new post-*Furman* death sentence laws have brought so much litigation in their train that the average length of time spent on death row rose. Among all prisoners executed between 1977 and 2005, the average time between the imposition of the most recent sentence received and execution was more than 10 years. Those executed during 2005 had been under a sentence of death for an average of 12 years and 3 months, 15 months longer than for inmates executed in 2004.[74]

But the United States is not the only country where prisoners languish for many years under sentence of death. For example, Pakistan reported that the average period between sentence and execution has been approximately six to eight years,[75] although other sources suggest that prisoners can stay on death row for up to 10 years.[76] In Japan, of the 61 persons who had received 'finalized' death sentences in mid-2004, 24 'had been eligible for execution for at least 10 years, the longest wait was 34 years and the average wait was nine years'.[77] The Japanese Federation of Bar Associations (JFBA) reported to the United Nations in 2004 that a prisoner was executed in 1999 18 years and 6 months after his conviction and 10 years after he was sentenced, although it also reported that 'the "waiting time" is becoming shorter these days'. But Okunishi Masaru (who was sentenced to death in 1961) is now 80 years old and Oohama Shouzou (sentenced to death in 1975) is 78. Both have spent decades in detention, living under the unrelenting strain of the threat of execution. It is not only those who are still pursuing appeals who languish in uncertainty: Oda Nobuo and Hakamada Iwao were convicted in the 1960s and exhausted their appeals in 1970 and 1980 respectively, but

---

[73] Amnesty International, *DP News*, May 2006, AI Index: ACT 53/002/2006. The actual figures given by Amnesty were between 19,474 and 25,546. We have rounded them to dispel any perception of accuracy. As far as we have been able to establish (the figures are often only estimates), at the end of 2005 substantial numbers of prisoners were known or thought to be under sentence of death: Algeria ('hundreds'), Bangladesh (655), Burundi (499), Cuba (50), Democratic Republic of Congo ('around 200'), Ethiopia (100), Ghana (113), India (267), Indonesia (90), Japan (around 100), Kenya (at least 1,000 but perhaps as many as 2,000), Malaysia (150), Morocco (100), Nigeria (530 in 2004), Pakistan (7,400), Palestine Authority (50), Philippines (1,100 prior to abolition in 2006), South Korea (63), Sri Lanka (approx 100), Tanzania (up to 400), Thailand (900), Uganda (555), Yemen ('hundreds'), and Zambia (230).

[74] Tracy L. Snell, *Capital Punishment 2005* (2006) pp. 10–11 (as of September 2007 there were no statistics available for 2006).

[75] *Seventh Quinquennial Survey*, UN Doc. E/2005/3, para. 122.

[76] Amnesty International, *Death Penalty blog* reporting the Human Rights Committee of Pakistan, 2 August 2006.

[77] David T. Johnson, 'Where the state kills in secret. Capital punishment in Japan' *Punishment and Society* 8 (2006), pp. 251–285 at 255.

remain under sentence of death today.[78] In Nigeria it has been reported that the 500 prisoners on death row had been there on average between 10 and 15 years.[79] There is some evidence to suggest that women are particularly affected, awaiting trial for prolonged periods of time, without access to legal representation, and are then kept in prison awaiting execution or clemency for up to 10 years.[80] The UN Special Rapporteur, Philip Alston, was told in 2006 that the average was 20 years, with at least one prisoner having been on death row since 1981.[81]

When a mission from FIDH visited Jordan in 2006 they found two prisoners who had been 'sentenced to death after summary proceedings before military courts in 1974 and 1976, respectively. They have therefore been on death row, anticipating execution for over 30 years'.[82] In Guyana some prisoners have been on death row for almost 22 years. A man convicted of rape and murder in India in 1990 was executed 14 years later in 2004. In Zambia there are apparently at least 30 prisoners who have been on death row between 8 and 25 years, and in Swaziland some prisoners have served at least 18 years on death row before being pardoned. Under Islamic law in Saudi Arabia offenders have sometimes had to wait for as long as 15 years until the victim's son had reached maturity and was able to make the decision whether to exact retaliation (*Qisas*) or accept compensation (*Diya*).[83] A Filipina woman, convicted in 1993 of murdering her employer, was reported to be still under sentence of death at the end of 2004.[84] And although the average period in Guatemala is now seven years, FIDH found prisoners who had been on death row for more than nine years.[85]

A curious and lamentable use of a separate 'death row' in which those sentenced to death are confined occurs in countries that are abolitionist *de facto* with a settled policy of not carrying out executions. In such circumstances confinement in the restricted and often overcrowded conditions of a death row becomes an additional punishment to what will eventually become life imprisonment, the only means of escape being a successful plea for clemency. This may not occur until many years of suffering have been endured. For example, in 2003, President Kibaki of Kenya granted clemency to several prisoners, one of whom, Francis Mbithi, had his death sentence commuted to life imprisonment after 23 years on death row.[86]

---

[78] Amnesty International, *Will this day be my last? The death penalty in Japan*, AI Index: ASA 2/006/2006.

[79] *Report of the National Nigerian Study Group on the Death Penalty* (2004) p. 81.

[80] Amnesty International, '*Nigeria: The death penalty and women under the Nigerian penal systems*', AI Index: AFR 44/007/2004, 10 February 2004.

[81] UN Doc. E/CN.4/2006/53/Add. 4, 7 January 2006, para. 30.

[82] FIDH mission to Jordan: *Abolition of the Death Penalty for Some Crimes Symbolic at Best*, 16 August 2006.

[83] It was reported that, owing to this, two men were executed in Saudi Arabia in 1983 for murders committed in 1966 and 1968: Sandra Mackey, *The Saudis: Inside the Desert Kingdom* (1987), pp. 270–271.

[84] Amnesty International, *Report 2005*, p. 216.

[85] FIDH report, *The Death Penalty in Guatemala: On the road towards abolition*, No. 422/2, p. 26.

[86] *The Nation*, 2 April 2007.

(c) Conditions on death row

Article 10 of the International Covenant on Civil and Political Rights states that 'All persons deprived of their liberty shall be treated with humanity and with respect for the inherent dignity of the human person'. It should be self-evident that this should apply in particular to those undergoing confinement while facing the prospect of execution. There can be no doubt that waiting to be executed, or wondering over a long period of time whether or not one will be successful in avoiding execution, must cause great stress. Indeed, it was argued twenty-five years ago that 'the death penalty in a legalistic society inevitably causes cruelty by the delay in carrying it out, and ... capital punishment therefore cannot be reconciled with constitutional rights and so is per se unlawful'.[87]

Various socio-psychological studies described the reactions of prisoners who have experienced a long period of uncertainty about their fate, as well as the problems posed for humane prison management. These reactions have been found to be similar to those of terminally ill hospital patients, but exacerbated by the physical conditions of cellular confinement for anything up to twenty-two hours a day, restricted visits, and, in many states, no access to prison jobs, educational classes, clubs, religious services, or recreational facilities or treatment programmes. Such conditions of despair and loneliness have been described as 'an austere world in which condemned prisoners are treated as bodies kept alive to be killed'.[88] As Margaret Vandiver has observed, it is not only condemned prisoners who suffer over this protracted period, but also their families, and sometimes the families of their victims too.[89]

Robert Johnson has described conditions on Oklahoma's death row H Unit as:[90]

[A] solitary and sterile, a cold, oppressive human wasteland in which prisoners are interred—confined underground—in utterly self-contained cell blocks replete with dimly lit and sparsely furnished concrete cages.

New York's death row is similar, with prisoners spending at least twenty-three hours alone in their cells every day.[91]

---

[87] David Pannick, *Judicial Review of the Death Penalty* (1982), p. 162.

[88] Robert Johnson and John L. Carroll, 'Litigating Death-Row Conditions, the Case for Reform' in Ira P. Robbins (ed.), *Prisoners and the Law* (1985), ch. 8, pp. 3–33. For the view of a correctional administrator, see Charlotte A. Nesbit, 'Managing Death Row', *Corrections Today* (July 1986), pp. 90–106; and for more personal and moving accounts, Jan Arriens (ed.), *Welcome to Hell: Letters and Other Writings by Prisoners on Death Row in the United States* (1991); Marie Mulvey Roberts (ed.), *Out of Night: Writings from Death Row* (1994); and see Richard M. Rossi, *Waiting to Die: Life on Death Row* (2004), and Kerry Max Cook, *Chasing Justice* (2007), for first-hand accounts.

[89] Margaret Vandiver, 'The Impact of the Death Penalty on the Families of Homicide Victims and of Condemned Prisoners' in J. R. Acker, R. M. Bohm, and C. S. Lanier (eds.), *America's Experiment with Capital Punishment* (2nd edn, 2003), pp. 613–645.

[90] Robert Johnson, 'Life under Sentence of Death: Historical and Contemporary Perspectives', in Acker, Bohm, and Lanier (eds.), *ibid.*, pp. 647–672 at 660.

[91] Johnson, *ibid.*, p. 665.

Only a few American states do not hold their prisoners separately on a death row. Most of them have only a handful of prisoners, but Missouri is an exception. All the state's condemned prisoners have, since 1991, been 'mainstreamed' into the general population of the prison in which they are held, the other prisoners nearly all being lifers convicted of similar crimes to those awaiting execution. It has been reported that this has 'humanized' the environment for 'capital offenders' by opening up to them normal prison facilities, and 'enhanced the ability of officials to justify current capital punishment inmate management practices'.[92] It may also be a means of legitimizing the long periods for which such prisoners are held waiting execution, without addressing the psychological impact of that very fact.

Over the past 30 years several prisoners in the United States have challenged their overall conditions of confinement on death row as an infringement of their rights under the Eighth Amendment of the Constitution not to suffer any 'cruel or unusual punishment'. Limited improvement in their conditions has resulted from litigation in several states, where the courts have recognized the special needs of the condemned and the psychological impact of unnecessarily harsh conditions. For example, in Texas, as a result of *Ruiz v Estelle* (1982), a class action in which the Fifth Circuit Court of Appeals found that the vastly overcrowded conditions under which all Texan prisoners were held violated the Eighth Amendment, agreement was reached in 1986 to improve conditions for death row prisoners. They were classified and those deemed 'work capable' (about 40 per cent of the inmates) were given jobs and granted all the privileges and freedom of movement enjoyed by ordinary prisoners. For the majority not considered to be capable of work (for security, physical, or psychological reasons) conditions were also somewhat improved. As a result they were guaranteed at least 15 hours a week out-of-cell recreation, although they were still housed separately.[93] Several other states have laid down minimum conditions for death row inmates, assuring them of stipulated hours of out-of-cell time, recreational facilities, and opportunities to work, dine, and attend religious services with the general prison population.

Despite these reforms, death rows 'freeze their prisoners in time, holding them captive in a sort of existential limbo until they are either executed or released to the prison world or the free world'.[94] In the second, impressive and moving, edition of his book *Death Work: A Study of the Modern Execution Process,* published in 1998, Robert Johnson defines death row as a species of 'torturous confinement' and concludes that:[95]

Aside from a smattering of essentially cosmetic reforms in a number of prisons—access to educational classes in some systems; the availability, on paper at least, of mental health

---

[92] George Lombardi, Richard L. Sluder, and Donald Wallace, 'Mainstreaming Death-Sentenced Inmates: The Missouri Experience and its Legal Significance' *Federal Probation* 61(2) (1997), pp. 3–11.

[93] Johnson, n. 90 above, pp. 658–660.

[94] *Ibid.*, p. 660.

[95] R. Johnson, *Death Work: A Study of the Modern Execution Process* (2nd edn., 1998), pp. 71 and 218.

counseling; modest increases of out-of-cell time and access to visitors; and, in a few states, the availability of part-time work—death rows today are essentially indistinguishable from their counterparts in earlier years.

Indeed, he remained of the opinion that 'The death penalty, when preceded by long confinement and administered bureaucratically, dehumanizes both the agents and recipients of this punishment and amounts to a form of torture'. Johnson provided an eerie and haunting description of these regimes:[96]

The peculiar silence of death row stems from the empty and ultimately lifeless regime imposed on the condemned. These offenders, seen as unfit to live in even the prison community, are relegated to this prison within a prison... Typical maximum security prisoners spend about eight to twelve hours a day in their cells; typically death row inmates spend twenty to twenty-two or twenty-three hours a day alone in theirs. Death row prisoners leave their cells to shower (often handcuffed) and to exercise (in a restricted area, sometimes fittingly called a 'recreation cage')... visits occur under heavy guard, are restricted in frequency and duration, and become increasingly rare as a prisoner's stay on death row continues... Deemed beyond correction, they typically are denied access to even meager privileges, amenities, and services available to regular prisoners... With only rare exceptions, condemned prisoners are demoralized by their bleak confinement and defeated by the awesome prospect of death by execution. Worn down in small and almost imperceptible ways, they gradually become less than fully human. At the end, the prisoners are helpless pawns in the modern execution drill. They give in, they give up, and submit: yielding themselves to the execution team and the machinery of death.

Johnson's analysis is summed up well by Willie Turner, who was seventeen years on Virginia's death row, and had experience of it as a reformed regime. Even under improved physical conditions, he described the psychological impact of waiting thus:[97]

It's the unending, uninterrupted immersion in death that wears on you so much. It's the parade of friends and acquaintances who leave for the death house and never come back, while your own desperate and lonely time drains away. It's the boring routine of claustrophobic confinement, punctuated by eye-opening dates with death that you helplessly hope will be averted. It's watching yourself die over the years in the eyes of family and friends... I've spent over 5000 days on death row. Not a single waking hour of any of those days has gone by without me thinking about my date with the executioner... All that thinking about it is like a little dying, even if you're on the best death row on earth... nothing could have prepared me for the despair and the frustration, for the loneliness and the abuse, for the shame and sorrow, for the hopes raised and dashed, for the dreams and nightmares of my death that my seventeen years facing my own advancing demise have served up.

[96] *Ibid.*, pp. 71 and 93.
[97] Johnson, n. 90 above, pp. 666.

Anyone who believes that this is merely a self-serving testament of self-pity should read the following evidence recently offered by the Warden of San Quentin Prison in California:[98]

I have observed that the weight and pressure of living as a condemned man on Death Row is extremely debilitating and wears a prisoner out both physically and emotionally. Every court decision brings a ray of hope and rescue...every court reprieve promises more and every court denial dashes that hope and engenders despair. The condemned prisoner must constantly adjust to these extremes of emotion, which grinds at his spirit. The process can be especially debilitating for prisoners who must contend with death warrants.

Death row conditions in some other countries must have even more traumatic effects on the prisoners. In Jordan, where some prisoners have been under sentence of death for as long as 30 years, they are 'only allowed one hour in the sun every day and have to spend the rest of their time in small prison cells with extremely poor ventilation under suffocating heat'.[99] According to the Cuban Commission for Human Rights and National Reconciliation, the approximately 50 prisoners on death row in March 2004 were held in their cells in 'inhuman conditions'.[100] In Japan, inmates are kept in solitary confinement in *tatami* mat cells about 8 square metres in size. They exercise alone and eat their meals alone. Virtually the only people who may visit or correspond with an inmate are attorneys and relatives. And even an inmate's reading material is strictly controlled.[101] In Nigeria things are even worse. An Amnesty International report describes Arthur Judah Angel's experience of nine years on death row in Nigeria's Enugu prison (after which his death sentence was commuted to life imprisonment):[102]

Arthur awaited trial for more than two years before being sentenced to death for murder in 1986. He was transferred to the notorious death row in Enugu prison, southern Nigeria. There, he waited in a windowless, 2 x 2.5m cell for his turn to be executed. He shared that space—its cardboard box beds and single bucket toilet—with as many as 13 other death row inmates. While on death row, Arthur witnessed numerous mass executions by firing squad or hanging. Groups of 25–50 people were executed on a monthly—sometimes weekly—basis especially under former military ruler General Ibrahim Babangida. Arthur also witnessed torture and other cruel, inhuman and degrading treatment on a regular basis. 'It was like hell. We were undergoing both mental and physical torture', he says. 'Some...died as a result of their injuries'.

---

[98]   Declaration of Daniel B. Vasquez in support of Ray Allen's Petition for Clemency and petition for Writ of Habeas Corpus, para. 14, quoted by Sandra L. Babcock, Co-chair, International Committee, National Association of Criminal Defense Lawyers at *Report on the Death Penalty*, Executive Summary, p. 11, para 36, <http://ohchr.org/english/bodies/hrc/docs/ngos/death%20penalty%20shadow%20rpt%20final.pdf>.

[99]   FIDH, *Jordan / Death Penalty: Abolition of the Death Penalty for Some Crimes Symbolic at Best*, 16 August 2006.

[100]   Amnesty International, *Annual Reports 2005* and *2006*.

[101]   *Japan Times*, 27 February 2007.

[102]   Amnesty International, 'Former death row prisoner in Nigeria describes torment' *The Wire* Vol. 35, No. 9, October 2005, AI Index: NWS 21/009/2005, at p. 9.

Angel's experiences are backed up by a recent report on a week-long visit to Nigeria in March 2007 by the UN's Special Rapporteur on Torture, Manfred Nowak. He concluded that there were only a 'few tangible results' from efforts to reform the justice system. A government-appointed committee on reform of the country's justice and prison system produced its first report in 2005. It recommended the release of all those who had been on death row for more than 10 years but Nowak found that one death row inmate had been waiting there for more than 20 years and that some 600 people are crammed into Nigeria's disease-infested death rows, with the many victims of police torture left without medical treatment for the injuries inflicted.[103] FIDH reported that in June 2006 at a prison in the Punjab in Pakistan there was 'an average of 7 to 8 persons incarcerated in death cells which measure 6 by 8 ft (1.8 x 2.4m)'[104] and in Kenya the cell block at Kamiti maximum security prison designed to hold 300 prisoners was, in June 2007, holding more than twice that number in cells that are 'poorly ventilated, dirty and stinking'.[105]

And lest it be forgotten, in December 2006 there were 50 women on death rows in America. Johnson notes that death row conditions for women are, in most states, much better: 'More often than not, condemned women are held in settings that are cozy and congenial, more like group homes or even private homes than like prisons or death rows'. However, he expects this to change if the execution of women begins to occur 'with any regularity'.[106] Furthermore, the American Civil Liberties Union contradicts his description, reporting that they 'live in virtual isolation, which often leads to psychosis and exacerbates existing mental illness'.[107]

It has been suggested that the physical conditions and, more importantly, the psychological stresses involved by being under sentence of death for protracted periods, with constant uncertainty as to one's eventual fate, is the reason why at least some of the approximately 115 people executed so far in the United States— more than 10 per cent—decided to forgo any further appeals and accept execution.[108] Some light has been shed on this through empirical research carried out by Professor John Blume. His study of 106 'volunteers' (which is what he calls those who withdrew their appeals) has shown that a high proportion of them had 'documented mental illness' (77%) or 'mental illness or severe substance abuse disorders' (88%) and that 'there are important similarities between persons who commit suicide and those who volunteer for execution'. Yet he found no evidence

---

[103] Toye Olori, 'Rights—Nigeria: Grim, Overflowing Death Rows' *IPS*, 19 March 2007.

[104] FIDH, *Slow March to the Gallows: the Death Penalty in Pakistan*, Report 464/2, January 2007, at p. 55.

[105] *The Nation*, 24 June 2007.

[106] Johnson, n. 88 above, at pp. 86–87. See also Jane Officer (ed.), *If I Should Die...A Death Row Correspondence* (1999).

[107] ACLU, '*The Forgotten Population: A look at death row in the United States through the experiences of women*' (2004).

[108] Amnesty International, *Death Penalty News*, June 2005, p. 5; Amnesty International, *United States of America: The illusion of control 'Consensual' executions, the impending death of Timothy McVeigh, and the brutalizing futility of capital punishment*, AI Index: AMR 51/053/2001, 24 April 2001.

that 'volunteer rates varied as a function of conditions of confinement'. On the other hand, he suggests that the differences between death row conditions are perhaps marginal and implies that it was the psychological stress of confinement that played a significant role in the decision to submit to execution in 26 of 44 respondents (59%) who made statements. Another 16 (44%) stated that acceptance of responsibility or of guilt was a factor.[109]

(d) Attempts to limit the time under sentence of death

International norms have been developing on the question of the so-called 'death row phenomenon' or 'syndrome' since the landmark case of *Soering v UK* was decided by the European Court of Human Rights in July 1989. The Court held that it would be a breach of Article 3 of the European Convention on Human Rights for the United Kingdom to extradite the prisoner, who would face the death sentence in Virginia, because his inevitably long wait on death row would amount to inhuman and degrading treatment and punishment.[110] The Judicial Committee of the Privy Council in London has gone some way to try to define what length of stay on death row is compatible with the human rights of the offender. Inmates had waited for up to twelve years in Jamaica and Trinidad and Tobago before being executed. Finding the conditions of confinement to be intolerable, the Privy Council ruled in 1993 in the cases of *Pratt and Morgan v Attorney General for Jamaica* that it would amount to inhuman and degrading punishment to execute a prisoner after a wait of five years, and even held out hope that a wait of over two years might be arguably inhumane treatment. Lord Griffiths, delivering the judgment, said:[111]

There is an instinctive revulsion against the prospect of hanging a man after he has been held under sentence of death for many years. What gives rise to this instinctive revulsion? The answer can only be our humanity; we regard it as an inhuman act to keep a man facing the agony of execution over a long extended period of time . . . To execute these men now after holding them in custody in an agony of suspense so many years would be inhuman punishment within the meaning of section 17(1) [of the Constitution of Jamaica].

This judgment applies to other Commonwealth countries in the Caribbean and to several more for whom the Judicial Committee of the Privy Council is the final court of appeal.

---

[109] John H. Blume, 'Killing the willing: "volunteers", suicide and competency' *Michigan Law Review* 103 (2005), pp. 939–1009 at 962–965 and 967–968.

[110] *Soering v United Kingdom*, Federal Republic of Germany intervening, 161 Eur Ct HR (Ser. A) 34 (1989).

[111] Pratt and Morgan had spent more than fourteen years on death row. The judgment affected 105 prisoners in Jamaica. *Pratt and Morgan v Attorney General for Jamaica* [1993] 4 All ER 769 and 783 (PC). A similar judgment on the unconstitutionality of long waits on death row was reached by the Zimbabwean Supreme Court in June 1993 in *Catholic Commission for Justice and Peace in Zimbabwe v Attorney General, Human Rights Law Journal* 14 (1993), p. 323. But William Schabas notes that a mere five months later a constitutional amendment negated this ruling: William A. Schabas, 'Execution Delayed, Execution Denied' *Criminal Law Forum* 5 (1994), pp. 180–193.

It was also not challenged in relation to Barbados in the first case to be heard by the newly constituted Caribbean Court of Appeal in July 2006 (see Chapter 3, page 109 n. 210).

Attitudes have changed. In February 2001, the Canadian Supreme Court in *Burns* held that unconditional extradition to the state of Washington, without assurance that the death penalty would not be imposed, would violate section 7 of the Canadian Charter of Rights and Freedom (see Chapter 1, pages 29–30). In part, this decision reflected a different judgment about the significance of the 'death row phenomenon' from that which the Court had reached a decade earlier in the *Kindler* case, when it had allowed extradition to Pennsylvania.[112] In *Burns* it held that:[113]

The finality of the death penalty, combined with the determination of the criminal justice system to try to satisfy itself that the conviction was not wrongful, inevitably produces lengthy delays, and the associated psychological trauma to death row inhabitants... The 'death row phenomenon' is not a controlling factor in s.7 [of the Canadian Charter of Rights and Freedoms] balance, but even many of those who regard its horrors as self-inflicted concede that it is a relevant consideration... we regard it as an inhuman act to keep a man facing the agony of execution over a long extended period of time.

In Uganda, in June 2005, *Susan Kigula and 416 others v The Attorney General* challenged the death penalty on four different aspects, one of which was the claim that long delays in carrying out executions, which led to 'death row syndrome', made the death penalty in Uganda unconstitutional.[114] The Constitutional Court held, after considering the international recognition of the death row phenomenon and hearing the harrowing evidence of Ben Ogwanga, who had spent 20 years on Uganda's death row, that, given the:[115]

very grim picture of the conditions in the condemned section of Luzira prison... coupled with the treatment meted out to the condemned prisoners during their confinement... [i]nordinate delays in such conditions constitute cruel, inhuman or degrading treatment prohibited by articles 24 and 44(a) of the Constitution of Uganda.

The Court held that a 'delay beyond three years after a condemned prisoner's sentence has been confirmed by the highest appellate court would tend towards unreasonable delay' and, therefore, that condemned prisoners who had 'been on the death row for five years and above after their sentences had been confirmed by the highest appellate court have waited longer than constitutionally permissible'.

In India the Supreme Court has laid down that an 'unduly long delay' after the conclusion of the judicial process would be relevant, but the period could not

---

[112] *Kindler v Canada* [1991] 2 SCR 779.

[113] *United States v Burns* [2001] 1 SCR 283.

[114] J. W. Katende, 'The Constitutional Challenge to the Death Penalty in Uganda', Death Penalty Conference 3–5 June 2005, Barbados, <http://www.deathpenaltyproject.org/DPP_BARBADOS_CONFERENCE_06.pdf>.

[115] The Republic of Uganda, in the Constitutional Court of Uganda, at Kampala. Constitutional Petition No. 6 of 2003 between *Susan Kigula and 416 others v The Attorney General*.

be fixed. It has taken into account overall periods in prison of 19 and 17 years in commuting a death sentence, but not 14 years 'even though most of the delay was caused by the State Government not acting, reportedly as the file relating to the prisoner had been lost'.[116]

In the United States the issue remains an 'important undecided one', yet to be fully tested by the Supreme Court.[117] But 18 years on death row was not regarded by a Federal Court of Appeals in 1998 as a situation that 'even begins to approach a constitutional violation' of cruel and unusual punishment prohibited by the Eighth Amendment.[118] In the cases of *Knight v Florida* and *Moore v Nebraska* the Court decided not to hear at that time (1999) an appeal from two death row inmates concerning the cruelty of the amount of time they had spent on death row. Justice Breyer dissenting stated: 'Both of these cases involve astonishingly long delays . . . The claim that time has rendered the execution inhuman is a particularly strong one'.[119] Similarly, when dissenting in the case of *Elledge v Florida* in 1998, Justice Breyer wrote that a lengthy delay between sentencing and execution may be unconstitutional: 'After such a delay, an execution may well cease to serve the legitimate penological purposes that otherwise provide a necessary constitutional justification for the death penalty'.[120]

Yet those who favour the death penalty claim that the prisoners have only themselves to blame for pursuing appeals. Thus, a paper prepared for the OSCE by two US Justice Department lawyers stated:[121]

The delay is typically the result of the convict's own insistence on the myriad of legal protections and layers of court review described above to ensure that his conviction and sentence were constitutionally determined and imposed. As Justice Thomas has stated [in *Knight v Florida*], 'I am unaware of any support in the American constitutional tradition or in this Court's precedent for the proposition that a defendant can avail himself of the panoply of appellate and collateral procedures and then complain when his execution is delayed'.

While far from sharing such a view, the UN Human Rights Committee, aware that a time limit could be used to truncate avenues for appeal or clemency, has so

---

[116] Bikram Jeet Batra, 'The Death Penalty in India—Issues and Aspects', paper given to the launch seminar of the China-EU project, 'Moving the Debate Forward—China's Use of the Death Penalty', 20–21 June, 2007, College for Criminal Law Science of Beijing Normal University and Great Britain-China Centre.

[117] In *Lackey v Texas*, 514 U.S. 1045, 115 S. Ct. 1421 (1995) the Supreme Court denied the petition for a writ of *certiorari* to a prisoner who sought to raise the question whether spending 17 years on death row violates the Eighth Amendment's prohibition against cruel and unusual punishment. Justice Stevens, in denying the writ, stated that this did not constitute a ruling on the merits but that 'a denial of *certiorari* on a novel issue will permit the state and federal courts to "serve as laboratories in which the issue receives further study before it is addressed by this Court"'.

[118] *Chambers v Bowersox*, 157 F.3d 560 at p. 570 (8th Cir. 1998).

[119] *Knight v Florida*, 528 U.S. 990 (1989); *Moore v Nebraska*, 528 U.S. 990 (1999).

[120] *Elledge v Florida*, 525 U.S. 944 (1998).

[121] Margaret Griffey and Laurence E. Rothenberg, 'The Death Penalty in the United States' in OSCE, *The Death Penalty in the OSCE Area* (2006), pp. 35–44 at 43.

far stood by its 'constant jurisprudence' that prolonged delays in the execution of a sentence of death do not *per se* constitute a violation of Article 7 in the absence of other 'compelling circumstances'.[122]

In our view, the evidence provided in this chapter of the suffering of prisoners over long periods of time, particularly in Japan, America, and Pakistan, often in very restricted circumstances and always under conditions of mortal uncertainty, as a result of *systemic* prerequisites for providing a fair and error-free system of capital punishment, must inevitably violate the spirit of Safeguard No. 9 which requires the infliction of 'the minimum possible suffering'.

(e) The treatment of relatives

The prisoners are not the only ones who may suffer. Many of the restrictions that make life on death row difficult for the prisoners also affect their families. Susan Sharp's research has shown that the harsh way in which society views those on death row affects the family members who feel socially isolated in their grief, rendering them hidden victims of the crime.[123] It has been found that family members of prisoners on death row also experience shame, stigma, fear and debilitating stress, leaving some suicidal.[124] They suffer a prolonged period of anticipatory grieving— often in a cycle of hope and despair, characterized by fear and uncertainty—and all the time in the knowledge that many people in their own community want the prisoner killed.[125] In some states in the United States this could last twenty years or more. While they wait many families have limited capacity to maintain supportive relationships with inmates on death row.[126] Whilst the rising political influence of the victims' rights movement has been demonstrated in local, state and national elections, with politicians making extensive use of victims and their experiences in speeches and campaign advertisements, no corresponding change has occurred for the families of homicide defendants, who remain largely invisible and unsupported.[127] There are advocacy groups across the United States in support of victims of murder, but almost none for the families of defendants.

The trauma for families is especially evident when the date of the execution draws near. In recognition of this, it appears to be common practice in most retentionist

---

[122] Communication No. 798/1998, *Howell v Jamaica* (views adopted on 21 October 2003, 79th session).

[123] Susan Sharp, *Hidden Victims: The effects of the death penalty on families of the accused* (2005).

[124] M. Costanzo, *Just revenge: Costs and consequences of the death penalty* (1997); J. O. Smykla, 'The Human Impact of Capital Punishment: Interviews with Families of Persons on Death Row' *Journal of Criminal Justice* 15 (1987), pp. 331–347.

[125] M. Vandiver, 'The Impact of the Death Penalty on the Families of Homicide Victims and of Condemned Prisoners' in J. R. Acker, R. M. Bohm, and C. S. Lanier (eds.), *America's Experiment with Capital Punishment* (2nd edn., 2003), pp. 613–645 at 614.

[126] M. Radelet, M. Vandiver, and F. M. Bernardo, 'Families, Prisons, and Men with Death Sentences: The Human Impact of Structured Uncertainty' *Journal of Family Issues* (1983) 4, pp. 593–612.

[127] Vandiver, n. 125 above, at 614.

countries to allow relatives to visit the condemned prior to execution, to inform them of the date of execution and to deliver to them the body for burial. Thus, in its reply to the UN Seventh Survey in 2004 Egypt mentioned that 'facilities were provided for relatives to visit on the day appointed for execution...and facilities must be provided for the observance of the religious duties necessary in accordance with the religious confession of the condemned person'. And Trinidad and Tobago stated that 'access to family and persons of like faith was provided prior to execution of the sentence'. However, this is not the case in several countries.

The UN Special Rapporteur has stigmatized the refusal of the Japanese authorities to provide convicted persons and their family members with advance notice of the date and time of execution as 'a clear human rights violation'.[128] The same can be said for Taiwan, where no notice is given to the condemned person and the family is not notified until after the execution has taken place, apparently 'in the interest of prison harmony'.[129] In Botswana a man was executed on 1 April 2006, with no notification of the execution being provided to his family who were not given access to him either before or after the execution. They heard news of his execution over the radio.[130]

According to the reports provided by OSCE, in Belarus, Tajikistan, Uzbekistan, and in Kazakhstan and Kyrgyzstan and the Russian Federation prior to the establishment of the moratoria, relatives were not informed of the date of the execution, the family only being informed afterwards. Many families told Amnesty International that the authorities had given official permission for the next monthly visit, only for the family to arrive at the prison to be told that their relative was already dead.[131] In several of these countries, the body has not been returned and the place of burial has been kept secret. The Human Rights Committee has criticized this, in cases involving Belarus and Uzbekistan, as having the effect of intimidating or punishing families by leaving them in a state of uncertainty and distress, amounting to a violation of Article 7 of the International Covenant on Civil and Political Rights.[132]

In their recent book, *In the Shadow of Death*, Beck *et al* estimated that there are currently approximately 13,532 individuals in the United States who are related to someone on death row.[133] Drawing on in-depth interviews with some of the

---

[128] 'Transparency and the Imposition of the Death Penalty' UN Doc. E/CN.4/2006/53/Add. 3, 24/03/06, para. 32.

[129] FIDH, *Report 450*, 2 June 2006, p. 34.

[130] Amnesty International, *Death Penalty News*, May 2006.

[131] Amnesty International, *Public Appeal: Deadly secrets: a heritage from the soviet union*, AI Index: EUR 04/011/2004.

[132] OSCE, *The Death Penalty in the OSCE Area*. Office of Democratic Institutions and Human Rights, *Background Paper 2006*, pp. 56–57. In addition, the UN Working Group on Arbitrary Detention, Report of Mission to Belarus, UN Doc. E/CN.4/2005/6/Add. 3, 25 November 2004; and *Report of the Special Rapporteur on the Situation of Human Rights in Belarus*, Adrian Severin, E/CN.4/2006/36, 16 January 2006, para. 20.

[133] E. Beck, S. Britto and A. Andrews, *In the Shadow of Death: Restorative Justice and Death Row Families* (2007), p. 8.

families of those under sentence of death, as well as the families of persons who were executed, they describe the severe depression, trauma, financial challenges, and other difficulties they faced when dealing both with other family members and with their local communities.[134] Like Sharp, they maintain that crime victims' and offenders' family members, although deeply divided in their feelings about the violent crime, have similar experiences, including grief (sometimes diagnosed as post-traumatic stress disorder), isolation, trauma, depression (the majority for more than a year, with the average for about five years), and frustration with the criminal justice system.[135] All this time they feel that their lives are 'on hold' and they cannot try to rebuild their shattered lives until either their loved one is executed or the sentence reversed.[136]

Murder Victims' Families for Human Rights (MVFHR), a Massachusetts-based organization representing the family members of the victims of murder and state executions, published a report in 2006 based on interviews with 36 families of executed prisoners, all of whom suffered from 'shame, increased isolation and feelings of personal failure', severe depression and suicide attempts. Some felt responsible for the crimes of their relatives or blamed themselves for their inability to save them from execution.[137] This study also found that children in particular remain confused and traumatized for a long time after the execution. It quotes one 10-year-old girl at the time of her father's execution in Texas in 2005: 'They're going to kill him because he killed somebody, so when they kill him, who do we get to kill?' As Sharp found, while such families often consider themselves also to be victims of the crime, they are treated as if they had committed the crime themselves.[138] In the moving BBC film of the execution of Edward Earl Johnson in Mississippi in 1987 (*14 days in May*) the prison warden, Don Cabana, in this, his first execution, reminded his prison officers that Johnson's family were guilty of no crime,[139] were decent people, and should be treated as such.[140] Yet it is not often recognized by those who support capital punishment that the pain experienced by the families of the person executed can be very similar to the pain experienced by the murderer's victim's family—as one mother interviewed by Susan Sharp made plain:[141]

[Outside the prisons]...they laugh at the families whose loved one has just been exterminated...They party, laugh and sing and cheer in front of a grieving family who loves

---

[134] *Ibid.*, p. 3.

[135] Vandiver, n. 125 above.

[136] Sharp, n. 123 above, p. 168.

[137] Susannah Sheffer and Renny Cushing, *Creating More Victims: How Executions Hurt the Families Left Behind* (2006).

[138] Sharp, n. 123 above.

[139] In fact, neither was Johnson, as evidence after his execution proved his innocence.

[140] The film, *14 Days in May*, is available at Reprieve: <http://www.reprieve.org.uk/getinvolved_products.htm>.

[141] Sharp, n. 123 above, p. 165.

their person no matter what he had done. I think the public should know that after they murder our loved one, we feel the same pain and rage as the family of a murder victim.

The Massachusetts report concluded that the needs of the families of the executed have not just been ignored, they have never been truly comprehended because these survivors are not recognized as victims and there are no execution victim families' support groups and no counselling services available to children left behind.[142]

Harsh or unsympathetic visitation policies can further add to the trauma experienced by families. Few prisons around the world have visitation facilities that go any way towards alleviating some of the pain and grief experienced by families. Prisons tend to be located away from public transport routes and many families cannot afford to visit often, even if this were allowed by the prison. When the family gets to the prison they are subject to somewhat degrading checks and searches consistent with the heightened security of death row which, whilst usually necessary, further add to their feelings of guilt and shame. Visiting areas are typically uncomfortable and the majority of death row prisoners are not allowed physical contact with their families. Even in the United States, where conditions are more civilized than in many other countries, the majority of states do not allow contact visits. As one woman, whose mother had a son on death row, told Susan Sharp:[143]

A mother of a Texas [death row] inmate will never touch their son again. There is no human contact allowed... There was a mother that begged to hold her son one last time before his execution and she was denied. They then let her hold her son's still warm but lifeless body. Don't they see that they are sentencing the family as well?

3. Conclusion

This chapter has demonstrated that, whatever justifications might be put forward for capital punishment, the process of inflicting it inevitably involves collateral abuses of human rights. The next three chapters provide additional evidence in support of this conclusion.

---

[142] Sheffer and Cushing, n. 137 above.
[143] Sharp, n. 123 above, p. 173.

6

Excluding the Vulnerable from Capital Punishment

Another very significant way in which the abolitionist movement to restrict the scope of capital punishment has progressed is by defining categories of persons who, because of their developmental status, are deemed not to be deserving of death. Thus, in 1984, Safeguard No. 3 of the ECOSOC resolution declared that 'persons below 18 years of age at the time of the commission of the crime shall not be sentenced to death, nor shall the death sentence be carried out on pregnant women, or on new mothers, or on persons who have become insane'. The categories to be exempted were broadened in 1989 when it was agreed that there should be 'a maximum age beyond which a person may not be sentenced to death or executed; and by eliminating the death penalty for persons suffering from mental retardation or extremely limited mental competence, whether at the stage of sentence or execution'. More recently, the UN Commission for Human Rights in Resolution 2004/67, followed by the Committee on Human Rights in Resolution 2005/5,[1] has called on all governments 'Not to impose the death penalty on a person suffering from *any* mental or intellectual disabilities or to execute such a person' (our emphasis). This chapter reviews the extent to which these attempts to narrow the use of capital punishment have been adopted in law and been adhered to in practice.

1. Juvenile Defendants

In addition to the force of the UN Safeguards, states that are party to the International Covenant on Civil and Political Rights (ICCPR) and the American Convention on Human Rights are prohibited (by Articles 6 (5) and 4 (5) respectively) from imposing capital punishment for offences committed by persons below 18 years of age, unless they have added a reservation to this effect—as the United States of America had done.[2] Moreover, this prohibition is embodied in

---

[1] *The question of the death penalty*, UN Doc. E/CN/.4/2005/L.77, 15 April 2005, p. 4.
[2] See the discussion in Ch. 1 above, p. 36.

the International Convention on the Rights of the Child (Article 37a),[3] which came into force in September 1990 and has now been ratified by every country except the United States and Somalia. In May 2002 Somalia signed the Convention and stated its intention to ratify it in the near future and the decision of the United States Supreme Court in *Roper v Simmons* in 2005, which declared that the imposition of the death penalty on 'juveniles' was unconstitutional (see below), has now removed the barrier to that country's ratification of the Convention.

At the beginning of the twenty-first century both the UN Sub-Commission on the Promotion and Protection of Human Rights (in Resolution 2000/17),[4] and the Inter-American Commission on Human Rights, in 2002,[5] were able confidently to declare that the *principle* that capital punishment should not apply to persons who committed a capital offence when under the age of 18 had been established as part of customary international law. In accordance with this, several countries brought their law into line with this practice. For example, Thailand did so in 2001 and in January 2005 the Legislative Yuan of Taiwan ratified an overhaul of the Criminal Code which included exempting people under the age of 18 or over 80 from the death penalty, even if they kill family members of direct lineage.[6]

Nevertheless, at least 17 countries that are parties to the Convention on the Rights of the Child have not yet formally abolished the powers to sentence juveniles to death.[7] In several of these countries the minimum age is fixed as low as 16 and, in a few, death sentences may be imposed on even younger children, sometimes because no distinction is drawn between adults and minors (as in Malaysia's 1975 Internal Security Act). In some of these countries youth is statutorily defined as a mitigating factor, but by no means in all. For example, in India the Supreme Court upheld the death sentence in May 2001 on a youth who had been convicted of murder at a time when he was suspected of being only 15 years of age, whereas under India's Juvenile Justice Act persons under the age of 16 cannot be sentenced to death.[8] The prisoner had been tried in an adult court, and the

---

[3] Adopted by General Assembly Resolution 44/125 of 20 November 1989, and currently ratified by 191 countries. Also in the Draft UN Standard Minimum Rules for the Administration of Juvenile Justice, which were adopted in 1984 (known as the Beijing Rules, and adopted by General Assembly Resolution 40/33, 29 November 1985). It is also forbidden by the African Charter on the Rights and Welfare of the Child, African Union OAU Doc. CAB/LEG/24.9/49 (1990), entered into force 29 November 1999, p. 3.

[4] UN Doc. E/CN.4/SUB.2/RES/2000/17 (17 August 2000). In 1999 the Sub-Commission (previously the sub-Commission on Prevention of Discrimination and Protection of Minorities) had, in Resolution 1999/4, condemned 'unequivocally the imposition and execution of the death penalty on those aged under 18 at the time of commission of the offence' and called on all states to commit themselves to abolishing the death penalty for such persons.

[5] Amnesty International, *The Exclusion Of Child Offenders From The Death Penalty Under General International Law*, ACT 50/004/2003, p. 1.

[6] Hands Off Cain, 1 January 2006.

[7] *Ibid.*

[8] Amnesty International, *Death Penalty News*, June 2001, AI Index: ACT.

Supreme Court in twice reviewing the sentence has declared that 'the awarding of a lesser sentence only on the ground of the appellant being a youth at the time of occurrence cannot be considered as a mitigating circumstance'.[9]

In several countries the law remains unclear. Pakistan, which ratified the Convention of the Rights of the Child in 1990, issued a Juvenile Justice System Ordinance in July 2000 prohibiting imposition of the death penalty on anyone under the age of 18 at the time of the offence, but this did not extend to the Provincially and Federally Administered Tribal Areas in the North and West.[10] Moreover, it was not applied to those juveniles already under sentence of death (in breach of UN Safeguard No. 2: see Chapter 4, n. 17), and in November 2001 it was reported that a young man was hanged for a murder he had allegedly committed when he was only 13 years of age. Although the President of Pakistan, Pervez Musharraf, commuted the death sentences of all the 100 or so juveniles on death row to life imprisonment in December 2001,[11] the decree was revoked by the Lahore High Court in 2004 as unconstitutional. Over two years later, an appeal to the Supreme Court of Pakistan was still under consideration. A recent report from Yemen indicates that a prisoner under sentence of death had been sentenced when he was only 15.[12]

The new constitution of Sudan states that 'The death penalty shall not be imposed on a person under the age of 18 or a person who has attained the age of 70 except in cases of retribution or *huddud*'. But, as the UN Special Rapporteur on Extrajudicial, Summary or Arbitrary Executions pointed out, 'This means that a child who has reached puberty (and is therefore an adult under Islamic Law) can be sentenced to death for such crimes as murder, rape or adultery'. She came across a number of persons in prison who had received a death sentence when they were under the age of 18, several of whom had been tried with adults. She was, however, assured by government officials that 'child prisoners would nevertheless not be executed'.[13]

The Nigerian Committee on Judicial and Legal Reform recommended (Chapter 10, Recommendation 7) in its final report in July 2005 that: 'capital and severe corporal punishment should be reserved only to those young persons

---

[9] *Ibid.*, p. 4.

[10] The Pakistan Penal Code and Code of Criminal Procedure do not establish an age limit below which the death penalty may not be imposed, but in 2000 the government of Pakistan restricted the use of the death penalty to adults when it issued the Juvenile Justice System Ordinance 2000, which prohibits the death penalty for anyone under the age of 18 at the time of committing the offence. Amnesty International, *Death Penalty News*, December 2000, AI Index: ACT 53/001/2001, and Amnesty International, News Release, *Pakistan: Young Offenders Taken off Death Row*, AI Index: ASA 33/029/2001.

[11] Reported in Amnesty International, News Release, *Pakistan: Young Offenders Taken off Death Row*, AI Index: ASA 33/029/2001, and Amnesty International, *Death Penalty News*, December 2001, AI Index: ACT 001/2002, p. 2.

[12] *News Yemen*, July 2007.

[13] *Report of the Special Rapporteur on Extrajudicial, Summary or Arbitrary Executions (Sudan)*, 2004, E/CN.4/2005/7Add. 2, paras. 51 and 52.

found to have been engaged in heinous offences such as armed robbery and cult-ism'. This statement, which was supported by the Nigerian Coalition on Death Penalty Abolition (NCDPA), the Human Rights Law Service (HURILAWS), and Legal Resources Consortium, is especially serious because the recommenda-tions are likely to influence a new Nigerian constitution.[14]

It appears that one reason why juveniles have occasionally, although rarely, been sentenced to death has been the failure of the authorities to have accurately determined the age of the accused, but this by no means accounts for all cases.[15] According to Amnesty International, 36 juvenile offenders have been executed in five countries since 2000—China (2), Democratic Republic of Congo (1, but none since 2000), Iran (19), Pakistan (2), Saudi Arabia (1), Sudan (2), and the United States of America (9, but none since 2003). Of these 36 individuals, six were executed in 2000, three in 2001, three in 2002, two in 2003, four in 2004, ten in 2005, five in 2006, and three had been executed up to the end of July 2007.[16] It is clear that Iran stands out among those countries where juveniles have been executed. According to Amnesty International, 71 persons convicted when under the age of 18 were, in June 2007, still facing execution.[17] So, yet again, it was necessary for the General Assembly of the United Nations, at its fifty-ninth session, to adopt a resolution (59/261, 23 November 2004) on children's rights, calling upon all states to abolish the death penalty for children below 18 years of age at the time of the offence.

Between 1990 and 2003 over half (19) of the 34 known executions of juvenile offenders were carried out in the United States. At the same time pressure had been mounting on the US Supreme Court to declare such executions uncon-stitutional. In the case of *Thompson v Oklahoma* (1988) the majority of the US Supreme Court had ruled that it was unconstitutional to impose the death pen-alty on a person who had committed the offence when aged 15, but over this age it was a matter for state legislatures to decide at what age the 'bright line' should be drawn. One year later, in *Stanford v Kentucky* and *Wilkins v Missouri*, the Court held, by a five to four majority, that it was not unacceptable to the values of con-temporary society and therefore did not violate the Constitution to sentence to death persons who had committed murders when aged 16 and 17.[18] This was

---

[14] Amnesty International, *Nigeria: Joint statement on the death penalty*, AI Index: AFR 44/015/2005.

[15] Committee on the Rights of the Child, E/CN.4/2004/86, para. 34 and E/CN.4/2004/7/ Add. 2, para. 57.

[16] Amnesty International, *Execution of Child Offenders since 1990*, 2007.

[17] Amnesty International, *Iran: the last executioner of children*, June 2007, AI Index: MDE 13/059/2007. Between August 2004 and March 2006 the UN Special Rapporteur on Extrajudicial, Summary or Arbitrary Executions sent 12 communications to Iran concerning nine boys and six girls, who had been sentenced to death for crimes committed when they were under 18, 'a wholly unacceptable situation': A/HRC/4/20, 29 January 2007, paras 16 and 17.

[18] It should be noted that in *Thompson v Oklahoma*, 487 U.S. 815 (1988), the Court had accepted that international practice was relevant to its decision, yet in *Stanford v Kentucky*, 492 U.S. 361 (1989), the majority held that 'it is *American* conceptions of decency that is dispositive' not the

so, even though opinion polls had shown that the majority of the population questioned had been opposed to the use of capital punishment for juveniles under the age of 18.[19] Furthermore, it should be noted that since 1983 the American Bar Association had declared itself in principle opposed to the imposition of capital punishment upon any person who committed the offence under the age of 18.[20] Yet, in 1999, the Supreme Court in the case of *Domingues v Nevada*[21] decided not to consider the issue of whether the execution of a person who was 16 at the time of the offence was a violation of customary international law and US treaty obligations. Despite the fact that the UN High Commissioner on Human Rights had appealed to the US authorities in June 1999 to prevent the execution of Chris Thomas in Virginia—calling upon them to 'reaffirm the customary international law ban on the use of the death penalty on juvenile offenders'[22]—the US Solicitor General filed a brief in the US Supreme Court setting out the government's view that the United States was not obliged under customary international law or US treaty obligations to exempt children. This was because the US government believed that it could continue to execute juveniles by virtue of its reservation to Article 6(5) of the ICCPR.[23] Following this, in 2001 the Court refused, by a majority of 5 to 4, to reconsider its 1989 judgment in the case of Kevin Stanford (who had been 17 when he committed murder) that the death sentence passed on him was not a violation of the Constitution. However, it was highly significant that the four dissenting justices declared that, in their opinion, the execution of juvenile offenders was a 'relic of the past and inconsistent with evolving standards of decency in a civilized society'.[24]

By the end of 2004, 20 of the 38 retentionist states had not set the minimum age at 18. In 14 it was specified at a lower age and in 6 no age limit was laid down by law. Eighteen states plus the federal jurisdiction (under the Violent Crime Control Act 1994) had specified the age at 18.[25] The only special protection provided in states where the lower age limit had been 16 or 17 or where no age limit was specified was the ruling in *Eddings v Oklahoma* (1982) that age, emotional

juvenile sentencing practices of other countries: Harold Hongju Koh, 'Paying "Decent Respect" to World Opinion on the Death Penalty' *UC Davis Law Review* 35 (2002), pp. 1085–1131 at 1100–1101.

[19] S. E. Skovoron, J. E. Scott, and F. T. Cullen, 'The Death Penalty for Juveniles: An Assessment of Public Support' *Crime and Delinquency* 35 (1989), pp. 546–561. A Gallup Poll in 1994 had found that 61% said that 'teenagers should not be spared the death penalty on account of their age'; Samuel R. Gross, 'Update: American Public Opinion on the Death Penalty—It's Getting Personal' *Cornell Law Review* 83 (1998), pp. 1448–1475 at 1466. But a poll taken in Arizona in July 2000 found that only 37% of respondents favoured the death penalty when the convicted murderer is a juvenile offender: <http://www.deathpenaltyinfo.org/article.php?scid=23&did=210#Arizona>.

[20] Victor Streib, 'Moratorium on the Death Penalty for Juveniles' *Law and Contemporary Problems* 61 (1998), pp. 55–74 at 56.

[21] 528 U.S. 963 (1999).

[22] Amnesty International, *United States of America: Failing the Future—Death Penalty Developments, March 1998–March 2000*, AI Index: AMR 51/03/00, p. 37.

[23] *Ibid.*, p. 41.

[24] In *Re Kevin Nigel Stanford*, 537 U.S. (2002), 21 October 2002.

[25] US Bureau of Justice Statistics, *Capital Punishment 2004* (2005), at p. 4.

upbringing, and childhood experiences should always be considered as mitigating factors. However, it is clear that courts in different states had varied a great deal in the consideration they had given to age as a mitigating factor.[26] Between 1976 and 2005 only 7 of the 38 states with the death penalty had executed a 'juvenile' offender and 13 of the 22 executed had been put to death in Texas, 3 in Virginia, 2 in Oklahoma and 1 each in South Carolina, Florida, Georgia, and Missouri.

The issue was again brought to the fore in 2003 when the Missouri Supreme Court held that the minimum age authorized in law for the imposition of capital punishment in that state, which was 16, was in violation of the Eighth Amendment of the United States Constitution and must be raised to 18. This decision was appealed to the US Supreme Court, which, on 1 March 2005, by a majority of 5 to 4, in *Roper v Simmons*, held that the Eighth and Fourteenth Amendments forbade imposition of the death penalty on offenders who were under the age of 18 when their crimes were committed. Seventy prisoners on death row had their death sentences commuted.

Why had there been such a turn-around in the position of the court? Of first importance was the Court's own ruling in 2002 in the case of *Atkins v Virginia* (see below, pages 200–203). The Court had held that a national consensus— due to 'evolving standards of decency that mark the progress of a maturing society' (*Trop v Dulles*)—had developed to the point that the execution of mentally retarded persons was 'so truly unusual' and disproportionate that it should be regarded as 'cruel and unusual'. This had set the precedent. Did not the same arguments apply to juveniles?[27] The majority of justices held that it did. They noted that five states since 1989 had outlawed the execution of persons who committed capital offences when under the age of 18 and only three states (Texas, Virginia, and Oklahoma) had executed a young offender in the previous 10 years. This was evidence of a consistent trend towards abolition of the practice. Despite the fact that more than half the states had not formally set the age limit for execution at 18, in practice there was evidence of an 'evolving standard of decency' prohibiting the sentence of death being imposed on persons who committed capital offences when under the age of 18.[28] The Court also held that there was an

[26] Dinah A. Robinson and Otis H. Stephens, 'Patterns of Mitigating Factors in Juvenile Death Penalty Cases' *Criminal Law Bulletin* 28 (1992), pp. 246–275.

[27] Jamie Hughes, 'For Mice or Men or Children? Will the expansion of the Eighth Amendment in *Atkins v Virginia* Force the Supreme Court to Re-examine the Minimum Age for the Death Penalty?' *Journal of Criminal Law and Criminology* 93 (2003), pp. 973–1008, pointing out that in *Atkins v Virginia* 'The Court has lowered its standards for defining a "national consensus", and this decision will have substantial future implications' (p. 973) and noting that 'only twenty of the thirty-nine death penalty jurisdictions (forty-six percent) have excluded mentally retarded offenders from death within their sentencing scheme. This is less than half of the states that had previously been required to establish a national consensus' (p. 998). Also, Victor L. Streib, 'Adolescence, Mental Retardation and the Death Penalty: The Siren Call of *Atkins v Virginia*' *New Mexico Law Review* 33 (2003), pp. 183–206.

[28] For a statistical analysis of the background to the *Simmons* decision regarding changes in the use of the death penalty for juveniles over time, see Jeffrey Fagan and Valerie West, 'The Decline of

abundance of evidence to suggest that persons under this age had 'diminished culpability' because they were susceptible to 'immature and irresponsible behavior'. Their 'vulnerability and lack of control over their immediate surroundings' gave them a greater claim than adults 'to be forgiven for failing to escape negative influences'. Nor were they 'irretrievably depraved' as they were still struggling to 'define their identity'. The majority of the justices therefore argued that neither of the two main justifications for capital punishment—retribution and deterrence—'provide adequate justification for imposing that penalty on juveniles'. They were 'categorically less culpable than the average criminal.' Thus:[29]

When a juvenile commits a heinous crime, the State can exact forfeiture of some of the most basic liberties, but the State cannot extinguish his life and his potential to attain a mature understanding of his own humanity. While drawing the line at 18 is subject to the objections always raised against categorical rules, that is the point where society draws the line for many purposes between childhood and adulthood and the age at which the line for death eligibility ought to rest. *Stanford* should be deemed to be no longer controlling on this issue.

In effect, the base-line had been moved up from 16 to 18 years of age.

It is important to recognize the influence of the international developments discussed in Chapter 1 in shaping this judgment. The majority of the Court (including Justice O'Connor, who dissented on another issue) declared that:[30]

The overwhelming weight of international opinion against the juvenile death penalty is not controlling here, but provides respected and significant confirmation for the Court's determination that the penalty is disproportionate punishment for offenders under the age of 18. The United States is the only country in the world that continues to give official sanction to the juvenile penalty. It does not lessen fidelity to the Constitution or pride in its origins to acknowledge that the express affirmation of certain fundamental rights by other nations and peoples underscores the centrality of those same rights within our own heritage and freedom.

This judgment has, however, not finally resolved all issues that concern the punishment of juveniles for capital offences. In July 2006, after having considered the second and third periodic reports submitted by the United States, the UN

the Juvenile Death Penalty: Scientific Evidence of Evolving Norms' *Journal of Criminal Law and Criminology* 95 (2005), pp. 427–497. They show (at 465–466) that there was a decline in the number of death sentences imposed on juveniles between 1990 and 2003 that was not simply explained by a decline in the number of juveniles per homicide or per homicide arrest, and (at 472–430) that the decline in the death sentencing rate per homicide was far greater than for adults, thus supporting the view that 'societal norms are shifting away from the use of the juvenile death penalty' (at 473).

[29] *Roper v Simmons*, 543 U.S. 551 (2005), at (b)(2), pp. 14–21.

[30] *Ibid.*, at (c), pp. 21–25. Note that Justices Scalia, Thomas and Chief Justice Rehnquist rejected the 'national consensus' argument and stated that 'More fundamentally, however, the basic premise of the Court's argument—that American law should conform to the laws of the rest of the world—ought to be rejected out of hand'. Justice Sandra O'Connor agreed with the first of these arguments but not the second (543 U.S. 2005).

Human Rights Committee noted with concern reports that 42 states and the federal government had laws allowing persons under the age of 18 at the time the offence was committed to receive sentences of life in prison without the possibility of parole, and that some 2,225 youth offenders were serving such sentences in US prisons.[31] The Committee ruled that sentencing children to life sentences without the possibility of parole was not in compliance with Article 24(1) of the ICCPR (provision on the protection of children) (see further Chapter 11). Nor, of course, does the discussion above on judicially imposed capital punishment tell the whole story. The number of 'juveniles' executed after conviction before a court of law is tiny compared with those who have been victims of extra-judicial executions and 'disappearances' in several countries during the last twenty years.

2. The Question of the Aged

ECOSOC has urged all member states to establish a maximum age beyond which persons may not be sentenced to death or executed, but only a few countries have done so. No one over 80 years of age may be executed in Taiwan, and over 70 in Sudan; in Kazakhstan and the Russian Federation no one over age 65; and in Mongolia, Uzbekistan, and Guatemala, no one over 60.[32]

The reason why this safeguard is not more widely embraced is probably because the rationale for exempting persons on the basis of age *per se* is less easy to accept than the rationale for exempting the young on the grounds of their lesser responsibility. Of course, age can bring lesser responsibility when senility can be established, but this can always be taken into account as an exculpating form of insanity or limited mental capacity. Also, age more generally may be a mitigating factor.

Very little information is available on the ages of persons executed worldwide, but it is known, for example, that in Japan a man of 70 was executed in 1993 and another in 1995 and currently there are several very elderly prisoners awaiting execution, the oldest being aged 86.[33] It has been reported that in Saudi Arabia a man aged 97 is under sentence of death.[34] In the United States John Nixon, aged 77, was executed in December 2005 for a crime committed 19 years earlier in 1986 and at the end of 2005 the oldest person on death row was a white male in Arizona who

---

[31] The Committee was relying on the Amnesty International and Human Rights Watch Joint Study, *The Rest of their Lives: Life without Parole for Child Offenders in the United States*, October 2005, <http://hrw.org/reports/2005/us1005/>.

[32] There are other exemptions. For example, in the Sudan, Islamic law exempts a father who kills his son or daughter.

[33] Okunishi Mauri (sentenced to death for poisoning five women in 1961) is now 80 years old and another prisoner on Japan's death row is 78. See Amnesty International, *Will this be my last? The Death Penalty in Japan*, 2006, <http://web.amnesty.org/library/index/engasa220062006>. According to another report, Ishida Tomizo, 'who had his request for a retrial denied in 2004, 13 years after he submitted it', is 86 years' old: Amnesty International, *Death Penalty News*, June 2004, AI Index: ACT 53/001/2004.

[34] *Agence France Presse*, 25 February 2007.

was aged 90, having been sentenced to death in 1983.[35] This is yet another aspect of the 'death row phenomenon', which was discussed in Chapter 4.

3. The Exemption of Pregnant Women

While it is not yet universally the case that pregnant women are exempted from the death penalty by law, or that they are spared as 'new mothers' after having given birth, these exemptions are becoming much more common. For example, new legislation came into force in Vietnam in 2000 allowing the death sentence on pregnant women and mothers of children aged up to 36 months to be changed to life imprisonment.[36] As a result, in January 2007 a judge spared the life of one of the worst offenders in a 21-member drug trafficking gang because she had become pregnant in prison, whilst five of the others faced the firing squad. Indeed, in recent years there have been no reports of pregnant women or mothers with recently born children being executed. The last reported instance was a death sentence imposed on a pregnant woman in the Democratic Republic of Congo in 1998.[37]

Once a woman has given birth, some countries (such as Kuwait) automatically commute the sentence to imprisonment for life. But 20 countries have informed the United Nations that they would not invariably do so, in other words that mothers of young children could be executed.[38] The laws of several countries specify no minimum period before a woman who has given birth may be executed: the execution is merely 'stayed'.[39] Some others set specific periods. In Indonesia the period is 40 days, in Egypt and Libya two months, in Jordan three months,[40] and in Yemen two years, provided that there is someone to support the child. In Antigua and Barbuda, Belarus, Indonesia, and in China the imposition of the death penalty is no longer allowed if a female offender is pregnant at the time of the trial.[41]

Although there is no international norm barring the sentencing to death and execution of women in general, they have been exempted altogether from capital

---

[35] Hands Off Cain, 14 December 2005: <http://www.handsoffcain.info/news/index.php?iddocumento=7413480>.

[36] Amnesty International, *Report 2001*, p. 266.

[37] *Special Rapporteur on Extrajudicial, Summary or Arbitrary Executions*, E/CN.4/1999/39/Add. 1, para. 68.

[38] Bahrain, Bangladesh, Barbados, Brunei Darussalam, Burundi, Cameroon, Egypt, Guatemala, Ghana, Guinea, Jamaica, Japan, Jordan, Lebanon, Niger, South Korea, Thailand, Togo, Trinidad and Tobago, and Tunisia.

[39] Barbados, Cameroon, Japan, Lebanon, Niger, South Korea, Thailand, Togo, and the United Arab Emirates.

[40] Art. 358 of the Penal Procedure Code of Jordan. However, Art. 17 of the Penal Code stipulates that 'in the event that a woman under sentence of death proves to be pregnant, the death penalty shall be commuted to hard labour for life'.

[41] Hans-Jörg Albrecht, 'The Death Penalty in China from a European Perspective', in M. Nowak and Xin Chunying (eds.), *EU-China Human Rights Dialogue: Proceedings of the Second EU-China Legal Experts Seminar Held in Beijing on 19 and 20 October 1998* (2000), pp. 95–118 at 97.

punishment in a few countries—mainly those associated with the former Soviet system—Belarus, Mongolia, Uzbekistan, and the Russian Federation. Nor has a woman been executed in Cuba since the revolution. Nevertheless, women are usually not categorically exempted, and indeed the case for exempting them as a matter of principle is not easy to establish. As Victor Streib has put it:[42]

Making women ineligible for the death penalty, as Russia has done expressly and as the United States has done in practice, seems harder [than for juveniles or the mentally retarded] to defend...One need not be a supporter of the death penalty to observe that if men are eligible for it, then women should be also. Otherwise women are lumped in with juveniles and the mentally retarded as not fully responsible human beings.

Reports of women sentenced to death have come from many retentionist countries, including China, Democratic Republic of the Congo, Indonesia, Iraq, Japan, Nigeria, Saudi Arabia, Thailand, and the United States. In 1998, when the state of Texas executed a woman, it was the first such execution in the United States since 1984, but since then another 10 women have been executed, but none since September 2005. Nine of the 11 women executed since 1976 were white non-Hispanic and two were black non-Hispanic.[43] Frances Newton, executed in Texas in September 2005, was the first black woman to be executed since 1977. Altogether, 50 women were on death row by the end of 2006 in the United States.

According to reports from Amnesty International and Hands Off Cain, women have also been executed recently in Iran (at least three women hanged in 2006), Vietnam (at least two were executed for selling drugs in 2006), Indonesia (2005), and more frequently in China (according to Amnesty International's *Death Penalty Log* at least 33 women were executed in 1999 and there have been numerous recent reports in 2005 and 2006 of women being executed, primarily for murder but in one case for smuggling babies). There have been reports every year of some women being executed in Saudi Arabia.

4. The Status of the Mentally Retarded

The Fifth UN Quinquennial Survey in 1995 asked for the first time whether the law eliminated the death penalty for persons suffering from mental retardation or extremely limited mental competence—a mental development disorder variously referred to in some countries as 'mental handicap' or 'learning disability'.[44]

[42] Victor L. Streib, 'Executing Women, Juveniles, and the Mentally Retarded: Second Class Citizens in Capital Punishment' in J. R. Acker, R. M. Bohm, and C. S. Lanier (eds.), *America's Experiment with Capital Punishment* (2nd edn, 2003), pp. 301–323 at 322.

[43] Victor L. Streib, *The Fairer Death: Executing Women in Ohio* (2006). For a very thorough state-by-state study relating to the 175 women sentenced to death between 1900 and 1998, see Kathleen A. O'Shea, *Women and the Death Penalty in the United States, 1990–1998* (1999).

[44] Amnesty International, *Mental Retardation and the Death Penalty*, AI Index: ACT 75/002/2001.

According to the replies from the latest, seventh, survey, Bahrain and Morocco have no laws to prohibit the execution of the mentally retarded. In Japan the 'weak-minded' cannot be sentenced to death, but the legal test of being able to distinguish right from wrong and the mental competence to act on that knowledge is so limited that the Japan Federation of Bar Associations (JFBA) reported that mental retardation is not necessarily included in the 'weak-minded' category. In fact, according to JFBA, the courts find even the most mentally retarded people are completely mentally competent. The reply from Trinidad and Tobago stated that the law did not allow the mentally retarded or those of extremely limited mental competence to be sentenced to death. But it appears that this is only insofar as mental retardation falls within the concept of 'abnormality of mind, defined as a condition of arrested or retarded development of mind of inherent causes or induced by disease or injury'. The condition would have to be such as to render the person 'unfit to plead or guilty but insane at the time the murder was committed'. Thailand replied that the mentally retarded or those of extremely limited mental competence may not be sentenced to death because section 78 of the Thai Penal Code allows extenuating circumstances to be taken into account by the court, which may 'if it thinks fit, reduce the punishment to be inflicted on the offender by not more than one half'. In Belarus and Tajikistan, according to reports from OSCE, if it is established that the defendant has a mental disorder resulting in inability to be aware of or control his actions, the court may suspend the execution.[45]

It is not merely that the mentally retarded have a lesser capacity to understand the meaning and consequences of their actions and are much less likely to be deterred by threats of punishment; they are also much more vulnerable when, as suspects, they fall into the hands of the criminal justice system. They are likely to be more suggestible, more ready to please by confessing, less knowledgeable about their right not to answer questions without the advice of a lawyer, and less adept at negotiating pleas: more likely, therefore, to be wrongly convicted.[46] A tragic example of this was the case of Earl Washington, a man with an IQ variously assessed as being between 57 and 69, who was convicted of the rape and murder of a young woman in Culpepper, Virginia, in 1982 on the basis of a confession he made to the police. It is not clear that all members of the jury were aware of his degree of mental retardation and they accepted that he had voluntarily waived his right to remain silent. Yet, sixteen years after he was sentenced to death—at one time he came within three days of execution—he was exonerated and pardoned when a DNA test proved that he was not guilty of the crime.[47]

---

[45] OSCE, *The Death Penalty in the OSCE Area, Background Paper*, 2003/1, pp. 33 and 37.

[46] Human Rights Watch, *Beyond Reason: The Death Penalty and Offenders with Mental Retardation* (March 2001), Pt. IV.

[47] *Ibid.*, Summary and Recommendations, p. 3. See also Margaret Edds, *An Expendable Man: the Near-Execution of Earl Washington Jr.* (2003).

The problem is that there appears to be no common agreement on how severe such retardation must be to lead to acquittal or the imposition of a lesser sentence than death. For instance, Article 18 of the Criminal Law of the People's Republic of China (1997) states that 'If a mental patient has not *completely* lost the ability of recognizing or controlling his own conduct… he shall bear criminal responsibility; however he *may* be given a lighter or mitigated punishment' (our emphasis). Presumably this refers not only to those of diminished responsibility due to mental illness but also to those who are not fully competent because of mental retardation. It does not, of course, absolutely bar the execution of those who have a degree of mental retardation, as the word 'may' signifies, and how it is interpreted in the practice of capital punishment is unknown owing to the official secrecy which surrounds the subject in China.[48] Given the speed with which cases are processed, especially during 'strike hard' campaigns, it is not difficult to imagine that there will not always have been a careful review of the accused's state of mental competence before an execution is carried out. However, the situation may improve a great deal now that the Supreme People's Court has undertaken the review of all death sentences (see Chapter 3, page 101).

It is impossible, therefore, on a worldwide basis, to gauge the extent to which the widespread prohibition on the execution of the mentally retarded has in fact provided a safeguard for all those to whom it might apply in principle. This is mainly because in most countries there have been no studies of the mental abilities of prisoners facing the death sentence, there is a shortage of experts to make the assessments, and in any case there may be differences between cultures in defining the level of mental functioning that constitutes 'retardation' and no reliable means of distinguishing between those who are 'learning disabled' and those who simply have very little learning.

Until the Supreme Court of the United States handed down its judgment in *Atkins v Virginia* in June 2002 there was no constitutional bar to sentencing to death mentally retarded persons convicted of murder in the United States. While the United States had not been entirely alone in continuing with this practice—there had been a report of one such execution in Japan[49] and another in Kyrgyzstan[50] in the mid-1990s—by the end of the twentieth century the USA was the only country officially continuing to execute such offenders.

In the late 1980s a groundswell of public opinion began in the United States that persuaded more and more legislatures to prohibit the execution of the mentally retarded.[51] In 1986 the Georgia Board of Pardons and Paroles refused

---

[48] See Albrecht, n. 40 above, pp. 97–98.

[49] *Report of the Special Rapporteur on Extrajudicial, Summary or Arbitrary Executions,* E/CN.4/1995/61 (December 1994), para. 380.

[50] *Report of the Special Rapporteur on Extrajudicial, Summary or Arbitrary Executions,* E/CN.4/1997/60 (December 1996), para. 90.

[51] For the position up to 1992, see Kent S. Miller and Michael L. Radelet, *Executing the Mentally Ill: The Criminal Justice System and the Case of Alvin Ford* (1993), pp. 175–176.

clemency to Jerome Bowden, a man with a full-scale IQ of 65, on the grounds that they considered it high enough for him to know right from wrong. In the furore pending his execution, in June 1986, a state-wide poll was conducted which found that two-thirds of respondents opposed the execution of the mentally retarded.[52] In 1988 Georgia became the first state to pass a Bill prohibiting the execution of the mentally retarded.

In *Penry v Lynaugh* (1989) the Supreme Court had decided that mentally disordered offenders were not 'categorically' exempt from capital punishment and that the appellant, who was mentally retarded, with an IQ of 50–65, organic brain damage, and a history of considerable physical and emotional abuse as a child, should not be spared the death penalty—because although it diminished his blameworthiness, it was held also to increase the probability of dangerous behaviour in the future.[53] The Court held that there was at that time no consensus of opinion in the United States that the execution of the mentally retarded amounted to cruel and unusual punishment, because only two states at that time—Georgia and Maryland—had enacted statutes barring it. This decision, according to a national opinion poll, was very unpopular: 71 per cent of those questioned believed that such retarded persons should not be executed.[54]

The controversy in the United States was fuelled by several high-profile cases.[55] It has been claimed that at least 44 prisoners with 'mental retardation or significant organic brain damage' were executed between 1984 and March 2001—some with intelligence quotients as low as 59 and the lower 70s—equivalent to the mental age of 7- to 10-year-olds.[56] However, the number of the mentally retarded executed each year began to decline substantially: from six in 1999 to only one in 2001,[57] although, according to a report by Human Rights Watch in 2001, experts believed that there may have been 'two or three hundred' mentally retarded persons on death row in the United States at that time.[58]

---

[52] In a Gallup Poll taken in 2001 it was similarly found that two-thirds of a sample of the American public were opposed to executing people with mental retardation, and only 16% of those who otherwise supported capital punishment supported the execution of a person who is mentally retarded; cited in *McCarver v State of North Carolina*, brief of Amici Curiae Diplomats (No. 00–8727), 8 June 2001, p. 17.

[53] William A. Schabas, 'International Norms on Execution of the Insane and the Mentally Retarded' *Criminal Law Forum* 4 (1994), pp. 95–117 at 108–109. Penry's death sentence was overturned by the US Supreme Court for a second time because the jury was still not properly instructed about mental retardation.

[54] Thomas R. Marshall, 'Public Opinion and the Rehnquist Court' *Judicature* 74 (6) (1991), pp. 322–329 at 324.

[55] *Report of the Special Rapporteur on Extrajudicial, Summary or Arbitrary Executions*, E/CN.4/2001/9 (2001), para. 82.

[56] See D. Keyes, W. Edwards, and R. Perske, 'People with Mental Retardation are Dying, Legally at least 44 have been Executed' *Journal of Mental Retardation* 40(3) (2002), pp. 243–244; also William J. Edwards, 'Capital Punishment and Mental Disability: *Amici Curiae Brief in Penry v Johnson*' *Criminal Law Forum* 12 (2001), pp. 267–276.

[57] See Keyes, *et al.*, at n. 56, above.

[58] Human Rights Watch, *Beyond Reason*, n. 46 above, Summary and Recommendations, p. 1.

By the beginning of the new millennium it had become clear that the time was ripe for a fresh constitutional assault on this practice. By December 2001 Georgia had been joined by 17 other states and the federal government, the District of Columbia, and Puerto Rico.[59] President George W. Bush had declared, perhaps in an off-guard moment, in June 2001 that 'we should never execute anybody who is mentally retarded': at least, one might say 'in principle'.[60] The issue was to be tested in the US Supreme Court in the case of *Ernest Paul McCarver v State of North Carolina* (No. 00–8727, 2000), a man with an IQ of 67. In briefs to the court it was argued that the execution of the mentally retarded had become 'manifestly inconsistent with evolving international standards of decency'. This was backed up by the testimonies of distinguished foreign diplomats on the negative reaction of foreign countries to America's failure to ban the 'cruel and uncivilized practice' of executing the mentally retarded. It was argued that to execute McCarver would 'strain diplomatic relations with close American allies, provide diplomatic ammunition to countries with worse human rights records, increase US diplomatic isolation, and impair other United States foreign policy interests'; furthermore, that the Supreme Court could not 'meaningfully evaluate "evolving standards of decency that mark the progress of a maturing society"[61] without weighing international as well as domestic opinion'.[62]

This effort became moot when North Carolina abolished capital punishment for the mentally retarded, and applied the Act retrospectively to cover all such cases under sentence of death. But in June 2002 the Court held, by a majority of 6 to 3, in the case of *Atkins v Virginia*,[63] a man with an IQ of 59 who had been convicted of kidnapping and murdering a 21-year-old airman when he was just 18, that 'evolving standards of decency' had now produced a 'national consensus' in opposition to the execution of the mentally retarded: a consensus that was backed by international condemnation of the practice. It was not just the fact that now twenty, rather than two, jurisdictions had abolished capital punishment of the mentally retarded: it was 'the consistency of the direction of change' that provided 'powerful evidence that today society views mentally retarded offenders as categorically less culpable than the average criminal'. Moreover, the fact that the majority gave weight to the overwhelming disapproval of the practice of sentencing the mentally retarded to death 'within the world community' was a significant shift away from the Supreme Court's previous stance on the relevance of international human rights opinion—despite the fact that the minority, as voiced by Justice Scalia, continued to 'fail to see...how the views of other countries

---

[59] *Mental Retardation and the Death Penalty*, on the Death Penalty Information Center website.

[60] Raymond Bonner, 'President Says the Retarded Should Never be Executed', *New York Times*, 12 June 2001.

[61] *Trop v Dulles*, 356 U.S. 101 (1958).

[62] Harold Hongju Koh, 'Paying "Decent Respect" to World Opinion on the Death Penalty' *U C Davis Law Review* 35 (2002), pp. 1085–1131.

[63] 56 US 304 (2002).

regarding the punishment of their citizens provide any support for the Court's ultimate determination'.

The decision in *Atkins* did not, however, lay down how mental retardation should be defined. The majority quoted the definitions of the American Association of Mental Retardation (AAMR) and the American Psychiatric Association, both of which stressed 'significant sub-average intellectual functioning'[64] but came to the conclusion that 'we leave to the States the task of developing appropriate ways to enforce the constitutional restriction upon its execution of sentences'.

However, there was no common statutory definition among those states that had already passed laws abolishing capital punishment for the mentally retarded. Although some had identified an IQ threshold, others did not. Some stipulated that the defendant's state of mental retardation must have been diagnosed by age 18, others by age 22, and yet others had no age limit. Thus, in July 2001, when Missouri banned execution of anyone convicted in future who is mentally retarded, the condition was defined as involving 'substantial limitations in general functioning characterized by significant sub-average intellectual functioning with . . . deficits and limitations in two or more adaptive behaviours such as communication, self-care, home living, or social skills . . . which conditions are manifested and documented before eighteen years of age'; no IQ level was specified.[65] Thus, prior to *Atkins* the state statutes contained varying weight of evidence and procedural standards,[66] although following *Atkins* there was a flurry of state legislative activity to amend death penalty statutes to prohibit the execution of mentally retarded offenders and to define who is and is not in that category.[67] Six American states stipulate that there is a rebuttable presumption that

---

[64] The AAMR defined mental retardation as 'substantial limitations in present functioning. It is characterized by significantly sub-average intellectual functioning, existing concurrently with related limitations in two or more of the following applicable adaptive skill areas: communication, self-care, home living, social skills, community use, self direction, health and safety, functional academics, leisure and work. Mental retardation manifests before 18'. The American Psychiatric Association's definition uses almost the same wording. It too stresses that the onset 'must occur' before age 18 years. Neither definition states an IQ level. In 2006 the American Bar Association (ABA) declared that 'Defendants should not be executed or sentenced to death if, at the time of the offense, they had significant limitations in both their intellectual functioning and adaptive behavior, as expressed in conceptual, social, and practical adaptive skills, resulting from mental retardation, dementia, or a traumatic brain injury': American Bar Association, Section of individual rights and responsibilities, Criminal Justice section, *Commission on mental and physical disability law*, ABA Death penalty moratorium implementation project, ABA death penalty representation project, Beverly Hills Bar Association, para. 1, p. 1.

[65] See Missouri Legislation, Bill SB 267 (2001).

[66] Victor L. Streib, n. 42 above, p. 315. For a valuable discussion of the problems involved in assessing mental retardation, especially in borderline cases, see Richard J Bonnie and Katherine Gustafson, 'The Challenge of Implementing *Atkins v Virginia*: How Legislators and Courts can Promote Accurate Assessments and Adjudication of Mental Retardation in Death Penalty Cases' *University of Richmond Law Review* 42 (2007), pp. 811–860.

[67] As was predicted by Streib, n. 42 above, p. 317.

the person is mentally retarded when the tested IQ level is 70 or below,[68] but the Federal Criminal Code has no definition of mental retardation. It thus remains to be seen whether the Supreme Court ruling will be the end of the matter. While there is strong opposition to capital punishment in general, there are likely to be continuing disputes about who is and who is not 'sufficiently' mentally retarded to benefit from the constitutional ruling that to execute the mentally retarded is 'cruel and unusual punishment' prohibited by the Eighth Amendment.[69] It is likely, therefore, that the focus will shift among abolitionists to broaden the definition of those who may benefit from this ruling.[70]

In February 2005 the California Supreme Court refused to define mental retardation simply by an IQ level of 70. Inmates can have a hearing 'as long as a qualified expert says they are retarded'. A judge would then decide whether it was more likely than not that the AMR standards have been met. And in Georgia, unlike any other state, the defendant is required to prove his or her mental retardation 'beyond reasonable doubt'. The ABA's Death Penalty Assessment Panel for Georgia points out that 'the effect of this rule is exacerbated by the failure of the Georgia Suggested Pattern Jury Instructions to explain that mental retardation is a mitigating circumstance that may be considered by the jury during the sentencing phase of a capital trial'.[71] Furthermore, Alabama has not passed a statute to protect people with mental retardation from execution. As a result, and despite repeated judicial requests for legislative guidance, the Alabama courts have been forced to fashion a stop-gap process for dealing with claims of mental retardation. The legislature's abdication of its responsibility has resulted in a legitimate and continuing risk that the State of Alabama may execute mentally retarded offenders, despite the constitutional prohibition against it.[72]

Shortly after the *Atkins* decision was handed down, a Texas jury found John Paul Penry, at his third trial, not to be mentally retarded and sentenced him once again to death, despite the fact that he had never tested above an IQ level of 70. But in October 2005 the Texas Court of Criminal Appeals overturned this decision and ordered a new trial, stating that jurors during his retrial may not have properly considered his claims of mental impairment beyond mental retardation as mitigating evidence.[73] It is even more ironic that in August 2005 a Virginia

[68] Kentucky, Maryland, and Nebraska stipulate that an IQ of 70 or below is presumptive evidence of mental retardation; Tennessee and Washington set a 'required' level of IQ at 70 or below; South Dakota's statute states that an IQ level exceeding 70 is presumptive evidence that the defendant does *not* have significant sub-average general intellectual functioning. Arkansas has set an IQ of 65 or below as the standard for a rebuttable presumption of mental retardation.

[69] Michael L. Perlin, 'Life as in Mirrors, Death Disappears: Giving Life to Atkins' *New Mexico Law Review* 33 (2003), pp. 315–348.

[70] For example, to individuals like Dalton Prejean, who was executed in 1990 and was widely regarded as mentally retarded although he had a measured IQ of 76, seen as equivalent to the mental functioning of a 13½-year-old.

[71] ABA, *The Georgia Death Penalty Assessment Report*, January 2006, p. iv.

[72] ABA, *The Alabama Death Penalty Assessment Report*, June 2006, p. iv.

[73] *Houston Chronicle*, 5 October 2005, cited on the Death Penalty Information Centre website.

Circuit Court jury found that Daryl Atkins had not proved mental retardation by a preponderance of the evidence and was therefore eligible for execution. In their most recent appeal to the Virginia Supreme Court, Atkins' attorneys argued that the jury should not have been told that Atkins had been convicted of capital murder and sentenced to death. The lawyers stated that this information distracted the jury from fairly carrying out its duty to decide whether Atkins was mentally retarded. The Virginia Supreme Court agreed, stating in its opinion, 'The fact that the jury knew that a prior jury had sentenced Atkins to death prejudiced his right to a fair trial on the issue of his mental retardation'. In June 2006 the Court therefore ordered a new mental retardation hearing.[74]

5. Protection of the Insane and Severely Mentally Ill

(a) The mentally ill at the time of conviction

It was established by both the Ancel (1962) and Morris Reports (1967) to the United Nations that in all retentionist countries there are provisions that, in one way or another, exclude the insane from liability to the death penalty. But Marc Ancel's caveat is as pertinent today as it was when he raised it 45 years ago: 'it would have been interesting to discover to what extent insanity or mental disturbance *in reality* barred death sentences' (our emphasis). There are still many examples where mentally ill defendants continue to be sentenced to death. Thus, the UN Special Rapporteur sent urgent appeals to Cuba in 2001 and to Singapore in 2003 urging these countries not to execute prisoners who, it was claimed, had been sentenced to death despite being mentally ill.[75] According to the Background Paper prepared by OSCE: 'On 21 April 2005, Bill Benefiel was executed in Indiana. He had been diagnosed with schizotypal personality disorder and had undergone a number of evaluations prior to his arrest for murder'.[76] A good example of how perceptions and assessments of insanity can vary depending on the decision-maker is the recent case of Andrea Yates in the United States. In 2001 she was convicted of murdering her five children by drowning them all and sentenced to life imprisonment with the possibility of parole after 40 years. But in July 2006, after a retrial, a Texas jury found her not guilty by reason of insanity and committed her to a secure state hospital for treatment.

---

[74] *Associated Press*, 8 June 2006. According to the Death Penalty Information Centre, James Lee Clark was executed in Texas in April 2007, despite reports that he had an IQ of 68.

[75] E/CN.4/2001/9/Add. 1, para. 157 and E/CN.4/2003/4/Add. 1 and Corr. 1, para. 450.

[76] OSCE, *The Death Penalty in the OSCE Area, Background Paper 2005*, quoting <http://www.internationaljustice.com>. The ABA, *Indiana Death Penalty Assessment Report* found (at p. 4) 'a significant number of people with severe mental disabilities on death row, some of whom were disabled at the time of the offence and others of whom became seriously [mentally] ill after conviction and sentence'.

In the United States a number of the retentionist states and the US federal government modified various features of the insanity defence in the wake of John Hinckley's acquittal in 1987, on grounds of insanity, of attempting to assassinate President Reagan. Notwithstanding these changes, all but three states and the federal government have retained the insanity defence as a ground of acquittal. Twelve states have also supplemented the insanity defence with an optional verdict of 'Guilty but Mentally Ill', which appears to preclude a death sentence. However, the US Supreme Court, in *Clark v Arizona* in 2006, held that unless 'the mental disease or defect [was] of such severity that he [or she] did not know that the criminal act was wrong' a severe mental illness was insufficient to negate the presumption of sanity and *mens rea*.[77]

While the impact of the various changes in the insanity defence on the proportion of defendants in capital cases who are sentenced to death is hard to gauge,[78] there is no doubt that psychiatric evidence is of growing importance *after* a finding of guilt to a capital charge. This is because diminished mental responsibility is specifically listed as a mitigating factor in the capital sentencing statutes of most American states, and psychiatric evidence of this nature must be admitted and considered by the sentencing jury (or judge in three states) under various constitutional rulings of the US Supreme Court, whether or not the factor is specified by statute. Typical formulations of the mitigating criteria refer to impairment of the defendant's capacity 'to appreciate the criminality of his conduct or to conform his conduct to the requirements of the law' or to the influence of 'extreme mental or emotional disturbance'. Nevertheless, in *Commonwealth v Moser* (1988) the Pennsylvania Supreme Court upheld the death penalty for a man found by the sentencing panel to have been under the influence of extreme mental or emotional disturbance at the time of the offence and to have no prior criminal record. And in *Commonwealth v Logan* (1988) it upheld the death penalty for a mentally ill man who instructed his attorney to present no mitigating evidence at the sentencing stage. Also, in *Commonwealth v Fahy* (1986) the court upheld a death sentence for the torture killing of a 12-year-old girl despite the fact that the jury found that the defendant 'was under the influence of extreme mental or emotional disturbance' and that 'the defendant's capacity to appreciate the criminality of his conduct or conform his conduct to the requirements of law was substantially impaired'.[79] It was hardly surprising, therefore, that a medical investigation in the 1980s of 15 death row inmates in the United States whose

---

[77] *Clark v Arizona*, No. 05–5966. 2006, 548 U.S. ___, 2006.

[78] R. D. Mackay, 'Post-*Hinckley* Insanity in the USA' *Criminal Law Review* (1988), pp. 88–96.

[79] Bruce Ledewitz, 'Sources of Injustice in Death Penalty Practice: The Pennsylvania Experience *Dickinson Law Review* 95 (1991), pp. 651–690 at 657–661, who also cites other cases. However, in Louisiana in 1990 a diagnosis of multiple personality disorder was 'recognized as a potentially mitigating factor in . . . granting of a new sentencing procedure for a man sentenced to death . . . and the subsequent commutation of his sentence': *Wilson v Smith*, quoted in Dorothy Otnow Lewis and Jennifer S. Bard, 'Multiple Personality and Forensic Issues' *Psychiatric Clinics of North America* 41 (3) (1991), pp. 741–756 at 747.

executions were imminent found that 'all had histories of severe head injuries, five had major neurological impairment and seven had other less serious neurological problems (eg. blackouts, soft signs) ... Six subjects had schizophreniform psychoses antedating incarceration and two others were manic depressive'.[80]

In practice it is very hard to draw a 'bright line' between mental illness that amounts to insanity and is therefore a defence to the crime, mental illness which diminishes responsibility for the crime to the extent that it can be regarded as grounds for mitigating the punishment, and mental illness that is not sufficient to save a person from the death penalty. Where the line is drawn can be dependent not only on the mental state of the person concerned at the time he or she is examined by a psychiatrist, but also on the sympathy of the jury, the heinousness of the crime, and the competence, authority, and persuasiveness of the psychiatrists before the court. It is made even more difficult to assess when psychiatrists appear for both the prosecution and the defence, each with a different interpretation of the defendant's mental state. Where a psychiatrist is asked to assess not only those features of the defendant's mental state that might mitigate the penalty but also those that might indicate his potential as 'a continuing serious threat to society' (see Chapter 8, pages 288–290), the testimony can obviously have quite opposite effects on the decision whether or not to impose the death penalty. Thus, psychiatric testimony has become a two-edged sword, such that 'efforts to show diminished capacity' may be 'self-defeating'.[81] It is for this reason that some writers have attempted to define the types of severe mental illness that should, categorically, not be eligible for the death penalty. For example, Professors Blume and Johnson state:[82]

It seems to us that all mental illness, or at least all major mental illness, such as schizophrenia, bipolar disorder, or even substance abuse disorders, diminish culpability in a significant way ... with respect to *statutory* reform, major mental illness is the standard we think legislatures ought to adopt for categorical exemption.

The judgment of the US Supreme Court in the *Atkins* case, which accepted that the mentally retarded should, *as a category*, be protected from capital punishment, plus the decision in *Simmons* that all juveniles should also be protected,

---

[80] Dr Dorothy O. Lewis *et al.*, 'Psychiatric, Neurological, and Psycho-educational Characteristics of 15 Death Row Inmates in the United States' *American Journal of Psychiatry* 143 (1986), pp. 838–845. Also, Marilyn Feldman, Kathleen Mallouh, and Dorothy O. Lewis, 'Filicidal Abuse in the Histories of 15 Condemned Murderers' *Bulletin of the American Academy of Psychiatry and Law* 14 (1986), pp. 345–352. Eight had been victims of potential filicidal assaults and there was evidence of extraordinary abuse in 12 cases.

[81] George E. Dix, 'Psychological Abnormality and Capital Sentencing: The New "Diminished Responsibility"' *International Journal of Law and Psychiatry* 7 (1984), pp. 249–267 at 265. Also, C. Robert Showalter and Richard J. Bonnie, 'Psychiatrists and Capital Sentencing: Risks and Responsibilities in a Unique Legal Setting', *Bulletin of the American Academy of Psychiatry and Law* 12 (1984), pp. 153–167.

[82] John H. Blume and Sheryl Lynn Johnson, 'Killing the non-willing: *Atkins*, the volitionally incapacitated, and the death penalty' *South Carolina Law Review* 55 (2003), pp. 93–143 at 143.

has therefore exposed an inconsistency in so far as the severely mentally ill are concerned. In July 2003, for example, Judge Robert Henry on the US Court of Appeals for the 10th Circuit noted the *Atkins* ruling and concluded that the imposition of the death penalty against Robert Bryan, a mentally ill Oklahoma death row inmate, 'contributes nothing' to the goals of retribution and deterrence. Although Judge Henry was joined by three other judges on the court, the majority prevailed and Robert Bryan was executed in June 2004.[83]

The problem facing those who believe that the severely mentally ill should be *categorically* excluded from being sentenced to death is that, unlike the situation when *Atkins* was decided, no state with the death penalty has changed its law so as to prohibit sentencing to death and executing the mentally ill but not insane, making it much more difficult to establish an 'evolving standards of decency' claim. However, a May 2002 Gallup poll found 72 per cent of Americans supported capital punishment in general, but that support dropped to 26 per cent for juveniles convicted of murder, 19 per cent for the mentally ill, and 13 per cent for the mentally retarded.[84]

In November 2004 two federal judges upheld the death sentence of Indiana death row inmate Arthur Baird, noting that whilst the US Supreme Court had prohibited the execution of offenders with mental retardation in *Atkins*, 'it has not yet ruled out the execution of persons who kill under an irresistible impulse' brought about by mental illness. The judges acknowledged that 'as an original matter, we might think it inappropriate to sentence to death a man as seemingly insane as Baird at the time of the murders. But it is not our judgment to make'. Arthur Baird's death sentence was commuted by Governor Mitch Daniels on 29 August 2005, just two days before Baird was due to be executed. While he based his decision on other factors involved in the case, Governor Daniels' commutation order referred to court findings that Baird was suffering from mental illness at the time of the crime and noted: 'it is difficult to find reasons not to agree' with the findings of an Indiana Supreme Court judge that Baird is 'insane in the ordinary sense of the word'.

In 2003 the American Bar Association Section on Individual Rights and Responsibilities set up a task force 'to consider mental disability and the death penalty'. It was inspired by the rationale in *Atkins v Virginia*, that the death penalty for the mentally retarded could neither serve as a useful deterrent nor be regarded as 'deserved' retribution, and that it was much more difficult to ensure a fair trial and accurate determination of the evidence where there was the possibility of coercion, false confessions, and the prejudicial responses of jurors to the demeanour and seeming callousness of the mentally incompetent. Would not the

[83] Christopher Slobogin, 'What *Atkins* could mean for people with mental illness' *New Mexico Law Review* 33 (2003), pp. 293–314.

[84] Tom W. Smith, Director of the General Social Survey, National Opinion Research Center, *Chicago Tribune*, 7 December 2003, cited on the Death Penalty Information Center website at: <http://www.deathpenaltyinfo.org/article.php?did=2163>.

same logic apply to the severely mentally ill? The Task Force was not being asked to extend the insanity defence, only to consider whether severe mental illness ought to be regarded as a *'per se* mitigating factor in capital cases'.[85]

Although the American Bar Association does not take an official position on the rights and wrongs of the death penalty, it passed a Resolution (122A) in 2006 which was supported by both the American Psychiatric Association and the American Psychological Association which 'urged each jurisdiction that imposes capital punishment to implement policies and procedures that would exclude persons for whom the death penalty would be disproportionate to their culpability'.[86]

Paragraph 2 of the Resolution states:[87]

Defendants should not be executed or sentenced to death if, at the time of the offense, they had a *severe* mental disorder or disability that significantly impaired their capacity (a) to appreciate the nature, consequences or wrongfulness of their conduct, (b) to exercise rational judgment in relation to conduct, or (c) to conform their conduct to the requirements of the law. A disorder manifested primarily by repeated criminal conduct or attributable solely to the acute effects of voluntary use of alcohol or other drugs does not, standing alone, constitute a mental disorder or disability for purposes of this provision.

But the recognition of mental illness of sufficient severity to justify a lesser penalty than death depends, of course, on the availability of experienced and independent psychiatric testimony. There are many parts of the world where this is unavailable. Thus, it has been accepted by the Judicial Committee of the Privy Council in London that the shortage of qualified forensic psychiatrists in certain Commonwealth Caribbean countries has meant that the mental health of defendants in murder cases is not routinely assessed, either on behalf of the state or by independent psychiatrists for the defence.[88] This must also be the case in other regions where there are few such experts, especially when combined with a shortage of financial resources available to the defence to obtain an independent mental assessment. According to research carried out in China by a team from the Law Institute of the Chinese Academy of Social Sciences and by Professor Hans-Jörg Albrecht of the Max Planck Institute for Foreign and International Criminal Law, lawyers applied for an evaluation of mental disorder in only two of 100 cases where a death sentence had been imposed at an Intermediate People's Court in a

---

[85] Ronald J. Tabak, 'Overview of Task Force Proposals on Mental Disability and the Death Penalty' *Catholic University Law Review* 54 (2004–2005), pp. 1123–1131 at 1125; Ronald S. Honberg, National Director for Policy and Legal Affairs at the National Alliance for the Mentally Ill (NAMI), 'The Injustice of Imposing Death Sentences on People with Severe Mental Illness' *Catholic University Law Review* 54 (2004–2005), pp. 1153–1167 at 1153.

[86] American Bar Association, Section on individual rights and responsibilities, Criminal Justice section, *Commission on mental and physical disability law*, ABA Death penalty moratorium implementation project, ABA death penalty representation project, Beverly Hills Bar Association, p. 5.

[87] *Ibid.*, para. 2, p. 1.

[88] See, for example, *Ramjattan v Trinidad and Tobago*, *The Times*, 1 April 1999, and *Campbell v Trinidad and Tobago*, 21 July 1999, unreported.

rural area of China. And in only one of 60 death-eligible cases appearing before an Intermediate Court in South-West China 'did a psychiatric expert evaluate the mental state of a defendant'. [89]

(b) Mental illness after conviction—competence to be executed

There is no reliable information on the extent to which retentionist countries take account of the mental state of a person sentenced to death *after* conviction when deciding whether or not to proceed with the execution. Subsequent mental illness is no bar to eventual execution in many countries, although it appears that it is often the practice to delay the execution until the person has sufficiently recovered. For example, in Japan, Morocco, and Trinidad and Tobago death-sentenced prisoners who have become insane can only be executed if they recover from their insanity. Yet, in practice, this must depend on whether the authorities deem the prisoner to be sufficiently recovered. Thus, in *Sahadath v Trinidad and Tobago*, the Human Rights Committee found that a warrant for execution had been issued to a prisoner who was known to be mentally ill, in violation of Article 7 of the International Covenant on Civil and Political Rights.[90] According to a leading Japanese lawyer, at least one prisoner has been executed despite suffering from schizophrenia.[91] This claim was backed up by Amnesty International, which reported that in 2005 it had received further evidence that persons suffering from mental illness have been sentenced to death and executed in that country.[92] On her visit to Jamaica in 2002, the Special Rapporteur on Extrajudicial, Summary or Arbitrary Executions was told by a number of inmates that some persons were convicted despite being mentally ill and she saw two persons on death row who appeared to be mentally ill.[93]

A survey, conducted in 1985, of the then 36 American states that authorized the death penalty revealed that each of them had a statutory, common law, case law, or executive clemency provision to ensure that the incompetent should not be executed. Yet in 2006 Amnesty International was able to draw up a list of 100 persons who had been executed since 1977 who had a history of serious mental illness either at the time of the offence for which they were convicted *or* at the time of their execution, and provided vivid illustrations.[94]

---

[89] Hans-Jörg Albrecht and Research Unit Of The Death Penalty Cases Survey Institute Of Law, *Strengthening the Defence in Death Penalty Cases in the People's Republic of China: Empirical Research into the Role of Defence Councils in Criminal Cases Eligible for the Death Penalty* (2006), pp. 112–114.

[90] Human Rights Committee Case No. 684/1996, *Sahadath v Trinidad and Tobago*: issuance of a warrant of execution to a mentally ill person was in violation of Article 7 of the ICCPR, views adopted 2 April 2002, A57/40 (Vol. II), p. 61.

[91] Referring to Testsuo Kawanaka, executed in 1993. Yoshihiro Yasuda, 'The Death Penalty in Japan' in *Death Penalty. Beyond Abolition* (2004), pp. 215–231.

[92] Amnesty International, *Report 2005*, p. 146.

[93] UN Doc. E/CN.4/2004/7/Add. 2, para. 58.

[94] Amnesty International, *United States of America. The Execution of Mentally Ill Offenders, Summary Report*, AI Index: AMR 51/002/2006, p. 5.

The case of Rickey Ray Rector, executed by the state of Arkansas in 1992, is often cited as an example,[95] but there have been several others. Jeremy Vargas Sagastegui was executed in Washington State in 1998 having waived his right to appeal and having represented himself at trial. Three months before he committed the crime he was diagnosed as suffering from schizophrenia and manic depression.[96] In November 2001 New Mexico resumed executions after more than four decades by putting to death an allegedly brain-damaged man who had given up his appeals after spending fourteen years on death row. Four urgent appeals were sent by the UN Special Rapporteur to states of the United States of America in 2003 concerning prisoners facing execution despite being mentally ill.[97] In May 2004 Kelsey Patterson was executed in Texas for double murder, despite having suffered from paranoid schizophrenia since 1981 and having been recommended for commutation of sentence by the Texas Board of Pardons. And, in 2005:[98]

Troy Kunkle was executed in Texas, despite suffering from serious mental illness, including schizophrenia, evidence of which was not presented to the jury that sentenced him to death. He was just over 18 at the time of the crime and had suffered a childhood of deprivation and abuse.

Amnesty International and the Death Penalty Information Center have highlighted a number of other cases where clearly mentally ill defendants have been allowed to represent themselves (e.g. Guy Le Grande in North Carolina and Scott Panetti in Texas, who is said by his attorney to have been 'in the full flower of schizophrenia'). In April 2007 the US Supreme Court, when hearing Panetti's appeal, was asked to answer the question:[99]

Does the Eighth Amendment permit the execution of a death row inmate who has a factual awareness of the reason for his execution but who, because of a severe mental illness,

[95] 'Rickey Ray Rector was a brain-damaged African-American who had been sentenced to death by an all-white jury. Rector had destroyed part of his brain when he turned his gun on himself after killing the police officer...Logs at the prison show that in the days leading to his execution, Rector was howling and barking like a dog, dancing, singing and laughing inappropriately, and saying that he was going to vote for Clinton (who was Governor of Arkansas and running for the Presidency of the USA). After the execution, guards found that Rector had put aside his pie thinking that he was coming back to eat it after the execution.' Quoted from Stephen B. Bright, 'The Politics of Capital Punishment: The Sacrifice of Fairness for Executions' in Acker, Bohm, and Lanier (eds.), n. 42 above, p. 120; see also Marshall Frady, 'Death in Arkansas', *The New Yorker*, 22 February 1993, pp. 105–125.
[96] Amnesty International, *United States of America: Failing the Future: Death Penalty Developments, March 1998–March 2000*, AI Index: AMR 51/03/00, p. 18.
[97] UN Doc. E/CN.4/2004/7, para. 55.
[98] Amnesty International, *Report 2005*, p. 275.
[99] *Panetti v Quarterman*, No. 06–6407. The US Court of Appeals for the 5th Circuit had previously ruled that Scott Panetti, who was allowed to defend himself in his Texas trial despite his schizophrenia and 14 stints in mental hospitals, and who says the devil compelled his actions, was aware that he committed a crime and that he was to be punished. The question for the Supreme Court is whether mere awareness of one's acts can be equated with mental competence, or whether the person also needs to rationally understand what is taking place. The National Alliance on Mental Illness had urged the Justices to take the case (Death Penalty Information Center).

has a delusional belief as to why the State is executing him, and thus does not appreciate that his execution is intended to seek retribution for his capital crime?

The US Supreme Court ruled, on 28 June 2007, that Panetti deserved a rehearing on his claim of mental incompetence, overturning the decision by the US Court of Appeals for the Fifth Circuit that had used an overly restrictive definition of what constitutes insanity.[100]

It is obvious that if persons are detained for long periods on death row awaiting execution, as they are in many countries (see Chapter 5 pages 173–174 above), their mental states may seriously deteriorate. Although no precise figures are available, it has been estimated that as many as five to ten per cent of persons on death rows at any one time in America are suffering from a serious mental illness.[101] According to the ABA *Death Penalty Assessment Report for Florida*, published in 2006, 'The State... has a significant number of people with severe mental disabilities on death row, some of whom were disabled at the time of the offense and others of whom became seriously ill after conviction and sentence'.[102]

In 1986 the US Supreme Court in the case of *Ford v Wainwright* ruled, as a matter of constitutional law, that a state may not execute an incompetent person, and that judicial procedures must be used to adjudicate the question. But what did incompetence mean? As Amnesty International has pointed out, Justice Powell 'suggested that the test should be whether the prisoner is aware of his or her impending execution and the reason for it'. Such a strict cognitive interpretation would save, at least for the time-being, only the truly insane, not those who were severely mentally ill. For, as Justice Powell put it, 'the only question raised' by Alvin Ford's claim was 'not whether, but when, his execution may take place'. Because if the 'petitioner is cured of his disease, the State is free to execute him'.[103]

In *Perry v Louisiana* (1990), where the state wanted to forcibly feed Mr Perry to render him competent for execution, the Supreme Court held that the rule laid down in *Washington v Harper* (1990) should be applied, which stated that although an inmate could refuse psychotropic drugs, this was not an absolute right. This meant that forced medication would be permitted under the Due Process Clause when the state could show that the inmate was likely to be dangerous in the future and that the medication is in the prisoner's medical

---

[100] Death Penalty Information Center website at: <http://www.deathpenaltyinfo.org/article.php?did=2412>. Not everyone, however, is optimistic that this represents a watershed in death penalty jurisprudence on this matter. For example, Michael Mello has argued that the USA is highly likely to go on executing the mentally ill after *Panetti*: M. Mello, 'Executing the Mentally Ill: When is Someone Sane Enough to Die?' *Criminal Justice* 22(3) (2007), pp. 30–41: <http://www.abanet.org/crimjust/cjmag/22–3/home.html>.

[101] Richard J. Bonnie, 'Mentally Ill Prisoners on Death Row: Unsolved Puzzles for Courts and Legislatures' *Catholic University Law Review* 54 (2004–2005), pp. 1169–1193 at 1192.

[102] ABA, *The Florida Death Penalty Assessment Report*, September 2006, p. ix.

[103] Amnesty International, *The United States of America: The Execution of Mentally Ill Offenders, Summary Report*, AI Index: AMR/51/002/2006, p. 3.

interest.[104] As a reflection of these serious concerns, the Texas legislature passed into law in 1999 a Bill that exempted the 'incompetent' from the death penalty, defined as 'One who does not understand that s/he is to be executed and that the execution is imminent, and the reason that s/he is being executed'. Only the insane would pass such a strict cognitive test. This is illustrated by the case of Steven Kenneth Staley, who had been on death row in Texas for 15 years. He had been diagnosed as a schizophrenic who refused medication and was therefore incompetent to be executed. In April 2006 State District Judge Wayne Salvant—following an earlier decision in 2003 by the US Court of Appeals for the Eighth Circuit, upheld by the Supreme Court of the United States, to allow Arkansas officials to forcibly medicate Charles Singleton, a mentally ill death row prisoner, so as to make him competent to be executed[105]—ordered that Staley should be forcibly medicated so as to render him competent to be executed. Singleton was executed in October 2003 and Judge Salvant's ruling on Staley was upheld by the Texas Court of Criminal Appeals in Texas in 2007. So far, only two death penalty states, Maryland and Montana, commute immediately and permanently a death sentence to life imprisonment without parole once a prisoner under sentence of death is certified to be insane.[106]

In an attempt to define the circumstances under which a mentally ill person cannot be executed, the American Bar Association resolved in 2006 that:[107]

(a) ... A sentence of death should not be carried out if the prisoner has a mental disorder or disability that significantly impairs his or her capacity (i) to make a rational decision to forgo or terminate post-conviction proceedings available to challenge the validity of the conviction or sentence; (ii) to understand or communicate pertinent information, or otherwise assist counsel, in relation to specific claims bearing on the validity of the conviction or sentence that cannot be fairly resolved without the prisoner's participation; or (iii) to understand the nature and purpose of the punishment, or to appreciate the reason for its imposition in the prisoner's own case.

---

[104] On the problem of finding an adequate terminology for the mentally incompetent, such as 'severe mental impairment', see Roberta M. Harding, ' "Endgame": Competency and the Execution of Condemned Inmates—A Proposal to Satisfy the Eighth Amendment's Prohibition against the Infliction of Cruel and Unusual Punishment' *Saint Louis University Public Law Review* 14 (1994), pp. 105–152. For discussions on 'synthetic sanity' and the competence to be executed, see G. Linn Evans, '*Perry v Louisiana* (1990): Can a State Treat an Incompetent Prisoner to Ready him for Execution?' *Bulletin of the American Academy of Psychiatry and Law* 19 (1991), pp. 249–270 at 256–258; and James R. Acker and Charles S. Lanier, 'Unfit to Live, Unfit to Die: Incompetence for Execution under Modern Death Penalty Legislation' *Criminal Law Bulletin* 33 (1997), pp. 107–150; also, Gary Fields 'Criminal Mind: On Death Row, Fate of Mentally Ill is a Thorny Problem—Can States Execute Inmates Made Sane Only by Drugs? Medical, Legal Quandary—A Test Case in Mr. Thompson' *The Wall Street Journal*, 14 December 2006.

[105] Amnesty International, *United States of America. The Execution of Mentally Ill Offenders. Summary Report*, AI Index: AMR 51/002/2006, p. 3.

[106] Eric M. Kniskern, 'Does *Ford v. Wainwright*'s Denial of Executions of the Insane Prohibit the State from Carrying out its Criminal Justice System?' *Southern University Law Review* 26 (1999), pp. 171–195, at 191–194; Md. Code Ann. Art. 27 §75A (1997); Mont. Code Ann. §46–19-201 (1997).

[107] See n. 86 above, para. 3, p. 1.

The Bar Association set out the procedures to be followed in each of these three categories of case:[108]

Procedure in Cases Involving Prisoners Seeking to Forgo or Terminate Post-Conviction Proceedings. If a court finds that a prisoner under sentence of death who wishes to forgo or terminate post-conviction proceedings has a mental disorder or disability that significantly impairs his or her capacity to make a rational decision, the court should permit a next friend acting on the prisoner's behalf *to initiate or pursue available remedies to set aside the conviction or death sentence* [our emphasis].

   Procedure in Cases Involving Prisoners Unable to Assist Counsel in Post-Conviction Proceedings. If a court finds at any time that a prisoner under sentence of death has a mental disorder or disability that significantly impairs his or her capacity to understand or communicate pertinent information, or otherwise to assist counsel, in connection with post-conviction proceedings, and that the prisoner's participation is necessary for a fair resolution of specific claims bearing on the validity of the conviction or death sentence, the court should suspend the proceedings. If the court finds that there is no significant likelihood of restoring the prisoner's capacity to participate in post-conviction proceedings in the foreseeable future, *it should reduce the prisoner's sentence to the sentence imposed in capital cases when execution is not an option* [our emphasis].

   Procedure in Cases Involving Prisoners Unable to Understand the Punishment or its Purpose. If, after challenges to the validity of the conviction and death sentence have been exhausted and execution has been scheduled, a court finds that a prisoner has a mental disorder or disability that significantly impairs his or her capacity to understand the nature and purpose of the punishment, or to appreciate the reason for its imposition in the prisoner's own case, *the sentence of death should be reduced to the sentence imposed in capital cases when execution is not an option* [our emphasis].

Richard Bonnie has identified the dilemma between protecting the prisoner and the State's right to enforce the law as one in which 'the underlying values at stake are the dignity of the condemned prisoner and the integrity of the law'.[109] Thus:[110]

The ABA Task Force's proposal would require that an offender not only must 'understand' the nature and purpose of punishment but also must 'appreciate' its personal application in his own case—that is, why it is being imposed *on him*. This formulation is analogous to the distinction often drawn between 'factual understanding' and a 'rational understanding' of the reason for the execution. If, as is generally assumed, the primary purpose of the competence-to-be-executed requirement is to vindicate the retributive aim of punishment, then offenders should have more than a shallow understanding of why they are being executed.

The assessment of 'mental competence to be executed' and the treatment of persons under sentence of death has placed psychiatrists in an acute ethical dilemma

---

[108] *Ibid.*, pp. 1–2.
[109] Richard J. Bonnie, 'Mentally Ill Prisoners on Death Row: Unsolved Puzzles for Courts and Legislatures' *Catholic University Law Review* 54 (2004–2005), pp. 1169–1193.
[110] *Ibid.*, at p. 1173.

and aroused considerable controversy. Should a psychiatrist use professional skills to treat a mentally ill person who, upon recovery, may be executed? If not, is the person to be allowed to suffer the pains of acute mental illness? And on what scientific evidence are judgments of competency to be executed based? Are they not inevitably likely to be influenced by the psychiatrist's own views on the morality and efficacy of the death penalty? Indeed there is evidence in the United States that psychiatrists who are willing to make competency assessments are also more likely to favour the death penalty than those who refuse to make such judgments.[111] Nor is it clear in the United States that an indigent defendant has any remedy in due process if his psychiatrist turns out to be incompetent: i.e. there is no right to competent psychiatric assistance.[112] A particular problem arises in relation to those who 'volunteer' to be executed. Are they acting rationally to escape the trauma of death row? Are they simply accepting their fate as one they deserve? Or are they seeking a form of state-assisted suicide? John Blume's study of 106 prisoners who had volunteered for execution revealed that 'Of the 106 volunteers, at least 93 (88%) of them had documented mental illness or severe substance-abuse disorders'. Blume proposed a standard for assessing whether there is suicide motivation but which would also protect the right of the mentally healthy inmate to forgo further appeals when motivated by acceptance of the justness of punishment.[113]

In the light of the evidence reviewed above, the UN Seventh Quinquennial Report on Capital Punishment, published in 2005, concluded that:[114]

[T]he safeguard to protect the insane and persons suffering from mental retardation or extremely limited mental competence from capital punishment will need to be reformulated to be in line with the recommendation of the Commission on Human Rights to include 'any form of mental disorder'.

---

[111] R. J. Bonnie, 'Dilemmas in Administering the Death Penalty: Conscientious Abstention, Professional Ethics, and the Needs of the Legal System' *Law and Human Behavior* 14 (1990), pp. 67–90; Stanley L. Brodsky, 'Professional Ethics and Professional Morality in the Assessment of Competence for Execution: A Response to Bonnie' *ibid.*, pp. 91–97; R. J. Bonnie, 'Grounds for Professional Abstention in Capital Cases: A Reply to Brodsky' *Law and Human Behavior* 14, pp. 99–102; M. A. Deitchman, W. A. Kennedy, and J. C. Beckham, 'Self-Selection Factors in the Participation of Mental Health Professionals in Competency for Execution Evaluations' *Law and Human Behavior* 15 (1990), pp. 287–303; and D. H. Wallace, 'The Need to Commute the Death Sentence: Competency for Execution and Ethical Dilemmas for Mental Health Professionals' *International Journal of Law and Psychiatry* 15 (1992), pp. 317–337. For a thorough study of the *Ford* case and its consequences, see Kent S. Miller and Michael L. Radelet, *Executing the Mentally Ill: The Criminal Justice System and the Case of Alvin Ford* (1993). See also Robert T. M. Phillips, 'Professionalism, Mental Disability, and the Death Penalty: The Psychiatrist as Evaluator: Conflicts and Conscience' *New York Law School Law Review* 41 (1996), pp. 189–199.

[112] Gordon B. Burns, 'The Right to Effective Assistance of a Psychiatrist under *Ake v. Oklahoma*' *Criminal Law Bulletin* 30 (1994), pp. 429–457.

[113] John Blume, 'Killing the Willing: Volunteers, Suicide and Competency' *Michigan Law Review* 103 (2005), pp. 939–1009 at 943 and 962.

[114] UN Doc. E/2005/3, para. 89.

6. Conclusion

The discussion of the factual evidence reviewed in this chapter shows that great progress has been made in excluding altogether from the threat of the death penalty those who were juveniles—defined as under the age of 18—at the time the capital crime was committed. Progress has also been made in gaining an international consensus against the death sentence being imposed on pregnant women and the 'mentally retarded', although problems of definition, and particularly of diagnosis in 'borderline' cases, remain a major concern. In all countries, the clearly insane are excused because they simply cannot be convicted, but the mentally ill pose a real problem because of failure to diagnose severe mental illness in many countries which do not have an adequate number of professional psychiatrists prepared to work in the forensic field. Furthermore, there are disputes about how mentally ill the person must be to earn mitigation of sentence and to be disqualified for execution; to what extent the mentally ill can be treated and then executed; and how much emphasis death penalty statutes should place on protecting the public from persons deemed to be 'dangerous' because of their mental illness (see Chapter 8).

7

Protecting the Accused and Ensuring Due Process

1. International Standards

International human rights conventions mandate that criminal sanctions can only be imposed against an individual who has been subject to due process of law which guarantees a presumption of innocence, a fair opportunity to answer the charges brought against him or her before a duly constituted court, and the assistance of a well-qualified defence counsel. In the context of capital punishment, because execution is irrevocable, due process protections become even more significant. For this reason the UN Economic and Social Council in 1989 called for:[1]

special protection to persons facing charges for which the death penalty is provided, by allowing time and facilities for the preparation of their defence, including the adequate assistance of counsel at every stage of the proceedings, *above and beyond* the protection afforded in non-capital cases [our emphasis].

United Nations Safeguard No. 4 for the protection of the rights of those facing the death penalty is aimed at avoiding any danger that an innocent person could be sentenced to death by providing that: 'capital punishment may be imposed only when the guilt of the person charged is based on clear and convincing evidence *leaving no room for an alternative explanation* of the facts' (our emphasis). Safeguard No. 5, which mentions the 'final judgment', makes it clear that the question of the safety of the conviction must be questioned throughout the process right up to appeal and clemency proceedings (see pages 257–264 below):[2]

capital punishment may only be carried out pursuant to final judgment rendered by a competent court after legal process which gives all possible safeguards to ensure a fair trial, at least equal to those contained in article 14 of the International Covenant on Civil and Political Rights, including the right of anyone suspected of or charged with a crime for which capital punishment may be imposed to adequate legal assistance at all stages of the proceedings.

---

[1] Economic and Social Council Resolution 1989/64 (1).
[2] The entire text of Art. 14 is reproduced in App. 3.

In 1996 the Economic and Social Council strengthened this safeguard by encouraging all member states in which the death penalty has not been abolished to ensure that each defendant facing a possible death sentence is given all guarantees to ensure a fair trial, as contained in Article 14 of the International Covenant on Civil and Political Rights (ICCPR), and bearing in mind the 'Basic Principles on the Independence of the Judiciary', the 'Basic Principles on the Role of Lawyers', the 'Guidelines on the Role of Prosecutors', the 'Body of Principles for the Protection of All Persons under Any Form of Detention or Imprisonment', and the 'Standard Minimum Rules for the Treatment of Prisoners' to ensure that defendants who do not sufficiently understand the language used in court are fully informed, by way of interpretation or translation, of all the charges against them and the content of the relevant evidence deliberated in court.[3]

Not surprisingly, when retentionist countries have been asked periodically through the United Nations Quinquennial Surveys whether they abide by the 4th and 5th Safeguards nearly all have said that they do comply, for no country would blatantly admit that it executed persons who could have been innocent. Indeed, they have all stated that there had been no instances where persons were executed without and/or outside the judicial process.

But, of course, these assurances cannot be taken at face value in all countries, for there may be a wide gap between the aspirations of procedural law and the actual practices of a criminal justice system.[4] This gap between the law in books and the law in action is probably even greater in some of the large number of retentionist countries which have never responded to the United Nations' requests for information. In other countries, such as the central Asian republics, Tajikistan and Uzbekistan, and Kyrgystan and Kazakhstan (prior to abolition), there may have been a formal adherence to the UN standards, but a critic, Botagoz Kassymbekova, has suggested that this was merely to appease the international donor community, whereas in practice the system was a legacy of 'an authoritarian social and political culture' in which citizens as well as their leaders 'value social order and stability over human life', which promotes a continuing view of due process as an impediment to eliminating their society of those who threaten its precarious order.[5] Thus, the UN Human Rights Committee (HRC) found Tajikistan to be in breach of Articles 7 and 14 of the ICCPR for

---

[3] Resolution 1996/15(3) and (4).

[4] For instance, the reply to the 7th Survey from Morocco stated that 'the principle of fair trial is established in the law of criminal procedure', which 'entitles the public prosecutor to supervise the conduct of investigations by the judicial police and control its operations, as well as to visit the places of custody of persons suspected of committing an offence'. In practice, however, as noted by a concerned HRC, suspects could be detained without counsel for as long as 96 hours before being brought before a judge, with the Crown Prosecutor General having the power to extend that time indefinitely: Official Records of the General Assembly, 55th session, Supp. No. 40 (1) I (A/55/40), para. 108.

[5] B. Kassymbekova, 'Capital Punishment in Kyrgyzstan: Between the Past, "Other" State Killings and Social Demands' in A. Sarat and C. Boulanger (eds.), *The Cultural Lives of Capital Punishment* (2005), pp. 171–194 at 191.

convicting and sentencing a defendant to death by military tribunal after a confession had been obtained through torture; he had been denied privileged access to his lawyer and had not been allowed to call witnesses on his behalf or a doctor to testify to his injuries received while under arrest and interrogation.[6] These were clear breaches of the right to a fair trial, to impartiality and independent determination, to the granting of reasonable requests needed to maintain an adequate defence, and, most importantly, to his right to life.[7] Likewise, a report to the Human Rights Council in 2006, on the theme of transparency and the imposition of the death penalty, recorded breaches of death penalty safeguards during 2005 in relation to Afghanistan, Bangladesh, Barbados, Burundi, Chad, China, Indonesia, Iraq, Japan, Lebanon, Pakistan, Philippines (prior to abolition), Saudi Arabia, Singapore, Sri Lanka, Sudan, Tanzania, Trinidad and Tobago, Uzbekistan, Yemen, and the Palestinian Authority.[8]

2. Ensuring a Fair Trial

(a) A question of evidence

Standards mandated for trial procedures apparently vary considerably. For instance, Egypt requires 'certitude and certainty stemming from conclusive evidence attributable to the act of the accused' and that 'The death penalty...must be passed by unanimous opinion, after having consulted the Mufti of the Republic [the official responsible for delivering legal opinions] on the legality of the sentence in accordance with the provisions of the Islamic *Shari'ā*'. By contrast, Chad and Madagascar apply a vaguer standard: 'any form of evidence may be brought to establish guilt', unless the law provides otherwise, and 'the judges shall decide according to their own (deep-seated) inner convictions'. In responding to the UN Fifth Survey Bahrain was the only country that did not require a presumption of innocence. Bangladesh reported that defendants can be compelled to testify in the witness box and compelled to confess guilt, with the burden of proof falling on the defendant, not the prosecution. This has been so also in India under the provisions of martial law. The Japanese '*daiyo Kangoku* system' relies heavily on confessions obtained during lengthy police detention, which can last up to

---

[6] Communication No. 1117/2002, *Khomidov v Tajikistan* (views adopted on 29 July 2004, eighty-first session) HRC A/59/40/ (II), pp. 363–368 at 367.

[7] Similar examples of injustice based on failure to follow international standards of due process in capital cases are not difficult to find. In *Arutyunyan v Uzbekistan* the HRC found breaches of Arts. 6 and 14 (Communication No. 917/2000, views adopted: 29 March 2004, HRC A/59/40 (II) 96–100 at 99). Similar observations were made by the Committee in: 811/1998 (*Mulai v Republic of Guyana*), 867/1999 (*Smartt v Republic of Guyana*), 964/2001 (*Saidov v Tajikistan*), and 1096/2002 (*Kurbanova v Tajikistan*).

[8] UNCHR, Report of the Special Rapporteur on Extrajudicial, Summary or Arbitrary Executions, *Transparency And The Imposition Of The Death Penalty*, E/CN.4/2006/53/Add. 3, 24 March 2006.

23 days before charge. The same is true in China. According to one study, in 58 of 60 death penalty eligible cases that were dealt with by an Intermediate People's Court in the South-West of China there was a confession and 'in almost all cases' in another rural area of China (94% of 54 murder convictions).[9] Furthermore, it is very rare in China for witnesses to appear in court and thus there is no prospect of cross-examination on the evidence, which is presented in writing. In effect, a system for producing confessions leaves the real 'trial' in the secret confines of the police station. In Iraq, many pre-trial confessions on television were reported in 2005 which violated the defendants' right to a fair trial based on the presumption of innocence.[10]

The prospects for a fair trial are at a minimum where the accused has been forced to confess through torture. Philip Alston, the current Special Rapporteur on Extrajudicial, Summary or Arbitrary Executions, found that torture is consistently used by the Nigerian police to extract confessions and that these confessions have often served as the evidentiary basis for the conviction of persons charged with capital offences.[11] Similarly, after a visit to Nigeria in March 2007, Manfred Nowak, the UN's Special Rapporteur on Torture, confirmed that the Nigerian police break the law with impunity and extract confessions and information by force. He determined that abuse of suspects was 'systemic' and 'routine', with some detainees being shot at, beaten, and even suspended from the ceilings for prolonged periods in order to extract confessions.[12] Similarly, following his visit to Uzbekistan in November and December 2002, the UN Special Rapporteur on Torture, Theo van Boven, concluded that torture or similar ill-treatment was systemic in Uzbekistan and 'appear[s] to be used indiscriminately against persons charged for activities qualified as serious crimes such as acts against State interests, as well as petty criminals and others', with many confessions being 'obtained through torture and other illegal means' and used in capital cases.[13] He also notified the government of Afghanistan that Abdullah Shah, who had been executed, had been forced to sign a confession, had been tortured, and that his trial fell below international fair trial standards in other respects. Not surprisingly, the

---

[9] H. J. Albrecht and Research Unit of the Death Penalty Cases Survey Institute of Law, *Strengthening the Defence in Death Penalty Cases in the People's Republic of China. Empirical Research into the Role of Defence Councils in Criminal Cases Eligible for the Death Penalty.* Research in Brief, No. 37 (2006), pp. 113–114.

[10] Amnesty International, *Unjust and Unfair: The Death Penalty in Iraq*, AI Index: MDE 14/014/2007, pp. 19–27.

[11] UN Doc. E/CN.4/2006/53Add. 4, January 2006, para. 28.

[12] Toye Olori, 'Rights—Nigeria: Grim, Overflowing Death Rows', Inter Press Service, 19 March 2007.

[13] UN Doc. E/CN.4/2003/68/Add. 2; also, International Federation for Human Rights (FIDH), *The Death Penalty in Uzbekistan: Torture and Secrecy*, Report 426/2 October 2005. See also Human Rights Watch, '"Empty Promises:" Diplomatic Assurances no Safeguard against Torture', 16 No. 4 (D), April 2004; Human Rights Watch, Uzbekistan ' "And It Was Hell All Over Again..."': Torture In Uzbekistan', 12 (12) (D) December 2000.

government refuted these allegations.[14] Torture and mistreatment in places of detention in Jordan is also well-documented.[15] Following a mission to Jordan in 2006, the UN Special Rapporteur on Torture, Manfred Nowak, concluded that 'there is general impunity for torture and ill-treatment in Jordan' and that 'torture is systematically practiced at both the [General Intelligence Department] and the [Criminal Investigation Department]'. He also noted that 'no functioning complaints mechanism exists to report and seek effective redress for acts of torture'.[16] According to Amnesty International, in trials in Saudi Arabia, which 'often take place behind closed doors', prisoners may have been convicted 'solely on the basis of confessions obtained under duress, torture or deception'.[17]

(b) Allowing sufficient time to prepare a defence

Several countries have enacted, sometimes by decree or under military law, legislation aimed at speeding up the trial process and expediting all processes of post-trial review. Thus, in China, when 'strike hard campaigns' have been in progress, such as the one in 2001 (see Chapter 4, page 147), police, prosecutors, and lawyers were urged to speed up the process of criminal trials even more, with the result that there was bound to be a greater risk of wrongful convictions.

Pakistan (in 1987) introduced 'speedy trial' courts and allowed only a short period for appeal to be lodged (seven days). The Special Rapporteur on Extrajudicial, Summary or Arbitrary Executions expressed concern that, under the Curbing of Terrorist Activities Act 1992 in Bangladesh, investigations of such offences had to be completed within 30 (exceptionally 45) days and that the trial, held before a special tribunal, was to be completed within 60 (exceptionally 90)

---

[14] UN Doc. E/CN.4/2005/62/Add. 1, paras. 7–8.

[15] Amnesty International, *Jordan: Death penalty/torture and ill-treatment, Sajida Rishawi Atrous (f)* AI Index: MDE 16/001/2007, 31 January 2007.

[16] UN Doc. E/CN.4/2006/6/Add. 1. Also, FIDH, *Abolition of the Death Penalty for Some Crimes Symbolic at Best* 16 August 2006. In 2004, van Boven sent a joint urgent appeal, with the Special Rapporteurs on Extrajudicial, Summary or Arbitrary Executions, the Independence of Judges and Lawyers, and Violence Against Women, regarding the situation of Alakor Lual Deng, from the Dinka ethnic group in Sudan, at risk of being executed by stoning following a conviction for adultery by the Criminal Court in Nahud in Western Kordofan State, Sudan, in July 2003. She was not represented by a lawyer at her trial nor was she provided with a Dinka interpreter, even though the trial was conducted in Arabic. Van Boven also received allegations concerning Abubaker Adam Osman, a 17-year-old Masalit from Hey Karari in Nyala, Sudan, who was arrested in May 2004 by the military, who detained him for four days. He alleges that they beat him, whipped him, and kicked him with their army boots while under their custody. He was then transferred to police custody and charged with murder, which carries the death penalty. No investigation is known to have been opened into his allegations of torture and, almost a year after his detention, he had still not yet been brought before a court: Amnesty International: *Sudan No one to complain to: No respite for the victims, impunity for the perpetrators*, AI Index: AFR 54/138/2004; E/CN.4/2005/62/Add. 1, para. 1668.

[17] Amnesty International, *Saudi Arabia, Defying World Trends*, AI Index: MDE 23/015/2001.

days. Of course, such time limits are likely to make it difficult to prepare an adequate defence.[18]

(c) Adequate legal representation

As mentioned at the start of this chapter, the fifth safeguard requires adequate legal assistance at *all stages* of capital proceedings (our emphasis). To what degree is such representation permitted, and if allowed, provided to indigent capital defendants who cannot afford it? In response to the Sixth UN Survey in 1999, Bahrain, Barbados, Comoros, Kazakhstan, Thailand, and Turkey stated that provision of counsel was more extensive than that which was afforded in non-capital cases. The reply to the Seventh Survey from Egypt indicated that although an indigent defendant could not choose his or her own lawyer:

> offences punishable by the death penalty are designated as serious crimes under article 10 of the Penal Code and consequently must be investigated by the Department of Public Prosecutions, an intrinsic part of the judiciary whose members enjoy legal immunity... If the accused has no counsel to defend him during investigations, the Department of Public Prosecutions appoints such counsel in the decision for committal for trial... If the accused fails to engage counsel for the trial the court is obliged by law to appoint a lawyer to undertake his defence at the expense of the State.

Thailand also reported to the Seventh Survey that 'the offender is able to defend his/her offence at every stage from investigation to court level'.

However, there is plenty of evidence that adequate legal representation is not provided in many countries that retain the death penalty. Trials have taken place where the defendant has had either no legal representation at all, whether at the investigative or trial stage of the proceedings; where the legal representation has been shown to be inadequate, whether because of the poor quality or motivation of lawyers or procedural barriers to them being able adequately to represent the defendant; or where they appear in the proceedings too late to make it possible to mount an adequate legal defence. The UN Special Rapporteur has expressed concern at the lack of counsel in a trial held behind closed doors in Libya;[19] lack of legal representation before special courts in the Darfur region of Sudan;[20] at lengthy pre-trial detention without legal assistance in Vietnam;[21] and lengthy detention incommunicado, including denial of legal representation in Yemen.[22] In Iran, in special jurisdictions like the Revolutionary Courts, Religious Courts,

---

[18] The Human Rights Committee (HRC) found Guyana in breach of its obligations under Art. 14(3) (b) and (d) of the ICCPR in the case of Lawrence Chan, in which the judge had allowed only two week-days for the defendant to consult with his lawyer, who was also engaged in another case: *Chan v Guyana*, views adopted 31 October 2005 CCPR/C/85/D/913/2000.

[19] UN Doc. E/CN.4/2003/3/Add.1, para. 338.

[20] *Ibid.*, paras. 474 and 475.

[21] UN Doc. E/CN.4/2002/74/Add. 2, para. 630.

[22] UN Doc. E/CN.4/2000/3/Add. 1, paras. 489 and 490.

and Military Courts, the only lawyers allowed to defend the accused are those named by these courts, which of course may include some lawyers who are less likely to challenge the authority of the court.

In response to the Seventh UN Survey, the Ministry of Justice of Japan stated that a person charged with a capital offence has the right to choose his or her own counsel at public expense, but it appears that this is true only after the person has been prosecuted. According to a report submitted by the International Federation for Human Rights on a mission to Japan, it is the defendant's responsibility to bring forth evidence in favour of their defence or to mitigate their responsibility, which is not always possible where defendants have limited means.[23] The Japan Federation of Bar Associations (JFBA) makes clear that 'The Japanese Criminal Justice System . . . doesn't adequately provide the right to counsel and the right to defence and fails to meet international human rights standards'.[24] It went on to assert 'it is obvious that there are wrongful convictions amongst capital cases'.[25] According to the official response, an amendment of Japan's Code of Criminal Procedure, which was due to enter into force on 27 November 2006, will allow a suspect who is arrested and detained but not prosecuted to have the right to choose his/her own counsel at public expense if he/she does not have the resources to pay for it.

A ruling of the Botswana High Court in 1999 had established that it was a violation of constitutional rights to deny prisoners who had been sentenced to death access to their lawyers.[26] Nevertheless, there have been reports of convicts being executed without the knowledge of their lawyers.[27] Concerns have also been raised about lack of legal representation at trials in Saudi Arabia, where 'the suspect is denied access to the outside world [including] legal assistance . . . until a confession is obtained'. And once this is obtained, the defendant is questioned by the judge or judges without a lawyer or legal representative present to defend him or her. In addition, no media or members of the public are given access to hearings. It remains to be seen whether the adoption of a new code of criminal procedure will guarantee the right to be defended by a lawyer in conformity with international standards.[28]

Under the Chinese Law of Criminal Procedure (1997), defence counsel must be appointed in cases where an indigent defendant is at risk of receiving a death

[23] FIDH, *The Death Penalty in Japan: A Practice Unworthy of a Democracy*, No. 359/2, May 2003, p. 14.

[24] Conference: 'Does Japan need the Death Penalty in the 21st Century?', Miyaziki City, Japan, 7 October 2004; report available from JFBA.

[25] Official Records of the General Assembly, 54th Session, Supp. No. 40, I (A/54/40), para. 164. As noted above, an accused citizen in Japan can be detained for up to 23 days prior to indictment, and even then only legal aid services are made available.

[26] Amnesty International, *Death Penalty Developments 1999*, AI Index: ACT 50/04/00, p. 21.

[27] Hands Off Cain, *2004 Report*, pp. 37 and 38.

[28] Lamri Chirouf, 'Defying World Trends: Saudi Arabia's Extensive Use of Capital Punishment', *1st World Congress against the Death Penalty*, Strasbourg, 21–23 June 2001.

sentence. Article 34 states that: 'If there is the possibility that the defendant may be sentenced to death and has not yet entrusted anybody to be his defender, the People's Court shall designate a lawyer that is obliged to provide legal aid to serve as a defender'. However, no lawyer is available to the defendant during the crucial stages of questioning and investigation prior to the trial while the evidence is being assembled. Furthermore, whilst the defender is allowed to 'meet and correspond with the criminal suspect in custody' (Article 36), this is vitiated by the rule which bars the lawyer from disclosing to the client the state's case against him or her, making it almost impossible for the lawyer to receive 'instructions' from the client in the way expected in Western legal systems. These procedures particularly disadvantage defendants who have little education and low socio-economic status, charged with capital offences.[29]

Further questions have been raised about China's provision of legal counsel because of constraints placed upon defence lawyers by the state.[30] As Albrecht *et al.* explain, 'access to the client is severely restricted and in particular during the investigation stage effective defence is not possible...: Lawyers may not discuss the case with their clients and conversations are monitored'.[31] In addition, capital defendants and their representatives do not have full access to case files, prosecutors do not disclose everything to the defence, and defence lawyers are at risk of prosecution and imprisonment if they present alternative evidence that is judged to be false. Fees paid under legal aid are very modest and many experienced lawyers would rather pay the fine for refusing to take a case. In practice, the work of most defence counsel begins once the case has emerged from the prosecutor and the accused has already made a confession. Defence counsel is therefore left in almost all cases with no other task than seeking mitigation of sentence. Yet even here his or her influence will be merely mediated through the trial judge, who reports to the Judicial Commission which decides the case, not all members of which will have attended the trial.[32]

In Iran, if the accused does not have his own lawyer, the state, according to the 1980 Constitution, is supposed to provide counsel. However, this is not common practice, perhaps because of the expense involved, and even when defence lawyers are appointed they cannot intervene in police or court investigations or interrogations without prior permission from the judge.

The situation in Nigeria is dire. The National Study Group on the Death Penalty summed up its investigation as follows:[33]

---

[29] Albrecht *et al.*, n. 9 above, pp. 35–38 and 100–103.
[30] Amnesty International, *People's Republic of China. Establishing the Rule of Law and Respect for Human Rights: The Need for Institutional and Legal Reforms*, AI Index: ASA 17/052/2002; and *Executed 'according to law'? The death penalty in China*, AI Index: ASA 17/003/2004.
[31] Albrecht *et al.*, n. 9 above, at p. 6.
[32] *Ibid.*, pp. 6–9.
[33] Nigeria, *Report of the National Study Group on the Death Penalty* (August 2004), p. 82.

We found that one of the most intractable problems in death penalty administration in Nigeria is the severe lack of competent and adequately compensated counsel for indigent defendants and death row inmates seeking appeals ... It is particularly noteworthy and of concern that the Legal Aid Council presently does not provide legal assistance and advise [sic] for persons facing capital offences.

Moreover, Philip Alston found that many defendants in capital trials in Nigeria have effectively had no legal representation and legal aid is not available for appeals.[34]

Brunei Darussalam and Tunisia reported to the Seventh Survey that the accused did not have the right to counsel of his or her own choosing from the moment of arrest, although legal representation was provided by the state. In Jamaica legal aid was provided but not all lawyers took part in the scheme. In South Korea assistance was provided only from the time of indictment but efforts were being made to amend the Penal Procedure Code to provide counsel from the time of arrest.[35] In many under-developed countries there is, in any case, a paucity of experienced lawyers able to defend persons facing the death penalty. For example, prior to the Legal Aid Act of 2001, Zambia employed only ten lawyers in its Department of Legal Aid, each of them having to cover up to 50 cases a year. The Legal Aid Act makes it possible for private lawyers to be paid on a case-by-case basis, but Amnesty International's scepticism of whether the new system 'will ensure adequate legal representation for defendants in capital cases',[36] has been proved right. According to research carried out in 2005 by the US Department of State, Zambia's legal aid office now employs a mere 14 attorneys.[37]

As with other breaches of international standards, the HRC receives evidence on cases where there has been inadequate legal representation. For example, in *Saidov v Tajikistan* the defendant, facing charges carrying the death penalty, was legally represented only towards the end of the investigation and had no opportunity to consult his representative. He had not been informed of his right to be represented by a lawyer upon arrest, and his lawyer was frequently absent during the trial: clear violations of Mr. Saidov's rights under Article 14, paragraphs 3 (b) and (d), of the Covenant.[38]

In a series of death penalty cases concerning Caribbean defendants, decided between 1987 and 1990, the UN HRC declared that defendants have an absolute right to effective counsel, including legal aid, under Article 14 (3) (d) of

---

[34] UN Doc. E/CN.4/2006/53Add. 4, January 2006, para. 28.

[35] UN Doc. E/2005/3/Add. 1.

[36] Amnesty International, *Zambia: Time to Abolish the Death Penalty*, AI Index: AFR 63/004/2001, pp. 3–4.

[37] US Department of State Bureau of Democracy, Human Rights, and Labor, *Country Reports on Human Rights Practices, 2005, Zambia*, 8 March 2006 at <http://www.state.gov/g/drl/rls/hrrpt/2005/61599.htm>.

[38] Case 964/2001 HRC 59/40 (Vol. 1, p. 114; Annex IX, sect. U, para. 6.8).

the ICCPR.[39] The case of *Smartt v Republic of Guyana* provided the HRC with evidence of failures to provide such legal representation in Guyana.[40] The issue before the Committee in this case was whether the absence of legal representation during committal hearings amounted to a violation of Article 14, paragraph 3 (d), of the Covenant. Because Smartt's pre-trial hearings took place after he had been charged with murder and so formed part of the criminal proceedings, the HRC found that the failure to secure legal representation for the defendant through legal aid or otherwise had certainly constituted a violation of the Covenant.[41]

The reply to the Seventh Survey from Trinidad and Tobago stressed that defendants would have counsel of their own choosing, at public expense if necessary, from the time of their arrest. Yet Trinidad and Tobago was found on a number of occasions during the period 1999–2003 by the HRC to be in violation of its obligations under Articles 9 and 14 of the ICCPR.[42] Specifically, the HRC cited the failure to ensure the timely provision of competent counsel, as well as excessive delays experienced by suspects and defendants in bringing their cases before a judge and in determining the outcome of trials and appeals.[43]

Even where counsel is provided to indigent defendants, there remains a question as to whether such representation is truly adequate, particularly given insufficient resources. The USA claims that its procedural safeguards include adequate legal counsel and other necessary resources,[44] yet it is widely accepted that those who are able to hire private lawyers rather than be served by a court-appointed attorney are considerably less likely to be sentenced to death. Over 20 years ago Professor Bowers found that, when all other relevant factors had been accounted for, the rate of death sentences in Georgia where the defendant had access only to a court-appointed defence counsel was 2.6 times higher.[45]

---

[39] *Robinson v Jamaica*, UNHRC Communication No. 223/1987, decided 30 March 1989; *Reid v Jamaica*, decided July 1990; *Pinto v Trinidad and Tobago*, decided July 1990; *Pratt and Morgan v Jamaica*, decided April 1989.

[40] Communication No. 867/1999, *Smartt v Republic of Guyana* (views adopted 6 July 2004, 81st session).

[41] HRC A 59/40 (II), pp. 41–46.

[42] Official Records of the General Assembly, 56th Session, Supp. No. 40 (I) (A/56/40), para. 72 (7); and *Kennedy v Trinidad and Tobago* (Communication No. 845/1998, views adopted 26 March 2002); *Teesdale v Trinidad and Tobago* (Communication No. 677/1996, views adopted 1 April 2002); and *Sooklal v Trinidad and Tobago* (Communication No. 928/2000, views adopted 21 March 2003).

[43] *Ashby v Trinidad and Tobago* (Communication No. 580/1994, views adopted 21 March 2002); *Wanza v Trinidad and Tobago* (Communication No. 683/1996, views adopted 26 March 2002); *Francis et al v Trinidad and Tobago* (Communication No. 899/1999, views adopted 25 July 2002); *Boodoo v Trinidad and Tobago* (Communication No. 721/1996, views adopted 2 April 2002); *Sextus v Trinidad and Tobago* (Communication No. 818/1998, views adopted 16 July 2001); and *Evans v Trinidad and Tobago* (Communication No. 908/2000, views adopted 21 March 2003). Also *Kennedy, Teesdale, and Sooklal*, cited in n. 42 above.

[44] UN Doc. E/2005/3/Add. 1.

[45] W. J. Bowers, 'The Pervasiveness of Arbitrariness and Discrimination under Post-*Furman* Capital Statutes' *Journal of Criminal Law and Criminology* 74 (1983), pp. 1067–1110 at

In 1984 the Supreme Court in *Strickland v Washington* established the bench-mark for judging any claim that counsel's conduct was so inadequate as to have violated the defendant's constitutional right to legal representation. However, the court cautioned lower courts to be highly deferential in their scrutiny of a law-yer's performance. In fact, this meant that it had to be so unreasonable as to have so undermined the proper functioning of the adversarial process that the trial could not be relied on as having produced a just result. Despite this consti-tutional requirement, many instances since then have been cited where court-appointed lawyers were evidently extremely ill equipped to handle the trial of a murder case. 'The case reports and academic literature are filled with countless accounts of inadequate legal representation in capital cases, both at the trial and sentencing phases', declared Justice Brennan of the US Supreme Court in 1994. 'Notwithstanding the heroic efforts of resource centers and appellate projects throughout the country, the meager hourly rates and expenditure caps that many states impose on appointed counsel in capital cases do not suggest that a solution to this crisis is imminent'.[46]

A Cincinnati newspaper investigation of Ohio capital cases found that more death sentences had been overturned in the state because of mistakes by defence lawyers than for any other reason, with 15 people on Ohio's death row winning federal appeals between 2000 and 2006 based entirely or in part on the poor per-formance of their lawyers. The review of appeals filed with the 6th Circuit found evidence that some capital defence attorneys never spoke to their clients, and oth-ers hired unqualified experts or none at all. In other instances, defence attorneys neglected to read key documents or conduct basic investigations or interviews with their own witnesses. In all, 19 people on death row in three states—includ-ing the 15 from Ohio, three from Tennessee, and one from Kentucky—received relief from the Sixth Circuit based on 'ineffective assistance of counsel claims' between 2000 and the end of 2006.[47]

A recent investigation by a newspaper found extensive problems of inad-equate counsel in Mississippi, Alabama, Georgia, and Virginia. In 73 of 80 cases reviewed, lawyers did little or nothing to defend their clients at the crit-ical stage where juries are weighing life and death. The attorneys often missed unspeakable abuse, abject poverty, and profound mental disabilities in their clients' backgrounds. Furthermore, the study found that appeal courts in the four states routinely refused to cite bad lawyering as a reason to overturn death

---

1078–1083; and D. C. Baldus, G. Woodworth, and C. A. Pulaski, *Equal Justice and the Death Penalty* (1990), p. 158.

[46] Justice William J. Brennan Jr, 'Neither Victims nor Executioners' *Notre Dame Journal of Law, Ethics and Public Policy* 8 (1994), pp. 1–9 at 3. Also, Vivian Berger, 'The Chiropractor as Brain Surgeon: Defense Lawyering in Capital Cases' *New York University Review of Law and Social Change* 18 (1990–91), pp. 245–254.

[47] *Cincinnati Enquirer*, 16 April 2007, reproduced on the Death Penalty Information Center (DPIC) website <http://www.deathpenaltyinfo.org/newsanddev.php?scid=68>.

sentences.[48] A similar study in Texas concluded that: 'Sheltered by an indifferent Texas Court of Criminal Appeals, lawyers appointed to handle appeals for death row inmates routinely bungle the job, submitting work that falls far below professional standards, frequently at taxpayer expense'. The study found that some appeals are incomplete, incomprehensible or improperly argued, whilst others are duplicated, poorly, from previous appeals.[49]

The recent report of the ABA's Penalty Assessment panel in Alabama stigmatized the indigent defence services as 'a mixed and uneven system that lacks level oversight and standards and does not provide uniform, quality representation to indigent defendants in all capital proceedings'.[50] With the exception of the recently established state capital post-conviction public defender office, the ABA determined that 'the State has failed to adopt a statewide public defender office, mandate the establishment of public defender offices providing coverage within each county, adequately fund indigent defense services in each county, or implement close oversight of indigent legal services at the county level'.[51] Furthermore, the ABA found that the compensation paid to appointed attorneys who represent capital defendants was insufficient for counsel to meet their obligations under the ABA 'Guidelines for the Appointment and Performance of Defense Counsel in Death Penalty Cases' (see below, page 230). Likewise, the ABA's study of the Alabama system[52] concluded that while many individual indigent defence lawyers in the state of Alabama are competent and effective, the state's indigent defence system had a similar 'patchwork' quality which, when, combined with the minimal qualifications and non-existent training required of attorneys representing capital defendants, had produced a system 'where serious fairness and accuracy breakdowns in capital cases are virtually inevitable'.[53]

Furthermore, the failure of Alabama, unlike most other states, to provide counsel in state post-conviction proceedings to indigent defendants sentenced to death exacerbated the problem of inadequate trial counsel and undermined further this critical constitutional safeguard.

---

[48] *North Carolina News & Observer*, 20 January 2007, reproduced on the DPIC website, *ibid*.

[49] Chuck Lindell, *Austin American-Statesman*, 29 October 2006; two-part series, 'Writs Gone Wrong,' 29–30 October 2006, at <http://www.statesman.com/news/content/news/interactive/10/102906_habeas.html> (also reproduced on the DPIC website).

[50] American Bar Association (ABA), *The Arizona Death Penalty Assessment Report*, July 2006, p. iii.

[51] *Ibid*.

[52] ABA, *The Alabama Death Penalty Assessment Report*, June 2006, pp. iii–iv.

[53] *Ibid*., p. iii. The Judicial Study Commission of the Alabama Supreme Court and a committee of the Alabama State Bar have proposed legislation at various times since 2000 to create a statewide indigent defence commission which would oversee indigent defence in Alabama. Thus far, efforts at getting such legislation passed have been unsuccessful. The Indiana assessment team also found that the provisions for the appointment, training, and monitoring of attorneys who represent indigent defendants 'falls far short of the requirements set out in the ABA guidelines': ABA: *The Indiana Death Penalty Assessment Report* (February 2007), p. 4. Also, *The Tennessee Death Penalty Assessment Report* (March 2007), p. vi.

Although a few states, such as Illinois and Louisiana, have attempted to raise the fees available to defence lawyers in capital cases, the situation in the United States has not markedly improved over the last decade, as the Columbia study of errors in capital cases has shown (see pages 270–271 below). Inadequate compensation for trial counsel and delays in payment has had an adverse impact in many states. Not only has it dissuaded some of the most experienced and qualified attorneys from taking capital cases, it may preclude those attorneys who do take these cases from having the funds necessary to present a vigorous defence. In Florida, for example, the 'registry attorneys' appointed for certain post-conviction proceedings[54] do not meet the requirements of the ABA guidelines for the appointment of counsel.[55] They need only minimal trial and appellate experience to qualify for appointment and are not adequately monitored. Their performance, according to Justice Raoul Cantero of the Florida Supreme Court, amounted to '[s]ome of the worst lawyering' he had ever seen.[56] Specifically, 'some of the registry counsel have little or no experience in death penalty cases. They have not raised the right issues . . . [and] [s]ometimes they raise too many issues and still haven't raised the right ones'.[57] Furthermore, in at least some instances, registry attorneys handling capital collateral cases have not been compensated at a rate that is commensurate with the provision of high quality legal representation. The Spangenberg Group (a research and consulting firm specializing in improving criminal justice programmes) has estimated that 'on average 3,300 "attorney hours" are required to take a case from denial of *certiorari* by the United States Supreme Court after direct appeal to the Florida Supreme Court to denial of *certiorari* from state post-conviction proceedings.[58] The compensation of registry attorneys during capital collateral proceedings in Florida, however, is subject to a statutory fee cap of $84,000 (or 840 hours at $100 an hour), which must cover fees of lead counsel as well as any attorney designated by lead counsel to assist him or her.[59]

[54] Capital collateral registry attorneys are private lawyers who are appointed from the state-wide registry to represent death-sentenced inmates during post-conviction proceedings in cases of a conflict of interest or when the defendant was convicted and sentenced to death in the northern region of Florida, which no longer has a Capital Collateral Regional Counsel Office.

[55] American Bar Association, 'Guidelines for the Appointment and Performance of Defense Counsel in Death Penalty Cases' *Hofstra Law Review* 31 (2003), pp. 913–1090.

[56] See his testimony to the Commission on Capital Cases, reported by Jan Pudlow, 'Justice Rips Shoddy Work of Private Capital Case Lawyers' *Florida Bar News*, 1 March 2005.

[57] *Ibid.* Former Florida Supreme Court Chief Justice Barbara Pariente has echoed Justice Cantero's concerns: American Bar Association, *The Florida Death Penalty Assessment Report*, Executive Summary, p. v at <http://www.abanet.org/moratorium/assessmentproject/florida/exec-utivesummary.pdf>.

[58] Spangenberg Group, *Amended Time and Expense Analysis of Post-Conviction Capital Cases in Florida* 16 (1998) quoted in the ABA Florida Death Penalty Assessment Report, Executive Summary, *ibid.*, at p. v.

[59] ABA, *The Florida Death Penalty Assessment Report* (September 2006), pp. iv–v. Although the most recent Spangenberg report noted the 'trend toward increased rates of compensation [which] serves to increase the number of qualified attorneys willing to handle capital trial cases . . . These rate increases across the country demonstrate that policy makers are recognizing that, in order to attract qualified counsel who are able to provide effective representation in capital cases, it is necessary to

Amnesty International lists at least 16 cases of people who were executed between 1985 and 2001 who had been defended by lawyers who were incompetent or who failed to mount an adequate case for the defence.[60] The degree of incompetence revealed by some investigative journalists has been truly shocking. According to an investigation by the *Chicago Tribune* of the 131 death row inmates executed during George Bush's tenure as Governor of Texas, 43 were represented by defence attorneys who had been publicly sanctioned for misconduct, 40 of them presented no evidence to the court or provided only one witness on their client's behalf, and 29 used psychiatric testimony condemned as untrustworthy by the American Psychiatric Association.[61] A similar study by the Common Sense Foundation found that more than one in six North Carolina death row inmates were represented at trial by lawyers who were disciplined by the North Carolina State Bar. Indeed, people on death row in North Carolina had often had the state's worst lawyers at trial. The Foundation released a further study in October 2006 which showed that at least 37 people now on death row had trial lawyers who would not have met today's minimum standards of qualification. Nearly a third of the cases where sufficient data was available fell into this substandard category.[62]

The most remarkable instance of this is the case of *Burdine v Johnson*.[63] Burdine was convicted of capital murder in Texas after a trial lasting three days. It was established that Burdine's defence counsel had slept during parts of the thirteen hours that the trial had taken up (the lawyer claimed that he was only concentrating). Yet the Federal Court of Appeal for the Fifth Circuit held, by a majority, that although counsel had slept, the appellant had failed to prove (and it was ten years after the trial) that the lawyer had slept during consequential parts of the trial and that there could therefore be a presumption of prejudice.[64] In August 2001 the Federal Court of Appeal for the Fifth Circuit considered the case again and decided that the defender's 'unconsciousness during Burdine's capital murder trial [did amount] to constructive denial of counsel for substantial periods of that trial'. The Court concluded that 'the Supreme Court's Sixth Amendment jurisprudence compels the presumption that counsel's

---

increase hourly rates of compensation': The Spangenberg Group (2007), *Rates of Compensation for Court-Appointed Counsel in Capital Cases at Trial: A State-By-State Overview*, p. 4.

[60] Amnesty International, *US: Arbitrary, Discriminatory or Cruel*, AI Index: AMR 51/003/2002, pp. 8 and 9; Amnesty International, *United States of America: updated briefing to the HR Committee on the Implementation of the ICCPR*, AI Index: AMR 51/111/2006.

[61] Amnesty International, *United States of America: The Death Penalty in Texas: Lethal Injustice*, AI Index: AMR 51/010/1998.

[62] Common Sense Foundation, October 2006, reproduced on the DPIC website: <http://www.deathpenaltyinfo.org/article.php?did=2110>. Also Michael Mello and Paul J. Perkins, 'Closing the Circle: The Illusion of Lawyers for People Litigating for their Lives at the Fin de Siècle', in J. R. Acker, R. M. Bohm, and C. S Lanier (eds.), *America's Experiment with Capital Punishment* (2nd edn., 2003), pp. 347–384 at 371–372.

[63] *Burdine v Johnson* (2000) 231 F.3d 950 (5th Cir. Texas).

[64] For a scathing comment on this judgment, see *Amicus Journal* 2 (2001), pp. 15–16.

unconsciousness prejudiced the defendant'.[65] As Stephen Bright has pointed out, the *Burdine* case is not unique. Another Texas prisoner, George McFarland, remains on death row having failed to get his death sentence quashed by the Texas Court Criminal Appeals on the grounds that his counsel had repeatedly fallen asleep and snored during his trial.[66] Furthermore, the decision of the Eleventh Circuit of the US Court of Appeals in the case of David Ronald Chandler appears to have set a very low standard for 'competent counsel'. Chandler's attorney admitted that he had hardly prepared for the sentencing part of the death penalty trial. He had concentrated on trying to prove his client innocent and did 'basically not anything explicitly' to bring forward mitigating circumstances to persuade jurors not to sentence his client to death.[67] In 2001 Chandler was granted clemency by President Bill Clinton.

A review of trial transcripts and appeal records of 80 recent (from 1997 to 2004) death penalty cases in the states of Mississippi, Georgia, Alabama, and Virginia, carried out by McClatchy Newspapers, found that 'in 73 of the 80 cases defense lawyers gave jurors little or no evidence to help them decide whether the accused should live or die. The lawyers routinely missed myriad issues of abuse and mental deficiency, abject poverty and serious psychological problems'.[68] The lawyers failed to meet the professional standards set by the ABA and the standards that the US Supreme Court has mandated in several cases yet in only two of the cases had the appeals courts overturned the sentences on the grounds of ineffective assistance of counsel; in eleven of the cases the defendant had already been executed—significant lapses in the defence attorney's performance not having caused any concern for the appeals courts; and the remaining cases are still on appeal. 'Overall, the 80 cases that McClatchy reviewed showed how poorly these four key death-penalty states fulfil a basic constitutional principle'.[69] In one Mississippi case, a lawyer had been given a report showing that his client was diagnosed as mentally retarded at age five, with an IQ of 68, but the lawyer threw away the report without ever presenting it as mitigating evidence.[70]

---

[65] *Burdine v Johnson* 262 F.3d (5th Cir 2001), 122 S. Ct 2347 (2002).

[66] Stephen N. Bright, 'Symposium: Restructuring Federal Courts: Habeas: Elected Judges and the Death Penalty in Texas. Why Full Habeas Corpus Review by Independent Federal Judges is Indispensable to Protecting Constitutional Rights' *Texas Law Review* 78 (2000), pp. 1805–1837 at 1811–1812. Also R. Copeland, Comment, 'Getting it Right from the Beginning: A Critical Examination of Current Criminal Defense in Texas and Proposal for a Statewide Public Defender System' *St. Mary's Law Journal* 32 (2001), pp. 493–540 at 523.

[67] *Chandler v United States of America* (2000) 218 F.3d 1305. See also for list of 16 cases where the prisoner had been executed, despite poor legal representation; Amnesty International, *United States of America. Arbitrary Discriminatory, and Cruel: An Aide-Memoire to 25 Years of Judicial Killing*, AI Index: AMR 51/003/2002, pp. 13–14.

[68] S. Henderson, 'Indefensible? Lawyers in key death penalty states often fall short', *McClatchy Newspapers*, 21 January 2007.

[69] *Ibid.*

[70] *Ibid.*

The ABA was so concerned about the inadequacies of legal representation that in 1989 it adopted *Guidelines for the Appointment and Performance of Counsel in Death Penalty Cases*. These emphasized the need for adequate compensation and support and for a 'concrete procedure for the appointment of attorneys with appropriate experience and training to represent defendants in capital cases'.[71] This effort did not have an immediate impact, for in 1997 the ABA called for a national moratorium on death sentences until this problem could be corrected. It was supported by the Attorney General of the United States, Janet Reno, who declared in 2000 that defendants should not be prosecuted 'for a capital crime until they have a lawyer who can properly represent them, and...the resources necessary to properly investigate the charges'.[72] This was cautiously echoed by Supreme Court Justice Sandra Day O'Connor in a speech in 2001 when she declared that 'perhaps it is time to look at minimum standards for appointed counsel in death penalty cases and adequate compensation for appointed counsel when they are used'.[73] Much more forcefully, in the same year, her colleague Justice Ruth Bader Ginsburg said that she had 'yet to see a death case, among the dozens coming to the Supreme Court...in which the defendant was well represented at trial' and that 'people who are well represented at trial do not get the death penalty'.[74] In 2003 the ABA issued a comprehensively revised and expanded version of its *Guidelines*, which made it clear not only that there should always be high quality legal representation for capital defendants but that it should:[75]

apply from the moment the client is taken into custody and extend to all stages of every case in which the jurisdiction may be entitled to seek the death penalty, including initial and ongoing investigation, pretrial proceedings, trial, post-conviction review, clemency proceedings and any connected litigation.

In recent years the US Supreme Court has begun to add some flesh to the *Strickland* bones, approvingly citing the ABA *Guidelines* when overturning death sentences based on inadequate preparation by capital defense counsel.[76] Thus in 2000, in *Williams v Taylor*, the US Supreme Court held that the *Strickland*

[71] American Bar Association, *Guidelines for the Appointment and Performance of Counsel in Death Penalty Cases* (1989).

[72] *USA Today*, 21 June 2000, cited on DPIC website, July 2000: <http://www.deathpenaltyinfo. org/article.php?did=1948>. See also the case of Exavious Lee Gibson, who through poverty had been forced to appear without legal representation at his post-conviction hearing in 1996. He had been sentenced to death in 1990 for a murder committed when he was 17; he had an IQ of between 76 and 82. In 1999 the US Supreme Court refused to consider his appeal: Amnesty International, *United States of America: Failing the Future—Death Penalty Developments, March 1998–March 2000*, AI Index: AMR 51/03/00, p. 18.

[73] Amnesty International, *Death Penalty News*, September 2001, AI Index: ACT 53/004/2001.

[74] Quoted in Stephen B. Bright, 'The Politics of Capital Punishment: The Sacrifice of Fairness for Executions' in Acker, Bohm, and Lanier (eds.), n. 62 above, pp. 127–146 at 137.

[75] American Bar Association, *Guidelines for the Appointment and Performance of Defense Counsel in Death Penalty Cases*, revised edn., February 2003.

[76] Carol Steiker and Jordan Steiker, 'The Shadow of Death: The Effect of Capital Punishment on American Criminal Law and Policy' *Judicature* 89 (5) (2006), pp. 250–253 at 253.

definition of effective assistance of counsel required counsel to investigate his client's background and to present reasonably discoverable mitigating evidence. The failure to do so in *Williams*, where the defendant's background included significant abuse and borderline mental retardation, violated the defendant's constitutional right to effective representation. Similarly, in 2003, in *Wiggins v Smith*, the US Supreme Court overturned a death sentence based on the failure of the defendant's lawyers to investigate fully his case.[77] The standard procedure in Maryland at the time of the *Wiggins* trial included preparation of a 'social history' report that would contain mitigation investigations regarding the case. As no such report was prepared or even requested by counsel, Justice O'Connor wrote that:[78]

Any reasonably competent attorney would have realized that pursuing such leads was necessary to making an informed choice among possible defenses, particularly given the apparent absence of aggravating factors from *Wiggins'* background.

Because of the failure by counsel to conduct an adequate investigation into *Wiggins'* very compelling social history, the Court concluded that the jury would have reached a different sentence had they been apprised of such mitigating evidence.[79] In 2005, in *Rompilla v Beard*,[80] a Pennsylvania defendant's lawyers were considered to have failed to review relevant records from his past.

Steps have been taken to try to improve the situation in several states, such as in Texas where the Fair Defence Act of 2002 facilitated the establishment of public defender offices. The Act explicitly states that 'counties must adopt and publish consistent county-wide indigent defence systems which meet basic minimum standards', meaning prompt access to counsel within five days of arrest for counties with a population greater than 250,000 and within seven days for smaller counties. The Act also adopted state-wide minimum qualifications for attorneys handling capital cases and provided research assistance to lawyers appointed in capital cases.[81] In Illinois, since 2000, fees for lawyers who defend death penalty cases have been raised[82] and in June 2001 an increase in the hourly rate for private counsel defending federal criminal defendants was agreed under the Criminal Justice Act. In 2005 the State of Georgia instituted a statewide capital

---

[77] No. 02–311 (26 June 2003).

[78] *Wiggins v Smith*, 539 U.S. 510 (2003).

[79] No. 04–5462 (20 June 2005).

[80] 545 U.S. 374 (2005).

[81] Texas Fair Defence Act of 2001, SB 7. It should be noted, however, that in January 2002 the Texas Court of Criminal Appeals had ruled that death row inmates had no right to capable counsel in their appeals, prompting dissenting Judge Price to remark that 'competent counsel' 'ought to require more than a human being with a law licence and a pulse': reported in the *Houston Chronicle*, 12 January 2002. For an evaluation of the implementation of this legislation, see The Public Policy Research Institute 'Study to Assess the Impacts of the Fair Defense Act on Texas Counties' Final Report, Texas A&M University, January 2005.

[82] FIDH, *The Death Penalty in the United States*, International Mission of Investigation No. 316/2 (May 2002).

defender system, which provides experienced attorneys for indigent defendants in capital proceedings at trial and on direct appeal. Since then, not one of their 23 defendants has been sentenced to death, but their future funding is insecure.[83] However, the state of Georgia remains virtually alone in not providing indigent defendants sentenced to death with counsel for state *habeas* proceedings.[84]

With the exception of three states—Arizona, California, and North Carolina—there is still no statutory right to payment for expert assistance, in addition to counsel, for assessing mitigating considerations relating to sentencing, the matter being left entirely to the discretion of the court. Whatever may be attempted by skilled and committed attorneys to seek remedies at the post-conviction stage, all may be lost if the initial defence fails to undertake its task effectively.

In 2006 the Constitution project, a Washington DC bipartisan organization, issued a report recommending that:[85]

Every jurisdiction that imposes capital punishment should create an independent authority to screen, appoint, train, and supervise lawyers to represent defendants charged with a capital crime. It should set minimum standards for these lawyers' performance [who] should be adequately compensated, and the defense should be provided with adequate funding for experts and investigators…The current Supreme Court standard for effective assistance of counsel (*Strickland v Washington*)…should be replaced in such cases by a standard requiring professional competence in death penalty representation.

While it appears that these efforts to bring about an improvement in the quality of representation in capital cases in the United States has resulted in some improvements, particularly in specifying that a higher quality of counsel is required in death penalty cases, there may not be, as Carol and Jordan Steiker point out, enough lawyers of the required quality who are 'willing and able to satisfy the demand'.[86] Consistent with the UN's fifth safeguard, these aspirations should not be confined to the US, but should be the goal of all retentionist countries.

---

[83] S. Henderson, 'Between life and death: A group of young lawyers is some prisoners' only hope' *McClatchy Newspapers*, 21 January 2007.

[84] ABA, *The Georgia Death Penalty Assessment Report* (January 2006), p. iii. See, more generally, Carol S. Steiker and Jordan M. Steiker, 'Judicial Developments in Capital Punishment Law', in Acker, Bohm, and Lanier (eds.), n. 62 above, pp. 72–73. Also Sheri Lynn Johnson, 'Wishing Petitioners to Death: Factual Misrepresentations in Fourth Circuit Capital Cases' 91 *Cornell Law Review* (2006), pp. 1105–1155.

[85] The Constitution Project, *Mandatory Justice: the Death Penalty Revisited*, Washington DC (2006), p. xvii.

[86] Carol Steiker and Jordan Steiker, 'A Tale of Two Nations: Implementation of the Death Penalty in "Executing" versus "Symbolic" States in the United States' *Texas Law Review* 84 (2006), pp. 1869–1927 at 1880 and 1889.; also, Scott Sunby, 'The Death Penalty's Future: Charting the Crosscurrents of Declining Death Sentences and the McVeigh Factor' *Texas Law Review* 84 (2006), pp. 1929–1972 at 1947.

(d) The plight of foreign nationals

All people in retentionist jurisdictions should have the right to a fair trial, including foreign nationals. ECOSOC added to its safeguards in 1996 an encouragement to Member States 'to ensure that defendants who do not sufficiently understand the language used in court are fully informed, by way of interpretation or translation, of all the charges against them and the content of the relevant evidence deliberated in court'.

The disadvantage suffered by foreigners has also raised the question of ensuring that consular assistance is provided for foreign nationals accused of crimes, as laid down in Article 36 (1b) of the Vienna Convention on Consular Relations. In 1993, according to the Special Rapporteur on Extrajudicial, Summary or Arbitrary Executions, [87] the following retentionist countries had failed to abide by the Vienna Convention: Egypt, Eritrea, Ethiopia, India, Iraq, Pakistan, Saudi Arabia (which has executed many migrant workers[88]), Sudan, and Yemen, thus depriving many of these foreigners of adequate legal assistance.

On 30 November 2004 the Special Rapporteur on Torture prepared a joint urgent appeal with the Chairperson-Rapporteur of the Working Group on Arbitrary Detention, the Special Rapporteur on the Human Rights of Migrants, and the Special Rapporteur on the Independence of Judges and Lawyers regarding thirteen Nigerian nationals and migrant workers residing in Jeddah, Saudi Arabia. They had been among hundreds detained in Jeddah on 29 September 2002 after a policeman was killed in a fight between local men and African nationals. All the others arrested were deported, but the 13 Nigerian nationals were alleged to have been tortured. On 22 November 2004 a hearing in the case of the 13 men took place before three judges in a closed session, without the assistance of a lawyer, a consular representative, or adequate translation facilities. They could not understand the proceedings, and were unable to understand whether the hearing concerned the prolongation of their detention or constituted their trial. One of them was sentenced to death and this was ratified by the Supreme Judicial Council. According to the report, if the victim had children (which is unknown), he could remain in prison until these children reach the age of 18, when they can accept or reject the payment of *Diya* (compensation) in place of the death penalty. Otherwise, he will be executed.[89]

---

[87] UN Doc. E/CN.4/1999/39/Add. 1, para. 213.

[88] Apparently more than half of those executed in Saudi Arabia in the 1990s were foreign nationals: Amnesty International, *Saudi Arabia, Defying World Trends: Saudi Arabia's Extensive Use of Capital Punishment*, AI Index: MDE 23/015/2001. In 2005 data suggested that this proportion remained high, at least two-thirds: Amnesty International, *Death Penalty News*, June 2005.

[89] UN Doc. E/CN.4/2005/62/Add. 1, para. 1444, Report of Theo van Boven. Amnesty International, 'Saudi Arabian at risk of execution', October 2007.

In March 2007 there were 124 foreign nationals from 33 countries on America's death rows, the largest number (54) being from Mexico.[90] Foreign nationals have been executed in the United States without ever being informed of their right to consular assistance, despite that country having ratified the Vienna Convention on Consular Rights in 1969.[91] The US Supreme Court did not halt the execution of a prisoner named Angel Breard, a citizen of Paraguay, by the Commonwealth of Virginia in 1998, despite clear evidence that he had not been informed of his right to consular assistance. This decision was in blatant disregard of an order to do so by the International Court of Justice (ICJ)—and despite a strongly worded appeal to stay the execution being sent to the Governor of Virginia by the United States Secretary of State, Madeleine Albright[92]—on the grounds that there was no constitutional remedy for the violation of Breard's right to be informed of consular assistance, because he had failed to raise the issue at an earlier stage of his appeals.[93] After receiving a comprehensive apology from the United States, Paraguay withdrew its case at the International Court of Justice (ICJ).

There was yet another high profile case. Two German citizens, the brothers Karl and Walter LaGrand (who had lived most of their lives in the United States), were convicted in 1984 of the murder of a bank manager in Arizona during an attempted robbery in 1982. They were not informed of their rights under the Vienna Convention and it was not until 1992 that they discovered that they had a right to consular assistance. Such was the delay that they were precluded under the doctrine of 'procedural default' from challenging their conviction and sentence on these grounds. After one of the brothers, Karl LaGrand, had been executed on 24 February 1999, and one day before Walter LaGrand was due to be executed on 3 March 1999, Germany brought the case to the ICJ. On 3 March 1999 the ICJ issued an Order (called a provisional measure but similar to an interim injunction) stating that the United States should take all measures at its disposal to ensure that Walter LaGrand was not executed pending a final decision of the ICJ. The US Solicitor General informed the US Supreme Court that 'an order of the International Court of Justice indicating provisional measures is not binding' and the Supreme Court refused to grant a stay of execution on

[90] Death Penalty Information Center website: <http://www.deathpenaltyinfo.org/article.php?did=198&scid=31>.

[91] Advisory Opinion of the Inter-American Court of Human Rights (OC-16/99 of 1 October 1999).

[92] Secretary Albright had written, 'The immediate execution of Mr Breard in the face of the Court's April 9 action could be seen as a denial by the United States of the significance of international law and the Court's processes in its international relations and thereby limit our ability to ensure that Americans are protected when living or traveling abroad'. However, the US Solicitor General opposed the stay: cited in Harold Hongju Koh, 'Paying "Decent Respect" to World Opinion on the Death Penalty' *UC Davis Law Review* 35 (2002), pp. 1085–1131 at 1112–1113.

[93] He was denied *certiorari* by the Supreme Court by 6 to 3: *Breard v Greene* (1998) 140 L.Ed2d 529.

the grounds of 'the tardiness of the pleas and the jurisdictional boundaries they implicate'. The Order from the ICJ was conveyed to the Governor of Arizona without comment. He ignored it, along with the recommendation of the Arizona Clemency Board for a stay of execution, and Walter LaGrand was executed on 3 March 1999. On 27 June 2001 the ICJ held that the United States had breached its obligations to the LaGrand brothers.[94]

The United States was again found by the ICJ to have failed to abide by its obligations to inform foreign nationals of their right to have their consulate informed of their detention in a case concerning Carlos Avena Guillen (*Avena and other Mexican nationals*).[95] On 31 March 2004 the Court held that the United States had violated its obligation under the Convention in 51 out of 52 cases brought before the Court in *Mexico v United States of America* and that the United States should review through the judicial process the convictions and sentences imposed in each case.[96] In its judgment the Court found by fourteen votes to one that the United States of America had breached the obligations incumbent upon it by not informing, without delay upon their detention, the 51 Mexican nationals of their rights,[97] and thereby depriving Mexico of its right to assist them. It found, in relation to 34 of the Mexican nationals, that America had deprived Mexico of the right to arrange for legal representation for those nationals. The Court ruled that America was now obliged to reconsider the sentences of these Mexican nationals and take into account the violation of their rights.

In February 2005 the US President directed state courts to hear the cases of all 57 Mexican nationals under sentence of death to decide whether 'actual prejudice' had occurred. But in order to avoid any such cases in the future, in March 2005 the US withdrew from the Optional Protocol to the Vienna Convention so that it would no longer be subject to adjudication by the International Court of Justice. Nevertheless, in autumn 2007 the US Supreme Court was due to issue its ruling in the case of Jose Ernesto Medellin. Medellin, a Mexican national held on death row in Texas, who has appealed his conviction on the grounds that his consular rights were violated. Medellin's case will enable the US Supreme Court to consider the *Avena* decision and choose whether to align its own jurisprudence with that of the International Court of Justice, by showing that the US takes seriously the rights of foreign nationals on its soil, or whether to ignore the international standards.

---

[94] LaGrand case, *Germany v United States of America*—Judgment, International Court of Justice, Press Release 2001/16, 27 June 2001, General List No. 104. See also Amnesty International, *United States of America: A Time for Action: Protecting the Consular Rights of Foreign Nationals Facing the Death Penalty*, AI Index: AMR 51/106/2001.

[95] United Nations, Treaty Series, Vol. 596, No. 8638.

[96] *Avena and other Mexican Nationals [Mexico v USA (Avena)]* 2004 ICJ 128, 31 March 2004, International Court of Justice, General List No. 128.

[97] Under Art. 36 of the Vienna Convention on Consular Relations, 24 April 1963.

(e) The right to be tried by an unbiased jury

In some countries trial is by jury and the jury may also recommend or determine the sentence, but very little is known about how juries reach their decisions in capital cases. It is an area almost entirely closed to the immediate scrutiny of researchers, and what is known is usually based on retrospective views of jurors.[98] Furthermore, such studies have only been carried out in the United States.

In June 2002, in *Ring v Arizona,* the US Supreme Court held that death sentences in five states imposed by a judge instead of a jury violated the constitutional right to trial by jury because the determination of proof of an aggravating circumstance (necessary to make the case 'capital') had been made by the judge, not the jury. In the majority opinion Justice Breyer explained that:[99]

Even in jurisdictions where judges are selected directly by the people, the jury remains uniquely capable of determining whether, given the community's views, capital punishment is appropriate...not 'cruel', 'unusual' or otherwise unwarranted...in the particular case in hand.

However, in *Schriro v Summerlin*[100] in June 2004 the Court decided that because its earlier decision had been on a point of procedure it would not be applied retroactively to those who had already been sentenced to death.[101]

Studies of capital punishment have exposed the controversies arising from the requirement that juries must be 'death-qualified'. Prospective jurors are questioned by the judge and attorneys in order to identify and reject those whose views on the death penalty are regarded as incompatible with their duty to apply the law conscientiously and to consider the 'full range' of penalties available to the court. It has been claimed that this has led to juries which are 'conviction-prone', less solicitous of a defendant's due process rights, and also unrepresentative of all sectors of society, particularly of women and black people.[102] There are substantial differences in the beliefs of 'excludable' and 'death-qualified' jurors on issues such as whether the death penalty is unfair to minorities, whether it

[98] On the need for research in this area, see Mark Constanzo and Sally Constanzo, 'Jury Decision Making in the Capital Penalty Phase: Legal Assumptions, Empirical Findings, and a Research Agenda' *Law and Human Behavior* 16 (1992), pp. 185–201.

[99] In three states, judges can still determine the sentence once a jury has found that an aggravating circumstance is present: *Ring v Arizona,* 536 US 584 (2002).

[100] *Schriro v Summerlin,* 542 US 348 (2004).

[101] The arguments accepted by the Supreme Court in *Ring* in 2002 had been rejected by it in a 1990 Arizona decision and also in a 1984 Florida case. 'The Supreme Court simply woke up to the arguments 10 years too late to save the 22 men who were put to death in Arizona between 1990 and 2002 under a procedure which the Court belatedly discovered was unconstitutional': Anthony. G. Amsterdam, 'Courtroom Contortions. How America's application of the death penalty erodes the principle of equal justice under law' *American Prospect* 15 (7) (2004), pp. 19–21.

[102] The 'death-qualified jury case' decided by the Supreme Court was *Lockhart v McCree* (1986). A large literature on this subject is cited in Marla Sandys and Scott McClelland, 'Stacking the Deck for Guilt and Death: The Failure of Death Qualification to Ensure Impartiality' in Acker, Bohm, and Lanier (eds.), n. 62 above, pp. 295–298.

deters murder, whether life without parole means really what it says, and in the weight given to various mitigating and aggravating factors.[103] In particular, there are strong race differences in the propensity to sentence persons to death. Eisenberg *et al.* found that whites were 'roughly twice as likely to vote for death on the first ballot as are blacks' but 'the dominant factor remains the will of the first-vote majority' and 'majority rule usually means white rule'. [104] This has been confirmed by the impressive Capital Jury Project in which Professor Bowers and his team analysed decision-making by jurors in 340 capital cases and interviewed 1,155 of the jurors in 14 states, which between them had executed 70 per cent of persons put to death between 1977 and 1 September 2002.[105] They found that the racial composition of the jury had a marked effect on whether or not the jury sentenced the defendant to death in cases where the defendant was black and the victim white. They isolated a 'white male dominance effect' and a 'black male presence effect' (blacks were almost always in a minority) although there was no such effect as regards women jurors. There was a 41 percentage points difference in the likelihood of a death sentence where there were four or fewer white males on the jury (30% sentenced to death) than where there were five or more (70% sentenced to death). Where there was no black member of the jury, 71.9 per cent of defendants in black-defendant/white-victim cases were sentenced to death, as opposed to 37.5 per cent in similar cases where there were one or more black male jurors. Significantly, these differences were not found in white/white and black/black cases.

By interviewing black and white male jurors from the same juries, the researchers discovered that, as the decision-making process progressed from stage to stage, the differences between the views of black and white male jurors on the appropriateness of imposing a death sentence grew wider, especially in the black-defendant/white-victim cases.

At the guilt phase [of the trial] whites were three times more likely than blacks to take a pro-death stand on punishment (42.3% versus 14.7%), and after sentencing instructions (from the judge) they were four times more likely to do so (58.5% versus 15.2%). By the first vote on punishment (when they were asked again by the researchers what they thought), the differential between white and black jurors on death reached more than seven to one (67.3% versus 9.1%).

By questioning the jurors further it was revealed that black male jurors were much more likely than white male jurors to have 'lingering doubts' about the defendant's degree of responsibility for the crime and therefore whether the

---

[103] Craig Haney, *Death by Design: Capital Punishment as a Social Psychological System* (2005), pp. 106–112.
[104] Theodore Eisenberg, Stephen P Garvey and Martin T. Wells, 'Forecasting Life and Death: Juror Race, Religion, and Attitude toward the Death Penalty, *Journal of Legal Studies*, 30 (2001) pp. 277–311 at 286, 305 and 309.
[105] William J. Bowers, Benjamin D. Fleury-Steiner, and Michael E. Antonio, 'The Capital Sentencing Decision: Guided Discretion, Reasoned Moral Judgment, or Legal Fiction' in Acker, Bohm, and Lanier (eds.), n. 62 above, pp. 413–467 at 424–425.

defendant was guilty of capital murder; to be much more sensitive to indications of remorse; and to be much less likely to take into account perceptions of future dangerousness in deciding on the imposition of the death penalty in black-defendant/white-victim cases.[106] In another study, carried out in Philadelphia, Baldus and his colleagues found that in the 110 cases where death sentences were imposed, the jury had failed to find a single mitigating circumstance in 59 of them, and that this was particularly unfavourable to black defendants, even where the juries had a preponderance of black members. They concluded therefore that 'the principal source of the racial disparities in Philadelphia is jury, rather than prosecutorial, decision making' and that 'the race-of-defendant effects we see in jury weighing decisions may reflect a tendency for juries in black defendant cases to give less mitigative weight to the mitigators they find than they do in the non-black defendant cases'.[107]

Further analyses of the thinking of black and white jurors, male and female, when confronted with cases involving a black defendant and a white victim, showed large differences in perception. Bowers *et al.* found that black and white males differ substantially, not only in respect to strong aggravating and mitigating considerations, such as dangerousness, remorse, and lingering doubt, but also in the ways that they see the crime (for example, ideas of crimes being particularly vicious as opposed to lacking in callousness) and in the extent to which they identify with the defendant and his family:[108]

The distinctiveness of their responses suggests why the presence of a single black male on the jury can have a very sizeable effect on sentencing outcomes...these data make it clear that identification or empathy with the defendant, and even more so with the defendant's family, is distinctive to black male jurors in these B/W cases...White jurors are much less receptive to mitigation than their black counterparts in these B/W cases.

The authors conclude that the *voir dire* authorized by the US Supreme Court in the case of *Turner* in 1986 has been a 'decisive failure' as a method of detecting

---

[106] William J. Bowers, Benjamin D. Steiner, and Marla Sandys, 'Death Sentencing in Black and White: An Empirical Analysis of the Role of Jurors' Race and Jury Racial Composition' *University of Pennsylvania Journal of Constitutional Law* 3 (2001), pp. 171–272. See also William Bowers, Marla Sandys, and Benjamin D. Steiner, 'Foreclosed Impartiality in Capital Sentencing: Juror's Predispositions, Guilt-Trial Experience, and Premature Decision-Making' *Cornell Law Review* 83 (1998), pp. 1476–1556.

[107] David C. Baldus *et al.*, 'Racial Discrimination and the Death Penalty in the Post-Furman Era: An Empirical and Legal Overview, with Recent Findings from Philadelphia' *Cornell Law Review* 83 (1998), pp. 1638–1770 at 1680, Table 3, 1715, 1721, and 1726.

[108] William J. Bowers, Marla Sandys, and Thomas W. Brewer, 'Crossing racial boundaries: A closer look at the roots of racial bias in capital sentencing when the defendant is black and the victim is white' *De Paul Law Review*, 53 (4) (2004), pp. 1497–1538 at 1513–15 (although note the small numbers in this study—30 white males, 15 black males). See also Haney's discussion of the 'empathic divide', which refers to 'otherness'; white people on juries find it much harder than black people to understand a black defendant's life in a human context, to understand and empathize with his personal history and therefore to be persuaded by mitigation evidence: Haney, n. 103 above, pp. 189–210.

'deeply ingrained and often unconscious racial attitudes'. They suggest that, short of abolition of the death penalty, 'affirmative jury selection', rather than exclusion, might help to resolve a problem for which there is no 'foolproof remedy . . . a remedy that enhances the likelihood that a black defendant can also have African Americans on his jury should at least help to reverse what is now an outrageous discrepancy in the treatment of defendants in such racial boundary crossing cases'.[109]

What is striking is that these findings related to cases nearly all of which were decided *after* the US Supreme Court, in the case of *Turner* (1986), had ruled that 'a capital defendant accused of an interracial crime is entitled to have prospective jurors informed of the race of the victim [specifically in Turner's case, a black defendant and white victim] and questioned on the issue of racial bias'.[110] As Bowers and his colleagues rightly assert, their evidence suggests that the *Turner* decision would do little to safeguard a black defendant in a white-victim case from racial bias. Thus, their research confirmed that the racial composition of a jury matters enormously in respect of a defendant's prospect of being sentenced to death. The inference to be drawn is that arbitrariness and discrimination in the application of the death penalty in black-offender/white-victim cases is bound up with different perceptions of persons drawn from different racial groups about whether a defendant deserves to die. As they point out, this question involves subjective judgments. And such judgments are inevitably affected by experience and prejudice. It appears, therefore, that leaving the resolution of such issues to citizens acting as jurors in a racially divided and discriminatory society is a fundamental flaw in the administration of capital punishment in the United States (the subject of Chapter 8, pages 303–308).

A number of studies for the Capital Jury Project have shown that the death qualification process does not weed out all those who think that death is the *only* appropriate penalty for capital murder—and thus are not capable of considering all factors, especially those in mitigation.[111] For example, capital juries in South Carolina have been found often to contain members whose support for the death penalty undermines their impartiality and renders them legally ineligible to serve. These jurors are very influential in bringing about death penalty verdicts.[112] Capital jurors, who have survived death qualification, often are

---

[109] See Bowers, Sandys and Steiner, 'Foreclosed Impartiality . . .', n. 106 above, at pp. 1532, 1534 and 1536.

[110] *Turner v Murray, Director, Virginia Department of Corrections*, 476 U.S. 28 (1986).

[111] Theodore Eisenberg, Stephen P. Garvey and Martin T. Wells, 'The Deadly Paradox of Capital Jurors' *Southern California Law Review* 74 (2) (2001), pp. 371–397 at 382.

[112] Theodore Eisenberg, Stephen P. Garvey and Martin T. Wells, 'Forecasting Life and Death: Juror Race, Religion, and Attitude toward the Death Penalty' *Journal of Legal Studies* 30, (2001), pp. 277–311.

unwilling or unable to consider mitigation evidence.[113] So, Bentele and Bowers have argued that:[114]

In addition to being more sensitive to jurors who find death to be the only proper punishment for murder, judges and lawyers should avoid requiring jurors to commit to being able to impose the death sentence. It should be sufficient for jurors to say that they can *consider* the death penalty as one of the possible options. [This is because f]or some jurors, the statement during *voir dire* seems to operate as a presumption of death—they see their role, their duty from the start, as one of involving a willingness and ability to perform the specific task of imposing a death sentence. Perhaps even more significantly, getting an assurance from all jurors that they can vote for death provides a powerful tool for pro-death members of a jury in persuading more reluctant members...failure to agree to a death sentence was seen as tantamount to violating their oath.

Of particular concern to black defendants in American murder trials has been the prosecution's use of peremptory challenges to exclude otherwise qualified and unbiased persons from the trial jury due to their race. This was forbidden by the Supreme Court in the case of *Batson v Kentucky* in 1986,[115] which held that 'specious reasons have been upheld for striking black jurors off the list' and that a person's race is simply 'unrelated to his fitness as a juror'. In 1992 this prohibition was extended, in the case of *Georgia v McCollum,* to defence counsel's use of peremptory challenges.[116] However, it would not, of course, be irrational for defence counsel to seek to obtain a jury that he or she believes would lessen the prospect of his client's conviction, and the same might be said with even more force about a prosecutor keen to ensure conviction.

Mere exhortation did not have the effect that the Supreme Court intended. A study by David Baldus and colleagues of the use of peremptory challenges to remove jurors in murder trials in Pennsylvania between 1981 and 1997 has shown that 'discrimination in the use of peremptory challenges on the basis of race and gender by both prosecutors and defence counsel was widespread' and that the *Batson* judgment had only had a marginal effect. Such discrimination was based

---

[113] The US Supreme Court in *Morgan v Illinois*, 504 U.S. 719 (1992), had ruled that the defence had the right to determine whether any juror would automatically vote for the death penalty, thus having the prospect of eliminating those that would never consider mitigating circumstances; see Sandys and McClelland, n. 102 above, at p. 408.

[114] Ursula Bentele and William J. Bowers, 'How Jurors Decide on Death: Guilt is Overwhelming; Aggravation requires Death; and Mitigation is no Excuse' *Brooklyn Law Review* 66 (2001), pp. 1011–1080 at 1062. See also the recent case of *Jeffrey Uttecht v Cal Coburn Brown*, in which the US Supreme Court upheld the decision of the Supreme Court of Washington, which had been reversed by the US Court of Appeals for the 9th circuit. Juror Z had been excused because the judge had held that he was substantially impaired in his ability to impose the death penalty because he appeared equivocal as to whether he could impose the death penalty if life without parole was a real option. Given the fact that half the American public appears to hold a similar view (see Ch. 10), this judgment has the potential to even further narrow the pool of potentially qualified jurors: Case No. 06–413, decided 4 June 2007.

[115] *Batson v Kentucky*, 476 U.S. 79 (1986).

[116] *Georgia v McCollum*, 505 U.S. 42 (1992).

on stereotypes 'that reflect fundamental differences in how male and female, black and non-black jurors view issues of criminal responsibility, culpability and punishment'. The prosecutors rather than defence counsel were most successful in obtaining a jury of their choice, for they were 'more successful in striking life-prone black venire [i.e. summoned] members than were defense counsel in striking death-prone non-black venire members'. Baldus and his colleagues concluded, 'the upshot of the [prosecutor's] comparative advantage in its use of peremptory strikes appears to be enhanced death-sentencing rates, particularly in cases involving black defendants'. This research had uncovered 'a significant source of injustice in the peremptory strike system, at least as used in Philadelphia capital trials' that could 'be justified neither legally nor morally'.[117] Such evidence led the Special Rapporteur on Extrajudicial, Summary or Arbitrary Executions to criticize the United States in 2003 for 'racist jury selection'.[118]

The US Supreme Court now appears to agree. In June 2005, in *Miller-El v Dretke*, the Court held by 6 to 3 that Thomas Miller-El, a Texas death row inmate, was entitled to a new trial in light of strong evidence of racial bias during jury selection at his original trial. In choosing a jury to try Miller-El, a black defendant, prosecutors struck 10 of the 11 qualified black panellists. The Supreme Court said that the selection process was replete with evidence that prosecutors were selecting and rejecting potential jurors because of race. And, furthermore, that the prosecutors took their cues from a manual on jury selection with an emphasis on race. Justice Souter, writing for the majority, set out the evidence that race governed who was allowed on the jury, including: disparate questioning of white and black jurors, jury shuffling, a culture of bias within the prosecutor's office, and the fact that the prosecutor's race-neutral explanations for the strikes were so far at odds with the evidence that the explanations themselves indicated discriminatory intent.[119] Some believe that the only effective remedy would be to ban peremptory challenges entirely so as to leave supervision of jury selection to the judge. That, of course, would require an assurance that judges were also not biased against black jurors.

Worrying also is the high level of jury misunderstanding of capital sentencing law, especially the factors which could be regarded as mitigating circumstances and the way in which they should be balanced against aggravating factors, such that for 'virtually three out of four jurors . . . sentencing instructions did not guide their decision-making on punishment but served instead as an after-the-fact façade for a decision made prior to hearing the instructions'.[120] Haney found,

---

[117] David C. Baldus, *et al.*, 'The Use of Peremptory Challenges in Capital Murder Trials: A Legal and Empirical Analysis', Symposium: Race, Crime, and the Constitution, *University of Pennsylvania Journal of Constitutional Law* 3 (2001), pp. 3–170 at 124–128.

[118] UN Doc. E/CN.4/2002/74/Add. 2, para. 590, and E/CN.4/2003/3/Add. 1, para. 510.

[119] *Miller-El v Dretke*, 545 U.S. 231 (2005): see, in particular, p. 7, fn. 2, and pp. 21–32.

[120] William J. Bowers and Benjamin D. Steiner, 'Choosing Life or Death: Sentencing Dynamics in Capital Cases' in Acker, Bohm, and Lanier (eds.), n. 62 above, pp. 309–349 at 321–328. In the case of *Weeks v Angelone*, 528 U.S. 225 (2000), the US Supreme Court ruled that a judge

from his own and other studies, 'a wide-spread lack of comprehension of capital sentencing instructions that compromises the jury's ability to engage in a process of fair and reliable decision making'.[121]

Numerous studies, reviewed by the ABA, similarly found that many capital jurors in Alabama, Georgia, and Florida did not understand their role and responsibilities when deciding whether to impose a death sentence. In Alabama:[122]

Over…53% erroneously believed that the defense had to prove mitigating factors beyond a reasonable doubt, and over 55% did not understand that they could consider any factor in mitigation regardless of whether other jurors agreed. In addition, a full 40% of capital jurors interviewed did not understand that they must find that one or more statutory aggravating circumstances exist beyond a reasonable doubt, over 56% incorrectly believed that they were required to sentence the defendant to death if they found the defendant's conduct to be 'heinous, vile, or depraved' beyond a reasonable doubt, and 52% erroneously believed that if they found the defendant to be a future danger to society, they were required by law to sentence him/her to death.

And in Georgia:[123]

Forty percent… of interviewed Georgia capital jurors did not understand that they could consider any evidence in mitigation and 62.2% believed that the defense had to prove mitigating factors beyond a reasonable doubt.

The ABA reports on Florida and Tennessee came up with similar findings.[124] The Florida Supreme Court recently noted that 'Florida is now the only state in the country that allows a jury to find that aggravators exist *and* to recommend a sentence of death by a mere majority vote'.[125] Consequently, the Court called upon the Florida legislature 'to revisit Florida's death penalty statute to require some unanimity in the jury's recommendations'.[126]

---

presiding over a death penalty case was not obliged to clarify a sentencing instruction that, while constitutional, left the jury confused: on the DPIC website, <http://www.deathpenaltyinfo.org/article.php?did=1052&scid=>. Also, Stephen P Garvey, Sheri Lynn Johnson, and Paul Marcus, 'Correcting Deadly Confusion: Responding to Jury Inquiries in Capital Cases' *Cornell Law Review* 85 (2000), pp. 627–651 at 639 and 642.

   [121] Haney, n. 102 above, pp. xiv and 163–188.

   [122] ABA, *The Alabama Death Penalty Assessment Report*, June 2006, p. 5.

   [123] ABA, *The Georgia Death Penalty Assessment Report*, January 2006, pp. iii–iv.

   [124] In one study, discussed by the *Florida Report*, over 35% did not understand that they could consider any evidence in mitigation and 49% believed that the defence had to prove mitigating factors beyond a reasonable doubt: ABA, *The Florida Death Penalty Assessment Report*, January 2006, pp. vi–vii. Also, William J. Bowers and Wanda D. Foglia, 'Still Singularly Agonizing: Law's Failure to Purge Arbitrariness from Capital Sentencing' *Criminal Law Bulletin* 39 (2003), pp. 51–86. The interviews conducted in this study took place after Florida reformed its jury instructions.

   [125] *State v Steele*, 921 So. 2d 538, 548–49 (Fla. 2005).

   [126] *Ibid.*

(f) The influence of victims

Another factor which may influence the fairness and impartiality of a trial for murder is evidence presented by the murdered person's family or close relatives of the impact of the death upon them and their evaluation of the 'worth' of the life of their loved one.

Prosecutors often consult with the families of homicide victims on the decision of whether or not to seek the death penalty,[127] although evidence suggests that they choose to ignore the victims' wishes if they are not in favour of capital punishment.[128] As we have noted (see Chapter 3, page 72), in jurisdictions which operate under Islamic law the relatives of the victim of a *Qesas* crime (which includes homicide) have the right to inflict or have inflicted upon the perpetrator the same harm as the victim has suffered, which may include death. Alternatively, the relative may accept *Diya* or victim compensation or, even more preferable according to the *Qu'ran*, may forgive the transgressor, so encouraging reconciliation between the families concerned.[129] In practice, however, as Cherif Bassiouni points out, many countries, including those which have declared their constitutions to be subject to the *Shari'a* as their supreme source of law, have interpreted *Qesas* as allowing the state to prosecute and punish these crimes in lieu of any compensation and forgiveness. Hence they have avoided total forgiveness in some cases but also avoided the death penalty in other cases where the victim might have chosen it.[130]

No statistical information on the extent to which *Diya* is accepted in lieu of execution seems to be available. However, since *Diya* depends on the family being available and able and willing to pay compensation, it is not surprising to find that foreign workers are rarely protected from execution by *Diya*. It appears that one pardon is granted in relation to every six executed Saudi citizens, but only one in relation to every 84 executed foreign workers.[131] It should be noted that the UN HRC has stated, with reference to Yemen, that '[t]he preponderant role of the victim's family in whether or not the [death] penalty is carried out on the basis of financial compensation' is 'contrary to Articles 6, 14 and 26 of the International Covenant'.[132]

---

[127] S. L. Karamanian, 'Victims' Rights and the Death-Sentenced Inmate: Some Observations and Thoughts' *Saint Mary's Law Journal* 29 (1998), pp. 1025–1036.

[128] W. A. Logan, 'Declaring Life at the Crossroads of Death: Victims' Anti-Death Penalty Views and Prosecutors Charging Decisions' *Criminal Justice Ethics* 18(2) (1999), pp. 41–57; J. H. Blume, 'Ten Years of Payne: Victim Impact Evidence in Capital Cases' *Cornell Law Review* 88 (2003), pp. 257–281.

[129] M. Cherif Bassiouni, 'Death as a Penalty in the Shari'a' in P. Hodgkinson and W. Schabas (eds.), *Capital Punishment: Strategies for Abolition* (2004), pp. 169–185.

[130] *Ibid.*, p. 183.

[131] Amnesty International, *Saudi Arabia, Defying World Trends: Saudi Arabia's Extensive Use of Capital Punishment*, AI Index: MDE 23/015/2001.

[132] Concluding observations of the HRC: Yemen, UN Doc. CCPR/CO/75/YEM, 26 July 2002, para. 15.

There is no doubt that survivors of homicide victims (what we might call 'secondary victims') experience extreme grief, feelings of pain, trauma, anger, guilt, isolation, confusion, and powerlessness.[133] Their emotional and psychological stress has been compared to that of rape victims and prisoners who have been tortured,[134] and defined by many as post-traumatic stress disorder. They also often feel they have been overlooked by the criminal justice system.[135] The academic literature is replete with empirical evidence of the ways in which the criminal justice response can aggravate and prolong families' distress.[136] Numerous studies have pointed to the need for such victims to be kept informed about the progress of the case—what has been referred to as 'service needs'.[137] But some have argued that secondary victims also need and deserve a more active role in the criminal process, in particular the opportunity to tell the court directly how they were affected by the crime.

Victim impact evidence was introduced into the United States as a result of local initiatives and endorsed by the President's 1982 Task Force on Victims of Crime, which sought to allow victims greater access to and participation in criminal proceedings with the aim of restoring the perceived imbalance between the rights of victims and defendants. In particular, it recommended that federal and state legislatures require victim impact statements at sentencing, and that prosecutors consult with victims and inform the court of their wishes regarding bail, pleas, sentencing, and restitution.[138] The 1987 case of *Booth v Maryland* tested the admissibility of victim impact evidence (VIE) in a capital case but the US Supreme Court ruled that such evidence is not relevant in the unique circumstance of a capital sentencing hearing in which it is the jury's function to 'express the conscience of the community on the ultimate question of life or death'[139] and that VIE was therefore cruel and unusual under the Eighth Amendment.[140]

---

[133] For authoritative personal accounts, see Part 1 of J. R. Acker and D. R. Karp (eds.), *Wounds that do not Bind: Victim-Based Perspectives on the Death Penalty* (2006); Martie P. Thompson, 'Homicide Survivors: A summary of the research' in R. C. Davis, A.J. Lurigio, and S. Herman (eds.), *Victims of Crime* (3rd edn., 2007); P. Rock, 'Murderers, Victims and "Survivors": The Social Construction of Deviance' *British Journal of Criminology* 38 (1998), pp. 185–200.

[134] E. Schlosser, 'A grief like no other' *Atlantic Monthly* (1997), pp. 37–76.

[135] M. Vandiver, 'The Impact of the Death Penalty on the Families of Homicide Victims and of Condemned Prisoners' in Acker, Bohm, and Lanier (eds.), n. 62 above, pp. 613–645.

[136] *Ibid.*

[137] C. Hoyle and L. Zedner, 'Victims, Victimization and Criminal Justice' in M. Maguire, R. Morgan, and R. Reiner (eds.), *The Oxford Handbook of Criminology* (4th edn., 2007), pp. 461–495.

[138] P. Tobolowsky, 'Victim Participation in the Criminal Justice Process: Fifteen Years after the President's Task Force on Victims of Crime' *New England Journal on Criminal and Civil Confinement* 25 (1999), pp. 21–106.

[139] *Booth v Maryland*, 482 U.S. 496, 502 (1987) at 504.

[140] D.E. Beloof, 'Constitutional Implications of Crime Victims as Participants' *Cornell Law Review* 88 (2003), pp. 282–305.

Two years later, in the 1989 case of *South Carolina v Gathers*,[141] the Supreme Court also ruled that VIE was inadmissible but left open the possibility that it might be admissible in future cases if it related directly to the circumstances of the offence. In 1991, in *Payne v Tennessee*,[142] a newly constituted Supreme Court overruled *Booth* with respect to (1) evidence of the victim's unique personal characteristics; and (2) evidence of the crime's impact on the victim's family and community; although it left unclear the admissibility of a victim's opinion about the appropriate sentence.[143] Hence, *Payne* cleared the way for capital sentencing juries to consider 'victim impact evidence'. Justice Rehnquist's justification was that this was 'simply another form or method of informing the sentencing authority about the specific harm caused by the crime' and provides 'a quick glimpse of the life [the defendant] chose to extinguish'. After *Payne* most state and federal courts have allowed extensive VIE,[144] but no court has revisited the issue of the victim's opinion on the appropriate sentence, leaving undisturbed the earlier *Booth* holding that opinion evidence is inadmissible as a matter of Eighth Amendment law. A few states, including Oklahoma, Alabama, and Kansas, do however expressly allow victims' opinions as to the appropriate sentence for capital defendants, although most jurisdictions deem this inadmissible.[145] Prosecutors also have broad discretion over how VIE is conveyed (e.g. videos, photos, poems, etc); who is permitted to testify (e.g. family, friends, co-workers, neighbours, rescue personnel); and the number of witnesses. For example, there were 55 victim witnesses at the trial of Oklahoma City bombing conspirator Terry Nichols, 38 appeared at the trial of Timothy McVeigh,[146] and 'about 45' victims gave VIE for the prosecution, with several giving impact statements against the death penalty, when Zacharias Moussaui, the 'twin towers' conspirator was tried in Virginia. These 45 represented less than 2 per cent of the nearly 3,000 people who died on September 11. In this high profile case the former New York City Mayor, Rudolph Giuliani, was the first to give a victim impact statement.[147] It is thus being used to provide far more than a mere 'quick glimpse' of victims and the loss resulting from a murder, as authorized by *Payne*: 'Jurors now regularly receive highly emotional, gripping evidence, with precious little in the way of substantive

---

[141] *South Carolina v Gathers*, 490 U.S. 805 (1989) at 810.

[142] 501 U.S. 808, 827 (1991).

[143] The *Payne* court expressly avoided re-examination of its earlier (*Booth*) bar on opinion evidence because, according to the Court, no evidence of the sort was presented in *Payne's* sentencing: W. A. Logan, 'Victims, Survivors and the Decisions to Seek and Impose Death' in J. R. Acker and D. R. Karp (eds.), '*Wounds That Do not Bind: Victim-Based Perspectives on the Death Penalty*' (2006), pp. 161–178.

[144] J. Blume, 'Ten Years of Payne: Victim Impact Evidence in Capital Cases' *Cornell Law Review* 88 (2003), pp. 257–281.

[145] D. E. Beloof, 'Constitutional Implications of Crime Victims as Participants', n. 140 above, pp. 282–305.

[146] Logan, n. 143 above, pp. 161–178; Blume, n. 128 above, pp. 257–281.

[147] CNN.com, 'Giving victims a voice in court' 15 May 2006: <http://www.sentencing.nj.gov/downloads/pdf/articles/2006/May2006/story13.pdf>.

limits and procedural controls, or guidance on how the potent evidence should influence their death decisions'.[148] Such highly wrought sentiments often leave no doubt as to what the victims believe to be the appropriate sentence.[149]

Victim impact evidence has proven to be politically popular. Many victims' rights groups and prosecutors argue that it promotes more informed and proportionate sentencing decisions and assists the sentencing goals of rehabilitation, by confronting the offender with the reality of the impact of his crime, and of retribution, by identifying the degree of harm done.[150] However, their main focus in homicide cases has been on the potential therapeutic effect on secondary victims.[151] Yet the evidence that making an impact statement reduces this secondary victimization, and reduces significantly the distress experienced by victims, is tenuous to say the least. Furthermore, empirical evidence as to whether VIE has the effect of increasing victim satisfaction more generally is also inconclusive. The provision of victim input has not been found to result in any significant increase in victims' satisfaction with the specific sentence imposed or with the criminal justice system generally.[152] In some cases it appears that giving evidence increases the satisfaction of victims whilst in others it decreases satisfaction.[153]

Whatever the claims may be of the satisfaction given to the relatives of homicide victims, the issue in so far as the UN Safeguards are concerned is whether such evidence prejudices the possibility of a fair trial and a fair consideration at the sentencing stage of all factors that might be weighed in mitigation of a possible death sentence.[154] Austin Sarat has argued that such statements legitimize vengeance: '*Payne* brought revenge out of the shadows and accorded it an honored place in the jurisprudence of capital punishment...'.[155]

Susan Bandes, one of the most ardent critics of VIE, argues that it interferes with the jury's ability to discharge its duty.[156] It deflects a jury already sympathetic towards the prosecution from its task of focusing on the defendant as an

---

[148] Logan, n. 143 above, at p. 8.

[149] J. L. Hoffmann, 'Revenge or Mercy? Some Thoughts About Survivor Opinion Evidence in Death Penalty Cases' *Cornell Law Review* 88(2) (2003), pp. 530–542.

[150] P. G. Cassell, 'Barbarians at the Gates? A Reply to the Critics of the Victims' Rights Amendment' *Utah Law Review* 2 (1999), pp. 479–544; E. Erez and L. Rogers, 'Victim Impact Statements and Sentencing Outcomes and Processes: The Perspectives of Legal Professionals' *British Journal of Criminology* 39 (1999), pp. 216–239; Tobolowsky, n. 138 above, pp. 21–106.

[151] R. P. Mosteller, 'Victim Impact Evidence: Hard to Find the Real Rules' *Cornell Law Review* 88 (2003), pp. 543–554; Cassell, n. 150 above; D. E. Beloof, *Victims in Criminal Procedure* (1999).

[152] Tobolowsky, n. 138 above.

[153] E. Erez, 'Victim Participation in Sentencing: And the Debate Goes On...' *International Review of Victimology* (3) (1994), pp. 17–32; see E. Erez and J. Roberts, 'Victim Participation in the Criminal Justice System', in R. C. Davis, A. J. Lurigio, and S. Herman (eds.), *Victims of Crime* (3rd edn., 2007), pp. 277–298.

[154] Mosteller, n. 151 above, pp. 543–554.

[155] A. Sarat, *When the State Kills: Capital Punishment and the American Condition* (2001), p. 45.

[156] S. Bandes, 'Empathy, Narrative, and Victim Impact Statements' *University of Chicago Law Review* 63 (1996), pp. 361–412.

individual. And it exacerbates existing inequalities in the jury's attitude towards the prosecution and the defendant. Certainly, some studies, using controlled experimental simulations, suggest that VIE which communicates greater harm to the 'survivors' increases the chance that the jury will impose a death sentence.[157] More controversially, research indicates that VIE encourages irrelevant or invidious distinctions about the comparative worth of different victims, based on the social position, articulateness, and race of the victims and their families, and that defendants in cases where victims are perceived by juries as 'worthy' are more likely to receive death sentences.[158] Burr maintains that:[159]

Victim impact evidence is lethal for capital defendants and often illusory for the witnesses who provide it...At best, victim impact testimony provides a momentary opportunity for survivors to give voice to their loss, be heard, and feel less isolated. At worst, victim impact testimony exploits the immense pain suffered by survivors—using the emotional reaction to their circumstances as a lever to produce a death sentence, while leaving them as onlookers in a criminal justice process whose focus is punishing the offender, not meeting the needs of survivors.

Thus, while VIE may provide some benefit to the victim, the accompanying risk of prejudicing the case against the defendant is likely almost always to outweigh such a benefit.[160]

(g) Special courts: independent and impartial tribunals?

Article 14 (1) of the Covenant provides for the right to equality before the courts and the right to a fair and public hearing by a competent, independent, and impartial tribunal established by law. It is difficult to assess the extent to which different jurisdictions guarantee this right when there is more than one type of court, just as it is difficult to compare the status of the courts in different countries that are empowered to impose the death sentence in the first instance. In most jurisdictions, only the highest level of criminal court or the Supreme Court has the power to impose a death sentence. But in several countries they are

[157] J. Luginbuhl and M. Burkhead, 'Victim Impact Evidence in a Capital Trial: Encouraging Votes for Death' *American Journal of Criminal Justice* 20 (1995), pp. 1–16; E. Greene, H. Koehring, *et al.*, 'Victim Impact Evidence in Capital Cases: Does the Victim's Character Matter?' *Journal of Applied Social Psychology* 28(2) (1998), pp. 145–156; B. Myers, and J. Arbuthnot, 'The Effects of Victim Impact Evidence on the Verdicts and Sentencing Judgments of Mock Jurors' *Journal of Offender Rehabilitation* 29(3/4) (1999), pp. 95–112; J. Nadler and M. R. Rose, 'Victim Impact Testimony and the Psychology of Punishment' *Cornell Law Review* 88(2) (2003), pp. 419–456.

[158] S. E. Sundby, 'The Capital Jury and Empathy: The Problem of Worthy and Unworthy Victims' *Cornell Law Review* 88 (2003), pp. 343–381.

[159] R. Burr, 'Litigating with Victim Impact Testimony: The Serendipity That Has Come from *Payne v Tennessee*' *Cornell Law Review* 88 (2003), pp. 517–529 at 517.

[160] Pioneering work by defense-based victim outreach seems to provide at least some of the benefits, but with reduced risks for due process: see Tammy Krause, 'Reaching Out to the Other Side: Defense-Based Victim Outreach in Capital Cases' in J. R. Acker and D.R. Karp (eds.), *Wounds That Do Not Bind: Victim Perspectives on the Death Penalty* (2006), pp. 379–396.

described vaguely as 'Court of Justice', 'Divisional', 'Regional', 'District', or even 'Competent' courts.

At various times in recent years—in Algeria, Bangladesh, Burundi, Democratic Republic of the Congo, Egypt, India, Indonesia, Iraq, Jordan, Palestine Authority, Sierra Leone, and Uganda for example—trials which resulted in the death penalty were held before military tribunals which afforded lesser rights than civilian courts.[161] There has been concern too about the powers given to Islamic courts to impose death sentences under a kind of summary jurisdiction, as in Chechnya, Afghanistan, and in northern Nigeria, where many of the judges are said to be virtually untrained in law.[162] In Somalia local 'clan' courts have sentenced people to death.[163] Amnesty International reported that in 2005 in Pakistan 'two men were executed by firing squad immediately after a tribal council—which has no powers to adjudicate criminal cases—convicted them of murder'.[164] From Iran, also, there have been reports of summary trials for drug offenders before Revolutionary Courts, with no defence counsel or right of appeal, even though these courts can impose the death sentence. In Jordan the exceptional State Security Court (SSC) has been responsible for issuing the majority of death sentences in recent years. Although its rulings are subject to review by the Court of Cassation, the SSC includes military judges and is presided over by an army officer. Furthermore, SSC judges are appointed by an executive order of the Prime Minister, which presents a clear violation of the principles of judicial independence and the separation of powers. Given this structural framework it should not be surprising that the SSC is notorious for its failure to investigate torture allegations and for admitting 'confessions' extracted by torture.[165]

The Special Rapporteur on Extrajudicial, Summary or Arbitrary Executions reported in 2004 that Emergency or Special Courts, staffed by one civilian and

---

[161] For Algeria, UN Doc. E/CN.4/1995/61, paras. 45–48; for the Democratic Republic of Congo, E/CN.4/1999/39/Add. 1, para. 66; for Burundi, Amnesty International, *Report 2001*, p. 61; for Egypt, E/CN.4/1995/61, paras. 119 and 126 (also, see Official Records of the General Assembly, 58th Session, Supp. No. 40, Vol. I (A/58/40), para. 77 and E/CN.4/1998/68/Add. 1, paras. 146–153); for Iraq, Report of the HRC, A/53/40, Vol. 1 (1998), p. 30; for Kuwait, E/CN.4/1995/61, paras. 202–205 (also E/CN.4/1996/4/Corr.1, para. 288); for Nigeria, E/CN.4/1996/4/Corr. 1, paras. 338–353 (also Report of the HRC, A/51/40, Vol. 1 (1997), para. 42); for Pakistan, Special Rapporteur's Report, E/CN.4/1998/68/Add. 1, para. 303; for Palestine, E/CN.4/2001/9/Add. 1, para. 436 (in June 2005 President Mahmoud Abbbas of the Palestinian Authority ordered the retrial of all who had been sentenced to death by the State Security Court); and for Sierra Leone, E/CN.4/1999/39/Add. 1, para. 216 and *Mansaraj et al v Sierra Leone* (Communication Nos. 839/1998, 840/1998 and 841/1998, views adopted 16 July 2001).

[162] Report of the Special Rapporteur on Extrajudicial, Summary or Arbitrary Executions, E/CN.4/1998/68, para. 85. Also, in the *Shari'a* Courts in northern Nigeria: Amnesty International, *BAOBAB for Women's Human Rights and Amnesty International Joint Statement on the Implementation of New Sharia-Based Penal Codes in northern Nigeria*, AI Index: AFR 44/008/2002.

[163] Amnesty International, *Report 2005*, p. 228.

[164] Amnesty International, *Report 2006*, p. 203.

[165] FIDH, *Abolition of the Death Penalty for Some Crimes Symbolic at Best*, 16 August 2006. Abolition of the SSC was recommended by the UN Committee Against Torture in 1995.

two military judges with no lawyers present, were established in Darfur, Sudan in 2001, dealing with offences of armed robbery, crimes against the state, murder and crimes related to drugs and public nuisance. At least one man was hanged after conviction and more than 30 people were under sentence of death. These courts were not abolished until March 2003.[166] In Bangladesh Speedy Trial Tribunals had sentenced 311 people to death between their formation in October 2002 and July 2005. And, according to Amnesty International, in 2004 a military commander was executed in Afghanistan after being sentenced to death for multiple murders by a special court, not open to the public, which denied him legal counsel and the right to cross-examine witnesses, and which failed to investigate his claim that he had been tortured.[167] In 2002 the HRC found, in *Kurbanov v Tajikistan*, that a death sentence pronounced by the Military Chamber of the Supreme Court violated Article 14, paragraph 1, as there was no valid reason for bringing a civilian before a military court (hence the tribunal was incompetent).[168] In the same year a military court in Uganda sentenced two soldiers to death for murder after a peremptory court martial lasting only two hours and thirty-six minutes. They were publicly executed by firing squad four days later, leading Amnesty International to condemn the proceedings for their lack of fair procedures and independence. There have, for some time, been concerns about 'the impartiality and independence of the Military Appeals Bureau in Egypt' and 'the lack of the effectiveness of this review procedure'.[169] Similar concerns have been expressed that military tribunals in the Democratic Republic of Congo have sentenced many to death without proper due process.

Following the attack on the United States on 11 September 2001, President George W. Bush decided to authorize by Executive Order on 13 November 2001 the establishment of Military Tribunals, sitting either inside or outside the United States, to try non-US citizens accused of terrorism, with the power to impose the death penalty.[170] There has been widespread concern that the tribunals might not meet the standards required for a fair trial, in particular that there would be no appeal of a death sentence to a civilian court of appeal independent of the executive branch of the government, because the Order limited appellate review to a specially created three-member panel appointed by the Secretary of Defense.[171] At its detention camp at Guantanamo Bay, Cuba, where there are just over 300 detainees from about forty countries, the United States is planning to conduct an unknown number of capital trials of alleged terrorists captured since 2002,

---

[166] UN Doc. E/CN.4/2005/7/Add. 2, para. 53, 6 August 2004.

[167] Amnesty International, *Report 2005*, pp. 36–37.

[168] No. 1096/2002, *Kurbanov v Tajikistan*, 59/40; Vol. 1, Annex IX, s. GG, para. 7.6.

[169] UN Doc. E/CN.4/1994/7, paras. 255–256.

[170] *Associated Press*, 26 November 2001.

[171] Military Commission Order No. 1, 'Procedures for trials by military commissions of certain non-United States citizens in the war against terrorism', 21 March 2002. See OSCE, *The Death Penalty in the OSCE Area, Background Paper*, 2004/1, p. 43.

although as of early November 2007, no one had gone to trial and only one man has pleaded guilty.[172]

The first set of rules of evidence and procedure for these commissions was struck down by the US Supreme Court in June 2006, and while the current regulations, contained in the Military Commissions Act signed into law on 17 October 2006, are not quite as onerous for defendants, they nevertheless make big inroads into normal due process protections. For example, the commissions will be able to consider evidence derived from physically and psychologically coercive interrogations, a more permissive use of hearsay evidence than would be allowed in the US federal courts and courts-martial, and testimony from secret sources which will not be subject to cross-examination.[173]

The failure to provide, in a timely fashion, competent legal representation constitutes one of the worst violations of the detainees' rights. Furthermore, the right to trial within a reasonable time, guaranteed in the US federal courts and courts-martial, is denied to 'unlawful enemy combatants'. These defendants do not have the right to an independent and impartial tribunal, which is essential to a fair trial, in part because there is no civilian component to the military commissions. The Act also provides for only a limited right of appeal, with respect to matters of law and not fact. Furthermore, only non-US nationals will be tried by the military commission; Americans accused of war crimes or terrorism-related offences will continue to be tried through the civilian courts or courts-martial. This is clearly discriminatory and in violation of international law. Finally, although the Act purports to adhere to the principle of 'innocent until proven guilty', this principle has been 'systematically undermined by persistent official commentary on their presumed guilt, including by the President', who would be the final authority to exercise clemency were anyone to be sentenced to death.[174]

3. The Right to Appeal

Article 14(5) of the ICCPR states: 'Everyone convicted of a crime shall have the right to his conviction and sentence being reviewed by a higher tribunal according to law'.[175] UN Safeguard No. 6, as amended in 1989, states that 'Anyone sentenced to death shall have the right to appeal to a court of higher jurisdiction, and steps should be taken to ensure that such appeals shall become mandatory'.

---

[172] An Australian pleaded guilty to material support of terrorism and was sentenced to nine months of confinement in his home country: *The New York Times*, 10 November 2007. See also, Amnesty International, *United States of America—Justice delayed and justice denied?: Trials under the Military Commissions Act*, AMR 51/044/2007, March 2007, p. 1.

[173] Clive Stafford Smith, *Bad Men: Guantanamo Bay and The Secret Prisons* (2007).

[174] Amnesty International, n. 172 above, p. 12.

[175] For an overview of the international safeguards pertaining to the right to appeal, see Amnesty International, *International Standards on the death penalty*, January 2006, AI Index: ACT 50/001/2006.

These mandatory provisions for appeal go beyond the 'right [of the convicted person] to his conviction and sentence being reviewed by a higher tribunal', set out in Article 14 (5) of the ICCPR. Furthermore, in resolution 2005/59, adopted in April 2005, the UN Commission on Human Rights urged all states that still maintain the death penalty '[t]o ensure that all legal proceedings, including those before special tribunals or jurisdictions, and particularly those related to capital offences, conform to the minimum procedural guarantees contained in Article 14 of the International Covenant on Civil and Political Rights'. The UN HRC has stated that the imposition of death sentences without the possibility of appeal is incompatible with the ICCPR.[176]

In most countries it is mandatory for death sentences to be automatically reviewed by a court of appeal on questions of law, procedure, fact, and severity of penalty. However, there is no right of appeal from the Revolutionary Courts in Iran, or Libya, or from courts dealing with exceptional cases in Jordan; nor is it automatic for appeals to be allowed by the Military Chamber of the Supreme Court in Tajikistan, and then only relating to questions of law.[177] In Egypt no appeal is allowed against sentences passed by the Emergency Supreme State Security Courts,[178] or from the criminal courts as such, except on consideration on points of law, not facts, by the Court of Cassation. But before pronouncing a death sentence the trial court has to submit case documents to the Mufti, the highest religious authority in the country, for his opinion. If he does not respond, in favour or against the death penalty, within ten days, the court is empowered to pronounce sentence of death. There is not a proper appeal process in Chad and in Oman there is no provision at all for appeal in cases of premeditated murder.[179] In both Lebanon and Togo an automatic right of appeal is provided on grounds of law and procedure only.

Appellate review is not automatic or mandatory in the following retentionist countries, where defendants have to exercise their right to initiate the process: Barbados, Belarus, Burundi, Guinea, Jamaica, Japan, Morocco,[180] Singapore, South Korea, Sri Lanka (although in that country the prison authorities are obliged by law to assist all prisoners to lodge an appeal against their sentence), Tonga, Trinidad and Tobago, and Zambia. The response from the Japanese

---

[176] HRC, Uganda, UN Doc. CCPR/CO/80/UGA, 4 May 2004, para. 13.

[177] HRC 59/40 (1), p. 116, Case 964/2001, *Saidov v Tajikistan*, Annex IX, s. V, para. 6.5. See also views of the HRC in *Maryam Khalilova v Tajikistan*, Communication No. 973/2001, UN Doc. CCPR/C/83/D/978/2001, 13 April 2005, paras. 7.5, 7.6.

[178] Carsten Jürgensen, '*Egypt: Death Penalty After Unfair Trials*', paper presented to the First World Congress against the Death Penalty, Strasbourg, 21–23 June 2001.

[179] UN Doc. E/CN.4/2001/9/Add. 1, para. 323; 'Civil and Political Rights Including the Questions of Disappearances and Summary Executions', Report of the Special Rapporteur 2001, Addendum E/CN.4/2001/9/Add. 1, para. 323.

[180] Official Records of the General Assembly, 55th session, Supp. No. 40, I (A/55/40), para. 110.

Federation of Bar Associations (JFBA) to the UN Seventh Survey in 2004 stated that:[181]

There is no official procedure to review the sentence. A death row prisoner can request a retrial, but in the course of this procedure the Court examines only if there is new and obvious evidence, which proves the applicant's innocence, or that the crime he/she committed deserves a lighter sentence…After the conviction of the death sentence, there is a possibility of execution even if the prisoner is requesting a retrial…In Japan even ongoing retrial procedure can be neglected for the execution.

The Japanese process is notoriously slow, and retrials are a rarity. There are inmates who have been on death row for decades, pleading their innocence and demanding retrials. Over the past 30 years, only four have been granted a retrial and subsequently acquitted. Masaru Okunishi, who is now 80 years old, and has been on death row since 1972, was set to be the fifth to go free when the Nagoya High Court granted him a retrial in April 2005. However, the court revoked its decision in December 2006.[182]

Until July 2006 the Supreme People's Court of China had delegated to the provincial High Courts its mandatory responsibility (under the Criminal Law of 1997) to verify and approve all death sentences, which was unsatisfactory given that the High Court was also the court of appeal (known in China as the 'trial of second instance') from sentences imposed by the Intermediate People's Courts. In effect, these High Courts were reviewing cases on the papers only, and approving their own decisions. Executions had usually been carried out speedily after final approval of the sentence.[183] In view of this, the acknowledged wide variations in the use of the death penalty, and the desire to reduce recourse to the supreme punishment, the trials of second instance in the High Courts will now be made open and the Supreme Court has taken back and exercised the power to review sentences at the end of this process, as from 1 January 2007, so as to ensure more uniformity and greater parsimony in the infliction of death sentences (see Chapter 3).[184]

Appellate review of the death penalty is automatic in all of the retentionist American states, as well as under federal law, and all but a few have statutes or rules of procedure that require a 'comparative proportionality review' of the sentence. It is not, however, a constitutional requirement',[185] and in some states

---

[181] UN Doc. E/2005/3, para. 104.

[182] *Japan Times*, 27 February 2007.

[183] Amnesty International, 'Killing Chickens to Scare Monkeys', paper presented to *First World Congress against the Death Penalty* (Strasbourg, June 2001).

[184] Amnesty International, *Executed 'according to law'?: the death penalty in China*, AI Index: ASA 17/003/2004.

[185] Richard van Duizend, 'Comparative Proportionality Review in Death Sentence Cases' *State Court Journal* 8(3) (Summer 1984), pp. 9–13 and 21–23.

(for example, Missouri and New Jersey) proportionality review is very limited. Those who have studied this approach have asserted that:[186]

The Court has not elected to use its available resources for a meaningful proportionality review process. Proportionality review as applied in this jurisdiction does little more than allow the reviewing court to justify a death sentence. [see Chapter 8, pages 308–310]

In 1996 the Economic and Social Council called upon member states in which the death penalty may be carried out:[187]

to allow adequate time for the preparation of appeals to a court of higher jurisdiction and for the completion of appeal proceedings, as well as petitions for clemency, in order to effectively apply rules 5 and 8 of the safeguards guaranteeing protection of the rights of those facing the death penalty.

The UN Special Rapporteur on Extrajudicial, Summary or Arbitrary Executions has recommended 'that States establish in their internal legislation a period of at least six months before a death sentence imposed by a court of first instance can be carried out, so as to allow adequate time for the preparation of appeals to a court of higher jurisdiction and petitions for clemency.'[188] The Special Rapporteur has also stated that 'Such a measure would prevent hasty executions while affording defendants the opportunity to exercise all their rights'.[189]

Most retentionist jurisdictions provide a mandatory waiting period between the time that a person is sentenced to death and the time allowed to lodge and prepare the case for appeal, with legal assistance provided. But the time allowed varies considerably. Some countries, such as Chad, Madagascar, and Mali, allow only three days to lodge an appeal; Bangladesh and Belarus only a week; Guatemala, Japan, Morocco, Sri Lanka, and Tunisia, two weeks or less. Only Bahrain, Burundi, Iran, Jamaica, Lesotho, Libya, Rwanda, Syria, Thailand, and Tonga allow thirty days or more. In its communication to the Commission on Human Rights in December 1998 the Government of Iran stated that anyone sentenced to death has the right to appeal to a court of higher jurisdiction including the Supreme Court, but that the sentence would be carried out: (a) if no protest or appeal has been made within the legal time limit of thirty days; (b) if the verdict is confirmed by the Supreme Court; or (c) where the request for appeal has been rejected or the appeal has been rejected in a final judgment.[190]

---

[186] Donald H. Wallace and Jonathon R. Sorensen, 'Missouri Proportionality Review: An Assessment of a State Supreme Court's Procedures in Capital Cases' *Notre Dame Journal of Law, Ethics and Public Policy* 8 (1994), pp. 281–315 at 313.

[187] Economic and Social Council Resolution 1996/15, reproduced in App. 3 below, page 418.

[188] Report of the Special Rapporteur on Extrajudicial, Summary or Arbitrary Executions: E/CN.4/1996/4, 25 January 1996, para. 556.

[189] Report of the Special Rapporteur on Extrajudicial, Summary or Arbitrary Executions: E/CN.4/1998/68, 23 December 1997, para. 118.

[190] Status of the International Covenants on Human Rights, Question of the Death Penalty, Report of the Secretary-General submitted pursuant to Commission Resolution 1998/8, Commission on Human Rights 55th Session, E/CN.4/1999/52/Add. 1.

In Texas a defendant has only thirty days after his conviction to present new evidence. Sixteen other American states require a new trial motion based on new evidence to be filed within sixty days of judgment. Eighteen US jurisdictions have time limits between one and three years, and only nine states have no time limits.[191] Thus, in general, the time allowed to lodge an appeal is short and in some countries very short indeed, especially when one recognizes that a successful appeal may have to rest upon the protracted process of uncovering new evidence. Furthermore, despite the existence of formal appeal procedures, it is apparent that in some countries persons have been executed within days of their conviction.

Safeguard 8 of the 'Safeguards Guaranteeing Protection of the Rights of Those Facing the Death Penalty', adopted by the UN Economic and Social Council in 1984, states: 'Capital punishment shall not be carried out pending any appeal or other recourse procedure or other proceeding relating to pardon or commutation of the sentence'. This position was further enforced by the UN Commission on Human Rights in resolution 2005/59, adopted on 20 April 2005, which urged all states that still maintain the death penalty 'not to execute any person as long as any related legal procedure, at the international or at the national level, is pending'. The UN HRC has made clear, in various cases, that the execution of a prisoner when the sentence was still under challenge in the courts of a state party to the ICCPR constitutes a violation of Article 6(1) and 6(2) of that Covenant.[192] The UN HRC requests interim measures of protection to stay executions pending their consideration of appeals. It has made clear, in such cases, that the execution of prisoners under consideration constitutes a grave breach of the state party's obligations under the ICCPR and the first Optional Protocol to the Covenant.[193]

Whilst no countries have admitted in recent years that they would allow anyone to be executed while an appeal was pending, early in 2000 a 14-year-old soldier was executed, alongside four other soldiers, in the Democratic Republic of the Congo within thirty minutes of being found guilty by a Military Court: with no time to lodge an appeal, let alone for consideration of clemency.[194] According to Amnesty International, executions in China used to occur within weeks of the

---

[191] See Amnesty International, *Fatal Flaws: Innocence and the Death Penalty in the USA* (1998), pp. 15–16. Also, for an argument advocating the repeal of all time limits, Vivian Berger, '*Herrera v Collins*: The Gateway of Innocence for Death-Sentenced Prisoners Leads Nowhere' *William and Mary Law Review* 35 (1994), pp. 943–1023.

[192] *Ashby v Trinidad and Tobago*, Views of the HRC, Communication No. 580/1994, UN Doc. CCPR/C/74/D/580/1994, para. 10.8.

[193] Concluding observations of the HRC: Uzbekistan, UN Doc. CCPR/CO/83/UZB, 26 April 2005, para. 6; Concluding observations of the HRC: Tajikistan, UN Doc. CCPR/CO/84/TJK, 18 July 2005, para. 8.

[194] Amnesty International, *The Death Penalty Worldwide: Developments in 2000*, AI Index: ACT 50/001/2001, p. 21.

alleged crime being prosecuted and 'within hours of final approval'.[195] Indeed, the executions usually take place the day after the mandatory one-month appeal period has expired. However, a more recent study relating to defence in death penalty cases concluded that there is 'a time-line of between 12 and 15 months from detention/arrest to execution'. And the data provided suggests that after the end of the trial of second instance (appeal) the execution occurs within two to three months.[196] Despite the fact that the review process has been returned to the Supreme People's Court, Zheng Xiaoyu, the disgraced former Head of the State Food and Drug Administration, was sentenced to death on 29 May 2007 and executed less than two months later, on 10 July.

Another procedural aspect that gives cause for concern is the time taken for appeals to be decided. As Amnesty International points out:[197]

Too short a time will not allow for an adequate appeals process or for further evidence of the possible innocence of the person to emerge. However prolonged periods on death row . . . leave the individual facing the constant strain of living with the fear of execution, almost always in harsh prison conditions.

In Jamaica the inordinately long time (in one case as long as seven years) that the Appeal Court had taken to deliver a written judgment was, as noted above, found by the UN HRC in *Pratt v Jamaica* (1989) to be a violation of due process and also cruel and unusual punishment.[198] In some other countries, such as America, Indonesia, Japan, and Pakistan, prisoners have also had to wait many years to learn of the outcome of their appeals.[199] Since 2000, 11 prisoners in Japan have been executed. In their cases the appeal process took between 10 to 16 years. Even when the appeal process is finalized, a prisoner can wait for years or even decades before being executed.[200]

In the United States the system of state and federal appeals almost inevitably allows many years to pass—often spent on a separate death row (as discussed in Chapter 5) before execution. In 1989 the Supreme Court ruled in *Teague v Lane*

---

[195] Amnesty International, *People's Republic of China: The Death Penalty: Killing Chickens to Scare Monkeys*, paper presented to the First World Congress against the Death Penalty, Strasbourg, 21–23 June 2001. A report, '10,000 Held in Strike Hard Drive', in the *South China Morning Post* (7 May 2001), noted that the *Lanzhou Morning Post* (Gansu province), announcing death sentences on eight persons convicted of violent crime and gang activities, had stated: 'The death sentences were expected to be carried out after appeals in 10 days'.

[196] Albrecht *et al.*, n. 9 above, pp. 105–109.

[197] Amnesty International, *'Will this day be my last?': The death penalty in Japan* (July 2006), AI Index: ASA 22/006/2006, p. 8.

[198] R. M. B. Antoine, 'The Judicial Committee of the Privy Council—An Inadequate Remedy for Death Row Prisoners' *International and Comparative Law Quarterly* 41 (1992), pp. 179–190 at 180; and William A. Schabas, 'Execution Delayed, Execution Denied' *Criminal Law Forum* 5 (1994), pp. 180–193 at 181–182, citing *Pratt v Jamaica*, Report of the HRC, UN, GAOR, 44th Session, Supp. No. 40 at 222, UN Doc. A/44/40 (1989).

[199] Amnesty International, *Indonesia: The Application of the Death Penalty* (November 1987), AI Index: ASA 21/27/87, p. 5. Amnesty International, n. 197 above.

[200] Amnesty International, n. 197 above.

that (with two narrow exceptions) federal *habeas corpus* petitioners would not be allowed to benefit from any new rules pertaining to the application of the death penalty unless they had been introduced prior to the defendant's conviction becoming final. In other words, new rules could no longer be retroactively applied to benefit prisoners on death row.[201] Two years later the Court in *McCleskey v Zant* held that federal courts would not henceforth entertain repetitive requests for writs of *habeas corpus*. Prisoners would be obliged to set forth all their legal arguments the first time round or show good cause why an argument had not been filed earlier. Furthermore, the Supreme Court required federal courts to reject all claims if the proper procedures had not been followed by the defendant in state courts.[202] An example was Roger Coleman, who filed in error (his attorney's error) his appeal in Virginia three days late. A federal court (*Coleman v Thompson,* 1991) decided that Coleman had thereby procedurally defaulted and refused to hear his constitutional claim—a decision affirmed by the US Supreme Court—before he was executed.[203]

The Anti-Terrorism and Effective Death Penalty Act of 1996 (AEDPA) responded to a perception that the statutory writ of *habeas corpus* was being abused by lawyers for death row prisoners by streamlining capital *habeas* and laying down specific time limits within which appeals in the United States had to be made: a one-year limit to apply for a writ of *habeas corpus* at a state court (section 101) and other time limits for courts to act on petitions. As a counter-balance it also imposed on states an obligation to provide mechanisms for appointing, compensating, and reimbursing competent state-appointed counsel to represent indigent defendants in their post-conviction proceedings, if their sentence has been upheld on direct appeal. If states wanted to benefit from the restrictions on the availability of *habeas*, they had to opt in to these new obligations. As Mello and Perkins put it: 'Texas gets to kill them faster, but only be giving them lawyers first'.[204]

The AEDPA was criticized in 1998 by the UN Special Rapporteur, who expressed concern that the Act, by severely limiting the ability of the federal courts to remedy errors and abuses in state proceedings, had 'further jeopardized

---

[201] Steven M. Goldstein, 'Chipping away at the Great Writ: Will Death Sentenced Federal Habeas Corpus Petitioners be Able to Seek and Utilize Changes in the Law?' *New York University Review of Law and Social Change* 18 (1990–91), pp. 357–414. Also, James S. Liebman, 'More than "Slightly Retro": The Rehnquist Court's Rout of Habeas Corpus Jurisdiction in *Teague v Lane*', *ibid.*, pp. 537–635; Richard Faust, Tina J. Rubinstein, and Larry W. Yackle, 'The Great Writ in Action: Empirical Light on the Federal Habeas Corpus Debate', *ibid.*, pp. 637–710.

[202] *McCleskey v Zant*, 499 U.S. 467 (1991).

[203] Amnesty International, *Fatal Flaws, Innocence and the Death Penalty in the USA*, p. 7. Also, Richard J. Bonnie, 'Preserving Justice in Capital Cases while Streamlining the Process of Collateral Review' *University of Toledo Law Review* 23 (1991), pp. 99–116. DNA evidence allowed by the outgoing Governor of Virginia showed that Coleman had been guilty, although this does not in any way render less abhorrent the procedural injustice.

[204] M. Mello and P. J. Perkins, 'Closing the Circle: The illusion of lawyers for people litigating for their lives at the fin de siècle' in Acker, Bohm, and Lanier (eds.), n. 62 above, pp. 347–384 at 381.

the implementation of the right to a fair trial as provided for in the ICCPR and other international instruments'.[205] Andrew Cantu was executed in 1999, after failing to obtain a further review of his case because he had not complied with the required one-year deadline for filing it.[206] Eric Freeman thought that the Supreme Court—regardless of what Congress may or may not have desired— would be unwilling 'to read AEDPA as imposing any significant additional limitations. Hence, it has consistently rejected restrictive readings proposed by the government'.[207] However, according to a forthcoming book by Eric Freedman and David Dow, the AEDPA has in fact led to a much lower percentage of successful *habeas corpus* petitions to federal courts: only 12 per cent in the years 2000 to 2006 compared with about 40 per cent before the passing of the Act.[208] Although there has been support in some quarters for attempts to speed up the appeals process even further,[209] as was proposed in the reauthorized Patriot Act in 2006, there is widespread concern among civil rights lawyers about how much further the courts can go in this direction without, as Franklin Zimring put it, 're-imagining fundamental principles of fairness and criminal justice'.[210]

4. The Right to Seek a Pardon, Clemency, or Commutation of Sentence

Article 6(4) of the ICCPR and UN Safeguard No. 7 both stipulate, in almost identical wording, that 'Anyone sentenced to death shall have the right to seek pardon, or commutation of sentence. Amnesty, pardon or commutation of the

---

[205] Amnesty International, *United States of America: Failing the Future—Death Penalty Developments, March 1998–March 2000*, AI Index: AMR 51/03/00, p. 30. Also, Larry W. Yackle, 'The American Bar Association and Federal Habeas Corpus' *Law and Contemporary Problems* 61 (1998), pp. 171–192.

[206] *Cantu-Tzin v Johnson*, (1998) 162 F.3d 295 (United States Court of Appeals for the 5th Cir). In 1999 the Mississippi legislature amended the code of criminal procedure, setting a time limit of one year within which a defendant must apply for post-conviction relief: see US Department of Justice, *Capital Punishment 2000* (2001), p. 3.

[207] Eric. M. Freedman, 'Federal Habeas Corpus in Capital Cases', in Acker, Bohm, and Lanier (eds.), n. 62 above, pp. 553–571 at 569.

[208] Cited on the Standdown Texas Project website: <http://standdown.typepad.com/weblog/federal_legislation/index.html>.

[209] B. Latzer and J. N. G. Cauthen, *Justice Delayed? Time Consumption in Capital Appeals: A Multistate Study* (May 2007), p. 18. They argue: 'Overall, the protracted capital appeals process presents several serious and costly problems for the administration of justice in the United States...we believe that those sentenced to death can be afforded the extraordinary review to which they are entitled in a much more efficient manner. As this study shows, some states have established more efficient appellate procedures while still maintaining guarantees of fairness and "super due process"'.

[210] Franklin E. Zimring, 'The Executioner's Dissonant Song: On Capital Punishment and American Legal Values' in Austin Sarat (ed.), *The Killing State: Capital Punishment in Law, Politics and Culture* (1999), pp. 137–147.

sentence of death may be granted in all cases of capital punishment'.[211] The Economic and Social Council (ECOSOC) further strengthened Safeguard No. 7 in 1989 by 'providing for automatic ... review with provisions for clemency or pardon in all cases'. Seven years later, in 1996, ECOSOC called upon member states in which the death penalty may be carried out 'to ensure that officials involved in decisions to carry out an execution are fully informed of the status of appeals and petitions for clemency of the prisoner in question'. The UN HRC has also stated that the imposition of death sentences without the possibility to seek pardon or commutation of the sentence is incompatible with the ICCPR[212] and in resolution 2005/59, adopted on 20 April 2005, the UN Commission on Human Rights urged all states that still maintain the death penalty 'to ensure ... the right to seek pardon or commutation of sentence'. As the ABA has made clear, 'Full and proper use of the clemency process is essential to guaranteeing fairness in the administration of the death penalty'.[213]

All the retentionist countries that responded immediately to the Seventh UN Survey (Bahrain, Egypt, Japan, Morocco, Thailand, and Trinidad and Tobago) stated that all persons sentenced to death had the right to seek a pardon or commutation or reprieve or act of clemency—the three latter terms being used interchangeably to mean the substitution of a lesser penalty than death—as did two countries that were abolitionist for ordinary crimes: El Salvador and Mexico. In most countries a request for pardon or commutation was automatically forwarded to the relevant person or body. While in Guatemala the right to seek a pardon or commutation of sentence has been eliminated, the HRC has noted that the President has nevertheless exercised his right to grant pardons based on the precedence of international treaties over domestic law.[214]

China is one of the few countries without an effective clemency procedure. In effect, the Supreme People's Court acts as the reviewing body after the death penalty has been affirmed after the 'trial of second instance' at the provincial High Court. But beyond that, the power granted to the President under the Constitution to grant pardons to persons under sentence of death must be approved by the Standing Committee of the National People's Congress. This is a dead letter, for as far as we can ascertain no Chinese prisoner has been pardoned since 1975.

In India the governor of a state and the President of India have constitutional powers to commute death sentences or grant pardons to those who submit clemency petitions. But they cannot exercise these powers on their own initiative; they

---

[211] 'Amnesty' is not mentioned in Safeguard No. 7.

[212] Concluding observations of the HRC: Uganda, UN Doc. CCPR/CO/80/UGA, 4 May 2004, para. 13. Also, Report of the Special Rapporteur on Extrajudicial, Summary or Arbitrary Executions: E/CN.4/2001/9, 11 January 2001, para. 88.

[213] ABA, *The Florida Death Penalty Assessment Report*, September 2006, p. vii.

[214] Official Records of the General Assembly, 56th session, Supp. No. 40, Vol. I (A/56/40), para. 85.

must act on the advice of the Council of Ministers. There is no limit on the number of petitions that a prisoner can submit and a great deal of time passes before such proceedings are concluded. In December 2006 the Minister of Home Affairs told the Indian Parliament that 'no mercy petition has been decided before six or seven years'.[215] When a decision is reached the President's views are not necessarily accepted. Thus, when President A. P. J. Abdul Kalam made a request in 2005, for the second time, to pardon approximately 50 prisoners under sentence of death, he was re-submitting an earlier recommendation for clemency in these cases which had been returned by the Home Ministry stating that they were not fit for a presidential pardon. Dissatisfied with this state of affairs, he called on the government to make a 'comprehensive [re]view' of the policy for granting pardons.[216]

In most retentionist countries clemency can be sought both while the various appeal and confirmation procedures are pending and after final judgment is announced. Sometimes there is a time limit. In Egypt, for example, the sentence is executed if no order for pardon or commutation is issued within fourteen days. In Thailand sixty days are allowed after final judgment for an appeal of clemency to the King.

According to the information provided by OSCE, in Belarus, Tajikistan, and Uzbekistan, cases of persons sentenced to death are automatically considered by the Clemency Commission irrespective of whether the person concerned seeks clemency. The case is then forwarded to the President for a final decision. No information on the outcome is published in Belarus and 'very few acts of clemency' appear to have been granted in Tajikistan prior to the establishment of the moratorium on executions, or in Uzbekistan, although no official statistics have ever been published.

The International Federation for Human Rights states that in Chad, 'if no cassation plea is made, or the Supreme Court denies the plea, the prisoner may appeal for pardon to the President of the Republic, but in reality the plea is automatic because even if the prisoner does not seek a pardon the prosecution must prepare a plea for pardon to send to the Ministry of Justice'.[217] The code of criminal procedure provides that a death sentence can only be enforced after the plea for pardon has been rejected. However, the Federation was unable to ascertain whether the clemency procedures were observed with regard to five persons executed in 2003.

---

[215] Quoted in B. J. Batra, 'The Death Penalty in India—Issues and Aspects', paper given to the launch seminar of the China-EU project, Moving the Debate Forward—China's Use of the Death Penalty, 20–21 June 2007, College for Criminal Law Science of Beijing Normal University and Great Britain-China Centre.

[216] Amnesty International, *Death Sentences and Executions in 2005*, AI Index: ACT 50/005/2006, April 2006.

[217] UN Doc. E/2005/3, para. 110.

The official Japanese reply to the Seventh UN Survey noted that a person sentenced to death had a right to seek commutation of the sentence or a pardon, but the JFBA stated that this was not the case: 'Only the warden, chief probation officer and public prosecutor have rights to make application for amnesty', although prisoners are allowed to request wardens to make such applications. No specific time is allowed for such procedures because, as the JFBA pointed out, 'a person cannot be informed of the date when he/she will be executed... it seems that the Government rejects the request [for an amnesty] just before the execution without any notice to the legal adviser. There is no recourse to confirm whether the prisoner him (her) self is informed of the fact of rejection, since the Government never discloses this type of information'. As far as we know, no prisoner has received a special pardon since 1975.[218]

It is apparent that in a number of retentionist countries the person who has been sentenced to death plays no part in the process nor is the pardoning process subject to the requirements of due process, or subject to review. In this regard, the decision of the Judicial Committee of the Privy Council in London in 2000 in the case of *Neville Lewis and others v the Attorney General of Jamaica and Another*[219] should be noted. This held that the exercise of the prerogative of mercy should, in the light of Jamaica's international obligations, be exercised by procedures that are fair and proper, such as disclosure to the applicant of all materials to go before the review committee, and amenable to judicial review.

In the United States the governor alone has the authority to decide clemency in 14 states;[220] in a further 10 he or she has discretion to decide, but only after considering a recommendation from the Pardons Board or Advisory Group.[221] In eight states the governor cannot commute a death sentence unless it has been recommended by the Board, although he or she may decline to follow a positive recommendation for clemency: Texas is such a state. In six states a Board or Advisory Group is solely responsible for making the determination, although in three of them the governor sits on the Clemency Board.[222] In many states the Pardons Board is appointed by the governor or appointed by procedures which

---

[218] Yoshihiro Yasuda, 'The death penalty in Japan' in *The Death Penalty—Beyond Abolition* (2004), p. 226.

[219] [2001] 2 AC 50; also Amnesty International, *Death Penalty Developments 2000*, AI Index: ACT 50/001/2001

[220] Although in California the governor may not grant a pardon or commutation to a person twice convicted of a felony except on recommendation of the state Supreme Court, with at least four judges concurring.

[221] The advisors to the governor can also play a role in the clemency process. Alberto Gonzales, as counsel to then-Governor George W. Bush, was responsible for presenting clemency applications of Texas death row defendants to Mr. Bush. It is said that his memos to Governor Bush regularly failed to include most mitigating circumstances, preventing a fair consideration of the clemency petition: People for the American Way, *Statement of Opposition to the Confirmation of Alberto Gonzales to the Office of Attorney General of the United States*, <http://www.pfaw.org/pfaw/general/default.aspx?oid=17608>.

[222] James R. Acker and Charles S. Lanier, 'May God—or the Governor—Have Mercy: Executive Clemency and Executions in Modern Death-Penalty Systems' *Criminal Law*

the governor can influence. In respect of federal prisoners only the President of the United States can grant clemency, and the procedures applying to prisoners under sentence of death are specified in the Code of Federal Regulations: 'No petition for clemency should be filed before proceedings on direct appeal have terminated, the prisoner should file a petition not later than 30 days after receiving notification on the scheduled day of execution'.[223] The President is assisted in his decision to grant clemency by the Office of the Pardon Attorney.

There is very little data available on the extent to which powers to pardon, commute, or reprieve are exercised in retentionist countries. In a few it appears to have been quite often granted. For example, in Russia in the period 1992–94, 98 per cent of those who appealed for pardon to, and were considered by, the Pardons Commission were granted it. However, the policy changed, and in 1995 only 9 per cent were pardoned.[224] In the years 1994–98, 133 prisoners in Thailand sought a pardon (including commutation of the sentence), of whom 50 were successful. In addition, 75 prisoners under sentence of death benefited from an amnesty granted by the King in 1996, and in 2000 a further 30 prisoners had their death sentences reduced to life imprisonment as part of another Royal Amnesty. In 2004, on the occasion of the Queen's 72nd birthday many prisoners in Thailand benefited from a Royal Pardon. All capital punishment penalties passed before 1999 were commuted to a life sentence.[225]

In 2000 President Yoweri Museveni commuted the sentences of 16 prisoners from death to life imprisonment in Uganda, and in Nigeria those prisoners awaiting execution for more than twenty years were pardoned and released and those who had been under sentence of death for between ten and twenty years had their sentence reduced to life imprisonment.[226] In Swaziland, in 2001, four murderers who had been on death row for between sixteen and eighteen years were pardoned by King Mswati, on the grounds that they had served sufficient time. In 2004 the President of Zambia commuted 'several' death sentences.[227]

In some countries, mass pardons or commutation orders have been signed by presidents. For example, in January 2001, on leaving office as President of the Philippines, Joseph Estrada signed commutation orders for 103 death row prisoners,[228] and in April 2006 President Arroyo ordered the commutation of all death sentences—more than 1,000—in what was in reality a mass amnesty, rather than an individual consideration of the grounds for clemency, as a prelude

---

Bulletin 36 (2000), pp. 200–237—updated information from the DPIC website: <http://www.deathpenaltyinfo.org/article.php?did=126&scid=13>.

[223] Title 28, Ch. 1, para. 1.10, revised 1 July 2001.

[224] Alexander Mikhlin, *The Death Penalty in Russia* (1999), pp. 7 and 103–122.

[225] FIDH, *The death penalty in Thailand*, Report No. 411/2, March 2005, p. 27.

[226] Amnesty International, *Report 2001*; Uganda: p. 252, Nigeria: p. 183.

[227] Commission on Human Rights, *The Question of the Death Penalty*, Report of the Secretary-General, E/CN.4/2006/83, 10 February 2006, para. 13.

[228] Amnesty International, *Report 2000*. In one case the President failed to get through on the telephone to the execution chamber in time to grant a last-minute reprieve, p. 193.

to abolition of capital punishment two months later. Similarly, the President of Malawi has commuted all death sentences to life imprisonment, whatever the individual circumstances, on the grounds of his opposition to capital punishment.

In the United States, in January 2003, Governor Ryan of the State of Illinois commuted the death sentences of all 167 inmates on death row on the grounds that the criminal justice system of the state could not guarantee that innocent persons were not amongst them (see Chapter 3, page 120). This decision to make a 'mass commutation' has not been without its critics, on the grounds that such power should have been employed on a discretionary case-by-case basis, but it nevertheless sent a very strong message about the flaws in the American capital punishment system.[229]

In several retentionist countries pardons are rarely granted: they include Bahrain, Indonesia,[230] and Singapore, where, according to Amnesty International, the commutation of a death sentence by the President of Singapore in 1998 was only the fifth to be granted in thirty-five years.[231]

In the United States clemency is thought to be the last chance to correct errors. The Supreme Court in *Herrera v Collins* (1993) noted that clemency 'is the historic remedy for preventing miscarriages of justice where judicial process has been exhausted...the "fail safe" in our criminal justice system'.[232] However, it has become exceptionally rare for the governor of the state or a Board of Pardons to exercise clemency in favour of the prisoner. Prior to the mass commutation by Governor Ryan of Illinois, as Professors Radelet and Bedau have shown, grants of clemency had become rarer: from about one in every four or five death row inmates in the 1970s to about one in 40 by the late 1980s. There were only 29 commutations of death sentences for humanitarian reasons in the twenty-year period 1973 to 1992,[233] and altogether only 40 between 1973 and June 1999: a ratio of 13.8 executions to every one commutation, 'or roughly three to nine times greater than the comparable ratios [according to the state concerned] during the pre-*Furman* years'.[234] Thirteen of these clemency decisions were in fact made by the Governors of New Mexico and Ohio—both of whom were opposed

---

[229] For a discussion of these opinions see Dan Markel, 'State, Be not Proud: A Retributivist Defense of the Commutation of Death Row and the Abolition of the Death Penalty' *Harvard Civil Rights-Civil Liberties Law Review* 40 (2005), pp. 409–480.

[230] Report of the Special Rapporteur on Extrajudicial, Summary or Arbitrary Executions E/CN.4/1996/4/Corr. 1, para. 244.

[231] Amnesty International, *Death Penalty News*, June 1998, AI Index: ACT 53/03/98, p. 4.

[232] 506 U.S. 390 (1993).

[233] Michael Radelet and Hugo Adam Bedau, 'The Execution of the Innocent' *Law and Contemporary Problems* 61 (1998), pp. 105–217 at 119.

[234] In 1971, Governor Winthrop Rockefeller commuted all death sentences in Arkansas (C. Burnett, *Justice Denied* (2002), p. 162); and, in 1965, Governor Frank Clement commuted all the death sentences in Tennessee after the legislature defeated an abolition bill by a single vote (M. Gottschalk, *The Prison and the Gallows* (2006), p. 213).

to the death penalty—as they left office.[235] Leaving aside the decisions of the outgoing governors of Illinois, New Mexico, and Ohio, there have only been 40 grants of clemency in the 30 years since 1976.

Texas has been particularly loath to grant clemency. For example, the single commutation recommended by the Pardons Board to the Governor in 1998 was the first for seventeen years.[236] In fact the Texas Clemency Board has voted 'yes' only five times since 1930, the last time in August 2007. The official reasons for clemency in the minority of cases where it is granted have been: doubt about guilt; reduced blameworthiness because of mental health issues; and disproportionate punishment among equally culpable offenders; but, as Victor Streib has remarked, 'clemency decisions are intensely political decisions, being made by political leaders beholden to the voting public for their present jobs and... re-election'.[237] It is thus not surprising that it is often an outgoing governor that grants a pardon or clemency. For example, in November 2005, the outgoing Governor of Virginia granted a pardon to Robin Lovitt on the day before his appointed execution, on the grounds that DNA evidence that might have exonerated Lovitt had been destroyed. In January 2005, the outgoing Governor of Indiana commuted the death sentence on death row inmate Michael Daniels to life imprisonment. The governor noted that Daniels had an IQ of 77, indicating borderline mental retardation, and that evidence casting doubt on his guilt had never been presented in court. Perhaps emboldened by his predecessor, later that year the new governor commuted the death sentence of Arthur Baird on grounds of mental illness.

In the United States due process is absent from reviews of appeals for clemency, for the American courts have refused to recognize clemency proceedings as anything more than 'a right to ask for mercy'. Thus, in 1998 the US Supreme Court affirmed in the case of *Ohio Adult Parole Authority v Woodard* that the 'heart of executive clemency [is]... to grant clemency as a matter of grace'.[238] In saying this, the Court relied on a 1981 judgment that commutation of sentence 'is simply a unilateral hope', not a due process right.[239] In *Woodard* it conceded only that 'some *minimal* procedural safeguards might apply'. Clemency proceedings have therefore been stigmatized as 'standard-less in procedure, discretionary in exercise, and unreviewable in result'[240] and there is increasing pressure to recognize

---

[235] Governor Toney Anaya in New Mexico in 1986 (for all inmates) and Governor Richard Celeste in Ohio in 1991(for 8 inmates). See Acker and Lanier, n. 222 above, p. 215.

[236] Amnesty International, *Killing without Mercy: Clemency Procedures in Texas*, AI Index: AMR 51/85/99, p. 6. Similarly, the pardoning of a mentally ill prisoner, who had committed the murder when aged 17, by the Georgia Board of Pardons and Paroles in February 2002, was the first such pardon granted by that body since 1994.

[237] V. L. Streib, *Death Penalty in a Nutshell* (2005), p. 209.

[238] *Ohio Adult Parole Authority v Woodard*, 523 U.S. 272 (1998).

[239] *Connecticut Board of Pardons v Dumschat*, 452 U.S. 458 (1981).

[240] Hugo Adam Bedau, 'The Decline of Executive Clemency in Capital Cases' *New York University Review of Law and Social Change* 18 (1990–91), pp. 255–272 at 257. And Michael L.

the need for due process and detailed guidelines to govern the exercise of discretion in such proceedings.[241] The lack of due process produces some inconsistent and arbitrary results, as an Amnesty International report makes clear: 'Across the USA as a whole, clemency authorities have stopped some executions and commuted sentences on the grounds of lingering doubt. In other cases, equally compelling cases have not led to clemency'.[242] The report gives the example of Darrell Mease, who was granted clemency by the Governor of Missouri on the grounds that Pope John Paul II, who was visiting the state, made a personal plea on his behalf.[243]

The ABA has criticized the lack of transparency in Florida's clemency decision-making process. For example, the factors considered by the Board of Executive Clemency are largely undefined and the Board is not required to provide its reasons for denying clemency. Indeed, the Governor can deny clemency at any time, for any reason, even without holding a public hearing on the death-sentenced inmate's eligibility for clemency. The ABA concluded that Florida's clemency process is inadequate.[244] Texas has also been criticized for failing to provide minimal due process for death-sentenced applicants. In fact, 'It does not have a uniform, well-understood set of criteria used to judge clemency petitions; nor does it have safeguards to ensure that the party making clemency recommendations are independent'.[245]

5. Finality of Judgment: Awaiting the Outcome of Legal Proceedings

In previous UN surveys those retentionist states that provided information claimed to have adhered to UN Safeguard No. 8, which is aimed to ensure that no one is executed while any appeal is pending to any authorized body, national or international: 'Capital punishment shall not be carried out pending any appeal or other recourse procedure or other proceeding relating to a pardon or commutation of sentence'. However, not all the responding retentionist countries

Radelet and Barbara A. Zsembik, 'Executive Clemency in Post-Furman Capital Cases' *University of Richmond Law Review* 27 (1993), pp. 289–314.

[241] Daniel T. Kobil, 'The Evolving Role of Clemency in Capital Cases', in Acker, Bohm, and Lanier (eds.), n. 62 above, pp. 673–692. Kobil provides a list of the due process procedures required and guidelines of the factors that might be regarded as possible grounds fort granting clemency at pp. 687–688.

[242] Amnesty International, *United States of America, The Experiment that Failed: A reflection on thirty years of executions*, AI Index: AMR 51/011/2007 p. 21.

[243] *Ibid.*, at p. 13.

[244] ABA, *The Florida Death Penalty Assessment Report*, September 2006, p. vii

[245] Texas Appleseed and Texas Innocence Network, 2005, 'The Role of Mercy: Safeguarding Justice in Texas through Clemency Reform' at <http://www.texasmoratorium.org/Report.pdf>, p. 1.

which replied to the Seventh Survey stated that they abided by the Eighth Safeguard. Only Jamaica replied that execution was suspended until all avenues of appeal through international bodies had been exhausted. Thailand and Brunei Darussalam both stated that international bodies were not involved in the matter.[246] The official reply from Japan was that 'an appeal to international bodies does not legally affect the procedure for execution of the death penalty'. The report of FIDH to Japan confirmed this.[247]

There have been disturbing cases of executions going ahead before all avenues of appeal or other proceedings before international bodies have been completed in Trinidad and Tobago while 'appeal procedures were still pending',[248] in Botswana,[249] in Nigeria,[250] and in Tajikistan.[251] Indeed, in 2005, the UN HRC recalled that in at least two cases Tajikistan had executed prisoners under sentence of death prior to the moratorium in 2004, even though their cases were pending before the Committee under the Optional Protocol to the ICCPR and requests for interim measures for protection had been addressed to the state party. The Committee concluded that the disregard of the Committee's requests for interim measures constituted a grave breach of Tajikistan's obligations under the ICCPR and the Optional Protocol.[252] There have also been reports of executions having taken place while petitions for clemency or review by an international body have been under way in the Bahamas in 2000, while the Inter-American Commission on Human Rights was due to hear a petition,[253] and in Botswana in 2001, where a woman was executed while her petition was pending before the African Commission on Human and Peoples' Rights[254] and without her family or lawyer being informed.[255] The OSCE reported that in Uzbekistan 'at least 14 death sentences have been executed despite requests of the HRC to stay the executions,... which reminded Uzbekistan that it amounts to a grave breach of the Optional Protocol' which the state party had acceded to and which recognizes the Committee's competence to receive and examine complaints from individuals

---

[246] UN Doc. E/2005/3. Add. 1.

[247] FIDH, 2003, No. 359/2.; Yasuda, n. 218 above, at p. 226.

[248] UN Doc. E/CN. 4/1995/61, para. 382.

[249] Amnesty International, *Botswana: Amnesty International Appalled by Secret Execution*, AI Index: AFR 15/002/2001.

[250] In the Nigerian case of *Nasiru Bello v Attorney General et al* (1985) 1 NWLR 828 the convict was executed while the appeal on the case was before the Supreme Court; *The Report of the National Study Group on Death Penalty*, Abuja, August 2004, p. 59 (cited in UN Doc. E/CN.4/2006/53/Add. 4).

[251] Amnesty International, *Concerns in Europe, January–June* 2001, AI Index: EUR 01/003/2001.

[252] OSCE, *The Death Penalty in the OSCE Area, Background Paper* (2006), p. 70. The HRC also found, prior to the abolition of the death penalty in 2006, that three people had been executed pending communications to the Committee: *Piandiong et al v the Philippines* (Communication No. 869/1999, views adopted 19 October 2000).

[253] Amnesty International, *Report 2001*, p. 40.

[254] Amnesty International, *Botswana*, AI Index: AFR 15/002/2001.

[255] OSCE, *The Death Penalty in the OSCE Area, Background Paper* 2004/1, p. 35.

under the state party's jurisdiction.[256] In a bizarre case a man was executed early in 2006 in Pakistan while a court was preparing to consider his appeal. This was due to 'negligence in the Registrar's office' because 'the information had not been communicated to the jail'.[257]

6. Wrongful Convictions and Innocent Persons Exonerated

Acquittal or later exoneration of the innocent is the main test of procedural safeguards. If due process works as it should, innocent men and women should never be executed. Nor should they be wrongly convicted because due process has not been observed. Therefore, having considered the procedural safeguards in place across the world it is crucial to examine, at this stage, the evidence on the extent to which convictions are set aside on appeal, the convicted are exonerated and released from death row, and persons who were truly innocent have been put to death.

Retentionist countries which have replied to the UN quinquennial surveys have all said that they know of no cases of persons having been executed when there were clear doubts about their guilt. This is not surprising, for two reasons. First, this is not something that is likely to be admitted even if doubts did exist in some quarters, but secondly while such doubts may not exist at the time of conviction and execution, they may be unearthed considerably later. It is more important to recognize that observing the safeguards against wrongful conviction is an aspiration, rather than a statement of what is, in reality, achieved in all cases. The real issues are how the rules of procedure are operated in practice and whether the activities of police, prosecutors, judges, and juries are such as to endeavour scrupulously to avoid any possibility of wrongful conviction. That can only be assessed by careful independent academic empirical research or in-depth case studies. As Stephen Bright notes:[258]

To understand the realities of the death penalty [in the USA], one must look to the states that sentence people to death by the hundreds and have carried out scores of executions. In those states, innocent people have been sentenced to die based on such things as mistaken eyewitness identifications, false confessions, the testimony of partisan experts who render opinions that are not supported by science, failure of police and prosecutors to turn over evidence of innocence, and testimony of prisoners who get their own charges dismissed by testifying that the accused admitted the crime to them.

---

[256] *Ibid.*, 2004/1, p. 47; HRC 2005 A/60/40 (Vol. 1) p. 56. The same complaint was made against Tajikistan at p. 70. See also Report of the Special Rapporteur on Torture, Theo van Boven: E/CN.4/2005/62/Add. 1, para. 1914, 30 March 2005.

[257] FIDH, *Slow March to the Gallows. Death Penalty in Pakistan*, Report No. 464/2, January 2007, p. 18.

[258] S. Bright, 'Why the United States will join the rest of the world in abandoning capital punishment' in H. Bedau and P. Cassell (eds.), *Debating the Death Penalty* (2004), pp. 152–182.

The exoneration of innocent people who have spent time on the death rows of retentionist nations is currently one of the most important matters of concern not only for those who care about the administration of justice in different jurisdictions, but also for abolitionists because, if we take the example of the USA, the relatively recent recognition that innocent people have been, and continue to be, sentenced to death and perhaps some executed for crimes they did not commit has arguably done more to bolster the abolitionist movement than anything else in the past few decades. Since the establishment of the first Innocence Project,[259] founded in 1992 by Barry C. Scheck and Peter J. Neufeld, there has been a proliferation of other Innocence Projects —currently forty—across the USA dedicated to the investigation of possible wrongful convictions.[260] Although, of course, this is not the only argument against the death penalty, and some think that it is overemphasized,[261] others like the British lawyer Clive Stafford Smith believe that in America, 'the risk of executing the innocent will eventually bring about the end of capital punishment'.[262]

Reports of persons being released from custody, often many years after their conviction, after proof has been forthcoming of their innocence, have regularly emanated from Amnesty International, Hands off Cain, and other human rights agencies.[263] For example, in 2006 cases were reported from Bangladesh (Shah Alam Babu, wrongfully convicted of murder and condemned to death in 2004); China (Gao Jinfa sentenced to death for the rape and murder of two girls in 2003); and Pakistan (four activists of the banned Lashkar-e-Jhangvi group, sentenced to death on charges of sectarian killing in 2001).[264] There have been some cases where there could be no doubt at all about innocence. For example, Nie Shubin, a young farmer from North China, was executed in 1995 for the rape and murder of a local woman. He had reportedly been tortured in police custody. In early 2005, a suspect detained in connection with another case reportedly confessed to the same crime, apparently describing the crime scene in detail. Judicial authorities later admitted their mistake, prompting Nie Shubin's family to seek compensation from the authorities. She Xianglin and Teng Xingshan were both

---

[259] The Innocence Project is a non-profit legal clinic affiliated with the Benjamin N. Cardozo School of Law at Yeshiva University, New York: <http://www.innocenceproject.org/about>.

[260] Plus a few other similar initiatives housed in public defenders' offices or university law schools. In addition, there are innocence projects in the UK (at the Universities of Bristol and Leeds) and in Australia (at Griffith and Melbourne law schools).

[261] C. S. Steiker and J. M. Steiker, 'The Seduction of Innocence: The attraction and limitations of the focus on innocence in capital punishment law and advocacy' *The Journal of Criminal Law and Criminology* 95 (2005), pp. 587–624 at 587.

[262] Clive Stafford Smith, Introduction to *The Exonerated*, a play by J. Blank and E. Jensen (2006).

[263] According to the Amnesty International *Fatal Flaws* report, n. 191 above, there had been reports not only from the USA, but also from Belize, China, Japan, Malawi, Malaysia, Pakistan, Papua New Guinea, the Philippines, Trinidad and Tobago, and Turkey.

[264] From Hands Off Cain website: <http://www.handsoffcain.info/bancadati/schedastato.php?idstato=9000041>.

convicted of the murder of their wives in two separate cases in 1994 and 1987 respectively. Both were sentenced to death despite pleas of innocence and allegations that both had confessed because they had been severely beaten during interrogations. In both cases, the alleged murder victims reappeared several years later—in April and June 2005 respectively. She Xianglin's sentence had been commuted to 15 years imprisonment after a re-trial; Teng Xingshan, however, had been executed in 1989.[265]

Others have been luckier in that their innocence was established before their execution date arrived. For example, in Nigeria the Court of Appeal acquitted Bodurin Baruwa in 1996 after he had spent 16 years in prison for a murder he did not commit. In his case, the Court of Appeal said that he would 'leave custody amazed at the way the law had been used to work extreme injustice and hardship on him and his family'.[266] In a similar case a Ugandan man, Eddie Mpagi, was on death row for 19 years in Luzira Maximum Security Prison for murdering a man who turned out to be alive.[267] Okunishi Masaru, who was sentenced to death in Japan in 1961, and is now 80 years old, has repeatedly protested his innocence. The Tsu District Court found him innocent on grounds of insufficient evidence but this verdict was reversed by a higher court which sentenced him to death. Following the finalization of Okunishi's sentence by the Supreme Court in 1972, Okunishi continued to appeal for a retrial; all six applications were rejected. In April 2005, the Nagoya High Court finally granted Okunishi a retrial, citing the existence of new evidence that could prove his innocence. Okunishi has spent 45 years in detention, and over 30 years on death row with the constant fear of execution.[268] In Israel the discovery of new evidence in the case of John Demjanjuk, who had been identified with such certainty as 'Ivan the Terrible', a camp guard responsible for mass murder of Jews during the Second World War, produced doubts where none hitherto had existed.[269]

Convictions that had resulted in executions have been posthumously overturned in the United Kingdom, Uzbekistan, and the Russian Federation, amongst other countries.[270] For example, the conviction of George Kelly, who

---

[265] Amnesty International, Asia Pacific office: *China: The Death Penalty, A Failure of Justice.*

[266] Nigeria, *Report of National Study Group on Death Penalty* (August 2004), p. 580.

[267] Quoted in *The Question of the Death Penalty in Africa*, African Union, African Commission on Human and People's Rights, 11/2004, at p. 12.

[268] Amnesty International, *'Will this day be my last?': The death penalty in Japan*, AI Index: ASA 22/006/2006.

[269] John Demjanjuk was sentenced to death on 18 April 1988. In July 1989 his sentence was overturned by the Supreme Court of Israel after the court examined exceptionally admitted, newly discovered, evidence at the appeals stage, and held that this created the possibility of reasonable doubt as to the identification of John Demjanjuk as 'Ivan the Terrible'.

[270] Amnesty International, *Fatal Flaws: Innocence and the Death Penalty in the USA*. In Britain the Court of Appeal in February 1998 quashed the conviction of Mahmoud Hussein Mattan, a Somali national who had been hanged for murder in 1952 (*R v Mattan*, transcript provided by Smith Bernal, *The Independent*, 4 March 1998). See also the references to the cases of Timothy Evans and Derek Bentley in Ch. 2, p. 45.

was hanged in England in 1950 for a murder he did not commit, was quashed by the Court of Appeal in 2003. In 2006 it was reported that his remains were to be exhumed from Walton Prison so they could be re-buried in consecrated ground.[271] In January 2007 eight South Korean pro-democracy activists were posthumously acquitted of treason charges, more than 30 years after they were executed.

Miscarriages of justice are especially likely when there are 'crackdowns' on crime or when particularly heinous crimes lead to pressure on the police to produce 'an offender'. This may lead over-zealous police to misinterpret or even fabricate evidence or to extract confessions by torture or other illegitimate methods. This may be exacerbated by poor legal defence and by an over-readiness of courts to convict. Thus, in China during the 'strike hard campaigns' of 1997 and 1998 there were several reports of wrongful convictions.[272] And in the Russian Federation Valerii Borshchev, the Chair of the President's Commission on Human Rights, estimated that when the President declared a 'war' on crime during 1995 and 1996, the proportion of those executed who were later found to be innocent increased from the already high rate of 15 per cent to 30 per cent.[273] Similar concerns had been expressed in Bangladesh and the Philippines (especially aroused by the allegation of torture of the suspects in the Rolando Abadilla murder)[274] where errors had been found in 70 per cent of the 511 cases involving 591 death-sentenced inmates that the Philippines Supreme Court had reviewed between 1994 and late in 2001.[275] There is a particular danger when suspects are rounded up by the authorities following attempted coups. Thus in Zambia, following a coup attempt in October 1997, 59 men were convicted and sentenced to death. An official inquiry ordered by the government following allegations made in court of the use of torture found that there had been beatings, burning, electric shocks, enforced painful postures, sexual harassment, mental torture—such as simulated execution—and other degradations. The Commission found that 'victims were both physically and mentally affected by these experiences to the extent that they had no choice but to make incriminating statements'.[276]

---

[271] *BBC News Online*, 10 March 2006.

[272] Hans-Jörg Albrecht, 'The Death Penalty in China from a European Perspective' in M. Nowak and Xin Chunying (eds.), *EU-China Human Rights Dialogue: Proceedings of the Second EU-China Legal Experts Seminar Held in Beijing on 19 and 20 October 1998* (2000), pp. 95–118 at 116, referring to reports in: *China Youth Daily*, 8 May 1998; *Oriental Daily*, 12 and 25 September 1997; *Xinjiang Legal News*, 24 October 1997; and *Xinmin Evening News*, 17 October 1997.

[273] Patrick Henry, 'Execution Foes Press for Moratorium', *Moscow Times*, September 1997, quoted in D. Barry and E. Williams, 'Russia's Death Penalty Dilemmas' *Criminal Law Forum* 8 (1997), pp. 231–258 at 253.

[274] Amnesty International, *Philippines: The Rolando Abadilla Murder Inquiry—An Urgent Need for Effective Investigation of Torture*, AI Index: ASA 35/08/00.

[275] Free Legal Assistance Group (FLAG), 'Position Paper on the Death Penalty Bills' *Flag Newsletter*, December 2001.

[276] Amnesty International, *Zambia: Time to Abolish the Death Penalty*, AI Index: AFR 63/004/2001, p. 14.

Claims that innocent people have been convicted of murder and some of them executed are not new in the United States—one has only to recall the notorious Sacco and Vanzetti case of 1927. More recently, a report issued in 1993 by the Subcommittee on Civil and Constitutional Rights, Committee on the Judiciary of the US Congress, entitled *Innocence and the Death Penalty: Assessing the Danger of Mistaken Executions,* noted that 'at least 48 people have been released from prison after serving time on death row since 1973 with significant evidence of their innocence'.[277] But until recently such exonerations of falsely convicted defendants were regarded as aberrations and the fact that they had been discovered was taken as reassurance that the system was able to correct its errors. What has changed is that 'these once-rare events have become disturbingly commonplace'.[278]

The full scale of 'serious reversible error' found in death penalty convictions in the United States was revealed for the first time in June 2000 by a study carried out at the Columbia Law School by Professor James Liebman and colleagues. This study, of every capital conviction and appeal between 1973 and 1995, found that in 68 per cent of cases that had reached the final third stage of state and federal appeal during this period (a process that on average took nine years), an error had been found sufficient to overturn the original capital conviction. Ninety per cent of these prejudicial errors had been discovered during appeals to the state courts, but even where cases proceeded to the federal appeal courts, a high error rate was still apparent. This high rate of 'reversal' persisted over the entire period covered by the study and across most states: three-fifths of the states had an error rate of 70 per cent or higher. The most common causes of these errors, accounting for 76 per cent of the cases, were found to be: 'egregiously incompetent defense lawyers' who did not even look for—and *demonstrably missed*—important evidence that the defendant was innocent or did not deserve to die (37 per cent of cases); police and prosecutors who *did* discover that kind of evidence but *suppressed* it, again keeping it from the jury (19 per cent of cases); and faulty instructions to jurors (20 per cent of cases). Furthermore, 82 per cent of those who had their death sentences overturned were not sentenced to death when the errors were cured on a retrial, and 7 per cent were found to be innocent of the capital crime. Thus, only 11 per cent of those originally sentenced to death were judged to deserve such a sentence when the errors of the original trial were corrected.[279] These data alone provide sufficient evidence that the checks and balances discussed above failed in the majority of cases in the US during this time.

[277] DPIC, *Innocence and the Death Penalty: Assessing the Danger of Mistaken Executions,* Staff Report by the Subcommittee on Civil and Constitutional Rights, Committee on the Judiciary, 103rd Congress, 1st Session (1993), pp. 2 and 8.

[278] Samuel R. Gross, Kristen Jacoby, Daniel J. Matheson, Nicholas Montgomery, and Sujata Patil, 'Exonerations in the United States 1989 through 2003' *Journal of Criminal Law and Criminology* 95 (2005), pp. 523–560 at 523.

[279] James S. Liebman, Jeffrey Fagan, Valerie West, and Jonathan Lloyd, 'Capital Attrition: Error Rates in Capital Cases, 1973–1995' *Texas Law Review* 78 (2000), pp. 1771–1803.

Further analysis of these data revealed that the proportion of errors was greatest in those states and counties which most often sentenced offenders to death: in other words, the percentage of errors increased in proportion to the percentage of homicides which resulted in a death sentence, especially in relation to cases that were not highly aggravated.[280] Professor Liebman and his colleagues concluded:[281]

The more often states succumb to pressures to inflict capital sentences in marginal cases, the higher is the risk of error and delay, the lower is the chance verdicts will be carried out, and the greater is the temptation to approve flawed verdicts on appeal. Among the disturbing sources of pressure to overuse the death penalty are political pressures on elected judges, well-founded doubts about the state's ability to convict serious criminals, and the race of the state's residents and homicide victims.

If such a large number of legal and factual errors made at trials for capital offences are found by appeals courts in the United States of America, where the scope of capital punishment is narrowly drawn and the legal system is well developed, it is hard to believe that they will not occur also in many other retentionist countries.

In the USA the Death Penalty Information Center (DPIC) publishes an 'Innocence list' of those who have been sentenced to death but subsequently had their conviction overturned and been acquitted at re-trial or had all charges dropped, or have been given an absolute pardon by the governor, based on new evidence of innocence. The list dates from 1973 and at the end of May 2007 it showed that there had been 124 people in 25 states exonerated after serving an average of 9.2 years on death row. Some served longer: Timothy Howard and Gary Lamar James were both released from Ohio in 2003 having served 26 years, whilst Laurence Adams, released in 2004, had served 30 years. The longest time before exoneration is 33 years, served by Peter Limone who was convicted in 1968 and released in 2001. A study by Professor Gross and colleagues of all 340 exonerations in the United States from 1989 to 2003 (205 of whom had been convicted of murder and 74 sentenced to death) found that the rate of exonerations increased sharply over the fifteen-year period of their study from an average

---

[280] Another study found that the largest category of inmates who were released from death row (n = 81) consisted of non-white defendants convicted of killing white victims (36 = 44.4% compared to 32 = 39.5% being white defendants/white victims, and 12=14.8%, non-white defendant/non-white victims): T. Roitberg Harmon, 'Race for your Life: An Analysis of the Role of Race in Erroneous Capital Convictions' *Criminal Justice Review* 29 (2004) pp. 76–96.

[281] James S. Liebman, Jeffrey Fagan, Andrew Gelman, Valerie West, Gareth Davies, and Alexander Kiss, *A Broken System, Pt. II: Why There Is So Much Error in Capital Cases, and What Can be Done About It?* (February 2002): see Columbia Law School, Broken System 2 website for the report and other links, <http://www2.law.columbia.edu/brokensystem2/index2.html>— quotation in text from 'Summary Explanation' in the Executive Summary. Also, Andrew Gelman, James S. Liebman, Valerie West, and Alexander Kiss, 'A Broken System: The Persistent Pattern of Reversals of Death Sentences in the United States' *Journal of Empirical Legal Studies* 1(2) (2004), p. 209.

of 12 a year from 1989 to 1994, to an average of 42 a year since 2000. They concluded:[282]

Exonerations from death row are more than twenty-five times more frequent than exonerations from other prisoners convicted of murder, and more than 100 times more frequent than for all imprisoned felons. This huge discrepancy must mean that false convictions are more likely for death sentences than for all murder cases, and much more likely than among felony convictions generally—an unavoidable and extremely disturbing conclusion.

Over half (56%) of murder exonerations included perjury: 'False confessions also play a large role in murder convictions that led to exonerations, primarily among two particularly vulnerable groups of innocent defendants: juveniles, and those who are mentally retarded or mentally ill'. It is therefore likely, given the demise of the death penalty for juveniles and the mentally retarded, that the rate of exonerations will fall in the future.[283]

As with most matters concerning the administration of justice in the USA, geography makes a difference. Florida appears to lead the USA in death row exonerations, having, since 1973, exonerated twenty-two death-row inmates. Combined, these death-row exonerees served approximately 150 years in prison before being released.[284]

The conservative response to all this evidence has been perhaps predictable, namely that it merely proves how thorough the American appeal process is in ensuring that innocent persons are not executed.[285] It is claimed that many whose convictions are reversed are only 'legally' or 'technically' innocent, rather than factually innocent; and that the miniscule risk of executing an innocent is far outweighed by the utilitarian benefits of the death penalty, namely retribution and deterrence. As Griffey and Rothenberg argue:[286]

the purported risk of executing an innocent person is most often predicated on the reversals of murder convictions for trial error, which simply do not correlate with or reflect actual innocence. Second, despite protracted and determined effort, abolitionists have been unable to identify a single factually innocent person who has been executed post-*Furman*. Finally, while a segment of American society views any possibility, however

---

[282] Samuel R. Gross, Kristen Jacoby, Daniel J. Matheson, Nicholas Montgomery, and Sujata Patil, 'Exonerations in the United States 1989 through 2003', n. 278 above, at 524, 527–529 and 552.

[283] The definition of innocence used by the DPIC in placing defendants on the list of exonerated individuals is that they had 'been convicted and sentenced to death, and subsequently either a) their conviction was overturned and they were acquitted at a re-trial, or all charges were dropped, or b) they were given an absolute pardon by the governor based on new evidence of innocence.' See DPIC, <http://www.deathpenaltyinfo.org/article.php?scid=6&did=110>.

[284] One inmate, Frank Lee Smith, was exonerated after he died of cancer while on death-row.

[285] In an article in *Wall Street Journal Europe*, 16 June 2000, Paul Cassell, Professor of Law at the University of Utah, argued that all the innocent people released from death row are merely proof that the criminal justice system is working efficiently: 'the 68% "error rate" in capital cases—might accordingly be viewed as a reassuring sign of the American judiciary's circumspection before imposing the ultimate sanction'.

[286] Margaret Griffey and Laurence E. Rothenberg, 'The Death Penalty in the United States' in *The Death Penalty in the OSCE Area, Background Paper* 2006, pp. 35–44 at 41–42.

slight, that even one innocent person may be executed to be an unacceptable risk, most Americans recognize that perfection in criminal justice matters cannot be absolutely guaranteed in relation to any sanction, and that any risk of error there may be relating to capital punishment is acceptable in light of the many protections that exist against such error and the deterrent and retributive value of the death penalty... To call someone 'innocent', even though they owe the reversal of their conviction simply to one of the many procedural protections afforded to capital defendants, cheapens the word and impeaches the moral authority of those who claim that a person has been 'exonerated'.

But the fact of the matter is that many of these cases have come to light not through the thoroughness of the state's review processes, but through the vagaries of luck, through confessions of other criminals, and by the hard effort of campaigners outside the official criminal justice system:[287]

In one way or another, virtually every case in which death row inmates are able to prove their innocence is a story of exceptional luck. Only when we realize how lucky the exonerated death row inmates have been can we realize how easy it is for fatal mistakes to go undetected.

Anthony Porter of Illinois only escaped the death penalty by the chance intervention of outsiders, rather than through any thorough investigation of his claims to innocence by the authorities. Peter Limone was sentenced to die in Massachusetts' electric chair, but was spared in 1974 when Massachusetts abolished the death penalty and his sentence was commuted to life in prison. Clearly, had he been sentenced in a retentionist state he would not have lived to see his conviction overturned, after compelling new evidence emerged that he and his co-defendants were actually innocent of the murder of which they were convicted.[288] As Hugo Bedau has put it: 'it is beyond reasonable doubt that innocent persons have been put to death, even if it cannot be proved'.[289] Rosen notes that:[290]

the day is approaching when the American criminal justice system will have to face the reality that it executed a person who was unquestionably innocent. Even before this grisly

---

[287] Radelet and Bedau, 'The Execution of the Innocent', n. 233 above at p. 118, and Michael L. Radelet and Hugo Adam Bedau, 'The Execution of the Innocent' in Acker, Bohm, and Lanier (eds.), n. 62 above, pp. 325–344 at 335. Also, S. Gross, 'Lost Lives: Miscarriages of Justice in Capital Cases' *Law and Contemporary Problems* 61 (1988), pp. 125–152.

[288] *Commonwealth v Limone*, 2001 Mass. Super. LEXIS 7 (2001).

[289] Michael L. Radelet, Hugo Adam Bedau, and Constance E. Putnam, *In Spite of Innocence* (1992). For criticisms of this book, claiming that no proof had been forthcoming of innocent persons being executed, see Stephen J. Markman and Paul G. Cassell, 'Protecting the Innocent: A Response to the Bedau-Radelet Study' *Stanford Law Review* 41 (1988), pp. 121–160; and the reply by Hugo Adam Bedau and Michael L. Radelet, 'The Myth of Infallibility: A Reply to Markman and Cassell', *ibid.*, pp. 161–170. It should be noted that Markman and Cassell argued that even if a few innocent persons had been executed this was a loss justified by the gains of capital punishment in terms of its utility in controlling murder; see also Richard A. Posner, 'The Economics of Capital Punishment' in *Economists' Voice* (March 2006), p. 2. Also, Kelli Hinson, 'Post-Conviction Determination of Innocence for Death Row Inmates' *SMU Law Review* 48 (1994), pp. 231–261 at 254. For strong support for Bedau and Radelet, see Lawrence C. Marshall, 'In Spite of Meese' *Journal of Criminal Law and Criminology* 85 (1994), pp. 261–280.

[290] R. A. Rosen, 'Innocence and Death' *North Carolina Law Review* 82 (2003), pp. 61–114 at 89.

moment, however, the more reflective observers know that the system has executed innocent people and will continue to do so in future.

To some proponents of the death penalty, such as the late Ernest van den Haag,
the execution of some innocent persons is regarded as inevitable: because 'judges
and juries are human and fallible we can minimize, but not altogether avoid such
miscarriages'. He argued that 'there is a trade-off in minimizing them. To avoid
convicting innocents we require so much evidence for conviction that many
guilty persons escape punishment—which is no less unjust than convicting the
innocent'. Furthermore, van den Haag argued, in true utilitarian vein, some
innocent persons have to suffer in order that sufficient guilty persons can be convicted to provide the general deterrent effect that he believed executions provide,
so saving many lives of yet unknown innocent victims.[291] Whatever else, this is
not a 'human rights' argument.

There is no doubt that the widespread availability of genetic fingerprint DNA
testing has played an enormous part in convincing people in the USA and elsewhere that some of the people released from death row are not just 'technically
innocent' because of some due-process violation, but truly innocent. For example,
Earl Washington Jr., who is mentally retarded, spent nearly a decade on death row
before DNA evidence convinced Virginia's governor that he was innocent.[292] On
11 April 2007 another man, Kenneth Tinsley, pleaded guilty to the 1982 rape
and murder of Rebecca Lynn Williams that Washington was nearly executed
for and was sentenced to two consecutive life terms.[293] In 15 of the death penalty exoneration cases recorded by the Death Penalty Information Center, DNA
had been a substantial factor in establishing innocence (for example, in 2005,
Harold Wilson's innocence was confirmed by DNA evidence). As Weisberg has
argued:[294]

Although death penalty supporters may have acknowledged, in principle, that mistakes
can happen in death penalty cases, the general assumption before these DNA acquittals
seems to have been that the legal system took its greatest care in cases in which execution
was possible, and the chances of error in capital cases was in fact minimal. We now know
that this is not so, and we can put faces on people who, but for the system's slowness and

[291] Ernest van den Haag, 'Justice, Deterrence and the Death Penalty' in Acker, Bohm, and
Lanier (eds.), n. 62 above, pp. 139–156 at 147. A similar view has been expressed by a Russian
scholar: 'It must be said that errors are committed in all spheres of human activities [for example
in medical operations] but this is not grounds to renounce such activity': Mikhlin, n. 224 above,
at p. 167.
[292] In the 1990s DNA results combined with the victim's statement all but exonerated
Washington and persuaded Governor Wilder to commute his sentence to life with the possibility
of parole, shortly before leaving office in 1994. In 2000 additional DNA tests were ordered and the
results again excluded Washington as the rapist. In October 2000 Virginia Governor Jim Gilmore
granted Earl Washington an absolute pardon.
[293] *Associated Press*, 11 April 2007.
[294] Robert Weisberg, 'The Death Penalty Meets Social Science: Deterrence and Jury Behavior
Under New Scrutiny' *Annual Review of Law and Social Science* 1 (2005), pp. 151–170 at 170.

their own good luck, might well have been executed for murders they did not commit. This human reality may prove to be more important than masses of social science evidence on deterrence and other issues in determining support for the death penalty in the long run.

An example from Arizona provides evidence that such cases are changing mindsets. In February 2006 several members of the Arizona House and Senate offered apologies to Ray Krone, a former Arizona death row inmate who was freed in 2002 following DNA tests. The Arizona Senate Judiciary Chairman said that Krone's case shows that corrections are needed to protect the innocent, noting, 'This is happening more frequently than we would like to admit', while another legislator, Representative Phil Lopes, said that Krone's case 'exemplifies why we should abolish the death penalty' in Arizona.[295]

Indeed, a comprehensive study by Brandon Garrett of all 200 persons who had by early 2007 been exonerated in the USA through the use of DNA evidence, which included 14 persons who had been sentenced to death (all but one for a rape murder, where such evidence is much more likely to be available), showed conclusively 'the inability of appeal courts to effectively review claims relating to the central unreliable and false evidence supporting these convictions'. In the 14 capital cases which were exonerated through DNA the evidence had been 'surprisingly weak', involving in six cases testimony of jailhouse informants and in five cases a false confession had been obtained (three had been mentally retarded prisoners).[296] As Liebman has put it, 'Suddenly and starkly, DNA reveals us and our institutions to be what they strive to escape notice for being: inherently but often unknowably—and thus—incurably—flawed, unreliable and untrustworthy'.[297]

There is a strong movement in the United States to make this DNA evidence statutorily available to defendants protesting their innocence in all retentionist states and the federal jurisdiction; and as of March 2007, 40 states had laws that allowed inmates access to post-conviction DNA testing.[298] The Justice for All Act of 2004[299] affects the death penalty by creating a DNA testing programme and authorizing grants to states for capital prosecution and capital defense improvement. Title IV of the Justice for All Act, entitled the Innocence Protection Act of 2004, includes these three subtitles that affect the death penalty: exonerating the innocent through DNA testing; improving the quality of

---

[295] *Associated Press*, 21 February 2006.

[296] Brandon L. Garrett, 'Judging Innocence' *Columbia Law Review*, forthcoming: January 2008, available at SSRN: <http://ssrn.com/abstract=999984> at pp. 25–27. See also: Barry Scheck, 'Innocence, Race and the Death Penalty' *Howard Law Journal* 50 (2007) pp. 445–469; and Jeffrey L. Kirchmeier, 'Dead Innocent: The Death Penalty Abolitionist Search for a Wrongful Execution' *Tulsa Law Review* 42 (2006), pp. 403–435.

[297] James S. Liebman, Comment: The New Death Penalty Debate: What's DNA got to do with it?', *Columbia Human Rights Law Review* 33 (2002), pp. 527–552 at 547.

[298] See <http://www.innocenceproject.org/fix/DNA-Testing-Access.php>.

[299] Public Law No. 108–405 became law on 30 October 2004.

representation in State capital cases; and compensation for the wrongfully convicted. It has to be recognized that DNA will not help in many cases of capital murder, for it is typically only useful in rape murders. On the other hand, it can be used to confirm guilt with near absolute confidence and this may well persuade advocates of capital punishment that only those who deserve to die are put to death, and thus rob the opponents of capital punishment of one of their most powerful and emotive arguments against it.[300] Yet it could have another effect, as Austin Sarat has pointed out. By being able to demonstrate conclusively that mistakes can occur in the types of crime where DNA evidence is most likely to be available, people may come to see that the probability of mistake may be even greater for those types of murder where the only evidence is eyewitness, from jailhouse informants, or circumstantial.[301] Indeed this is just what has happened in Illinois where the Commission set up to examine the administration of capital punishment persuaded the legislature that such uncorroborated evidence should be barred.

7. Conclusions

This review of the evidence relating to the extent to which retentionist countries have abided (or perhaps it would be better to say, for some, have in practice been able to abide) by the safeguards established by the United Nations and the ICCPR for the provision of fair and impartial trials, the protection of the innocent, and the provision of effective appeals and clemency proceedings, shows how easy it is for abuses of human rights to occur when capital punishment is left on the statute book and put into effect.

Furthermore, very few retentionist countries appear to have put in place a systematic means for ensuring that all persons in the criminal justice system, including defendants and their legal representatives, are made familiar with the ECOSOC Safeguards and those provided by Articles 6 and 14 of the ICCPR. Most appear to assume that all concerned will be aware of the protections that are available under domestic law and procedure through the normal training they receive and that, as a matter of course, defendants will be made aware of safeguards by their counsel. Clearly, this is often not the case.

[300] Steiker and Steiker, 'The Seduction of Innocence', n. 261 above, at p. 622.

[301] Ronald J. Tabak, Commentary, 'Finality without Fairness: Why we are Moving towards Moratoria on Executions, and the Potential Abolition of Capital Punishment' *Connecticut Law Review* 33 (2001), pp. 733–763 at 751. See also the website of the Innocence Project at Cardozo Law School, which reviews cases where defendants say that they have been wrongfully convicted and, where appropriate, arranges for DNA tests to be carried out: <http://www.innocenceproject.org>. Also the interview with Barry Scheck at <http://www.pbs.org/wgbh/pages/frontline/shows/case/interviews/scheck.html>.

Yet while all must be done, where and while capital punishment persists, to make sure that the realities of criminal procedure match up to the international standards for the protection of those facing the sentence of death, it needs to be realized that many of the situations and practices reviewed in this chapter, and the next, arise by virtue of the very existence of the death penalty and the emotions it arouses. Reform of procedures will simply never be sufficient to meet the human rights objections to capital punishment.

8

Deciding Who Should Die: Problems of Inequity, Arbitrariness, and Racial Discrimination

1. Mandatory or Discretionary?

(a) The attack on mandatory death sentences

Marc Ancel noted forty-five years ago that 'in general the modern tendency is more and more to drop the mandatory character of the death penalty. It is provided as the ultimate punishment but replaceable by another penalty'. Since then, and especially in recent years, the mandatory death penalty has come under sustained attack as the international jurisprudence on capital punishment has developed.

In the 1960s, 22 of the 42 American states still had a mandatory death penalty for murder. After the *Furman* decision in 1972 held all existing death penalty statutes to be unconstitutional, several states again enacted statutes which made death a mandatory sanction for a limited group of specifically defined categories of murder such as the killing of a law enforcement officer and killing while carrying out a robbery. The Supreme Court, however, in a series of cases beginning with *Woodson v North Carolina*[1] and *Roberts v Louisiana*[2] in 1976, struck down mandatory statutes of this kind as unconstitutional under the Eighth Amendment. They were regarded as both too broad, as they mandated death in cases where it was not warranted, and too rigid, as they precluded an individualized consideration of the facts of the case at sentencing. By not allowing the introduction of any mitigating circumstances they were liable both to invite juries to acquit, thereby reintroducing an undesirable element of arbitrariness into the system, and, where imposed, to be in some cases disproportionate to the circumstances of the case.[3]

---

[1] 428 U.S. 280 (1976).
[2] 428 U.S. 325 (1976).
[3] *Columbia Law Review*, Note, 'Distinguishing among Murders when Assessing the Proportionality of the Death Penalty' 85 (1985), pp. 1786–1807 at 1790. And for an interesting study of the effects of a mandatory death penalty in the period prior to the *Furman* decision, see

The Court had left the question open as to whether, in principle, a state could define a much more limited class of murder for which the death penalty might be applied mandatorily, and many commentators thought that this might be upheld for murder committed while serving a life sentence of imprisonment. However, the Nevada statute which provided for this was ruled unconstitutional in 1987 in the case of *Sumner v Shuman*.[4] Since then it has been widely accepted in the United States that no specific class of murder can be defined in statute for which it would always be right, whatever the circumstances in which it had been committed, to impose the death penalty.

In 1983 the Supreme Court of India, in the case of *Mithu v The State of Punjab*, ruled that section 303 of the Indian Penal Code, which made the death penalty mandatory for a person convicted of murder if they were already undergoing a sentence of life imprisonment, was unconstitutional. Indeed, the Court stated that by making the penalty mandatory, the sentencing process was reduced to a 'farce'.[5] This has not finally settled the matter because since *Mithu* the mandatory death penalty has been appointed under a section of the Narcotics Drugs and Psychotropic Substances Act 1985 and of the Prevention of Atrocities Act 1989. But no case has yet come before the Indian Supreme Court to test its constitutionality.[6]

The death penalty is still mandatory for some crimes in less than a third (31) of the 95 retentionist and abolitionist *de facto* countries that at present (December 2007) retain the death penalty on their statute books, even if no persons have been, or are very rarely, executed for them.[7] Whilst it is usually only mandatory for 'capital murder', it is still the only sentence available for armed robbery in several African countries, including Kenya (ADF), Nigeria, Tanzania (ADF), and Zambia.[8] Furthermore, 12 of the 26 countries which introduced the death penalty for producing, or trading in, illicit drugs have made it mandatory on conviction of possessing quantities over certain prescribed (and sometimes relatively modest) amounts. This is the case in Brunei Darussalam (ADF), Egypt,

H. A. Bedau, 'Felony Murder Rape and the Mandatory Death Penalty: A Study in Discretionary Justice' *Suffolk University Law Review* 10 (1976), pp. 493–520.

[4] 486 U.S. 66 (1987).

[5] *Mithu v State of Punjab*, AIR 1983 SC 483; 2 SCR 690 (1983).

[6] We are grateful to Bikram Jeet Batra for allowing us to draw on his excellent, as yet unpublished, paper 'The Death Penalty in India—Issues and Aspects'.

[7] Barbados, Bahrain, Brunei Darussalam (abolitionist *de facto*–ADF), China (for two Articles of the Criminal Code, see Ch. 4, pp. 144–145), Comoros (for offences against the state, treason, and espionage), Egypt, Ghana (ADF), Guatemala (rape of a child), Guinea, Guyana, India (Arms Act, drugs, and prevention of atrocities), Iran, Jordan, Kenya (ADF), Kuwait (drugs offences), Lebanon (for treason and collaboration with the enemy), Malaysia, Morocco (ADF), Nigeria, Pakistan, Qatar, Saudi Arabia (for drug importers, smugglers, and recidivist distributors), Singapore, Taiwan (in the military code and for 'causing major disturbance of the financial order or counterfeiting'), Tanzania (ADF), Thailand, Togo (ADF), Trinidad and Tobago, United Arab Emirates, Yemen, Zambia, and Zimbabwe.

[8] Similarly, the death penalty in Guinea is mandatory not just for murder but for a 'wide range of offences'. Amnesty International, *Report 2006*, p. 129.

Guyana (ADF), India, Iran, Jordan, Malaysia, Qatar, Saudi Arabia, Singapore, Thailand, and the United Arab Emirates (see Chapter 4, pages 137–139). These laws have been supported by the governments concerned on the grounds that the threat of the imposition of capital punishment in all circumstances has a potent deterrent effect, and that to make exceptions would limit that effect. Opponents of the mandatory death penalty have strongly criticized the arbitrariness of these laws because they quite often depend on the chance factor of how much of the drug the offender had in his or her possession or how much the police could trace. And they quite often fall upon persons who had a relatively low involvement or peripheral role in the organization of trading, rather than those who were the 'kingpins'.[9]

Some countries have devised an attenuated form of mandatory death sentence by invoking the principle of 'exceptional circumstances'. In Africa several countries—Botswana, Lesotho, Swaziland, and Zimbabwe—have imported Roman-Dutch common law with its concept of 'extenuating circumstances', sufficient proof of which gives the court the discretion to reduce a capital to a non-capital offence and impose a sentence other than death.[10] A similar provision exists also in Belize. Nevertheless, the failure of legislation to give any guidance as to what can constitute an extenuating circumstance means that there is a 'danger involved in making such a vital matter as extenuation depend upon the exercise of subjective moral judgment based on rather nebulous factors'.[11] In Japan, where the death penalty for ordinary offences is discretionary, it is mandatory for 'conspiring with foreign States to cause the use of armed force against Japan', but according to Japan's reply to the UN Seventh Survey there are circumstances where this punishment can be mitigated. Under the provisions of the Military Code of El Salvador, the death penalty is mandatory for treason, espionage, rebellion, and conspiracy to desert, but the judge has discretion to decide to apply it to a few of the most culpable ringleaders.

Elsewhere the approach has been to try to evade the objections to mandatory sentencing by defining only certain types of murder, regarded as particularly heinous as 'capital murder'—the premeditated murder of a police officer in Bahrain, for instance. Jamaica, and other British Commonwealth Caribbean countries, attempted to do this, following the pattern of the British Homicide Act of 1957 (see Chapter 2, pages 45–46), but even this more restrictive approach has been judged to be unlawful (see below, page 283).

United Nations institutions have made their opposition to the mandatory death penalty abundantly and repeatedly clear. In her interim report to the

---

[9] Ezzat Fattah, 'The Use of the Death Penalty for Drug Offences and Economic Crime' *Revue Internationale de Droit Pénal* 58 (1987), pp. 723–736 at 732–734.

[10] E. Dumbutshena, 'The Death Penalty in Zimbabwe' *Revue Internationale de Droit Pénal* 58 (1987), pp. 521–532.

[11] See Geoffrey Feltoe, 'Extenuating Circumstances: A Life and Death Issue' *Zimbabwe Law Review* 4 (1987), pp. 60–87.

General Assembly in 2000, the Special Rapporteur on Extra-judicial, Summary and Arbitrary Executions stated her belief that the death penalty 'should under no circumstances be mandatory'.[12] The reason for this was very fully set out by her successor Philip Alston in January 2007:[13]

[T]he proper application of human rights law—especially of its provisions that '[n]o one shall be arbitrarily deprived of his life' and that '[n]o one shall be subjected to...cruel, inhuman or degrading...punishment'—requires weighing factors that will not be taken into account in the process of determining whether a defendant is guilty of committing a 'most serious crime'. As a result, these factors can only be taken into account in the context of individualized sentencing by the judiciary in death penalty cases...The conclusion, in theory as well as in practice, was that respect for human rights can be reliably ensured in death penalty cases only if the judiciary engages in case-specific, individualized sentencing that accounts for all of the relevant factors...It is clear, therefore, that in death penalty cases, individualized sentencing by the judiciary is required to prevent cruel, inhuman or degrading punishment and the arbitrary deprivation of life.

Both the UN Human Rights Committee[14] and the Inter-American Commission on Human Rights[15] have also held that the mandatory death penalty is a violation of their respective conventions. These decisions have included cases emanating from the Bahamas, Jamaica, the Philippines, and Trinidad and Tobago, as well as Grenada and St Vincent and the Grenadines. In *Baptiste v Grenada*, for instance, the Inter-American Commission on Human Rights explained:[16]

International and domestic authorities suggest that individualized sentencing or the exercise of guided discretion by sentencing authorities to consider potential mitigating circumstances of offenders and offences is a condition *sine qua non* for the non-arbitrary and humane imposition of capital punishment.

As explained above (Chapter 3, page 104), Trinidad and Tobago, and Barbados, because of the 'savings clause' in their Constitutions, cannot consider any legal challenge to the application of capital punishment as such, including the

---

[12] See UN Doc. A/55/288, para. 34.

[13] UN Doc. A/HRC/4/20, Report of the Special Rapporteur on Extra-judicial, Summary, and Arbitrary Executions, 29 January 2007, para. 55.

[14] See *Kennedy v Trinidad and Tobago*, 28 March 2002, CCPR/C/74/D/845/1998; and *Thompson v St Vincent and the Grenadines* (2000) UN Doc. CCPR/C/70/D906/1998, which held that the mandatory death penalty breached Art. 6 (1)—the right to life—of the International Covenant on Civil and Political Rights. Also, *Chan v Guyana* UN Doc. CCPR/C/85/D/913/2000, views adopted 31 October 2005.

[15] *Hilaire v Trinidad and Tobago*, Inter-American Commission Report 66/99 (1999). In *Hilaire, Constantine and Benjamin and Others v Trinidad and Tobago* (21 June 2002, Ser. C No. 94 (2002) the Inter-American Court held that the mandatory death penalty in Trinidad and Tobago was contrary to the provisions of Art. 4(2) of the American Convention. See also *Carpo v The Philippines* (No. 1077/2002, views adopted 28 March 2003) where the Human Rights Committee held that the mandatory imposition of the death penalty (prior to abolition in 2006) for the broadly defined offence of murder by Art. 48 of the Revised Penal Code of the Philippines violated Art. 6 of the ICCPR.

[16] *Baptiste v Grenada*, CR 38/00 (2000), para. 59.

mandatory death sentence. As a consequence, it can only be abolished by the legislators of these countries.[17] However, in a landmark judgment in April 2001, the East Caribbean Court of Appeal held, in the case of *Spence and Hughes v The Queen*, that the mandatory death penalty in St Vincent and the other island states covered by the Court[18] was an arbitrary deprivation of the right to life that was not protected by the 'savings clause'. Justice J. Saunders, delivering judgment, said:[19]

The mandatory death penalty robs those upon whom sentence is passed of any opportunity whatsoever to have the court consider mitigating circumstances even as an irrevocable punishment is meted out to them. The dignity of human life is reduced by a law that compels the court to impose death by hanging upon all convicted of murder, granting none an opportunity to have the individual circumstances of his case considered by the court that is to pronounce sentence.

In March 2002 appeals on behalf of the Crown in the case of *Hughes* and also from St Christopher and Nevis (also affected by the judgment of the East Caribbean Court of Appeal) in the case of *Berthill Fox* were dismissed by the Judicial Committee of the Privy Council, which held that the imposition of a mandatory sentence of death on conviction for murder was in contravention of the offender's constitutionally guaranteed right not to be subject to inhuman or degrading punishment or treatment at the hands of the state.[20]

At the same time, the Judicial Committee of the Privy Council decided the case of *Patrick Reyes v The Queen*, which sought to clarify whether a mandatory death penalty was acceptable under the Constitution of Belize, because it was applied only to a specific class of capital murder and was always subject to review by the Board of Pardons. The Judicial Committee (in a judgment delivered by Lord Bingham of Cornhill, the senior Law Lord) declared that the fact that there existed a well-established Board of Pardons in Belize, which could mitigate the imposition of a mandatorily imposed death sentence, did not suffice. For while the act of clemency (see Chapter 7, page 260) was a proper part of the 'constitutional process of conviction, sentence and the carrying out of the sentence', it was nevertheless 'an executive act' of mercy which could not be 'a substitute for the judicial determination of the appropriate sentence'. Furthermore, the Committee accepted the argument that even a mandatory sentence imposed for a restricted

---

[17] Saul Lehrfreund, 'The Commonwealth Caribbean and Evolving International Attitudes towards the Death Penalty' in Penal Reform International *et al.*, *Commonwealth Caribbean Human Rights Seminar, Belize, 12–14 September 2000* (2001), pp. 79–82.

[18] The countries covered by this judgment are: Anguilla, Antigua and Barbuda, the British Virgin Islands, Dominica, Grenada, Montserrat, St Lucia, St Kitts and Nevis, and St Vincent and the Grenadines.

[19] *Spence and Hughes v The Queen*, Criminal Appeal No. 20 of 1998, East Caribbean Court of Appeal, Judgment (2 April 2001). See Saul Lehrfreund, 'International Legal Trends and the "Mandatory" Death Penalty in the Commonwealth Caribbean' *Oxford University Commonwealth Law Journal* 1 (2001), pp. 171–194.

[20] *The Queen v Peter Hughes* [2002] UKPC 12, para. 30; *Berthill Fox v Queen* [2002] 2 AC 284.

category of capital murder (the applicant had been sentenced on conviction of murder by shooting) 'precluded any consideration of the humanity of sentencing him to death', given the wide range of circumstances under which a shooting could occur.[21]

In November 2004 the Jamaican Senate passed an amendment to remove the mandatory death sentence for capital murder following the Privy Council's decision in *Lambert Watson v The Queen* which held that the death penalty could not be mandatorily applied even to a narrow range of 'capital' murders.[22] Only four of the 45 under sentence of death resulting from the application of the mandatory death penalty were re-sentenced to death. The mandatory death penalty was abolished in the Bahamas in March 2006 in the case of *Forrester Bowe Jr. and Trono Davis* because the Privy Council found that it violated human rights principles. The Court accepted the argument that the mandatory death penality was already a violation of international customary law when the Constitution of the Bahamas had come into force in 1973. Thus, they declared that 'The appellants should not be denied such protection because, a quarter century before they were condemned to death, the law was not fully understood'.[23] In similar vein, the Privy Council in February 2007 upheld the appeal of 13 prisoners who had been mandatorily sentenced to death in 1986 following the murders of Maurice Bishop and 10 others in the unsuccessful coup in Grenada in the Caribbean in 1983. Drawing on their decision in *Bowe*, the Privy Council held that at the time the mandatory sentences were imposed they were already unconstitutional and had been so since the Constitution came into force in 1974.[24]

The same arguments against the mandatory death penalty have been successfully employed in former British colonies in Africa. In 2005 the Constitutional Court of Uganda in the case of *Susan Kigula and 416 others*, brought by all the prisoners on death row at the time, held the mandatory death penalty to be unconstitutional for the same reasons as so many other courts have done so: namely, that it does not provide the court with the opportunity, nor the defendant the right, to put forward any mitigating circumstances, to show whether, in the particular case before it, the death penalty is the appropriate punishment.[25] Two years later, in April 2007, the Malawi High Court in the case of *Francis Kafantayeni*—the State having remained neutral on the issue—came to the same conclusion. As a result, the mandatory death sentences of all 30 prisoners on death row were vacated and the defendants remitted for sentence.[26] It is difficult to see on what

[21] *Patrick Reyes v The Queen* [2002] UKPC 11, para. 43.

[22] *Lambert Watson v The Queen* [2005] 1AC 400. In this case the panel of the Privy Council decided that the mandatory death penalty was not subject to a savings clause.

[23] *Forrester Bowe Jr. and Trono Davis v The Queen* [2006] UKPC 10, at para. 42.

[24] *Bernard Coard and others v The Attorney General of Grenada* [2007] UKPC 7.

[25] *Susan Kigula and 416 others v The Attorney General of Uganda*, Constitutional Petition No. 6 of 2003.

[26] High Court of Malawi, Constitutional Case No. 12 of 2005, *Kafantayeni v Attorney General*, 27 April 2007.

grounds similar arguments will not win the day when they are contested in Kenya (in a case already listed), Nigeria, and Tanzania.

These developments clearly indicate that international standards have become yet more firmly set against the mandatory imposition of capital punishment, and those countries which maintain such penalties are in breach of a widely accepted human rights norm.

Yet the abolition of mandatory sentences has not, and will not, resolve the problem of inequity or disproportionality in the administration of capital punishment. For the paradox is that when the death penalty is *not* mandated for a crime, it inevitably introduces 'a large element of uncertainty and discretion into the selection of who will die'.[27] In other words, whether the death penalty is mandatory or discretionary, arbitrariness and discrimination may still remain. The circumstances in which capital crimes are committed and the degree of culpability of their perpetrators varies so widely that truly equitable enforcement of the death penalty remains a 'chimera', as the British Royal Commission on capital punishment concluded over 50 years ago (see Chapter 2, pages 44–45).

(b) The exercise of discretion in capital cases

In many retentionist nations whether or not the death penalty is imposed for a capital offence is left to the discretion of the court and it is the judge who pronounces the sentence of death. But in the United States it has now been established, since the Supreme Court handed down its decision in *Ring v Arizona* in June 2002, that it is the jury that must first find the facts beyond a reasonable doubt (as opposed to the judge by a preponderance of the evidence) when such facts increase the maximum penalty available, including any determinations that would make a convicted murderer eligible for the death penalty.[28] This holding does not preclude the judge from making the ultimate sentencing decision; it simply requires that all factual findings that could make the defendant 'death-eligible' be made by a jury. As explained by John Douglass: '*Ring* attempts to draw a bright line, assigning the death-eligibility fact-finding to the jury, while leaving the ultimate exercise of sentencing discretion—the selection process—beyond the reach of the sixth amendment'.[29] In addition, '*Ring* means that a defendant contesting facts which may expose him to death is entitled not just to a jury, as *Ring* explicitly decided, but to the Sixth Amendment rights of notice, confrontation, compulsory process, and speedy and public trial as well'.[30] At present judges decide the sentence only in Montana and Nebraska (3 judge panel), while in Alabama, Delaware and

[27] Bryan Stevenson, 'Capital Punishment in the United States' in Penal Reform International *et al.*, n. 17 above, at p. 68.

[28] *Ring v Arizona*, 122 S.Ct. 2428 (2002).

[29] John G. Douglass, 'Confronting Death: Sixth Amendment Rights at Capital Sentencing' 105 *Columbia Law Review* (2005), pp. 1967–2028 at 1971.

[30] *Ibid.*, at p. 1997.

Florida the judge has the power to override a jury decision. In all other states the jury decides whether capital punishment is or is not imposed.

Whoever is empowered to decide whether or not a death sentence is imposed, some mechanisms usually exist that aim to ensure that it is not inflicted on persons at random or in an obviously discriminatory fashion. One way to ensure this is to use it *only* for the gravest of offences. It has been suggested by the British barrister, Edward Fitzgerald that the right approach towards exercising discretion in capital cases is to start from a strong presumption *against* the death penalty. He argues that 'the presence of *any significant mitigating* factor justifies exemption from the death penalty even in the most gruesome cases' and explains that:[31]

such a restrictive approach can be summarized as follows: The normal sentence should be life imprisonment. The death sentence should only be imposed instead of the life sentence in the 'rarest of rare' cases where the crime or crimes are of exceptional heinousness and the individual has no significant mitigation and is considered beyond reformation.

The policy in India since the landmark case *Bachan Singh v State of Punjab* (1980) has been to reserve the death penalty for the 'rarest of rare', meaning the most extreme cases. In *Bachan Singh* the Supreme Court listed a number of aggravating and mitigating circumstances that should be taken into account, emphasizing as aggravating factors the brutality or depravity of the murder, whether it was of a police officer, a public servant or a member of the armed forces while on duty, or a person assisting a law enforcement officer, and as mitigating circumstances, extreme mental or emotional disturbance, mental defect, age, unlikely future dangerousness, the probability of being reformed, whether the accused believed that he was morally justified or was acting under duress.[32] Three years later another bench of the Supreme Court, in *Machhhi Singh and Others v State of Punjab* (1983), developed a sort of typology of cases, with examples where the 'collective conscience' of a community may be shocked, such as 'when the murder was committed in an extremely brutal, grotesque, diabolical, revolting or dastardly manner'; 'When a murder is committed for a motive which evinces total depravity and meanness'; 'Anti-social or socially abhorrent murder' including 'dowry deaths or killings due to infatuation with another woman'; 'multiple murders of members of a particular family'; and 'where the victim

---

[31] Edward Fitzgerald, 'The Mitigating Exercise in Capital Cases' in *Death Penalty Conference 3–5 June 2005, Barbados: Conference Papers and Recommendations*, pp. 9–40 at 13, 15 and 24. See also, Edward Fitzgerald QC and Keir Starmer QC, *A Guide to Sentencing in Capital Cases* (2007) at p. 13. This is quite the opposite of the procedure in Pakistan, where a Supreme Court ruling in 2003 stated, in relation to murder, that 'the normal penalty of death should be awarded and leniency in any case should not be shown, except where strong mitigating circumstances for lesser sentence could be gathered'. According to an attorney the standard required for mitigating circumstances has since this judgment become 'preposterously high' and '*de facto* impossible to reach': quoted in FIDH, *Slow March to the Gallows: Death Penalty in Pakistan*, Report No. 464/2 January 2007, pp. 16–17.

[32] See *Bachan Singh v State of Punjab* 2 SCJ [1980] 474 at 524 and *Bachan Singh v State of Punjab* [1983] 1 SCR 145 at 252 and 256. Also Chiranjivi J. Nirmal, 'Setting an Agenda' in C. J. Nirmal (ed.), *Human Rights in India* (2000), pp. 234–269 at 252.

is an innocent child, helpless woman, aged or infirm person, a public figure whose murder is committed other than for personal reasons'.[33]

Given the range of circumstances listed and the different emphases of these two judgments, it is perhaps understandable that the courts have been inconsistent in drawing the dividing line between ordinary cases of murder and those that are regarded as the 'rarest of rare'.[34]

Japan also has a policy of only executing those who commit 'extremely heinous offences'[35] and the death penalty for murder in Egypt is said to be reserved for cases with 'certain aggravating circumstances', such as where the murder is premeditated or planned, as in poisoning.[36]

In China most crimes for which there is a discretionary death penalty stipulate the alternative sentence to be not less than ten years' imprisonment. But the use of this discretion has not been restricted or guided except by the very general and vague statement in Article 61 of the 1997 Criminal Code that 'punishment shall be meted out on the basis of the facts, nature and circumstances of the crime, the degree of harm done to society and the relevant provisions of this Law'.[37] Consequently, there appears to have been considerable arbitrariness in the imposition of capital punishment in China.[38] Now that the final review of all death sentences has been returned to the Supreme People's Court it is expected that guidelines will be drawn up.

The issue that arises from this general development towards a more restrictive use of a discretionary death penalty is whether, in practice, this has made it possible to impose it in a sufficiently even-handed and non-discriminatory manner for it to be acceptable, either under the law or constitution of the country concerned or under the generally accepted principles of proportionate and equitable treatment of persons convicted of offences of equivalent gravity. On the other hand, the experience of those American states that have retained the death penalty under new statutes, which aim to limit and guide the discretion of the court so as to make its imposition no longer arbitrary or discriminatory, casts considerable doubt on the ability of draughtsmen or criminal justice systems to achieve this aim. The American experience, which has been subject to critical legal as well as detailed empirical analysis to an extent unknown in other countries, is worth reviewing for the lessons it offers.

---

[33] *Machhi Singh and Others v State of Punjab* (1983) 3 SCR 413.

[34] Bikram Jeet Batra, 'The Death Penalty in India—Issues and Aspects' unpublished paper, 2007.

[35] Japan, National Statement on *Crime Prevention for Freedom, Justice, Peace and Development* (1985), p. 139.

[36] N. Hosni, 'La Peine de mort en droit égyptien et en droit islamique' *Revue Internationale de Droit Pénal* 58 (1987), pp. 407–420 at 412.

[37] Criminal Law of the People's Republic of China (1997), Ch. 4, 'The Concrete Application of Punishments'. Also, Hans-Jörg Albrecht, 'The Death Penalty in China from a European Perspective' in M. Nowak and Xin Chunying (eds.), *EU-China Human Rights Dialogue: Proceedings of the Second EU-China Legal Experts' Seminar Held in Beijing on 19 and 20 October 1998* (2000), pp. 95–118 at 96.

[38] Marina Svensson, 'State Coercion, Deterrence, and the Death Penalty in the PRC', paper presented to the Annual Meeting of the Association of Asian Studies, Chicago, 22–25 March 2001.

2. Legal Analyses: The American Experience

As is well known, the US Supreme Court held by a majority in *Furman v Georgia* (1972) that the death penalty statute of the state of Georgia was unconstitutional because it was being applied in an arbitrary and capricious fashion, and in a way that discriminated against the poor and especially African-Americans. The death penalty was being inflicted more and more rarely, and the circumstances in which persons were sentenced to the supreme penalty were often indistinguishable from many others where the defendant received a lesser penalty. In the oft-quoted words of Justice Stewart, for anyone to be sentenced to death was such a freakish event that it was 'cruel and unusual in the same sense that being struck by lightning is cruel and unusual'.[39] As a result, all the outstanding death sentences in the retentionist states were commuted to life imprisonment.

Although many believed that capital punishment would not be resurrected, 38 states and the federal government subsequently passed new statutes aimed at meeting the requirements of the equal protection clause of the Fourteenth Amendment and the prohibition against cruel and unusual punishment of the Eighth Amendment of the US Constitution. As mentioned above, the Supreme Court refused to endorse any statutes that laid down a mandatory death penalty.[40] Thus, the new statutes had to define the categories of persons who could be sentenced to death sufficiently narrowly and with such constraints as to avoid its arbitrary or discriminatory infliction and yet, at the same time, sufficiently broadly to allow the discretion necessary to treat each case on its specific merits.

(a) The reformed statutes

The solution, which had been offered by the Model Penal Code, was to enumerate a specific list of aggravating and mitigating circumstances.[41] The procedures, according to this 'blueprint', were to be as follows:[42]

A capital sentence is excluded if the court is satisfied that none of the aggravating circumstances was established by the evidence at the trial or would be established on a

---

[39] *Furman v Georgia*, 408 U.S. 238, 309 (1972).

[40] *Woodson v North Carolina*, 428 U.S. 280 (1976).

[41] Franklin Zimring maintains that these 'death penalty provisions are arguably the element of the original [Model Penal] Code most in need of redrafting' (p. 1398), and regrets that the American Law Institute in its proposals for revising the Code's provisions on sentencing and punishment, have not included capital punishment—because it is a 'politically charged terrain' (p. 1399). He argues that the original Code's list of felonies for automatic eligibility for a death penalty 'is probably responsible...for more death sentences and executions than all other aggravating factors combined' (p. 1403). Franklin E. Zimring, 'The Unexamined Death Penalty: Capital Punishment and Reform of the Model Penal Code' 105 *Columbia Law Review* (2005), pp. 1396–1415.

[42] Quoted from Herbert Wechsler, 'The Model Penal Code and the Codification of American Criminal Law' in R. Hood (ed.), *Crime, Criminology, and Public Policy: Essays in Honour of Sir Leon Radzinowicz* (1974), pp. 419–468 at 452–453.

further proceeding to determine sentence; that substantial mitigating circumstances calling for leniency were established at the trial; that the defendant was under eighteen years of age at the time of the crime; that his mental or physical condition calls for leniency; or that the evidence does not foreclose all doubt respecting the defendant's guilt. If no such finding is made, a further proceeding is initiated before the court or court and jury. Much scope is given to the evidence admissible in that proceeding. The court or jury is directed to take into account the enumerated aggravating and mitigating circumstances and any other facts considered relevant. Capital sentence is again excluded unless the tribunal finds that one of the aggravating circumstances and no mitigating circumstance sufficiently substantial to call for leniency are established. Apart from this, the sentence is discretionary but if the jurisdiction puts the issue to the jury, it must be unanimous for penalty of death and the court must concur in its opinion for the sentence to be passed.

In implementing the suggestion of the Model Penal Code, post-*Furman* statutes have adopted one of three basic approaches in their procedure for taking account of aggravating and mitigating circumstances. 'Balancing Schemes' 'require the judge or jury to identify the aggravating and mitigating factors associated with the offence and offender, [and to] to balance or weigh these factors against one another', while 'Threshold Schemes' state that 'proof of at least one statutory aggravating factor makes the offender eligible for death' before the judge or jury is to 'consider' other aggravating and mitigating circumstances.[43] Three states, Oregon, Texas, and Virginia, require 'special sentencing issue' determinations before a defendant can be sentenced to death, with Oregon and Texas requiring a finding concerning the defendant's future dangerousness and Virginia requiring a finding of future dangerousness or of 'outrageously or wantonly vile, horrible or inhumane conduct'.[44] In addition, the post-*Furman* statutory provisions of another 21 states also include a defendant's potential for future violence among the aggravating factors that jurors *may* take into account if invited to do so. In other words, juries are required when considering aggravating circumstances to predict the likelihood of future serious violence.[45]

In a series of cases in 1976 the US Supreme Court upheld the statutes of Georgia, Florida, and Texas, all of which in one way or another provided legislative guidelines for the exercise of the discretion of judge and jury and conformed to several features of the Model Penal Code's draft statute.[46] They all listed a number of specific aggravating circumstances, such as murder carried out during

---

[43] See James R. Acker and Charles S. Lanier, 'Beyond Human Ability? The Rise and Fall of Death Penalty Legislation' in J. R. Acker, R. M. Bohm and C. S. Lanier (eds.), *America's Experiment with Capital Punishment* (2nd edn., 2003), pp. 85–125 at 109–113.

[44] *Ibid.*, at p. 112.

[45] Jonathan R. Sorenson and Rocky L. Pilgrim, 'An Actuarial Risk Assessment of Violence Posed by Capital Murder Defendants' *Journal of Criminal Law and Criminology* 90 (2000), pp. 1251–1270 at 1252.

[46] *Gregg v Georgia*, 428 U.S. 153 (1976); *Proffitt v Florida*, 428 U.S. 242 (1976); *Jurek v Texas*, 428 U.S. 262 (1976). For a more detailed discussion of the way in which these statutes differed from

a felony and murder of law enforcement personnel; provided for a bifurcated trial, with a separate hearing before a jury to determine sentence; and ensured an automatic review by the State Supreme Court or Court of Criminal Appeals.

Yet, in other important ways the statutes differed quite widely both in their objectives and in their specific form.[47] For example, 27 states, including Georgia and Florida, provided that the appellate review should include what is known as a 'proportionality review' to assess 'whether the death sentence is excessive or disproportionate to the penalty imposed in similar cases, considering both the crime and the defendant'. Four states included no such legal obligation but have nevertheless carried out such reviews, and seven states, including Texas, have no provisions for a proportionality review.

Florida listed in its statute seven *mitigating* circumstances (as did some other states, such as Kentucky). Georgia, Ohio, and three other states did not, leaving the range of mitigating factors completely unspecified.[48] The Georgia statute (and the Florida statute in similar terms) included within its list of specified *aggravating* circumstances whether the crime was committed by a person involved in one or more contemporaneous offences, such as a rape or an armed robbery, and whether the crime was 'outrageously or wantonly vile, horrible or inhuman in that it involved torture, depravity of mind, or an aggravated battery of the victim'.

In 1978 the Supreme Court invalidated Ohio's death penalty statute in *Lockett v Ohio*, because it violated the principle that the sentencer 'not be precluded from considering, *as a mitigating factor*, any aspect of the defendant's character or record and any of the circumstances of the offense that the defendant proffers as a basis for a sentence less than death'.[49] Based on this principle, the Court set aside a death sentence in *Hitchcock v Dugger*,[50] under the Florida statute previously upheld in *Proffitt*, because the statute did not allow for consideration of *all* mitigating circumstances. Recently, the Supreme Court reaffirmed this principle in *Abdul-Kabir v Quarterman*,[51] where it invalidated the 'special issues' procedure in Texas because the procedure prevented the jurors from giving meaningful consideration to the defendant's mitigating evidence, namely his abused childhood. The procedure required the judge to impose a death sentence based on the

---

the Model Penal Code, see F. E. Zimring and G. Hawkins, *Capital Punishment and the American Agenda* (1986), pp. 77–92.

[47] See, for example, James A. Acker and Elizabeth R. Walsh, 'Challenging the Death Penalty under State Constitutions' *Vanderbilt Law Review* 42 (1989), pp. 1299–1363 at 1362. And James A. Acker and Charles S. Lanier, 'Matters of Life and Death: The Sentencing Provisions of the Capital Punishment Statutes' *Criminal Law Bulletin* 31 (1995), pp. 19–60.

[48] J. A. Acker and C. S. Lanier, 'In Fairness and Mercy: Statutory Mitigating Factors in Capital Punishment Laws' *Criminal Law Bulletin* 30 (1994), pp. 299–345.

[49] 438 U.S. 536. This principle was reiterated in *Eddings v Oklahoma*, 455 U.S. 104 (1982) and *Skipper v South Carolina*, 476 U.S. 1 (1986).

[50] 481 U.S. 393 (1987).

[51] No. 05-11284 (2007).

affirmative jury response to two questions, one concerning the severity of the crime and the other concerning future dangerousness, neither of which allowed for the consideration of the mitigating evidence presented by the defendant.

In 1991, pursuant to the Supreme Court's decision in *Payne v Tennessee*, prosecutors were allowed for the first time to introduce evidence that the victim was 'an individual whose death represents a unique loss to society', thus making it possible to present to the court a 'victim-impact statement' (see Chapter 7, pages 244–247).[52]

(b) Legal critiques of the post-*Furman* statutes

The post-*Furman* death penalty statutes have been subjected to critical scrutiny by many legal scholars, most of whom have concluded that they 'represent only the most modest advance towards formality over the old pre-*Furman* statute(s)'.[53] Further:[54]

Although contemporary post-*Furman* statutes represent a wholesale revision of earlier capital punishment laws, the new legislation in practice has delivered little more than a series of empty promises. Serious and perhaps inexorable problems linger in the administration of modern death-penalty statutes.

James Acker and Charles Lanier have noted that in 23 states (or three-fifths of those with the death penalty) capital punishment can be imposed in cases of felony murder,[55] even though the offender had himself or herself no intention to kill.[56] In a few jurisdictions a death sentence *must* be imposed if the sentencer finds that aggravating circumstances outweigh mitigating factors, or if it is found that one or more aggravating factors exist but no mitigating features have been established, as in Pennsylvania.[57] In 1990 the US Supreme Court ruled in *Blystone v Pennsylvania* that this did not violate the ruling against a mandatory death

---

[52] *Payne v Tennessee*, 501 U.S. 808 (1991). See Michael Vitiello, '*Payne v Tennessee*: A "Stunning Ipse Dixit"' *Notre Dame Journal of Law, Ethics and Public Policy* 8 (1994), pp. 165–280 at 167.

[53] See, for example, Robert Weisberg, 'Deregulating Death' *Supreme Court Review* (1983), pp. 305–395 at 321; and R. A. Bonner, 'Death Penalty' *Annual Survey of American Law* (1984), pp. 493–513 at 498–499. Also Michael Hintze, 'Tinkering with the machinery of death: Capital Punishment's toll on the American Judiciary' *Judicature* 89(5) (2006), pp. 254–257 at 257.

[54] Acker and Lanier, 'Beyond Human Ability? The Rise and Fall of Death Penalty Legislation', n. 43 above, at p. 115.

[55] For example, Georgia law allows for the imposition of a death sentence when the defendant has been convicted either of malice murder or of felony murder. Malice murders are those murders committed with express malice (intent to kill) or implied malice (an abandoned and malignant heart or a reckless disregard for human life). Felony murder is a killing in the commission of a felony irrespective of malice. The Georgia ABA report has recommended that the death penalty should only be imposed where the jury has found the defendant acted with either express or implied malice: ABA, *The Georgia Death Penalty Assessment Report* (January 2006), p. iv.

[56] J. A. Acker and C. S. Lanier, 'The Dimensions of Capital Murder' *Criminal Law Bulletin* 29 (1993), pp. 379–417 at 385.

[57] Acker and Lanier, 'Matters of Life and Death', n. 47 above, p. 27.

penalty so long as the jury was allowed to review all mitigating factors.[58] It is obvious that if avoiding the death penalty is based on finding at least one mitigating factor, there must be much room for subjective assessment of the circumstances in which murders are carried out—which in Pennsylvania can be anything pertaining to the circumstances of the crime or the character and record of the defendant. Most state statutes require that the aggravating circumstances *outweigh* the mitigating circumstances, but this is not always the case. In 2006, the Supreme Court upheld a Kansas statute that mandated a death sentence where aggravating and mitigating circumstances were in *equipoise*.[59]

When weighing aggravating and mitigating circumstances, there is much room for different perceptions, subjective judgments, and theories of crime causation which can influence the interpretation of events on which a life-or-death decision rests. This is particularly so where the jury is required to consider as an aggravating factor whether the murder was 'heinous, atrocious or cruel' or some similar test.[60] 'Far from ensuring that the class of the "death-eligible" is meaningfully narrowed, factors that focus on whether an intentional murder was "especially heinous" or manifested an "utter disregard for human life" invite an affirmative answer in every case'.[61]

The recent Death Penalty Assessment Reports issued by the ABA for Arizona and Alabama raised concerns about such legal provisions. The Arizona report noted that in 2002 the Arizona Capital Case Commission had expressed concern about the ambiguity of the (F)(6) statutory aggravating circumstance (a murder committed in an 'especially cruel, heinous or depraved manner'), but no change has yet been introduced. The report concluded that 'given the inherent vagueness of this aggravating circumstance, it is of utmost importance that the State of Arizona adopt a uniform and specific definition of this aggravating circumstance when instructing jurors during the aggravation phase of a capital trial'.[62]

In addition, critics have pointed to cases where death sentences were imposed and upheld after appellate review where the circumstances of the offence were by no stretch of the imagination the most egregious.[63] John Spinkelink, the first

---

[58] Joan Biskupic, *The Supreme Court Yearbook, 1989–1990* (1991), p. 39. This is the case also under Arizona law. See *Walton v Arizona, ibid.*, p. 40. Also, Acker and Lanier, n. 47 above, pp. 29–30.

[59] *Kansas v Marsh*, 04–1170 (2006) held that the Eighth Amendment allowed the imposition of the death penalty as long as the mitigating circumstances did not outweigh the aggravating circumstances.

[60] J. A. Acker and C. S. Lanier, ' "Passing this Lexicon of Death", Aggravating Factors in Capital Sentencing Statutes' *Criminal Law Bulletin* 30 (1994), pp. 107–152 at 124–130.

[61] Carol S. Steiker and Jordan M. Steiker, 'Judicial Developments in Capital Punishment Law' in Acker, Bohm, and Lanier (eds.), n. 43 above, pp. 55–83 at 65.

[62] ABA, *The Arizona Death Penalty Assessment Report* (July 2006), p. iv. Also, ABA, *The Alabama Death Penalty Assessment Report* (June 2006), p. v.

[63] B. L. Ledewitz, 'The New Role of Statutory Aggravating Circumstances in American Death Penalty Law' *Duquesne Law Review* 22 (1984), pp. 317–396 at 391–392, discussing the case of *Godfrey v Georgia*; and *American University Law Review*, Note, 'The Death Penalty in Georgia: An Aggravating Circumstance' 30 (1981), pp. 835–861 at 853–854.

person to be executed by Florida after the *Furman* decision was, according to the Assistant Attorney General who represented the state, 'the least obnoxious person on death row in terms of the crime he committed'.[64] Perhaps the former Chief Justice of Florida's Supreme Court had such a case in mind when he conceded that 'We certainly have executed those people who...didn't fit the criteria for execution in the state of Florida'.[65]

Statutes which make an assessment of the convicted murderer's future dangerousness relevant to consideration of the death penalty have also been severely criticized.[66] Psychiatrists are called upon in these circumstances to say whether or not the prisoner will commit further homicides, yet all the evidence suggests that, despite their apparent certainty in individual cases, they are much more often wrong than correct. For example, a comparison was made between 92 death-sentenced, but commuted, Texas prisoners (who had been found to be very likely to commit criminal acts of violence that would constitute a continuing threat to society) and a group of life-sentenced prisoners convicted in capital murder trials. This comparison showed that the former 'dangerous murderers' had no higher incidence of prison violence: only one committed a gang murder in prison. Of 12 such 'dangerous murderers' who were released, one did commit a further murder but 11 did not. This is a very high rate of false positives (that is, persons predicted to be dangerous who turned out not to be so) and other studies have produced similar findings.[67] There is no doubt that jurors when asked to estimate the dangerousness of persons convicted of capital murder greatly overestimate the likelihood that they will commit further violent acts.[68]

A bizarre application of 'categorical' rather than clinical risk assessment was made in a Texas capital murder case in 1996. The jury, at the penalty phase of the trial, was asked to assess the defendant's risk of violence. The statutory question was whether the defendant, if not executed, 'would commit criminal acts of violence that would constitute a continuing threat to society'. The Attorney General of Texas introduced as an expert witness a psychologist who found that the defendant, Victor Saldano, possessed many risk factors for violence, including Hispanic ethnicity (based on the over-representation of Hispanics in the prison population), which the witness testified was 'a factor weighing in favor of future

---

[64] Quoted in J. Greenberg, 'Capital Punishment as a System' *Yale Law Journal* 91 (1982), pp. 908–936 at 926–927.

[65] *The Spectator*, 21 March 2001.

[66] Jon Sorensen and James Marquart, 'Future dangerousness and Incapacitation' in Acker, Bohm, and Lanier (eds.), n. 43 above, pp. 283–300 at 283, argue that 'Statutes which demand, as well as those which allow death penalty decisions to be based on future dangerousness, result in the same sort of standard-less sentencing denounced by the Court in *Furman*'.

[67] See James W. Marquart, Sheldon Ekland-Olson, and Jonathan R. Sorensen, 'Gazing into the Crystal Ball: Can Jurors Accurately Predict Dangerousness in Capital Cases?' *Law and Society Review* 23 (1989), pp. 449–468; J. W. Marquart and J. R. Sorensen, 'Institutional and Post-release Behavior of *Furman*-Commuted Inmates in Texas' *Criminology* 26 (1988), pp. 677–693, which found a ratio of true to false positives among those regarded as dangerous of 1:20.

[68] Sorensen and Pilgrim, n. 45 above.

dangerousness'. The jury subsequently sentenced Saldano to death. The Texas Court of Criminal Appeals upheld the sentence, one of the judges stating: 'I am convinced that, the reference by [the witness] to the fact that Hispanics and African-Americans are incarcerated at a rate greater than their percentage of the general population of this country did not harm [the] appellant'. He nevertheless did not deny that 'The danger that such testimony could be interpreted by a jury in a particular case as evidence that minorities are more violent than non-minorities is real'. The defendant petitioned for *certiorari* to the US Supreme Court, and at the hearing in 2000 the Texas Attorney General conceded that 'because the use of race in Saldano's sentencing seriously undermined the fairness, integrity, or public reputation of the judicial process, Texas confesses error and agrees that Saldano is entitled to a new sentencing hearing'.[69] As a result, an amendment to the Texas Code of Criminal Procedure, effective from 1 September 2001, laid down that 'Evidence may not be offered by the state to establish that the race or ethnicity of the defendant makes it likely that the defendant will engage in future criminal conduct'.

Also to be considered is the constitutional propriety of making the death penalty dependent upon uncertain future actions which may fall short of causing death and thus are not, in themselves, liable to the death penalty, or dependent on judgments of future dangerousness based on past actions which were not at the time considered dangerous. Thus in the case of Steve Roach, executed in Virginia in January 2000 for shooting Mary Ann Hughes, assessment of his future dangerousness was based in part on a parole violation for possessing a shotgun, despite the fact that no adult, including the police, had seen fit to remove it from him.[70]

Furthermore, judgments might be based merely on the prisoner's 'record', as in the case of Thomas Barefoot, whose death sentence was upheld by the US Supreme Court in 1983 even though the psychiatric evidence of dangerousness was given by two practitioners who had not personally examined the defendant.[71]

Another problematic issue is the extent to which jurors are able to make informed judgments between a death sentence or life imprisonment based on their knowledge of the real effects of being sentenced to life without parole or to a specific minimum period before consideration of parole. In an important judgment, *Simmons v South Carolina* (1994), the Supreme Court ruled that the jury must be told about the possibility of sentencing a defendant to prison for life without parole *if* the prosecution uses the defendant's dangerousness as an argument for the death penalty, so that a choice can be made between death and lifetime incarceration.[72]

[69] *Saldano v Texas*, 530 U.S. 1212 (2000). For a description of the case, see *Texas Lawyer*, 12 June 2000, 13 November 2000, and 5 March 2001.

[70] Amnesty International, *Death Penalty Developments March 1998–March 2000*, AI Index: AMR 51/03/00.

[71] *Barefoot v Estelle*, (1983) 463 U.S. 880.

[72] *Simmons v South Carolina*, 512 US 154 (1994). Also, *The Supreme Court Yearbook, 1993–1994* (1995), p. 74.

Despite this ruling, in *Brown v Texas*, decided in 1997, the Supreme Court denied *certiorari* in a case where the jury was denied information about how long the defendant would serve in prison if not sentenced to death. Also, in *Weeks v Angelone* (2000), the Supreme Court upheld a death sentence despite the fact that the jury had not understood that it was entitled to sentence the defendant to life imprisonment.[73] It was not until 2001 that the Supreme Court, in *Shafer v South Carolina*,[74] affirmed that whenever dangerousness is an 'issue' at the sentencing stage, due process requires that, under the sentencing statutes of that state, the jury must be informed that a life sentence carries no possibilities of parole. However what probably matters most is what juries believe about the possibilities of release (see Chapter 11, page 390).[75]

Furthermore, a study based on interviews with 240 jurors who had made decisions in 58 cases across six states (California, Kentucky, Missouri, North Carolina, South Carolina, and Texas) provided convincing evidence that 'for many jurors, the decision about guilt is so overwhelming that it precludes a separate decision about what a proper sentence might be'.[76] In other words, the juries' involvement in the guilt trial so influenced them that they were not in a frame of mind to give due weight to mitigation evidence. The authors concluded that 'A different kind of sentencing hearing is needed, with a new jury not committed to the prosecution's story from the outset, and with the defense taking the stage first to present its story of mitigation in terms of the defendant's character and background'.[77]

Many legal scholars have also pointed out that the US Supreme Court has endorsed statutes which, in certain ways, appear likely to loosen the constraints on the discretion of judges and juries and so once more give them wide, maybe too wide, discretionary scope. It decided, in *Lockett v Ohio* (1978) and other cases, that all mitigating factors should be considered and weighed in the balance, even if they are not among those specifically listed in the statute. Under the law of several states, such as Florida, only statutory aggravating factors may be taken into account by the jury, but this is not required constitutionally, for in *Zant v Stephens*

---

[73] *Weeks v Angelone*, 528 U.S. 225 (2000).

[74] *Shafer v South Carolina*, 532 US 348 (2001).

[75] See Julian Killingley, 'Note on *Shafer v South Carolina*' *Amicus Journal* 3 (2001), pp. 20–21.

[76] Ursula Bentele and William J. Bowers, 'How Jurors Decide on Death: Guilt is Overwhelming; Aggravation requires Death; and Mitigation is no Excuse' *Brooklyn Law Review* 66 (2001), pp. 1011–1080 at 1030. Also, Wanda D. Foglia, 'They know not what they do: unguided and misguided discretion in Pennsylvania Capital Cases' *Justice Quarterly* 20 (2003), pp, 187–211 at 197–198 and 205.

[77] Bentele and Bowers, n. 76 above, at 1061. This practical suggestion is part of the ongoing assessment of the role of the capital jury in the sentencing process and the shortcomings of the current system. See, e.g., Susan D. Rozelle, 'The Principled Executioner: Capital Juries' Bias And The Benefits Of True Bifurcation' *Arizona State Law Journal* 38 (2006) pp. 769–807 (advocating a repeal of the unitary jury requirement in capital cases in some jurisdictions); see, more generally, Nancy J. King, *et al.*, 'Panel Discussion on The Capital Jury' *Indiana Law Journal* 80 (2005) pp. 47–67 (discussing the role of, and the problems with, capital juries in a bifurcated system).

(1983) the Court declared that all aggravating circumstances could be considered regardless of whether they related to the aggravating circumstance which had brought the defendant within the scope of the death penalty provisions of the statute. The argument was that the statutory aggravating factor merely acted to narrow the class of persons eligible for the death sentence, and that once such narrowing had taken place all factors of aggravation and mitigation should be considered. But this, of course, undermines the policy of controlling the degree of discretion to impose a death sentence.[78]

In addition, in *Pulley v Harris* (1984), a Californian case, the Supreme Court confirmed that there was no constitutional requirement for the appeal court to compare the sentence of death with sentences imposed in similar cases: it was an additional safeguard but not a critical one.[79] Furthermore, the Court held that in Louisiana, where a proportionality review is mandatory,[80] it was sufficient for the appeal court to compare the death sentence with cases from the same narrow judicial district rather than make a state-wide comparison with other cases (*Maggio v Williams*, 1983).[81]

The Supreme Court has declared that it is 'unwilling to say that there is any one right way for a State to set up its capital sentencing scheme'.[82] Nevertheless, the conclusion reached by legal scholars is that the attempts made by the various states and the decisions reached by the Supreme Court have nowhere produced a system that reduces the scope of discretion to a level where arbitrariness will not result. In 1994, in the case of *Callins v Collins*, Justice Blackmun, a former strong supporter of the death penalty, came to a similar conclusion about the efforts since *Gregg* in 1976 to fashion 'legal formulas and procedures that would sufficiently control arbitrariness in the infliction of the death penalty by capital juries'. He said[83]:

The death penalty remains fraught with arbitrariness, discrimination, caprice, and mistake ... Experience has taught us that the constitutional goal of eliminating arbitrariness and discrimination from the administration of death ... can never be achieved without compromising an equally essential component of fundamental fairness—individualized sentencing ... It is virtually self-evident to me now that no combination of procedural rules

---

[78] Bonner, n. 53 above, pp. 498–499. And for a succinct summary of the law, see Acker and Lanier, 'Beyond Human Ability', n. 43 above.

[79] It had, in effect, decided this when upholding the Texas statute, which does not provide for proportionality review, in *Jurek v Texas*, 428 U.S. 262 (1976).

[80] Bonner, n. 53 above, pp. 493–494; Barry Nakell and Kenneth A. Hardy, *The Arbitrariness of the Death Penalty* (1987), p. 66; and *Howard Law Journal*, Note, 'Safeguarding Eighth Amendment Rights with a Comparative Proportionality Review in the Imposition of the Death Penalty, *Pulley v Harris'* 28 (1985), pp. 331–333.

[81] The ABA Death Penalty Assessment Reports for Alabama, Georgia, and Arizona all found the proportionality review of death sentences to be inadequate.

[82] Stephen Gillers, 'The Quality of Mercy: Constitutional Accuracy at the Selection Stage of Capital Sentencing' *University of California Davis Law Review*, 18 (1985), pp. 1037–1111, quoting the judgment in *Spaziano v Florida* (1984) at 1111.

[83] *Callins v Collins*, 510 US 1141 (1994), pp. 1129–1130.

or substantive regulations can ever save the death penalty from its inherent constitutional deficiencies. The basic question—does the system accurately and consistently determine which defendants 'deserve' to die?—cannot be answered in the affirmative... The problem is that the inevitability of factual, legal, and moral error gives us a system that fails to deliver the fair, consistent, and reliable sentences of death required by the Constitution.

In an oft-quoted passage, Blackmun further declared:[84]

From this day forward, I no longer shall tinker with the machinery of death... to continue to coddle the Court's delusion that the desired level of fairness has been achieved and the need for regulation eviscerated, I feel morally and intellectually obligated simply to concede that the death penalty experiment has failed.

It is a conclusion that many academic lawyers believe has been borne out by experience over the last twenty years. In numerous books and articles they have emphasized the impossibility of concurrently maximizing both flexibility and non-arbitrariness; or of encapsulating in legal rules decisions that ultimately rest upon the subjective moral evaluations of prosecutors, juries, and judges.

Furthermore, it has been argued that the apparently restrictive death penalty laws enacted in the United States in response to *Furman* have, in fact, 'legitimated capital punishment' by creating 'a false aura of rationality', thereby giving the *impression* that the imposition of the death penalty is highly regulated and carefully monitored, even when it is not. 'The Court's death penalty law thus leaves sentencing judges and juries with a false sense that their power is safely circumscribed'.[85] Yet, in his 1998 report on the death penalty in the United States, the UN Special Rapporteur on Extra-judicial, Summary, and Arbitrary Executions wrote that laws increasing the number of crimes which are eligible for the death penalty contravened the restrictive intent of Article 6 (2) of the ICCPR. For the truth is that aggravating factors, widening the potential scope of capital punishment, continue to be added to statutes across the United States.

Between 1998 and 2007 some further aggravating factors have been included in state death penalty statutes.[86] These include: murder of two or more persons in the course of one 'scheme' and murder that was one of a series committed by the defendant (Alabama); 'murder committed to promote a street gang or criminal syndicate', 'murder with the intent to prevent cooperation with law enforcement or to prevent or retaliate for court testimony', 'murder committed in a cold, calculated manner', and 'murder committed by using a "remote stun gun"' (Arizona);

---

[84] *Callins v Collins*, p. 1130.

[85] Steiker and Steiker, n. 61 above, pp. 75–78. Also Roger Hood, 'Capital Punishment' in M. Tonry (ed.), *The Handbook of Criminology* (1998), pp. 739–776 at 767–768.

[86] Amnesty International, *United States of America: Failing the Future—Death Penalty Developments, March 1998–March 2000*, AI Index: AMR 51/03/00, p. 9. Also, US Department of Justice, *Capital Punishment 1999* (2000), *Capital Punishment 2000* (2001), *Capital Punishment 2001* (2002), *Capital Punishment 2002* (2003), *Capital Punishment 2003* (2004), and *Capital Punishment 2005* (2006).

'murder of a child under the age of 12' (Arkansas); 'where the victim was a peace officer at a state hospital' (California); murder 'because of the victim's race, color, ancestry, religion, or national origin', 'use of a weapon during a Class 1 felony when use of the weapon itself constituted a felony under State or Federal Law' including 'use of chemical, biological or radiological weapons', 'intentional killing of more than one person in more than one criminal episode' (Colorado); 'murder to avoid arrest or prosecution' (Connecticut); 'murder of a person in retaliation for providing court testimony' (Delaware); 'murder of conservation officers' (Georgia and Mississippi); 'murder committed on school property or in any venue related to a school-sponsored activity when the perpetrator intended to cause death or substantial bodily harm to more than one person by means of a weapon, device or course of action that would normally be hazardous to the lives of more than one person' (Nevada); 'any murder where the victim had a domestic violence restraining order filed against the defendant' (New Jersey); 'killing a pregnant woman' (Colorado and Indiana); 'intentional killing of an under 14 year old boy by an over 21 year old', 'deliberate killing of any person in the commission of an act of terrorism', and 'the murder of judges and witnesses' (Virginia); and 'murder in the commission of abuse against a child under 16 years of age' (Wyoming).[87] California may have the most aggravating circumstances of all. A 1977 statute first increased the number of 'special circumstances' that could be used to justify a death sentence from 10 to 12, then added 14 new special circumstances in 1978 (proposition 7), and several more since then, bringing the total to 25 or 36 when various subsections are also included.[88]

Jonathan Simon and Christina Spaulding have called these often 'symbolic' additions to the list of aggravators 'tokens of our esteem...that legislators could use to serve constituencies interested in capital punishment'.[89] They conclude that when all these new aggravating circumstances are taken into account, some 80 to 90 per cent of defendants who were death-eligible before the *Furman* decision were still death-eligible.[90] This movement to extend the categories of persons and situations for which the death penalty may be imposed was, however, seriously challenged by

[87] The following legislative attempts failed: California (1998, murder of victim under 14 or murder by arson or kidnapping; 1999, murder of a victim protected by restraining order, or during rape or/molestation of child); Connecticut (murder with torture); Florida (murder of a victim protected by restraining order); Georgia (death caused by distribution, etc. of drugs); Maryland (murder of a victim protected by court order, murder involving drug trafficking); Missouri (murder of child under 13); Texas (murder where victim protected by court order, where victim tortured); and Washington (1999, murder where victim was pregnant). *Ibid.*

[88] Glenn L. Pierce and Michael L. Radelet, 'The Impact of Legally Inappropriate Factors on Death Sentencing for California Homicides, 1990–1999' 46 *Santa Clara Law Review* (2005), pp. 1–47 at 3. An increase in available aggravating circumstances does not always correspond with an increase in the number of capital sentences. Pierce and Radelet point out that 'less than 1% of all homicides result in a death sentence': *ibid.*, at p. 19.

[89] Jonathan Simon and Christina Spaulding, 'Tokens of our Esteem: Aggravating Factors in the Era of Deregulated Death Penalties' in Austin Sarat (ed.), *The Killing State: Capital Punishment in Law, Politics, and Culture* (1999), pp. 81–136.

[90] *Ibid.*, p. 87.

the report of Governor Ryan's Commission to investigate the use of capital punishment in Illinois. The report, published in April 2002, recommended that 'the current list of 20 factual circumstances under which a defendant is eligible for a death sentence should be eliminated in favor of a simpler and narrower group of eligibility criteria'. In doing this, the majority of the Commission boldly advocated the abolition of the felony-murder category altogether, so that the death penalty could only be applied in five types of case: 'where the defendant has murdered two or more persons, or where the victim was either a police officer or a firefighter; or an officer or inmate of a correctional institution; or was murdered to obstruct the justice system; or was tortured in the course of the murder'. This selection of crimes was, it seems, chosen because those who wished to retain capital punishment believed that 'it retains an important role in...expressing on behalf of the community, the strongest condemnation of a small number of the most heinous crimes'.[91] While any abolitionist would welcome, as a step in the right direction, the reduction in the categories of crime to which capital punishment can apply, there is nevertheless no reason to believe that the selection of crimes chosen by the Commission is any more defensible, in terms of morality or social policy, than a list that would include other crimes. Nor will it avoid unsupportable anomalies—for example, it will not be obvious why killing a firefighter is intrinsically worse than killing an ambulance worker, or why killing a prison inmate is worse than killing a child.

The Council on Capital Punishment, appointed by Governor Mitt Romney of Massachusetts, which reported in 2005, recommended that any statute should include only a 'narrowly defined list of death-eligible murders...so that only "the worst of the worst" murders, and murderers, will be eligible for the ultimate punishment'.[92] The five categories of murder chosen on the basis that 'the overwhelming majority of such murders are among the most heinous of all crimes' were: '(1) murder as an act of political terrorism, (2) murder to obstruct justice, and (3) narrowly defined torture-murder...(4) multiple murder in a single episode, (5) multiple murder in more than one episode, and (6) murder by a defendant who is already subject to a sentence of life imprisonment without possibility of parole for a prior murder'.[93] It has been disputed whether this list does include cases in which the overwhelming majority of defendants deserve death—take, for example, murders of multiple intra-family members—and also that there would inevitably be 'legislative' or 'aggravator' 'creep' as categories were added in response to particularly heinous cases of other types of murder.[94]

---

[91] *Report of the Governor's Commission on Capital Punishment: George H. Ryan Governor* (April 2002), pp. ii, iii, and 65–67.

[92] See 'Report of the Governor's Council on Capital Punishment—Introduction' *Indiana Law Journal* 80 (2005), pp. 1–27 at 2–3. The Constitution project, a Washington DC bipartisan organization, issued a report in 2006 which also recommended a restricted list of criteria for determining death penalty eligibility: The Constitution Project Death Penalty Initiative, *Mandatory Justice: the Death Penalty Revisited* at pp. xxiv–xxv.

[93] Report of the Governor's Council on Capital Punishment, *ibid.*, p. 11.

[94] Franklin E. Zimring, 'Symbol and Substance in the Massachusetts Commission Report' *Indiana Law Journal* 80 (2005), pp. 115–129 at 120.

In any event, the foregoing clearly illustrates that the post-*Furman* statutes have serious flaws that demand reform and call into question the ability to devise a system that can administer the death penalty in a way that is not arbitrary, unfair, and cruel. This 'broken system' is another strong justification for the abolition of the death penalty.[95]

3. Criminological Investigations

(a) Methodological considerations

The validity of the legal case-based criticisms discussed above has, to some extent, been put to the test of empirical inquiry. Many such endeavours have been made in recent years to examine the extent to which the post-*Furman* statutes in the United States have led to a reduction or even elimination of arbitrariness and discrimination in the application of the death penalty. However, the problem that arises in any study that seeks to compare those sentenced to death with those who are not is to find a way of matching cases that are truly alike. While it is true to say that each crime has its own particular configuration of circumstances and each offender his or her own prior history, motivations, and personal characteristics it is nevertheless possible to devise ways of controlling for those factors that are of legal relevance in weighing the aggravating and mitigating circumstances of each particular case.[96]

In an imaginative and sophisticated attempt to overcome the objection that 'matching' has been based on too few factors to be able to prove conclusively that the different rates of death penalty observed were due to arbitrariness or discrimination, Professors Baldus, Woodworth, and Pulaski embarked in the late 1970s and early 1980s on a major study of the imposition of the death penalty in Georgia—a state that had executed more offenders than any other in the previous thirty years and whose practice had been the subject of close scrutiny and rejected as in violation of the Constitution of the United States in *Furman v Georgia* in 1972. Baldus and his colleagues compared the practice of the Georgia criminal justice system with regard to the imposition of the death penalty under the pre-*Furman* statute with its imposition under the post-*Furman* statute, which was approved by the Supreme Court in 1976 in the case of *Gregg v Georgia*.

They recognized that it would be impossible, given the relatively small number of cases, to match each with another on more than three or four salient factors, and they therefore chose to develop a regression analysis, based on the 20–30 most statistically significant legitimate variables (out of 150 used in the initial analysis),

---

[95] For a recent trenchant critique of the Supreme Court's 'doctrinal incoherence' on the question of the death penalty, see James S. Liebman, 'Slow dancing with death: The Supreme Court and Capital Punishment, 1993–2006' *Columbia Law Review* 107 (2007), pp. 1–130.

[96] Some earlier studies using other methods are discussed in Ch. 6 of the third edition of this book.

in order to produce a 'culpability index'. Six groups of cases were identified by statistical analysis, within each of which the cases had a similar rate of death sentences, ranging from a group among whom less than one in ten were predicted to get the death sentence to a group in which all were predicted to be sentenced to death. The cases in each group were therefore not necessarily factually similar but were similarly 'culpable' in the sense that a particular combination of aggravating and mitigating circumstances produced a similar probability—for example, whether low, medium, or high—of them being sentenced to death. On this basis it was possible to assess the extent to which the new legislation has reduced the incidence of arbitrary and discriminatory death sentences among cases of similar culpability.[97]

This approach inevitably raises the question: what degree of variation in the infliction of the death sentence, when various legally relevant factors are accounted for, is evidence of *unacceptable* arbitrariness or discrimination? Baldus and his colleagues made the judgment that it would be presumptively 'excessive' if a death sentence were imposed on an offender when not more than 35 per cent of like cases were sentenced to death; and that it would only be 'presumptively even-handed' to sentence someone to death if the death-sentencing rate among similar cases was 80 per cent and over. This, like many other issues concerning the death penalty, is ultimately a matter for moral and political judgment.

It has also to be recognized that findings relating to disparities in the rate of death sentencing do not in themselves provide evidence of disparities in the rate of executions. It is necessary to study the entire post-conviction process, from appeal to clemency, in order to establish whether at the end of the day whatever arbitrariness may have existed at the time of sentence in the court of first instance still remains.

(b) Probabilities of being sentenced to death

As already shown, there is no doubt that the new capital statutes have drawn the bounds of eligibility to include a far greater number of cases than prosecutors, judges, or juries are willing to see sentenced to death. It has been found, however, that there is a great deal of variability between states and between counties in the same state in the proportion of death-eligible murders in which the prosecution seeks the death penalty and juries or judges impose it. A comparison between Georgia and California, for instance, showed that in the former state 40 per cent of persons indicted for murder who had no prior record, who killed one person, and who killed the person in the commission of a serious contemporaneous felony were sentenced to death, yet in California no case of this kind received the death penalty.[98] There are similar variations within states. For

---

[97] David Baldus, George Woodworth, and Charles A. Pulaski Jr., *Equal Justice and the Death Penalty: A Legal and Empirical Analysis* (1990).

[98] Quoted in G. M. Stein, 'Distinguishing among Murders when Assessing the Proportionality of the Death Sentence' *Columbia Law Review* 85 (1985), pp. 1786–1807 at 1806.

example, a study carried out in 2001 for the Virginia Joint Legislative Audit and Review Commission found that 'geographic location more so than any other factor, including race, was the overwhelming variable in Virginia's death penalty system'. Indeed 48 of the 120 counties and cities in Virginia had not had a conviction which led to an execution since 1908. Tony Poveda studied 85 such areas in Virginia which had had at least three potential capital crimes between 1978 and 2001 and found that in 38 of them not a single death sentence had been imposed.[99] Likewise, research carried out for the Illinois Commission showed marked variations in the proportion of cases charged as first-degree murder that resulted in a death sentence in Illinois over the years 1988 to 1997, ranging from 8.4 per cent in rural counties and 3.4 per cent in urban counties, to only 1.5 per cent of cases in Cook County, which includes Chicago.[100] In Maryland it was found that:[101]

of the 76 death sentences handed down in Maryland since 1978, 34 (45 percent) were imposed in Baltimore County, a jurisdiction in which the prosecutor regularly seeks the death penalty despite only 12 percent of the State's death-eligible cases occurring in Baltimore County...By comparison, 44 percent of the State's death eligible cases occur in Baltimore City, yet Baltimore City only hands down 13 percent of the state's death sentences.

In Colorado the prosecutors accepted a guilty plea to a lesser charge or waived the death penalty in 104 of 171 cases (61%) where defendants were initially charged with capital murder: only 11 were eventually committed for a penalty trial, and four of these were sentenced to death.[102] Similarly, in Georgia, only 23 per cent of eligible defendants convicted of murder after trial were sentenced to death and no more than 37 per cent of those who had been convicted of murder along with a contemporaneous felony. This is because the prosecutors sought the death penalty in over half the eligible cases only if three or more statutory aggravating factors were present.[103] In their studies of Philadelphia and Nebraska, Baldus' team found that only 14 and 17 per cent respectively of the death-eligible cases they

---

[99] Tony G. Poveda, 'Geographical location, death sentences and executions in post-*Furman* Virginia' *Punishment and Society* 8 (2006), pp. 423–442 at 424. The ABA *Tennessee Death Penalty Assessment Report* (2007) noted at p. vi that '44.7 percent of all Tennessee capital cases from 1993 to 2003 originated in Shelby County' and that 'no statewide standards exist to guide the exercise of this discretion [of prosecutors] and there is a wide variance of attitudes among the different attorneys among different parts of the State'.

[100] Glenn Pierce and Michael Radelet, 'Race, Region and Death Sentencing in Illinios 1988–1997' p. 17, para. 3 on 'Geographic Region' S. 1(A), of Research Reports, Illinois, (2002); *Report of the Governor's Commission on Capital Punishment: George H. Ryan Governor* (2002), Technical Appendix.

[101] Michael A. Millemann and Gary W. Christopher, 'Preferring white lives: the racial administration of the death penalty in Maryland' *University of Maryland Law Journal of Race, Religion, Gender and Class* 5(1) (2005), pp. 1–26 at 6.

[102] David Baldus, George Woodworth, and Charles A. Pulaski Jr., 'Arbitrariness and Discrimination in the Administration of the Death Penalty: A Challenge to State Supreme Courts' *Stetson Law Review* 15 (1986), pp. 133–261 at 147–148.

[103] Baldus, *et al.*, n. 97 above, p. 107.

studied were actually sentenced to death.[104] A study in North Carolina found an even lower rate: only 2.8 per cent of all homicide cases recorded during the period 1993 to 1997 resulted in a death sentence being imposed.[105] And in Maryland, Raymond Paternoster's study estimated that 'a person charged with a death eligible crime has roughly a one-in-six (16 percent) chance of being a defendant in a capital proceeding, and one in seventeen (5.8 percent) chance of receiving a death sentence'.[106] The chances of being executed were, of course, even lower (see Chapter 9, pages 322–325).

All these studies suggest that prosecutors 'weed out' the less serious cases and proceed only to pursue the death penalty for the more egregious types of murder. To what extent, then, is there evidence that prosecutors and courts have been even-handed in their judgments and confined death sentences to those who have committed the gravest of crimes?

(c) Who is selected for death?

Only one study, that of Baldus, *et al.*, has collected comparative data which throws light on whether the post-*Furman* statutes have led to a more homogeneous selection of the most egregious cases for the death sentence. They compared the 'culpability scores' of those sentenced both to death and to life imprisonment in pre- and post-*Furman* samples. The death sentence rate had, in fact, under the new law, increased by over a half, from 15 per cent of eligible convicted cases to 23 per cent. But the large overlap between death and 'life' cases which had existed prior to *Furman* had decreased: 'only 29 per cent of the post-*Furman* death sentence cases possessed culpability scores equal to or less than the culpability score of the 95th percentile life-sentence case, a decline from the pre-*Furman* figure of 61 percent'. In other words, post-*Furman*, 7 out of 10 death-sentenced cases were more serious than all but the 5 per cent of most serious life-sentenced cases.[107] Furthermore, while pre-*Furman* 40 per cent of sentences were judged to be presumptively 'excessive' (in the sense that fewer than 35 per cent in that category were sentenced to death), after *Furman* only 13 per cent were 'excessive', although a further third of the death-sentenced cases had characteristics that put them in a category where between 35 and 70 per cent of 'like' offenders were sentenced

[104] David Baldus, George Woodworth, David Zuckerman, Neil Alan Weiner, and Barbara Broffit, 'Racial Discrimination and the Death Penalty in the post-*Furman* Era: An Empirical and Legal Overview, with Recent Findings from Philadelphia' *Cornell Law Review* 83 (1998), pp. 1638–1770; and D. Baldus, G. Woodworth, G. L. Young, and A. M. Christ, 'Arbitrariness and Discrimination in the Administration of the Death Penalty: A Legal and Empirical Analysis of the Nebraska Experience (1973–1999)' *Nebraska Law Review* 81 (2002), pp. 486–756.

[105] Issac Unah and John Charles Boger, *Preliminary Report on the Findings of the North Carolina Death Penalty Study 2001* (April 2001).

[106] See Millemann and Christopher, n. 101 above, p. 7, quoting from p. 20 of the Paternoster report.

[107] Baldus, *et al.*, *Equal Justice*, n. 97 above, p. 91.

to death.[108] And while pre-*Furman* only 23 per cent were 'even-handed' (at least 80 per cent in that category being sentenced to death), after *Furman* the proportion was 51 per cent. They therefore concluded that the reform of the capital statutes had created a more selective and less arbitrary system,[109] although half of those who received a death sentence were still not in the category where the expectation of getting such a sentence was at least 80 per cent.[110] Detailed comparisons of those sentenced to death with those who were spared revealed the same pattern. The case of Warren McCleskey, an African-American man sentenced to death for shooting a white policeman during a robbery (whose case, according to Baldus, was in a 'culpability' band where the probability of a death sentence was 31 per cent), was compared with 16 other cases of police killings in the same county in Georgia. None of the defendants in these cases had been sentenced to death and only one of them had advanced to a penalty trial.[111]

(d) Is there still evidence of racial discrimination?

One of the major reasons why the Justices of the Supreme Court held in *Furman v Georgia* that the death penalty was, as administered, unconstitutional, was that it was not only imposed arbitrarily, but also inequitably depending upon the race of the defendant. There had been a long history of racial bias, especially in the southern states.

It must have been assumed that the statutes, whose constitutionality was affirmed by the Supreme Court in the *Gregg* decision of 1976, would largely eliminate racial bias, but significant discrepancies have remained between the proportion of cases sentenced to death according to whether the defendant or victim was white or black. Of all persons executed between 1976 and the end of July 2007, 34 per cent were black, 57 per cent were white, seven per cent Hispanic and two per cent of other ethnic origin. Between 1976 and 2004, 86 per cent of white homicide victims were killed by whites and 94 per cent of black victims were killed by black perpetrators. Murder in the USA is clearly mostly intra-racial.[112] Yet, of the 1,057 persons executed in the USA between 1977 and the end of 2006, almost 80 per cent had been convicted of killing a white victim,[113] although whites accounted for only half

---

[108] *Ibid.*, p. 92. Over a quarter of cases fell into a category with a predicted death- sentencing rate of 38 per cent or lower.

[109] *Ibid.*, p. 131.

[110] Another study of the Georgia experience, using a rather different methodology, revealed that, in nearly two-thirds of cases, less than a quarter of 'like' offenders were sentenced to death—resembling 'strikes of lightning'—while, at the other end of the spectrum, there was a relatively small group of especially egregious cases (but only 13 per cent of the total) where over 8 out of 10 received the death penalty. See Arnold Barnett, 'Some Distribution Patterns for the Georgia Death Sentence' *University of California Davis Law Review* 18 (1985), pp. 1327–1363.

[111] Baldus, *et al.*, n. 97 above, pp. 334–335.

[112] US Bureau of Justice Statistics, *Homicide Trends in the USA: Trends by Race* (2006), US Department of Justice.

[113] NAACP Legal Defense and Educational Fund Inc, *Death Row, U.S.A.* (Winter 2007).

of all homicide victims over the same period.[114] Furthermore, of the 1,057 persons executed, only 15 involved white defendants who had killed black victims.[115]

But, obviously, any differences in the types of murder which are intra-racial and those committed across racial boundaries have to be taken into account. For example, it appears that a considerably higher proportion of black-defendant/white-victim cases are committed in circumstances (such as murders in the course of committing a felony) that make them death-eligible. When this and other factors are taken into account, the question still remains: to what extent do racial factors play a part in determining the odds of receiving a death sentence?

In a sample of pre-*Furman* Georgia cases, Baldus *et al.* found that the odds of a black defendant receiving the death penalty were 12 times that of a comparable white defendant. Yet the post-*Furman* sample revealed no state-wide race-of-defendant effect at all. This was confirmed by Gross and Mauro's study of post-*Furman* cases from Georgia, Florida, and Illinois, where the race-of-defendant differences disappeared once the number of aggravating factors was controlled for.[116]

However, many inquiries have found a race-of-victim effect. Those who kill white persons are considerably more likely to be sentenced to death than those who kill blacks, regardless of the race of the defendant. Nonetheless, there is some evidence to suggest that the race of the victim has played a lesser role under the post-*Furman* statutes. In Georgia, Baldus *et al.* found that prior to *Furman* the gap between the death sentence rate of white defendants-white victims and black defendants-white victims, which had been 23 percentage points (8% versus 31%), had narrowed after *Furman* to 13 percentage points (22% versus 35%). Furthermore, in the earlier period knowledge of the race of the victim had improved predictive accuracy of the likelihood of a death sentence being imposed by 21 percentage points (from 43% to 64%), whereas under the new statutes it only added 8 percentage points to predictive accuracy (72% to 80%). Both of these findings were strong indicators of a lessening of the race-of-victim effect. But there has been evidence forthcoming to show that it is still not an insignificant factor.

A review of 28 studies by the US General Accounting Office (GAO) published in 1990 concluded that 'in 82 per cent of the studies, race-of-victim [white] was found to influence the likelihood of being charged with capital murder or receiving the death penalty... This finding was remarkably consistent across data sets, states,

---

[114] US Bureau of Justice Statistics, n. 112 above.

[115] NAACP, n. 113 above.

[116] There was some evidence of a race-of-defendant effect in Illinois which showed up in a regression analysis, but none for Georgia and Florida; S. Gross and R. Mauro, 'Patterns of Death: An Analysis of Racial Disparities in Capital Sentencing and Homicide Victimization' *Stanford Law Review* 37 (1984), pp. 27–153 and their book, *Death and Discrimination: Racial Disparities in Capital Sentencing* (1989).

data collection methods, and analytical techniques... [However]... the race of offender influence is not so clear cut'.[117]

In 2003, when Baldus and his colleagues reviewed 18 empirical studies (ranging from 'simple tabulations demonstrating unadjusted racial disparities to well-controlled multivariate analyses') conducted since the GOA report, they concluded that:[118]

The post-1990 results are consistent with those summarized in the GAO report, i.e. two document no race effects at all [Nebraska and New Jersey[119]]; three report both race-of-defendant and race-of-victim effects [Philadelphia, Federal, and Connecticut] two report disparities in black defendant/white victim cases [Kentucky and Maryland] and twelve report race-of-victim effects but no race-of-defendant effects [Arizona, California, Florida, Illinois Indiana, Maryland (2), Missouri, North Carolina, South Carolina, Texas and Virginia].

In addition to the variability of these findings from jurisdiction to jurisdiction, it has been found that all the 'racial disparities were *stronger* in well-controlled studies than in the less-well-controlled studies'.[120] Professor Baldus and his team followed up their ground-breaking research in Georgia with studies of death sentencing in New Jersey (1982–96), Philadelphia (1983–93) and Nebraska (1973–99). The New Jersey study revealed race-of-victim effects in prosecutorial decision-making, but less pronounced than in studies carried out in southern states. Yet this study, in contrast to those in the south, 'revealed substantial disparate treatment of black defendants by penalty-trial juries'. These effects were equivalent to an average 8 percentage points difference between black and non-black defendants after controlling for the defendants' culpability that was estimated by the regression analysis. But they were much wider in the 'mid-range' of cases, where the average disparity between the rate of being sentenced to death was 30 percentage points (52% for black defendants and 22% for white defendants), a difference which was statistically significant.[121] The findings in Philadelphia were similar:[122]

---

[117] US General Accounting Office, 'Death Penalty Sentencing: Research Indicates Pattern of Racial Disparities' (1990), GAO/GDD-90-57, at 6.

[118] David C. Baldus and George Woodworth, 'Race Discrimination and the Death Penalty: An Empirical and Legal Overview' in Acker, Bohm, and Lanier (eds.), n. 43 above, pp. 501–551 at 518–19. Also, David C. Baldus, G. Woodworth, D. Zuckerman, N. A. Weiner, and B. Broffitt, 'Racial Discrimination and the Death Penalty in the *Post-Furman* Era: An Empirical and Legal Overview, with Recent Findings from Philadelphia' *Cornell Law Review* 83 (1998), pp. 1638–1770, App. B at 1742–1745. Also Jon Sorenson, Donald H. Wallace, and Rocky L. Pilgrim, 'Empirical Studies on Race and Death Penalty Sentencing: A Decade after the GAO Report' *Criminal Law Bulletin* 36 (2001), pp. 395–408 at 403.

[119] Hon David S. Baime, *Report to the Supreme Court Systematic Proportionality Review Project 2000*, pp. 4–5. Also: David Weisbud and Joseph Naus, 'Report to the Special Master David Baime: re Systematic Proportionality review' *Report to the New Jersey Supreme Court* (June 2001).

[120] Baldus *et al.*, 'Racial Discrimination and the Death Penalty in the *Post-Furman* Era', n. 104 above, p. 1661.

[121] At the p < 0.006 level. Baldus, *et al.*, 'Racial Discrimination and the Death Penalty in the *Post-Furman* Era', n. 104 above, pp. 1663 and 1664, fn. 79.

[122] Baldus *et al.*, *ibid.*, App., pp. 1713–1715.

Among the unanimously decided cases, the race-of-defendant effects were substantial, consistent, and statistically significant, or nearly so, in both the overall models of jury death-sentencing and in the analyses of jury weighing decisions...The race-of-victim results are also substantial and statistically significant, or nearly so, across a range of analyses, but they are somewhat weaker than the race-of-defendant effects...In the light of these results and of our methodology, we consider it implausible that the estimated disparities are either a product of chance or reflect a failure to control for important omitted case characteristics.

Confirmation of the race of defendant effect has come from an ingenious study by psychologist Jennifer Eberhardt and colleagues who tested the hypothesis that black defendants who fitted the racial stereotype of a black male who had killed a white victim were more likely to be sentenced to death than such a person who had killed a white victim. By employing the Baldus database from his Philadelphia study they obtained photographs of black defendants who killed white victims and black defendants who killed black victims. They then asked Stanford University students to rate the black defendants according to the degree to which they fitted the stereotypical image of a black person (for example, broad nose, thick lips, and dark skin), without the students knowing that these were convicted murderers or what the purpose of the study was. Using stereotypicality (above and below the median) as an independent variable and taking into account through an analysis of covariance (ANCOVA) six non-racial factors which are known to influence death sentencing as controls, they found that '24.4% of those Black defendants [who had killed white victims] who fell in the lower half of the stereotypicality distribution received a death sentence, whereas 57.7% of those Black defendants who fell in the upper half received a death sentence'. When the exercise was repeated on the black defendant/black victim cases they found no difference at all between the death sentence rates for the more or less stereotypical black defendants. 'Thus, defendants who were perceived to be more stereotypically Black were more likely to be sentenced to death [indeed more than twice as likely] only where their victims were white'.[123]

Because Georgia was the focus for the first most detailed research on disparities in capital sentencing, it is of interest to note that a more recent study of death sentences imposed in the state between 1989 and 1998 revealed that little appears to have changed. Raymond Paternoster, Glen Pierce, and Michael Radelet found that both the race of the defendant and the race of the victim predict who is sentenced to death in the State of Georgia, with white suspects and those who kill white victims being more likely to be sentenced to death than black suspects and

[123] Jennifer L. Eberhardt, Paul G. Davies, Valerie J. Purdie-Vaughns, and Sheri Lynn Johnson, 'Looking Deathworthy. Perceived Stereotypicality of Black Defendants Predicts Capital Sentencing Outcomes' *Psychological Science* 17 (5) (2006), pp. 383–386.

those who kill black victims.[124] 'The data show that among all homicides with known suspects, those suspected of killing whites are 4.56 times as likely to be sentenced to death as those who are suspected of killing blacks.' Furthermore, white suspects with white victims were significantly more likely than black suspects with black victims to be sentenced to death. 'In short, the widespread disparities documented by researchers with data from the 1970s have continued in the 1990s.'[125]

Two studies by Glenn Pierce and Michael Radelet have reinforced the over-riding impact of race of victim on capital sentencing, first in Illinois where an analysis of all first-degree murder convictions between 1988 and 1997 produced a 'robust race-of-victim effect' even after aggravating factors, such as previous criminal history, were controlled for, but no statistically significant evidence of race-of-defendant effects once the same sort of factors had been taken into account.[126] Then in California, where only 11 persons had been executed between 1972 and 1 November 2005, all but two of them for killing white victims, they found that 'homicides involving non-Hispanic white victims were 3.7 times more likely to result in a death sentence, than those with non-Hispanic African American victims'.[127]

In face of all this evidence it is interesting to note the interpretation of it made by two US Justice Department officials in a paper written for the Organisation for Security and Cooperation in Europe (OSCE), which claimed that 'the extent of racial disparities in capital cases in the United States has been vastly exaggerated'

---

[124] Raymond Paternoster, Glen Pierce and Michael Radelet, 'Race and Death Sentencing in Georgia, 1989–1998' in American Bar Association, *Evaluating Fairness and Accuracy in State Death Penalty Systems: The Georgia Death Penalty Assessment Report*, App. at S–T (2006). Evidence suggests that this is also true of the federal system. A recent ACLU report shows that the risk of a case being authorized for the death penalty is 84% higher in cases where the victim is white, regardless of the race of the defendant; American Civil Liberties Union, *The Persistent Problem of Racial Disparities in the Federal Death Penalty*, 25 June 2007: <http://www.aclu.org/pdfs/capital/racial_disparities_federal_deathpen.pdf>.

[125] ABA, *The Georgia Death Penalty Assessment Report*, p. iv and App. at P–T. See also, for similar findings, Raymond Paternoster, Robert Brame, *et al*, 'An Empirical Analysis of Maryland's Death Sentencing System with respect to the Influence of Race and Legal Jurisdiction' Final Report (1999), at p. 36. And, in relation to South Carolina, Michael J. Songer and Isaac Unah, 'The Effect of Race, Gender and Location on Prosecutorial Decision to Seek the Death Penalty in South Carolina' *South Carolina Law Review* 58 (November 2006), stating that 'South Carolina prosecutors are three times more likely to seek the death penalty in White victim cases than in Black victim cases' at p. 60, and in relation to North Carolina, Issac Unah and John Charles Boger, *Preliminary Report on the Findings of the North Carolina Death Penalty Study 2001* (April 2001).

[126] Illinois, *Report of the Governor's Commission*, n. 100 above, p. 196, and App. by Glenn R. Pierce and Michael L. Radelet, 'Race, Region, and Death Sentencing in Illinois, 1988–1997', p. 18.

[127] Glenn L. Pierce and Michael L. Radelet, 'The Impact of Legally Inappropriate Factors on Death Sentencing for California Homicides, 1990–1999' 46 *Santa Clara Law Review* (2005), pp. 1–47 at 19, 25 and 34. See also Catherine Lee, 'Hispanics and the Death Penalty: Discriminatory Charging Practices in San Joaquin County, California' *Journal of Criminal Justice* 35 (2005) pp. 7–27 who found that defendants accused of killing Hispanic victims were less likely to face a capital charge than those accused of killing a white victim, having controlled for whether the killing was committed during a contemporaneous felony.

because very few studies were of sufficiently 'high-quality'. They quoted the testimony given by their department to Congress on the findings of the GAO report:[128]

[T]he high-quality studies support the conclusion that legally relevant considerations overwhelmingly account for any apparent race-of-the-victim effect. Since that time, evidence is equivocal; some studies show no effect of the race of the victim when characteristics of the crime are controlled for, while some continue to show effects. (Again, no studies show statistically significant effects based on race of the defendant.) Finally, it should also be noted that even if the claim of race of the victim were valid, it would prove only that some crimes against black victims are punished less severely than comparable crimes against white victims, not that black defendants are treated more harshly than white defendants. The solution to such a problem would not be to abolish the death penalty—resulting in greater leniency for murderers of both black and white victims, and eliminating retribution and deterrence for society as a whole—but rather to ensure that murderers of black victims are more consistently sentenced to death.

But of course this would undermine the rationale of the post-*Furman* statutes and greatly increase the number of black people executed in the United States.[129]

(e) The effectiveness of proportionality review

To what extent has the requirement for state Supreme Courts to carry out a 'proportionality review' of death sentences—as a means of eliminating inequities—in fact eradicated any arbitrariness or racial differences that may have resulted from the decisions of juries and judges at the trial courts? Detailed analysis by David Baldus and colleagues of the way in which proportionality review had been conducted by the Georgia Supreme Court revealed that between 20 and 25 per cent of death sentences were vacated, but this was nearly always on procedural grounds, and not because they were deemed to be 'excessive and disproportionate'. Indeed, in a study of Supreme Court proportionality reviews in five states, it was found that the death penalty had been considered to be comparatively excessive in only one case, and similarly, in a ten-year period, the Missouri Supreme Court reversed only one of 70 cases on grounds of disproportionality.[130] Baldus *et al.* concluded that proportionality review had not eliminated disparities: 17–25 per cent of the death sentences affirmed were in the presumptively 'excessive' category (less than 35% probability that similar cases would have been

---

[128] Margaret Griffey and Laurence E. Rothenberg, 'The Death Penalty in the United States' in *The Death Penalty in the OSCE Area*, Background Paper (2006), pp. 35–44 at 39–41.

[129] Randall Kennedy, '*McCleskey v. Kemp*: Race, Capital Punishment and The Supreme Court' *Harvard Law Review* 101 (1988), pp. 1388–1443.

[130] George E. Dix, 'Appellate Review of the Decision to Impose Death' *Georgetown Law Journal* 68 (1979), pp. 97–161 at 111. Also, Donald H. Wallace and Jonathan R. Sorensen, 'Missouri Proportionality Review: An Assessment of a State Supreme Court's Procedures in Capital Cases' *Notre Dame Journal of Law, Ethics and Public Policy* 8 (1994), pp. 281–315 at 286.

sentenced to death) and nearly half were in the mid-category of culpability. Thus, only 20–30 per cent were in the 'presumptively even-handed' category (80% or higher probability).[131]

Several inquiries suggested that proportionality review had done nothing to correct race-of-victim disparities. Killing a white victim still increased the odds of receiving a death penalty in Georgia, Florida, and Illinois, even after proportionality review. Although reversal of cases on procedural grounds had reduced the race-of-victim difference by 35 per cent, it still remained a substantial factor affecting death sentences.[132]

All the research so far conducted has attributed the failure of proportionality review to remedy both arbitrariness and discrimination to the fact that comparisons have been made with only a narrow range of cases: the smaller 'the pool' the less likely is the court to find aberrant cases. Thus, in comparing the case under review with other cases, state Supreme Courts have either searched for similar cases among those in which the death penalty had been imposed (eight states), or 'first degree murder convictions in which the death sentence was an issue, whether or not the sentence was imposed' (14 states). This, of course, excludes all those cases that were death-eligible under the statute, but where a guilty plea to a lesser charge was accepted. For this reason, the National Center for States Courts project on comparative proportionality review recommended that 'the pool of eligible cases...should contain, as a minimum, all cases in which the indictment included a death-eligible charge, and a homicide conviction was obtained (including manslaughter)'.[133] Professor Baldus and his colleagues found that the Georgia Supreme Court's procedures were 'biased in favor of findings that death sentences are not excessive or disproportionate' and that, as a consequence, 'it has never vacated a death sentence because of the infrequency with which death sentences occur in other similar cases'. Excessive sentences were only reversed as a side-effect of procedural argument, not as a result of comparative proportionality review. Nevertheless, they argued that if state Supreme Courts were to approach the task in a more systematic and empirically based manner, with or without the help of quantitative methods, it might be possible for them, when conducting proportionality reviews, to produce an even-handed result.[134] However, it appears that there is

---

[131] For a less sophisticated but instructive study, which weighed aggravating and mitigating circumstances and found that cases were upheld after proportionality review, even though few were 'presumptively even-handed' see D. H. Wallace and J. R. Sorenson, 'Missouri Proportionality Review: An Assessment of a State's Supreme Court's Proceedings in Capital Cases' *Notre Dame Journal of Law, Ethics and Public Policy: Symposium on Capital Punishment* 8 (1994), pp. 281–315.

[132] Baldus, *et al.*, *Equal Justice*, n. 97 above, p. 216.

[133] Richard van Duizend, 'Comparative Proportionality Review in Death Sentence Cases' *State Court Journal* 8(3) (1984), pp. 9–23 at 11.

[134] D. C. Baldus, C. A. Pulaski Jr, G. Woodworth, and F. D. Kyle, 'Identifying Comparatively Excessive Sentences of Death: A Quantitative Approach' *Stanford Law Review* 33 (1980), pp. 1–74 at 68, and D. C. Baldus, G. Woodworth, and C. A. Pulaski, 'Reflections on the "Inevitability" of

still a long way to go before this is achieved. For example, the ABA's Tennessee Death Penalty Assessment Report, published in March 2007, criticized[135] the Tennessee Supreme Court for having:

limited the court's duty for ensuring that 'no aberrant death sentence is confirmed'. Accordingly, neither the Tennessee Supreme Court nor the Tennessee Court of Criminal Appeals engages in a meaningful review of death-eligible and death-imposed cases to ensure that similar defendants who commit similar crimes are receiving proportional sentences.

The evidence so far available suggests that there is more reason to be sceptical whether proportionality review alone can ever eliminate all traces of arbitrariness and capriciousness in the choice of the very few who are eventually put to death. Baldus and his colleagues conclude their recent study by suggesting that 'the empirical findings from Philadelphia and New Jersey . . . indicate that the problem of arbitrariness and discrimination in the administration of the death penalty is a matter of continuing concern and is not confined to southern jurisdictions'.[136]

(f) Concerns at the federal level

All the data so far reviewed about arbitrariness in the imposition of capital punishment in the United States has referred to the practice of certain states. More recently, however, the question has been raised whether similar variations exist within the federal system. Former President Clinton, when in office, declared:[137]

I am concerned also at the federal level related more to the disturbing racial composition of those who've been convicted. And the apparent fact that almost all the convictions are coming out of just a handful of states.

The review that he ordered the Department of Justice to carry out did, in fact, reveal marked geographical and racial disparities but also a good deal of controversy about whether they did or did not reveal racial bias. The Justice Department regarded the findings as conclusive evidence that the federal death penalty system operated without racial bias, affirming that its prosecutors were all 'professionals' who would never take such extraneous and legally irrelevant factors into account, and that the much higher proportion of ethnic minorities found among federal

---

Racial Discrimination in Capital Sentencing and the "Impossibility" of its Prevention, Detection and Correction' *Washington and Lee Law Review* 51 (1994), pp. 359–430 at 404 and 408–419.

[135] At p. v.

[136] Baldus *et al.*, *Cornell Law Review* 83 (1998), n. 118 above, at p. 1738. On the other hand, it should be noted that their analysis of 175 death-eligible homicide cases in Nebraska, resulting in 29 death-sentenced defendants, found no significant differences in treatment based on the race of the defendant or the race of the victim: *Nebraska Law Review* 81 (2002), n. 104 above.

[137] *New York Times*, 29 June 2000.

capital cases, and variations between federal prosecutorial districts, was due to the nature of the crime (such as drug-related murder) in which ethnic-minority defendants were more often involved than were whites.[138] But the study was met with profound academic scepticism, voiced especially by Professor Baldus, that such a research method had provided data adequate to refute the charge of racial bias, especially because no study was made of how cases were selected for federal prosecution from the pool of cases that could be eligible, nor did the research design take into account the race-of-victim effect as an explanation of why the death sentence was sought more often for white defendants, whose victims were likely to be predominantly white.[139]

So, a further detailed study was carried out for the National Institute of Justice by the Rand Corporation, using an innovative strategy. Three teams of researchers, each working independently with their preferred method and choice of variables to be included in the analysis, studied 312 cases, with 652 defendants, which had been received by the Department of Justice Capital Case Unit, from Assistant Attorney Generals between 1 January 1995 and 31 July 2000. Each of the teams found, 'despite substantial differences in their analytical methods' that race disparities disappeared when the heinousness of the crime was taken into account. With this information they were able to predict the decision to 'seek' the death penalty with 85 to 90 per cent accuracy 'without considering defendant or victim race'. '[G]iven the inherent problems in using statistical models under these circumstances', the authors stressed that their results should be interpreted cautiously.[140] Even so, it appears that race effects, whether of defendants or victims, do not have the same impact on charging decisions at the federal level—perhaps because of the gravity of the crimes concerned—as they have in the majority of state systems that have been subject to rigorous analysis.

4. Policy Implications

The US Supreme Court by a majority of 5 to 4 affirmed the death sentence in *McCleskey v Kemp*,[141] despite the evidence of institutionalized race-of-victim bias provided by the Baldus research. The majority held that an appellant sentenced to death would have to prove that intentional discrimination had occurred in his

---

[138] US Department of Justice, *The Federal Death Penalty System: A Statistical Survey (1988–2000)* (12 September 2000). Also US Department of Justice, *The Federal Death Penalty System: Supplementary Data, Analysis and Revised Protocols for Capital Case Review* (6 June 2001).

[139] Cited at the Death Penalty Information Center website, 11 June 2001.

[140] Stephen Klein, Richard Berk, and Laura Hickman, *Race and the Decision to Seek the Death Penalty in Federal Cases* (US Department of Justice, 2006). See also, American Civil Liberties Union, *The Persistent Problem of Racial Disparities in the Federal Death Penalty* (2007).

[141] 481 U.S. 279 (1987).

or her specific case. How difficult it is to prove this was illustrated by the case of *Dobbs v Zant* in 1991, in which the appellant failed to convince the 11th Circuit of the US Court of Appeals that the death penalty imposed on him for killing a white victim had been influenced by racial prejudice despite the fact that he had brought forward evidence of the use of the word 'nigger' by the prosecutor, several of the jurors, and even by his own court-appointed attorney, who voiced derogatory opinions about the black community.[142]

According to Justice Powell, *McCleskey* 'cannot prove a constitutional violation by demonstrating that other defendants who may be similarly situated did not receive the death penalty'. Yet, the 'systemic' statistical evidence presented in *McCleskey* was precisely the sort of evidence that has been accepted by the Supreme Court as providing sufficient proof of discrimination in other fields. As Baldus and Woodworth pointed out, this means 'that equal protection claims of purposeful race discrimination in death penalty cases are now subject to a far heavier burden of proof than is applied to evaluate claims in ordinary jury and employment discrimination cases'.[143]

The issue has continued to arouse controversy. Some have argued that the fact that the death penalty is not administered fairly in relation to the race of the victim is not a reason to abolish capital punishment. They interpret the findings as indicating that capital punishment is not used enough in black-victim cases because black lives are not prized as highly as white lives. So they would like to see an 'evening up' of the scales of justice (see above, page 308).[144]

On the other hand, it seemed to abolitionists unreasonable that the majority of the US Supreme Court would not accept that the evidence presented, which went unchallenged, was sufficient to show an inherent and systemic racial bias in the death penalty system as a whole. The majority of the Court was reluctant to admit this, because they feared that to concede this argument in relation to capital punishment would open up a challenge to discretionary decision-making throughout the criminal justice system.[145] There can be no doubt that the failure of the Court

---

[142] *Dobbs v Zant*, 963 F.2d 1403 (11th Circuit 1991).

[143] However, the New Jersey Supreme Court in *State v Marshall* (1992) ruled that under the equal protection clause of the New Jersey Constitution, claims of race-of-victim and race-of-defendant discrimination are cognizable. However, no remedies were discussed because in this case the court did not find evidence of unconstitutional racial discrimination: see Baldus and Woodworth, in Acker, Bohm, and Lanier, n. 43 above, pp. 407 and 411–412.

[144] John C. Adams, 'Racial Disparity and the Death Penalty' *Law and Contemporary Problems* 61 (1998), pp. 153–170. Also, Ashutosh Bhagwat, 'The McCleskey Puzzle: Remedying Prosecutorial Discrimination against Black Victims in Capital Sentencing' in D. J. Hutchinson, D. A. Strauss, and G. R. Stone (eds.), *The Supreme Court Review 1998* (1999), pp. 145–192 at 149.

[145] *McCleskey v Kemp* (1987). On the Supreme Court's attitude towards empirical research, see James R. Acker, 'Research on the Death Penalty: A Different Agenda: The Supreme Court, Empirical Research Evidence, and Capital Punishment Decisions, 1986–1989' *Law and Society Review* 27 (1993), pp. 65–87, and Franklin E. Zimring, 'Research on the Death Penalty: The Liberating Virtues of Irrelevance', *ibid.*, pp. 9–17.

to uphold, under the equal protection clause, a class-wide claim of racial discrimination, based on uncontested social science research, was a setback for abolitionists. They had, after all, relied in the past upon such evidence as a means of combating capital punishment, most notably in the famous *Furman* judgment. It appears, moreover, that since *McCleskey,* courts have routinely 'summarily dismissed... contentions [based on statistical evidence of differential treatment on the grounds of race] on the grounds that the Supreme Court... had precluded this type of challenge to a death sentence' altogether. This appears to be a very narrow interpretation, and it reinforces the claim that unrealistic demands for 'statistical proof' have been made, of a kind not called for in other areas of discrimination law.[146] It appears that the courts have simply not wanted to confront the issue. Indeed, in concluding the majority opinion in *McCleskey v Kemp,* Justice Powell held that arguments about systemic discrimination were 'best presented to the legislative bodies'.[147]

Since 1988 the US Congress has considered two very similar measures to allow defendants to challenge their death sentence (although not convictions) on the grounds of racial bias: the Fairness in Death Sentencing Act and the Racial Justice Act, the latter being incorporated in 1994 into the Violent Crime Control and Law Enforcement Act of 1994 as Title IX 'Racially Discriminatory Capital Sentencing'. The objective was to allow courts 'to consider evidence showing a consistent pattern of racially discriminatory death sentences in the sentencing jurisdiction, taking into account the nature of the cases being compared, the prior records of the offenders, and other statutorily appropriate non-racial characteristics'. The appellant would have had to show statistically that the disparity was significant and that his particular case fitted the pattern of racially discriminatory sentencing, and the prosecution would have been able to rebut the evidence and the inferences drawn from it.[148] This would have been a tough test for defendants to respond to. Nevertheless, the threat it was believed to pose to the operation of the death penalty was such that this Title was thrown out of the 1994 Violent Crime Control Act as it passed through the Senate.

---

[146] For a valuable discussion of this issue, see John H. Blume, Theodore Eisenberg, and Sheri Lynn Johnson, 'Post-*McCleskey* Racial Discrimination Claims in Capital Cases' *Cornell Law Review* 83 (1998), pp. 1771–1810 at 1798–1806.

[147] See Baldus, *et al., Equal Justice,* n. 97 above, p. 415; F. J. Bendremer, G. Bramnick, J. C. Jones, and S. C. Lippman, '*McCleskey v Kemp*: Constitutional Tolerance for Racially Disparate Capital Sentencing' *University of Miami Law Review* 41 (1986), pp. 295–355; Keith A. Green, 'Statistics and the Death Penalty: A Break with Tradition' *Creighton Law Review* 21 (1987), pp. 265–301.

[148] 103rd Congress, 2nd Session, House Report, pp. 103–458, *Racial Justice Act* (24 March 1994), mimeo. And Ronald J. Tabak, 'Is Racism Irrelevant? Or should the Fairness in Death Sentencing Act be Enacted to Substantially Diminish Racial Discrimination in Capital Sentencing?' *New York University Review of Law and Social Change* 18 (1990–91), pp. 777–806.

However, in 1998 Kentucky became the first state to pass a Racial Justice Act (RJA). Although it was not made retroactive, section 1 of the Act reads as follows:[149]

(1) No person shall be subject to or given a sentence of death that was sought on the basis of race.
(2) A finding that race was the basis of the decision to seek a death sentence may be established if the court finds that race was a significant factor in decisions to seek the sentence of death in the Commonwealth at the time the death sentence was sought.
(3) Evidence relevant to establish a finding that race was the basis of the decision to seek a death sentence may include statistical evidence or other evidence, or both, that death sentences were sought significantly more frequently:
    (a) Upon persons of one race than upon persons of another race; or
    (b) As punishment for capital offenses against persons of one race than as punishment for capital offenses against persons of another race.
(4) The defendant shall state with particularity how the evidence supports a claim that racial considerations played a significant part in the decision to seek a death sentence in his or her case. The claim shall be raised by the defendant at the pre-trial conference. The court shall schedule a hearing on the claim and shall prescribe a time for the submission of evidence by both parties. If the court finds that race was the basis of the decision to seek the death sentence, the court shall order that a death sentence shall not be sought.
(5) The defendant has the burden of proving by clear and convincing evidence that race was the basis of the decision to seek the death penalty. The Commonwealth may offer evidence in rebuttal of the claims or evidence of the defendant.

Similar legislation was recommended in 1999 by the *Final Report of the Pennsylvania Supreme Court Committee on Racial and Gender Bias in the Justice System* and also brought before the Georgia General Assembly in 2003, but to date neither measure has made progress into legislation. Early in 2007 a Racial Justice Act was under consideration by the North Carolina General Assembly.

Although less progress has been made than some had hoped, Professor Baldus and his colleagues believe that mechanisms such as these Acts can make the infliction of the death penalty fair: 'the problems of discrimination in the use of the death penalty are as susceptible to identification, adjudication, and correction as are the practices of discrimination in other areas of American life that the civil rights movement has already addressed'.[150] Indeed, in their article in the *Nebraska Law Review*, they put forward a set of proposals for reform, including, a 'Fairness

---

[149] See also, Justin R. Arnold 'Race and the Death Penalty after *McCleskey*: A Case Study of Kentucky's Racial Justice Act' *Washington and Lee Journal of Civil Rights and Social Justice* 12 (2005), pp. 93–107.

[150] Baldus and Woodworth, in Acker, Bohm, and Lanier (eds.), n. 43 above, pp. 501–551 at 536. See further D. C. Baldus, G. C. Woodworth, and C. A. Pulaski, 'Reflections on the "Inevitability" of Racial Discrimination in Capital Sentencing and the "Impossibility" of its Prevention, Detection and Correction' *Washington and Lee Law Review* 51 (1994), pp. 359–430. Also, David C. Baldus, 'The Death Penalty Dialogue between Law and Social Science' *Indiana Law Journal* 70 (1995), pp. 1033–1041.

in Death Sentencing Act for Nebraska'.[151] Yet, others believe that capital punishment will probably remain a 'lottery' in which the system selects a few cases for execution on unacceptable social and moral criteria.[152] Indeed, in a recent review and summing up of the experiences under the post-*Furman* capital statutes, James Acker and Charles Lanier concluded that because they had failed to eliminate 'problems of race discrimination, erroneous convictions, and unequal justice' they may signal 'the beginning of the end of capital punishment in America'.[153]

It remains debatable whether any legislative formula or judicial practice can be devised that can satisfactorily eliminate the objectionable features of discrimination or other forms of arbitrariness from the enforcement of capital punishment without undermining the whole institution of the death penalty. Indeed, it is the belief that it is impossible to eliminate these problems 'in a manner that is compatible with our [American] legal system's fundamental commitment to fair and equal treatment' that underlines what has been dubbed 'the new abolitionism' in America.[154]

Those who have the power to shape policy must face the fact that in any discretionary system, even one with statutory guidelines, some persons will be sentenced to death whose cases it is impossible to distinguish from some of those who escape it. What degree of even-handedness is expected and what degree of capriciousness will be tolerated? Is it sufficient that 'even when viewed in the most favourable light, only 50 per cent to 60 per cent of the death sentences in [Georgia were] presumptively even-handed; and approximately one-quarter appear[ed] to be excessive'?[155] Or will it be agreed that 'a capital punishment system that provides arbitrary leniency for some defendants by definition is responsible for arbitrary execution of others',[156] and that this is neither morally nor politically acceptable? As Professor Baldus and his colleagues have put it:[157]

Many consider it insensitive and unseemly, if not immoral, for a country with our historical record on slavery and racial discrimination to persist in using a punishment that whites almost exclusively administer and control, that serves no demonstrated penological function, and has a profound adverse impact—physically, psychologically, and symbolically—on its black citizens.

---

[151] David C. Baldus, G. Woodworth, G. L. Young, and A. M. Christ, 'Arbitrariness and Discrimination in the Administration of the Death Penalty: A Legal and Empirical Analysis of the Nebraska Experience (1973–1999)' *Nebraska Law Review* 81 (2002), pp. 486–756 at 658–659.

[152] See, for example, the debate on the extent to which the death penalty might be regarded as a form of lottery: Richard A. Berk, Jack Boger, and Robert Weiss, 'Research on the Death Penalty: Chance and the Death Penalty' *Law and Society Review* 27 (1993), pp. 89–110; the response from Raymond Paternoster, 'Assessing Capriciousness in Capital Cases' *ibid.*, pp. 111–123; and 'Rejoinder' by Berk, Boger, and Weiss, pp. 125–127.

[153] J. R. Acker and C. S. Lanier, 'Introduction: America's Experiment with Capital Punishment' in Acker, Bohm, and Lanier (eds.), n. 43 above, pp. 3–23 at 9.

[154] Sarat, n. 89 above, p. 251.

[155] Baldus *et al.*, *Equal Justice*, n. 97 above, p. 400.

[156] B. A. Nakell and K. A. Hardy, *The Arbitrariness of the Death Penalty* (1987), p. 161.

[157] Baldus *et al.*, in Acker, Bohm, and Lanier, n. 43 above, p. 1651.

The evidence reviewed in this chapter clearly illustrates the great value of empirical criminological inquiry in shedding light on the actual administration of death penalty statutes. Several retentionist countries have, in the past, informed the United Nations that they are carrying out research on the death penalty, but none, as far as can be determined, have done so. It behoves them to make available the funds, and provide the access to the data, that are necessary to carry out inquiries into the realities of how the death penalty is administered so that there is a firm factual basis to guide discussions on the question of abolition.

9

The Question of Deterrence

1. Reliance on the Deterrent Justification

It may appear self-evident that to be threatened with death will provoke more fear and therefore be a greater deterrent than to be threatened with imprisonment, even if for the rest of one's natural life. As the Victorian English judge Sir James Fitzjames Stephen put it: 'The plain truth is that statistics are no guide at all...the question as to the effect of capital punishment on crime must always be referred, not to statistics, but to the general principles of human nature'.[1] This 'gut reaction' is still widely shared and appears to lie behind the scepticism expressed by supporters of capital punishment towards social science data that appear to have failed conclusively to prove that there is an inverse relationship between the use of capital punishment and the rate of murder.[2] And this is why any new study that appears to provide evidence that the rate of executions reduces the rate of murder is greeted so enthusiastically, and often uncritically, by those who favour the retention of the death penalty.

A study by James and John Galliher of the death penalty debates that took place in the New York State Senate and Assembly in nineteen consecutive years between 1977 and 1995 showed that the ' "ordinary knowledge" of the deterrent effects of capital punishment on homicides [was]...by far the most frequent justification [advanced] for the reinstatement of capital punishment in these legislative debates'. As one Assemblyman put it: 'Instinct and experience tells me that the threat of execution is a deterrent to murder'. Galliher and Galliher provide further similar examples from other Assemblymen.[3] Similarly, George W. Bush, when debating

---

[1] J. F. Stephen, 'Capital Punishments' *Fraser's Magazine* 69 (1864), pp. 753–772 at 753 and 759. Also, Leon Radzinowicz and Roger Hood, *A History of English Criminal Law, Vol. V, The Emergence of Penal Policy* (1986), pp. 674–676.

[2] Louis P. Pojman and Jeffrey Reiman, *The Death Penalty, For and Against* (1998): views 'for' by Louis P. Pojman, pp. 44–51, and 'against' by Jeffrey Reiman, pp. 139–140. And, Michael Davis, *Justice in the Shadow of Death: Rethinking Capital and Lesser Punishments* (1996), pp. 9–31; Gary Wills, 'The Dramaturgy of Death' *New York Review of Books* (21 June 2001), quoting William Weld, Governor of Massachusetts, 'My gut is that...capital punishment is a deterrent' and Bob Graham, former Governor of Florida, 'This is an issue that is inherently beyond what empirical research can validate'.

[3] James M. Galliher and John F. Galliher, 'A "Commonsense" Theory of deterrence and the "Ideology" of Science: the New York Death Penalty Debate' *Journal of Criminal Law and Criminology* 92 (2002), pp. 307–333 at 312 and 326 (Assemblyman Greenberg in 1977).

with Senator Al Gore in the Presidential hustings of 2000, appeared to have no doubt that 'the reason to support the death penalty is because it saves other people's lives', adding that this was 'the only reason to be for it'.[4] To the late Ernest van den Haag, who spoke so strongly in favour of capital punishment, 'The salient question about the death penalty [was] not: Could innocents be executed by mistake? (The answer is yes—courts are fallible) but: Does the death penalty save more innocent lives than it takes? Is there a net gain or loss?'[5] He had no doubt that the answer was 'a net gain'.[6]

If it does not have such a utility—or if it does not control crime through incapacitation of the criminal beyond what can be achieved by life imprisonment—it would be, in the words of the US Supreme Court in *Coker v Georgia*, 'nothing more than the purposeless and needless imposition of pain and suffering', and thus an unconstitutional punishment.[7] As Peterson and Bailey note: 'During the past 25 years a number of justices of the United States Supreme Court have emphasized the fundamental importance of the deterrent question to the constitutionality of capital punishment'. For example, in the 1984 case of *Spaziano v Florida* Justice White stated that 'a majority of the Court has concluded that the general deterrence rationale adequately justifies the imposition of capital punishment at least for certain classes of offences for which the legislature may reasonably conclude that the death penalty has a deterrent effect'.[8]

Similarly, in *Roper v Simmons* in 2005, Justice Scalia argued, even in relation to juveniles, that the death penalty had a deterrent effect, on the grounds that Simmons had apparently—wrongly—informed his co-accused that they would not be executed if they assisted him with the murder because the state did not have the death penalty for juvenile offenders.[9] Cass Sunstein and Adrian Vermeule have argued that if a recent study is correct in showing that each execution leads to an average of 18 fewer murders being committed (see pages 340–343 below), a case can be made for regarding capital punishment as 'morally obligatory—above

---

[4] Quoted in John J. Donohue and J. Wolfers, 'The Death Penalty: No Evidence for Deterrence' *Economists' Voice* (April 2004), p. 1.

[5] Ruth D. Peterson and William C. Bailey, 'Is Capital Punishment an Effective Deterrent for Murder? An Examination of Social Science Research' in J. R. Acker, R. M. Bohm, and C. S. Lanier (eds.), *America's Experiment with Capital Punishment* (1st edn., 1999), pp. 157–182 at 175; quoting Justice White in *Spaziano v Florida*, 468 U.S. 447 (1984).

[6] Ernest van den Haag, 'Justice, Deterrence and the Death Penalty' in Acker, Bohm, and Lanier, n. 5 above, pp. 233–249 at 241.

[7] *Coker v Georgia*, quoted in *Thompson v Oklahoma* (29 June 1988), No. 86–6169, 108, *Supreme Court Reporter*, pp. 2687–2700 at 2700.

[8] Ruth D. Peterson and William C. Bailey, 'Is Capital Punishment an Effective Deterrent for Murder? An Examination of Social Science Research' in J. R. Acker, R. M. Bohm, and C. S. Lanier (eds.), *America's Experiment with Capital Punishment* (2nd edn., 2003), p. 275, quoting Justice White in *Spaziano v Florida*, 468 U.S. 447 (1984).

[9] 'Before committing the crime, Simmons encouraged his friends to join him by assuring them that they could "get away with it" because they were minors.' Justice Scalia, with whom the Chief Justice and Justice Thomas joined, dissenting, *Roper v Simmons*, 543 U. S. 551 (2005), on writ of *certiorari* to the Supreme Court of Missouri, 1 March 2005, pp. 15–16.

all from the standpoint of those who wish to protect life'.[10] This utilitarian calculus has been supported by the leading economist Gary Becker and the distinguished judge, Richard Posner,[11] but condemned by supporters of abolition who regard it as unethical for the state to take the lives of its captives.[12] It is, nevertheless, the essence of the argument of those who support capital punishment in many countries, such as China, Japan, Indonesia, Malaysia, Singapore, by many nations in the Middle East and some in Africa. The Chinese authorities, for example, held strongly to the opinion that the use of the death penalty, by 'striking severely at the gravest crimes', increased public security. Similarly, in 1980 it was claimed that the imposition of Islamic law, including the death penalty, had been an essential factor in the transformation of Saudi Arabia into a society with a high degree of public order and a low rate of crime.[13]

But although it must undoubtedly be the case that there have been instances when people have refrained from murder, in particular circumstances, for fear of execution, this in itself is an insufficient basis on which to conclude that the existence of the death penalty on the statute book, plus the (often remote) threat of execution, will lead to a lower rate of murder per head of population than would be the case without the threat of this ultimate penalty. In other words, the issue is not whether the death penalty deters some—if only a few—people where threat of a lesser punishment would not, but whether, when all the circumstances surrounding the use of capital punishment are taken into account, it is associated with a *marginally* lower *rate* of the kinds of murder for which it has been appointed. The reason why one must take account of, and weigh, all its effects is that capital punishment has several drawbacks to counter its supposed 'obvious' advantages. For example, an offender threatened with death could have an added incentive to kill witnesses to his crime. Furthermore, it may be much less easy to convict persons where the punishment may be death than where it is less draconian. In other words, *severity* of punishment may run counter to the more effective *certainty* of

[10] C. R. Sunstein and A. Vermeule, 'Is capital punishment morally required? Acts, omissions, and life-life tradeoffs' *Stanford Law Review* 58 (2006), pp. 703–750 at 705 and 750. This view was quoted with approval by Justice Department members Margaret Griffey and Laurence E. Rothenberg in their paper 'The Death Penalty in the United States' in *The Death Penalty in the OSCE Area*, Background Paper 2006, pp. 35–44 at 36.

[11] For accessible examples of their work see Richard A. Posner, 'The Economics of Capital Punishment' and Gary S. Becker, 'On the Economics of Capital Punishment', both published in *Economists' Voice*, March 2006, p. 2.

[12] Carol. S. Steiker, 'No, Capital punishment is not morally required: deterrence, deontology, and the death penalty' *Stanford Law Review* 58 (2006), pp. 751–789; and C. R. Sunstein and A. Vermeule, 'Deterring Murder: A Reply' *Stanford Law Review* 58 (2006), pp. 847–857.

[13] Farouk Abdul Rahman Mourad, 'Effect of the Implementation of the Islamic Legislation on Crime Prevention in the Kingdom of Saudi Arabia: A Field Research' in UNSDRI, *The Effects of Islamic Legislation in Crime Prevention in Saudi Arabia* (1980), pp. 494–567. This study was based on the testimony of 22 aged people about the state of crime before and after the establishment of the Saudi Kingdom. It made no attempt to disentangle the supposed influence of the death penalty from the influence of other changes in law enforcement and in social, economic, and political conditions over this period.

punishment. Evidence to support this comes from both England and Wales and Canada, where since abolition of the death penalty it has proven easier to convict persons charged with a homicide of the more serious offence of murder rather than manslaughter. In fact, the proportion convicted of murder among all those convicted of a homicide in England and Wales increased from 28 per cent in 1965 (the year that capital punishment was abolished) to 61 per cent in 2002–2003.[14] The same has been true in Canada, where the conviction rate for first-degree murder, rather than second-degree murder or a lesser charge, has doubled from under 10 per cent, when execution would result, to about 20 per cent, 'now they [juries] are not compelled to make life-and-death decisions'.[15]

Furthermore, capital punishment at the hands of the state is not the only threat that the offender faces: it may pale into insignificance compared with the risk that the police may intervene with deadly force, the intended victim may successfully strike back, or associates of the victim may seek swift revenge, as can happen in 'drug wars'.

It must be recognized that, because it would be morally offensive to conduct any random experiments in the use of capital punishment, it remains very difficult, if not impossible, to find empirical data relating to the deterrent effects of the threat of capital punishment that would utterly convince a committed proponent of the death penalty to change his or her mind. Indeed, as far as some crimes threatened by capital punishment in several countries are concerned, such as importing or trading in illegal drugs, economic crimes, or politically motivated violence, there simply is no reliable evidence of any kind relating to the deterrent effects of executions. Nor have any empirical studies investigated the impact of capital punishment when used on a more extensive scale as an exemplary punishment in law and order campaigns, such as have occurred in China[16] and Iran. The only exception is an interesting, but inevitably, given the available data, rather rudimentary, study of armed robbery carried out in Nigeria many years ago (see pages 328–329 below). Consequently, almost all the studies available for review are concerned with the deterrent effect of capital punishment on the rate of murder in the United States.

What can be done, however, with regard to the crime of murder, is to weigh all the evidence carefully and attempt to reach a balanced conclusion. And that is the purpose of this chapter. But in doing so, it must be remembered that the utilitarian justification of deterrence is only one factor to weigh in the balance. Issues of proportionality, desert, humanity, respect for human rights, of arbitrariness

---

[14] Kathryn Coleman, Krista Jannson, Peter Kuiza, and Emma Reed, *Homicide, Firearm Offences and Intimate Violence*, Home Office Research Bulletin, 2 July 2007, table 1.08, p. 23.

[15] Mark Warren, *The Death Penalty in Canada: Facts, Figures and Milestones* (2001).

[16] It has been claimed that the 'war waged on criminal elements' in China in 1983 (when many executions took place) led to a drop of 36% in criminal offences. There is no means of knowing, however, what the effect of so many executions was on the willingness of citizens to report crime: Yao Zaohiu, *New Crimes Emerging in the Process of China's Development and the Strategic Policies and Measures to be Taken*, UNAFEI Resource Material Series No. 30 (1986).

and discrimination, and the dangers of wrongful convictions must all be weighed against whatever claims might be made in the name of general deterrence. Indeed, as the discussion on public opinion and the death penalty shows (see Chapter 10, page 373), the number of supporters of capital punishment in the United States who say that they favour it because of its deterrent effect is now remarkably low.

2. Conceptual Issues: The Need for Clarification

It is necessary first to remind readers that when we speak of deterrence we mean *general* deterrence, the effects of the threat of being punished by death, not the effect of having received a death sentence (known as specific deterrence). As far as general deterrence is concerned, one must distinguish between two different, although often related, conceptions. The usual sense in which it is used in discussions of the death penalty implies that the threat of the capital sanction, or to be more precise the perceived risk of being executed, causes those who are about to commit a capital offence to desist in more cases than would the alternative sanction of life imprisonment. It is therefore hypothesized that there will be an observable and regular relationship between the risk of execution (i.e. the probability of being executed following conviction) and the rate of capital offending. The second sense in which the concept of deterrence has emerged implies that the existence of the death penalty for a crime has a 'moralizing' influence on people's perceptions of the gravity of that crime, and therefore reinforces their inhibitions against committing it. This has been called 'general prevention' or 'long-term deterrence'.[17] Thus, it is argued that if the death penalty for a type of crime were to be abolished, this would lower perceptions of the seriousness of that crime (say, murder) and thus, over a period of some time (not necessarily in the short term), the incidence of that crime would rise. It is indicative of a lack of confidence in the rational calculation of risk theory that van den Haag came to embrace the general prevention thesis[18]:

Many criminologists believe deterrence requires that prospective criminals calculate the advantages of crime and compare them with disadvantages, including punishment. Criminals usually do not do that. Nor does deterrence theory require that they calculate... [Rather t]he major impact of criminal justice is on habit formation, not on habits already formed.

Indeed, the fact that some countries retain the death penalty but rarely, if ever, execute offenders, is testimony to their belief in the symbolic power of the death penalty to repress the incidence of murder.

---

[17] J. Andenaes, *Punishment and Deterrence* (1974), especially Ch. 2; Nigel Walker, 'The Efficacy and Morality of Deterrence' *Criminal Law Review* (1979), pp. 125–144; and Deryck Beyleveld, 'Identifying, Explaining and Predicting Deterrence' *British Journal of Criminology* 19 (1979), pp. 205–224.

[18] van den Haag, n. 6 above, at p. 247.

The alternative hypothesis, which has, in recent years, gained a number of adherents, is that capital crimes (here, specifically homicide) may be stimulated, not suppressed, by the execution of offenders. This has been called the 'brutalization' hypothesis.[19] Like general deterrence, the theory might work on two levels. In the short term, executions would stimulate the would-be killer by releasing inhibitions because he or she would be able to identify with the state as an 'enforcer' and 'executioner' seeking lethal vengeance.[20] It has also been suggested that the drama surrounding executions stimulates certain people to seek such notoriety or to see this as an alternative to suicide. If any of these effects were evident, one would find that in the aftermath of executions there would be an increase, rather than a decrease, in murders. In its other sense, brutalization theory implies that the moral message given by executions stimulates, rather than inhibits, violence by specifically condoning killing as vengeance. It is common to quote Cesare Beccaria's dictum: 'the death penalty cannot be useful because of the example of barbarity it gives men... It seems to me absurd that the laws, which are an expression of the public will, which detest and punish homicide, should themselves commit it'.[21] It follows that those jurisdictions that retain the death penalty and use it would be expected, other things being equal, to have higher homicide rates than those that do not, and that a general increase in executions would be followed at some later date by an increase in homicides.

Thus, while a general deterrent effect would be supported by negative correlations between executions and the homicide rates, brutalization would be supported by positive correlations. It is, of course, possible that both effects work on different segments of the 'threatened population', and that what will be measured is the marginal impact of one against the other, or perhaps a 'balancing out' of these contrary effects. Indeed, this has been the interpretation of findings that a small number of executions is positively correlated with murder rates (i.e. they 'brutalize' citizens, leading to more murders) whereas above a 'threshold' a larger number of executions is negatively related to the murder rate (i.e. they act as a deterrent), as has recently been put forward by Joanna Shepherd (see pagse 341–342 below).

3. General Deterrence in Context

Virtually all studies of general deterrence have assumed that whatever the general preventive effects of the death penalty may be, they will not be sustained in the longer term if no executions take place. Most empirical studies have therefore concentrated

---

[19] See in particular, William J. Bowers, with G. L. Pierce and J. F. McDevitt, *Legal Homicide: Death as Punishment in America, 1864–1982* (1984), pp. 271–335; and W. J. Bowers, 'The Effect of Executions is Brutalization, not Deterrence' in K. C. Haas and J. A. Inciardi (eds.), *Challenging Capital Punishment* (1989), pp. 49–89.
[20] Bowers, *ibid.*, at pp. 53–54.
[21] Cesare Beccaria, *On Crimes and Punishment* (1764), trans. Henry Paolucci (1963), p. 50.

on estimating the effect of changes in the probability of being executed on the incidence of homicide. Intuition suggests that the policy of deterrence is only likely to
have any impact if it is enforced with a sufficient degree of certainty against persons
who, in the course of their conduct, calculate the probable penal consequences.[22]

It has to be recognized that in the United States the probability of being executed if charged with a culpable homicide is very low. Even restricting the calculation to those murders that are statutorily 'death-eligible' the probability of
being sentenced to death is only about 1 in 10 and of being executed between 0.6
and 1.25 per 100. Indeed, of the 7,320 persons who went into prison under sentence of death in the United States between 1977 (after the Supreme Court reaffirmed the death penalty) and the end of 2005, only 14 per cent had been executed
whilst 37 per cent had had the death sentence removed and received 'other dispositions'.[23] And as Donohue and Wolfers point out, 'In 2003 there were 16,503
homicides in the USA but only 144 persons sentenced to death... Moreover of
the 3,374 inmates on death row at the beginning of the year [2003], only 65 were
executed'.[24] In fact, low probabilities of execution have been found even in those
countries that use capital punishment the most. South Africa was a good example
when it had the death penalty: in 1978–79, just over two in every 100 alleged
murders resulted in an execution.[25]

For any rational calculation of these probabilities to affect the offender's decision
whether or not to commit the offence he or she must know whether the act is likely
to be classed as a capital offence, whether or not the prosecutor will place it in that
limited class which is likely to attract the death penalty, and whether he or she will
be among that tiny group of offenders who eventually will be put to death.

The assumption upon which guided discretionary statutes rest is that the death
sentence will be applied only to those from whom society needs the greatest protection and/or those who have committed crimes that are regarded as particularly

---

[22] T. Sellin, *The Penalty of Death* (1980), p. 100. It must be recognized that in reaching a decision people may take into account grave consequences even when the probability of them occurring
is very low. There is a large literature on this phenomenon; none of it, however, relates to the question of capital punishment: Daniel Kahneman, Paul Slovic, and Amos Tversky (eds.), *Judgment
under Uncertainty: Heuristics and Biases* (1982). It has frequently been pointed out that these
consequences are often far more remote than being killed by a potential victim, a rival criminal, or
the police.

[23] Tracy L. Snell, *Capital Punishment 2005* (2006), US Department of Justice, Bureau of
Justice Statistics. This confirms an earlier estimate that it was unlikely in the longer term that more
than 10% would be executed: C. A. Nesbit, P. L. Howard, and S. M. Wallace, *Managing Death-
Sentenced Inmates: A Survey of Practices* (1989), p. 26. In Illinois only 12 persons were executed
between 1977 and 2002, although over 5,300 were convicted of first-degree murder between 1988
and 1997 alone; of whom, 115 were sentenced to death: Illinois, *Report of the Governor's Commission
on Capital Punishment: George H. Ryan Governor* (April 2002), p. 188.

[24] J. J. Donohue and J. Wolfers, 'Uses and Abuses of Empirical Evidence in the Death Penalty
Debate' *Stanford Law Review* 58 (2006), pp. 791–846 at 795.

[25] M. C. J. Olmesdahl, 'Predicting the Death Sentence' *South African Journal of Criminal Law
and Criminology* 6 (1982), pp. 201–218 at 202. Mr. Delroy Chuck's report to the Fraser Committee
in Jamaica noted that 'the 93 men whom we have hanged since 1958... represent less than four
per cent of the killers since then' (1981), p. 120.

repulsive because of the aggravating circumstances surrounding the murder. Fagan, Zimring, and Geller, having examined the FBI's Supplemental Homicide Reports, found that[26]:

across all states, a total of 24.5% of all reported killings were potentially death-eligible types of cases, with the lion's share of these being forcible felony killings (11.8%) and killings with multiple victims (7.8%)…and a small number…were killings of children (3.4%).

Among the forcible felony killings, nearly 80 per cent occurred during a robbery. This confirms the assumption that the majority of death-eligible crimes are the actions of rational 'calculating criminals', not those that have arisen from emotional outbursts among the ordinary population. Any study of deterrence should seek to test whether those who rationally calculate their crimes are more likely to be deterred by threat of death than those who act on impulse. On the other hand, several of the aggravating circumstances that make a person liable for the death penalty in many jurisdictions relate to crimes that intuitively do not appear likely to be affected by rational calculation of the marginally increased probability of execution. The murders that are described as 'especially heinous, atrocious, or cruel' are likely to be carried out by psychopathic personalities or persons who have lost control of their normal inhibitions. Those who go on a spree of killings appear immune to the threats that follow each one of them.

Thus, the restrictive policies now being pursued by most retentionist nations, reserving capital punishment for the 'worst of the worst' or the 'rarest of the rare' have made the intuitive arguments in favour of the deterrent impact of the death penalty less plausible, and made it more necessary than ever to seek to test its assumptions through empirical research. Yet this does not mean that if countries returned to past practices of using capital punishment more frequently a deterrent effect would be found. At whatever period studies have been carried out over the past seventy years or so, no completely convincing evidence has been forthcoming that capital punishment is marginally more effective as a deterrent to murder than the threat of long-term imprisonment.[27]

In 1967 Norval Morris observed[28]:

There are three standard methods by which the deterrent effect of the death penalty may be tested. First, the commission of capital crimes such as murder may be measured in a given jurisdiction before and after the abolition or reintroduction of capital punishment. Secondly, the rate of crime of two or more jurisdictions—similar except that at least one has abolished the death penalty—may be compared. Thirdly, the commission of a crime such as murder within a single jurisdiction may be measured before and after widely publicised executions of murderers.

---

[26] Jeffrey Fagan, Franklin E. Zimring, and Amanda Geller, 'Capital Punishment and Capital Murder: Market Share and the Deterrent Effects of the Death Penalty' *Texas Law Review* 84 (2005–2006), pp. 1803–1868 at 1821.

[27] Peterson and Bailey, n. 5 above, pp. 251–282 at 277.

[28] United Nations, *Capital Punishment, Developments 1961 to 1965* (1967), pp. 40–41.

Since the mid-1970s a further method has been introduced, namely the sophisticated statistical theory and techniques of econometric and other multivariate statistical analyses. These have been employed to calculate over time and/or across jurisdictions the association between the rate of executions and the rate of homicides, once other factors that may affect both the 'supply' of murders and the use of executions have been controlled for through the use of multiple regression analysis.

4. Assessing Homicide Trends

Both Marc Ancel and Norval Morris discussed at length what Ancel called 'the criminality curve' as a means of assessing whether a reduction in the use of capital punishment, or its complete abolition, appeared *prima facie* to produce a rise in the rate of murder or, conversely, whether the introduction of the death penalty had reduced it. It is obvious, however, that any change in the use of the death penalty may itself be associated with social changes, changes in life-saving medical practices, and changes in penal practice that affect the rate of murder, and that unless these are taken into account no definite conclusions can be drawn about the impact of the death penalty alone. Nevertheless, although a rise in homicide might not necessarily be caused by the removal of the deterrent, one would expect there to be a consistent fall in homicides if it were true that executions of those guilty of murder have a unique power as a restraint on committing homicides or those kinds of murder classed as 'capital'.

The fact that the statistics, cited below, continue to point in the same direction is persuasive evidence that countries need not fear sudden and serious changes in the curve of crime if they reduce their reliance upon the death penalty. In Australia, for example, where the last executions occurred in the mid-1960s, the reported murder rate per 100,000 of the population has, a few fluctuations aside, fallen as Table 9.1 shows for the years 1993–2005.[29]

Prior to the abolition of the death penalty in Canada the homicide rate had been rising, yet in 2003, twenty-seven years after the abolition of the death penalty, the rate had fallen to 1.73 per 100,000 population, 44 per cent lower than it had been in 1975 (3.02 per 100,000), the year before abolition.[30] Its sharp decline following abolition was a potent argument used by the Canadian Prime Minister in 1987 when opposing the reintroduction of capital punishment.[31] Apparently, there has also been no correlation between the number of death sentences imposed and the number of aggravated murders in Belarus as the use of

---

[29] In South Australia 'abolition of the death penalty had no effect on homicide trends in that state': Ivan Potas and John Walker, *Capital Punishment* (1987), p. 3.

[30] See <http://canadaonline.about.com/od/crime/a/abolitioncappun.htm>.

[31] Speech in the Canadian House of Commons, 22 June 1987, by the Rt. Hon. Brian Mulroney, Prime Minister of Canada, *Commons Debates*, p. 7477.

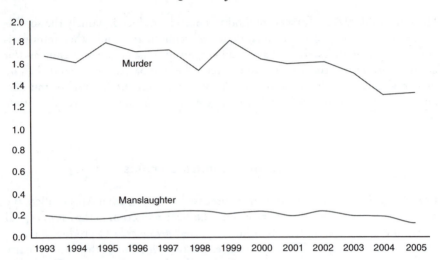

Table 9.1 Australia: Murder and manslaughter, rate per 100,000 persons, 1993–2005

Source: Australian Bureau of Statistics 2006. Recorded crime, victims, Australia [various issues]. ABS Cat. No. 4510.0. Canberra: ABS, <http://www.aic.gov.au/stats/crime/homicide.html>.

the death penalty has fluctuated and then declined in recent years. As Vasilevich and Sarkisova have pointed out[32]:

> On the contrary, the number of murders committed with aggravating circumstances— which are grounds under law for the possibility of applying the death penalty—increased in years when the punishment was used on a significant number of occasions.

Yet, if there are social factors creating an increase in violence as a whole in society, one would expect the rate of murder to rise irrespective of capital punishment. And if the removal of the threat of executions reduced the comparative 'cost' of committing murder in relation to the 'costs' of committing other kinds of violent crime, one would expect murders to rise at a rate equivalent to, or more steeply than, other violent crimes.[33] We have not come across a situation where this has been the case. For example, while the number of recorded homicides per million population has doubled in England and Wales since the abolition of the death penalty—from around an average of 7.1 per million in the years 1966 to 1970 to about 14 per million in 2005–06—the increase has been far less than the increase in serious violent offences. Just the last thirteen years has seen a six-fold increase in violent crime and a five-fold increase in violence against the person.[34] Furthermore, while the number of persons convicted of *murder* has risen five-fold over these years, from 64 in 1967 to 323 in 2003–04, the number convicted of all

[32] Gregory A. Vasilevich and Elissa A. Sarkisova, 'Prospects for Abolition of the Death Penalty in the Republic of Belarus' in *The Death Penalty in the OSCE Area, Background Paper 2006*, at p. 15.

[33] Bowers, with Pierce and McDevitt, n. 19 above, pp. 113–114.

[34] Home Office Crime Statistics for England and Wales: <http://www.crimestatistics.org.uk/output/page38.asp>.

homicides has increased only 2.3 times from 251 to 588.[35] But the reason for this, as noted above (pages 319–320), is that without capital punishment an increasing proportion of those prosecuted for homicide have been convicted of the more serious charge of murder. In other abolitionist countries which have been experiencing a rise in crime, homicide rates have also lagged a long way behind increases in violent offences in general.[36]

In the United States the homicide (murder and non-negligent manslaughter) rate surged from 4.8 per 100,000 in 1960 to 8.8 per 100,000 in 1977, when the first execution took place after a ten-year moratorium. It continued to rise to a peak of 10.2 per 100,000 in 1980, after which it fell to 7.9 by 1985, only to rise again to 9.8 in 1991. Since then the rate declined sharply, to 5.7 per 100,000 by 1999, after which it has remained steady at around 5.5 per 100,000 while the number of executions has declined from 98 in 1999 to 53 in 2007.[37] Moreover, there had been no clear relationship between the number of executions in one year and the rate of murder and non-negligent manslaughter in the following year.[38] In order to assess whether, as some had claimed,[39] the higher rate of homicides in the United States after the moratorium on executions was introduced in 1972 was evidence that murders rose when fear of execution ceased, Donohue and Wolfers compared the trends in the United States with those in neighbouring Canada. They found that the trends in the two homicide rates had moved in 'virtual lockstep' even though the two countries have had different policies on capital punishment. For example, the homicide rate did increase after 1972, when the moratorium on executions began in the United States but it did so too in Canada where there had been no executions since 1962.[40] Similarly, when Donohue and Wolfers re-analysed Dale Cloninger and Robert Marchesini's studies of the moratoria on executions in Illinois and Texas, which claimed that in both periods homicide rates had risen, they were able to show that the monthly homicide count in these areas had, in fact, followed almost exactly the trend

---

[35] Kathryn Coleman, Krista Jannson, Peter Kuiza, and Emma Reed, *Homicide, Firearm Offences and Intimate Violence*, Home Office Research Bulletin, 02/07, 2007, table 1.08, p. 23.

[36] A study of crime trends in 12 of the countries (and two of their major cities) which had abolished capital punishment *de jure* revealed that, in general, the homicide rate in the longer term was more likely to fall than to rise relative to other non-capital crimes: D. Archer and R. Gartner, *Violence and Crime in Cross-National Perspective* (1994), p. 136. For a similar finding, see E. A. Fattah, *A Study of the Deterrent Effects of Capital Punishment with Special Reference to the Canadian Situation* (1972). There have been very few attempts to assess the effects of capital punishment on the rate of other felonies. For an interesting example, which found no instances of a negative relationship between the use of capital punishment and felony rates, see William C. Bailey, 'The General Preventive Effect of Capital Punishment on Non-Capital Felonies' in R. M. Bohm (ed.), *The Death Penalty in America: Current Research* (1991), pp. 21–38.

[37] US Department of Justice, *Homicide Trends in the U.S.—Long Term Trends and Patterns*, <http://www.ojp.gov/bjs/homicide/hmrt.htm>.

[38] For information on recorded homicides in the USA see the Annual US Department of Justice publication, *Crime in the United States*.

[39] Referring to H. Dezhbakhsh and J. M. Shepherd, 'The Deterrent Effect of Capital Punishment: Evidence from a Judicial Experiment' *Economic Inquiry* 44(3) (2006), pp. 512–535.

[40] Donohue and Wolfers, n. 24 above, p. 799.

in the rest of the country.[41] The same was found when there was a short-term suspension of executions in Texas from 1996 to early 1997: 'again we find no evidence of an abnormal rise (or fall) in Texas homicides during this period'.[42]

Individual time-series studies of six states—California, New York, North Carolina, Ohio, Oregon, and Utah—carried out by William Bailey in the 1980s used regression analysis in an attempt to control for the effects of various socio-demographic variables on changes in the homicide rate, such as: the proportion of the population that is male, the proportion 20 to 40 years of age, the proportion non-white, the proportion in urban areas, and the proportion unemployed, in order to isolate better the effect of the death penalty, in particular execution rates, on homicide rates.[43] In some instances, the execution rates were found to be negatively correlated with the homicide rates, but not significantly so. For example, the largest correlation found in a time-series analysis of Utah covering the years 1910–62 suggested that 'a one percent increase in the certainty of the death penalty is associated with an approximate reduction in homicides of only eight hundredths of a person per 100,000 population'. In other words, a doubling of the execution rate would reduce the homicide rate by only eight-tenths of a person.[44] Such studies, however, have been regarded as inconclusive for three reasons. First, they have controlled for very few of the variables that might explain the 'supply' of murders: in particular, they have generally included no other law enforcement variables than the execution rate. Secondly, their level of statistical sophistication cannot account for all the possible interrelationships between variables. Thirdly, the execution rate in most states has been very low for many years, and this has made statistical tests rather suspect.

A study in Nigeria published in 1987 (the only relatively recent inquiry into the deterrent effects of capital punishment outside the United States) found no consistent pattern in the relationship between the average number of executions carried out and the incidence of either murder or armed robbery. In some periods an increase in executions was matched by an increase in crime, in other periods by

[41] Referring to: Dale O. Cloninger and Roberto Marchesini, 'Execution moratoriums, commutations and deterrence: the case of Illinois' *Applied Economics* 38(9) (2006), pp. 967–973, (for Illinois); and Dale O. Cloninger, Edward R. Waller, Yvette Bendeck, and Lee Revere, 'Returns on negative beta securities: implications for the empirical SML' *Applied Financial Economics* 14(6) (2004), pp. 397–402 for Texas.

[42] Donohue and Wolfers, n. 24 above, p. 821.

[43] W. C. Bailey, 'The Deterrent Effect of the Death Penalty for Murder in California' *Southern California Law Review* 52 (1979), pp. 743–764; 'Murder and Capital Punishment in the Nation's Capital' *Justice Quarterly* 1–2 (1984), pp. 211–223; 'An Analysis of the Deterrent Effect of the Death Penalty in North Carolina' *North Carolina Central Law Journal* 10 (1978), pp. 29–51; 'The Deterrent Effect of the Death Penalty for Murder in Ohio' *Cleveland State Law Review* 28 (1979), pp. 51–81; 'Deterrence and the Death Penalty for Murder in Oregon' *Williamette Law Review* 16 (1979), pp. 67–85; 'Deterrence and the Death Penalty for Murder in Utah' *Journal of Contemporary Law* 5 (1978), pp. 1–20; Scott H. Decker and Carol W. Kohfeld, 'A Deterrence Study of the Death Penalty in Illinois, 1933–1980' *Journal of Criminal Justice* 12 (1984), pp. 367–377.

[44] Bailey, 'Deterrence and the Death Penalty for Murder in Utah', n. 43 above, p. 15.

a decline. Furthermore, the introduction of the death penalty for armed robbery in 1970 was followed by an increase rather than a decrease in armed robberies. The author, Professor Adeyemi, concluded therefore that there was no evidence to support the general deterrent efficacy of the death penalty in Nigeria.[45] As a matter of fact, the opposite appears to be the case. According to the report of the National Study Group on the Death Penalty, which reported in 2004, 'Since Nigeria began to impose the death penalty on convicted armed robbers, the crime has increased and become more daring and heinous'.[46] This suggests that it is dangerous to appoint the death penalty for such crimes, as it encourages the killing of witnesses.

Such studies provide valuable indicators, but they cannot of course settle the question in a way that would convince a staunch retentionist because many of them provide no means of controlling for those variables (other than the rate of executions) which may cause fluctuations in the rate of crime over time.

5. The Comparative Method

The renowned early studies by Professor Thorsten Sellin attempted to control for such factors by comparing the rates of wilful homicides in five groups of three contiguous states: three groups in the Mid-West, and two in New England. The states were chosen so that the three in each group resembled each other as closely as possible in 'social organization, composition of population, economic and social conditions, etc.', but differed in that at least one of the three states had the death penalty. The results showed unambiguously that the average annual rate of homicide in these states for the years 1940 to 1955 bore no relationship to whether or not death was the maximum penalty for murder.[47] A later review of such comparisons carried out between 1919 and 1969 showed that, in the majority of cases, abolitionist states had lower rates of homicide than their retentionist neighbours and that states that abolished the death penalty generally tended to have a smaller increase in homicides than did retentionist neighbouring states.[48]

Sellin's conclusions were criticized on two grounds. First, that his method was far too crude to take into account, and attach the appropriate weight to, the wide range of social factors and law enforcement and penal practices that might

---

[45] A. A. Adeyemi, 'Death Penalty: Criminological Perspectives. The Nigerian Situation' *Revue Internationale de Droit Pénal* 58 (1987), pp. 485–502 at 490–494.

[46] *Report of the National Study Group on Death Penalty*, Abuja, August 2004 (Chair, Prof. Omyemisi Bangbose), p. 57.

[47] Thorsten Sellin (ed.), *The Death Penalty* (1959), pp. 22–28. See also his contribution to *The Death Penalty: Retribution or Deterrence?*, UNAFEI Resource Material Series No. 13 (1977), pp. 41–52.

[48] Bowers, with Pierce and McDevitt, n. 19 above, pp. 279–280.

influence the homicide rates of the neighbouring states. And, of course, in some parts of the United States, notably the south, West Virginia is the only abolitionist state to compare with retentionist states. Secondly, that comparing states in relation to whether or not death was the maximum penalty was too weak a test to ascertain whether the perceived risk of execution affected the conduct of those contemplating murder. This could only be done by taking into account the execution rates. Nevertheless, a well-conducted study by Richard Lempert of the same neighbouring states, which correlated differences in the number of executions with differences in the murder rate, also found 'no linear relationship between a state's willingness to execute and the number of lives that a state loses to homicides'.[49] A later analysis of the homicide rates in groups of contiguous states for the years 1980 to 1995 has confirmed that 'for most of the six groupings, the evidence is contrary to the deterrent hypothesis'.[50] Similarly, a study of differences in homicide and other violent crime rates between 293 counties which crossed a state line and therefore had different jurisdictions operating on either side of the border found that whether the jurisdiction did or did not have the death penalty or carry out executions had no significant effect on the level of violent crime, and what effect there was turned out to be positive not negative.[51]

An analysis conducted by the *New York Times* in 2000 also showed that 10 of the 12 states without the death penalty had lower homicide rates than the national average, while half the states with the death penalty had homicide rates above the national average. Indeed, over the past twenty years states with the death penalty had homicide rates varying between 48 and 101 per cent higher than those states without capital punishment.[52] According to the Illinois Coalition to Abolish the Death Penalty, states without the death penalty had an average homicide rate of 4.9 per 100,000 population, which is a third lower than the rate of 7.4 homicides per 100,000 in states with the death penalty. But, of course, to a convinced retentionist such comparisons would not mean much in themselves: they would probably argue that where murder rates were highest the need for capital punishment as a deterrent was greatest.

A state-by-state analysis also revealed that there is no pattern that would suggest that those states which have executed offenders have experienced any greater decline in their homicide rates than have states which have no death penalty at all. For example, between 1980 and 1985 the homicide rate fell by 21 per cent in Florida and 25 per cent in Georgia, both of them jurisdictions with relatively high rates of execution at the time; but over the same period the homicide rate in

[49] Richard Lempert, 'The Effect of Executions on Homicides: A New Look in an Old Light' *Crime and Delinquency* 29 (1983), pp. 88–115 at 100–101.

[50] Peterson and Bailey, n. 8 above, p. 255.

[51] D. Cheatwood, 'Capital Punishment and the Deterrence of Violent Crime in Comparable Counties' *Criminal Justice Review* 18 (2) (1993), pp. 165–181.

[52] Raymond Bonner and Ford Fessenden, *States with no Death Penalty Share Lower Homicide Rates* (22 September 2000), reproduced at <http://www.deathpenaltyinfo.org/article.php?did=437&scid=>.

New York, a state then without the death penalty, also fell by 26 per cent. More recently, Donohue and Wolfers also found that the same trends in homicide rates were evident in both death penalty and non-death penalty states and concluded: 'Clearly, most of the action in homicide rates in the United States is unrelated to capital punishment'.[53]

Several studies have used the cross-sectional method to study changes over time, taking into account other variables that might have affected the homicide rate. One of the first was carried out by William Bailey who studied homicide rates in 39 states over 28 selected years between 1910 and 1962 and found only small negative correlations between executions and homicide rates. He concluded that socio-demographic indicators and the length of imprisonment were both better determinants of murder rates than were executions.[54]

Brian Forst used a different test. He employed a cross-sectional approach combined with a time-series analysis in 32 states, in order to see whether those states in which the execution rate declined the most between 1960 and 1970 also had the largest increases in the homicide rate. Forst included in his regression analysis social and demographic factors and also other punishment variables—the rate of conviction for murder and the average prison term served by convicted murderers. This produced no evidence that 'those states in which the actual use of capital punishment ceased during the 1960s experienced (any) greater increase in the murder rate than did those states that did not use capital punishment in the first place'. The inference drawn was that the upsurge in the rate of homicide of 53 per cent during this period was coincidental with the moratorium on capital punishment, not caused by it, the most significant factor being the rate of conviction and the rate of imprisonment for homicide. The data is thus consistent with the deterrent hypothesis, but really supports the view that certainty of punishment is the factor that has the greatest impact, not the severe sanction of execution.[55]

An imaginative analysis of comparative and time-series data has recently been carried out by Jeffrey Fagan, Franklin Zimring, and Amanda Geller[56] who studied homicide rates and executions over the years 1976 to 2003 to test whether executions had an effect on the rate of murders which they are meant to deter, namely capital 'death-eligible' murders. They hypothesized that if executions result in a decrease in the murder rates over and above the effect of any other factors that affect murder rates, then they should affect 'capital murders' more than any other type. This would mean that 'any increase in execution risk should reduce the proportion of killings that are death eligible *if* it is the change in death risk that is

---

[53] Donohue and Wolfers, n. 24 above, p. 810.

[54] William Bailey, 'A Multivariate Cross-Sectional Analysis of the Deterrent Effect of the Death Penalty' *Sociology and Social Research* 64 (1980), pp. 183–207.

[55] Brian E. Forst, 'The Deterrent Effect of Capital Punishment: Cross-Sectional Analysis of the 1960s' *Minnesota Law Review* 61 (1977), pp. 743–767 at 754–764.

[56] Jeffrey Fagan, Franklin Zimring, and Amanda Geller, 'Capital Homicide and Capital Punishment: A Market Share Theory of Deterrence' *Texas Law Review*, 84 (2006), pp. 1803–1868.

operating net of other factors that may be influencing homicide rates'.[57] In other words, they measured changes in what they called the 'market share' of cases that would be death eligible, 'both over time and between states at various points of time'.[58] Their findings provided no support for the deterrence hypothesis. Indeed, the market-share of death-eligible murders had risen 'from a low of approximately 22 per cent in 1975 to a peak of nearly 32 per cent in 1995, decline[d] to about 28 per cent in 2000 before rising again to more than 30 per cent through 2004' while the number of executions had risen from 21 in 1984 to 98 in 1999.[59]

Furthermore, the market share of capital-eligible homicides was 'nearly identical in states without the death penalty'. So, they concluded: 'Rates of death-eligible killings don't go down any faster than non-death eligible killings when execution rates go up, and the death eligible types of killings is no greater share of the total in states with no penalty'. Turning their attention to Texas, where a high proportion of the executions in the USA have been carried out, and to Harris County in particular (which includes the city of Houston), they discovered the same pattern over the years 1996 through to 2003. While the number of executions increased, the rate of capital-eligible homicides remained virtually unchanged and therefore, as murders as a whole declined, the 'market share' of the murders which were threatened by execution increased, rather than fell. This they confirmed by regression analyses which took into account a wide variety of variables that might have affected the homicide rate both in the USA as a whole and in Texas counties, concluding that 'the marginal deterrent effect of the threat or example of execution on those cases at risk for such punishment is invisible'.[60]

Attempts have also been made, using the comparative method, to test whether the availability of the death penalty better protects the police and leads to fewer instances where they have to resort to deadly force for self-protection. Thorsten Sellin claimed that this was not so, and indeed that the opposite was true: police, slayers, and suspects were all more likely to be killed in retentionist than in abolitionist states.[61] But this, again, provided no convincing proof that without the death penalty the rates would not have been higher in the retentionist states. In two more sophisticated analyses of 50 states, for the period 1961 to 1971, and 1973 to 1984, William C. Bailey noted that there had been a decline in the number of policemen killed. He used regression analysis to partial out the effects of a wide range of social variables on the level of those serious crimes that might be associated with police deaths, and also to control for the time-lag between police killings and a possible death sentence. This revealed no evidence that police killings were lower in those jurisdictions that provided for capital punishment than in those that did not, or in those that had a relatively high level of executions as opposed to a low rate.[62]

---

[57] *Ibid.*, p. 1811.			[58] *Ibid.*, p. 1812.			[59] *Ibid.*, p. 1826.

[60] *Ibid.*, p. 1860.

[61] Sellin, n. 22 above, pp. 89–102.

[62] William C. Bailey and Ruth D. Peterson, 'Police Killings and Capital Punishment: The Post-*Furman* Period' *Criminology* 25 (1987), pp. 1–25; W. C. Bailey, 'Capital Punishments

Yet another study by Peterson and Bailey, which analysed police killings in the United States over the years 1976 to 1989, 'found no evidence that overall and specific types of police killings were responsive to the provision of capital punishment, execution rates or television news coverage devoted to executions'.[63] Indeed, as Jeffrey Fagan has recently pointed out, of the 52 police officers reported by the FBI to have been feloniously killed in the USA in 2003, 28 occurred in the South where the death penalty is most often employed and only three policemen were killed in the northeast where most states do not have the death penalty or, if they do, very rarely use it.[64]

Sellin's comparative analysis had also found that the rate of homicides of persons in custody, either inmates or officers, was no higher in abolitionist than retentionist states. Some more recent comparisons have confirmed this still to be the case. In 1980 there were no differences in prison homicides between the 16 abolitionist and 36 retentionist states once the size of their prison populations was taken into account.[65]

It has been argued that the comparative approach has not paid sufficient attention to controlling for variables other than the existence of the death penalty or the rate of executions. Whilst this is true of the earlier studies, this cannot be said of the most recent work in this genre such as that of Bailey and Peterson or Fagan, Zimring, and Geller. Furthermore, these new more sophisticated attempts, using the comparative method, have confirmed the solidity of the earlier findings that used less sophisticated techniques. Taken together, it can still be said that their strength lies 'not in individual studies but on the work taken as a whole'.[66]

6. Measuring the Immediate Impact

Since the mid-1930s attempts have been made to see whether it could be shown that an execution, particularly in a well-publicized and notorious case, had an impact on the subsequent number of homicides. The usual method has been to compare the number of reported cases in the week(s) before and after the

and Lethal Assaults against Police' *Criminology* 19 (1982), pp. 608–625; W. C. Bailey and R. D. Peterson, 'Murder, Capital Punishment and Deterrence: A Review of the Evidence and an Examination of Police Killings' *Journal of Social Issues* 50(2) (Summer 1994), pp. 53–74.

[63] Peterson and Bailey, n. 8 above, p. 273.

[64] Jeffrey Fagan, 'Public Policy Choices on Deterrence and the Death Penalty: A Critical Review of New Evidence', Testimony before the Joint Committee on the Judiciary of the Massachusetts Legislature on House Bill 3834, 'An Act Reinstating Capital Punishment in the Commonwealth' (14 July 2005), p. 12.

[65] James A. Acker, 'Mandatory Capital Punishment for the Life Term Inmate who Commits Murder: Judgments of Fact and Value in Law and Social Sciences' *Criminal and Civil Confinement* 11–12 (1985), pp. 267–327 at 295.

[66] Richard Lempert, 'Desert and Deterrence: An Assessment of the Moral Bases of the Case for Capital Punishment' *Michigan Law Review* 79 (1981), pp. 1177–1231 at 1205.

execution. The early studies showed no decline, but rather an increase in homicides. However, they had too many flaws for much confidence to be placed in them.[67] Attempts to improve the methodology have not been entirely successful, producing conflicting findings and stirring up considerable controversy. In a study published in 1980 David Phillips analysed the effects on the weekly murder rate in London of 22 notorious executions listed in *The Times* newspaper between 1858 and 1921. He compared the number of homicides in the week before the execution took place with those in the week of the execution and in the weeks afterwards, and came to the conclusion that the execution had a marked effect in reducing the number of homicides both in the week of the execution and in the two weeks following. After that, the decline in numbers was cancelled out by an equivalent increase in the following few weeks.[68]

The most that can be said for this finding is that publicized executions 'defer' homicides, but do not, over the longer term, reduce them. Phillips's study of executions in London was vigorously criticized on a number of grounds, particularly for not specifying precisely the period over which the execution was expected to have an impact as well as for failing to control for seasonal and other factors. William Bowers therefore extended the number of reported homicides to ten weeks either side of the week of execution and reanalyzed the data. This produced a substantial increase in the number of post-execution over pre-execution homicides, suggesting that each execution was associated with an average increase of 2.4 homicides. The increase was at least twice as high after the most publicized cases (measured by news space) as after the less publicized cases. There was no evidence that this was due to an 'anticipatory deterrent effect' producing a lower than normal level of homicides prior to the execution. Bowers interpreted these data as clearly consistent with the 'brutalization' hypothesis, specifically over the shorter-term period.[69] These findings appear to confirm an earlier study of the monthly execution rates and monthly rates of homicides in New York State between 1906 and 1963 which came to the conclusion that each execution had the effect of increasing the number of homicides by two in the first month after the execution.[70]

In a later study Phillips and Hensley showed that in the United States between 1973 and 1979 highly publicized news stories of death sentences passed on persons who had killed whites led to a decline in the number of white-victim murders in the four-day period after the story. But again the effect was very short-lived. More

---

[67] Bowers, 'The Effect of Executions is Brutalization, not Deterrence', n. 19 above, pp. 66–67.

[68] David P. Phillips, 'The Deterrent Effect of Capital Punishment: New Evidence on an Old Controversy' *American Journal of Sociology* 86 (1980), pp. 139–148; Hans Zeisel, Comment, *ibid.*, at 168–169. Also, David P. Phillips, 'Strong and Weak Research Designs for Detecting the Impact of Capital Punishment on Homicide' *Rutgers Law Review* 33 (1981), pp. 790–798 at 797.

[69] Bowers, 'The Effect of Executions is Brutalization, not Deterrence', n. 19 above. See also the criticisms in Larry Tifft, 'Capital Punishment Research, Policy and Ethics: Defining Murder and Placing Murderers' *Crime and Social Justice* 21 (Summer 1982), pp. 61–68 at 63–64.

[70] Bowers, with Pierce and McDevitt, n. 19 above, p. 299.

significantly, there was no evidence that life sentences had a weaker deterrent effect than either death sentences or executions.[71] Yet claims of substantial deterrent effects from highly publicized executions have been made. Steven Stack calculated that as many as 480 innocent lives had been saved due to the impact of 16 such executions between the years 1950 and 1980. However, a careful and sophisticated time-series analysis of his and other data 'provided no indication that national media attention to executions had the hypothesized deterrent effect on homicides during 1940–1986... For periods ranging through one year after executions, the overall effect of executions on homicide rates was essentially zero'.[72]

It might be thought that there would be a strong impact when a jurisdiction returned to capital punishment after a long period of suspension. Thus, an assessment was made of the effects on the homicide rate of the first four executions to take place in the United States after the ten-year moratorium ended in 1977. This showed that in only one instance, the notorious execution of Gary Gilmore, did the national homicide rate subsequently decline in the following two weeks. However, further analysis revealed that no effect could be found in Utah (where the execution took place) or in other western states. The decline appears to have been mostly in the north-eastern and south-eastern states, which were immobilized by one of the worst ever blizzards. This is an instructive reminder of how variables not normally taken into account in studies of this sort can bias the findings.[73] A study of the impact of Oklahoma's first execution for twenty-five years in 1990 came to the conclusion that it had had no effect on felony-murders but had produced an abrupt increase in the number of homicides in which a stranger was killed. The authors interpreted this as support for the brutalizing effect of the death penalty, through lowering inhibitions against killing.[74] On the other hand, Godfrey and Shiraldi showed a mixed outcome relating to murder rates before and after the widely publicized executions of Robert Alton Harris and David Mason in California (the first such executions in California for eighteen years). The comparative murder rates in the four months prior to and following Harris's execution in 1992 were 306 and 333. This suggested a 'brutalization effect'. The comparative figures for Mason's execution a year later were 362 prior to and 348 following his death. This would suggest a deterrent effect if the same logic were

[71] David P. Phillips and John E. Hensley, 'When Violence is Rewarded or Punished: The Impact of Mass Media Stories on Homicide' *Journal of Communications* (1984), pp. 101–116.

[72] William C. Bailey and Ruth D. Peterson, 'Murder and Capital Punishment: A Monthly Time-Series Analysis of Execution Publicity' *American Sociological Review* 54 (1989), pp. 722–743 at 739. This study was undertaken in response to Steven Stack's article 'Publicized Executions and Homicide' *American Sociological Review* 52 (1987), pp. 532–540.

[73] Sam G. McFarland, 'Is Capital Punishment a Short-Term Deterrent to Homicide? A Study of the Effects of Four Recent American Executions' *Journal of Criminal Law and Criminology* 74 (1983), pp. 1014–1032 at 1025 and 1032.

[74] John K. Cochran, Mitchell B. Chamlin, and Mark Seth, 'Deterrence or Brutalization? An Impact Assessment of Oklahoma's Return to Capital Punishment' *Criminology* 32 (1994), pp. 107–134.

followed, or alternatively that homicide rates are, in fact, unaffected one way or another by an execution.[75]

In a recent article, Stolzenberg and d'Alessio attempted to identify 'the nature and direction of the causal relations among execution risk, execution newspaper publicity, and murder incidents'. That is, they wanted to know whether a rise in murder rates lowered, 'at least in the short term, the probability of execution following a murder' *or* whether the rise in murder would 'bring pressure to bear on prosecutors more often to seek the death penalty'. After analysing all recorded first-degree murder incidents in Harris County, Texas, from 1990 to 1994, and the amount of publicity given to each of them in the most-read local paper, *The Houston Chronicle,* and employing sophisticated multi-variate regression analyses, they found:[76]

no empirical evidence that frequency of executions influences murder incidents in the negative direction. Additionally and contrary to predictions derived from the brutalization hypothesis, this insignificant coefficient fails to render credence to the importance of executions as a factor in escalating murder incidents... of particular salience is the negative and statistically significant delayed and sustained effect of murder incidents on execution risk... As the number of murder incidents in Houston rises, the number of executions in Texas decreases substantially the following month and to a lesser extent each month thereafter.

Their findings shed light on the importance of understanding the causal direction of correlations, for if it supports anything it supports the 'overload hypothesis', namely, that more murders are associated with fewer executions, not that fewer executions cause more murders.

This review has demonstrated one thing at least. None of these researchers were able to overcome the formidable methodological problems of relating executions to homicides over such a short time-span within a longer time-series, so as to be able to *prove* the existence of a 'brutalization' *or* a deterrent effect. Certainly, evidence from such short-term studies should not be used to sustain the contention that executions either raise or depress the rate of homicide in the longer run. And, indeed, the findings have not impressed the leading American academic experts. A survey of all living former Presidents of the American Society of Criminology, the Academy of Criminal Justice Sciences, and the Law and Society Association, published in 1995, found that 88 per cent of the 67 respondents believed (on the basis of their knowledge of the literature and research) that the death penalty does not *lower* the murder rate and 80 per cent of them believed that a significant increase in the number or speed of executions would not deter more homicides. On the

---

[75] Michael J. Godfrey and Vincent Shiraldi, 'The Death Penalty may Increase Homicide Rates' reproduced in David L. Bender, *et al.* (eds.), *Does Capital Punishment Deter Crime?* (1999), pp. 47–52.

[76] Lisa Stolzenberg and Stewart J. D'Alessio, 'Capital Punishment, Execution Publicity and Murder in Houston Texas' *Journal of Criminal Law and Criminology* 94 (2004), pp. 351–379, at 352, 357, 369, and 374.

other hand, two-thirds of them disagreed or strongly disagreed with the statement that 'overall the presence of the death penalty tends to *increase* a state's murder rate rather than to *decrease* it'. It appears therefore that most of these experts believe that capital punishment has a neutral effect on such crime, and that politicians who argue that capital punishment is a unique deterrent are really 'support[ing] the death penalty as a symbolic way to show they are tough on crime'.[77]

7. The Econometric Model

Beginning in the 1970s, attempts have been made to try to use the methods developed in econometrics 'to use multiple regression analysis to isolate through a process of mathematical purification, the effect of one variable upon the other, under conditions that exclude the interference of all other variables'.[78] One method is to analyse the fluctuations over time in the rates of executions and homicides and various 'control' variables. Such *time-series* may cover one jurisdiction only, but more commonly have either aggregated all jurisdictions or, more recently, analysed all jurisdictions at a state or even at the county level, in order to obtain sufficient data upon which a reliable analysis can be based. The other method is to analyse the variations between states in executions and homicides at particular periods of time. Such *cross-sectional* studies set out to test whether the variations in homicide rates are explained by the different patterns of executions in the different states or by other factors. This has brought to the study of deterrence a greater sophistication of method, but one which has raised questions about the appropriateness as well as the reliability and validity of the inferences that have been drawn from the data they have produced.

These studies have produced conflicting results with at least as many estimates of negative effects (consistent with deterrence) as positive effects (consistent with 'brutalization'). According to Janet Chan and Deborah Oxley's recent analysis of '61 studies [not all of them strictly using an econometric model] that involved regression or ARIMA analysis (autoregressive integrated moving average, a statistical modeling technique for time series data), only 14 (23%) found evidence consistent with a deterrent effect, while 40 (66%) concluded there was no deterrent effect, and the rest (11%) were inconclusive or found contradictory results'.[79] A fierce controversy continues. So we shall first summarize the major findings of this research and the major critiques of them before attempting to reach a

[77] Michael L. Radelet and Ronald L. Akers, 'Deterrence and the Death Penalty: The Views of Experts' *Journal of Criminal Law and Criminology* 87(1) (1996), pp. 1–11.
[78] Hans Zeisel, 'The Deterrent Effects of the Death Penalty: Facts v Faith' *Supreme Court Review* (1976), pp. 317–343 at 332–332.
[79] Janet Chan and Deborah Oxley, 'The deterrent effect of capital punishment: A review of the research evidence' *Crime and Justice Bulletin* 84 (2004), New South Wales Bureau of Crime Statistics and Research, p. 4.

balanced judgment on the methodological strengths and weaknesses of this attempt to isolate the 'general deterrent effect'.

Isaac Ehrlich's well-known study of the relationship between the homicide rate and the rate of executions in the United States over the period 1935 to 1969 lit the fuse. It produced a large negative correlation: in other words, the higher the rate of executions, the lower the homicide rate. It led him to estimate that 'an additional execution per year over the period in question may have resulted, on average, in seven or eight fewer murders'.[80] In a later study Ehrlich employed a cross-sectional rather than a time-series method. Instead of aggregating the data from all states over a long period, he computed the homicide rates for each state separately for two different years, 1940 and 1950, distinguishing those states that executed offenders from those that did not. In addition to the probability of conviction, and the probability of execution given conviction, Ehrlich included a number of control variables that might explain the 'supply' of murders: the percentage of families with incomes below half the medium income for the state; the percentage of non-whites in the population; the percentages of the population aged 15–24 and 25–34; and the percentage living in urban areas. Ehrlich found that this cross-sectional analysis corroborated his earlier time-series study. There was 'a statistically significant difference between the mean rates of murder in executing and non-executing states after the effect of the other variables [entering] the equation had been accounted for' and he calculated '*tentative estimates*' of a 'trade-off' in executing states of between 20 and 24 fewer murders for each execution:[81] an effect up to three times greater than that found in his time-series study. Furthermore, Ehrlich argued that executions *per se* did not necessarily produce the lower rates of murder; it depended on the *size* of the risk of being executed once convicted. More precisely, it would really depend on the *perceived* risk of execution amongst those who might be candidates to commit a murder. But a study of actual executions would not, of course, be able to measure perceptions of risk of executions—only to infer that the two were related.

Some other studies using the same methodology have come to similar conclusions. An analysis of homicides in England and Wales over the period 1929 to 1968 by Kenneth Wolpin had estimated that 'with no adaptations by the police, juries or potential offenders which alter other deterrent variables, executing

[80] Isaac Ehrlich, 'The Deterrent Effect of Capital Punishment: A Question of Life and Death' *American Economic Review* 65 (1975), pp. 397–417. Ehrlich found that the coefficients for the murder rate and two different measures of the execution risk were -0.06 and -0.065 respectively. This means that a 0.06% decrease in the homicide rate was associated with a 1% increase in execution risk. Thus over the 35-year period 1933–67, when there was a yearly average of 8,965 murders and 75 executions, the marginal trade-offs were approximately 8,965 divided by 75 x 0.06 = 7.17 or 8,965 divided by 75 x 0.065 = 7.77. In some years, for example 1959 and 1966, he found the coefficients produced a trade-off of one execution for 17 fewer murders. See Ehrlich, 'Deterrence: Evidence and Inference' *Yale Law Journal* 85 (1975), pp. 209–227.

[81] Isaac Ehrlich, 'Capital Punishment and Deterrence: Some Further Thoughts and Additional Evidence' *Journal of Political Economy* 85 (1977), pp. 741–788 at 757–758 and 778–779.

an additional convicted murderer...would reduce the number of homicides by...4.08 potential victims'. However, he noted that increasing the proportion of homicides cleared as murder, rather than manslaughter, reduced the number of homicides, and 'such a change far exceeds that of any other "deterrent" variable'.[82] And, as we have shown, when capital punishment was abolished in England, the certainty of being convicted of murder increased sharply (see page 320 above). In 1986 Stephen Layson published his replication of Ehrlich's time-series analysis, using the homicide figures from both the US Vital Statistics and the FBI, first for the period 1936–77,[83] and later for 1934–84 (to include the period when executions had resumed after the moratorium of 1968–76).[84] Both studies found a negative and statistically significant relationship between the homicide rate and the probabilities of arrest, of conviction, and of execution given a conviction. In other words, increases in the probabilities of these punishment variables were associated with decreases in the homicide rate. Again, the effect was greatest for the probability of conviction, and least powerful for the probability of execution once convicted. Nevertheless, Layson estimated that the trade-off was larger than the seven or eight homicides found in Ehrlich's time-series—varying from 8.5 to as many as 28 fewer homicides for each execution.[85] This, until recently, was undoubtedly the strongest and most uncompromisingly presented evidence of a possible deterrent effect of the death penalty.

At the time, these studies were subject to rigorous criticism. In particular, other researchers, using the same methods, failed to replicate the findings. Thus, when William Bowers and Glenn Pierce repeated Ehrlich's time-series analysis they found that when the last five years of his series (from 1964 onwards) were excluded, during which there were very few executions and a sharply rising homicide rate, 'all empirical support for the deterrent effect of executions disappears'.[86] Indeed, there were more positive than negative coefficients of the relationship between executions and homicide for the years 1935 to 1964 when executions

---

[82] Kenneth A. Wolpin, 'Capital Punishment and Homicide in England: A Summary of Results' *American Economic Review* 68 (1978), pp. 422–427 at 426. Wolpin controlled for the proportion of males aged 20–29; the UK unemployment rate net of temporary lay-offs; the proportion of the population in rural areas; the real gross domestic product per capita for the UK; and dummy variables to distinguish before and after the Second World War, before and after the Homicide Act 1957, and a continuous time trend corresponding to the years 1929–68, exclusive of the years of the Second World War. Because the author did not provide all the data it is impossible to gauge the validity of the findings.

[83] Stephen A. Layson, 'Homicide and Deterrence: A Re-examination of the United States Time-Series Evidence' *Southern Economic Journal* 52 (1985), pp. 68–99.

[84] Stephen A. Layson, 'United States Time-Series Homicide Regressions with Adaptive Expectations' *Bulletin of the New York Academy of Medicine* 62 (1986), pp. 589–600.

[85] Layson, n. 83 above, p. 80. In his study covering the later years up to 1984, Layson estimated a 'trade-off' of 15 murders for each execution. However, he does sound a note of caution because 'there is always the possibility that some important variable has been omitted from the analysis'. The relative 'trade-off' of 15 should therefore be treated as 'a rough estimate': Layson, n. 84 above, p. 599.

[86] W. L. Bowers and G. L. Pierce, 'The Illusion of Deterrence in Isaac Ehrlich's Research on Capital Punishment' *Yale Law Journal* 85 (1975), pp. 187–208 at 197–198.

were at their most frequent.[87] Both Passell,[88] and Black and Orsagh, using cross-sectional designs for the years 1950 and 1960 (the latter differentiating between southern and northern states), were unable to find a consistent relationship between sanctions and homicide. This was a period when very few executions were carried out—less than 2 per cent of those convicted of first-degree homicide in 1960. They concluded, therefore, 'that a similar policy of executing a very small percentage of persons convicted of first-degree homicide should again have no appreciable effect on the homicide rate'.[89]

However, in 2002 news of new econometric American studies, this time claiming to have overcome some of the methodological objections to the earlier work, emerged in the press. They all claimed to have found a 'deterrent effect' of executions. In addition, claims were made that only executions by electrocution had a deterrent effect, that shorter periods of time spent on death row prior to execution were associated with fewer murders, and—in the opposite direction—an increase in the number of persons whose sentences were 'commuted' caused an increased rate of subsequent homicides.

Using techniques similar to those employed by Ehrlich and Layson, H. Naci Mocan and R. Kaj Gittings, two economists at the University of Colorado, claimed to have found[90] 'statistically significant relationships between homicide and executions, commutations, and removals':[91]

Using the average of the coefficients estimated, we found that each additional execution or commutation results in a reduction or increase of about five murders. The impact of total removals is smaller. Each removal from death row other than execution and death yields about one additional homicide.

Yet Mocan and Gittings calculated the execution rate as the ratio of executions to the number of death row inmates, which, given the length of time which inmates in the United States spend on death row and the high proportion of cases which are successful on appeal, appears to be a very suspect measure of the probability of being executed once convicted.

Another team of economists at Emory University in Georgia—Hashem Dezhbakhsh, Paul H. Rubin, and Joanna M. Shepherd—also published their analysis of 'panel data' based on homicide and execution rates for over 3,000 counties in the United States for the period 1977 to 1996. The use of 'panel data' from each county was to get round the problem identified in the earlier research

---

[87] *Ibid.*, pp. 197–98; and Bowers, with Pierce and McDevitt, n. 19 above, pp. 320–322.

[88] P. Passell, 'The Deterrent Effect of the Death Penalty: A Statistical Test' *Stanford Law Review* 28 (1975), pp. 61–80 at 80.

[89] Theodore Black and Thomas Orsagh, 'New Evidence on the Efficacy of Sanctions as a Deterrent to Homicide' *Social Science Quarterly* 58 (1978), pp. 616–630 at 629.

[90] H. Naci Mocan and R. Kaj Gittings, 'Getting Off Death Row: Commuted Sentences and the Deterrent Effect of Capital Punishment' *Journal of Law and Economics* 46 (2003), pp. 453–478 at 456.

[91] *Ibid.*, at p. 466.

of 'aggregating' the data, which meant that executions in one jurisdiction would be correlated with the homicide rate not just in the same jurisdiction but over the country as a whole. Panel data examined the relationship between executions and homicide rates in the same area, although, of course, the problem with this is that in many areas there were no executions at all. Claiming to have used more sophisticated statistical controls than either Ehrlich or his critics, Dezhbakhsh and his colleagues stated that they had found a 'substantial deterrent effect of both sentences to death and executions', with a 'conservative estimate...that each execution results in, on average, eighteen fewer murders'. In fact, the findings reveal that 18 was the average with a margin of error of 10. This meant that they could be 95 per cent confident that the 'deterrent effect' lay between 8 and 28 fewer murders.[92] Paul Zimmerman, another economist, using similar methods to examine the period 1978 to 1997, estimated that each execution deterred an average of fourteen murders.[93]

Joanna Shepherd has examined whether the evidence of a 'deterrent effect' found in her earlier study with Dezhbakhsh and Rubin varied according to the type of murder and found that the combination of 'death row sentences' and executions deterred all types of murder, estimating the size of the effect to be that each death row sentence deters approximately 4.5 murders and that each execution deterred approximately three murders.[94] But, in her detailed discussion of her findings, Shepherd states that her analysis of monthly data on homicides, executions, and other variables at the state level over the years 1977 to 1999 revealed that:[95]

executions deter murders by intimates and crimes-of-passion murders [the murder rates per 100,000 population all decrease in execution months] and do not cause increases in stranger murders [they neither increase or decrease in execution months]. So of the three murders deterred per execution approximately one is a murder by an intimate and two are acquaintance murders. Three crimes of passion are deterred.

Not only is this finding counter-intuitive, but her other finding that 'stranger murders' are unaffected by executions, supports the work of Fagan *et al.* (see pages 331–332 above), who have shown that the rates of murder most likely to be 'death-eligible' (whereas crimes of passion or between intimates rarely are) are not affected by the rate of executions.

Joanna Shepherd also analysed her data to test whether 'capital punishment's impacts on murder rates differ among states'. She concluded that it did. Indeed,

---

[92] H. Dezhbakhsh, *et al.*, 'Does Capital Punishment have a Deterrent Effect? New Data from Postmoratorium Panel Data' *American Law and Economics Review* 5 (2003), pp. 344–376 at 369. See also J. M. Shepherd, 'Deterrence versus Brutalization: Capital Punishment's Differing Impacts among States' *Michigan Law Review* 104 (2005), pp. 203–255.

[93] Quoted in Shepherd, *ibid.*, p. 216.

[94] J. M. Shepherd, 'Murders of Passion, Execution Delays, and the Deterrence of Capital Punishment' *Journal of Legal Studies* 33 (2004), pp. 283–321.

[95] *Ibid.*, at 305, 308 and 318.

she reported that 'executions deter murder in only six states. Capital punishment, however, actually *increases* murder in thirteen states... In eight states, capital punishment has no effect on the murder rates... In seventy-eight per cent of states, executions do not deter murder'. She claimed that 'a threshold number of executions for deterrence exists, which is approximately nine executions during the [20 year] sample period' between 1977 and 1996, but that 'in states that conducted fewer executions than the threshold, the average execution increased the murder rate or had no effect'. This, she hypothesized, was due to:[96]

two opposing effects. First the execution creates a brutalizing effect: it contributes to creating a climate of brutal violence... Second the execution creates some deterrence: potential criminals recognise that the state is willing to wield the ultimate penalty... When the number of executions exceeds the threshold, the deterrence effect begins to outweigh the brutalization effect.

It is hard to imagine that citizens would be more brutalized by fewer executions than by a greater number, or that fear could replace brutalization, when the number exceeded one every 30 months, in such a calculated manner.

In yet another study, Dezhbakhsh and Shepherd, using state-level panel data from 1960 to 2000, so as to cover the period prior to, during, and after the moratorium on executions between 1972 and 1976, reported that 'about ninety-one per cent of states experienced an increase in murder rates after they suspended the death penalty and in about sixty per cent of the cases the murder rate dropped after the state reinstated the death penalty'.[97]

Paul R. Zimmerman's analysis, again using state level panel data for the years 1978–2000, purported to show that only executions that had been carried out by electrocution were associated with a deterrent effect: none of the other four methods was found to have a statistically significant impact on the *per capita* incidence of murder. Since 84 per cent of executions carried out since 1976 have been by lethal injection, and only 8 per cent by electrocution, between 1995 and 2000 when the number of homicides was declining, Zimmerman's finding would seem to challenge the argument that the decline had been due to the deterrent effects of executions.[98] Because so few executions were by electrocution, his finding that this was the only method that deterred murder seems in strange contrast to his other study which reported that each execution was associated with 14 fewer homicides. Certainly, one thing that stands out from this batch of studies, all of which have used a similar method and studied the same or closely similar time frames, is that the size of the estimated deterrent effect varies so much, from an average of 18 murders not committed for each execution in one study to 5 and to 3 in two other studies. And as the use of the term 'deterrent effects' shows, the assumption

[96] Shepherd, n. 92 above, pp. 206–207.
[97] Quoted in Shepherd, n. 92 above, pp. 215–216.
[98] Paul R. Zimmerman, 'Estimates of the Deterrent Effect of Alternative Execution methods in the United States: 1978–2000' *American Journal of Economics and Sociology* 65 (2006), pp. 909–941.

has been made that because an inverse relationship has been found between executions and homicide rates this is proof that executions *cause* the lower rates rather than higher homicide rates producing a lower proportion of them being executed. As Donohue and Wolfers remind us, even if the findings are accepted at face-value, 'the direction of the causal arrow remains an open question'.[99]

As with Ehrlich's momentous publications, the new batch of studies has also come under fierce criticism and has been treated with scathing scepticism. They have been attacked from both a theoretical and a methodological perspective, been subject to attempts to repeat and verify the findings, and been faulted for their logic and the inferences that have been drawn from the correlations they have produced. Donohue and Wolfers repeated the analysis of Dezhbakhsh and Shepherd and found 'a standard error nearly three times larger than theirs and hence [they concluded] our coefficient is statistically insignificant'. Indeed they found it 'difficult to isolate any causal effects with confidence'.[100]

In another paper they say that Dezhbakhsh, Rubin, and Shepherd (DRS) had not, in fact, run the regression that they claimed to have run. When Donohue and Wolfers did this they found the opposite result: 'each execution is associated with 18 *more* executions!'. They also stated that 'the DRS study mis-used a sophisticated econometric technique—instrumental variables estimation' and that when they made the 'most minor tweaking of the DRS instruments, one can get estimates ranging from 429 lives saved per execution to 86 lives lost'. They concluded that a variation so wide was 'outside the bounds of credibility'.[101]

Similarly, Jeffrey Fagan found that Mocan and Gittings had used a 'substitution algorithm' when calculating the relationship between executions, death sentences and homicide rates, because it would not have been possible to divide by zero when no executions had occurred—a common situation. They had therefore replaced zero with .99, a decision Fagan points out, that 'increases the size of the deterrence coefficient by approximately the value of 1 rather than a value of zero'. When he re-ran the Mocan and Gittings regression models correcting for this coding decision, he found that the 'deterrence variable is no longer statistically significant'.[102] He also found a problem with missing information in the FBI homicide data set, and when he substituted the more complete homicide victim data contained in the National Center for Health Statistics, 'regression model results change dramatically and the magnitude of the putative deterrent effect is significantly reduced'.[103] Fagan also noted that it

---

[99] Donohue and Wolfers, n. 4 above, at p. 5.
[100] Donohue and Wolfers, n. 24 above, at pp. 805 and 806–807.
[101] Donohue and Wolfers, n. 4 above, p. 3.
[102] Jeffrey Fagan, 'Death and Deterrence Redux: Science, Law and Causal Reasoning on Capital Punishment' *The Ohio State Journal of Criminal Law* 4 (2006) pp. 255–321 at 309.
[103] *Ibid.*, p. 282.

matters what measure of homicide is used as the dependent variable. He found that:[104]

when one narrows the search for deterrence by focusing not on general homicide trends and rates, but on the subset of homicides that are eligible for the death penalty, any evidence of deterrence disappears...from 1976—2003 in death penalty states, using a variety of econometric models, [the study] shows that there is no significant effect of executions on the rate of capital-eligible murders.

8. Methodological Problems in Measuring the Deterrent Effect

This chapter has already pointed to the serious methodological problems that face anyone who tries to test the hypothesis that the number of death sentences and executions carried out *causes* a lower rate of homicides of the kind that are threatened by the sanction than if they were not carried out, or that death sentences and executions *subsequently* reduce the rate of such murders. It is nevertheless essential to assess the extent to which the findings provide a sound basis for any policy decisions. Whilst criticisms have not been directed at the technical skills of those who have used regression analysis and, more specifically, the models of econometric research, the appropriateness of applying such a methodology to the issue of capital punishment has generated great controversy.[105]

What follows is a brief review of some of the more general theoretical and methodological issues which have dogged the attempts to prove or disprove the existence of the deterrent effect of executions in the USA. Readers who are interested in a more detailed critique, specifically of the earlier work of Ehrlich and Layson, will find it in the third edition of this book.

First, there is the problem of sufficient data. As Robert Weisberg has put it:[106]

Whatever measures of statistical significance one uses...[s]ocial scientists face a couple of blunt facts about [the] death penalty and deterrence. First, the percentage of people sentenced to death in the United States who actually are executed is minute, so if research is

---

[104] *Ibid.*, pp. 278–279.

[105] See Professor James Fox's testimony to the Subcommittee on Criminal Justice, Committee on the Judiciary, US House of Representatives, on 7 May 1986, entitled 'Persistent Flaws in Econometric Studies of the Death Penalty: A Discussion of Layson's Findings' mimeo: 'None of my criticisms here should suggest any deficiency in Professor Layson's skill. Even the most expert econometrician could not derive reliable estimates of the deterrent effect of capital punishment with these data and with this approach' at p. 8. Fox's criticisms have since been published: James Alan Fox and Michael L. Radelet, 'Persistent Flaws in Econometric Studies of the Deterrent Effect of the Death Penalty' *Loyola of Los Angeles Law Review* 23 (1989), pp. 29–44.

[106] Robert Weisberg, 'The Death Penalty Meets Social Science: Deterrence and Jury Behavior Under New Scrutiny' *Annual Review of Law and Social Science* 1 (2005), pp. 151–170 at 154. See also J. J. Donohue and J. Wolfers, 'Uses and Abuses of Empirical Evidence in the Death Penalty Debate' *Stanford Law Review* 58 (2006), pp. 791–846.

concerned with the actual or perceived likelihood of a death-sentenced murderer suffering the ultimate penalty, the data will always seem insufficient. Second...the executions that do occur are disproportionately centered in a few states—indeed, close to a majority in a single state—so the various effects of skewing hamper sound empirical inference-drawing.

Indeed, Richard Berk has shown that executions in states other than Texas are so infrequent, that when Texas is removed from the data-set there is no evidence that executions are negatively and significantly related to the rate of homicide.[107]

Second, there is the question of whether the theory of rational choice upon which the econometric model is based is an appropriate one for studying the relationship between the act of murder and the existence of a threat of execution. Ehrlich and those who have followed him believe that it is. As Ehrlich put it: 'Being emotional does not preclude the ability to make self-serving choices...the prospect of punishment...still may prevail upon individuals to avoid situations in which "loss of control" is likely to occur'.[108] Abolitionists have commonly rejected the deterrence argument on the grounds that most murders are not committed for large gains by professional or calculating criminals, but are the outcome of innumerable woes: the murderers are 'characteristically uneducated, impoverished social misfits whose crimes appear to be the stupid or senseless manifestations of anger or fear'.[109] The inference drawn is that the fear of capital punishment rather than long imprisonment will not restrain those who are apt to commit murder, because murder usually arises from an explosion of temper or loss of control, from mental illness or defective personality, or from panic when faced with imminent capture.

The alternative interpretation of these undeniable facts has commonly been that the low number of well-adjusted persons among known murderers proves that such persons calculate the odds and draw back for fear of suffering death. On the other hand, if fear of executions would cause a substantial number of people to draw back from violence that leads to death, one would also expect it to cause them to draw back from violence that when begun has the potential to lead to death. Here the findings are counter-intuitive. For example, Shepherd, reporting on the findings of a study by Lawrence Katz, Steven Levitt, and Eileen Shustorovich, notes that 'As expected, the execution rate had no statistically significant relationship with overall violent crime rates (which consist mainly of robbery and aggravated assault rates) and property crime rates; that is, executions had no effect on non-capital crimes'.[110] Although this may make sense as far

[107] Richard Berk, 'New Claims about Executions and General Deterrence: Déjà Vu All Over Again?' *Journal of Empirical Legal Studies* 2 (2) (2005), pp. 303–330.

[108] Ehrlich, n. 81 above, pp. 742–743. Also, I. Ehrlich, 'On Positive Methodology, Ethics, and Polemics in Deterrence Research' *British Journal of Criminology* 22 (1982), pp. 124–139 at 124.

[109] Bowers, with Pierce and McDevitt, n. 19 above, p. 273.

[110] Shepherd, 'Deterrence versus Brutalization', n. 92 above, p. 217, citing L. Katz, S.D. Levitt, and E. Shustorovich, 'Prison Conditions, Capital Punishment, and Deterrence' *American Law and Economics Review*, 5 (2003), pp. 318–343, which concludes, at p. 339, that 'there is little evidence in support of a deterrent effect of capital punishment as presently administered'.

as property crimes are concerned, as they are not threatened with execution, the assumption about violent crimes, including robbery, is counter-intuitive. This is because many murders arise from such crimes and many serious violent offences do not result in murder only because of unforeseen circumstances, especially the availability of medical assistance. The claim that those violent acts that result in murder can be deterred but not those that do not result in death rests upon no sound social science theory.

Third, have the appropriate statistical methods and models been employed to estimate the deterrent effects? The substantial variations in the findings of the early statistical studies suggest that this may be so. Indeed, in their trenchant criticism of recent studies, Donohue and Wolfers stated that:[111]

We find that the existing evidence for deterrence is surprisingly fragile, . . . The estimated effects of capital punishment on homicide rates change dramatically even with small changes in econometric specifications. Aggregating over all of our estimates, it is entirely unclear even whether the preponderance of evidence suggests that the death penalty causes more or less murder.

Thus, after reanalysing Dezhbakhsh and Shepherd's data, they found that small changes in the specification of how the data are coded[112]

lead to very different results from those using the minor variation that they actually implemented . . . an equally likely interpretation [for Shepherd's findings] . . . is that the differences across states also reflect different degrees of misspecification, or simply noise. In sum, given the sensitivity of these results to rather small and sometimes arbitrary changes one has little reason to prefer the conclusion that the death penalty will save lives to the conclusion that scores will die as a result of each execution.

They therefore conclude that what they call statistical 'pyrotechnics' had led the authors of the article to sacrifice plausibility on 'the altar of sophistication'.[113]

Fourth, have all the relevant variables been taken into account when attempting to control for those other factors that might affect both the homicide rate and the execution rate? The answer to this, of course, depends to a great extent on the theory which it is believed best explains homicide rates. An example is gun ownership, which one study found to have a statistically significant effect upon the homicide rate.[114] Other factors that may affect the homicide rate are difficult to measure because they are facets of the more general social climate and culture, such as migration, the effectiveness of informal social controls, the extent of alcohol abuse, the availability and price of illegal drugs, the degree of communal integration, and the extent to which there is a 'sub-culture of violence' or alternative modes of relieving frustrations other than violence. Of course, it is not possible to

---

[111] Donohue and Wolfers, n. 106 above, at pp. 794 and 843.
[112] *Ibid.*, at pp. 826–827.
[113] *Ibid.*, at p. 842.
[114] Gary Kleck, 'Capital Punishment, Gun Ownership, and Homicide' *American Journal of Sociology* 84 (1979), pp. 882–908.

state *a priori* what effect their inclusion would have on the relationship between homicide and execution rates, whether negative or positive.

Jeffrey Fagan has drawn particular attention to the effects of other punishments, not solely death sentences and executions, on the homicide rate, because increases in the rate and length of sentences of imprisonment for those crimes associated with death-eligible murders, especially robbery, will have an incapacitative effect. They may also deter such robberies. He drew attention to the fact that the recent econometric research has omitted the impact of the increasing use of life sentences without the option of parole: 'Accordingly, the omission of LWOP from research on legal interventions to reduce homicide is a potentially biasing omission'.[115] This is because LWOP sentences (life imprisonment without the possibility of parole) have been 'more than three times more frequent in murder cases than were death sentences and nearly 10 times more frequent than executions'.[116] He also noted that 'Through mechanisms that connect drug sales and gun violence, the crack epidemic exerted a strong push on murder rates'.[117] Yet, 'None of the new deterrence studies consider the epidemics of drug use and related violence'.[118]

9. Implications for Policy

The evidence reviewed in this chapter should lead any dispassionate analyst to conclude that it is not prudent to accept the hypothesis that capital punishment, as practised in the United States, deters murder to a marginally greater extent than does the threat and application of the supposedly lesser punishment of life imprisonment. Indeed, it is quite incorrect to conclude, when statistically significant negative coefficients have been found, that they constitute *proof of deterrence*. It is therefore not correct, as Professor Shepherd has done, to refer to all statistically significant negative correlations between the number of executions and the number of homicides as 'deterrence', and positive correlations as 'brutalization'. Such correlations may be *consistent* with a deterrent or brutalization hypothesis, but there are often alternative explanations.

The conclusion reached by the Panel set up by the American National Academy of Sciences, published nearly 30 years ago, has stood the test of time:[119]

[A]ny policy use of scientific evidence on capital punishment will require extremely severe standards of proof. The non-experimental research to which the study of the

---

[115] Jeffrey Fagan, 'Death and Deterrence Redux: Science, Law and Causal Reasoning on Capital; Punishment' *The Ohio State Journal of Criminal Law* 4 (2006), pp. 255–321 at 269.
[116] *Ibid.*, at p. 270.
[117] *Ibid.*, at p. 275.
[118] *Ibid.*, at p. 276.
[119] A. Blumstein, J. Cohen, and D. Nagin (eds.), *Deterrence and Incapacitation: Estimating the Effects of Criminal Sanctions on Crime Rates*, Washington D.C., National Academy of Sciences (1978) at p. 63.

deterrent effects of capital punishment is necessarily limited will almost certainly be unable to meet those standards of proof.

Jeffrey Fagan's conclusion after his thorough examination of the most statistically sophisticated studies in the modern era seems to us to be eminently sound:[120]

The only scientifically and ethically acceptable conclusion from the complete body of existing social science literature on deterrence and the death penalty is that it is impossible to tell whether deterrent effects are strong or weak or whether they exist at all...In fact, this work fails the test of rigorous replication and robustness of analysis that are the hallmarks of good science.

Nor is there any reason to change the judgment made in 1985 that the data 'are not sufficiently strong to lead researchers with different prior beliefs to reach a consensus regarding the deterrent effects of capital punishment'.[121] The implications of this conclusion for policy depend ultimately on moral and political views of what standards of proof are required. Most of those who favour abolition (assuming that they are not opposed to execution under any circumstances) would demand proof that executions have a substantial marginal deterrent effect. Thus, the leading American academic abolitionist Professor Hugo Adam Bedau has stated that, although it is hard to find a moral argument why the most atrocious of killers should not forfeit their lives, the evidence of research strongly supports the view that capital punishment 'exceed [s] what is necessary to achieve whatever legitimate goals a system of punishment has'—in other words, as much deterrence as can be achieved can be achieved without resorting to capital punishment. His argument is very persuasive:[122]

Anyone who studies the century and more of experience without the death penalty in American abolitionist jurisdictions must conclude that these jurisdictions have controlled criminal homicide and managed their criminal justice system, including their maximum security prisons with life-term violent offenders, at least as effectively as have neighbouring death penalty jurisdictions. The public has not responded to abolition with riot and lynching; the police have not become habituated to excessive use of lethal force; prison guards, staff and visitors are not at greater risk; surviving victims of murdered friends and loved ones have not found it more difficult to adjust to their grievous loss.

Those retentionist countries that rely on the deterrent justification should face the fact that if capital punishment were to be used to try to obtain its maximum possible deterrent effect, it would have to be enforced mandatorily, or at least with a high degree of probability, and therefore on a substantial scale across most categories of homicide. This is not an option for democratic states bound by the rule

---

[120] Fagan, n. 115 above, at p. 315.

[121] W. S. McManus, 'Estimates of the Deterrent Effect of Capital Punishment: The Importance of the Researcher's Prior Beliefs' *Journal of Political Economy* 93 (1985), pp. 417–425 at 425.

[122] Hugo Adam Bedau, 'Abolishing the Death Penalty even for the Worst Murderers' in Austin Sarat (ed.), *The Killing State: Capital Punishment in Law, Politics, and Culture* (1999), pp. 40–59 at 47–49.

of law, concern for humanity, and respect for human rights. For, as Dezhbakhsh and Shepherd recognize, executions also have costs: 'these include the harm from the death penalty's possibly discriminatory application and the risk of executing innocent people. Policy makers must weigh the benefits and costs to determine the optimal use of the death penalty'.[123] There is no doubt that all these costs would increase heavily if the execution rate were to be increased dramatically in all retentionist states. One wonders, therefore, whether those states that do retain the death penalty for some limited class of murders and murderers, imposed in a somewhat haphazard and arbitrary way on only a few of those that are death-eligible, and even then only execute a few from time to time, can really claim that such a policy is justified by its general deterrent effects. Looked at this way, the balance of evidence clearly favours the abolitionist position.

[123] H. Dezhbakhsh and J. M. Shepherd, 'The Deterrent Effect of Capital Punishment: Evidence from a Judicial Experiment' *Economic Inquiry* 44 (2006), pp. 512–525 at 534.

10

A Question of Opinion or a Question of Principle?

In this chapter we review findings from research which has attempted to measure attitudes of the public towards capital punishment, including various subsections of the public who may have distinctive views on the subject because of their knowledge of the issues involved, their religious beliefs, or their position in the social structure. We pay particular attention to retentionist jurisdictions, and explore the relationship between public opinion and government justifications for retaining or abolishing capital punishment. We go on to consider how opinions are affected by knowledge about the use of the death penalty, and how opinions about capital punishment may change in the short and long term after it has been abolished. One of the main justifications for the death penalty is that the families of victims may consider that it is the only just response to heinous crimes and, furthermore, that they cannot 'move on' from the grieving without the execution of the perpetrator. In the United States in particular, pressure groups formed by family members of the murdered victim have supported capital punishment on the grounds that it is necessary to provide 'closure' for the kin of the deceased. We explore the influence of such groups and conclude with a consideration of the extent to which legislatures and constitutional courts should be influenced by public opinion in its various forms.

1. Public Opinion and the Politics of Abolition

(a) The appeal to popular opinion

Retentionist countries, both democratic and autocratic, frequently fall back on the argument that the 'public' are not ready for abolition. Indeed, that citizens regard execution as the just, deserved, response to murder and/or that it is necessary for the protection of the public because of its unique deterrent power and final incapacitative effect. On the other hand, where abolition has come about it has not been as a result of the majority of the general public supporting it. The issue of what weight should be placed on popular opinion remains at the heart of the controversy over the abolition of capital punishment. Sometimes it is argued that abolition without public support would undermine confidence in the law and perhaps lead to private vengeance.[1] Others argue, more generally, that the state must express 'the will of the people'.[2] Opposed to this, abolitionists assert that the public needs to be educated about the realities of capital punishment and the human rights issues involved. Furthermore, that those who may be subject to capital punishment need their human rights protected against the sentiments of a vengeful public. In the end, they would argue, public opinion is shaped by the use made of capital punishment, not vice versa, so that when capital punishment is abolished public support for it begins to wither away.

There are plenty of examples of the appeal to public opinion. Thus, at the end of 2006, the Justice Minister of Japan, Jinen Nagase, told reporters: 'I am aware of various opinions on the issue, but nearly 80% of the people in this country have no objection to the existence of the death penalty. I don't have any plan to change the current justice system'.[3] In April 2007, to cite another example, Malawi's Special Law Commission, reporting on its review of the Constitution, recommended that the death penalty should be retained. It had considered a 'number of written submissions praying for the abolition of the death penalty on the understanding that it does not serve any meaningful purpose' and that it was 'inconsistent with section 44(1) of the Constitution which recognises the right to life as a non-derogable right'. The Commission, which nevertheless held to the view 'that there are certain offences which require retribution for offenders to protect society', maintained that 'the general populace of Malawi [particularly in the rural areas] was not ready to have the death penalty abolished as this would be taken to mean that murder was being sanctioned by the law'.[4]

Taiwan provides an example where the President and the Minister of Justice have made a commitment to abolish the death penalty to enhance human rights but are faced with a population 80% of whom would apparently not be in favour of such a move.[5] It has therefore devised a policy to shape public opinion towards acceptance of gradual abolition. The Ministry of Justice document, *The Policy of Gradual Abolition of the Death Penalty* (2005), made it clear that 'a *popular*

---

[1] In the debate leading to abolition in France this argument was used by the then Minister of Justice, M. Peyrefitte; see G. Picca, 'La peine de mort: Un problème politique et social' *Revue Internationale de Droit Pénal* 68 (1987), pp. 435–450 at 448. It was also employed by the government of Tanzania in 1994 to head off a challenge to capital punishment; it was said that if 'progressive' criminal policy 'jumped too far ahead of the population' the people would resort to 'mob justice': *Republic v Mbushuu et al.* [1994] 2 LRC 335 (High Court of Tanzania), at 349.

[2] A view expressed by Botswana, for example (see Marc J. Bossuyt, *The Administration of Justice and the Human Rights of Detainees*, Report to the United Nations (1987), E/CN.4/Sub.2/1987/20, p. 24) and more recently by Zambia (see Ch 3, p. 77).

[3] *Mail & Guardian Online*, 26 December 2006. He failed to mention another poll of over 2,000 people conducted in December 2004 which showed that 32% of the respondents thought that there may be a case for abolition in future 'if circumstances changed': CPOD Global Scan, 22 February 2005, cited at *Angus Reid Global Monitor*.

[4] *The Daily Times*, 24 April 2007, and the feature article 'Constitutional Review' in *The Daily Times*, 1 May 2007.

[5] *Taipei Times*, 2 January 2006.

consensus on abolition must be established' before the government 'will propose significant legislative change' (our emphasis).[6] Thus, the government has announced that it would solicit views from all sectors of society during 2007 on the issue of whether to abolish capital punishment.[7]

It is said that deep-seated support for the death penalty among the Chinese people is based on traditional values of Chinese culture, disseminated through history books or vernacular novels, as well as oral traditions, which proclaim that 'the killer should be killed'.[8] Failure to take this into account, it is argued, would have serious consequences for political and social stability.[9] Even one of the most vocal abolitionists in China today, law professor Qiu Xinglong, has pessimistically declared: 'judging by the specific state of affairs of today's China, it is impossible to have capital punishment abolished in China in the near future'.[10] However, it should be remembered that similar views—'a life for a life'—were often strongly held in European culture before the death penalty was abolished.[11]

The extent to which governments base their penal policy on the attitudes expressed by the population depends upon their political ideology and the sources from which they believe the authority of law should emanate. Most of the countries of the Middle East and North Africa, for example, are adamant that retention of the death penalty is the clear commandment of Islam. On the other hand, in Western liberal parliamentary democracies, where laws are based on the mandate given to elected representatives, it is not incumbent on legislators to follow popular opinion. In France, Germany, the United Kingdom, and Canada abolition of the death penalty took place even though popular opinion was opposed to it.[12]

---

[6] International Federation of Human Rights (FIDH), *The Death Penalty in Taiwan; Towards Abolition?* Report 450/2 (June 2006), pp. 11–12. Also *Central News Agency English News*, 12 October 2006.

[7] Amnesty International, *Death Penalty blog*, 12 January 2007.

[8] Liu Hainan, 'The Effect on the Capital Punishment by the Chinese Traditional Theory of the Criminal Law' in M. Nowak and Xin Chunying (eds.), EU-*China Human Rights Dialogue: Proceedings of the Second EU-China Legal Experts, Seminar, Beijing, 19–20 October 1998* (2000), pp. 99–120 at 120.

[9] Virgil K. Y. Ho, 'What is Wrong with Capital Punishment?: Official and Unofficial Attitudes Toward Capital Punishment in Modern and Contemporary China' in A. Sarat and C. Boulanger (eds.), *The Cultural Lives of Capital Punishment* (2005), pp. 274–290.

[10] Qiu Xinglong (2001) at p. 97, cited in Ho, *ibid.*, at p. 286.

[11] A well-known example was John Stuart Mill's speech supporting capital punishment in the British House of Commons in 1868, when he stated that by taking the life of a man who has taken another's life 'we show most emphatically our regard for it, by the adoption of a rule that he who violates that right in another forfeits it for himself'. (quoted in Leon Radzinowicz and Roger Hood, *A History of English Criminal Law, Vol. 5, The Emergence of Penal Policy* (1986), p. 686.

[12] On the situation in France, see Picca, n. 1 above, and Robert Badinter, *L'Abolition* (2000), who notes on p. 301 that on the morning of the debate on abolition *Le Figaro* (17 September 1981) published an opinion poll which showed that 62% of respondents favoured the death penalty, with 33% against. When asked whether they were in favour of capital punishment for particularly atrocious crimes, 73% replied 'yes'. On Germany, see M. Mohrenschlager, 'The Abolition of Capital Punishment in the Federal Republic of Germany: The German Experience' *Revue Internationale de Droit Pénal* 58 (1987), pp. 509–519 at 513; and Richard J. Evans, *Rituals of Retribution: Capital Punishment in Germany 1600–1987* (1996), pp. 801–804, and Statistical App. at 935; on Canada,

Indeed, François Mitterrand's campaign for President of France in 1981, only four years after the last execution had taken place, included a pledge to abolish the death penalty even though the majority of voters supported capital punishment. Mitterrand was elected and the death penalty abolished. He was then re-elected, thus showing that capital punishment was not the most salient issue amongst voters and that his political leadership had been accepted. All these countries have held steadfastly to the view—despite strong differences of opinion—that popular sentiment alone should not determine penal policy, that task being the responsibility of elected representatives exercising their own judgment. The parliaments of Canada and the United Kingdom both rejected several attempts to reinstate capital punishment before it was finally abolished for all crimes in all circumstances, despite the fact that in both countries the polls showed substantial majorities at the time in favour of reinstatement.[13]

The early chapters of this book made it clear that in many jurisdictions the death penalty has become a focus of human rights dialogues, and a number of them have abolished the death penalty partly as a result of the concerted efforts of influential and well-informed bodies. Opinion has often been mediated through the authoritative pronouncements of official Commissions of Inquiry, in so far as they have dispassionately reviewed the evidence. Effective campaigns have drawn the attention of the public and of policy-makers to those defects of capital punishment that create the greatest unease; namely, the inevitability of mistakes (see Chapter 7), and an unacceptable degree of arbitrariness in its infliction (see Chapter 8). It is therefore important for abolitionist movements to gain the support of elite opinion-formers, especially among those who influence and administer the criminal justice system. In various retentionist countries, recent years have witnessed the emergence of anti-death penalty and broader human rights pressure groups, even within regimes not normally sympathetic to human rights discourse. For example, in Cuba a moderate dissident group (Arco Progresista), which has proposed a charter of human rights for public consideration, raised public awareness of the issue by carrying out, in 2003, an opinion survey which indicated widespread opposition to the death penalty. Out of 35,209 people interviewed, only 1,842 disagreed with the text of the proposed charter, the first article of which stated that 'no Cuban shall be sentenced to death or executed'. Of the total number of respondents, just 4% (1,400) believed that the death penalty should be kept on the books, and then only for exceptional crimes.[14]

see Ezzat A. Fattah, 'Canada's Successful Experience with the Abolition of the Death Penalty' *Canadian Journal of Criminology* 25 (1987), pp. 421–431.

[13] *British Social Attitudes: Who Shares New Labour Values? The 16th Report* (1999); *Report of Canadian Commons Debates*, 5 June, col. 6803, 18 June, col. 7309, 25 June, 1987, col. 7594; AI, *Death Penalty News*, September 1995, AI Index: ACT 43/03/95.

[14] *Inter Press Service*, 28 April 2007, cited at <http://www.lanuevacuba.com/nuevacuba/notic-06-04-2805.htm>.

It will be recalled that abolition has sometimes been linked specifically with the overthrow of totalitarian and repressive regimes and the establishment of new democratic constitutions which promote the 'right to life'; such as in Italy and Germany after the Second World War, in Romania after the fall of Ceausescu, and in Cambodia after the demise of Pol Pot's infamous reign. In several 'new' states, as mentioned in Chapters 2 and 3, it has been the President or the Minister of Justice who has, through an act of political leadership, promulgated the abolition of the death penalty on the grounds that it was a violation of human rights, whatever the majority of the public might claim to want. Hence capital punishment has been abolished on these grounds by a number of supreme courts, such as in Hungary, Ukraine, and South Africa. When the Constitutional Court of South Africa abolished capital punishment, on the grounds that it was incompatible with a human rights culture enshrined in the country's new constitution, it did so even though it recognized that 'the majority of South Africans agree that the death penalty should be imposed in extreme cases of murder'.[15]

(b) The role of public opinion in a populist democracy: the case of the United States

Quite a different view of representative government has been taken in the United States. A good deal of recent work has tried to explain why America, a country that in most respects has similar political values and a legal culture to other countries in the West, retains the death penalty when its allies, in Canada, Europe, Australia, and New Zealand have abolished it. Carol Steiker explores various theoretical accounts of 'American exceptionalism', including different homicide rates, the salience of crime as a political issue, and public opinion. For example, she reviews the argument that 'American populism' as compared to European 'elitism', 'best accounts for "American exceptionalism" as regards differences in death penalty policy'.[16] This theory has two dimensions to it, one institutional and one cultural. As for the first, certain features of American electoral politics can fairly be described as distinctively populist in comparison to most European parliamentary democracies. For example, the use of the primary system to select party candidates in both federal and state elections and the availability of 'direct democracy tools', such as referenda and initiatives, tends to increase the power of voters and to promote populist tendencies in political debates. Discussing the cultural dimension, Steiker points to differences in political culture between the United States and Europe, with

---

[15] *State v Makwanyane* [1995] (3) SA 391, quoted in William A. Schabas, 'Public Opinion and the Death Penalty', paper presented to the EU-China Seminar on Human Rights, Beijing, 10–12 May 2001, reprinted in Peter Hodgkinson and William A. Schabas (eds.), *Capital Punishment: Strategies for Abolition* (2004), pp. 309–331.
[16] Carol Steiker, 'Capital Punishment and American Exceptionalism' *Oregon Law Review* 81 (2002), pp. 97–130, at 114.

American politicians being conspicuously anti-elitist in their self-presentation, which creates a strong tendency to defer to majority sentiment, not merely as a matter of political expediency, but also as a reflection of how elected officials interpret their role.[17] Added to this is 'criminal justice populism' with a much greater degree of lay participation in the criminal process than in most other jurisdictions, and the election, rather than appointment, of prosecutors and, in many states, judges. Steiker concluded that:[18]

These clearly 'exceptional' institutional arrangements, like populism in electoral politics, provide a mechanism through which popular support for the use of capital punishment can influence institutional decision making... Elected officials who campaigned on a death penalty platform, or reelected officials who were vigorous advocates for the use of available capital sanctions while in office, no doubt perceive a mandate to use the death penalty in a way that European judges and prosecutors, more isolated products of an elite bureaucracy, could not possibly... American criminal justice populism may indeed present a serious impediment to American abolition.

In some American states the question of capital punishment has been put to the popular vote in referenda; for example, it was reinstated in California and Oregon in 1977 and 1978 respectively. In approving the legislation of states under the revised capital statutes in *Gregg v Georgia* and other cases in 1976, the majority of the United States Supreme Court clearly held the view that the fact that state legislators had revised their laws in order to ensure that capital punishment could be enforced against the most egregious types of murderer was taken to be an expression of public sentiment that could not be overridden by an abstract judgment that capital punishment was 'cruel and unusual punishment' *per se*. This is because the Court considers American public opinion as one of the barometers for deciding whether the death penalty violates 'evolving standards of decency'—a criterion used to determine whether punishments should be regarded as 'cruel and unusual'.

Post-1976, as Jonathan Simon argues:[19]

The death penalty, as it began to renew itself after *Furman*, was coming to represent a kind of populism in governance, that is, a willingness to define key aspects of law to accommodate popular feelings and fears, with implications far beyond criminal justice, and for the role of courts themselves.

In recent years leading politicians in the United States, from candidates for the Presidency and state governorships downwards, have felt inhibited from taking a stand against capital punishment for fear of its impact on their chances of election. The fact that candidates for the posts of public prosecutor as well as judge in

---

[17] *Ibid.*
[18] *Ibid.*, pp. 119–121.
[19] Jonathan Simon, *Governing Through Crime: How the war on crime transformed American democracy and created a culture of fear* (2007), p. 119.

many states must stand for election favours those who respond positively to public sentiments on the death penalty,[20] as Justice Penny White found to her cost when she was voted off the Tennessee Supreme Court in 1996 in a retention election that effectively became a referendum on the death penalty. She became the target of a vitriolic public campaign led by the Tennessee Conservative Union after she overturned the death sentence of a man convicted of raping and murdering an elderly woman.[21] Conversely, district attorneys like Bob Macy of Oklahoma succeeded in being re-elected after campaigning on this issue (his campaign poster boasted that he had put 44 murderers on death row). As an article written after his re-election, and at a time when he could boast having put 53 defendants on death row, put it: 'In the court of law, Macy meets with constant and sometimes severe criticism. But in the court of public opinion he consistently wins re-election—usually with more than 70% of the vote'.[22] Political pressure also pertains at the federal level. A report in 2002 made clear that the then Attorney General, John D. Ashcroft, frequently overruled his own federal prosecutors, reversing their recommendations 12 times in just his first year in office, ordering them to seek the death penalty in cases where they had recommended not doing so. The evidence suggests that he was often responding to demands from the victims' families.[23]

Yet, the American Bar Association's *Standards for Criminal Justice: Prosecution Function and Defense Function* provides that 'in making the decision to prosecute, the prosecutor should give no weight to the personal or political advantages or disadvantages which might be involved or a desire to enhance his or her record of convictions'.[24] Of course, in practice 'the burden of proving that a district attorney has abused his or her discretion in seeking the death penalty because of political ambition or community pressure will be extremely difficult to prove'.[25] But when the Supreme Court directly addressed the unrestrained power of

---

[20] S. B. Bright, 'Political Attacks on the Judiciary: Can justice be done amid efforts to intimidate and remove judges from office for unpopular decisions?' *New York University Law Review* 72 (1997), p. 308. Also Richard Brooks and Steven Raphael, 'Life terms or death sentences; the uneasy relationship between judicial elections and capital punishment' *Journal of Criminal Law and Criminology*, 92 (2003), pp. 609–639 at 638.

[21] J. Woods, 'Public outrage nails a judge' *Nashville Banner*, 2 August 1996; V. Wyatt, 'Give them death' *The Nashville Tennessean*, 22 July 1996.

[22] K. Armstrong, 'Cowboy Bob ropes win but at considerable cost' *Chicago Tribune*, 10 January 1999.

[23] D. Eggen, 'Ashcroft pursues death penalty' *The Washington Post*, 1 July 2002; A. Tilghman, 'Attorney General overrules local prosecutors in case of three Binghamton men accused in murder of alleged drug dealer' *Albany Times-Union*, 17 August 2002; W. Glaberson, 'Judge denounces Attorney-General's death-penalty push' *New York Times*, 24 December 2003; D. Hechler, 'U.S. death penalty in wake of Ashcroft' *The National Law Journal*, 29 November 2004.

[24] Cited by E. M. McCann, 'Opposing Capital Punishment: A prosecutor's perspective' 79 *Marquette Law Review* (1996), pp. 649–706 at 671 (The NDAA National Prosecution Standards provide similar rules).

[25] *Ibid.*, p. 668.

prosecutors to decide whether to seek the death penalty in a capital case in *Gregg v Georgia* in 1966, it ruled that it was constitutional.[26]

Political leaders such as George Pataki in New York and Governor George Deukmejian in California famously campaigned on the death penalty and once in office ensured that it would be imposed. Governors, like those lower down the political ladder, know that in most states, and nationally, the appetite of the majority is for capital punishment. And, as Jonathan Simon notes, no governor from a state that outlawed executions has been elected president since the reintroduction of capital punishment.[27] George Bush's 1988 presidential campaign was something of a watershed in this respect, with Democrat nominee Michael Dukakis being made to look weak and ineffective because of his principled opposition to the death penalty. Rather than rejecting this position, his successor, Bill Clinton, not only embraced the 'war against crime' mantra of his predecessor, but interrupted his campaign to oversee the execution of Rickey Ray Rector, a mentally retarded Arkansas prisoner.[28]

However, there are signs that public opinion on a candidate's stand on the issue of the death penalty may be beginning to change. For example, Senator John Kerry, who was the nominee of the Democratic Party to challenge Republican incumbent President George W. Bush in the US presidential election of November 2004, was the first major party presidential candidate in more than 15 years to declare himself to be opposed to capital punishment. His abolitionist stance did not seem to be an issue in the campaign, and almost certainly was not the main reason why he did not win.[29]

But, of course, politicians do not only pay attention to popular opinion polls; very important also is the expression of opinion by elites, especially those with practical knowledge and theoretical understanding of the issues involved, in this case lawyers. There is some evidence that attitudes of American lawyers are beginning to change too. A survey of 600 lawyers in the mid-1980s found two-thirds to be in favour of executing those persons currently on death row.[30] Yet, just over a decade later, in 1997, the powerful American Bar Association passed a resolution calling for a moratorium on executions 'until the jurisdiction implements policies and procedures... intended to (1) ensure that death penalty cases are administered fairly and impartially, in accordance with due process, and (2) minimize

---

[26] For a discussion of this prosecutorial power to seek the death penalty, and a recommendation to spread the power across committees of seven elected members, see J. A. Horowitz, 'Prosecutorial discretion and the death penalty: creating a committee to decide whether to seek the death penalty' *Fordham Law Review*, 65 (1997), pp. 2571–2610.

[27] Simon, n. 19 above, p. 69 (for an interesting discussion of the relationship between executive power and punitive policies in the USA see Simon, Ch. 2).

[28] M. Frady, 'Death in Arkansas' *New Yorker*, 22 February 1993.

[29] Professor Jordan M. Steiker, 'Federal Constitutional Regulation of the American Death Penalty: Past, Present, and Prospects for Judicial Abolition', lecture given at the Manor Road Social Sciences Building, University of Oxford, 27 April 2007.

[30] American Bar Association, *ABA Journal* 71 (1985), at p. 44.

the risk that innocent people may be executed'.[31] If the Commissions set up to examine this issue in several states all conclude, as did the Illinois Governor's Commission in April 2002, that 'no system given human nature and frailties, could ever be devised that would work perfectly and guarantee absolutely that no innocent person is ever again sentenced to death',[32] then American lawyers as a professional group may well come to embrace the principled human rights position against capital punishment.

2. The Nature of Public Opinion

(a) The social construction of opinion data

The concept of public opinion is undoubtedly open to a number of interpretations involving different means of gathering the data.[33] In Malawi, for instance, the Special Law Commission on the Review of the Constitution sought the 'views of stakeholders through district consultations, national television, radios, newspapers, brochures, banners and posters'.[34] Such an approach recognizes that there may be differing opinions among different sectors of the population, and that the opinions of some persons or sectors of the population may have more weight in the legislative process than the opinions of others. In South Korea, for example, research conducted in 2003, by the National Human Rights Commission of Korea, indicated that 80% of professionals in non-governmental organizations and members of correctional committees and 60% of members of the National Assembly and lawyers were willing to support abolition, as compared with less than half of the people reached by a public opinion poll.[35] But it is this latter sort of opinion which is generally referred to when politicians make claims about the public's attitude towards capital punishment and the possibility of its abolition. It is meant to measure what the general public will tolerate or, in democracies, what policy they will support in elections.

It is this meaning of 'public opinion', gathered through 'polls' of representative samples of the general population, that has dominated discourse on the death penalty, rather than the opinions of elites. Such polls record immediate opinions and responses, which are inevitably affected by the nature and specificity of the questions posed, the sequence of questioning, the socio-political context within which the survey takes place, and the socio-economic, race, and gender

---

[31] Quoted in A. Sarat, *The Abolition of the Death Penalty in International Law* (1997), at p. 254.

[32] Illinois, *Report of the Governor's Commission on Capital Punishment: George H. Ryan Governor* (April 2002), p. 207.

[33] See David A. Green, 'Public Opinion Versus Public Judgment About Crime: Correcting the "Comedy of Errors"' *British Journal of Criminology* 46 (2006), pp. 131–154; N. Walker and M. Hough (eds.), 'Limits of Tolerance' in *Public Attitudes to Sentencing* (1988).

[34] See 'Constitutional Review' *The Daily Times* (Malawi) 1 May 2007.

[35] Gallup Korea/Chosun Ibo, 7 October 2003, cited at *Angus Reid Global Monitor*.

composition of the sample, and knowledge of the issues involved. In the United States capital punishment is favoured more often by whites, the more wealthy, by males, Republicans, and conservatives, than it is by black people, poorer people, women, Democrats, and liberals.[36] It has been suggested that the degree of support will depend, at least in part, on the relative confidence of citizens from different social strata or ethnic groups that they, or people like them, will be treated fairly by the criminal justice system (see below).[37]

Even within socio-economic groups, attitudes towards the death penalty are more complex than has been often supposed: 'opinion can best be viewed as a set of ordered priorities, the order of which changes with time and circumstances'.[38] Indeed, there would appear to be a substantial body of non-ideologically committed opinion in the United States that can be affected in one direction or another by information about crime and the impact of punishment. Certainly, both Professor Hans Zeisel and the Gallup organization expressed the view that such changes are more emotional than rational, linked to 'the widely observed increase in personal fears, dissatisfaction with society in general, and feelings of helplessness'.[39] For example, people may generally oppose the death penalty yet be in favour of it when shocked by a particularly horrifying crime. There is evidence from Germany and Spain that the proportion of people favouring the death penalty has fluctuated considerably when questions have been asked in the aftermath of outbreaks of terrorist violence.[40] Thus the outrage caused by the Bali terrorist

[36] For example, the May 2006 American Gallup poll showed that Republicans preferred the death penalty to life imprisonment without parole (by a 64% to 31% margin); Democrats preferred life without parole (with only 31% preferring the death penalty and 63% LWOP); men preferred the death penalty (by a 56% to 39% margin) and women preferred life without parole (with only 39% of women preferring the death penalty and 55% LWOP): Jeffrey M. Jones, 'Two in Three Favor Death Penalty for Convicted Murderers' *Gallup*, 1 June 2006 <http://poll.gallupcom>. *Note:* throughout this chapter we report findings which rely on polls using representative surveys with known confidence limits, unless otherwise indicated.

[37] Robert M. Bohm, 'American Death Penalty Opinion, 1936–1986: A Critical Examination of the Gallup Polls' in R. M. Bohm (ed.), *The Death Penalty in America: Current Research* (1991), pp. 113–143 at 135; Steven E. Barkan and Steven F. Cohn, 'Racial Prejudice and Support for the Death Penalty by Whites' *Journal of Research in Crime and Delinquency* 31 (1994), pp. 202–209; Robert L. Young, 'Race, Conceptions of Crime and Justice, and Support for the Death Penalty' *Social Psychology Quarterly* 54 (1991), pp. 67–75; James Alan Fox, Michael J. Radelet, and Julie L. Bonsteel, 'Death Penalty Opinion in the Post-*Furman* Years' *New York University Review of Law and Social Change* 18 (1990–91), pp. 499–528 at 506–508; Samuel R. Gross, 'Update: American Public Opinion on the Death Penalty—It's Getting Personal' *Cornell Law Review* 83 (1998), pp. 1448–1475 at 1451.

[38] M. Warr and M. Stafford, 'Public Goals of Punishment and Support for the Death Penalty' *Journal of Research in Crime and Delinquency* 21 (1984), pp. 95–111 at 106.

[39] H. Zeisel and A. M. Gallup, 'Death Penalty Sentiment in the United States' *Journal of Quantitative Criminology* 5 (1989), pp. 285–296 at 294–295.

[40] M. Mohrenschlager, 'The Abolition of Capital Punishment in the Federal Republic of Germany: The German Experience' *Revue Internationale de Droit Pénal* 58 (1987), pp. 509–519 at 513; Evans, n. 12 above, p. 802; and A. Beristain, 'La sanction capitale en Espagne: Référence spéciale à la dimension religieuse Chrétienne' *Revue Internationale de Droit Pénal* 58 (1987), pp. 613–636, at 620–622.

bombing in 2002, which killed 202 people, some 164 of them foreign nationals, including 88 Australians, was reflected in polls in Australia in the following months, when support for capital punishment ranged up to 56% of respondents, although this was short-lived and by October 2007 it was down to less than a quarter.[41]

Indeed, according to some leading researchers:[42]

Increased support for the death penalty may be more of a reflection of the desire for the execution of a Ted Bundy [a notorious serial killer] and other celebrity criminals than for the execution of more typical and more obscure condemned inmates.. We suspect, therefore, that recent trends in survey data on death penalty opinions are largely a function of changes in the way respondents conceptualize a particular crime.

This was certainly the case in relation to the 'Oklahoma bomber', Timothy McVeigh. Researchers have insisted, therefore, that 'pollsters should clearly delineate the elements of the crime when soliciting a respondent's attitude to the death penalty, rather than leaving it to the respondent to 'fill in' the gory details'.[43] So, when the Gallup organization asked a national sample of American citizens whether they believed that Timothy McVeigh should be executed for the murders he committed in the Oklahoma bombing, 79% said 'yes' including 22% who, although generally opposed to capital punishment, thought that McVeigh nevertheless deserved to be executed.[44]

---

[41] The 2003 figures showed a statistically significant drop of almost 10% in support for the death penalty in the year after the Bali bombings. In 2003 less than half (46.8%) agreed that the death penalty should be reintroduced for murder, with a third saying that it should not (33.6%): New South Wales Council for Civil Liberties, *The Death Penalty in Australia and Overseas*, Background Paper 2005/3, 29 March 2005. By 2007 only 24% of respondents to an opinion poll stated that the penalty for murder should be death; *Angus Reid Global Monitor*, 22 October 2007, cited at the Death Penalty Information Centre website: <http://www.deathpenaltyinfo.org/article.php?did=2165#aus1007>. Furthermore, such events do not always lead to a surge in punitive opinions. For example, a poll in 2005 showed that support for capital punishment in Russia had declined to 65% from 79% in 2002, despite rising crime rates and terrorist attack's, such as at the theatre in Moscow in 2002, and the three-day siege and ultimate carnage at a school in Belsan in 2004: Yory Levada Analytic Centre Poll, 11 July 2005, cited at *Angus Reid Global Monitor*.

[42] James Alan Fox, Michael J. Radelet, and Julie L. Bonsteel, 'Death Penalty Opinion in the Post-*Furman* Years' *New York University Review of Law and Social Change* 18 (1990–91), pp. 499–528 at pp. 510–511. This may be particularly so when a notorious case sparks prolific responses on the internet, where the nuances of proponents' and opponents' positions are often lost. Mona Lynch has argued that internet discussions on the death penalty almost inevitably become reduced to a battle between good (as represented by innocent victims) and evil (the capital murderers): Mona Lynch, 'Capital Punishment as Moral Imperative: pro-death penalty discourse on the internet' *Punishment and Society* 4(2) (2002), pp. 213–236.

[43] Fox, *et al.*, *ibid.*, p. 515.

[44] *USA Today*, 20 June 2001: <http://www.usatoday.com/news/nation/2001-05-03-mcveigh-cappunish.htm>. McVeigh represents an 'extreme case' which no doubt tests the consciences of many who are opposed to the death penalty. It was, for example, reported that Professor Hugo Adam Bedau admitted that he personally was willing to see McVeigh and those like him executed so long as all others not like McVeigh were spared the death penalty: Robert J. Lifton and Greg Mitchell, *Who Owns Death? Capital Punishment, the American Conscience, and the End of Executions* (2000), pp. 220–221.

Opinions may also vary according to the political context, as well as the stage in the criminal process that has been reached, as was seen in the case of the former Iraqi dictator Saddam Hussein. When a poll was carried out in nine countries prior to his conviction 57% of Americans wanted him executed, compared to between 14% and 38% of respondents from the eight other countries, listed in Table 10.1 (below).[45] The majority of respondents from these countries thought he should be sentenced to prison without the possibility of parole. However, once he had been sentenced to death, an opinion poll conducted in December 2006 showed that a higher proportion in all countries thought that he should be executed: 82% of Americans, 69% of respondents from Britain, and 58% from France. In Germany (53%) and Spain (51%) there was a very slight majority in favour of execution and only in Italy did those in favour (46%) fall below half.[46] His execution was followed around the world by both jubilation and outrage, with the latter sentiment being expressed across Europe where the video-recording of the unruly scenes of mocking and baiting of the former dictator by those present caused particular offence. In comparison, jubilation was generally expressed in the United States of American, Iran, and among the Kurdish and Shia populations of Iraq.

(b) The strength of opinion

Strength of feelings or commitment to capital punishment may also vary in intensity. For example, David Johnson, who has studied capital punishment in Japan in depth, observes:[47]

the depth of citizen's support for capital punishment seems shallower in Japan than in countries such as the United States... there is little public clamour for capital punishment... either as a general criminal justice policy or as a sanction in specific cases... the role of the Japanese public may be less an activator or motivator of death sentences and executions than as 'passive assenter'.

To take another example, in Great Britain 74% of all respondents to a survey carried out in 1992 agreed with the statement that death was 'the most appropriate penalty for some crimes', but only 43% 'agreed strongly'.[48] Seven years later support had dropped to 57%, with only 28% agreeing 'strongly'.[49] Comparisons therefore between the support for capital punishment in various countries that do not take account of the *intensity* of feelings on the subject and how high or low it

---

[45] A more recent poll of the same nine countries, also by *Ipsos Public Affairs*, asked the same question about Osama bin Laden and, whilst the proportion of Americans in support of the death penalty for bin Laden was even higher (63%), the data were similar in that the majority of respondents from abolitionist countries thought that he should receive life in prison without the possibility of parole.

[46] *Harris Interactive/France 24/Le Monde*, December 2006, cited at *Angus Reid Global Monitor*.

[47] David T. Johnson, 'Where the state kills in secret. Capital punishment in Japan' *Punishment and Society* 8 (2005), pp. 251–285 at 269.

[48] *British Social Attitudes Cumulative Sourcebook* (1992), Table B-2.

[49] *British Social Attitudes: Who Shares New Labour Values? The 16th Report* (1999).

ranks among citizens' concerns are likely to be very misleading.[50] It is also the case that support for the death penalty in abstract gives no indication of what rate of executions respondents expect or what rate they would be willing to tolerate. The public might support the occasional execution of someone for a particularly egregious crime, but be opposed to a policy of executing a large proportion of murderers in order to try to enhance the deterrent effect of punishment. In this respect it needs to be emphasized that while opinion in the United States suggests that there is considerable support for the death penalty in abstract, and for particularly heinous murderers, there is very little clamour for executions in most cases of murder. Rather, very often persons awaiting death may evoke a good deal of sympathy.[51]

Indeed, research shows that very few would support the death penalty as a mandatory punishment to be applied to every case of murder and that questions therefore need to be carefully targeted towards specific categories of offences and the circumstances in which they have been committed.[52] Polls in Russia, for example, have shown that while only a very small proportion of those questioned (6.6%) favoured the complete abolition of capital punishment, the majority (69.1%) 'believed that the death penalty should be applied only in the most extreme instances and as infrequently as possible'.[53] In a study carried out in America some 20 years ago when support for the death penalty as shown by opinion polls was strong, people were given descriptions of three cases in which the defendants had been sentenced to death. Despite the fact that the majority stated that they were in favour of capital punishment in general, no more than 15% of the respondents recommended that any one of the defendants in these cases should be sentenced to death.[54] Some indication of what members of the public who declare themselves in favour of capital punishment might think when faced with the realities of inflicting capital punishment can also be inferred from the actions of those who have to make the life or death decision after hearing all the details of the case and the aggravating and mitigating circumstances when acting as jurors. As Hugo Bedau has pointed out, although jurors in America have to be 'death eligible'—that is, willing to bring in a death sentence—their 'views may be less predictable in concrete cases than they seem in the abstract'. Jurors picked because they support capital punishment in general still only hand down death sentences in about one in 10 capital cases.[55]

---

[50] Steiker, n. 16 above, pp. 97–130 at 111, hypothesizes that Europeans 'simply do not share Americans' fervor on the issue'.

[51] Hugo Adam Bedau, *Death is Different* (1987), pp. 153–163.

[52] Frances Cullen, Bonnie S. Fisher, and Brandon Applegate, 'Public Opinion about Punishment and Corrections' in M. Tonry (ed.), *Crime and Justice: A Review of Research* Vol. 27 (2000), pp. 1–79 at 17–18.

[53] A. S. Mikhlin, *The Death Penalty in Russia* (1999), pp. 8–22.

[54] This study by Phoebe Ellsworth is quoted in Phoebe C. Ellsworth and Lee Ross, 'Public Opinion and Capital Punishment: A Close Examination of the Views of Abolitionists and Retentionists' *Crime and Delinquency* 29 (1983), pp. 116–169 at 139.

[55] H. A. Bedau, 'The Controversy over Public Support for the Death Penalty: The Death Penalty versus Life Imprisonment' in H. A. Bedau (ed.), *The Death Penalty in America: Current Controversies* (1997), pp. 84–89 at 86.

(c) The importance of providing response alternatives

Polls have also shown that whether respondents support capital punishment or not depends on what the alternative to the death penalty might be, for example life imprisonment, with or without the possibility of parole (see below and Chapter 11). They may be most concerned that abolition would send the wrong message, by reducing the punishment so much that the crime would appear to be being treated too leniently; that the distinctions between the punishment for the gravest of crimes would be indistinguishable from the punishment for other grave but still less serious crimes; or that criminals who are potentially dangerous would be released while still a threat to members of the public. Thus, while 80% of Taiwanese say that they are opposed to abolishing the death penalty, another poll has revealed that 40% would accept abolition if Taiwan toughened jail terms for criminals and made it harder for them to receive parole.[56]

A series of American studies, begun by William Bowers,[57] has shown that 'only 19 to 43 percent of the public (depending on the sample), prefers the death penalty over the alternative of life imprisonment without the possibility of parole and with restitution to the relatives of the victim'.[58] This now appears also to be the case in many countries that have already abolished capital punishment.

In February 2007 Associated Press-Ipsos polled about 1,000 adults by telephone in each of nine countries: Britain, Canada (in April), France, Germany, Italy, Mexico (where 1,200 were interviewed in person), South Korea, Spain, and the United States.[59] The data for each country derives from one poll, in which respondents were asked a series of questions to ascertain more than just a general support for capital punishment. The death penalty exists in only two of these nine countries: the United States and South Korea (where it has not been enforced since December 1997). Table 10.1 presents the data in a way which makes it easy for the reader to compare preferences across jurisdictions. Hence we report data only from countries where the questions have been asked in the same way.

---

[56] *Webindia123*, 7 August 2005 cited at: <http://www.handsoffcain.info/news/index.php?iddocumento=7111677>.

[57] W. J. Bowers and M. Vandiver, *New Yorkers want an Alternative to the Death Penalty* (1991); W. J. Bowers and M. Vandiver, *Nebraskans want an Alternative to the Death Penalty* (1991); Edmund F. McGarrell and Marla Sandys, 'The misperception of public opinion toward capital punishment: examining the spuriousness explanation of death penalty support' *American Behavioral Scientist (Special Issue: Public Opinion on Justice in the Criminal Justice System)* 39:4 (February 1996), pp. 500–514.

[58] W. J. Bowers, 'Capital punishment and contemporary values: People's misgivings and the court's misperceptions' *Law and Society Review* 27 (1993), pp. 157–175; R. M. Bohm, 'American Death Penalty Opinion: Past, Present, and Future' in J. A. Acker, R. M. Bohm, and C. S. Lanier (eds.), *America's Experiment with Capital Punishment* (2nd edn., 2003), pp. 27–54 at 45. However, it has been suggested that, because of the way the question was posed, these findings may have exaggerated the decline in support for the death penalty when offered an alternative: see Gross, n. 37 above, at pp. 1456–1457.

[59] *The Associated Press International Affairs Poll*, conducted by Ipsos Public Affairs: <http://www.ipsos-mori.com/polls/2007/associatedpress.shtml>. Each poll had a margin of sampling error of plus or minus 3 percentage points.

Table 10.1 Public opinion on the death penalty in selected countries in 2007

Countries surveyed	Favoured death penalty for murder[60]	Preferences between prison and death penalty for murder[61]
Canada	44%	DP : 25% LWOP : 51% Prison/parole : 20%
France	45%	DP : 21% LWOP : 55% Prison/parole : 22%
Germany	35%	DP : 11% LWOP : 59% Prison/parole : 27%
Italy	31%	DP : 16% LWOP : 60% Prison/parole : 15%
Mexico	71%	DP : 46% LWOP : 43% Prison/parole : 7%
South Korea	72%	DP : 35% LWOP : 44% Prison/parole : 21%
Spain	28%	DP : 12% LWOP : 64% Prison/parole : 20%
United Kingdom	50%	DP : 34% LWOP : 44% Prison/parole : 19%
United States	69%	DP : 52% LWOP : 37% Prison/parole : 9%

Table 10.1 shows that although between a third and a half of respondents in five European countries thought that the death penalty was an appropriate penalty for murder, support dropped significantly, usually by more than half, when the possibility of life without parole (LWOP) was introduced in a further question as an alternative punishment. Indeed, in all of the European countries, with the exception of the UK, the majority of respondents chose life without parole

[60] The first question was 'Do you favour or oppose the death penalty for people convicted of murder?'. This combines two original categories ('strongly favour' and 'somewhat favour'); for disaggregated data see the original report, cited at n. 59 above.
[61] The second question, asked of the same people, was 'Which punishment do you prefer for people convicted of murder?'. The options were: death penalty; life in prison without the possibility of parole (LWOP); a long prison sentence with the chance of parole. Where percentages do not add up to one hundred, the rest replied that they were 'not sure'.

over other penalties. In the UK almost half (44%) chose LWOP, still significantly more than the proportion who chose the death penalty (34%). The Canadian respondents were very similar to the Europeans, perhaps reflecting their similar abolitionist histories. Respondents in Mexico and South Korea expressed the greatest support for the death penalty, with over two-thirds favouring it for murder, but the majority of respondents also preferred prison to the death penalty, when presented with a choice, and a comparatively high proportion of South Korean respondents (21%) favoured prison *with* the possibility of parole. The United States was the only country where a majority, but only a very slight majority (52%), favoured the death penalty over life imprisonment (47%).

Some nations, such as China, cite the use of capital punishment in the United States to justify retention. For this reason the recent decline in support for this punishment in the United States deserves further attention. First, overall support (69% in the poll cited in Table 10.1 and around two-thirds in a Gallup poll conducted in May 2006) is well below the support found in 1994 when 80% favoured capital punishment.[62] Second, support has further declined when those polled are given the alternative of LWOP. Between 2005 and 2006, according to the Gallup polls taken in those years, support for LWOP increased from 39% to 48% and support for the death penalty fell from 56% to 47% (the lowest percentage in two decades).[63] In Maryland, for example, support for life without parole as the alternative to the death penalty has jumped 18 percentage points in less than a decade: from 43% to 61% in 2007.[64] Even in Harris County, Texas, which includes Houston, where the highest number of executions have been carried out, polls have revealed that the proportion of residents that would prefer the sentence of life without parole rather than the death penalty for those who commit murder has increased from 53% in 2003 to 64% in 2005.[65]

Bowers has argued that these findings suggest that many people do not support the death penalty *per se*, but rather are concerned that they should be sufficiently protected. In other words, their opinions are based more on utilitarian than on retributive considerations. There is some support for this from studies of jurors. For example, in South Carolina it was found that amongst those in a sample of jurors who said that they 'strongly or moderately' supported the death penalty, 79% strongly or moderately agreed with the statement, 'You wish we had a better way of stopping murderers than the death penalty'.[66] Over half (52%) said they

---

[62] This draws on six opinion polls, all cited at *Angus Reid Global Monitor* between 2005 and 2006.

[63] Telephone interviews with 500 respondents aged 18 and older. Jones, n. 36 above; these data are slightly different from those gathered in February 2007 by *Ipsos Public Affairs*, n. 59 above.

[64] *Maryland Catholic Conference Press Release*, 'Maryland Voters Support Life without Parole as Replacement for the Death Penalty by More Than 2-to-1 Margin' 28 February 2007, quoted at the Death Penalty Information Center (DPIC) website: <http://deathpenaltyinfo.org/article.php?did=2266>.

[65] 2005 Houston Area Survey conducted by Rice University (2005), cited at DPIC website: <http://www.deathpenaltyinfo.org/article.php?&did=2147>.

[66] Theodore Eisenberg, Stephen P. Garvey, and Martin T. Wells, 'The Deadly Paradox of Capital Jurors' *Southern California Law Review* 74 (2000–2001), pp. 371–397 at 389.

would prefer it if murderers could be sentenced to life without parole and that proportion rose to 73% when the following phrase was added: 'and also required to work in prison for money that would go to the victims of families'.[67] Similarly, according to a study in Tennessee, 95% of a sample of 40 state legislators had said that they favoured the death penalty, but only 53% said that they would not prefer the alternative of life without parole plus work and payments of restitution.[68] These data need to be considered alongside studies which suggest that retribution is the main reason why the public supports the death penalty.[69]

3. Changing Public Opinion

How malleable are public attitudes to the death penalty? A number of factors and influences have been found to shape views on this subject, in particular: knowledge about the administration of capital punishment; racial animus, religion[70] and political predispositions, especially punitiveness; the influence of the homicide rate and of specific high profile cases, etc. What follows is not an exhaustive list of these variables but an indication of some of the more prominent factors that appear to influence opinion.[71]

(a) Knowledge of the administration and effects of capital punishment

As with other research on people's attitudes, there is a gap between the sort of 'off the top of the head opinion', which is tapped by opinion polls conducted on the

---

[67] *Ibid.*, at p. 391. See also William J. Bowers and Benjamin D. Steiner, 'Death by Default: An Empirical Demonstration of False and Forced Choices in Capital Sentencing' *Texas Law Review* 77 (1999), pp. 605–717 at 706.

[68] John T. Whitehead, ' "Good Ol' Boys" and the Chair: Death Penalty Attitudes of Policy Makers in Tennessee' *Crime and Delinquency* 44 (1998), pp. 245–256. It should be noted that 33% definitely preferred the alternative and 16% said they didn't know. Also, that support for the death penalty fell far less among a sample of prosecutors, 67% of whom did not prefer the alternative sentence; p. 251.

[69] A comparative study of college students' attitudes towards the death penalty in China and America found that retribution is the strongest predictor of support for capital punishment in America, whereas deterrence is the strongest predictor in China: Shanhe Jiang, Eric G. Lambert, and Jin Wang, 'Capital Punishment View in China and the United States: A preliminary study among college students' *International Journal of Offender Therapy and Comparative Criminology* 51(1) (2007), pp. 84–97.

[70] K. Mulligan, 'Pope John Paul II and Catholic opinion toward the death penalty and abortion' *Social Science Quarterly* 87: 3 (September 2006).

[71] Most of the literature on the variables that shape public opinion on the death penalty is American and we must warn against the assumption that these findings would be replicated in other jurisdictions. However, Steven Stack's analysis of sixteen other nations found that their data on indicators of public opinion on the death penalty largely confirmed US-based research: Steven Stack, 'Public Opinion on the Death Penalty: Analysis of Individual-level data from 17 Nations' *International Criminal Justice Review* 14 (2004), pp. 69–98.

telephone or in the street, and the complex weighing-up of considerations of the kind that juries have to undertake.[72]

Most members of the public possess very limited knowledge about the circumstances in which murders are committed, the characteristics of murderers, and all aspects of the administration of capital punishment.[73] As Haney remarks:[74]

This has allowed many citizens to support the death penalty without really understanding how it operates overall, and many courts to give their imprimatur to a system that is repeatedly but often incorrectly represented as fair, reliable and necessary.

For instance, opponents of the death penalty in Japan, such as Hosaka Nobuto, Secretary-General of the Parliamentary League for the Abolition of the Death Penalty, argue[75] that strong support for the death penalty in Japan is merely a reflection of the government's efforts to conceal information from the public and to deprive citizens of the opportunity for serious debate on the system:[76]

There is no discussion about this in the media...Even in the Diet, the death penalty is something of a taboo because most lawmakers know the abolitionist cause is unpopular. It has become a vicious circle: Politicians don't discuss it and the public doesn't hear the abolitionist case, so the politicians continue to avoid it.

Empirical investigations to assess the so-called 'Marshall hypothesis' have arisen from Justice Marshall's opinion in *Furman v Georgia* that 'it is imperative for constitutional purposes to attempt to discern the probable opinion of an informed electorate', for, as Robert Bohm has pointed out, Marshall believed that, given information about the death penalty, 'the great mass of citizens would conclude...that the death penalty is immoral and therefore unconstitutional', and public opinion would shift towards the abolitionist position.[77] When this view has been tested by empirical research, several studies have found evidence to support the Marshall hypothesis,[78] but other research has not. For example, a series of studies of students in a mid-western university by Robert Bohm and

---

[72] In relation to punishment and sentencing in general see P. Mayhew and J. van Kesteren, *Cross-national attitudes to punishment* (2002) in J. V. Roberts and M. Hough (eds.), *Changing Attitudes to Punishment: Public Opinion, Crime and Justice*, pp. 62–93; F. Cullen, B. Fisher, and B. Applegate, 'Public Opinion about Punishment and Corrections' in M. Tonry (ed.), *Crime and Justice. A Review of Research* (2000), pp. 1–79.

[73] Ellsworth and Ross, n. 54 above, pp. 139–145.

[74] Craig Haney, *Death by design: Capital Punishment as a Social Psychological System* (2005), p. 6.

[75] *The Japan Times*, 27 February 2007.

[76] *The Japan Times*, 8 April 2007.

[77] Bohm, n. 58 above, p. 35.

[78] A. Sarat and N. Vidmar, 'Public Opinion, the Death Penalty and the 8th Amendment: Testing the Marshall Hypothesis' *Wisconsin Law Review* 17 (1976), pp. 171–206; N. Vidmar and T. Dittenhoffer, 'Informed public opinion and death penalty attitudes' *Canadian Journal of Criminology* 23 (1981), pp. 43–56; Ellsworth and Ross, n. 54 above. All of these studies are discussed fully in A. D. Mitchell, 'The Effect of the Marshall Hypothesis on Attitudes Towards the Death Penalty' *Race, Gender and Class* 13 (2006), pp. 221–239.

his colleagues revealed that, despite taking a special class on the death penalty, increased knowledge had little effect on the opinions of students who supported capital punishment on the grounds of retribution, because the knowledge was often assimilated in a biased way, with the effect of shoring-up previously held emotionally based beliefs. The researchers concluded that opinions on the death penalty are far more difficult to change through instruction than is often assumed.[79] Furthermore, when there is change it tends to be short-lived: students questioned some two to three years later about whether they were in favour of or against the death penalty had 'rebounded to near their initial pre-test opinion'. Bohm hypothesized that 'perhaps it was because death penalty opinions are based primarily on emotion rather than on cognition and that, in the long run, cognitive influences on death penalty opinions give way to emotional factors'.[80]

However, the suggestion that attitudes to the death penalty are so deeply embedded that they are impervious to the impact of information about its administration and effects has to be placed alongside the fact that, in many countries, opinions for and against the death penalty have fluctuated quite markedly over relatively short periods of time. A prime example is the United States. In 1953 opinion polls showed 66% in favour of the death penalty but this had fallen to only 40% by 1965. According to the Gallup poll the proportion in favour of capital punishment reached a peak of 80% in 1994 before support fell back to 65% in 2001, only to rise somewhat to around 74% in 2005. These national trends were found also in California, where support for capital punishment changed from 49% in 1956 to 83% in 1985, and yet 10 years later stood at a much more modest 63%.[81]

(b) Concerns about the administration of justice

Some of the shift in public opinion noted above is no doubt attributable to increased knowledge and concern about how the death penalty is being administered. The last decade or so has witnessed increasing fears about the arbitrariness of the capital punishment system (see Chapter 8), evidence that some defence attorneys have been incompetent (see Chapter 7), and concern about the lethal injection procedure (see Chapter 5). Furthermore, the 'innocence movement' has attracted considerable media attention as persons sentenced to death have been found to be incontrovertibly innocent (see Chapter 7).

---

[79] R. M. Bohm, L. J. Clark, and A. F. Aveni, 'Knowledge and Death Penalty Opinions: A Test of the Marshall Hypotheses' *Journal of Research in Crime and Delinquency* 28 (1991), pp. 360–387; R. M. Bohm, R. E. Vogel, and A. A. Maisto, 'Knowledge and Death Penalty Opinion: A Panel Study' *Journal of Criminal Justice* 21 (1993), pp. 29–45; R. M. Bohm and R. E. Vogel, 'A Comparison of Factors Associated with Uninformed and Informed Death Penalty Opinions' *Journal of Criminal Justice* 22 (1994), pp. 125–143.

[80] Bohm, Vogel, and Maisto, *ibid.*, at p. 44.

[81] The Field Research Corporation, 2006.

Whilst a 2006 Gallup poll showed that a majority of Americans (60%) believed that the death penalty was fairly applied in their country and many said that it should be used more often,[82] a national public opinion poll conducted in 2007 found that:[83]

the American public is losing confidence in the death penalty. People are deeply concerned about the risk of executing the innocent, about the fairness of the process, and about the inability of capital punishment to accomplish its basic purposes.

Furthermore, this growing disillusionment is reflected in different states across America. Hence, whilst Californian's general support for the death penalty has remained quite high, at about 63% in 2006, less than half (48%) felt that when it is imposed it is generally fair and free of error. This is a significant decline from the proportion just two years before when 58% said that it was administered fairly.[84]

In particular, concern about the execution of innocent people has grown over the past decade or so. For example, Craig Haney found in a survey carried out in California in 1989 that 'Only 23% of our respondents told us that they thought there was a possibility that innocent people were too often executed' and 64% 'believed that innocent persons were so rarely executed that it was an unimportant issue in the death penalty debate'. Yet a decade later '73% of those surveyed said they were concerned enough about the risk of wrongful conviction that they were in favor of asking the governor to "halt all executions" until a study of the fairness of capital punishment in California could be completed'. As Haney rightly remarks, this illustrates people's responsiveness to information about how the system actually works.[85]

Furthermore, Unnever and Cullen's analysis of Gallup poll data reveals that three-quarters of Americans believe that innocent defendants have been executed within the last five years,[86] and this belief is associated with lower levels of support for the death penalty, especially among African Americans who were also more likely to believe that it was applied in a discriminatory manner (see pages 371–372 below).[87] Even supporters of capital punishment recognize that the execution

---

[82] Only about 1 in 5 believe that it is imposed too often and just over a half (51%) thought that it is not imposed enough: Jones, n. 36 above.

[83] R. C. Dieter, *A Crisis of Confidence: American's Doubts about the Death Penalty*, A Death Penalty Information Center Report (2007), p. 1.

[84] Field Poll, report by M. DiCamillo and M. Field, Field Research Corporation, 3 March 2006.

[85] Haney, n. 74 above, pp. 88–89.

[86] State polls replicate this finding. For example, in the high-executing state of Texas, a Scripps Howard poll in November 2004 showed that 70% of Texans believed that the state has executed innocent people.

[87] J. D. Unnever and F.T. Cullen, 'Executing the innocent and support for capital punishment: Implications for public policy' *Criminology & Public Policy* 4 (2005), pp. 3–38. Also, Austin Sarat, 'Innocence, Error, and the "New Abolitionism": A Commentary' *Criminology and Public Policy* 4 (1) (2005), pp. 45–54.

of innocent people is unacceptable, whatever other benefits they think capital punishment provides.[88] Hence the search for a 'fool-proof' system[89] because, as Richard Dieter has put it, 'Although the dissatisfaction with capital punishment has many roots, the common and principal concern heard throughout the country is the risk that innocent people may be caught up with the guilty'.[90] As Kaufman-Osborn has pointed out:[91]

If support for capital punishment has waned in recent years, this is not so much because new abolitionist arguments have been articulated and widely accepted, but because publicity has recently been lavished upon individualized stories of capital defendants represented by sleeping, intoxicated, or disbarred attorneys, of persons on death row proven innocent by undergraduate journalism students at Northwestern University, and of exonerations of the condemned on the basis of DNA testing.

Influential newspapers in a number of states that have traditionally supported the death penalty have both reflected and fed these growing concerns about the way capital punishment is being administered. For example, in April 2007 the *Dallas Morning News* called on Texas to abandon capital punishment, because the death penalty 'is both imperfect *and* irreversible'. The paper's traditional support for the death penalty had changed after reflection on increasing evidence that Texas has wrongly convicted a number of defendants in capital trials. The editorial announcing the paper's policy shift stated:[92]

This board has lost confidence that the state of Texas can guarantee that every inmate it executes is truly guilty of murder. We do not believe that any legal system devised by inherently flawed human beings can determine with moral certainty the guilt of every defendant convicted of murder.

In the same month, *The Sentinel* newspaper of Pennsylvania published an editorial, based upon an investigative article which had found the state's capital punishment laws to be 'useless', arguing that capital punishment should be abolished because it had failed to deter crime, had lost favour with the public, risked innocent lives, and prolonged the suffering of victims' family members who must endure years of legal appeals.[93]

---

[88] David Weinstock and Gary E. Schwartz, 'Executing the Innocent: Preventing the Ultimate Injustice' *Criminal Law Bulletin* 34 (1998), pp. 328–347 at 335–341.

[89] A survey carried out in 2005 found that 65% of respondents in Massachusetts were in favour of reinstating the death penalty if it could be made 'fool-proof' (i.e. only for heinous crimes and incorporating specific guidelines, such as verifiable scientific evidence and a 'no doubt' standard from juries). KRC Communications Research, May 2005, cited at *Angus Reid Global Monitor*.

[90] Dieter, n. 83 above, p. 2.

[91] T. V. Kaufman-Osborn, 'Regulating Death: Capital Punishment and the Late Liberal State' *Yale Law Review* 111 (2001), pp. 681–722 at 683.

[92] *Dallas Morning News*, 15 April 2007.

[93] *The Sentinel*, 3 April 2007.

(c) Race, religion and political predispositions

It was noted above that support for the death penalty as shown by opinion polls varies across sectors of the population, according to the race, gender, and religious or political affiliations of the respondents. This is important because it reveals another facet of the issue, namely: Whose opinions count? A lower proportion of black Americans, females, and supporters of the Democratic Party support the death penalty than do white Americans, males, and Republicans.[94] Over half (58%) of all respondents to a national public opinion poll of 1,000 Americans conducted in 2007 believed it was time for a moratorium on the death penalty but this proportion was much higher (75%) among African American respondents. Furthermore, whilst nearly 40% of all respondents expressed their moral objection to the death penalty, this proportion rose to 68% of African Americans.[95] In addition, Messner and his colleagues found that 'the presence of a "vigilante tradition", as indicated by a history of lynching, promotes death penalty support among whites but not blacks'.[96]

Polls conducted prior to the abolition of the death penalty in South Africa showed a similar racial division in support for capital punishment: approximately 80% of whites but only 49% of black Africans supported it.[97] It has been suggested that higher support amongst white Americans is fuelled by racial animus[98] but it may also be related to the fear of inter-racial homicide which much more often takes the form of black offender and white victim than vice-versa. Black respondents' lesser support for capital punishment appears to be linked to their view that it is applied in a racially discriminatory way.[99]

---

[94] Mitchell, n. 78 above. Also J. D. Unnever, F. T. Cullen, and V. Roberts, 'Not everyone strongly supports the death penalty: Assessing weakly-held attitudes toward capital punishment' *American Journal of Criminal Justice* 20 (2005), pp. 187–216. A time-series study by Jacobs and Kent shows that public support and Republican strength in the states influence capital sentencing and executions; D. Jacobs and S. L. Kent, 'The Determinants of Executions since 1951: How Politics, Protests, Public Opinion, and Social Divisions Shape Capital Punishment' *Social Problems* 54(3) (2007), pp. 297–318.

[95] Dieter, n. 83 above.

[96] Steven F. Messner, Eric P. Baumer, and Richard Rosenfield, 'Distrust of Government, the Vigilante Tradition, and Support for Capital Punishment' *Law and Society Review* 40(3) (2006), pp. 559–589.

[97] Another poll showed support varied across ethnic groups, from only 42% of Southern Sotho's to 79% of Afrikaans in favour of the death penalty: R. Garland, 'Capital Punishment' *South African Human Rights Year Book* 1 (1996), p. 5.

[98] J. Soss, L. Langbein, and A.R. Metelko, 'Why do white Americans support the death penalty?' *The Journal of Politics* 65 (2003), pp. 396–421. Also, S. Barkan and S. Cohn, 'On Reducing White Support for the Death Penalty: A Pessimistic Appraisal' *Criminology & Public Policy* 4 (2005), pp. 39–44 at 42. A recent experimental study by Peffley and Hurwitz suggests that while African Americans who oppose the death penalty are influenced by evidence that it discriminates against ethnic minorities, as well as evidence that innocent people are executed, whites are highly resistant to such arguments and in fact become more supportive of the death penalty upon learning that it discriminates against blacks: M. Peffley and J. Hurwitz, 'Persuasion and Resistance: Race and the Death Penalty in America' *American Journal of Political Science* 51(4) (2007), pp. 996–1012.

[99] David N. Baker, Eric G. Lambert, and Morris Jenkins, 'College Students' Racial Differences in Death Penalty Support and Opposition: A Preliminary Study of White and Black' *Journal of Black Studies* 35 (2005), pp. 201–224.

Support for capital punishment has also been found to vary according to the respondent's religious beliefs.[100] Broadly speaking, in America liberal religious groups are opposed to the death penalty, while conservative faith groups support it. The Mennonites, Amish, and Quakers have traditionally been the most active opponents of the death penalty, supported by the Methodist and Presbyterian Churches and Jewish congregations. On the other hand, Southern Baptists, Muslims, and Mormons tend to be retentionist.[101] The Roman Catholic Church through the Catholic Bishops' Conference[102] is opposed to capital punishment, but lay Catholics are more divided; some support conservative and punitive policies, such as Supreme Court Justice Antonin Scalia, while others, notably Sister Helen Prejean, author of the powerful book *Dead Man Walking*, passionately support abolition.[103] Overall, however, support for the death penalty amongst Catholics is on the wane. For example, according to a Zogby poll in November 2004, Catholic support for the death penalty had fallen to 48% from a peak of 68% in 2001. And a recent poll of 1,000 Americans found that a moral objection to the death penalty was higher amongst Catholics (47%) than the general population (39%). The 2005 Gallup poll of America's 'Moral Values and Beliefs' found that 70% of Catholics and also the same proportion of Protestants (69%) believed that the death penalty was morally wrong, indicating a sharp divide between those who apply Christian moral values to the question of capital punishment and those who take a more utilitarian view of the matter.[104]

(d) The homicide rate

At first glance there appears to be no necessary connection between the degree of public support for the death penalty and the incidence of homicide. For example, the majority of the public in favour of capital punishment is much higher in Japan, which has a comparatively low homicide rate (approximately 0.5 per 100,000 inhabitants) than it is in Sweden, where the homicide rate is about 2.39 per 100,000 inhabitants. Furthermore, among those countries with relatively low homicide rates, some are abolitionist, like Spain (1.25), Austria (0.81), and Germany (0.98),

---

[100] Thomas C. Berg, 'Religious Conservatives and the Death Penalty' in 'Symposium: Religious Role in the Administration of the Death Penalty' *William and Mary Bill of Rights Journal* 9 (2000), pp. 31–60.

[101] <http://www.religioustolerance.org/execut7.htm>.

[102] *A Culture of Life and the Penalty of Death*, <www.usccb.org/sdwp/national/penaltyofdeath. pdf>. See also the Amicus Curiae Brief of the United States Conference of Catholic Bishops and Other Religious Organizations (2004) WL 1617400 to *Roper v Simmons* 125 S.Ct. 1183 (2005). A recent study showed that those Catholics who esteemed Pope John Paul II, who died in 2005, were more likely to oppose the death penalty, suggesting that they may well have taken their cues from him directly, rather than simply reflecting the Catholic line on the sanctity of life: K. Mulligan, 'Pope John Paul II and Catholic opinion toward the death penalty and abortion' *Social Science Quarterly* 87:3 (2006).

[103] See also, Sister Helen Prejean, *The Death of Innocents: An Eyewitness Account of Wrongful Executions* (2006).

[104] J. D. Unnever, F. T. Cullen and J. P. Bartkowski, 'Images of God and Public Support for Capital Punishment: Does a Relationship with a Loving God Matter?' *Criminology* 44(4) (2006).

whilst others retain the death penalty, such as Indonesia (1.05). Thus we cannot assume that a relatively low homicide rate automatically means that the population will not be particularly concerned about murder, or that they do not worry about relatively small increases in rates of homicide.

Short-term changes in crime rates might have some temporary impact on the public's liberal or punitive attitudes, although it is likely that people will revert back to their natural 'predispositions'. The dramatic rise in the homicide rate in the United States in the late 1980s and early 1990s undoubtedly increased popular support for capital punishment and other punitive measures, not, it appears, because more people came to believe in their deterrent effect,[105] but because it created a 'retributive' surge'.[106] Hence, after a clear decrease in support for the death penalty during the 1960s and 1970s, to about 47%, it started to rise again and by the early 1990s it was between 75% and 80%.[107] The subsequent sharp decline in the homicide rate (from a high of 10.2 per 100,000 inhabitants in the 1980s and early 1990s to 5.5 in 2000, where it has remained since) has resulted in a lessening of support for capital punishment. Only 38% of respondents in a poll conducted in 2007 believed that the death penalty is a deterrent; 60% said it was not[108] (see also Table 10.1) but, as Julian Roberts points out, as recently as 1986 fully 61% held this view.[109]

In trying to explain this shift in opinion a number of researchers in the 1980s suggested that deterrence was given as the justification because it appeared to provide a scientific, and therefore socially acceptable, rationale, when what actually underlay support for capital punishment was the sorts of predispositions discussed above,[110] and that it was during the early 1990s that people became increasingly willing to endorse retribution.[111] This switch away from deterrence as the main justification may be the reason why, in a period of much lower homicide rates, American public opinion has been affected by other issues, most importantly by the question of fairness and justice in the administration of capital punishment.[112]

---

[105] A point noted by Ellsworth and Gross in 1994, n. 54 above, p. 27. Also, more generally, David Jacobs and Jason T. Carmichael, 'Ideology, Social Threat, and the Death Sentence: Capital Sentences across Time and Space' *Social Forces* 83 (2004), pp. 249–278.

[106] See Bohm, n. 58 above, p. 31.

[107] Schabas, n. 15 above, p. 314

[108] Dieter, n. 83 above.

[109] J. V. Roberts, 'Capital Punishment, Innocence, and Public Opinion' *Criminology and Public Policy* 4:1 (2005), p. 1. However, opinion polls have differed, according to the questions asked—as to whether deterrence is the *primary* reason why people favour capital punishment or only one among a number of other reasons, most notably retribution. See also Jones, n. 36 above.

[110] For example, T. R. Tyler and R. Weber, 'Support for the Death Penalty: Instrumental Response to Crime, or Symbolic Attitude?' *Law and Society Review* 17 (1982), pp. 21–46; E. A. Fattah, 'Perceptions of Violence, Concern about Crime, Fear of Victimization and Attitudes to the Death Penalty' *Canadian Journal of Criminology* 21 (1979), pp. 22–38; Ellsworth and Ross, n. 54 above, pp. 145–157.

[111] Phoebe C. Ellsworth and Samuel R. Gross, 'Hardening of the Attitudes: Americans' Views on the Death Penalty' *Journal of Social Issues* 50(2) (Summer 1994), pp. 19–25.

[112] Samuel R. Gross and Phoebe C. Ellsworth, 'Second Thoughts: Americans' Views on the Death Penalty at the Turn of the Century' in Stephen P. Garvey (ed.), *Capital Punishment and the American Future* (2001), Ch. 6.

Nevertheless, it is clear that in retentionist countries that are experiencing very high rates of violence public opinion is usually unsympathetic to abolition. This has been the case in the English-speaking Caribbean where lethal violence has reached epidemic proportions, especially in Jamaica and Trinidad. For example, in Trinidad, murders recorded by the police increased from 7.6 per 100,000 of the population of approximately 1.26 million in 1993 to 30.7 per 100,000 in 2005, one of the highest incidents of culpable homicide in relation to population in the world. Each day the national newspapers report on homicides and the frequent failures of the justice system to prosecute and convict murderers,[113] thus feeding the climate of fear. Not surprisingly, an opinion poll carried out by the Trinidad *Sunday Guardian* in November 2003 found that 62% of respondents were fearful of being murdered, and two years later a further poll revealed that 55% of respondents put crime as the major problem facing the country, citing the murder rate as their main concern.[114]

Rising crime rates in some other countries have been correlated with increased support for the death penalty (in general, and for specific offences), regardless of their abolitionist status. For example, in Mexico, following a record reporting of 3,706 kidnappings in the year 2003–2004, an opinion poll found that 65% of respondents would support applying the death penalty to those found guilty of kidnapping.[115] Similarly, just over two-thirds (67%) of respondents to a survey in the Dominican Republic considered the death penalty to be an appropriate punishment for people convicted of sexual abuse against children, although their country abolished capital punishment in 1924.[116] An opinion poll conducted in 2007 shows that the people of Peru (where the death penalty was abolished for ordinary crimes in 1979) have similar concerns about sexual abuse of children: 81% of respondents in the capital city of Lima endorse the death penalty as the appropriate penalty for those convicted of raping young children. In addition, 69% of respondents supported capital punishment for rape in general, with 61% for premeditated murder and, rather alarmingly, over a quarter (28%) considered the death penalty appropriate for theft.[117] These data may well reflect, to some extent, the unsuccessful efforts of the Peruvian president just a few months earlier to persuade the country's lawmakers to support his proposal to allow the death penalty for child abusers and murderers, although public opinion may also have influenced that very campaign.

South Africa has one of the highest crime rates in the world, with particularly high rates of homicide (approximately 47,000 a year) and physical and sexual violence. This might explain why 75% of persons polled in early 2007[118] wanted their

---

[113] At the same time the number of persons committed for trial charged with murder fell from a high of 88 in 1999 to only 38 in 2002, a decline of over 50%.

[114] Roger Hood and Florence Seemungal, 'A Rare and Arbitrary Fate: Being Mandatorily Sentenced to Death in Trinidad and Tobago—A Summary of the Report to the Death Penalty Project' *Amicus* (17) 2007, pp. 7–16.

[115] Indermerc Louis Harris poll, 18 June 2004, cited at *Angus-Reid Global Monitor,*

[116] Gallup poll, cited at *Angus Reid Global Monitor*, 22 April 2006.

[117] Apoyo/El Comercio, cited at *Angus Reid Global Monitor*, 25 January 2007.

[118] <http://www.athlone.co.za/community/opinions/pastpoll.php?pollid=5>.

government to bring back capital punishment, 12 years after it was abolished. Again, particularly heinous crimes seemed to agitated public support for its reintroduction[119]. At the first court appearance in April 2007 of Andrew Jordaan, charged with the murder of seven-year-old Sheldean Human, an angry mob assembled in front of the Pretoria Magistrates' Court, waving posters demanding: 'Hang hom!' ('Hang him!').[120] Rising crime rates in Poland, which fuelled increasing fear, and a lack of faith in the criminal process, helped to secure the election of a government which campaigned for the reintroduction of the death penalty (see Chapter 2).[121]

On the other hand, there are countries where there is no evidence that increasing rates of serious crime have led many more citizens to favour the reintroduction of capital punishment. Brazil, which abolished capital punishment for ordinary crimes in 1979, is currently suffering from extraordinary levels of violence, and yet support for capital punishment has not increased significantly over the last few years. After various high-profile crime 'sprees'—for example, in Sao Paulo, where more than 200 people were killed in May 2006 when a prison-based gang unleashed a wave of attacks against police and other symbols of government authority—support for the death penalty has fluctuated within a relatively narrow band: 55% in 1993, 48% in 2000, 51% in 2006, and, most recently, 55% in 2007.[122]

The evidence reviewed above suggests that there is not an immutable relationship between rising levels of homicide and increased support for the death penalty. Much will depend on the extent to which citizens believe in the general deterrent power of executions, their faith in alternative punishments, and the ability of the political system to tackle the roots of the increase through social reforms and a more effective response by the agencies of criminal justice to increase the certainty, rather than the severity, of punishment.

4. Abolition and its Effect on Public Opinion

Robert Badinter, who played a vital role in ensuring that the death penalty was abolished in France in 1981, has suggested that it takes about ten to fifteen years following abolition for the public to stop thinking of it as useful and to realizes that it makes no difference to the level of homicide.[123] Support for Badinter's hypothesis has been found in various jurisdictions across the world.

---

[119] Garland, n. 97 above, p. 5.

[120] Opinion, *Business Day*, 8 April 2007.

[121] Although at least some of this increase is due to more reliable criminal statistics since the demise of communist rule: A. Fijalkowski, 'Capital Punishment in Poland: An aspect of the "cultural life" of death penalty discourse' in A. Sarat and C. Boulanger, *The Cultural Lives of Capital Punishment: Comparative Perspectives* (2005), pp. 147–168 at 157.

[122] Datafolha survey, *Associated Press*, 8 April 2007, cited at the DPIC website: <http://www.deathpenaltyinfo.org/article.php?did=2165#brazil>.

[123] R. Badinter, Amnesty International lecture, 1 March 2007, Taylorian Institute, Oxford.

Steven Stack's analysis of support for the death penalty across 17 countries, after controlling for several variables,[124] came to two interesting conclusions. First, 'that residence in a retentionist nation significantly increases the odds of an individual supporting the death penalty'.[125] This suggests that people on the whole support what has been the norm in their culture. Secondly, he found that each year of abolition reduced the level of support for the death penalty.[126] This also supports the same hypothesis: when the death penalty has been abolished, more and more citizens come in time to regard it as a punishment 'of the past'. The data tend to support this interpretation, with just a few exceptions to the rule, such as Peru (see page 374 above).

Britain has experienced declining support for the death penalty as time has passed since abolition, from 74% in favour in 1986 to 65% in 1996 and just 54% in 2004.[127]

In many countries the public continue to support capital punishment for some years following abolition, resulting in dissonance between the political discourse and the norms and values of the electorate. For example, when the new Czech Republic was instituted in 1993 abolition was enshrined in its constitution, but just twelve years later an opinion poll revealed that over half of the respondents (57%) wanted capital punishment reintroduced.[128]

But, in time, popular attitudes tend to conform more closely to the political lead and ensuing political processes.[129] Over a quarter of a century ago France abolished the death penalty, even though 62% of the French people supported it at that time. Currently, only 42% favour reinstating it.[130] Whilst a substantial majority of German citizens supported capital punishment just prior to and after abolition in 1949, support had fallen to only 24% by 1992.[131] In New Zealand, where capital punishment was abolished in 1961, a poll in 2004 showed that only 28% of respondents thought that the death penalty should be reinstated.[132] In Australia too only 25% think that the death penalty is the appropriate

---

[124] He controlled for instrumental variables (such as national homicide rates, punitiveness, and confidence in courts) and symbolic variables (such as authoritarianism and fundamentalism) as well as gender, age, and marital status: Stack, n. 71 above, at pp. 87–88.

[125] 'Persons residing in a retentionist state are fully 2.88 times as likely to support the death penalty as persons residing in an abolitionist nation': *ibid.*, p. 86.

[126] Lowering the odds of an individual's death penalty support by 46%: *ibid.*, pp. 87–88.

[127] British Social Attitude Surveys, data available at the *British Social Attitudes* website: <http://www.britsocat.com/Body.aspx?control=BritSocAtHome>.

[128] *Angus Reid Global Monitor*, 24 November 2005.

[129] D. Garland, *Punishment and Modern Society: A Study in Social Theory* (1990), p. 246.

[130] *TNS Sofres* at <http://tempsreel.nouvelobs.com>, 18 September 2006, cited at the DPIC website: <http://www.deathpenaltyinfo.org/article.php?did=2165#France>.

[131] Hans-Jörg Albrecht, 'The Death Penalty in China from a European Perspective' in Manfred Nowak and Xin Chunying (eds.), *EU-China Human Rights Dialogue: Proceedings of the Second EU-China Legal Experts' Seminar Held in Beijing, 19–20 October 1998* (2000), pp. 95–118 at 115. Also, Evans, n. 12 above, pp. 797, 802–804, and 935–937.

[132] Colmar Brunton poll, 16 July 2004, cited at *Angus Reid Global Monitor*.

punishment for murder.[133] Similarly, a survey in 2006 indicated that only 29% of Finns would approve of the death penalty as a punishment for certain crimes committed during peacetime.[134] And in Italy, where capital punishment was abolished for ordinary crimes after the Second World War, the proportion is even lower, with 76% of a poll conducted in 2005 being against the death penalty.[135] Perhaps the most extreme example of this trend is to be found in Norway, where capital punishment was abolished in 1905: only 17% of the population now supports the death penalty, which is well below the world average.[136] The evidence from other northern European countries also suggests that once abolitionist policies become embedded in the national consciousness sentiments in favour of the death penalty gradually diminish in the general population, irrespective of changes in the homicide rate, and whilst there are differences in support for different types of murder the general trend is clear.[137]

A poll of 1,001 British adults in 2006, which asked whether respondents supported the death penalty in various 'scenario' situations, found none where the majority chose the death penalty. Support ranged from 46% for murder in a terrorist attack, 43% for murder of a child, 38% for murder of a police officer on duty,[138] 34% for murder committed while already serving a life sentence, 23% for murder of an adult stranger, 7% for murder of a spouse in a fit of rage, to just 3% for mercy killing/euthanasia.[139] Just across the water, most Irish people have turned resolutely against capital punishment. A referendum held in June 2001 produced a majority of 62% to 37% in favour of an amendment to the Constitution prohibiting the Irish Parliament from enacting 'any law providing for the imposition of the death penalty'.[140]

Of particular significance are the age differentials in support of the death penalty in abolitionist countries. Those who are younger and have never lived in a country which executes its prisoners appear far less likely to support the death penalty. In Finland, for example, almost 41% of those aged 35 to 49 remained in favour of capital punishment, but younger respondents showed far less support (just 20% of students).[141] An examination of recent Gallup surveys in Great Britain, Canada, and in the United States found that in all three nations support for capital punishment was lowest among those who were 18–29 years old.[142]

---

[133] Roy Morgan International, 24 December 2005, cited at *Angus Reid Global Monitor*.

[134] Helsingin Sanomat, Suomen Gallup, 21 November 2006, cited at the DPIC website: <http://www.deathpenaltyinfo.org/article.php?did=2165#fin>.

[135] *Angus Reid Global Monitor*, 9 October 2005.

[136] Stack, n. 71 above, p. 73.

[137] Franklin E. Zimring and Gordon Hawkins, *Capital Punishment and the American Agenda* (1986), pp. 10–15 and 21–22.

[138] In January 1960 a Gallup poll had found that 70% of people surveyed believed that killers of police officers should hang.

[139] An Ipsos-MORI poll, *Angus Reid Global Monitor*, 1 February 2006.

[140] Amnesty Interntional, *Death Penalty News*, June 2001, AI Index: ACT 53/003/2001, p. 2.

[141] Helsingin Sanomat, Suomen Gallup: 21 November 2006, cited at the DPIC website.

[142] Gallup Poll press release, *Death Penalty Gets Less Support From Britons, Canadians Than Americans*, 20 February 2006, cited at the DPIC website.

For example, a *YouGov* poll of 2,616 British adults commissioned by the *Daily Telegraph* at the end of 2005 found only 31% of 'the young' supported capital punishment, compared with 59% of older respondents.[143] *British Social Attitudes* survey data show stronger support across all age groups, but still a significant difference between them: in 1986, 23 years after abolition, support for capital punishment was at 70% for young people aged 17 to 34, but at 79% for those aged over 55. By 2005 only 53% of young people supported it, compared to 65% of older people.[144] The new generation, growing up without capital punishment, would seem to have significantly less desire for it than their elders, although the general trend is for declining support across all age groups.

5. The Impact of Victims' Advocates on Support for the Death Penalty

Another factor which may have shaped opinion in recent years is concern for the victims of homicide, or rather those who are collateral or 'secondary' victims—in particular the parents, spouses, siblings, and others closely related to the victim—sometimes referred to as 'the survivors'. This is put bluntly in the question often posed to abolitionists: 'What about the victim. Don't they have rights too?'. In a zero sum game, it is argued, you have to be *either* for the offender *or* for the victim. The position of offenders who have lawyers and other supporters campaigning for their rights has been contrasted with that of collateral victims who have traditionally had no one to represent them, especially in Western societies that define crime as an offence against the state or the Crown. Proponents of victims' rights have therefore come to argue that retribution is needed to heal the hurt felt by those who are left to mourn: execution, it is claimed, is necessary to bring 'closure' to the survivors of murder victims, and other *potential* victims need *potential* murderers to be deterred.

In most Western nations the victims' rights movement has sought to enhance the place of victims in the criminal process and has successfully advocated that specific legal rules be modified to give the interests of victims greater weight and to provide victims with restitution, compensation, counselling, consultation before plea bargains are finalized, and a chance to give victim impact evidence at sentencing (see Chapter 7). Nowhere has this movement been more influential than in the United States. In his dissenting opinion in *Furman v Georgia* in 1972, Justice Blackmun chided the majority for failing to 'make reference to the misery the petitioners' crimes occasioned to the victims, to the families of the victims,

---

[143] *Daily Telegraph*, 3 January 2006 <http://www.telegraph.co.uk/news>.
[144] *British Social Attitude Surveys*, data available at the British Social Attitudes website: <http://www.britsocat.com/Body.aspx?control=BritSocAtHome>.

and to the communities where the offenses took place'.[145] Blackmun's warning of a populist backlash, at a time when the victims' rights movement was just emerging, was prescient. Ever since, supporters of the death penalty have sought to remind decision-makers of the misery inflicted upon innocent citizens by those people who find themselves on death row. Groups such as 'The National Organization for Parents of Murdered Children' and local groups like the Texas-based 'Justice for All' have fought successfully for procedural rights for victims as an effective means of securing severe punishments for defendants and further generating public support for the death penalty.[146] When victims' groups are explicit in their demand for the death penalty they may influence at least some criminal justice practitioners, governors, and elected legislators, especially in the United States, where the political system responds more readily to the views of the electorate.

The American media regularly provide evidence of the impact of victims on criminal justice decision-making. For example, in an interview with the *New York Times* in 1995, Lynne Abraham, referred to as 'the deadliest DA in Philadelphia' because of her aggressive support for the death penalty, explained: 'I've looked at those sentenced to be executed. No one will shed a tear. Prison is too good for them. They don't deserve to live. I represent the victim and the family. I don't care about killers'.[147] The emphasis in many news reports is on the supposed benefits of 'closure' when a person has been put to death, a term that was not used by the media to describe a major objective of the death penalty until 1989. Since then its use, in American print media in particular, has increased significantly, even though research has not shown whether there are psychological advantages for families of homicide victims when the defendant is executed, or whether the adjustment to the loss of a loved one in a homicide is any different across different jurisdictions.[148] In 1993, there were ten stories a year combining the topic 'death penalty' and the word 'closure', whereas in 2001 there were more than 500 such stories.[149] Closure became part of American consciousness when Timothy McVeigh, the Oklahoma bomber, was convicted in 1997 and a Texas paper ran a headline, 'Verdict brings sense of closure for families'.[150] The then Attorney-General, John Ashcroft, said that allowing hundreds of family members to view the execution via a television monitor would help to 'close this chapter in their lives'. The importance that began to be attached to closure was evident when,

---

[145] 408 U.S. 238 at 413–414, Blackmun dissenting.

[146] P. Hodgkinson, 'Meeting the needs of the families of the homicide victim and the condemned' in P. Hodgkinson and W. Schabas, *Capital Punishment: Strategies for Abolition* (2004), pp. 332–358.

[147] T. Rosenburg, 'The Deadliest D.A.' *New York Times Magazine*, 16 July 1995, p. 9.

[148] See, in relation to the literature on 'closure': M. Vandiver, 'The Impact of the Death Penalty on the Families of Homicide Victims and of Condemned Prisoners' in Acker, Bohm, and Lanier, n. 58 above, pp. 613–646; also, Vandiver's discussion of E. Schlosser, 'A Grief Like No Other' *The Atlantic Monthly* (September 1997), pp. 37–76; David Spiegel, 'Closure? The Execution Was Just The Start' *Washington Post*, 29 April 2001.

[149] F. E. Zimring, *The contradictions of American capital punishment* (2003), pp. 59–61.

[150] Cited in Vandiver, n. 148 above.

in 2002, the *ABC News/Washington Post* poll included the statement: 'The death penalty is fair because it gives satisfaction and closure to the families of murder victims'. Sixty percent of the respondents agreed either strongly or somewhat with that statement.[151] And in a detailed study of newspaper reports of the responses of victims' families following a homicide, Gross and Matheson found that the most common issue—mentioned in over a third of these reports—was 'closure'.[152]

Yet the last decade has witnessed the emergence of a number of victims' groups speaking out against the death penalty. 'Murder Victims' Families for Reconciliation' is one high profile example. The group published a report in 2002 documenting the ways in which victims' families who opposed capital punishment have been ignored, marginalized, and denied support and information by many victim service providers and prosecutors.[153] Others victims' rights groups include 'Murder Victims' Families for Human Rights',[154] 'Journey of Hope...from Violence to Healing',[155] and the 'Lamp of Hope' project.[156] The slogan common to all of these groups is 'Not in our name': they oppose the death penalty but, more importantly, they are offended by politicians' use of victims as justification for capital punishment.[157]

When the issue was raised before the New Jersey Death Penalty Commission in 2006, it found that 'Family members of murder victims and other witnesses expressed a wide range of views... The overwhelming majority of witnesses testified that life without parole is the appropriate alternative to the death penalty'.[158] Indeed, a large number of family members testified that they opposed the death penalty on moral grounds. Lorry Post, the father of a murder victim told the Commission that 'the death penalty...just creates more killing and is a horrible thing which almost matches the horror of what some of us have lost by murder'.[159] Another witness challenged the 'closure thesis' when she said: 'We believe the death penalty is harmful and already interferes with a difficult healing process.

---

[151] G. Langer, 'Public Ambivalence Fuels Support For a Halt in U.S. Executions' *ABC News/Washington Post* poll, 'The Death Penalty Revisited', 2 May 2001.

[152] S. R. Gross and D. J. Matheson, 'What They Say at the End: Capital Victims' Families and the Press' *Cornell Law Review* 88(2) (2003), pp. 486–516.

[153] R. R. Cushing and S. Sheffer, *Dignity Denied: The Experience of Murder Victims' Family Members Who Oppose the Death Penalty* (2002).

[154] An international, non-governmental organization of family members of victims of criminal murder, terrorist killings, state executions, extra-judicial assassinations, and 'disappearances' which opposes the death penalty from a human rights perspective: <http://www.murdervictimsfamilies.org>.

[155] An organization, represented in a number of US states, led jointly by murder victim family members who oppose the death penalty, by death row family members and family members of the executed and the exonerated: <http://www.journeyofhope.org>.

[156] Founded by Texas Death Row prisoners to educate the public about the death penalty and alternatives, support victims' families by promoting healing and reconciliation, and to support prisoners' families to help break the cycle of violence: <http://www.lampofhope.org>.

[157] See, for example, R. King, *Don't Kill in Our Names: Families of Murder Victims Speak Out Against the Death Penalty* (2003).

[158] New Jersey Death Penalty Study Commission Report, January 2007, p. 56.

[159] *Ibid.*, p. 59.

For us, that harm is exacerbated by our belief that responding to one killing with another does not honor our loved one'.[160]

For the past two decades or so victims' organizations have pressed their support for the death penalty as if the relatives of victims would only have one opinion on the subject. As we have shown, victims are a heterogeneous group and the idea of an execution as therapeutic justice has been strongly challenged.

6. A Question of Principle

Ultimately, public opinion on the death penalty—meaning, essentially, an expression of 'off the top of the head' *sentiment* by the electorate who may or, as is more usual, may not be aware of all the facts and arguments relating to the issue—cannot determine an issue which many believe must be dealt with on the basis of a principled interpretation of human rights.

Reflecting on this issue, William Schabas pointed to a paradox: 'Democracy leans towards abolition, but retentionists defend the death penalty in the name of the will of the people. Do human rights need to be protected from public opinion?'[161] His answer to this question is unequivocal:[162]

While it is desirable that the human rights norms that are enshrined in international instruments and national constitutions find a favourable echo in public opinion, they surely cannot be dependent on it. Human rights instruments . . . are, first and foremost, aimed at protection of individuals from the state . . . If public opinion were to be canvassed each time individual rights were in jeopardy, there would be little doubt that human rights would come out the loser. Yet it would contradict the *raison d'être* of human rights law to make its efficacy contingent on public opinion, one of the very forces it is aimed at counteracting and neutralising.

Moreover, as we have shown in this chapter, opinions about capital punishment are diverse amongst different sectors of the population, which may be related to their relative status in society, their political ideology or religious beliefs, and how well they are informed about the issue, including what the effects of abolition might be. The experience of nearly all abolitionist countries is that opinions change and support for capital punishment withers as it comes to be seen as a 'thing of the past'. In other words, abolition can lead to changes in opinion that might not be imagined prior to abolition, by creating a different climate for the discourse on the limits of state punishment.

In this regard, the outstanding judgment of South Africa's Constitutional Court comes to mind. In 1995, its President, Arthur Chaskalson declared:[163]

---

[160] *Ibid.*, p. 60.
[161] Schabas, n. 15 above, p. 309.
[162] *Ibid.*, p. 328.
[163] *State v Makwanyane* (1995) (3) SA 391, para. 88.

Public opinion may have some relevance to the enquiry, but in itself is no substitute for the duty vested in the Courts to interpret the Constitution and to uphold its provisions without fear or favour. If public opinion were to be decisive, there would be no need for constitutional adjudication. The protection of rights could then be left to parliament, which has a mandate from the public, and is answerable to the public for the way its mandate is exercised . . . The very reason . . . for vesting the power of judicial review in the courts, was to protect the rights of minorities and others who cannot protect their rights adequately through the democratic process. Those who are entitled to claim this protection include the social outcasts and marginalized people in our society. It is only if there is a willingness to protect the worst and weakest amongst us that all of us can be secure that our own rights will be protected.

As we noted in Chapter 1, not every country has subscribed to the view that there should be an international human rights norm banning capital punishment for serious crimes in all circumstances, and this is undoubtedly a serious bone of contention in international deliberations on the subject. However, the abundant and growing evidence reviewed in this book about how the death penalty is enforced—which has revealed degrees of cruelty, violating human rights, and many breaches of the legal principles that demand the equitable, proportionate, impartial, and unbiased administration of criminal justice—may one day convince even those governments that would (in their ideal world) favour capital punishment that it cannot safely and properly be administered in human societies founded on the principles of human rights, equality, and justice.

11

The Challenge of a Suitable Replacement

1. The Nature of the Challenge

Countries that seek to abolish the death penalty face the task of establishing viable alternatives that sufficiently satisfy the demands of retribution while remaining proportionate to the gravity of the crime; that appear not to greatly lessen any possible marginal deterrent effect; that incapacitate those who continue to pose a genuine threat to public safety; and that provide a humane environment with opportunities for the prisoner to be rehabilitated, or at least not made more dangerous by the conditions of confinement.

In considering what should replace the death penalty they will, of course, need to bear in mind that there is a difference between:

(i) providing a suitable penalty in cases where the executive reprieves or commutes a death sentence;
(ii) replacing the death penalty for crimes of lesser seriousness than murder when the scope of capital punishment is being retracted;
(iii) finding a replacement penalty for murder when a mandatory death sentence is abolished and the courts are allowed discretion as to punishment; and
(iv) replacing capital punishment *de jure* at what is often the last cycle of the abolition process, when executions have been reserved for a small number of the most egregious murders: in other words, replacing the death penalty for what are commonly called the 'worst of the worst' or the 'rarest of the rare' murders.

Retentionist countries, whether they are considering partial or total abolition, will naturally turn to examine the experience of countries that have already gone through this process. It is, as Hugo Bedau stated, 'the oldest of all the issues raised by the two-century struggle in Western civilization to end the death penalty'.[1] It is also a large and complex subject, far beyond the scope of one chapter. All we have attempted here is to describe the range of solutions that different countries have adopted and point to some of the problems they have revealed, in

---

[1] H. Bedau, 'Imprisonment vs Death: Does Avoiding Schwarzschild's Paradox lead to Sheleff's Dilemma?' *Albany Law Review* 54 (1990), pp. 481–495 at 481.

particular those raised by the sentence of life imprisonment without the possibility of parole—commonly referred to by the acronym LWOP.

In all jurisdictions that had a mandatory death penalty, there were always means, where there were strong mitigating circumstances, of substituting a lesser sentence through the exercise of mercy. For example, in England, before abolition of capital punishment for murder, mandatory death sentences upheld after appeal were always considered for reprieve.[2] Statistics collected by the Royal Commission on Capital Punishment showed that, between 1900 and 1949, 46 per cent of the 1,080 people sentenced to death for murder in England and Wales were reprieved, and 90 per cent of the 130 women.[3] Indeed, 'in some types of cases—such as "mercy killings" and "suicide pacts"—reprieve had become a foregone conclusion'.[4] In these cases, the alternative chosen was typically a sentence to life imprisonment to be reviewed at a time fixed by the Home Secretary according to the nature of the case. By virtue of the special circumstances surrounding the reprieve, the time spent in custody in the years prior to the abolition of capital punishment was usually between eight and twelve years.[5] In countries which are today abolitionist *de facto*, the practice normally is to commute all death sentences to life imprisonment with the possibility of release on parole.[6]

During the period when the capital statutes relating to crimes other than murder were being repealed in the nineteenth century in Europe and America, the punishment substituted for death was either transportation overseas for a specific period or imprisonment for a determinate period, usually with some remission of sentence for good behaviour. Offences which previously had all been threatened with death were graded by their seriousness and the maximum punishments appointed for each of them were also graded in conformity with the principle of proportionality. The death penalty was therefore replaced by maximum periods of imprisonment suited to the particular gravity and circumstances of the offence and offender.

It became more problematic when mandatory death sentences were replaced by a discretionary punishment and the death penalty was reserved for the 'worst of the worst' murders. The choice was between sentencing all persons convicted of murder who were not sentenced to death to a mandatory indeterminate life sentence, subject to review, or to give the judge power to sentence to whatever

---

[2] Leon Radzinowicz and Roger Hood, *The Emergence of Penal Policy in Victorian and Edwardian England* (1990), p. 677–681.

[3] Cmd. 8932, 1953, p. 13. In the first half of the twentieth century women convicted of murder in South Africa were also almost always reprieved: Robert Turrell, *White Mercy: A study of the death penalty in South Africa* (2004).

[4] Stephen Shute, 'Punishing Murderers: Release Procedures and the "Tariff", 1953–2004' *Criminal Law Review* (November 2004), pp. 873–895 at 873.

[5] *Ibid.*

[6] Lilian Chenwi, *Towards the Abolition of the Death Penalty in Africa: A Human Rights Perspective* (2007).

penalty, determinate or indeterminate, that was considered appropriate. It is these options that most retentionist countries now face.

In modern times, in all countries, the penalty chosen to replace capital punishment for murder has been imprisonment of varying duration, usually for an indeterminate period but sometimes for a determinate period, and under varying conditions of confinement. Indeterminate sentences, known as life-imprisonment, as well as determinate ones, are usually not served for the full term, being subject to review at varying proportions of the time served and release under supervision on licence if the offender is no longer regarded as a threat to the community. Inevitably, some prisoners have been found to constitute a continuing threat and therefore have remained in custody for the rest of their life, but there is a big difference between their situation, where they have had the opportunity to earn release, and those of prisoners in a few countries—the United States in particular—where a life sentence can from the outset be for a full-life period with no possibility of review or parole. In some jurisdictions in the United States it is the mandatory sentence for capital murder; in others, it is discretionary. The implications of the introduction of LWOP as an alternative to capital punishment, in particular when it is the mandatory punishment for capital murder, will be critically examined. We shall argue that the experiences of other countries show that it is unnecessary for retentionist states to adopt LWOP to replace the death penalty, and that many of the human rights arguments that apply to capital punishment apply just as much to LWOP, especially when it is used as the mandatory penalty for capital murder, let alone when it is employed for less serious offences.

2. The Range of Alternative Penalties

The seventh United Nations survey of capital punishment, covering the period 1999 to 2003, asked abolitionist countries about the maximum punishment that had been substituted for the crimes that had previously been sanctioned by capital punishment.[7] None of the 38 abolitionist countries that completed the questionnaire had instituted life imprisonment without the possibility of parole as the mandatory penalty for murder to replace the death penalty.[8] And only one (the United Kingdom) provided for it, under statutory guidelines, for murder of the most serious kind. The replies revealed a great deal of variability, 'both in the type of penal sanction (whether life imprisonment or a determinate sentence of imprisonment) and in the period that in reality has to be served before there

---

[7] UN Doc. E/2005/3, para. 12.

[8] Thirty-three of which had completely abolished capital punishment for all crimes under all circumstances, and five of which had abolished capital punishment for murder and all other 'ordinary' crimes, before 1 January 1999.

can be any consideration of early release', as well as in the mechanisms to allow prisoners to be released.[9]

In a minority of retentionist countries the penalty for murder is a mandatory sentence to life imprisonment with the possibility of release on parole. For example, persons convicted of first-degree murder in Canada (who were formerly those sentenced to death) are not eligible for parole until 25 years. After 15 years they can, however, apply to have the eligibility date brought forward and become eligible for unescorted temporary leave and 'day parole' three years before their full parole eligibility date.[10] In Ireland, where the penalty for murder is also a mandatory life sentence, the Parole Board initially reviews prisoners after they have served seven years, and regularly thereafter, but the final decision on when the prisoner should be released rests with the Minister of Justice. Apparently,[11]

the length of time spent in custody by offenders serving life sentences can vary substantially. Of those prisoners serving life sentences who have been released, the average sentence served in prison is approximately twelve years. However, this is only an average and there are prisoners serving life sentences in Ireland who have spent in excess of thirty years in custody.

Life imprisonment is also the mandatory penalty for murder in Israel but the President usually commutes it to 30 years and the Prisons Service Parole Board has the power to reduce this by one-third for good conduct. In Finland, a life-sentenced prisoner can only be released through clemency granted by the President, but this is usually, even if not always, granted after an average of 13 years.

In England and Wales the system has undergone several changes since capital punishment for murder was abolished in 1965—changes which have lengthened the period spent in custody. Under current law the judge announces the minimum period of life imprisonment that must be served in custody in order to satisfy the demands of retribution and deterrence (called the 'tariff'). Minimum periods are laid down in Sentencing Guidelines, the lowest period being 15 years rising to 30 years for the murder of a police officer or a murder committed in the course of burglary or where firearms are used.[12] However, in rare cases of premeditated killings of two or more people, sexual or sadistic child murders, or political murders, the judge is expected to impose a 'whole life' sentence, with no prospect of release. For all other 'lifers', once the tariff has been served, the offender is eligible for consideration of release on licence by the Parole Board, under the supervision of the Probation Service with the potential for recall to prison if there are indications that he or she poses a risk to the public. The 'lifer' will have been prepared for eventual rehabilitation through the various levels of

---

[9] UN Doc. E/2005/3, para. 12.
[10] Government of Canada, *Parole: Contributing to Public Safety*, <http://www.npb-cnlc.gc.ca>.
[11] Citizens Information Board of Ireland, *Sentencing at Criminal Trials in Ireland*, <http:www. citizensinformation.ie>.
[12] A. Ashworth, *Sentencing and Criminal Justice* (2005), p. 117.

security and available programmes offered by the Prison Service until he or she is 'tested for freedom' in an open prison. The Parole Board's task is to make a risk assessment of the possible danger posed by the prisoner before releasing him or her into the community and to set up a series of requirements (for example, relating to accommodation, or continuing drug, alcohol, or anger management treatment) that he or she will have to adhere to while under supervision.

This system has been criticized by the judges on two grounds. First, that murders differ so greatly in their heinousness and the circumstances surrounding them that a mandatory life sentence is inappropriate.[13] They have therefore called for the discretion to sentence some persons convicted of murder to determinate periods of imprisonment or even, in very rare cases, to a community-based sentence. Secondly, the high minimum periods of custody fixed by the Criminal Justice Act of 2003 have been criticized, most recently by the Lord Chief Justice of England, for being far too long.[14]

Many more countries have replaced the death penalty with a discretionary maximum sentence of life imprisonment, with the alternative being a determinate sentence. The prisoner can obtain release on parole but the period to be served before becoming eligible varies considerably, as do the conditions under which early release is granted and implemented. For example, New Zealand sets no minimum for a life sentence but in Australian states it is set by the judge at the time the sentence is imposed: recently a judge in South Australia fixed the 'non-parole' term at 30 years for two lovers who hired a 'hit-man' to kill the man's wife. Elsewhere, the minimum varies from 10 years in Belgium, 12 years in Denmark, 15 years in Austria, Monaco, Romania, and Switzerland, to 20 or 25 years in Lithuania, 25 years in South Africa, 26 years in Italy, 30 years in Estonia, and two-thirds of the original determinate term of 20–25 years in Slovakia and the Netherlands (where life imprisonment is used very sparingly). A life sentence in France means at least 20 years in 'security detention' with no chance of early release for good conduct or a presidential amnesty. In Germany, a prisoner convicted of murder must be sentenced to a mandatory 15 years' imprisonment and serve at least two-thirds of the sentence or, if sentenced to a discretionary life imprisonment, serve at least 15 years. Those Eastern European countries (such as Slovakia and Poland) that replaced the death penalty with determinate sentences of imprisonment set a maximum ranging from 15 to 25 years.[15]

Life imprisonment is prohibited in various jurisdictions including Brazil, Colombia, Croatia, El Salvador, Mexico, Nicaragua, Norway, Peru, Portugal,

---

[13] Prison Reform Trust, *Report of the Committee on the Penalty for Homicide (The Lane Committee)* (1995); JUSTICE, *Sentenced to Life: reform of the law and procedures for those sentenced to life imprisonment* (1996).

[14] 'Chief Judge calls for shorter murder sentences' *The Guardian*, 9 March 2007.

[15] H. Albrecht, 'Post-Adjudication Dispositions in Comparative Perspective' in M. Tonry and R. Frase (eds.), *Sentencing and Sanctions in Western Countries* (2001).

Slovenia, Spain, and Venezuela,[16] primarily because of the emphasis, in principle even if not always in practice, on rehabilitation or re-education of prisoners in these countries.[17] So strongly opposed to indeterminate sentences are some of them (Brazil and Portugal, for example) that they fiercely objected—on human rights grounds—to the provision for life imprisonment when the Statute of the International Criminal Court was being finalized in 1998.[18] However, the Rome Statute did stipulate that sentences for even the gravest forms of crimes, such as crimes against humanity and genocide, should be reviewed after 25 years.

Yet in some of the countries that have replaced the death penalty with a determinate sentence it can be as long in practice as a life sentence in other countries. In Spain, for example, the maximum penalty for murder is 30 years.[19] Where there is discretionary release the minimum period before this can be considered varies from one-half to three-quarters of the sentence imposed, which can be as long as 20 years in Croatia (Croatia has a 40-year maximum but in practice it is rarely exercised), 21 years in Norway, 30 years in Slovenia, and 40 years in Colombia. Long-term prisoners in Portugal have to serve a longer proportion of their sentence in prison. Anyone sentenced to over six years, up to the maximum of 30 years, must serve five-sixths of the sentence before release can be considered.

3. The Ascendancy of Life Without Parole in America

Fear that dangerous murderers would be released on parole was behind the creation of LWOP statutes in many states, such as Alabama, Illinois, and Louisiana, in the immediate wake of the temporary abolition of capital punishment brought about by the *Furman* judgment in 1972.[20] This penalty was held to be constitutional by the US Supreme Court in *Schick v Reed* in 1974.[21] Since 1976 there has been an enormous rise in LWOP statutes as well as increasing restrictions on

---

[16] Marc Mauer, Ryan S. King, and Malcolm C. Young, 'The Meaning of "Life": Long Prison Sentences in Context' (May 2004): <http://www.sentencingproject.org/PublicationDetails.aspx?PublicationId=348>. N. Newcomen, 'Managing the Penal Consequences of Replacing the Death Penalty in Europe' in N. Browne and S. Kandelia (eds.), *Centre for Capital Punishment Studies Occasional Paper Series Three: Managing effective alternatives to capital punishment* (2005). Also, Penal Reform International Briefing No. 1, *Alternatives to the Death Penalty: The Problems with Life Imprisonment* (2007).

[17] D. van Zyl Smit, 'Life imprisonment: Recent issues in national and international law' *International Journal of Law and Psychiatry* 29 (2006) pp. 405–421 at 411.

[18] Life imprisonment is also the ultimate penalty for the International Criminal Tribunals of Rwanda and the former Yugoslavia, even though there had been no provision for it in Yugoslavian sentencing law: see D. van Zyl Smit, 'International Imprisonment' *International and Comparative Law Quarterly* 54 (April 2005), pp. 357–386 at 366–367.

[19] A. Coyle, 'Management of Long-term and Life-Sentenced Prisoners Internationally in the Context of a Human Rights Strategy' in Browne and Kandelia (eds.), n. 16 above.

[20] Julian H. Wright, Jr., Note, 'Life-Without-Parole: An alternative to death or not much of a life at all?' *Vanderbilt Law Review* 43 (1990) pp. 529–568 at 548.

[21] *Schick v Reed*, 419 U.S. 256, 267 (1974).

parole in both the federal[22] and the state systems. Prior to the mid-1990s LWOP was used infrequently and was available in only about half the states.[23] Today it is provided for by all but two states (New Mexico, which currently has the death penalty,[24] and Alaska, which does not) and it is also the maximum penalty under federal law for serious drug offences.[25] In addition, in some states LWOP is the mandatory penalty on a third conviction (the so-called 'three-strikes' rule) for specific felony offences of varying seriousness.[26]

Thus LWOP is now available in all but one death penalty state as a discretionary sentence available to the judge or jury when considering whether or not to impose a death sentence, and in some of these states, such as Kansas, 'every defendant who is possibly eligible for the death penalty but is not executed must be given life without parole'.[27] This means that those with strong mitigating circumstances who were not likely to be sentenced to death have been caught in the LWOP net. It therefore exists both alongside—as an alternative to—the death penalty in retentionist states *and* in place of it in abolitionist states.

In recent years more life sentences without the possibility of parole have been imposed in the United States than life imprisonment that allows for parole, thus increasing the proportion of lifers in prison who have no hope at all of release. Furthermore, in six states—Illinois, Iowa, Louisiana, Maine, Pennsylvania, and South Dakota—*all* life sentences are imposed without the possibility of parole. Seven states—Alabama, California, Florida, Illinois, Louisiana, Michigan, and Pennsylvania—have more than 1,000 prisoners serving LWOP sentences. The increase in those serving LWOP is clearly a result of changes in state policies rather than an increase in violent crime. This change of policy has had a dramatic influence on the size and structure of the prison population. Although the general prison population in the United States has risen considerably in the last few decades (as it has in the United Kingdom), the LWOP population has risen much more dramatically. From 1992 to 2003 the number of prisoners incarcerated for LWOP jumped by 170 per cent, from 12,453 to 33,633. Overall, one of every six lifers in 1992 was serving a sentence of life without parole but by 2003 that

---

[22] Comprehensive Crime Control Act (1984).

[23] M. Gottschalk, *The Prison and the Gallows: The politics of Mass Incarceration in America* (2006), p. 233; Wright, n. 20 above.

[24] In February 2007 the New Mexico House of Representatives approved legislation that would repeal the death penalty and replace it with a sentence of life without parole. The Bill is now due to go to the Senate for consideration: *Associated Press*, 12 February 2007.

[25] The American military courts can also sentence to LWOP. For example, in 2000 a US military court sentenced an Army sergeant to the maximum LWOP for the sexual assault and murder of an 11-year-old ethnic Albanian girl in Kosovo, while he was on peacekeeping duty: *CNN.com*, 1 August 2000.

[26] In Washington only for violent offences, but in California for less serious offences. See T. Jones and T. Newburn, 'Three strikes and you're out: Exploring Symbol and Substance in American and British Crime Control Policies' *British Journal of Criminology*, 46 (2006), pp. 781–802.

[27] Note, 'A matter of life and death: the effect of life-without-parole statutes on capital punishment' *Harvard Law Review* 119 (2006), pp. 1838–1845 at 1842.

proportion had increased to one in four, according to the report by Mauer and his colleagues.[28]

While many abolitionists shied away from recommending LWOP as a replacement for capital punishment, considering it to be just as offensive to human dignity, others have seen it as a political necessity if the public is to accept the abolition of capital punishment: 'Abolitionists have blitzed both legislatures and the media with pleas to adopt life-without-parole statutes in order to reduce executions, arguing that [it] . . . is a stronger, fairer, and more reliable punishment'.[29] An empirical study of jurors (as part of the Capital Jury Project) found that 'most jurors believed that capital murders would be back on the street even before they [could] become eligible for parole' and that the more the alternative to the death penalty was underestimated, the greater the likelihood that jurors would vote for the death penalty as the case came to be considered in the sentencing phase of the trial. This was true whether or not the defendant was alleged by the prosecutor to be dangerous.[30] Similarly, a study of 74 jurors in Pennsylvania (which does not require the jury to be told in every case that there is no possibility of parole) found that 'most of the jurors interviewed in that state did not think a life sentence truly meant life in prison' and indeed the majority significantly underestimated the time defendants were likely to spend in prison.[31] As the evidence suggested that 'The existence of parole . . . led more juries to sentence defendants to death . . . death penalty abolitionists hope[d] to force that number back down' through the introduction of the alternative of LWOP.[32]

However, as critics of this approach have argued, this strategy has proven to be a serious misjudgment, because:[33]

Twenty years of experience with life-without-parole statutes shows that although they have only a small effect on reducing executions . . . they have doubled and tripled the lengths of sentences for offenders who never would have been sentenced to death or even been eligible for the death penalty.

While the number of prisoners serving LWOP sentences increased dramatically, between 1992 and 2003, 'the death row population [also] grew by 31%'.[34]

---

[28] Mauer *et al.*, n. 16 above, at p. 11; and for a brief summary of the report see DPIC website: <http://www.deathpenaltyinfo.org/article.php?scid=67&did=1025>.

[29] Note, n. 27 above, p. 1838.

[30] William J. Bowers and Benjamin D. Steiner, 'Death by Default: An Empirical Demonstration of False and Forced Choices in Capital Sentencing' *Texas Law Review* 77 (1999), pp. 605–717, especially 645–671.

[31] The odds of those with low estimates of the time that would be served in prison were nearly five times the odds of those with high estimates. Wanda D. Foglia, 'They know not what they do: guided and misguided discretion in Pennsylvania Capital Cases' *Justice Quarterly* 20 (2003), pp. 187–211 at 204.

[32] Note, n. 27 above, at pp. 1838–1839.

[33] *Ibid.*, at p. 1839.

[34] *Ibid.*, at pp. 1851–1852.

To refuse to look at the effect of life-without-parole statutes on non-capital defendants [including those capital defendants who would not have been sentenced to death] is to sanction or encourage a law that holds twenty-five men in prison until their natural deaths in order to spare one man the death penalty.

Given the fact that such a small proportion of persons indicted for capital murder are eventually sentenced to death (see Chapter 4, page 146), any policy that substitutes life without parole as the mandatory penalty for all formerly death-eligible murders will save the lives of only a few at the cost of condemning a very much larger proportion of defendants to incarceration without any hope of ever being released.[35]

The Death Penalty Information Centre's 2006 Year End Report reminds us that the US Gallup polls now show support for LWOP trumping the death penalty.[36] As Richard Dieter explains, 'Life without parole sentences are becoming more attractive to many Americans, and it is the preferable choice over the death penalty for major subgroups of the population'.[37] In April 2007 an editorial in the *Dallas Morning News* spoke for many in Texas, in America, and even beyond its borders, in criticizing the death penalty for being unsafe and arbitrary and in recommending the alternative:[38]

Justice demands a punishment that is fair yet revocable, one that provides a sense of finality while allowing for the fallibility of the system. Life without parole meets that bar. It's harsh. It's just. And it's final without being irreversible. Call it a living death… [It protects] society from violent criminals and ensur[es] that every day of a murderer's life is a miserable existence. Our standards of punishment have evolved over time, from the gallows to firing squads, from the electric chair to lethal injection. Life without parole, essentially death by prison, should be the new standard.

The idea that LWOP should be the replacement for persons who have been or would have been sentenced to death has had its appeal beyond the United States. In 2006, when President Arroyo of the Philippines announced the commutation of all death sentences, they were replaced with life imprisonment without the possibility of parole. Other countries are contemplating introducing LWOP, for example South Korea, Sweden, Bulgaria, Ukraine, and Georgia have all

---

[35] For an excellent discussion of the issues involved see Catherine Appleton and Bent Grøver, 'The Pros and Cons of Life without Parole' *British Journal of Criminology* 47 (2007), pp. 597–615.

[36] At the Death Penalty Information Center (DPIC) website: <http://www.deathpenaltyinfo.org/2006YearEnd.pdf>.

[37] R. C. Dieter, *A Crisis of Confidence: American's Doubts about the Death Penalty* (2007), p. 2.

[38] 'Death No More: Life without parole should be new standard' *Dallas Morning News*, 16 April 2007. 'The overwhelming majority' of family members of murder victims testified to the New Jersey Death Penalty Study Commission that 'life without parole is the appropriate alternative to the death penalty', The Commission concluded that 'Replacing the death penalty with life without parole would be a certain punishment, not subject to lengthy delays of capital cases; it would incapacitate the offenders; and it would provide finality for victims' families': *New Jersey Death Penalty Study Commission Report* (2007), pp. 56 and 61.

introduced the possibility of LWOP for murder, although it is a discretionary penalty and prisoners have the right to petition for clemency.[39]

4. Life Without Hope: The New Challenge to Human Dignity

One hundred and forty years ago, John Stuart Mill compared the death penalty with life in prison and argued that the former was less cruel:[40]

What comparison can there really be, in point of severity, between consigning a man to the short pang of a rapid death, and immuring him in a living tomb, there to linger out what may be a long life in the hardest and most monotonous toil, without any of its alleviations or rewards—debarred from all pleasant sights and sounds, and cut off from all earthly hope, except a slight mitigation of bodily restraint, or a small improvement of diet?

Mill's critique struck at the heart of the problem of devising a replacement punishment for the death penalty. What penalty could be regarded as sufficiently severe to meet the demands of punishment for the worst of crimes and yet not be so inhumane in its length and in its administration as to be no improvement on being put to death?

Thirty years ago the Council of Europe ruled that 'it is inhuman to imprison a person for life without the hope of release' and that it would 'be compatible neither with modern principles on the treatment of prisoners . . . nor with the idea of the reintegration of offenders into society'.[41] More recently the European Court of Human Rights, in *Einhorn v France* (2001), did not rule out the possibility that the imposition of 'an irreducible life sentence may raise an issue under Article 3 of the European Convention on Human Rights', but did not reach a judgment on the matter. The European Union is currently considering whether to extend its extradition policy to apply to cases where the offences carry the sentence of LWOP.[42]

The non-governmental organisation Penal Reform International argues:[43]

Life sentences without the possibility of parole should not be used for any category of offender because the removal of the possibility of release not only amounts to inhuman

---

[39] P. Hodgkinson, 'Alternatives to the Death Penalty: The United Kingdom Experience' in Council of Europe Publishing (ed.), *Death Penalty: Beyond Abolition* (2004).

[40] This is from a speech given before Parliament on 21 April 1868 in opposition to a bill banning capital punishment, reproduced at Ethics Update: <http://ethics.sandiego.edu/Mill.html>.

[41] Council of Europe, *Treatment of long-term prisoners* (1977), p. 22.

[42] Catherine Appleton and Bent Grøver, n. 35 above, at p. 609. Also: P. Hodgkinson, 'Alternatives to the death penalty—the United Kingdom Experience' in Council of Europe (ed.), *Death Penalty: beyond abolition* (2004); van Zyl Smit, n. 17 above, at pp. 411–412.

[43] Penal Reform International, *Alternatives to the Death Penalty: The problems with life imprisonment*, Penal Reform Briefing No. 1, 2007(1), at p. 10.

and degrading treatment, but denies the offender a meaningful opportunity for rehabilitation, and is thus in contravention of Articles 10(1) and 10(3) of the *International Covenant on Civil and Political Rights*.

The question of whether LWOP breaches human rights norms has not been finally settled in Europe,[44] although in France, Italy, and Germany whole life sentences have been held to be unconstitutional.[45] As the German Federal Constitutional Court put it in 1977, 'The essence of human dignity is attacked if the prisoner, notwithstanding his personal development, must abandon any hope of ever regaining his freedom'.[46] LWOP has also been prohibited in Mexico, where the Supreme Court ruled it to be unconstitutional because it was considered to amount to cruel and unusual punishment,[47] and also in Namibia, where in *S v Nehemia Tjijo,* the Namibian High Court held that life imprisonment was simply a sentence of death, a form of cruel, inhuman, and degrading punishment and therefore unconstitutional. As Justice Levy put it, '[life imprisonment] removes from a prisoner all hope of his or her release... Take away his hope and you take away his dignity and all desire he may have to continue living'.[48]

On the other hand, supporters of LWOP argue that it is 'capable of accruing several important philosophical and practical advantages' over capital punishment.[49] Julian Wright, for example, has asserted that LWOP incapacitates, preserves the innocent lives of those who have been convicted unjustly for murder, and is an effective prosecutorial tool in murder trials—in that it helps to secure plea bargains and convictions—while the death penalty remains.[50] While acknowledging some of the problems, such as prison overcrowding, an ageing prison population and discipline problems brought about by trying to control inmates who have no incentives to behave, he believes these can be dealt with by 'adequate planning and foresight'.[51] He concluded that 'life-without-parole's philosophical and practical advantages outweigh its potential problems'.[52] Yet,

---

[44] In Europe, there are basically three models of conditional release: a 'discretionary release system' typical on the Continent, a 'mandatory release system' found in Sweden, and the 'mixed release system' in England and Wales, which combines automatic early release proceedings for prisoners serving a short sentence and individual proceedings for long sentences: Pierre Victor Tournier, 'Systems of Conditional Release (Parole) in the Member States of the Council of Europe' (2006), <http://champpenal.revues.org/document378.html>.

[45] At some stage the European Convention on Human Rights will have to settle this: van Zyl Smit, n. 17 above, at pp. 409–410; also D. van Zyl Smit, *Taking life imprisonment seriously in national and international law* (2002).

[46] Cited in van Zyl Smit, n. 17 above, at p. 409.

[47] Hodgkinson, n. 39 above.

[48] D. Van Zyl Smit, 'The death penalty in Africa' *African Human Rights Law Journal* 4 (2004), pp. 13–34 at 13.

[49] J. Wright, 'Life without Parole: An Alternative to Death or not Much of a Life at All?' *Vanderbilt Law Review* 43 (1990), pp. 529–568 at 556–557. Also Appleton and Grøver, n. 35 above.

[50] Wright, *ibid.*, at pp. 558–559.

[51] *Ibid.*, at pp. 565–566.

[52] *Ibid.*, at p. 566.

given Wright's other research which has shown that those awaiting execution on America's death rows consider LWOP to be a harsher sanction than the death penalty,[53] his promotion of LWOP as a *moral* alternative to the death penalty is curious.

Given that mandatory death sentences have been ruled unconstitutional, on the grounds that each case must be judged on its merits, taking into account all relevant mitigating as well as aggravating circumstances (see Chapter 8, pages 278–279), it is difficult to see how this argument could not equally apply to mandatory sentences of life imprisonment without the option of parole.[54] The question arises therefore of what punishment would be appropriate for the most heinous of murders should the death penalty be abolished. In order to adhere to the principle of proportionality, not all capital murders should be dealt with in the same way.[55] The matter has been further complicated by making LWOP the mandatory sentence under some 'three-strikes' laws and for certain drug offences, so destroying, as Hugo Bedau has pointed out, the principle of proportionality that the most severe punishments should be reserved for the most egregious crimes.[56]

Of all the justifications for LWOP, incapacitation is the most persuasive, but it is well established that it is very difficult to predict future dangerousness.[57] A system which applies LWOP mandatorily to capital murder (not just to the minority among them who would have been formerly sentenced to death) will inevitably sweep up in its scope a large proportion of prisoners who in some years' time will no longer present a danger.[58] As the warden of Louisiana's Angola Prison has said, most of his ageing charges serving LWOP have long since gone through 'criminal menopause'.[59]

All the evidence therefore suggests that to replace the death penalty with a mandatory sentence of life without parole is unnecessary, is liable to punish too severely persons who formerly would not have been sentenced to death and executed, and is arbitrary in its infliction of the same punishment on persons whose crimes and punishments should be individually assessed.

---

[53] J. Wright, 'Life without Parole: The View from Death Row' *Criminal Law Bulletin* 27 (3) (1991), pp. 34–57, discussed in Appleton and Grøver, n. 35 above.

[54] W. A. Logan, 'Proportionality and Punishment: Imposing Life Without Parole on Juveniles' *Wake Forest Law Review* 33 (1998), pp. 681–725 at 697.

[55] In America the proportionality principle was confirmed in *Weems v United States*, 217 U.S. 349, 367 (1910).

[56] H. A. Bedau, 'Abolishing the death penalty in the United States: an analysis of institutional obstacles and future prospects' in P. Hodgkinson and W. A. Schabas, *Capital Punishment: Strategies for Abolition* (2004), pp. 186–207 at 203. In Louisiana, for example, about 150 of the state's 3,800 LWOP prisoners were convicted of dealing heroin, most of them being low-level dealers.

[57] There is a vast literature on this subject. For an excellent overview, see: J. Monahan, 'The prediction of violent behavior: Toward a second generation of theory and policy' *American Journal of Psychiatry* 141 (1984), pp. 10–15; and John Monahan, 'Violence Risk Assessment: Scientific Validity and Evidentiary Admissibility' *Washington and Lee Law Review* 57 (2000), pp. 901–916.

[58] Shute, n. 4 above, at p. 887.

[59] Sasha Abramsky, 'Lifers: Prisoners Dilemma' *Legal Affairs* (April 2004), pp. 1–45.

There are also practical objections, particularly the enormous cost implications of housing increasing numbers of elderly people in prisons who will inevitably need medical and geriatric care.[60] Although it is true that the cost of life imprisonment without parole is at present less than that of pursuing a case to execution,[61] this is largely due to the 'super due process' required for death penalty cases but not, at present, for life sentences.[62] When the death penalty is abolished and LWOP becomes the most severe penalty that can be inflicted it is likely that there will be very strong pressure to ensure that those sentenced to perpetual imprisonment will also benefit from super due process. Pressure will then mount to reserve LWOP only for the most egregious cases.

5. Conditions of Confinement

At the beginning of the abolitionist movement at the end of the eighteenth century, before the establishment of long-term prison systems, punishments that replaced the death penalty were especially punitive. They could include transportation for life with no chance of return or, as Leon Radzinowicz pointed out, severe corporal punishment or banishment to the galleys. When Catherine the Great of Russia suspended capital punishment, for example, it was replaced with 333 lashes of the *knout*, which in practice virtually amounted to a death sentence, and in Austria, under the reign of Joseph II, prisoners were saved from execution only to be sentenced to the galleys. With the rise of imprisonment the American state of Louisiana replaced the death penalty with permanent solitary segregation, 'frightening in its inhuman physical and soul-destroying regime'.[63] As Radzinowicz put it, there was a disturbing disparity between the humane ethos of the Enlightenment and the 'sombre reality' of the punishments inflicted. These early examples are still germane when alternatives to execution are discussed because if the death penalty is to be replaced by very long periods of imprisonment, such that some persons will remain behind bars for the rest of their natural lives, the conditions under which they are kept in confinement become a matter of great importance. For example, the Minister of Justice of Rwanda, in the

[60] Mauer, *et al.* (2004), n. 16 above. The New Jersey Death Penalty Study, published in January 2007, pointed out (at p. 92) that the long-run costs associated with an increased number of prisoners serving life without parole, in particular 'the rising health care costs of aging prisoners', 'may very well offset the cost savings of abolishing the death penalty'.

[61] According to the Californian journalist, Jake Armstrong, the cost of the case against Michael Morales, sentenced to death in 1981, has so far amounted to approximately $250 million, compared with $4.8 million for his co-defendant Ricky Ortinga, sentenced to life imprisonment without the option of parole: *The New Sentinel*, March 2006.

[62] With full protections against wrongful convictions, appeals allowed for, and the best available legal assistance (see Ch. 7): Robert M. Bohm, 'The Economic Costs of Capital Punishment: Past, Present and Future' in J. R. Acker, R. M. Bohm, and C. S. Lanier (eds.), *America's Experiment with Capital Punishment* (2nd edn., 2003), pp. 573–594.

[63] L. Radzinowicz, *Adventures in Criminology* (1999), p. 282.

wake of that country's abolition of the death penalty in June 2007, stated that life imprisonment would have a 'special provision for recidivists for capital crimes', with several measures for 'those who will commit genocide or extermination in the future'. He was reported as saying 'They will be tough in that they [the criminals] will regret not having been hanged'.[64] The Council of Europe is concerned for such prisoners across the world:[65]

Life sentence prisoners who are unlikely to be released and will probably spend the rest of their natural life in prison must also be considered a vulnerable category of prisoner . . . Sentence planning for these prisoners will make great demands on imagination and flexibility in devising activities and psycho-social support that help the prisoner to come to terms with the hard reality of spending the rest of his or her natural life in prison. This will give rise to both ethical and practical problems when serious illness, age-related incapacitation and imminent death occur. Consideration should then be given to releasing the prisoner, or, if this is not possible, to allow the continued imprisonment to be carried out under compassionate conditions.

Luisa Bascur, Central Asian regional project director for the International Federation for Human Rights, has also expressed fears about what may happen in those Central Asian countries which have abolished or are in the process of abolishing the death penalty. Discussing the transfer of death row prisoners to regular prisons to spend decades in prison serving life sentences, she pointed out that reforming the penal systems is now a priority for activists:[66]

They don't get proper food there . . . Many die from tuberculosis and disease because there is no access to medical treatment . . . We are striving for more humane conditions in prisons and the rehabilitation of those having served their sentences. Sometimes even NGOs think the battle is won once the death penalty has been abolished. It is an important step. But the battle ahead of us is even greater.

In Chapter 5 we reported on how life on death row for most people in most jurisdictions was intolerable. But research suggests that for those serving life sentences, particularly those without the prospect of parole, it can be almost as bad. Van Zyl Smit refers to life imprisonment as 'particularly destructive to human dignity',[67] and Prison Reform International reports on the 'profound sociological and psychological impact on prisoners . . . [These p]risoners . . . can experience differential treatment and worse conditions of detention compared to other categories of

---

[64] *The New Times*, 25 January 2007.

[65] Council of Europe Report, Committee of Ministers, 'Recommendation of the Committee of Ministers to Member States on the managment by prison administrations of life-sentence and other long-term prisoners' (2003).

[66] Quoted in Kuban Abdymen, 'Death Penalty: Central Asia Nearing Abolition' *Inter Press Service (IPS) News*, 29 March 2007.

[67] D. van Zyl Smit, 'Abolishing Life Imprisonment?' *Punishment and Society*, 3 (2001), pp. 299–306 at 301.

prisoner'.[68] The European Council for the Prevention of Torture and Inhuman or Degrading Treatment or Punishment has found that such prisoners are subject to restrictions such as: separation from the rest of the prison population; handcuffing when they are taken out of their cells; prohibition of communication with other prisoners; and limited visit entitlements, all likely to exacerbate the deleterious effects inherent in long-term imprisonment. In the Russian Federation, for example, the Council found that life-sentenced prisoners are prohibited from associating with other prisoners and are kept in cells of less than two square metres. They are kept under surveillance day and night as they are considered to be a far greater threat than other categories of prisoner. In Kenya, too, life-sentenced prisoners are held in maximum security prisons, separate from other prisoners, and restricted from engaging in certain types of work.[69] Coyle informs us that punitive conditions of detention and less favourable treatment are particularly prevalent for reprieved death row prisoners:[70]

Singling long-term prisoners out for harsh treatment is a particular problem in countries that are in the process of adjusting their penal policy to deal with those prisoners who would have previously been executed.

A Florida newspaper reported in July 2007 that 11 years after supervising his first execution, a former Florida prison warden, Ron McAndrew, has argued for the abandonment of capital punishment, in favour of LWOP. But it is instructive that he does so on the grounds that as a punishment it is worse than the death penalty, yet protects states from executing an innocent person. He is quoted as saying 'the most severe punishment you could ever give anyone would be to lock them in a little cage made out of concrete and steel...with a steel cot, a mattress that is 2 inches thick, a stainless steel toilet that does not have a lid, and you leave them there for the rest of their natural life. There can't be a more severe punishment than that'.[71] But in reality, whilst there is a heightened level of appellate review for those sentenced to death in the United States, LWOP sentences have received no special consideration from appellate tribunals so that 'the vast majority of life-without-parole prisoners have almost no chance of having their sentences reversed'.[72]

Prisoners living in such conditions who have no prospect of release may find no disincentive from committing crimes or engaging in unacceptable behaviour while in prison, something which affects their fellow inmates and those charged with looking after them. Research conducted by Beck *et al.* suggests that 'life is different' in that a sentence other than death instils hope in the lives of the

---

[68] Penal Reform International, *Alternatives to the Death Penalty: The problems with life imprisonment*, Penal Reform Briefing No. 1 (2007) (1), p. 6.

[69] European Council for the Prevention of Torture and Inhuman or Degrading Treatment, *11th General Report on the CPT's activities* (2001).

[70] Coyle, n. 19 above, at p. 44.

[71] *Tallahassee Democrat*, 29 June 2007, cited at the DPIC website.

[72] Note, n. 27 above, p. 1852.

families of prisoners and awakens 'a capacity for productivity and compassionate contributions to the lives of others' and that offenders can make positive contributions to society, even from behind bars—but rarely while on death row.[73] But this is surely only true if both the families and the defendants have the prospect of eventual release to motivate their continued relationships with, and commitment to, each other and the wider community. If they know that no matter what they do they will die while incarcerated they are much less likely to feel motivated and the experiences of their families and friends are going to be very similar to those we described at the end of Chapter 5.

Anatoly Pristavkin, the eminent Russian writer and advisor to the President of the Russian Federation, reported on a visit by a parliamentary delegation headed by the Minister of Justice to a penal colony where former death row prisoners were serving their commuted sentences of life imprisonment:[74]

[It] gave a first-hand insight into the unbelievably difficult conditions in which these lifers exist. No radio, no newspapers, no opportunities for family visits. Incarcerated in former monastic cells on a lonely island in the northern forests their letters beg us to reinstate the death penalty.

Although the conditions of confinement in France cannot be compared with those in Russia, nevertheless, the long periods of indefinite confinement have taken their toll. Recently it was reported that ten prisoners condemned to life terms (who would have been sentenced to death before abolition) wrote in an open letter: 'We'd prefer an immediate end to our lives rather than being cooked slowly under a flame'. The signatories compared life in French prisons with the prospect of freedom only far into the future with 'slow execution'.[75] A similar story emerged in May 2007, when 300 Italian prisoners serving life sentences signed a letter to the President of Italy urging him to bring back the death penalty. The author of the letter, in prison for 17 years, explained that he is tired of 'dying a little bit every day'.[76] When prisoners are given no hope, the penalty becomes one of civil death.

6. The Challenge of Sentencing Juveniles Convicted of Murder

The International Covenant on Civil and Political Rights, to which the United States became a party in 1992, specifically addresses the need for special treatment

[73] E. Beck, S. Britto, and A. Andrews, *In the Shadow of Death: Restorative Justice and Death Row Families* (2007), p. 155.

[74] Anatoly Pristavkin, 'The Russian Federation and the death penalty' in *Death Penalty. Beyond Abolition* (2004), pp. 191–204 at 201.

[75] Julio Godoy, '*RIGHTS—Death Penalty Better, Say Some, Than Slow Execution*' *Inter Press Service (IPS) News*, 22 January 2007.

[76] Christian Fraser, 'Italy inmates seek death penalty' *BBC News*, 31 May 2007.

of children in the criminal justice system. Article 14(4), which was co-sponsored by the United States, mandates that criminal procedures for children charged with crimes 'take account of the age and the desirability of promoting their rehabilitation':[77]

The ICCPR, the CRC [the Convention on the Rights of the Child] and the Beijing Rules provide that deprivation of liberty for child offenders be a 'measure of last resort' and that juvenile justice includes rehabilitation as a core component.

In July 2006 the Human Rights Committee expressed concern in its Concluding Observations that in America the treatment of children as adults is not exclusively applied in 'exceptional circumstances', as provided in the ICCPR, and therefore that America is in violation of its treaty obligations.[78] Furthermore, the European Court of Human Rights has ruled that the principle of proportionality demands that any young person sentenced to life imprisonment must always have the prospect of release.[79] International human rights law prohibits life without parole for those who commit their crimes before the age of eighteen. The UN Convention on the Rights of the Child states explicitly that:[80]

No child who was under the age of 18 at the time he or she committed an offence should be sentenced to life without the possibility of release or parole . . . the Committee strongly recommends the States parties to abolish all forms of life imprisonment for offences committed by persons under the age of 18.

However, the United States (along with Somalia) has failed to ratify the United Nation's Convention on the Rights of the Child. Outside America, there are only about 13 juvenile offenders serving LWOP. About 13 other countries allow for minors to be given lifetime sentences with no provision for eventual release,[81] but of these, only three actually have any juveniles serving such sentences: Israel,

---

[77] Child Rights Information Network, 'Human Rights Advocates Juvenile Sentencing: Written statement for the fourth session of the Human Rights Council' (2007).

[78] Stating that sentencing children to LWOP is not in compliance with Art. 24(1) of the Covenant.

[79] *Weeks v United Kingdom* A 114 (1987), (1988) 10 EHRR 293; *Hussain v United Kingdom* 1996-I 252, (1996) 22 EHRR 1; and *V v United Kingdom* 1999-IX III, (2000) 30 EHRR 121, cited in D. van Zyl Smit, 'The Abolition of Capital Punishment for Persons Under the Age of Eighteen Years in the United States of America. What Next?' *Human Rights Law Review* 5:2 (2005), pp. 393–401 at 400, fn. 27.

[80] Art. 37 UN Convention on the Rights of the Child, Committee on the Rights of the Child, General Comment No. 10 (2007), 'Children's rights in juvenile justice' GE.07–41351 (E) 270407, April 2007, para. 77, p. 21.

[81] It is provided for in criminal legislation in Antigua and Barbuda, Australia, Brunei, Burkina Faso, Cuba, Dominica, Israel, Kenya, St Vincent and the Grenadines, the Solomon Islands, South Africa (pending abolition in a Criminal Justice Bill), Sri Lanka, Tanzania, and the United States: Human Rights Watch/Amnesty International, 2005. Ten American states set no minimum age, and 12 states set a minimum of 10 to 13 years of age; see Child Rights Information Network, n.77 above.

South Africa, and Tanzania—each of them only a handful, but nevertheless in violation of the Convention.

Not one of the original fifteen member states of the European Union allows young offenders to be sentenced to life without parole, [82] and on the African continent 31 countries prohibit life without parole for youth in their penal laws.[83] In all, at least 132 countries have objected on principle to the sentence of LWOP for juveniles. Within the United States a petition has been submitted on behalf of child offenders sentenced to life without parole to the Inter-American Court of Human Rights, showing how LWOP violates principles of international law.[84] Despite international treaties, America incarcerates more juveniles for life without parole, by far, than all other nations combined and critics argue that its increased use for juveniles reflects a particularly troubling consequence of the recent punitive shift in American policy towards prosecuting and punishing juveniles as adults.[85]

A recent report by Human Rights Watch and Amnesty International[86] points out that in 42 states and under federal law, the commission of a serious crime by juveniles under 18, in some states as young as 10, can result in them being treated as adults by the criminal justice system.[87] Therefore:[88]

[I]f the crime they committed was serious enough for an adult to get a life without parole sentence it has been imposed on them. Where such a sentence is mandatory, for, say, an adult committing first degree murder, children tried in adult courts for the same crime have not been able to argue that their youth should be a mitigating factor.

Partly as a consequence, the rate of LWOP sentencing for juveniles in America increased dramatically over the 1990s, from three per cent of convictions for murder in 1990 to nine per cent in 2000. Hence the Human Rights Watch and

---

[82] Austria, Belgium, Denmark, Finland, France, Germany, Greece, Ireland, Italy, Luxembourg, Netherlands, Portugal, Spain, Sweden, and United Kingdom.

[83] Algeria, Angola, Benin, Botswana, Burundi, Cameroon, Cape Verde, Chad, Cote d'Ivoire, Democratic Republic of the Congo, Djibouti, Egypt, Eritrea, Guinea, Guinea-Bissau, Lesotho, Liberia, Libya, Madagascar, Mali, Mauritius, Morocco, Mozambique, Namibia, Niger, Rwanda, Sao Tome and Principe, Togo, Tunisia, Uganda, and Zimbabwe.

[84] National Center for Youth Law, *Youth Law News*, 27 No. 3, July–September 2006.

[85] Logan, n. 54 above, at pp. 683–684.

[86] Human Rights Watch and Amnesty International, *The Rest of their Lives: Life without Parole for Child Offenders in the United States*, October 2005.

[87] In the 1990s, 40 states made it easier for juveniles to be tried in an adult court: Logan, n. 54 above, at pp. 690–691. Whilst New York and North Carolina are currently the only remaining states to automatically transfer 16-year-olds who commit crimes to adult courts, most other states have laws that *encourage* prosecutors to try juveniles as adults. However, in July 2007 Connecticut, following a trend set by other states, introduced a bill that removes 16 and 17 year-old offenders from the adult courts and puts them back into the juvenile justice system: Editorial, 'Back where they Belong' *New York Times*, 5 July 2007.

[88] Van Zyl Smit, n. 17 above.

Amnesty International study found that there are at least 2,225 juvenile offenders serving life without parole in the United States, compared with only about a dozen in the rest of the world. These juveniles are predominantly male, 60 per cent are African American and the majority (59%) received the sentence for their first ever criminal conviction of any sort. There is a great deal of variation across states, with 109 per 100,000 juveniles aged 14–17 serving life without parole in Louisiana but none in Vermont, Utah, New Jersey, or Idaho.

Whilst the case of *Roper v Simmons* in 2005 rendered the death penalty unconstitutional for those who committed the offence when under the age of 18, the Supreme Court has not considered the constitutionality of incarcerating juveniles for their natural lives. Indeed, as van Zyl Smit points out, the majority opinion in *Roper* was disingenuous in failing to tackle the constitutionality of life without parole, which was, after all, the sentence subsequently imposed on Simmons. This was despite the fact that, in arguing against the death penalty, Justice Kennedy had stated that, 'even a heinous crime committed by a juvenile is not evidence of irretrievably depraved character'. In other words, juveniles, even more than adults, can be rehabilitated and so permanent incarceration cannot be justified on the grounds of incapacitation. As Justice Scalia pointed out in his minority opinion, if the court was to take note of international opinion regarding the death penalty for juveniles, it should be consistent and accept that the Convention also prohibits life without parole for juveniles.[89]

In recognition of this, some states have recently introduced legislation to abolish this penalty for juveniles.[90] In April 2007 the California Senate Committee on Public Safety passed the Juvenile Life Without Parole Reform Act to make it impossible for state judges to sentence offenders younger than 18 to LWOP.[91] The state senator behind it, who has a doctorate in child psychology, argued that the human brain is still maturing during adolescence, and that therefore minors are more likely to be rehabilitated.[92] This, of course, is a similar position to that argued in the Amicus Curiae Brief of the American Psychological Association submitted in *Roper v Simmons* (2005). However, the elimination of life without parole will be of little consequence if states follow the example of Colorado which, in 2006, replaced its mandatory LWOP sentence for certain crimes for juveniles

[89] Justice Scalia's dissenting opinion in *Roper v Simmons*, 543 U.S. 551.

[90] Van Zyl Smit, 'The Abolition of Capital Punishment for Persons Under the Age of Eighteen Years in the United States of America. What Next?' *Human Rights Law Review* 5:2 (2005), pp. 393–401 at 400.

[91] A vote before the full state Senate was expected to take place in mid-May 2007, but by the end of 2007 this had not been reported.

[92] A. Paul, 'America's Imprisoned Kids' *American Prospect*, 11 May 2007 (web only): <http://www.prospect.org/cs/articles?article=americas_imprisoned_kids>.

with a sentence of 40 years before the possibility of parole.[93] As the American law professor, Babe Howell, has put it:[94]

Given current politics it is not clear to me that there are any promising arguments against these sentencing norms but human rights law. International embarrassment may some-day put us in a position where life sentences for juveniles become as embarrassing as Jim Crow did in the 1950s and 1960s.

7. Implications for Policy

We agree with Andrew Coyle, an authority on international prison systems, that 'Abolitionists cannot content themselves with arguing the negative aspects of capital punishment. They must also have a clear idea about what *should* happen to people who commit terrible offences'.[95] We have shown that most countries that have abolished the death penalty have put in its place a system where an in-determinate life sentence is available for the worst of the worst murders, in nearly all instances subject to review by the executive through a Parole Board or similar body. The expectation is that the prisoner will be fit for release after serving a minimum period of time in custody to mark the seriousness of the crime, but that in a few cases the offence may be so outrageous and the offender so likely to be dangerous that he or she will have to remain in custody, possibly until death. The sentence to life without parole is an entirely different matter because it forecloses any future decision as to the character and dangerousness of the person punished, and therefore extinguishes all hope. We, like Coyle and others, such as Robert Badinter, regard this as inhumane. To replace the death penalty by life impris-onment without any prospect of release is to replace one human rights abuse, the lack of respect for the dignity of the individual, with another.

Nor do we believe that the fact that some, but by no means all, prison systems in retentionist countries (and even some that are abolitionist) are ill-adapted at present to provide a positive regime for the long-term confinement of prison-ers who would formerly have been executed, ought to be used as an argument to delay abolition. Again to quote Andrew Coyle, there is something 'logically and morally wrong with the argument that criminals should be exterminated to save them from the inevitable suffering that accompanies long sentences in overcrowded prisons'.[96] In other words, alongside the goal of abolition, those who

---

[93] Previously, offenders as young as 12 were eligible for life without parole. The law was not made retroactive so does not affect the sentences of Colorado's 45 juveniles currently serving LWOP: Child Rights Information Network, n. 77 above.

[94] Quoted in Paul, n. 92 above.

[95] Andrew Coyle, 'Replacing the death penalty: the vexed issue of alternative sanctions' in Peter Hodgkinson and William A. Schabas (eds.), *Capital Punishment. Strategies for Abolition* (2004), pp. 92–115 at 93.

[96] Coyle, *ibid*.

campaign for the humane treatment of prisoners will need to refocus their attention on creating for life-sentenced (and very long determinate sentenced) prisoners a humane prison environment, accompanied by an effective and judicious system for reviewing suitability for release that adequately protects the public while respecting the humanity of the prisoner. In our opinion, sentences of life imprisonment which from the outset preclude any possibility of parole are not only inhumane, they are unnecessary and counter-productive. They raise many of the human rights issues that have been at the heart of the attack on the death penalty itself. They too should be abolished.

Appendix 1
Lists of Retentionist and Abolitionist Countries

TABLE A1.1

Countries that still retained the death penalty on 31 December 2007 and have carried out at least one judicial execution within the past 10 years (1997–2007)

51 'actively retentionist' countries

Afghanistan	Indonesia	Saint Kitts and Nevis
Bahamas	Iran	Saudi Arabia
Bahrain	Iraq	Sierra Leone
Bangladesh	Japan	Singapore
Belarus	Jordan	Somalia
Botswana	Korea, Democratic	Sudan
Burundi	People's Republic of	Syria
Chad	(North Korea)	Taiwan
China	Kuwait	Thailand
Comoros	Lebanon	Trinidad and Tobago
Congo, Democratic	Libya	Uganda
Republic of	Malaysia	United Arab Emirates
Cuba	Mongolia	United States of America
Egypt	Nigeria	Uzbekistan[2]
Equatorial Guinea	Oman	Vietnam
Ethiopia	Pakistan	Yemen
Guatemala[1]	Palestinian Authority	Zimbabwe
Guinea	Qatar	
India		

[1] In 2005 the President announced he would seek abolition of the death penalty.
[2] In 2005 the President signed a decree abolishing the death penalty, which came into effect on 1 January 2008.

TABLE A1.2

Countries that have abolished the death penalty for all crimes in all circumstances, in peacetime and wartime—by 31 December 2007

91 completely abolitionist countries

Country or territory	Date of abolition for all crimes	Date of abolition for ordinary crimes	Date of last execution
Albania	2007	2000	1995
Andorra	1990		1943
Angola	1992		n.k.
Armenia	2003		1991
Australia	1985	1984	1967
Austria	1968	1950	1950
Azerbaijan	1998		1993
Belgium	1996		1950
Bhutan	2004		1964
Bolivia[1]	1997	1995	1974
Bosnia and Herzegovina	2001	1997	n.k.
Bulgaria	1998		1989
Cambodia	1989		n.k
Canada	1998	1976	1962
Cape Verde	1981		1835
Colombia	1910		1909
Costa Rica	1877		n.k.
Côte d'Ivoire	2000		1960
Croatia	1991		1987
Cyprus	2002	1983	1962
Czech Republic	1990		n.k.
Denmark	1978	1933	1950
Djibouti	1995		1977
Dominican Republic	1966		n.k.
Ecuador	1906		n.k.
Estonia	1998		1991
Finland	1972	1949	1944
France	1981		1977
Georgia	1997		1994
Germany	1949		1948

TABLE A1.2 (*Continued*):

Country or territory	Date of abolition for all crimes	Date of abolition for ordinary crimes	Date of last execution
(Former German Democratic Republic)[2]	(1987)		(n.k.)
Greece	2004	1993	1972
Guinea-Bissau	1993		1986
Haiti	1987		1972
Holy See (Vatican City State)	1969		n.k.
Honduras	1956		1940
Hungary	1990		1988
Iceland	1928		1830
Ireland	1990		1954
Italy	1994	1947	1947
Kiribati	1979		1979*
Kyrgyzstan	2007		1998
Liberia	2005		1993
Liechtenstein	1987		1785
Lithuania	1998		1995
Luxembourg	1979		1949
Macedonia (Former Yugoslav Republic of)	1991		n.k.
Malta	2000	1971	1943
Marshall Islands	1986		1986*
Mauritius	1995		1987
Mexico	2005		1937
Micronesia (Federated States of)	1986		1986*
Moldova	1995		1989
Monaco	1962		1847
Montenegro (when Serbia and Montenegro)	2002		1989
Mozambique	1990		1986
Namibia	1990		1988
Nepal	1997	1990	1979
Netherlands	1982	1870	1952
New Zealand	1989	1961	1957

TABLE A1.2 (*Continued*):

Country or territory	Date of abolition for all crimes	Date of abolition for ordinary crimes	Date of last execution
Nicaragua	1979		1930
Norway	1979	1905	1948
Palau	1994		1994*
Panama	1922		1903
Paraguay	1992		1928
Philippines	2006		2000
Poland	1997		1988
Portugal	1976	1867	1849
Romania	1989		1989
Rwanda	2007		1998
Samoa	2004		1962
San Marino	1865	1848	1468
Sao Tome and Principe	1990		1975
Senegal	2004		1967
Serbia (when Serbia and Montenegro)	2002		1989
Seychelles	1993		1976
Slovakia	1990		1989
Slovenia	1989		1957
Solomon Islands	1978	1966	1966
South Africa	1997	1995	1991
Spain	1995	1978	1975
Sweden	1972	1921	1910
Switzerland	1992	1942	1944
Timor-Leste (East Timor)	1999		1999*
Turkey	2004	2002	1984
Turkmenistan	1999		1997
Tuvalu	1976		1976*
Ukraine	1999		1997
United Kingdom	1998	1965[3]	1964
Uruguay	1907		n.k.
Vanuatu	1980		1980*
Venezuela	1863		n.k.

n.k. = information not available.

* = date of independence, date of last execution under colonial rule not available.

Notes:

[1] According to the Constitution of Bolivia of 1967, amended in 1995, Article 17 prohibits the use of the death penalty. Despite this prohibition, the Penal Code of 1973 provided for capital punishment. To bring the law into line with the amended Constitution of 1995, the Bolivian Congress formally abolished the death penalty in 1997.

[2] The death penalty was abolished in the Federal Republic of Germany (FRG) in 1949 and in the German Democratic Republic (GDR) in 1987. The last execution in the FRG was in 1949; the last execution in the GDR was 1981.

[3] Capital punishment for ordinary crimes was abolished in Northern Ireland in 1973.

TABLE A1.3

Countries that have abolished the death penalty but only for all
ordinary crimes—by 31 December 2007

10 countries

Country	Date of abolition for ordinary crimes	Date of last execution
Argentina	1984	1916
Brazil	1979	1855
Chile	2001	1985
Cook Islands[1]	1965	n.k.
El Salvador	1983	1973
Fiji[2]	1979	1964
Israel	1954	1962
Kazakhstan	2007	2003
Latvia	1999	1996
Peru	1979	1979

Notes:
[1] The Cook Islands became self-governing (in free association with New Zealand) in 1965. The date of the last execution in the islands is not known.
[2] Capital punishment was abolished in Fiji in 2002 for treason, instigating foreign invasion with military force, and genocide, but remains under Military Code.

*Countries that retain the death penalty in law but which may be regarded
as abolitionist de facto on the grounds that no executions have been carried
out for at least 10 years or an official moratorium was in place on 31 December 2007*

Note: this does not mean that all of these countries are committed to not resuming executions. The 33 countries regarded as 'abolitionist in practice' by Amnesty International are in bold.

44 countries

Country or territory	Date of last execution
Algeria	1993
Antigua and Barbuda	1991
Barbados	1984
Belize	1985
Benin	1987
Brunei Darussalam	1957
Burkina Faso	1988
Cameroon	1997
Central African Republic	1981
Congo (Brazzaville) Republic of	1982
Dominica	1986
Eritrea[1]	1989
Gabon[2]	1989
Gambia[3]	1981
Ghana	1993
Grenada	1978
Guyana	1996
Jamaica	1988
Kenya	1987
Korea, Republic of (South Korea)	1997
Lao People's Democratic Republic	1989
Lesotho	1995
Madagascar	1958
Malawi	1992
Maldives	1952

TABLE A1.4 (*Continued*):

Country or territory	Date of last execution
Mali	1980
Mauritania	1989
Morocco	1993
Myanmar	1989
Nauru	1968
Niger	1976
Papua New Guinea	1950
Russian Federation (moratorium since May 1996)	1996
Sri Lanka	1976
St. Lucia	1995
St. Vincent and the Grenadines	1995
Suriname	1982
Swaziland	1983
Tajikistan (moratorium since April 2004)	2004
Tanzania	1994
Togo	1978
Tonga	1982
Tunisia	1991
Zambia	1997

Notes:
[1] Eritrea became independent in 1993.
[2] In September 2007 the Cabinet of Gabon announced that it would abolish the death penalty.
[3] Gambia abolished the death penalty in April 1993: it was reinstated by the military regime in August 1995.

Appendix 1

TABLE A1.5

*Countries and territories that abolished capital punishment between
1 January 1989 and 31 December 2007*

Note: this table lists a total of 59 countries—56 for all crimes and 3 for ordinary crimes only. Of these 59 countries, seven had already abolished the death penalty for ordinary offences prior to 1989: Canada, Cyprus, Italy, Malta, New Zealand, Switzerland, and the United Kingdom.

Year	Country or territory	Offences for which capital punishment was abolished		Whether abolitionist *de facto* (last execution at least 10 years prior to first abolition)
		All offences	Ordinary offences	
1989	Cambodia	X	–	No
1989	New Zealand	X	1961	Yes
1989	Romania	X	–	No
1989	Slovenia	X	–	Yes
1990	Andorra	X	–	Yes
1990	Croatia	X	–	No
1990	Czech Republic	X	–	No
1990	Hungary	X	–	No
1990	Ireland	X	–	Yes
1990	Mozambique	X	–	No
1990	Namibia	X	–	No
1990	São Tomé and Principe	X	–	Yes
1990	Slovakia	X	–	No
1991	Macedonia (Former Yugoslav Republic of)	X	–	No
1992	Angola	X	–	No
1992	Paraguay	X	–	Yes
1992	Switzerland	X	1942	No
1993	Guinea Bissau	X	–	No
1993	Seychelles	X	–	Yes
1994	Italy	X	1947	No
1994	Palau	X	–	No
1995	Djibouti	X	–	Yes
1995	Mauritius	X	–	No
1995	Moldova, Republic of	X	–	No
1996	Belgium	X	–	Yes
1997	Bolivia[1]	X	1995	Yes
1997	Georgia	X	–	No
1997	Nepal	X	1990	Yes
1997	Poland	X	–	No

TABLE A1.5 (*Continued*):

Year	Country or territory	Offences for which capital punishment was abolished		Whether abolitionist *de facto* (last execution at least 10 years prior to first abolition)
		All offences	Ordinary offences	
1997	South Africa	X	1995	No
1998	Azerbaijan	X	–	No
1998	Bulgaria	X	–	No
1998	Canada	X	1976	Yes
1998	Estonia	X	–	No
1998	Lithuania	X	–	No
1998	UK, GB & Northern Ireland	X	1965	No
1999	Timor Leste (East Timor)	X	–	No
1999	Latvia		X	No
1999	Turkmenistan	X	–	No
1999	Ukraine	X	–	No
2000	Côte d'Ivoire	X	–	Yes
2000	Malta	X	1971	Yes
2001	Bosnia-Herzegovina	X	1997	No
2001	Chile		X	Yes
2002	Cyprus	X	1983	Yes
2002	Serbia-Montenegro[2]	X	2001	Yes
2003	Armenia	X	–	Yes
2004	Greece	X	1993	Yes
2004	Turkey	X	2002	Yes
2004	Bhutan	X	–	Yes
2004	Samoa	X	–	Yes
2004	Senegal	X	–	Yes
2005	Liberia	X	–	Yes
2005	Mexico	X	–	Yes
2006	Philippines	X	–	No
2007	Albania	X	2000	No
2007	Rwanda	X	–	No
2007	Kazakhstan		X	No
2007	Kyrgyzstan	X	–	No

[1] See Table A1.2 n. 1.
[2] Montenegro became independent in 2006.

Appendix 2
Ratification of International Treaties

Countries that have signed or ratified the Second Optional Protocol to the International Covenant on Civil and Political Rights (ICCPR) and/or Protocol No. 6 to the European Convention for the Protection of Human Rights and Fundamental Freedoms (ECHR), Protocol No. 13 to the ECHR, and the Protocol to the American Convention on Human Rights (ACHR). Also, countries that have already abolished the death penalty completely or for ordinary crimes and have ratified the American Convention on Human Rights (Art. 4.3 bars the re-imposition of the death penalty once it has been abolished).

TABLE A 2.1

Countries bound by ratification (R) of at least one of these instruments = 76 plus 6 that have acceded by signature (S) = 82 (at 31 December 2007)

Country	Second Optional Protocol to the ICCPR	Protocol No. 6. ECHR	Protocol No. 13 ECHR	Protocol to the ACHR	ACHR
Albania	R (2007)	R (2000)	R (2007)		
Andorra	R (2006)	R (1996)	R (2003)		
Antigua				S (2006)	
Argentina	S (2006)				
Armenia		R (2003)	S (2006)		
Australia	R (1990)				
Austria	R (1993)	R (1984)	R (2004)		
Azerbaijan	R (1999)	R (2002)			
Belgium	R (1998)	R (1998)	R (2003)		
Bolivia					R (1979)
Bosnia-Herzegovina	R (2001)	R (2002)	R (2003)		
Bulgaria	R (1999)	R (1999)	R (2003)		
Brazil				R (1996)	R (1992)
Canada	R (2005)				
Cape Verde	R (2000)				
Chile	S (2001)			S (2001)	R (1990)
Colombia	R (1997)				R (1973)
Costa Rica	R (1998)			R (1998)	R (1970)
Croatia	R (1995)	R (1997)	R (2003)		

TABLE A2.1 (*Continued*):

Country	Second Optional Protocol to the ICCPR	Protocol No. 6. ECHR	Protocol No. 13 ECHR	Protocol to the ACHR	ACHR
Cyprus	R (1999)	R (2000)	R (2003)		
Czech Republic	R (2004)	R (1992)	R (2004)		
Denmark	R (1994)	R (1983)	R (2002)		
Djibouti	R (2002)				
Dominican Republic					R (1993)
Ecuador	R (1993)			R (1998)	R (1977)
El Salvador					R (1978)
Estonia	R (2004)	R (1998)	R (2004)		
Finland	R (1991)	R (1990)	R (2004)		
France	R (2007)	R (1986)	R (2007)		
Georgia	R (1999)	R (2003)	R (2003)		
Germany	R (1992)	R (1989)	R (2004)		
Greece	R (1997)	R (1998)	R (2005)		
Guinea-Bissau	S (2000)				
Haiti					R (1977)
Honduras	S (1990)				R (1977)
Hungary	R (1994)	R (1992)	R (2003)		
Iceland	R (1991)	R (1987)	R (2004)		
Ireland	R (1993)	R (1994)	R (2002)		
Italy	R (1995)	R (1988)	S (2002)		
Latvia		R (1999)	S (2002)		
Liberia	R (2005)				
Liechtenstein	R (1998)	R (1990)	R (2002)		
Lithuania	R (2002)	R (1999)	R (2004)		
Luxembourg	R (1992)	R (1985)	R (2006)		
Macedonia (FYROM)	R (1995)	R (1997)	R (2004)		
Malta	R (1994)	R (1991)	R (2002)		
Mexico	R (2007)			R (2007)	R (1981)
Moldova	R (2006)	R (1997)	R (2006)		
Monaco	R (2000)	R (2005)	R (2005)		
Montenegro[1]	R (2006)	R (2006)	R (2006)		
Mozambique	R (1993)				
Namibia	R (1994)				
Netherlands	R (1986)	R (2006)	R (1991)		
Nepal	R (1998)				
New Zealand	R (1990)				

TABLE A2.1 (*Continued*):

Country	Second Optional Protocol to the ICCPR	Protocol No. 6. ECHR	Protocol No. 13 ECHR	Protocol to the ACHR	ACHR
Nicaragua	S (1990)			R (1999)	R (1979)
Norway	R (1988)	R (2005)	R (1991)		
Panama	R (1993)			R (1991)	R (1978)
Paraguay	R (2003)			R (2000)	R (1989)
Peru					R (1978)
Philippines	S (2006)				
Poland	S (2000)	R (2000)	S (2002)		
Portugal	R (1990)	R (1986)	R (2003)		
Romania	R (1991)	R (1994)	R (2003)		
Russian Federation		S (1997)			
San Marino	R (2004)	R (1989)	R (2003)		
Saō Tomé and Principe	S (2000)				
Serbia	R (2001)	R (2004)	R (2004)		
Seychelles	R (1994)				
Slovak Republic	R (1999)	R (1992)	R (2005)		
Slovenia	R (1994)	R (1994)	R (2003)		
South Africa	R (2002)				
Spain	R (1991)	R (1985)	S (2002)		
Sweden	R (1990)	R (1984)	R (2003)		
Switzerland	R (1994)	R (1987)	R (2002)		
Timor Leste	R (2003)				
Turkey	R (2006)	R (2003)	R (2006)		
Turkmenistan	R (2000)				
Ukraine	R (2007)	R (2000)	R (2003)		
UK	R (1999)	R (1999)	R (2003)		
Uruguay	R (1993)			R (1994)	R (1985)
Venezuela	R (1993)			R (1992)	R (1977)
TOTAL RATIFIED	64	46	40	9	18
TOTAL SIGNED	8	1	5	2	

[1] Formerly part of Serbia-Montenegro.

Appendix 3
International Instruments

Safeguards Guaranteeing Protection of the Rights of those Facing the Death Penalty[1]

1. In countries which have not abolished the death penalty, capital punishment may be imposed only for the most serious crimes, it being understood that their scope should not go beyond intentional crimes with lethal or other extremely grave consequences.
2. Capital punishment may be imposed only for a crime for which the death penalty is prescribed by law at the time of its commission, it being understood that if, subsequent to the commission of the crime, provision is made by law for the imposition of a lighter penalty, the offender shall benefit thereby.
3. Persons below 18 years of age at the time of the commission of the crime shall not be sentenced to death, nor shall the death sentence be carried out on pregnant women, or on new mothers, or on persons who have become insane.
4. Capital punishment may be imposed only when the guilt of the person charged is based upon clear and convincing evidence leaving no room for an alternative explanation of the facts.
5. Capital punishment may only be carried out pursuant to a final judgment rendered by a competent court after legal process which gives all possible safeguards to ensure a fair trial, at least equal to those contained in article 14 of the International Covenant on Civil and Political Rights, including the right of anyone suspected of or charged with a crime for which capital punishment may be imposed to adequate legal assistance at all stages of the proceedings.
6. Anyone sentenced to death shall have the right to appeal to a court of higher jurisdiction, and steps should be taken to ensure that such appeals shall become mandatory.
7. Anyone sentenced to death shall have the right to seek pardon, or commutation of sentence; pardon or commutation of sentence may be granted in all cases of capital punishment.
8. Capital punishment shall not be carried out pending any appeal or other recourse procedure or other proceeding relating to pardon or commutation of the sentence.
9. Where capital punishment occurs, it shall be carried out so as to inflict the minimum possible suffering.

---

[1] Economic and Social Council resolution 1984/50.

Additions to Safeguards as Agreed by the Economic and Social Council Resolution 1989/64

1. Affording special protection to persons facing charges for which the death penalty is provided by allowing time and facilities for the preparation of their defence, including the adequate assistance of counsel at every stage of the proceedings, above and beyond the protection afforded in non-capital cases.
2. Providing for mandatory appeals or review with provisions for clemency or pardon in all cases of capital offence.
3. Establishing a maximum age beyond which a person may not be sentenced to death or executed.
4. Eliminating the death penalty for persons suffering from mental retardation or extremely limited mental competence, whether at the stage of sentence or execution.

Strengthening of the Safeguards as Agreed by the Economic and Social Council Resolution 1996/15.

The Council:

1. Encouraged Member States in which the death penalty had not been abolished to ensure that each defendant facing a possible death sentence was given all guarantees to ensure a fair trial, as contained in article 14 of the International Covenant on Civil and Political Rights, and bearing in mind the Basic Principles on the Independence of the Judiciary the Basic Principles on the Role of Lawyers, the Guidelines on the Role of Prosecutors, the Body of Principles for the Protection of All Persons under Any Form of Detention or Imprisonment, and the Standard Minimum Rules for the Treatment of Prisoners.
2. Also encouraged Member states in which the death penalty had not been abolished to ensure that defendants who did not sufficiently understand the language used in court were fully informed, by way of interpretation or translation, of all the charges against them and the content of the relevant evidence deliberated in court.
3. Called upon Member States in which the death penalty might be carried out to allow adequate time for the preparation of appeals to a court of higher jurisdiction and for the completion of appeal proceedings, as well as petitions for clemency, in order to effectively apply rules 5 and 8 of the safeguards guaranteeing protection of the rights of those facing the death penalty.
4. Also called upon Member States in which the death penalty might be carried out to ensure that officials involved in decisions to carry out an execution were fully informed of the status of appeals and petitions for clemency of the prisoner in question.
5. Urged Member States in which the death penalty might be carried out to effectively apply the Standard Minimum Rules for the Treatment of Prisoners, in order to keep to a minimum the suffering of prisoners under sentence of death and to avoid any exacerbation of such suffering.

International Covenant on Civil and Political Rights, G.A. res. 2200A (XXI), 21 U.N. GAOR Supp. (No. 16) at 52, U.N. DOC. A/6316 (1966), 999 U.N.T.S. 171, Entered Into Force Mar. 23, 1976 (Articles 6, 7, 10, 14, and 15).

Article 6

1. Every human being has the inherent right to life. This right shall be protected by law. No one shall be arbitrarily deprived of his life.
2. In countries which have not abolished the death penalty, sentence of death may be imposed only for the most serious crimes in accordance with the law in force at the time of the commission of the crime and not contrary to the provisions of the present Covenant and to the Convention on the Prevention and Punishment of the Crime of Genocide. This penalty can only be carried out pursuant to a final judgement rendered by a competent court.
3. When deprivation of life constitutes the crime of genocide, it is understood that nothing in this article shall authorize any State Party to the present Covenant to derogate in any way from any obligation assumed under the provisions of the Convention on the Prevention and Punishment of the Crime of Genocide.
4. Anyone sentenced to death shall have the right to seek pardon or commutation of the sentence. Amnesty, pardon or commutation of the sentence of death may be granted in all cases.
5. Sentence of death shall not be imposed for crimes committed by persons below eighteen years of age and shall not be carried out on pregnant women.
6. Nothing in this article shall be invoked to delay or to prevent the abolition of capital punishment by any State Party to the present Covenant.

Article 7

No one shall be subjected to torture or to cruel, inhuman or degrading treatment or punishment. In particular, no one shall be subjected without his free consent to medical or scientific experimentation.

Article 10

1. All persons deprived of their liberty shall be treated with humanity and with respect for the inherent dignity of the human person.
2. (a) Accused persons shall, save in exceptional circumstances, be segregated from convicted persons and shall be subject to separate treatment appropriate to their status as unconvicted persons;
   (b) Accused juvenile persons shall be separated from adults and brought as speedily as possible for adjudication.
3. The penitentiary system shall comprise treatment of prisoners the essential aim of which shall be their reformation and social rehabilitation. Juvenile offenders shall be segregated from adults and be accorded treatment appropriate to their age and legal status.

Article 14

1. All persons shall be equal before the courts and tribunals. In the determination of any criminal charge against him, or of his rights and obligations in a suit at law, everyone shall be entitled to a fair and public hearing by a competent, independent and impartial tribunal established by law. The press and the public may be excluded from all or part of a trial for reasons of morals, public order (ordre public) or national security in a democratic society, or when the interest of the private lives of the parties so requires, or to the extent strictly necessary in the opinion of the court in special circumstances where publicity would prejudice the interests of justice; but any judgement rendered in a criminal case or in a suit at law shall be made public except where the interest of juvenile persons otherwise requires or the proceedings concern matrimonial disputes or the guardianship of children.
2. Everyone charged with a criminal offence shall have the right to be presumed innocent until proved guilty according to law.
3. In the determination of any criminal charge against him, everyone shall be entitled to the following minimum guarantees, in full equality:

   (a) To be informed promptly and in detail in a language which he understands of the nature and cause of the charge against him;
   (b) To have adequate time and facilities for the preparation of his defence and to communicate with counsel of his own choosing;
   (c) To be tried without undue delay;
   (d) To be tried in his presence, and to defend himself in person or through legal assistance of his own choosing; to be informed, if he does not have legal assistance, of this right; and to have legal assistance assigned to him, in any case where the interests of justice so require, and without payment by him in any such case if he does not have sufficient means to pay for it;
   (e) To examine, or have examined, the witnesses against him and to obtain the attendance and examination of witnesses on his behalf under the same conditions as witnesses against him;
   (f) To have the free assistance of an interpreter if he cannot understand or speak the language used in court;
   (g) Not to be compelled to testify against himself or to confess guilt.
4. In the case of juvenile persons, the procedure shall be such as will take account of their age and the desirability of promoting their rehabilitation.
5. Everyone convicted of a crime shall have the right to his conviction and sentence being reviewed by a higher tribunal according to law.
6. When a person has by a final decision been convicted of a criminal offence and when subsequently his conviction has been reversed or he has been pardoned on the ground that a new or newly discovered fact shows conclusively that there has been a miscarriage of justice, the person who has suffered punishment as a result of such conviction shall be compensated according to law, unless it is proved that the non-disclosure of the unknown fact in time is wholly or partly attributable to him.
7. No one shall be liable to be tried or punished again for an offence for which he has already been finally convicted or acquitted in accordance with the law and penal procedure of each country.

Article 15

1. No one shall be held guilty of any criminal offence on account of any act or omission which did not constitute a criminal offence, under national or international law, at the time when it was committed. Nor shall a heavier penalty be imposed than the one that was applicable at the time when the criminal offence was committed. If, subsequent to the commission of the offence, provision is made by law for the imposition of the lighter penalty, the offender shall benefit thereby.
2. Nothing in this article shall prejudice the trial and punishment of any person for any act or omission which, at the time when it was committed, was criminal according to the general principles of law recognized by the community of nations.

Bibliography

References to UN documents, such as resolutions and reports of committees and of the Special Rapporteur, as well as those of the Council of Europe and the European Community, were too numerous to include and can be found in the footnotes, as can the citations to reports from Amnesty International, the Death Penalty Information Center, and other organizations. Amnesty International reports can be easily traced by country or subject matter by using the AI Index reference. Only major reports from organizations are included in the Bibliography.

Abramsky, S., 'Lifers: Prisoners' Dilemma', *Legal Affairs* (April 2004), pp. 1–45.

Acker, J. R., 'Mandatory Capital Punishment for the Life Term Inmate who Commits Murder: Judgments of Fact and Value in Law and Social Sciences', *Criminal and Civil Confinement* 11–12 (1985), pp. 267–327.

—— 'Research on the Death Penalty: A Different Agenda: The Supreme Court, Empirical Research Evidence, and Capital Punishment Decisions, 1986–1989', *Law and Society Review* 27 (1993), pp. 65–87.

—— Bohm, R. M. and Lanier, C. S. (eds.), *America's Experiment with Capital Punishment* (1st edn., 1998; 2nd edn., 2003), Durham North Carolina: Carolina Academic Press.

—— and Karp, D. R. (eds.), *Wounds that do not Bind: Victim-Based Perspectives on the Death Penalty* (2006), Durham, North Carolina: Carolina Academic Press.

—— and Lanier, C. S., 'The Dimensions of Capital Murder', *Criminal Law Bulletin* 29 (1993), pp. 379–417.

—— —— 'In Fairness and Mercy: Statutory Mitigating Factors in Capital Punishment Laws', *Criminal Law Bulletin* 30 (1994), pp. 299–345.

—— —— "Parsing this Lexicon of Death", Aggravating Factors in Capital Sentencing Statutes', *Criminal Law Bulletin* 30 (1994), pp. 107–152.

—— —— 'Matters of Life and Death: The Sentencing Provisions of the Capital Punishment Statutes', *Criminal Law Bulletin* 31 (1995), pp. 19–60.

—— —— 'Unfit to Live, Unfit to Die: Incompetence for Execution under Modern Death Penalty Legislation', *Criminal Law Bulletin* 33 (1997), pp. 107–150.

—— —— 'May God—or the Governor—Have Mercy: Executive Clemency and Executions in Modern Death-Penalty Systems', *Criminal Law Bulletin* 36 (2000), pp. 200–237.

—— —— 'Beyond Human Ability? The Rise and Fall of Death Penalty Legislation' in J. R. Acker, R. M. Bohm, and C. S. Lanier (eds.), *America's Experiment with Capital Punishment* (2nd edn., 2003), pp. 85–125.

—— and Walsh, E. R., 'Challenging the Death Penalty under State Constitutions', *Vanderbilt Law Review* 42 (1989), pp. 1299–1363.

Adams, J. C., 'Racial Disparity and the Death Penalty', *Law and Contemporary Problems* 61 (1998), pp. 153–170.

Adeyemi, A. A., 'Death Penalty: Criminological Perspectives. The Nigerian Situation', *Revue Internationale de Droit Pénal* 58 (1987), pp. 485–502.

Albrecht, H., 'The Death Penalty in China from a European Perspective', in M. Nowak and Xin Chunying (eds.), *EU-China Human Rights Dialogue: Proceedings of the Second EU-China Legal Experts Seminar, Beijing, 19–20 October 1998* (2000).

—— 'Post-Adjudication Dispositions in Comparative Perspective', in M. Tonry and R. Frase (eds.), *Sentencing and Sanctions in Western Countries* (2001), Oxford: Oxford University Press.

—— and Research Unit Of The Death Penalty Cases Survey, Cass Institute Of Law, *Strengthening the Defence in Death Penalty Cases in the People's Republic of China* (2006), Freiburg-im-Breisgau: Max Plank Institute for Foreign and International Criminal Law.

Al-hewesh, S. M., 'Shari'ā Penalties and Ways of their Implementation in the Kingdom of Saudi Arabia', in *The Effects of Islamic Legislation on Crime Prevention in Saudi Arabia* (1980), Rome: Kingdom of Saudi Arabia in collaboration with UNSDRI, pp. 349–400.

American Bar Association, *A Gathering Momentum: Continuing Impacts of the American Bar Association Call for a Moratorium on Executions* (January 2000).

—— 'ABA Guidelines for the Appointment and Performance of Defense Counsel in Death Penalty Cases', *Hofstra Law Review* 31 (2003), pp. 913–1090.

——American Civil Liberties Union, *The Persistent Problem of Racial Disparities in the Federal Death Penalty* (2007), Durham NC: ACLU Capital Punishment Project.

American Medical Association, 'Council on Ethical and Judicial Affairs. American Medical Association: Physician Participation in Capital Punishment', *Journal of the American Medical Association* 270 (1993), pp. 365–368.

American University Law Review, Note, 'The Death Penalty in Georgia: An Aggravating Circumstance', 30 (1981), pp. 835–861.

Amnesty International, *The Death Penalty Amnesty International Report* (1979), London: Amnesty International, AI Index: ACT 05/03/79.

Amsterdam, A. G., 'Courtroom Contortions. How America's application of the death penalty erodes the principle of equal justice under law', *American Prospect* 15 (7) (2004), pp. 19–21.

Anagnostopoulos, I. G. and Magliveras, K. D., *Criminal Law in Greece* (2000), London: Kluwer Law International.

Ancel, M., *The Death Penalty in European Countries* (1962), Strasbourg: Council of Europe.

Andenaes, J., *Punishment and Deterrence* (1974), Ann Arbor: University of Michigan Press.

Antoine, R. M. B., 'The Judicial Committee of the Privy Council—An Inadequate Remedy for Death Row Prisoners', *International and Comparative Law Quarterly* 41 (1992), pp. 179–190.

Appleton, C. and Grøver, B., 'The Pros and Cons of Life Without Parole', *The British Journal of Criminology* 47 (2007), pp. 597–615.

Archer, D. and Gartner, R., *Violence and Crime in Cross-National Perspective* (1994), New Haven CT: Yale University Press.

Arendt, H., *Eichmann in Jerusalem: A Report on the Banality of Evil* (new edn., 1994), Harmondsworth: Penguin Books Ltd.

Arriens, J. (ed.), *Welcome to Hell: Letters and Other Writings by Prisoners on Death Row in the United States* (1991), Cambridge: Ian Faulkner Publishing.

Ashworth, A., *Sentencing and Criminal Justice* (4th edn., 2005) Cambridge: Cambridge University Press.

Badinter, R., *L'Abolition* (2000), Paris: Fayard.

Bailey, V., 'The Shadow of the Gallows: the Death Penalty and the British Labour Government, 1945–1951', *Law and History Review* 18 (2), 2000, pp. 305–350.

Bailey, W. C., 'An Analysis of the Deterrent Effect of the Death Penalty in North Carolina', *North Carolina Central Law Journal* 10 (1978), pp. 29–51.

—— 'Deterrence and the Death Penalty for Murder in Utah', *Journal of Contemporary Law* 5 (1978), pp. 1–20.

—— 'Deterrence and the Death Penalty for Murder in Oregon', *Williamette Law Review* 16 (1979), pp. 67–85.

—— 'The Deterrent Effect of the Death Penalty for Murder in California', *Southern California Law Review* 52 (1979), pp. 743–764.

—— 'The Deterrent Effect of the Death Penalty for Murder in Ohio', *Cleveland State Law Review* 28 (1979), pp. 51–81.

—— 'A Multivariate Cross-Sectional Analysis of the Deterrent Effect of the Death Penalty', *Sociology and Social Research* 64 (1980), pp. 183–207.

—— 'Capital Punishments and Lethal Assaults against Police', *Criminology* 19 (1982), pp. 608–625.

—— 'Murder and Capital Punishment in the Nation's Capital', *Justice Quarterly* 1–2 (1984), pp. 211–223.

—— 'The General Preventive Effect of Capital Punishment on Non-Capital Felonies', in R. M. Bohm (ed.), *The Death Penalty in America: Current Research* (1991), pp. 21–38.

—— and Peterson, R. D., 'Police Killings and Capital Punishment: The Post-*Furman* Period', *Criminology* 25 (1987), pp. 1–25.

—— —— 'Murder and Capital Punishment: A Monthly Time-Series Analysis of Execution Publicity', *American Sociological Review* 54 (1989), pp. 722–74.

—— —— 'Murder, Capital Punishment and Deterrence: A Review of the Evidence and an Examination of Police Killings', *Journal of Social Issues* 50(2) (Summer 1994), pp. 53–74.

Baker, D. N., Lambert, E. G., and Jenkins, M., 'College Students Racial Differences in Death Penalty Support and Opposition: A Preliminary Study of White and Black', *Journal of Black Studies* 35 (2005), pp. 201–224.

Baldus, D. C., 'The Death Penalty Dialogue between Law and Social Science', *Indiana Law Journal* 70 (1995), pp. 1033–1041.

—— Pulaski, C., A., Woodworth, G., and Kyle, F. D., 'Identifying Comparatively Excessive Sentences of Death: A Quantitative Approach', *Stanford Law Review* 33 (1980), pp. 1–74.

—— and Woodworth, G., 'Race Discrimination and the Death Penalty: An Empirical and Legal Overview', in J. R. Acker, R. M. Bohm, and C. S. Lanier (eds.), (2nd. edn., 2003), *America's Experiment with Capital Punishment*, pp. 501–551.

—— —— 'Race Discrimination and the Legitimacy of Capital Punishment: Reflections on the Interaction of Fact and Perception', *DePaul Law Review* 53 (2004), pp. 1411–1489.

—— —— and Pulaski, C., A., 'Arbitrariness and Discrimination in the Administration of the Death Penalty: A Challenge to State Supreme Courts', *Stetson Law Review* 15 (1986), pp. 133–261.

—— —— ——, *Equal Justice and the Death Penalty* (1990), Boston: Northeastern University Press.

—— —— —— 'Reflections on the "Inevitability" of Racial Discrimination in Capital Sentencing and the "Impossibility" of its Prevention, Detection and Correction', *Washington and Lee Law Review* 51 (1994), pp. 359–430.

—— —— Young, G. L., and Christ, A. M., 'Arbitrariness and Discrimination in the Administration of the Death Penalty: A Legal and Empirical Analysis of the Nebraska Experience (1973–1999)', *Nebraska Law Review* 81 (2002), pp. 486–756.

—— —— Zuckerman, D., and Weiner, N. A., 'The Use of Peremptory Challenges in Capital Murder Trials: A Legal and Empirical Analysis' Symposium: Race, Crime, and the Constitution', *University of Pennsylvania Journal of Constitutional Law* 3 (2001), pp. 3–170.

—— —— Zuckerman, D., Weiner, N. A., and Broffitt, B., 'Racial Discrimination and the Death Penalty in the *Post-Furman* Era: An Empirical and Legal Overview, with Recent Findings from Philadelphia', *Cornell Law Review* 83 (1998), pp. 1638–1770.

Bandes, S., 'Empathy, Narrative, and Victim Impact Statements', *University of Chicago Law Review* 63 (1996), pp. 361–412.

Banner, S., *The Death Penalty: An American History* (2002), Cambridge, Mass: Harvard University Press.

Bantekas, I. and Hodgkinson, P., 'Capital Punishment at the United Nations: Recent Developments', *Criminal Law Forum* 11(1) (2000), pp. 23–34.

Barkan, S. E. and Cohn, S. F., 'Racial Prejudice and Support for the Death Penalty by Whites', *Journal of Research in Crime and Delinquency* 31 (1994), pp. 202–209.

—— —— 'On Reducing White Support for the Death Penalty: A Pessimistic Appraisal', *Criminology and Public Policy* 4(1) (February 2005), pp. 39–44.

Barnett, A., 'Some Distribution Patterns for the Georgia Death Sentence', *University of California Davis Law Review* 18 (1985), pp. 1327–1363.

Barry, D. and Williams, E., 'Russia's Death Penalty Dilemmas', *Criminal Law Forum* 8 (1997), pp. 231–258.

Bassiouni, M. C., 'Death as a Penalty in the Shari'ā', in P. Hodgkinson and W.A. Schabas (eds.), *Capital Punishment: Strategies for Abolition* (2004), pp. 169–185.

Batra, B. J. 'The Death Penalty in India—Issues and Aspects', paper given to the launch seminar of the China-EU project, *Moving the Debate Forward—China's Use of the Death Penalty* 20–21 June 2007, College for Criminal Law Science of Beijing Normal University and Great Britain-China Centre.

Bayer, R., 'Lethal Injections and Capital Punishment: Medicine in the Service of the State', *Journal of Prison and Jail Health* 4(1) (1984), pp. 7–15.

Beccaria, C., *On Crimes and Punishments* (1764), trans. H. Paolucci (1963), Indianapolis: Bobbs-Merrill.

Beck, E., Britto. S., and Andrews, A., *In the Shadow of Death: Restorative Justice and Death Row Families* (2007), Oxford: Oxford University Press.

Bedau, H. A., 'Felony Murder Rape and the Mandatory Death Penalty: A Study in Discretionary Justice', *Suffolk University Law Review* 10 (1976), pp. 493–520.

—— *Death is Different* (1987), Boston: Northeastern University Press.

——'Imprisonment vs Death: Does Avoiding Schwarzschild's Paradox lead to Sheleff's Dilemma?', *Albany Law Review* 54 (1990), pp. 481–95.

—— 'The Decline of Executive Clemency in Capital Cases', *New York University Review of Law and Social Change* 18 (1990–91), pp. 255–272.

—— 'The United States', in P. Hodgkinson and A. Rutherford (eds.), *Capital Punishment: Global Issues and Prospects* (1996), pp. 45–76.

—— 'The Controversy over Public Support for the Death Penalty: The Death Penalty versus Life Imprisonment', in H. A. Bedau (ed.), *The Death Penalty in America: Current Controversies* (1997), Oxford: Oxford University Press, pp. 84–89.

—— 'Abolishing the Death Penalty even for the Worst Murderers' in A. Sarat (ed.), *The Killing State: Capital Punishment in Law, Politics, and Culture* (1999), pp. 40–59.

—— 'Abolishing the death penalty in the United States: an analysis of institutional obstacles and future prospects', in P. Hodgkinson and W.A. Schabas (eds.), *Capital Punishment: Strategies for Abolition* (2004), Cambridge: Cambridge University Press, pp. 186–207.

——and Cassell, P. (eds.), *Debating the Death Penalty* (2004), New York: Oxford University Press.

—— and Radelet, M. L., 'The Myth of Infallibility: A Reply to Markman and Cassell', *Stanford Law Review* 41 (1988), pp. 161–170.

Beloof, D. E., *Victims in Criminal Procedure* (1999), North Carolina: Carolina Academic Press.

—— 'Constitutional Implications of Crime Victims as Participants', *Cornell Law Review* 88 (2003), pp. 282–305.

Bendremer, F. J., Bramnick, G., Jones, J. C., and Lippman, S.C., '*McCleskey v Kemp*: Constitutional Tolerance for Racially Disparate Capital Sentencing', *University of Miami Law Review* 41 (1986), pp. 295–355.

Bentele, U. and Bowers, W. J., 'How Jurors Decide on Death: Guilt is Overwhelming; Aggravation requires Death; and Mitigation is no Excuse', *Brooklyn Law Review* 66 (2001), pp. 1011–1080.

Berger, V., 'The Chiropractor as Brain Surgeon: Defense Lawyering in Capital Cases', *New York University Review of Law and Social Change* 18 (1990–91), pp. 245–254.

—— '*Herrera v Collins*: The Gateway of Innocence for Death-Sentenced Prisoners Leads Now Here', *William and Mary Law Review* 35 (1994), pp. 943–1023.

Berg, T. C., 'Religious Conservatives and the Death Penalty', in 'Symposium: Religious Role in the Administration of the Death Penalty', *William and Mary Bill of Rights Journal* 9 (2000), pp. 31–60.

Beristain, A., 'La sanction capitale en Espagne: Reférénce spéciale à la dimension religieuse Chrétienne', *Revue Internationale de Droit Pénal* 58 (1987), pp. 613–636.

Berk, R., New Claims about Executions and General Deterrence: Déjà Vu All Over Again?', *Journal of Empirical Legal Studies* 2 (2) (2005), pp. 303–330.

—— Boger, J. and Weiss, R., 'Research on the Death Penalty: Chance and the Death Penalty', *Law and Society Review* 27 (1993), pp. 89–110.

—— —— 'Rejoinder', *Law and Society Review* 27 (1993), pp. 125–127.

Beyleveld, D., 'Identifying, Explaining and Predicting Deterrence', *British Journal of Criminology* 19 (1979), pp. 205–224.

Bhagwat, A., 'The *McCleskey* Puzzle: Remedying Prosecutorial Discrimination against Black Victims in Capital Sentencing', in D. J. Hutchinson, D. A. Strauss, and G. R. Stone (eds.), *1998 The Supreme Court Review* (1999), pp. 145–192.

Bienen, L. B., 'A Good Murder', *Fordham Urban Law Journal* 20 (1993), pp. 585–607.

—— Weiner, N. A., Allison, P. D., and Mills, D. L., 'The Reimposition of Capital Punishment in New Jersey: Felony Murder Cases', *Albany Law Review* 54 (1990), pp. 709–817.

Black, T. and Orsagh, T., 'New Evidence on the Efficacy of Sanctions as a Deterrent to Homicide', *Social Science Quarterly* 58 (1978), pp. 616–630.

Blackshield, A. R., 'Capital Punishment in India', *Journal of the Indian Law Institute* 21 (1979), pp. 137–226.

Blume, J. H., 'Ten Years of *Payne*: Victim Impact Evidence in Capital Cases', *Cornell Law Review* 88 (2003), pp. 257–281.

—— 'Killing the Willing: 'Volunteers, Suicide and Competency', *Michigan Law Review* 103 (2005), p. 939–1009.

—— and Johnson, S. L., 'Killing the non-willing: *Atkins*, the volitionally incapacitated, and the death penalty', 55 *South Carolina Law Review* (2003), pp. 93–143.

—— —— and Eisenberg, T., 'Post-*McCleskey* Racial Discrimination Claims in Capital Cases', *Cornell Law Review* 83 (1998), pp. 1771–1810.

Boaz, J. E., 'Summary Processes and the Rule of Law: Expediting Death Penalty Cases in Federal Courts', *Yale Law Journal* 95 (1985), pp. 349–370.

Bohm, R. M. (ed.), *The Death Penalty in America: Current Research* (1991), Cincinnati: Anderson Publishing Co.

Bohm, R. M., 'American Death Penalty Opinion, 1936–1986: A Critical Examination of the Gallup Polls', in R. M. Bohm (ed.), *The Death Penalty in America: Current Research* (1991), pp. 113–143.

—— 'American Death Penalty Opinion: Past, Present, and Future', in J. R. Acker, R. M. Bohm, and C. S. Lanier (eds.), *America's Experiment with Capital Punishment* (2nd edn., 2003), pp. 27–54.

—— 'The Economic Costs of Capital Punishment: Past, Present and Future' in J. R. Acker, R. M. Bohm, and C. S. Lanier (eds.), *America's Experiment with Capital Punishment* (2nd edn., 2003), pp. 573–594.

—— Clark, L. J. and Aveni, A. F., 'Knowledge and Death Penalty Opinions: A Test of the Marshall Hypotheses', *Journal of Research in Crime and Delinquency* 28 (1991), pp. 360–387.

—— and Vogel, R. E., 'A Comparison of Factors Associated with Uninformed and Informed Death Penalty Opinions', *Journal of Criminal Justice* 22 (1994), pp. 125–143.

—— —— and Maisto, A. A., 'Knowledge and Death Penalty Opinion: A Panel Study', *Journal of Criminal Justice* 21 (1993), pp. 29–45.

Bonner, R., 'Death Penalty', *Annual Survey of American Law* (1984), pp. 493–513.

Bonnie, R. J., 'Dilemmas in Administering the Death Penalty: Conscientious Abstention, Professional Ethics, and the Needs of the Legal System', *Law and Human Behavior* 14 (1990), pp. 67–90.

—— 'Grounds for Professional Abstention in Capital Cases: A Reply to Brodsky', *Law and Human Behavior* 14 (1990), pp. 99–102.

—— 'Preserving Justice in Capital Cases while Streamlining the Process of Collateral Review', *University of Toledo Law Review* 23 (1991), pp. 99–116.

—— 'Mentally Ill Prisoners on Death Row: Unsolved Puzzles for Courts and Legislatures', *Catholic University Law Review* 54 (2004–2005), pp. 1169–1193.

Borg, M. J. and Radelet, M., 'On botched executions', in P. Hodgkinson and W. A. Schabas (eds.), *Capital Punishment: Strategies for Abolition* (2004), pp. 143–168.

Bossuyt, M. J., *The Administration of Justice and the Human Rights of Detainees* (1987), United Nations.

Bowers, W. J., 'The Pervasiveness of Arbitrariness and Discrimination under Post-Furman Capital Statutes', *Journal of Criminal Law and Criminology* 74 (1983), pp. 1067–1110.

—— 'The Effect of Executions is Brutalization, not Deterrence', in K. C. Haas and J. A. Inciardi (eds.), *Challenging Capital Punishment* (1988), pp. 49–89.

—— 'Capital punishment and contemporary values: People's misgivings and the court's misperceptions', *Law and Society Review* 27 (1993), pp. 157–175.

—— and Foglia, W. D., 'Still Singularly Agonizing: Law's Failure to Purge Arbitrariness from Capital Sentencing', *Criminal Law Bulletin* 39(1) (2003), pp. 51–86.

—— and Pierce, G. L., 'The Illusion of Deterrence in Isaac Ehrlich's Research on Capital Punishment', *Yale Law Journal* 85 (1975), pp. 187–208.

—— —— and McDevitt, J. F., *Legal Homicide: Death as Punishment in America, 1864–1982* (2nd edn., 1984), Boston: Northeastern University Press.

—— Fleury-Steiner, B. D., and Antonio, M. E., 'The Capital Sentencing Decision: Guided Discretion, Reasoned Moral Judgment, or Legal Fiction', in J. R. Acker, R. M. Bohm, and C. S. Lanier (eds.), *America's Experiment with Capital Punishment* (2nd edn., 2003), pp. 413–467.

—— Sandys, M., and Brewer, T. W., 'Crossing racial boundaries: A closer look at the roots of racial bias in capital sentencing when the defendant is black and the victim is white', *De Paul Law Review* 53(4) (2004), pp. 1497–1538.

—— Sandys, M., and Steiner, B. D. 'Foreclosed Impartiality in Capital Sentencing: Juror's Predispositions, Guilt-Trial Experience, and Premature Decision-Making', *Cornell Law Review* 83 (1998), pp. 1476–1556.

—— and Steiner, B. D., 'Death by Default: An Empirical Demonstration of False and Forced Choices in Capital Sentencing', *Texas Law Review* 77 (1999), pp. 605–717.

—— —— and Sandys, M., 'Death Sentencing in Black and White: An Empirical Analysis of the Role of Jurors' Race and Jury Racial Composition', *University of Pennsylvania Journal of Constitutional Law* 3 (2001), pp. 171–272.

—— and Vandiver, M., *New Yorkers Want an Alternative to the Death Penalty*, (1991) Boston: Northeastern University Press.

—— —— *Nebraskans Want an Alternative to the Death Penalty*, (1991) Boston: Northeastern University Press.

Boxer, J. T., 'China's Death Penalty: Undermining Legal Reform and Threatening National Economic Interest', *Suffolk Transnational Law Review* 22 (1999), pp. 593–618.

Brennan, W. J., Jr., 'Neither Victims nor Executioners', *Notre Dame Journal of Law, Ethics and Public Policy: Symposium on Capital Punishment* 8 (1994), pp. 1–9.

Bright, S., 'Political Attacks on the Judiciary: Can justice be done amid efforts to intimidate and remove judges from office for unpopular decisions?', *New York University Law Review* 72 (1997), pp. 308–330.

—— 'Symposium: Restructuring Federal Courts: Habeas: Elected Judges and the Death Penalty in Texas. Why Full Habeas Corpus Review by Independent Federal Judges is Indispensable to Protecting Constitutional Rights', *Texas Law Review* 78 (2000), pp. 1805–1837.

—— 'The Politics of Capital Punishment: The Sacrifice of Fairness for Executions', in J. R. Acker, R. M. Bohm, and C. S. Lanier (eds.), *America's Experiment with Capital Punishment* (2nd edn., 2003), pp. 127–146.

—— 'Why the United States will join the rest of the world in abandoning capital punishment' in H. Bedau and P. Cassell (eds.), *Debating the Death Penalty* (2004), pp. 152–182.

British Medical Association, *Medicine Betrayed: The Participation of Doctors in Human Rights Abuses*, Report of a Working Party (1992), London: Zed Books.

Brodsky, S. L., 'Professional Ethics and Professional Morality in the Assessment of Competence for Execution: A Response to Bonnie', *Law and Human Behavior* 14 (1990), pp. 91–97.

Brooks, R. W. and Raphael, S., 'Life terms or death sentences: the uneasy relationship between judicial elections and capital punishment', *Journal of Criminal Law and Criminology*, 92 (2003), pp. 609–639.

Browne, N. and Candelia, S. (eds.), *Managing effective alternatives to capital punishment: Centre for Capital Punishment Studies Occasional Paper Series Three:* (2005), London: CCPS University of Westminster.

Burnett, C., *Justice Denied* (2002), Boston: Northeastern University Press.

Burnham, M. A., 'Saving Constitutional Rights from Judicial Scrutiny: the Savings Clause in the Law of the Commonwealth Caribbean', *The University of Miami Inter-American Law Review*, 36 (2&3) (2005), pp. 249–269.

Burns, G. B., 'The Right to Effective Assistance of a Psychiatrist under *Ake v Oklahoma*', *Criminal Law Bulletin* 30 (1994), pp. 429–457.

Burr, R., 'Litigating with Victim Impact Testimony: The Serendipity That Has Come from *Payne v Tennessee*', *Cornell Law Review* 88 (2003), pp. 517–529.

Byers, K. A., 'Incompetency, Execution, and the Use of Antipsychotic Drugs', *Arkansas Law Review* 47 (1994), pp. 361–391.

Calabresi, S. G. and Lawson, G., 'Equity and Hierarchy: Reflections on the Harris Execution', *Yale Law Journal* 102 (1992), pp. 255–279.

Callinan, I. D. F. Hon., 'Capital Punishment' <http://www.nswccl.org.au/docs/pdf/speech%20callinan%202005.pdf>.

Caminker, E. and Chemerinsky, E., 'The Lawless Execution of Robert Alton Harris', *Yale Law Journal* 102 (1992), pp. 225–254.

Carroll, J. E., Note, 'Images of Women and Capital Sentencing among Female Offenders: Exploring the Outer Limits of the Eighth Amendment and Articulated Theories of Justice', *Texas Law Review 75* (1997), pp. 1413–1451.

Cascells, W., Curran, W. J., and Hyg, S. M., 'Doctors, the Death Penalty and Lethal Injections', *New England Journal of Medicine* 307 (1982), pp. 1532–1533.

Cassell, P. G., 'Barbarians at the Gates? A Reply to the Critics of the Victims' Rights Amendment', *Utah Law Review* 2 (1999), pp. 479–544.

Cerna, C. M., 'The Death Penalty and the Jurisprudence of the Inter-American System for the Protection of Human Rights', paper presented to the *Conference on the Death Penalty*, University of Galway, September 2001.

Chan, J. and Oxley, D., 'The deterrent effect of capital punishment: A review of the research evidence', *Crime and Justice Bulletin* No. 84 (2004), New South Wales Bureau of Crime Statistics and Research.

Cheatwood, D., 'Capital Punishment and the deterrence of Violent Crime in Comparable Counties', *Criminal Justice Review* 18(2) (1993), pp. 165–181.

Chenwi, L., *Towards the Abolition of the Death Penalty in Africa: A Human Rights Perspective* (2007), Pretoria, SA: Pretoria University Law Press.

Chirouf, L., 'Defying World Trends: Saudi Arabia's Extensive Use of Capital Punishment', paper presented to the *First World Congress against the Death Penalty*, Strasbourg, 21–23 June 2001.

Cho, B., 'The death penalty in South Korea and Japan: "Asian values" and the debate about capital punishment', in P. Hodgkinson and W. A. Schabas (eds.), *Capital Punishment: Strategies for Abolition* (2004), pp. 253–272.

Cloninger, D. O. and Marchesini, R., 'Execution moratoriums, commutations and deterrence: the case of Illinois', *Applied Economics* 38(9) (2006), pp. 967–973.

—— and Waller, E. R., Bendeck, Y., and Revere, L., 'Returns on negative beta securities: implications for the empirical SML', *Applied Financial Economics* 14(6) (2004), pp. 397–402.

Cochran, J. K., Chamlin, M. B., and Seth, M., 'Deterrence or Brutalization? An Impact Assessment of Oklahoma's Return to Capital Punishment', *Criminology* 32 (1994), pp. 107–134.

Cohen, J., *The Criminal Process in the People's Republic of China 1949–1963* (1968), Cambridge, MA: Harvard University Press.

Coleman, K., Jannson, K., Kuiza, P., and Reed, E., *Homicide, Firearm Offences and Intimate Violence*, Home Office Research Bulletin 02/07 (2007).

Columbia Law Review, Note, 'Distinguishing among Murders when Assessing the Proportionality of the Death Penalty' 85 (1985), pp. 1786–1807.

Constanzo, M., *Just revenge: Costs and consequences of the death penalty* (1997), New York: St. Martin's Press.

—— and Constanzo, S., 'Jury Decision Making in the Capital Penalty Phase: Legal Assumptions, Empirical Findings, and a Research Agenda', *Law and Human Behavior* 16 (1992), pp. 185–201.

Constitution Project, The, *Mandatory Justice: the Death Penalty Revisited* (2006), Washington DC.

Cook, K. M., *Chasing Justice* (2007), New York: Harper Collins.

Copeland, R., Comment, 'Getting it Right from the Beginning: A Critical Examination of Current Criminal Defense in Texas and Proposal for a Statewide Public Defender System', *St. Mary's Law Journal* 32 (2001), pp. 493–540.

Council of Europe, *The Death Penalty: Abolition in Europe* (1999), Strasbourg: Council of Europe Publications.

—— *Death Penalty: Beyond Abolition* (2004), Strasbourg: Council of Europe Publications.

Coyle, A., 'Replacing the death penalty: the vexed issue of alternative sanctions', in P. Hodgkinson and W. A. Schabas (eds.), *Capital Punishment. Strategies for Abolition* (2004), pp. 92–115.

—— 'Management of Long-term and Life-Sentenced Prisoners Internationally in the context of a Human Rights Strategy', in N. Browne and S. Candelia (eds.), *Managing effective alternatives to capital punishment* (2005).

Cullen, F., Fisher, B., and Applegate, B., 'Public Opinion about Punishment and Corrections', in M. Tonry (ed.), *Crime and Justice. A Review of Research* (2000), Chicago: University of Chicago Press, pp. 1–79.

Curran, W. J. and Cascells, W., 'The Ethics of Medical Participation in Capital Punishment by Intravenous Drug Injection', *New England Journal of Medicine* 302 (1980), pp. 226–230.

—— and Hyg, S. M., 'Psychiatric Evaluations and Mitigating Circumstances in Capital Punishment Sentencing', *New England Journal of Medicine* 307 (1982), pp. 1431–1432.

Cushing, R. and Sheffer, S., *Dignity Denied: The Experience of Murder Victims' Family Members Who Oppose the Death Penalty* (2002), Cambridge, MA: Murder Victims' Families for Reconciliation.

Davis, M., 'What is Unethical about Physicians Helping at Executions?,' in *Justice in the Shadow of Death: Rethinking Capital and Lesser Punishments* (1996), pp. 65–94.

Decker, S. H. and Kohfeld, C. W., 'A Deterrence Study of the Death Penalty in Illinois, 1933–1980', *Journal of Criminal Justice* 12 (1984), pp. 367–377.

Deitchman, M. A., Kennedy, W. A., and Beckham, J. C., 'Self-Selection Factors in the Participation of Mental Health Professionals in Competency for Execution Evaluations', *Law and Human Behavior* 15 (1990), pp. 287–303.

Denno, D. W., 'Is Electrocution an Unconstitutional Method of Execution? The Engineering of Death over a Century', *William and Mary Law Review* 35 (1994), pp. 551–692.

—— 'Testing *Penry* and its Progeny', *American Journal of Criminal Law* 22 (1994), pp. 1–75.

—— 'Getting to Death: Are Executions Constitutional?', *Iowa Law Review* 82 (1997), pp. 319–417.

—— Execution and the Forgotten Eighth Amendment', in J. R. Acker, R. M. Bohm, and C. S. Lanier, (eds.), *America's Experiment with Capital Punishment* (1998), pp. 547–577.

—— 'Adieu to Electrocution', *Ohio Northern University Law Review* 26 (2000), pp. 655–688.

—— 'When Legislatures Delegate Death: The Troubling Paradox behind State Uses of Electrocution and Lethal Injection and what it Says about Us', *Ohio State Law Journal* 63 (2002), pp. 63–260.

—— 'Lethally Humane? The Evolution of Executions in the United States', in J. R. Acker, R. M. Bohm, and C. S. Lanier, (eds.), *America's Experiment with Capital Punishment* (2nd edn., 2003), 693–762.

Dezhbakhsh, H., Rubin, P. H., and Shepherd. J. M., 'Does Capital Punishment have a Deterrent Effect? New Data from Postmoratorium Panel Data', *American Law and Economics Review* 5 (2003), pp. 344–376.

—— and Shepherd, J. M., 'The Deterrent Effect of Capital Punishment: Evidence from a Judicial Experiment', *Economic Inquiry*, 44 (2006), pp. 512–525.

Dieter, R. C., *A Crisis of Confidence: American's Doubts about the Death Penalty*, A Death Penalty Information Center Report (June 2007).

Dix, G. E., 'Appellate Review of the Decision to Impose Death', *Georgetown Law Journal* 68 (1979), pp. 97–161.

—— 'Psychological Abnormality and Capital Sentencing: The New "Diminished Responsibility"', *International Journal of Law and Psychiatry* 7 (1984), pp. 249–267.

Dobryninas, A., 'The experience of Lithuania's journey to abolition'. in P. Hodgkinson and W. A. Schabas (eds.), *Capital Punishment: Strategies for Abolition* (2004), pp. 233–252.

ue, J. J. and Wolfers, J., 'The Death Penalty: No Evidence for Deterrence', *onomists' Voice* (April 2004).

—— Uses and Abuses of Empirical Evidence in the Death Penalty Debate', *Stanford Law Review* 58 (2006), pp. 791–846.

Douglass, J. G., 'Confronting Death: Sixth Amendment Rights at Capital Sentencing', 105 *Columbia Law Review* (2005), pp. 1967–2028.

Drewry, G., 'The Politics of Capital Punishment' in G. Drewry and C. Blake (eds.), *Law and the Spirit of Inquiry* (1999) The Hague: Kluwer Law International, pp. 137–159.

Dumbutshena, E., 'The Death Penalty in Zimbabwe' *Revue Internationale de Droit Pénal* 58 (1987), pp. 521–532.

Eberhardt, J. L., Davies, P. G., Purdie-Vaughns, V. J., and Johnson, S. L., 'Looking Deathworthy. Perceived Stereotypicality of Black Defendants Predicts Capital Sentencing Outcomes', *Psychological Science* 17 (5) (2006), pp. 383–386.

Edds, M., *An Expendable Man: the Near-Execution of Earl Washington Jr.* (2003), New York: New York University Press.

Edwards, W. J., 'Capital Punishment and Mental Disability: *Amici Curiae* Brief in *Penry v Johnson*', *Criminal Law Forum* 12 (2001), pp. 267–276.

Ehrlich, I., 'The Deterrent Effect of Capital Punishment: A Question of Life and Death', *American Economic Review* 65 (1975), pp. 397–417.

—— 'Deterrence: Evidence and Inference', *Yale Law Journal* 85 (1975), pp. 209–227.

—— 'Capital Punishment and Deterrence: Some Further Thoughts and Additional Evidence', *Journal of Political Economy* 85 (1977), pp. 741–788.

—— 'On Positive Methodology, Ethics, and Polemics in Deterrence Research', *British Journal of Criminology* 22 (1982), pp. 124–139.

Eisenberg, T., Garvey, S. P., and Wells, M. T., 'Forecasting Life and Death: Juror Race, Religion, and Attitude toward the Death Penalty', *Journal of Legal Studies* 30 (2001), pp. 277–311.

—— —— —— 'The Deadly Paradox of Capital Jurors', 74 *Southern California Law Review* (2001), pp. 371–397.

Ellsworth, P. C. and. Gross, S. R., 'Hardening of the Attitudes: Americans' Views on the Death Penalty', *Journal of Social Issues* 50(2) (Summer 1994), pp. 19–25.

—— and Ross, L., 'Public Opinion and Capital Punishment: A Close Examination of the Views of Abolitionists and Retentionists', *Crime and Delinquency* 29 (1983), pp. 116–169.

Engel, P., *The Abolition of Capital Punishment in New Zealand* (1977), Wellington: Department of Justice.

Erez, E., 'Victim Participation in Sentencing: And the Debate Goes On. . . .', *International Review of Victimology* 3 (1994) pp. 17–32.

—— and Roberts, J. V., 'Victim Participation in the Criminal Justice System' in R. Davis, A. J. Lurigio, and S. Herman (eds.), *Victims of Crime* (3rd edn., 2007), Los Angeles: Sage, pp. 277–298.

—— and Rogers, L., 'Victim Impact Statements and Sentencing Outcomes and Processes: The Perspectives of Legal Professionals', *British Journal of Criminology* 39 (1999), pp. 216–239.

Evans, G. L., '*Perry v. Louisiana* (1990): Can a State Treat an Incompetent Prisoner to Ready him for Execution?', *Bulletin of the American Academy of Psychiatry and Law* 19 (1991), pp. 249–270.

Evans, R.J., *Rituals of Retribution: Capital Punishment in Germany 1600–1987* (1996), Oxford: Oxford University Press.

Ewing, C. P., '"Above all Do No Harm"': The Role of Health and Mental Health Professionals in the Capital Punishment Process', in J. R. Acker, R. M. Bohm, and C. S. Lanier (eds.), *America's Experiment with Capital Punishment* (2nd edn., 2003), pp. 597–612.

Fagan, J., '*Public Policy Choices on Deterrence and the Death Penalty: A Critical Review of New Evidence*', Testimony before the Joint Committee on the Judiciary of the Massachusetts legislature on House Bill 3834, 'An Act Reinstating Capital Punishment in the Commonwealth' (14 July 2005).

—— 'Death and Deterrence Redux: Science, Law and Causal Reasoning on Capital; Punishment', *The Ohio State Journal of Criminal Law* 4 (2006), pp. 255–321.

—— and West, V., 'The Decline of the Juvenile Death Penalty: Scientific Evidence of Evolving Norms', *Journal of Criminal Law and Criminology* 95 (2005), pp. 427–497.

—— Zimring, F. E., and Geller, A., 'Capital Homicide and Capital Punishment: A Market Share Theory of Deterrence', *Texas Law Review* 84 (2006), pp. 1803–1868.

Farber, N. J., Aboff, B. M., Weiner, J., Davis, E. B., Boyer, E. G., and Ubel, P. A, 'Physicians' Willingness to Participate in the Process of Lethal Injection for Capital Punishment', *Annals of International Medicine* 135(10) (2001), pp. 884–888.

Fattah, E. A., 'Perceptions of Violence, Concern about Crime, Fear of Victimization and Attitudes to the Death Penalty', *Canadian Journal of Criminology* 21 (1979), pp. 22–38.

—— 'The Use of the Death Penalty for Drug Offences and for Economic Crime', *Revue Internationale de Droit Pénal* 58 (1987), pp. 723–736.

—— 'Canada's Successful Experience with the Abolition of the Death Penalty', *Canadian Journal of Criminology* 25 (1987), pp. 421–431.

Feldman, M., Mallouh, K., and Lewis, D. O., 'Filicidal Abuse in the Histories of 15 Condemned Murderers', *Bulletin of the American Academy of Psychiatry and Law* 14 (1986), pp. 345–352.

Feltoe, G., 'Extenuating Circumstances: A Life and Death Issue', Zimbabwe Law Review 4 (1987), pp. 60–87.

Fijalkowski, A., 'Capital Punishment in Poland: An aspect of the "cultural life" of death penalty discourse', in A. Sarat and C. Boulanger (eds.), *The Cultural Lives of Capital Punishment: Comparative Perspectives* (2005), pp. 147–168.

Finks, T. O., 'Lethal Injection: An Uneasy Alliance of Law and Medicine', *Journal of Legal Medicine* 4 (1983), pp. 383–403.

Fitzgerald, E., 'Commonwealth Caribbean', in P. Hodgkinson and A. Rutherford (eds.), *Capital Punishment: Global Issues and Prospects* (1996), pp. 143–153.

—— 'Savings Clauses and the Colonial Death Penalty Regime', in *Penal Reform International*, Simons Muirhead and Burton, Foreign and Commonwealth Office, Attorney General's Ministry (Belize), *Commonwealth Caribbean Human Rights Seminar, 12–14 September 2000* (2001), pp. 113–126.

—— 'The Mitigating Exercise in Capital Cases', in *Death Penalty Conference 3–5 June 2005, Barbados: Conference Papers and Recommendations*, London: The Death Penalty Project Ltd., pp. 9–40.

—— and Starmer, K., *A Guide to Sentencing in Capital Cases* (2007), London: The Death Penalty Project Ltd.

Fitzpatrick, J. and Miller, A., 'International Standards on the Death Penalty: Shifting Discourse', *Brooklyn Journal of International Law* 19 (1993), pp. 273–366.

Foglia, W. D., 'They know not what they do: unguided and misguided discretion in Pennsylvania Capital Cases', *Justice Quarterly* 20 (2003), pp. 187–211.

Foley, T. J., 'The New Arbitrariness: Procedural Default in Federal Habeas Claims in Capital Cases', *Loyola of Los Angeles Law Review* 23 (1989), pp. 193–212.

Forst, B. E., 'The Deterrent Effect of Capital Punishment: Cross-Sectional Analysis of the 1960s', *Minnesota Law Review* 61 (1977), pp. 743–767.

Fox, J. A. and Radelet, M. L., 'Persistent Flaws in Econometric Studies of the Deterrent Effect of the Death Penalty', *Loyola of Los Angeles Law Review* 23 (1989), pp. 29–44.

Freedman, E. M., 'Federal Habeas Corpus in Capital Cases', in J. R. Lanier, R. M. Bohm, and C. S. Lanier (eds.), *America's Experiment with Capital Punishment* (2nd edn., 2003), pp. 553–571.

Galliher, J. M. and Galliher, J. F., 'A "Commonsense" Theory of Deterrence and the "Ideology" of Science: the New York Death Penalty Debate', *Journal of Criminal Law and Criminology* 92 (2002), pp. 307–333.

—— Koch, L. M., Keys, D. P., and Guess, T. J., *America without the Death Penalty: States Leading the Way* (2002), Boston: Northeastern University Press.

Gao, Ming Xuan., *The Main Idea in General Provisions of the Criminal Law* (in Chinese) (1986), Tianjin.

—— 'A Brief Dissertation on the Death Penalty in the Criminal Law of the People's Republic of China', *Revue Internationale de Droit Pénal* 58 (1987), pp. 399–405.

Garland, D., *Punishment and Modern Society: A Study in Social Theory* (1990), Oxford: Clarendon Press.

—— 'The Cultural Conditions of Capital Punishment', *Punishment and Society* 4 (2002) 459–487.

—— 'Capital punishment and American culture: some critical reflections', *Punishment and Society* 7 (2005), pp. 347–376.

—— 'Death, Denial, Discourse: On the Forms and Functions of American Capital Punishment' in D. Downes, P. Rock, C. Chinkin, and C. Gearty (eds.), *Crime, Social Control and Human Rights: From Moral Panics to States of Denial, Essays in Honour of Stanley Cohen* (2007), Cullompton: Willan Publishing, pp. 136–144.

—— 'The Peculiar Forms of American Capital Punishment', *Social Research* 74 (2007), pp. 435–464.

Garland, R., 'Capital Punishment', *South African Human Rights Year Book* (7)1 (1996), pp. 1–16.

Garrett, B. L., 'Judging Innocence', *Columbia Law Review* 108, January 2008.

Garvey, S. P. (ed.), *Capital Punishment and the American Future* (2001), Durham, N.C.: Duke University Press.

—— Johnson, S. L., and Marcus, P., 'Correcting Deadly Confusion: Responding to Jury Inquiries in Capital Cases', *Cornell Law Review* 85 (2000), pp. 627–651.

Gatrell, V., *The Hanging Tree. Execution and the English People 1770–1868* (1994) Oxford: Oxford University Press.

Gawande, A., 'When Law and Ethics Collide—Why Physicians Participate in Executions', *New England Journal of Medicine* 354 (12) (23 March 2006), pp. 1221–1229.

Gaylord, M. and Galliher, J. F., 'Death Penalty Politics and Symbolic Law in Hong Kong', *Howard Journal of Criminal Justice* 33 (1994), pp. 19–37.

Gelman, A., Liebman, J. S., West, V., and Kiss, A., 'A Broken System: The Persistent Pattern of Reversals of Death Sentences in the United States', *Journal of Empirical Legal Studies* 1(2) (2004), p. 209.

——— *A Broken System, Pt. II: Why There Is So Much Error in Capital Cases, and What Can be Done About It?* (February 2002), Columbia Law School Publications.

Gemalmaz, M.S., 'The Death Penalty in Turkey (1920–21): Facts, Truths and Illusions', *Criminal Law Forum* 13 (2002), pp. 91–122.

Gewirth, K. E. and Dorne, C. K., 'Imposing the Death Penalty on Juvenile Murderers: A Constitutional Assessment', *Judicature* 75(1) (1991), pp. 6–15.

Gibeaut, J., 'A Painful Way to Die?', *ABA Journal* April 2006.

Gillers, S., 'The Quality of Mercy: Constitutional Accuracy at the Selection Stage of Capital Sentencing', *University of California Davis Law Review* 18 (1985), pp. 1037–1111.

Girling, E., 'European Identity and the Mission against the Death Penalty in the United States' in A. Sarat and C. Boulanger (eds.), *The Cultural Lives of Capital Punishment: Comparative Perspectives* (2005), pp. 112–128.

Gliszczynska, A., Sekowska, K. and Wieruszewski, R., 'The Abolition of the Death Penalty in Poland', in *The Death Penalty in the OSCE Area* (2006), OSCE Background Paper, pp. 19–26.

Godfrey, M. J. and Shiraldi, V., 'The Death Penalty May Increase Homicide Rates', reprinted in D. L. Bender *et al.* (eds.), Does Capital Punishment Deter Crime? An Opposing Viewpoints Series (1999), San Diego: Greenhaven Press, pp. 47–52.

Goldstein, S. M., 'Chipping away at the Great Writ: Will Death Sentenced Federal Habeas Corpus Petitioners be Able to Seek and Utilise Changes in the Law?', *New York University Review of Law and Social Change* 18 (1990–91), pp. 357–414.

Goodman, D. S., 'Demographic Evidence in Capital Sentencing', *Stanford Law Review* 39 (1987), pp. 499–543.

Gottschalk, M., *The Prison and the Gallows: The Politics of Mass Incarceration in America* (2006), Cambridge: Cambridge University Press.

Green, D. A., 'Public Opinion Versus Public Judgment About Crime: Correcting the "Comedy of Errors"', *British Journal of Criminology* 46 (2006), pp. 131–154.

Green, K. A., 'Statistics and the Death Penalty: A Break with Tradition', *Creighton Law Review* 21 (1987), pp. 265–301.

Greene, E. and Koehring, H., 'Victim Impact Evidence in Capital Cases: Does the Victim's Character Matter?', *Journal of Applied Social Psychology* 28(2) (1998), pp. 145–156.

Greenberg, J., 'Capital Punishment as a System', *Yale Law Journal* 91 (1982), pp. 908–936.

Griffey, M. and Rothenberg, L. E., 'The Death Penalty in the United States', in *The Death Penalty in the OSCE Area*, OSCE Background Paper 2006, pp. 35–44.

Gross, S., 'Race and Death: The Judicial Evaluation of Evidence of Discrimination in Capital Sentencing', *University of California, Davis, Law Review* 18 (1985), pp. 1275–1325.

——— 'Lost Lives: Miscarriages of Justice in Capital Cases', *Law and Contemporary Problems* 61 (1988), pp. 125–152.

——— 'Update: American Public Opinion on the Death Penalty—It's Getting Personal', *Cornell Law Review* 83 (1998), pp. 1448–1475.

—— and Ellsworth, P. C., 'Second Thoughts: Americans' Views on the Death Penalty at the Turn of the Century' in Garvey, S. P. (ed.), *Capital Punishment and the American Future* (2001), pp. 7–57.

—— and Jacoby, K. Matheson, D. J., Nicholas Montgomery, N., and Patil, S., 'Exonerations in the United States 1989 through 2003', *Journal of Criminal Law and Criminology* 95 (2005) pp. 523–560.

—— and Matheson, D. J., 'What They Say at the End: Capital Victims' Families and the Press', *Cornell Law Review* 88(2) (2003), pp. 486–516.

—— and Mauro, R., 'Patterns of Death: An Analysis of Racial Disparities in Capital Sentencing and Homicide Victimization', *Stanford Law Review* 37 (1984), pp. 27–153.

—— —— *Death and Discrimination: Racial Disparities in Capital Sentencing* (1989), Boston: Northeastern University Press.

Grzeskowiak, A., 'Capital Punishment in Polish Penal Law', *United Nations Crime Prevention and Criminal Justice Newsletter* 12 and 13 (1986), pp. 43–46.

Gupta, S.C., *Capital Punishment in India* (1986), New Delhi: Deep and Deep Publications.

Haas, K. C. and Inciardi, J. A. (eds.), *Challenging Capital Punishment* (1988), Newbury Park: Sage.

Hainan, L., 'The Effect on the Capital Punishment by the Chinese Traditional Theory of the Criminal Law', in M. Nowak and Xin Chunying (eds.), EU-*China Human Rights Dialogue: Proceedings of the Second EU-China Legal Experts*, Seminar Held in Beijing on 19 and 20 October 1998 (2000), pp. 99–120.

Haines, H. H., *Against Capital Punishment. The Anti-Death Penalty Movement in America, 1972–1994* (1996), New York: Oxford University Press.

Hall, D. J., 'Victims' Voices in Criminal Court: The Need for Restraint', 28 *American Criminal Law Review* (1991), pp. 233–261.

Haney, C., *Death by Design: Capital Punishment as a Social Psychological System.* (2005), New York: Oxford University Press.

Harding, R. M., '"Endgame": Competency and the Execution of Condemned Inmates—A Proposal to Satisfy the Eighth Amendment's Prohibition against the Infliction of Cruel and Unusual Punishment', *Saint Louis University Public Law Review* 14 (1994), pp. 105–152.

Harvard Law Review, Note, 'A matter of life and death: the effect of life-without-parole statutes on capital punishment', *Harvard Law Review* 119 (2006), pp. 1838–1852.

Hatchard, J. and Coldham, S., 'Commonwealth Africa', in P Hodgkinson and A. Rutherford (eds.), *Capital Punishment: Global Issues and Prospects* (1996), pp. 155–191.

Hechler, D., 'U.S. death penalty in wake of Ashcroft' *The National Law Journal*, 29 November 2004.

Hillman, H., 'The Possible Pain Experienced during Execution by Different Methods', *Perception 22* (1993), pp. 745–753.

Hinson, K., 'Post-Conviction Determination of Innocence for Death Row Inmates', *SMU Law Review* 48 (1994), pp. 231–261.

Hintze, M., 'Tinkering with the machinery of death: Capital Punishment's toll on the American Judiciary', *Judicature* 89(5) (2006), pp. 254–257.

Ho, V. K. Y., 'What is Wrong with Capital Punishment?: Official and Unofficial Attitudes Toward Capital Punishment in Modern and Contemporary China', in A. Sarat and C. Boulanger (eds.), *The Cultural Lives of Capital Punishment* (2005), pp. 274–290.

Hodgkinson, P., 'Meeting the needs of the families of the homicide victim and the con-demned' in P. Hodgkinson and W. A. Schabas (eds.), *Capital Punishment: Strategies for Abolition*, (2004), pp. 332–358.

Hodgkinson, P. and Rutherford A. (eds.), *Capital Punishment: Global Issues and Prospects* (1996), Winchester: Waterside Press.

Hodgkinson, P., and Schabas, W A. (eds.), *Capital Punishment: Strategies for Abolition*, (2004), Cambridge: Cambridge University Press.

Hoffman, L. J., Note, 'The Madness of the Method: The Use of Electrocution and the Death Penalty', *Texas Law Review* 70 (1992), pp. 1039–1062.

—— 'Justice Dando and the "Conservative" Argument for Abolition', *Indiana Law Review* 72 (1996), pp. 21–24.

Holovatiy, S., 'Abolishing the Death Penalty in Ukraine: Difficulties Real or Imagined?', in Council of Europe, *The Death Penalty: Abolition in Europe* (1999), pp. 139–151.

Honberg, R. S., 'The Injustice of Imposing Death Sentences on People with Severe Mental Illness'. *Catholic University Law Review* 54 (2004–05), pp. 1153–1167.

Hood, R., Capital Punishment', in M. Tonry (ed.), *The Handbook of Crime and Punishment* (1998), New York: Oxford University Press, pp. 739–776.

—— 'The Value of Statistical Returns and Empirical Research in Discussions on the Death Penalty', paper presented to the *EU-China Human Rights Seminar*, Beijing, 11–12 May 2001.

—— *The Death Penalty: A Worldwide Perspective* (3rd edn., 2002), Oxford: Oxford University Press.

—— and Seemungal, F., *A Rare and Arbitrary Fate. Conviction for Murder, the Mandatory Death Penalty and the Reality of Homicide in Trinidad and Tobago* (2006), London: The Death Penalty Project Ltd.

Horvath, T., 'L'Abolition de la peine de mort en Hongrie', *Revue Internationale de Criminologie et de Police Technique* 2 (1992), pp. 167–179.

Hosni, N., 'La Peine de mort en droit égyptien et en droit islamique', *Revue Internationale de Droit Pénal* 58 (1987), pp. 407–420.

Howard Law Journal, Note, 'Safeguarding Eighth Amendment Rights with a Comparative Proportionality Review in the Imposition of the Death Penalty, *Pulley* v. *Harris*', 28 (1985), pp. 331–333.

Horowitz, J. A., 'Prosecutorial discretion and the death penalty: creating a committee to decide whether to seek the death penalty', 65 *Fordham Law Review* (1997), pp. 2571–2575.

Hoyle, C. and Zedner, L. 'Victims, Victimization and Criminal Justice', in M. Maguire, R. Morgan and R. Reiner (eds.), *The Oxford Handbook of Criminology* (4th. edn., 2007), Oxford: Oxford University Press, pp. 461–495.

Hu, Yunteng, 'On the Death Penalty at the Turning of the Century' in M. Nowak and Xin Chunying (eds.), *EU-China Human Rights Dialogue: Proceedings of the Second EU-China Legal Experts, Seminar Held in Beijing, 19–20 October 1998* (2000), pp. 88–94.

Hughes, J., 'Supreme Court Review. For Mice or Men or Children? Will the expansion of the Eighth Amendment in *Atkins v Virginia* Force the Supreme Court to Re-examine the Minimum Age for the Death Penalty?', *Journal of Criminal Law and Criminology* 93 (2003), pp. 975–1008.

Illinois, *Report of the Governor's Commission on Capital Punishment. George H. Ryan Governor* (April 2002).

Indiana Law Journal, *Report of the Governor's [of Massachusetts] Council on Capital Punishment - Introduction*' 80 (2005), pp. 1–27.

Jackson, B. and Christian, D., *Death Row* (1980), Boston: Beacon Press.

Jacobs, D. and Carmichael, J. T., 'The Political Sociology of the Death Penalty: a Pooled Time-Series Analysis', *American Sociological Review* 67(1) (2002), pp. 109–131.

—— —— 'Ideology, Social Threat, and the Death Sentence: Capital Sentences across Time and Space', *Social Forces*, 83 (2004), pp. 249–278.

—— —— and Kent, S. L. 'Vigilantism, Current Racial Threat and Death Sentences', *American Sociological Review* 70 (2005), pp. 656–677.

—— and Kent S. L. 'The Determinants of Executions since 1951: How Politics, Protests, Public Opinion, and Social Divisions Shape Capital Punishment', *Social Problems* 54(3) (2007), pp. 297-318.

Japan, *National Statement on Crime Prevention for Freedom, Justice, Peace and Development* (1985).

Johnson, D. T., 'Where the state kills in secret. Capital punishment in Japan', *Punishment and Society* 8 (2006), pp. 251–285.

Jeffries Jr., J. C., *Justice Lewis F. Powell, Jr.: A Biography* (1994), New York: University of Virginia Press, C. Scribner's & Sons.

Jiang, S., Lambert, E. G., and Wang, J., 'Capital Punishment View in China and the United States: A preliminary study among college students', *International Journal of Offender Therapy and Comparative Criminology* 51(1) 2007, pp. 84–97.

Johnson, R., 'Under Sentence of Death: The Psychology of Death Row Confinement', *Law and Psychology Review* 5 (1979), pp. 141–158

—— *Condemned to Die: Life under Sentence of Death* (1981), Prospect Heights, Ill.: Waveland Press.

—— 'Institutions and the Promotion of Violence', in A. Campbell and J. J. Gibbs (eds.), *Violent Transactions* (1986), Oxford: Blackwell, pp. 181–205.

—— *Death Work: A Study of the Modern Execution Process* (2nd edn., 1998), Belmont, Calif.: Wadsworth Publishing.

—— 'Life under Sentence of Death: Historical and Contemporary Perspectives', in J. R. Acker, R. M. Bohm, and C. S. Lanier (eds.), (2nd edn., 2003) *America's Experiment with Capital Punishment*, pp. 647–671.

—— and Carroll, J. L., 'Litigating Death-Row Conditions, the Case for Reform', in I. P. Robbins (ed.), *Prisoners and the Law: Prisoners' Rights Sourcebook* (1985), New York: Clark Boardman, Chapter 8, pp. 3-33.

Johnson, S. L., 'Wishing Petitioners to Death: Factual Misrepresentations in Fourth Circuit Capital Cases', *Cornell Law Review* 91 (2006), pp. 1105–1155.

Jones, T. and Newburn, T., 'Three strikes and you're out: Exploring Symbol and Substance in American and British Crime Control Policies', *British Journal of Criminology* 46 (2006), pp. 781–802.

Jürgensen, C., 'Egypt: Death Penalty After Unfair Trials', paper presented to the *First World Congress against the Death Penalty*, Strasbourg, 21–23 June 2001.

Justice, *Sentenced to Life: reform of the law and procedures for those sentenced to life imprisonment* (1996), London: Justice.

Kahneman, D., Slovic, P., and Tversky, A. (eds.), *Judgment under Uncertainty: Heuristics and Biases* (1982), Cambridge: Cambridge University Press.

Kaiser, G., 'Capital Punishment in a Criminological Perspective', *United Nations Crime Prevention and Criminal Justice Newsletter* 12 and 13 (1986), pp. 10–18.

Kaplan, P. J., 'American Exceptionalism and Racialized Inequality in American Capital Punishment', *Law and Social Inquiry* 31 (2006), pp. 149–175.

Karamanian, S. L., 'Victims' Rights and the Death-Sentenced Inmate: Some Observations and Thoughts', *Saint Mary's Law Journal* 29 (1998), pp. 1025–1036.

Kassymbekova, B., 'Capital Punishment in Kyrgyzstan: Between the Past, "Other" State Killings and Social Demands', in A. Sarat and C. Boulanger (eds.), *The Cultural Lives of Capital Punishment* (2005), pp. 171–194.

Katende, J. W., 'The Constitutional Challenge to the Death Penalty in Uganda', *Death Penalty Conference* 3–5 June 2005, Barbados, London: The Death Penalty Project Ltd.

Katz, L., Levitt, S. D., and Shustorovich, E., 'Prison Conditions, Capital Punishment, and Deterrence', *American Law and Economics Review* 5 (2003), pp. 318–343.

Kaufman-Osborn, T. V., 'Regulating Death: Capital Punishment and the Late Liberal State', *Yale Law Review* 111 (2001), pp. 681–733.

Keating, J., 'Out of Sight, Out of Mind', *Amicus Journal* 3 (2001), pp. 15–19.

Keil, T. J., and. Vito, G. F., 'Kentucky Prosecutor's Decision to Seek the Death Penalty: A Lisrel Model' in R.M. Bohm (ed.), *The Death Penalty in America: Current Research* (1991), pp. 53–68.

Keyes, D., Edwards, W. and Perske, R. 'People with Mental Retardation are Dying, Legally at least 44 have been Executed', *Journal of Mental Retardation* 40(3) (2002), pp. 243–244.

Khamidov, K., 'International Experience and legal Regulation of the Application of the Death Penalty in Tajikistan', in *The Death Penalty in the OSCE Area* (2006), *Background Paper 2006*, pp. 27–34.

Killingley, J., 'Note on *Shafer v South Carolina*', *Amicus Journal* 3 (2001), pp. 20–21.

King, R., *Don't Kill in Our Names: Families of Murder Victims Speak Out Against the Death Penalty* (2003), New Jersey: Rutgers University Press.

King, N. J. *et al.*, 'Panel Discussion on The Capital Jury', *Indiana Law Journal* 80 (2005) pp. 47–67.

Kirkpatrick, J., 'The Relevance of Customary International Norms to the Death Penalty in the United States', *Georgia Journal of International and Comparative Law* 25 (1995), pp. 1–16.

Kirchmeier, J. L., 'Another Place Beyond Here: The Death Penalty Moratorium Movement in the United States', *University of Colorado Law Review* 73 (2002), pp. 2–116.

Kleck, G., 'Capital Punishment, Gun Ownership, and Homicide', *American Journal of Sociology* 84 (1979), pp. 882–908.

Klein, L. R., Forst, B., and Filatov, V., 'The Deterrent Effect of Capital Punishment: An Assessment of the Evidence' in A. Blumstein, J. Cohen, and D. Nagin (eds.). *Deterrence and Incapacitation* (1978), Washington D.C.: National Academy of Sciences, pp. 336–360.

Klein, S., Berk, R., and Hickman, L., *Race and the Decision to Seek the Death Penalty in Federal Cases* (2006), Washington D.C.: US Department of Justice.

Kniskern, E. M., 'Does *Ford v. Wainwright's* Denial of Executions of the Insane Prohibit the State from Carrying out its Criminal Justice System?', *Southern University Law Review* 26 (1999), pp. 171–195.

Knowles, J., 'Capital Punishment in the Commonwealth Caribbean: Colonial Inheritance or Colonial Remedy?', in P. Hodgkinson and W. A. Schabas (eds.), *Capital Punishment: Strategies for Abolition* (2004), pp. 282–308.

Kobil, D. T., 'The Evolving Role of Clemency in Capital Cases' in J. R. Acker, R. M. Bohm, and C. S. Lanier (eds.), *America's Experiment with Capital Punishment* (2nd edn., 2003), pp. 673–692.

Koh, H. H., 'Paying "Decent Respect" to World Opinion on the Death Penalty', *UC Davis Law Review* 35 (2002), pp. 1085–1113.

Koniaris, L. G., Zimmers, T, A., Lubarsky, D. A., and Sheldon, J. P., 'Inadequate anaesthesia in lethal injection for execution', *The Lancet*, Vol. 365, Iss. 9468 (16–22 April 2005), pp. 1412–1414.

Kozinski, A., 'Tinkering with Death' in H. Bedau and P. Cassell (eds.), *Debating the Death Penalty* (2004), pp. 1–14.

Krause, T., 'Reaching Out to the Other Side: Defense-Based Victim Outreach in Capital Cases, in J. R. Acker and D. R. Karp (eds.), *Wounds That Do Not Bind: Victim Perspectives on the Death Penalty* (2006), pp. 379–396.

Kruger, H. C., 'Protocol No. 6 to the European Convention on Human Rights', in Council of Europe, *The Death Penalty: Abolition in Europe* (1999), pp. 69–78.

Latzer, B. and Cauthen, J. N. G., *Justice Delayed? Time Consumption in Capital Appeals: A Multistate Study* (May 2007), US National Archive of Criminal Justice Data, NCJRS.

Layson, S. A., 'Homicide and Deterrence: A Re-examination of the United States Time-Series Evidence', *Southern Economic Journal* 52 (1985), pp. 68–69.

—— 'United States Time-Series Homicide Regressions with Adaptive Expectations', *Bulletin of the New York Academy of Medicine* 62 (1986), pp. 589–600.

Ledewitz, B. L., 'The New Role of Statutory Aggravating Circumstances in American Death Penalty Law', *Duquesne Law Review* 22 (1984), pp. 317–396.

—— 'Sources of Injustice in Death Penalty Practice: The Pennsylvania Experience', *Dickinson Law Review* 95 (1991), pp. 651–690.

Lehrfreund, S., 'The Commonwealth Caribbean and Evolving International Attitudes towards the Death Penalty', in Penal Reform International *et al.*, *Commonwealth Caribbean Human Rights Seminar*, Belize, 12–14 September 2000 (2001), pp. 79–82.

—— 'International Legal Trends and the "Mandatory" Death Penalty in the Commonwealth Caribbean', *Oxford University Commonwealth Law Journal* 1 (2001), pp. 171–194.

Lempert, R., 'Desert and Deterrence: An Assessment of the Moral Bases of the Case for Capital Punishment', *Michigan Law Review* 79 (1981), pp. 1177–1231.

—— 'The Effect of Executions on Homicides: A New Look in an Old Light', *Crime and Delinquency* 29 (1983), pp. 88–115.

Lesser, W., *Pictures at an Execution* (1993), London: Harvard University Press.

Lewis, D. O., Feldman, M., Jackson, L., and Bard, B., 'Psychiatric, Neurological, and Psycho-educational Characteristics of 15 Death Row Inmates in the United States', *American Journal of Psychiatry* 143 (1986), pp. 838–845.

—— and Bard, J. S., 'Multiple Personality and Forensic Issues', *Psychiatric Clinics of North America* 41(3) (1991), pp. 741–756.

Liebman, J. S., 'More than "Slightly Retro": The Rehnquist Court's Rout of Habeas Corpus Jurisdiction in *Teague v Lane*', *New York University Review of Law and Social Change* 18 (1990–91) pp. 537–635.

—— 'Opting for Real Death Penalty Reform', 63 *Ohio State Law Journal* (2002), pp. 315–331.

—— 'Comment: The New Death Penalty Debate: What's DNA got to do with it?', *Columbia Human Rights Law Review* 33 (2002), pp. 527–552 .

—— Fagan, J., Gelman, A., West, V., Davies, G., and Kiss, A., *A Broken System, Pt. II: Why There Is So Much Error in Capital Cases, and What Can be Done About It?* (February 2002), Columbia Law School, <http://www2.law.columbia.edu/brokensystem2/>.

—— Fagan, J., West, V., and Lloyd, J., 'Capital Attrition: Error Rates in Capital Cases, 1973–1995', *Texas Law Review* 78 (2000), pp. 1771–1803.

Lifton, R. J., and Mitchell, G., *Who Owns Death? Capital Punishment, the American Conscience, and the End of Executions* (2000), New York: HarperCollins.

Liu, J., 'Crime Patterns During the Market Transition in China', *British Journal of Criminology* 45 (2005), pp. 613–633.

Logan, W. A., 'Proportionality and Punishment: Imposing Life Without Parole on Juveniles', *Wake Forest Law Review* 33 (1998), pp. 681–725.

—— 'Declaring Life at the Crossroads of Death: Victims' Anti-Death Penalty Views and Prosecutors Charging Decisions', *Criminal Justice Ethics* 18(2) (1999), pp. 41–57.

—— 'Victims, Survivors and the Decisions to Seek and Impose Death' in J. R. Acker and D. R. Karp (eds.), *'Wounds That Do Not Bind: Victim-Based Perspectives on the Death Penalty'* (2006), pp. 161–178.

Lombardi, G., Sluder, R. L., and Wallace, D., 'Mainstreaming Death-Sentenced Inmates: The Missouri Experience and its Legal Significance', *Federal Probation* 61(2) (1997), pp. 3–11.

Luginbuhl, J. and Burkhead, M., 'Victim Impact Evidence in a Capital Trial: Encouraging Votes for Death', *American Journal of Criminal Justice 20* (1995), pp. 1–16.

Lynch, M., 'Capital Punishment as Moral Imperative: pro-death penalty discourse on the internet', *Punishment and Society* 4(2) (2002), 213–236.

McCann, E. M., 'Opposing Capital Punishment: A prosecutor's perspective', *Marquette Law Review* 79 (1996), pp. 649–706.

McFarland, S. G., 'Is Capital Punishment a Short-Term Deterrent to Homicide? A Study of the Effects of Four Recent American Executions', *Journal of Criminal Law and Criminology* 74 (1983), pp. 1014–1032.

McGarrell, E. F. and Sandys, M., 'The misperception of public opinion toward capital punishment: examining the spuriousness explanation of death penalty support', *American Behavioral Scientist (Special Issue: Public Opinion on Justice in the Criminal Justice System)* 39 (February 1996), pp. 500–514.

McManus, W. S., 'Estimates of the Deterrent Effect of Capital Punishment: The Importance of the Researcher's Prior Beliefs', *Journal of Political Economy* 93 (1985), pp. 417–425.

Mackay, R. D., 'Post-Hinckley Insanity in the USA', *Criminal Law Review* (1988), pp. 88–96.

Mackey, S., *The Saudis: Inside the Desert Kingdom* (1987), London: Harrap.

Magee, D., *Slow Coming Dark: Interviews on Death Row* (1982), London: Quartet.

Mailer, N., *The Executioner's Song* (1979), Boston Mass.: Little, Brown and Company.

Mandon, A., *'Kindler* and the Courage to Deal with American Convictions', *Criminal Reports* 8 C.R. (4th) (1991), pp. 68–81.

Markel, D., 'State, Be not Proud: A Retributivist Defense of the Commutation of Death Row and the Abolition of the Death Penalty', *Harvard Civil Rights-Civil Liberties Law Review* 40 (2005), pp. 409–480.

Markman, S. J. and Cassell, P. G., 'Protecting the Innocent: A Response to the Bedau-Radelet Study', *Stanford Law Review* 41 (1988), pp. 121–160.

Marshall, L.C., 'In Spite of Meese', *Journal of Criminal Law and Criminology* 85 (1994), pp. 261–280.

Marshall, T. R., 'Public Opinion and the Rehnquist Court', *Judicature* 74 (6) (1991), pp. 322–329.

Marquart, J. W., Ekland-Olson, S., and Sorensen, J. R., 'Gazing into the Crystal Ball: Can Jurors Accurately Predict Dangerousness in Capital Cases?', *Law and Society Review* 23 (1989), pp. 449–468.

—— and Sorensen, J. R., 'Institutional and Postrelease Behavior of Furman-Commuted Inmates in Texas', *Criminology* 26 (1988), pp. 677–693.

Mauer, M., King, R. S., and Young, M. C., *The Meaning of 'Life': Long Prison Sentences in Context* (2004), The Sentencing Project: <http://www.sentencingproject.org/PublicationDetails.aspx?PublicationId=348>.

Mayhew, P. and van Kesteren, J., *Cross-national attitudes to punishment*, in J. V. Roberts and M. Hough (eds.), *Changing Attitudes to Punishment. Public Opinion, Crime and Justice* (2002), Cullompton: Willan Publishing, pp. 62–93.

Mello, M., 'Executing the Mentally Ill: When is Someone Sane Enough to Die?', *Criminal Justice* 22(3) (2007), pp. 30-41, <http://www.abanet.org/crimjust/cjmag/22-3/home.html>.

—— and Perkins, P. J., 'Closing the Circle: The illusion of lawyers for people litigating for their lives at the fin de siècle', in J. R. Acker, R. M. Bohm, and C. S. Lanier (eds.), *America's Experiment with Capital Punishment* (2nd edn., 2003), pp. 347–384.

Meltsner, M., *Cruel and Unusual: The Supreme Court and Capital Punishment* (1973), Random House, pp. 106–148.

Mendes, D. and Delzin, D., 'Using the Bill of Rights to halt executions: a reply to Peter Hodgkinson', *Amicus Journal* 15 (2005), pp. 18–21.

Messner, S.F., Baumer, E. P., and Rosenfield, R., 'Distrust of Government, the Vigilante Tradition, and Support for Capital Punishment', *Law and Society Review* 40(3) (2006), pp. 559–589.

Mikhlin, A. S., *The Death Penalty in Russia* (1999), London: Simmonds & Hill and Kluwer Law International, pp. 8–22.

Millemann, M. A. and Christopher, G. W., 'Preferring white lives: the racial administration of the death penalty in Maryland', *University of Maryland Law Journal of Race, Religion, Gender and Class* 5(1) (2005), pp. 1–26.

Miller, K. S. and Radelet, M. L., *Executing the Mentally Ill: The Criminal Justice System and the Case of Alvin Ford* (1993), London: Sage.

Miller, R. D., 'Evaluation of and Treatment to Competency to be Executed: A National Survey and an Analysis', *Journal of Psychiatry and Law* (Spring 1988), pp. 67–90.

Mitchell, A. D., 'The Effect of the Marshall Hypothesis on Attitudes Towards the Death Penalty', *Race, Gender and Class* 13 (2006), pp. 221–239.

Mocan, H., N. and Gittings, K. R., 'Getting Off Death Row: Commuted Sentences and the Deterrent Effect of Capital Punishment', *Journal of law and Economics* 46 (2003), pp. 453–478.

Mohrenschlager, M., 'The Abolition of Capital Punishment in the Federal Republic of Germany: The German Experience', *Revue Internationale de Droit Pénal* 58 (1987), pp. 509–519.

Moldrich, D., *Hangman—Spare that Noose* (1983), Colombo: D. Moldrich .

Monahan, J., 'The prediction of violent behavior: Toward a second generation of theory and policy', *American Journal of Psychiatry* 141 (1984) pp. 10–15.

—— 'Violence Risk Assessment: Scientific Validity and Evidentiary Admissibility', *Washington and Lee Law Review* 57 (2000), pp. 901–916.

Mossman, D., 'Assessing and Restoring Competency to be Executed: Should Psychiatrists Participate?', *Behavioral Sciences and the Law* 5 (1987), pp. 397–405.

—— 'The Psychiatrist and Execution Competency: Fording Murky Ethical Waters', *Case Western Law Review* 43 (1992), pp. 1–95.

Mosteller, R. P., 'Victim Impact Evidence: Hard to Find the Real Rules', *Cornell Law Review* 88 (2003), pp. 543–554.

Mourad, F. A. R., 'Effect of the Implementation of the Islamic Legislation on Crime Prevention in the Kingdom of Saudi Arabia: A Field Research', in *The Effects of Islamic Legislation in Crime Prevention in Saudi Arabia* (1980), Rome: UNSDRI, pp. 494–567.

Mulligan, K., 'Pope John Paul II and Catholic opinion toward the death penalty and abortion', *Social Science Quarterly* 87 (2006), pp. 739-753.

Murphy, E. L., 'Application of the Death Penalty in Cook County', *Illinois Bar Journal* (October 1984), pp. 90–95.

Myers, B. and Arbuthnot, J., 'The Effects of Victim Impact Evidence on the Verdicts and Sentencing Judgments of Mock Jurors', *Journal of Offender Rehabilitation* 29(3/4) (1999), pp. 95–112.

Nakell, B.A. and Hardy, K. A., *The Arbitrariness of the Death Penalty* (1987), Philadelphia, PA: Temple University Press.

Naude, B., *Criminal Justice and the Death Penalty in South Africa: A Criminological Study* (1992), Pretoria, S. A.: Pretoria Institute of Criminology.

Nesbit, C. A., 'Managing Death Row', *Corrections Today* (July 1986), pp. 90–106.

—— Howard, P. L., and Wallace, S. M., *Managing Death-Sentenced Inmates: A Survey of Practices* (1989), Washington: American Correctional Association.

Neumayer, E., *Death penalty: the political foundations of the global trend towards abolition* (2005), <http://ssrn.com/abstract=489628>.

Newcomen, N., 'Managing the Penal Consequences of Replacing the Death Penalty in Europe' in N. Browne and S. Candelia (eds.), *Managing effective alternatives to capital punishment.* (2005), London: CCPS.

Nirmal, C. J., 'Setting an Agenda', in C. J. Nirmal (ed.), *Human Rights in India* (2000), New York: Oxford University Press, pp. 234–269.

Nowak, M., 'Is the Death Penalty an Inhuman Punishment?', in T. S. Orlin, A. Rosas, and M. Scheinin (eds.)., *The Jurisprudence of Human Rights Law: A Comparative Interpretive Approach* (2002), Abo Akademi University Institute of Human Rights, pp. 27–45.

Nsereko, D. D. N., '*The Death Penalty in Botswana'* (1987), Mimeo.

—— and Glickman, M. J. A., 'Capital Punishment in Botswana', *United Nations Crime Prevention and Criminal Justice Newsletter* 12 and 13 (November 1986), pp. 51–53.

NSW Council for Civil Liberties, *The Death Penalty in Australia and Oversees*, Background Paper 2005/3 (2005), p. 2.

Officer, J. (ed.), *If I should die... A Death Row Correspondence* (1999), Cheltenham: New Clarion Press.

Olmesdahl, M. C. J., 'Predicting the Death Sentence', *South African Journal of Criminal Law and Criminology* 6 (1982), pp. 201–218.

O'Shea, K. A., *Women and the Death Penalty in the United States, 1990–1998* (1999), London: Praeger.

Palmer, M., 'The People's Republic of China', in P. Hodgkinson and A. Rutherford (eds.), *Capital Punishment: Global Issues and Prospects* (1996), pp. 105–141.

Pannick, D., *Judicial Review of the Death Penalty* (1982), London: Duckworth.

Passell, P., 'The Deterrent Effect of the Death Penalty: A Statistical Test', *Stanford Law Review* 28 (1975), pp. 61–80.

Pastore, A. L. and Maguire, K. (eds.), *Sourcebook of Criminal Justice Statistics—1999* (2000), Washington D. C.: US Department of Justice.

Paternoster, R., 'Prosecutorial Discretion and Capital Sentencing in North and South Carolina', in R. M. Bohm. (ed.), *The Death Penalty in America: Current Research* (1991), pp. 39–52.

—— 'Assessing Capriciousness in Capital Cases', *Law and Society Review* 27 (1993), pp. 111–123.

—— Pierce, G. and Radelet, M. L., *Race and Death Sentencing in Georgia, 1989–1998*, in *American Bar Association, Evaluating Fairness and Accuracy in State Death Penalty Systems: The Georgia Death Penalty Assessment Report* (2006).

Patten, C., Speech delivered to the *First World Congress Against the Death Penalty* in Strasbourg, June 2001.

Peffley, M. and Hurwitz, J., 'Persuasion and Resistance: Race and the Death Penalty in America', *American Journal of Political Science* 51(4) (2007), pp. 996–1012.

Penal Reform International, *Alternatives to the Death Penalty: The problems with life imprisonment*, Penal Reform Briefing No. 1 2007(1): 2.

Peterson, R. D. and Bailey, W. C., 'Is Capital Punishment an Effective Deterrent for Murder? An Examination of Social Science Research', in J. R. Acker, R. M. Bohm, and C. S. Lanier (eds.), *America's Experiment with Capital Punishment* (1998), pp. 157–182.

Phillips, D. P., 'The Deterrent Effect of Capital Punishment: New Evidence on an Old Controversy', *American Journal of Sociology* 86 (1980), pp. 139–148.

—— 'Strong and Weak Research Designs for Detecting the Impact of Capital Punishment on Homicide', *Rutgers Law Review* 33 (1981), pp. 790–798.

—— and Hensley, J. E., 'When Violence is Rewarded or Punished: The Impact of Mass Media Stories on Homicide', *Journal of Communications* (1984), pp. 101–116.

Phillips, R. T. M., 'Professionalism, Mental Disability, and the Death Penalty: The Psychiatrist as Evaluator: Conflicts and Conscience', *New York Law School Review* 41 (1996), pp. 189–199.

Picca, G., 'La peine de mort: Un problème politique et social', *Revue Internationale de Droit Pénal* 68 (1987), pp. 435–450.

Pierrepoint, A., *Executioner Pierrepoint: An Autobiography* (1974) London: Harrap Publishing, 1974; and (2005), Orpington: Eric Dobby Publishing Ltd.

Pierce, G. and Radelet, M. L., *Race, Region and Death Sentencing in Illinois 1988–1997*, Appendix 1A to Illinois, *Report of the Governor's Commission on Capital Punishment: George H. Ryan Governor*, (2002).

—— —— 'The Impact of Legally Inappropriate Factors on Death Sentencing for California Homicides, 1990–1999', 46 *Santa Clara Law Review* (2005), pp. 1–47.

Pojman, L.P., 'Why the Death Penalty is Morally Permissible' in H. Bedau and P. Cassell (eds.), *Debating the Death Penalty* (2004), New York: Oxford University Press, pp. 51–75.

—— and Reiman, J., *The Death Penalty, For and Against* (1998), Lanham, Md.: Rowman & Littlefield.

Posner, R. A., 'The Economics of Capital Punishment', *Economists' Voice* (March 2006).

Potas, I. and Walker, J., *Capital Punishment, Trends and Issues in Criminal Justice No. 3* (1987), Canberra: Australian Institute of Criminology.

Poveda, T. G., 'Geographical location, death sentences and executions in post-*Furman* Virginia', *Punishment and Society* 8 (2006), pp. 423–442.

Prejean, H., *Dead Man Walking* (1993), London: Fount.

—— *The Death of Innocents: An Eyewitness Account of Wrongful Executions* (2006), Vintage Books.

Pridemore, W. A., 'Change and Stability in the Characteristics of Homicide Victims, Offenders and Incidents During Rapid Social Change', *British Journal of Criminology*, 47 (2007), pp. 331–345.

Prison Reform Trust, *Report of the Committee on the Penalty for Homicide (The Lane Committee)* (1995).

Pristavkin, A., 'A vast place of execution—the death penalty in Russia', in Council of Europe, *The Death Penalty: Abolition in Europe* (1999), pp. 129–137.

—— 'The Russian Federation and the death penalty', in Council of Europe, *Death Penalty. Beyond Abolition* (2004), pp. 191–204.

Prokosch, E., 'The Death Penalty versus Human Rights', in Council of Europe, *The Death Penalty: Abolition in Europe* (1999), pp. 17–27.

QUI, Shengui, 'Strike hard' *China Review* 33 (Summer 2005), pp. 6-9.

Radelet, M .L., 'Physician Participation', in P. Hodgkinson and A. Rutherord (eds.), *Capital Punishment: Global Issues and Prospects* (1996), pp. 243–260.

—— 'More Trends toward Moratoria on Executions', *Connecticut Law Review* 33 (2001), pp. 845–860.

—— and Akers, R. L., 'Deterrence and the Death Penalty: The Views of Experts', *Journal of Criminal Law and Criminology* 87(1) (1996), pp. 1–11.

—— and Bedau, H. A., 'The Execution of the Innocent', *Law and Contemporary Problems* 61 (1998), pp. 105–217.

—— —— and Putnam, C. E., *In Spite of Innocence: Erroneous Convictions in Capital Cases* (1992), Boston: Northeastern University Press.

—— and Pierce, G., 'Race and Prosecutorial Discretion in Homicide Cases', *Law and Society Review* 19 (1985), pp. 587–621.

—— Vandiver, M. and Bernardo, F. M., 'Families, Prisons, and Men with Death Sentences', *Journal of Family Issues* 4 (1983), pp. 593–612.

—— and Zsembik, B.A., 'Executive Clemency in Post-Furman Capital Cases', *University of Richmond Law Review* 27 (1993), pp. 289–314.

Radzinowicz, L., *A History of English Criminal Law*, Vol. 1 (1948), London: Stevens and Sons.

—— *A History of English Criminal Law*, Vol. 4 (1948), London: Stevens and Sons.

—— *In Search of Criminology* (1962) Cambridge, MA: Harvard University Press.

—— *Adventures in Criminology* (1999), London: Routledge.

—— and Hood, R., *A History of English Criminal Law and its Administration, Vol. 5 The Emergence of Penal Policy* (1986), London: Stevens, also published as *The Emergence of Penal Policy in Victorian and Edwardian England* (1990), Oxford: Clarendon Press.

Raoul Wallenberg Institute of Human Rights and Humanitarian Law, *The Abolition of the Death Penalty in South Africa*, Report No. 23 (1997), Lund.

Redmond, L. M., 'Sudden Violent Death', K. J. Doka. (ed.), *Living with Grief after Sudden Loss* (1996), pp. 53–71.

Redo, S. M., *United Nations Position on Drugs Crimes* (1985), UNAFEI Resource Material No. 27.

Reinhardt, S., 'The Supreme Court, the Death Penalty, and the *Harris* Case', *Yale Law Journal* 102 (1992), pp. 205–223.

Roberts, J. V., 'Capital Punishment, Innocence, & Public Opinion', *Criminology & Public Policy* 4 (2005), pp. 1–54.

Roberts, J. V. and Hough, M. (eds.), *Changing Attitudes to Punishment: Public Opinion, Crime and Justice* (2002), Cullompton: Willan Publishing.

Roberts, M. M. (ed.), *Out of Night: Writings from Death Row* (1994), Cheltenham: New Clarion Press.

Robinson, D. A. and Stephens, O. H, 'Patterns of Mitigating Factors in Juvenile Death Penalty Cases', *Criminal Law Bulletin* 28 (1992), pp. 246–275.

Rock, P., 'Murderers, Victims and "Survivors": The Social Construction of Deviance', *British Journal of Criminology* 38 (1998), pp. 185–200.

Rodley, N., 'The United Nation's work in the field of the death penalty', in Council of Europe *The Death Penalty—Beyond Abolition* (2004), pp. 125–157.

Roitberg, H. T., 'Race for your Life: An Analysis of the Role of Race in Erroneous Capital Convictions', *Criminal Justice Review* 29 (2004) pp. 76–96.

Rosen, R. A., 'Innocence and Death', *North Carolina Law Review* 82 (2003), pp. 61–114.

Rossi, R. M., *Waiting to Die: Life on Death Row* (2004), Vision Paperbacks.

Rozelle, S. D., 'The Principled Executioner: Capital Juries' Bias And The Benefits Of True Bifurcation', *Arizona State Law Journal* 38 (2006), pp. 769–807.

Sadler, J. and Rose, M. R., 'Victim Impact Testimony and the Psychology of Punishment', *Cornell Law Review* 88(2) (2003), pp. 419–456.

Sandys, M. and McClelland, S., 'Stacking the Deck for Guilt and Death: The Failure of Death Qualification to Ensure Impartiality' in J. R. Acker, R. M. Bohm, and C. S. Lanier (eds.), *America's Experiment with Capital Punishment* (2nd edn., 2003), pp. 295–298.

Sarat, A., 'Violence, Representation, and Responsibility in Capital Trials: The View from the Jury', *Indiana Law Journal* 70 (1995), pp. 1103–1135.

—— *The Killing State: Capital Punishment in Law, Politics and Culture* (1999), New York: Oxford University Press.

—— *When the State Kills: Capital Punishment and the American Condition* (2001), Princeton N.J: Princeton University Press.

—— 'The "New Abolitionism" and the Possibilities of Legislative Action: the New Hampshire Experience', 63 *Ohio State Law Journal* (2002), pp. 343–359.

—— 'Innocence, Error, and the "New Abolitionism": A Commentary', *Criminology and Public Policy* 4 (1) (2005), pp. 45–54.

Sarat, A. and Boulanger, C. (eds.), *The Cultural Lives of Capital Punishment: Comparative Perspectives* (2005), Stanford Calif: Stanford University Press.

—— and Vidmar, N., Public Opinion, the Death Penalty and the 8th Amendment: Testing the Marshall hypothesis', *Wisconsin Law Review*, 17 (1976), pp. 171–206.

Schabas, W. A., 'Note on *Kindler* v. *Canada* (Minister of Justice)', *American Journal of International Law* 87 (1993), pp. 128–133.

—— *'Soering's* Legacy: The Human Rights Committee and the Judicial Committee of the Privy Council Take a Walk down Death Row', *International and Comparative Law Quarterly* 43 (1994), pp. 913–923.

—— 'Execution Delayed, Execution Denied', *Criminal Law Forum* 5 (1994), pp. 180–193.

—— 'Les réserves des États-Unis d'Amérique au pacte international relatif aux droits civils et politiques en ce qui a trait à la peine de mort', *Revue Universelle des Droits de l'Homme* 6 (1994), pp. 137–150.

—— 'International Norms on Execution of the Insane and the Mentally Retarded', *Criminal Law Forum* 4 (1994), pp. 95–117.

—— 'Symposium. Religion's Role in the Administration of the Death Penalty: Islam and the Death Penalty', *William and Mary Bill of Rights Journal*, 9 (2000), pp. 223–236.

—— 'From *Kindler* to *Burns:* International Law is Nourishing the Constitutional Living Tree', paper presented at a *Conference on Capital Punishment and International Human Rights Law*, Galway, 20 September 2001.

—— *The Abolition of the Death Penalty in International Law* (3rd edn., 2002), Cambridge: Cambridge University Press.

—— 'International Law, Politics, Diplomacy and the Abolition of the Death Penalty', 13 *William and Mary Bill of Rights Journal* (2004), pp. 417–444.

—— 'International Law and the Death Penalty: reflecting or promoting change?' in P. Hodgkinson and W. A. Schabas (eds.), *Capital Punishment: Strategies for Abolition* (2004), pp. 36–62.

——'Public Opinion and the Death Penalty', in P. Hodgkinson and W. A. Schabas (eds.), *Capital Punishment: Strategies for Abolition* (2004), pp. 309–331.

Schalock, R. L., Luckasson, R. A., and Shogren, K. A., 'The Renaming of Mental Retardation: Understanding the Change to the Term Intellectual Disability', *Intellectual and Developmental Disabilities*, 45(2) (2007), pp. 116-124.

Shah, S., 'How Lethal Injection Reform Constitutes Impermissible Research on Prisoners', *American Criminal Law Review* 45(3) (2008), <http://papers.ssrn.com/sol3/papers.cfm?abstract_id=1028127>.

Scheck, B., Neufeld, P., and Dwyer, P., *Actual Innocence: Five Days to Execution and other Dispatches from the Wrongfully Convicted* (2000), New York: Doubleday.

Scheinin, M., 'Capital Punishment and the International Covenant on Civil and Political Rights: Some Issues of Interpretation in the Practice of the Human Rights Committee', paper presented to the *EU-China Human Rights Seminar*, Beijing, 10–12 May 2001.

Schlosser, E., 'A grief like no other', *Atlantic Monthly* (1997), pp. 37–76.

Schwartz, B., 'Death TV? Is there a Press Right of Access to News that Allows Television of Executions?', *Tulsa Law Journal* 30 (1994), pp. 305–353.

Scott, G. R., *The History of Capital Punishment* (1950, reissued 1965), London: Torchstream Books.

Sellin, T., *The Penalty of Death* (1980), Beverly Hills, Calif.: Sage.

Sharp, S., *Hidden Victims: The effects of the death penalty on families of the accused* (2005), New Brunswick, New Jersey: Rutgers University Press.

Sheffer, S. and Cushing, R., *Creating More Victims: How Executions Hurt the Families Left Behind* (2006), Murder Victims' Families for Human Rights.

Shepherd, J. M., 'Deterrence versus Brutalization: Capital Punishment's Differing Impacts among States', *Michigan Law Review* 104 (2005), pp. 203–255.

Showalter, C. R. and Bonnie, R. J., 'Psychiatrists and Capital Sentencing: Risks and Responsibilities in a Unique Legal Setting', *Bulletin of the American Academy of Psychiatry and Law* 12 (1984), pp. 153–167.

Shute, S., 'Punishing Murderers: Release Procedures and the "Tariff", 1953–2004', *Criminal Law Review* (2004), pp. 873–895.

Shutong, Y., 'Le système de la peine capitale dans le droit pénal chinois', *Revue Internationale de Droit Pénal* 58 (1987), pp. 689–695.

Simon, J., *Governing Through Crime: How the war on crime transformed American democracy and created a culture of fear* (2007), Oxford: Oxford University Press.

—— and Spaulding, C., 'Tokens of our Esteem: Aggravating Factors in the Era of Deregulated Death Penalties', in A. Sarat (ed.), *The Killing State: Capital Punishment in Law, Politics, and Culture* (1999), pp. 81–136.

Singh, M. P., 'Capital Punishment: Perspective and the Indian Context' in R. Agarwal and S. Kumar (eds.), *Crimes and Punishment in New Perspective* (1986), Delhi: Mittal Publications, pp. 28–39.

Skolnick, A. A., Note 'Physicians in Missouri (but not Illinois) Win Battle to Block Physician Participation in Executions', *Journal of the American Medical Association* 274(7) (1995), pp. 524–526.

Skovoron, S. E., Scott, J. E., and Cullen, F. T., 'The Death Penalty for Juveniles: An Assessment of Public Support', *Crime and Delinquency* 35 (1989), pp. 546–561.

Slobogin, C., 'What *Atkins* could mean for people with mental illness', *New Mexico Law Review* 33 (2003), pp. 293–314.

Small, M. A. and Otto, R. K., 'Evaluations of Competency to be Executed: Legal Contours and Implications for Assessment', *Criminal Justice and Behavior* 18 (1991), pp. 146–158.

Smykla, J. O., 'The Human Impact of Capital Punishment: Interviews with Families of Persons on Death Row', *Journal of Criminal Justice* 15 (1987), pp. 331–347.

Snell, T L., *Capital Punishment 2000* (2001), Washington D. C.: US Department of Justice, Bureau of Justice Statistics.

—— *Capital Punishment 2005*, US Department of Justice, Bureau of Justice Statistics (December 2006), NCJ 215083, pp. 10–11.

Songer, M. J. and Unah, I., 'The Effect of Race, Gender and Location on Prosecutorial Decision to Seek the Death Penalty in South Carolina', *South Carolina Law Review* 58 (2006), pp. 161–209.

Sorenson, J. R., and Marquart, J. W., 'Prosecutorial and Jury Decision-Making in *Post-Furman* Texas Capital Cases', *New York University Review of Law and Social Change* 18 (1990–91), pp. 743–776.

—— —— 'Future dangerousness and Incapacitation', in J. R. Acker, R. M. Bohm, and C. S. Lanier (eds.), *America's Experiment with Capital Punishment* (2nd edn., 2003), pp. 283–300.

—— Pilgrim, R. L., 'An Actuarial Risk Assessment of Violence Posed by Capital Murder Defendants', *Journal of Criminal Law and Criminology* 90 (2000), pp. 1251–1270.

—— Wallace, D. H. and Pilgrim, R. L., 'Empirical Studies on Race and Death Penalty Sentencing: A Decade after the GAO Report', *Criminal Law Bulletin* 36 (2001), pp. 395–408.

Soss, J., Langbein, L., and Metelko, A. R., 'Why do white Americans support the death penalty?', *The Journal of Politics* 65 (2003), pp. 396–421.

Spangenberg Group, *A Study of Representation of Capital Cases in Texas* (1993), Boston Mass.

—— *Amended Time and Expense Analysis of Post-Conviction Capital Cases in Florida* (1998), Boston Mass.

—— *Rates of Compensation for Court-Appointed Counsel in Capital Cases at Trial: A State-By-State Overview*, (2007), Boston Mass.

Stack, S., 'Publicized Executions and Homicide', *American Sociological Review* 52 (1987), pp. 532–540.

—— 'Public Opinion on the Death Penalty: Analysis of Individual-level data from 17 Nations' *International Criminal Justice Review* 14 (2004), pp. 69–98.

Stafford Smith, C., 'Introduction', to J. Blank and E. Jensen *The Exonerated*, a play (2006), London: Faber and Faber.

—— *Bad Men: Guantanamo Bay and The Secret Prisons* (2007), London: Weidenfeld & Nicolson.

Starkweather, D. A., 'The Retributive Theory of "Just Deserts" and Victim Participation in Plea Bargaining', *Indiana Law Journal* 67 (1992), pp. 864–67.

Steiker, C. S., 'Capital Punishment and American Exceptionalism', *Oregon Law Review*, 81 (2002), pp. 97–130.

—— 'No, Capital punishment is not morally required: deterrence, deontology, and the death penalty', *Stanford Law Review* 58 (2006), pp. 751–789.

—— and Steiker, J. M., 'Should Abolitionists Support Legislative Reform?', 63 *Ohio State Law Journal* (2002), pp. 417–432.

—— —— 'Judicial Developments in Capital Punishment Law' in J. R. Acker, R. M. Bohm, and C. S. Lanier (eds.), *America's Experiment with Capital Punishment* (2nd edn., 2003), pp. 72–73.

—— —— 'The Seduction of Innocence: The attraction and limitations of the focus on innocence in capital punishment law and advocacy', *The Journal of Criminal Law and Criminology* 95 (2005), pp. 587–624.

—— —— 'The shadow of death: The Effect of Capital Punishment on American Criminal Law and Policy', *Judicature*, 89(5) (2006), pp. 250–253.

—— —— 'A Tale of Two Nations: Implementation of the Death Penalty in "Executing" Versus "Symbolic" States in the United States', *Texas Law Journal* (84) 2006, pp. 1869–1927.

Stein, G. M., 'Distinguishing among Murders when Assessing the Proportionality of the Death Sentence', *Columbia Law Review* 85 (1985), pp. 1786–1807.

Stephen, F., 'Capital Punishments', *Fraser's Magazine* 69 (1864), pp. 753–772.

Stolzenberg, L. and D'Alessio, S. J., 'Capital Punishment, Execution Publicity and Murder in Houston Texas', *Journal of Criminal Law and Criminology* 94 (2004), pp. 351–379.

Streib, V. L., 'Moratorium on the Death Penalty for Juveniles', *Law and Contemporary Problems* 61(1998), pp. 55–74.

—— 'Executing Women, Children, and the Retarded: Second Class Citizens in Capital Punishment', in J. R. Acker, R. M. Bohm, and C. S. Lanier (eds.), *America's Experiment with Capital Punishment* (2nd edn., 2003), pp. 301–323.

—— *Death Penalty in a Nutshell* (2005), St. Paul, MN: Thomson West.

—— *The Fairer Death: Executing Women in Ohio* (2006), Athens, Ohio: Ohio University Press.

Sundby, S. E., 'The Death Penalty's Future: Charting the crosscurrents of declining death sentences and the McVeigh factor', *Texas Law Review* 84 (2000), pp. 1929–1972.

—— 'The Capital Jury and Empathy: The Problem of Worthy and Unworthy Victims', *Cornell Law Review* 88 (2003), pp. 343–381.

Sunstein, C. R. and Vermeule, A., 'Is capital punishment morally required? Acts, omissions, and life-life tradeoffs' 58 *Stanford Law Review* (2006), pp. 703–750.

—— 'Deterring Murder: A Reply', *Stanford Law Review*, 58 (2006), pp. 847–857.

Svandize, E., 'Georgia, former republic of the USSR: managing abolition', in P. Hodgkinson and W. A. Schabas (eds.), *Capital Punishment: Strategies for Abolition* (2004), pp. 273–308.

Svensson, M., 'State Coercion, Deterrence, and the Death Penalty in the PRC', paper presented to the *Annual Meeting of the Association of Asian Studies*, Chicago, 22–25 March 2001.

Tabak, R. J., 'The Death of Fairness: The Arbitrary and Capricious Imposition of the Death Penalty in the 1980s', *New York University Review of Law and Social Change* 14 (1986), pp. 797–848.

—— 'Is Racism Irrelevant? Or should the Fairness in Death Sentencing Act be Enacted to Substantially Diminish Racial Discrimination in Capital Sentencing?', *New York University Review of Law and Social Change* 18 (1990–91), pp. 777–806.

—— Commentary; 'Finality without Fairness: Why we are Moving towards Moratoria on Executions, and the Potential Abolition of Capital Punishment', *Connecticut Law Review* 33 (2001), pp. 733–763.

—— 'Overview of Task Force Proposals on Mental Disability and the Death Penalty', *Catholic University Law Review* 54 (2004–05) pp. 1123–1131.

Tay, S. C., 'Human Rights, Culture, and the Singapore Example', *McGill Law Journal* 41 (1996), pp. 743–780.

Thompson, M. P., 'Homicide Survivors: A summary of the research' in R. C. Davis, A. J. Lurigio, and S. Herman (eds.), *Victims of Crime* (3rd edn., 2007), Los Angeles: Sage, pp. 109–124.

Tifft, L., 'Capital Punishment Research, Policy and Ethics: Defining Murder and Placing Murderers', *Crime and Social Justice* 21 (Summer 1982), pp. 61–68.

—— 'Reflections on Capital Punishment and the "Campaign against Crime" in the People's Republic of China', *Justice Quarterly* 2 (1985), pp. 127–137.

Timmons, P., 'Seed of Abolition: Experience and Culture in the Desire to End Capital Punishment in Mexico, 1841–1857', in A. Sarat and C. Boulanger (eds.), *The Cultural Lives of Capital Punishment: Comparative Perspectives* (2005), pp. 69–91.

Tobolowsky, P., 'Victim Participation in the Criminal Justice Process: Fifteen Years after the President's Task Force on Victims of Crime', *New England Journal on Criminal and Civil Confinement* 25 (1999), pp. 21–106.

Tournier, P. V., 'Systems of Conditional Release (Parole) in the Member States of the Council of Europe' (2006), <http://champpenal.revues.org/document378.html>.

Toussaint, P., 'The Death Penalty and the "Fairy Ring"', in Council of Europe, *The Death Penalty: Abolition in Europe* (1999), pp. 29–34.

Trevaskes, S., 'Severe and Swift Justice in China', *British Journal of Criminology* 47 (2007), pp. 23–41.

Trombley, S., *The Execution Protocol* (1993), London: Century.

Truog, R. D. and Brennan, T. A., 'Participation of Physicians in Capital Punishment', *New England Journal of Medicine* 329 (1993), pp. 1346–1349, and correspondence 330 (1994), pp. 935–937.

Turack, D. C., 'The New Chinese Criminal Justice System', *Cardozo Journal of International and Comparative Law* 7 (1999), pp. 49–70.

Turrell, R., *White Mercy: A Study of the Death Penalty in South Africa'* (2004), Westport, CT: Praeger Publishers.

Tyler, T. R. and Weber, R., 'Support for the Death Penalty: Instrumental Response to Crime, or Symbolic Attitude?', *Law and Society Review* 17 (1982), pp. 21–46.

Unah, I. and Boger, J. C., *Preliminary Report on the Findings of the North Carolina Death Penalty Study 2001* (April 2001).

United Kingdom, *Royal Commission on Capital Punishment 1949–1953*, Report (Cmd 8932, 1953), London: HMSO.

United Nations, *Capital Punishment* (Ancel Report), (1962).

United Nations, *Capital Punishment, Developments* 1961 to 1965 (Morris Report), (1967).

United States of America, Department of Justice, *Capital Punishment*, Bureau of Justice Statistics (Annual), Washington D.C.

—— *Sourcebook of Criminal Justice Statistics*, Bureau of Justice Statistics (Annual), Washington DC.

—— *Crime in the United States* (Annual), Washington DC: US Department of Justice.

—— *The Federal Death Penalty System: A Statistical Survey (1988–2000)* (12 September 2000), Washington DC.

—— US Department of Justice, *The Federal Death Penalty System: Supplementary Data, Analysis and Revised Protocols for Capital Case Review* (6 June 2001), Washington D.C.

Unnever, J. D. and Cullen, F. T., 'Executing the innocent and support for capital punishment: Implications for public policy', *Criminology & Public Policy* 4 (2005), pp. 3–38.

—— —— and Bartkowski, J. P., 'Images of God and Public Support for Capital Punishment: Does a Relationship with a Loving God Matter?', *Criminology* 44 (2006), pp. 833–864.

—— —— and Roberts, V., 'Not everyone strongly supports the death penalty: Assessing weakly-held attitudes toward capital punishment', *American Journal of Criminal Justice* 20 (2005), pp. 187–216.

Van Den Berg, G. P., 'The Soviet Union and the Death Penalty', *Soviet Studies* 35 (1983), pp. 154–174.

Van Den Haag, E., 'Justice, Deterrence and the Death Penalty' in J. R. Acker, R. M. Bohm, and C. S. Lanier (eds.), *America's Experiment with Capital Punishment* (2nd edn., 2003), pp. 233–249.

Vandiver, M., 'The Impact of the Death Penalty on the Families of Homicide Victims and of Condemned Prisoners', in J. R. Acker, R. M. Bohm, and C. S. Lanier (eds.), *America's Experiment with Capital Punishment* (2nd edn., 2003), pp. 613–645.

Van Duizend, R., 'Comparative Proportionality Review in Death Sentence Cases', *State Court Journal* 8(3) (1984), pp. 9–23.

Van Zyl Smit, D., 'Abolishing Life Imprisonment?', *Punishment and Society* 3 (2001), pp. 299–306.

—— *Taking life imprisonment seriously in national and international law* (2002), The Hague: Kluwer.

—— 'The death penalty in Africa', *African Human Rights Law Journal* 4 (2004), pp. 13–34.

—— 'The Abolition of Capital Punishment for Persons Under the Age of Eighteen Years in the United States of America. What Next?', *Human Rights Law Review* 5:2 (2005), pp. 393–401.

—— 'International Imprisonment', *International and Comparative Law Quarterly* 54 (April 2005), pp. 357–386.

—— 'Life imprisonment: Recent issues in national and international law', *International Journal of Law and Psychiatry* 29 (2006), pp. 405–421.

Virginia Law Review, Note, 'The Executioner's Song: Is there a Right to Listen?', 69 (1983), pp. 373–401.

Vasilevich, G. A. and Sarkisova E. A., 'Prospects for Abolition of the Death Penalty in the Republic of Belarus', *The Death Penalty in the OSCE Area, Background Paper 2006* (2006), pp. 9–17.

Vidmar, N. and Dittenhoffer, T., 'Informed public opinion and death penalty attitudes', *Canadian Journal of Criminology*, 23 (1981) pp. 43–56.

Vitiello, M., '*Payne v Tennessee*: A "Stunning Ipse Dixit"', *Notre Dame Journal of Law, Ethics and Public Policy* 8 (1994), pp. 165–280.

Vogelman, L., 'The Living Dead: Living on Death Row', *South African Journal on Human Rights* 5(2) (1989), pp. 183–195.

Walker, N., 'The Efficacy and Morality of Deterrence', *Criminal Law Review* (1979), pp. 125–144.

—— and Hough, M., 'Limits of Tolerance' in N. Walker and M. Hough, *Public Attitudes to Sentencing*, Cambridge Studies in Criminology (1988), Aldershot: Gower.

Wallace, D. H., 'The Need to Commute the Death Sentence: Competency for Execution and Ethical Dilemmas for Mental Health Professionals', *International Journal of Law and Psychiatry* 15 (1992), pp. 317–337.

—— and Sorensen, J. R., 'Missouri Proportionality Review: An Assessment of a State Supreme Court's Procedures in Capital Cases', *Notre Dame Journal of Law, Ethics and Public Policy* 8 (1994), pp. 281–315.

Warden, R., 'Illinois Death Penalty Reform: How it happened, what it promises', *Journal of Criminal Law and Criminology* 95 (2005), pp. 381–426.

Warren, M., *The Death Penalty in Canada: Facts, Figures and Milestones* (2001). London: Amnesty International.

—— 'Death, Dissent and Diplomacy: the U.S. Death Penalty as an Obstacle to Foreign Relations', 13 *William and Mary Bill of Rights Journal* (2004), pp. 309–337.

Wechsler, H., 'The Model Penal Code and the Codification of American Criminal Law', in R. Hood (ed.), *Crime, Criminology, and Public Policy: Essays in Honour of Sir Leon Radzinowicz* (1974), pp. 419–468. London: Heinemann.

Weinstock, D. and. Schwartz, G. E., 'Executing the Innocent: Preventing the Ultimate Injustice', *Criminal Law Bulletin* 34 (1998), pp. 328–347.

Weisberg, R., 'Deregulating Death', *Supreme Court Review* (1983), pp. 305–395.

—— 'The Death Penalty Meets Social Science: Deterrence and Jury Behavior Under New Scrutiny', *Annual Review of Law and Social Science* 1 (2005), pp. 151–170.

Whitehead, J. T., '"Good Ol' Boys" and the Chair: Death Penalty Attitudes of Policy Makers in Tennessee', *Crime and Delinquency* 44 (1998), pp. 245–256.

Whitman, J. Q., *Harsh Justice: Criminal Punishment and the Widening Divide Between America and Europe* (2003), New York: Oxford University Press.

Williams, C. W., 'The Federal Death Penalty for Drug-Related Killings', *Criminal Law Bulletin* 27 (1991), pp. 387–415.

Wills, G., 'The Dramaturgy of Death', *New York Review of Books* (21 June 2001).

Wilson, R. J., 'The Influence of International Law and Practice on the Death Penalty in the United States', in J. R. Acker, R. M. Bohm, and C. S. Lanier (eds.). *The American Experiment* (2nd edn., 2003), pp. 147–165.

Windlesham, Lord., *Responses to Crime*, Vol. 3 (1996), Oxford: Oxford University Press, pp. 60–61.

Wohlwend, R., 'The Efforts of the Parliamentary Assembly of the Council of Europe' in Council of Europe, *The Death Penalty: Abolition in Europe* (1999), pp. 55–67 and Appendix II, 'Europe a Death Penalty Free Continent' at pp. 171–184.

Wolpin, K. A., 'Capital Punishment and Homicide in England: A Summary of Results', *American Economic Review* 68 (1978), pp. 422–427.

Wright, J. H., 'Note, Life-Without-Parole: An alternative to death or not much of a life at all?', *Vanderbilt Law Review* 43 (1990), pp. 529–568.

Xinliang, C., *The Death Penalty in the United Nations Standards and China's Legal System of Criminal Justice* (1998), United Nations.

Yackle, L. W., 'The Great Writ in Action: Empirical Light on the Federal Habeas Corpus Debate', *New York University Review of Law and Social Change* 18 (1990–91), pp. 637–710.

—— 'The American Bar Association and Federal Habeas Corpus', *Law and Contemporary Problems* 61 (1998), pp. 171–192.

Yasuda, Y., 'The death penalty in Japan', in Council of Europe *The Death Penalty: Beyond Abolition* (2004), pp. 215–231

Yorke, J., 'The Evolving European Union Strategy Against the Death Penalty: from Internal Renunciation to Global Ideology—Part 1', *Amicus Journal* No. 16 (2006), pp. 23–28.

—— 'The Evolving European Union Strategy Against the Death Penalty: From Internal renunciation to a Global Ideology—Part 2', *Amicus Journal* No. 17 (2007), pp. 26–33.

Young, R. L., 'Race, Conceptions of Crime and Justice, and Support for the Death Penalty', *Social Psychology Quarterly* 54 (1991), pp. 67–75.

Zaohiu, Y., *New Crimes Emerging in the Process of China's Development and the Strategic Policies and Measures to be Taken,* UNAFEI Resource Material Series No. 30 (1986).

Zeisel, H., 'Comment', *American Journal of Sociology* 86 (1980), pp, 168–169.

—— 'Race Bias in the Administration of the Death Penalty: The Florida Experience', *Harvard Law Review* 95 (1981), pp. 456–468.

—— and Gallup, A. M., 'Death Penalty Sentiment in the United States', *Journal of Quantitative Criminology* 5 (1989), pp. 285–296.

Zhao, Bingzhi (ed.), *The Road of the Abolition of the Death Penalty in China. Regarding the Abolition of the Non-Violent Crime at the Present Stage*, Renmin University of China, Series of Criminal Jurisprudence (44) (2004), Beijing: Press of the Chinese People's Public Security University.

Zhao, Bingzhi., 'Existing State and Prospect of Death Penalty Reform in China at Present Time', *Working Papers, Launch Seminar of the China-EU project: Moving the Debate Forward: China's Use of the Death Penalty,* June 2007, Beijing: College for Criminal Law Science of Beijing Normal University and Great Britain-China Centre, pp. 162–168.

Zimmerman, P. R., 'Estimates of the Deterrent Effect of Alternative Execution methods in the United States: 1978–2000', *American Journal of Economics and Sociology* 65 (2006), pp. 909–941.

Zimring, F. E., 'Research on the Death Penalty: The Liberating Virtues of Irrelevance', *Law and Society Review* 27 (1993), pp. 9–17.

—— 'The Executioner's Dissonant Song: On Capital Punishment and American Legal Values', in A. Sarat (ed.), *The Killing State: Capital Punishment in Law, Politics and Culture* (1999), pp. 137–147.

—— *The Contradictions of American Capital Punishment* (2003), New York: Oxford University Press.

—— 'Symbol and Substance in the Massachusetts Commission Report', *Indiana Law Journal* 80 (2005) pp. 115–129.

—— 'The Unexamined Death Penalty: Capital Punishment and Reform of the Model Penal Code', 105 *Columbia Law Review* (2005), pp. 1396–1415.

—— and Hawkins, G., *Capital Punishment and the American Agenda* (1986), Cambridge: Cambridge University Press.

Cases Cited

Abu-Ali Abdur'Rahman v. Phil Bredesen	2005 Tenn. LEXIS 828
Arutyunyan v. Uzbekistan	HRC Communication No. 917/2000, UN Doc. CCPR/C/80/D/917/2000 (2004)
Ashby v. Trinidad and Tobago	HRC Communication No. 580/1994, UN Doc. A/57//40 Vol. II Annex IXA (2002)
Atkins v. Virginia	56 U.S. 304 (2002)
Bachan Singh v. State of Punjab	2 SCJ 474 (1980); AIR 1980 SC 898; AIR 1982 SC 1325; 1 SCR 145 (1983)
Baptiste v. Grenada	CR 38/00 (2000)
Barefoot v. Estelle	463 U.S. 880 (1983)
Batson v. Kentucky	476 U.S. 79 (1986)
Blystone v. Pennsylvania	494 U.S. 299 (1990)
Boodoo v. Trinidad and Tobago	HRC Communication No. 721/1996, UN Doc. CCPR/C/74/D/721/1996 (2002)
Booth v. Maryland	482 U.S. 496, 502 (1987)
Bowe and Davis v. The Queen	[2006] UKPC 10; [206] 1 WLR 1623
Boyce and Joseph v. The Queen	(2004) UKPC 32; [2005] 1 AC 400
Breard v. Greene	523 U.S. 371 (1989)
Brown v. Texas	443 U.S. 47 (1979)
Bryan v. Moore	528 U.S. 960 (1999); 528 U.S. 1133 (2000); 145 L.Ed.2d 927 (2000)
Burdine v. Johnson	231 F.3d 950 (5th Cir 2000); 262 F.3d 336 (5th Cir 2001); 122 S.Ct. 2347 (2002)
Callins v. Collins	114 S.Ct. 1127 (1994); 510 U.S. 1141 (1994)
Campbell v. Wood	18 F.3d 662 (1994)
Campbell v. Trinidad and Tobago	UKPC Appeal No. 6321 July 1999, unreported
Cantu-Tzin v. Johnson	162 F.3d 295 (5th Cir. 1998)
Carpo v. The Philippines	HRC Communication No. 1077/2002, UN Doc. CCPR/C/77/D/1077/2002 (2003)
Catholic Commission for Justice and Peace in Zimbabwe v. Attorney General	14 Human Rights Law J., 323 (1993)
Chambers v. Bowersox	157 F.3d 560 (8th Cir. 1998)
Chandler v. United States of America	218 F.3d 1305 (2000)
Clark v. Arizona	540 U.S. _ (2006)
Clark v. Arizona	No. 05–5966. 2006, 548 U.S. _2006
Coard and others v. The Attorney General of Grenada	UKPC 7 [2007]
Coker v. Georgia	433 U.S. 584 (1977)
Coleman v. Thompson	111 S.Ct. 2546 (1991); 510 U.S. 1141 (1994)
Commonwealth v. Fahy	737 A.2d 214, 217 (Pa. 1999)
Commonwealth v. Limone	2001 Mass. Super. LEXIS 7 (2001)
Commonwealth v. Logan	404 Pa. Super. 100, 590 A.2d 300 (1991)
Commonwealth v. Moser	No. 98002520, CC 9800585, 9802270, (1998)
Connecticut Board of Pardons v. Dumschat	452 U.S. 458 (1981)
Cooper v. Rimmer	379 F.3d 1029, 1033 (9th Cir. 2004)
Dawson v. The State	274 Ga. 327 (2001) Supreme Court of Georgia

Dobbs v. Zant	963 F.2d 1403 (11th Cir. 1991); 506 U.S. 357 (1993)
Domingues v. Nevada	526 U.S. 1156 (1999)
Eddings v. Oklahoma	455 U.S. 104 (1982)
Einhorn v. France	House of Lords Application No. 71555/01, 16 October 2001, unreported
Elledge v. Florida	525 U.S. 944 (1998)
Evans v. Trinidad and Tobago	HRC Communication No. 908/2000, UN Doc. CCPR/C/77/D/908/2000 (1999)
Fierro v. Gomez	(1994) 865 F.Supp. 1387 (N.D.Cal.)
Fierro v. Gomez	(1996), 77 F.3d 301 (9th Cir 1996)
Ford v. Wainwright	477 U.S. 399 (1986)
Fox v. The Queen	[2002] 2 AC 284
Francis and others v. Trinidad and Tobago	HRC Communication No. 899/1999, UN Doc. CCPR/C/75/D/899/1999 (2002)
Furman v. Georgia	408 U.S. 238 (1972)
Georgia v. McCollum	505 U.S. 42 (1992)
Germany v. United States of America, LaGrand Case	International Court of Justice, Judgment 27 July 2001, Press Release 2001/16
Godfrey v. Georgia	446 U.S. 420 (1980)
Gregg v. Georgia	428 U.S. 153 (1976)
Herrera v. Collins	506 U.S. 390 (1993)
Hilaire v. Trinidad and Tobago	Inter-American Commission Report 66/99 (1999).
Hilaire, Constantine and Benjamin v. Trinidad and Tobago	1 ACHR 2, Ser. C No. 94 (2002)
Howell v. Jamaica	HRC Communication No. 798/1998, UN Doc. CCPR/C/79/D/798/1998 (2003)
Hussain v. United Kingdom	Application 1996-I 252 (1996) 22 EHRR 1
Judge v. Canada	HRC Communication No. 829/1998, UN Doc. CCPR/C/78/D/829/1998 (2003)
Jurek v. Texas	428 U.S. 262 (1976)
Kansas v. Marsh	548 U.S. (2006)
Kennedy v. Trinidad and Tobago	RC Communication No. 845/1998, UN Doc. CCPR/C/74/D/845/1998 (2000)
Khalilova v. Tajikistan	HRC Communication No. 973/2001, UN Doc. CCPR/C/85/D/973/2001 (2005)
Khalilova v. Tajikistan	Annex IX, s. V, para. 6.5. Communication No. 973/2001, UN Doc. CCPR/C/83/D/978/2001
Khomidov v. Tajikistan	RC Communication No. 1117/2002, UN Doc. CCPR/C/81/D/1117/2002 (2004)
Kigula and 416 others v. The Attorney General	Constitutional Court of Uganda, Constitutional Petition No. 6 of 2003
Kindler v. Canada	[1991] 2 SCR 779
Kindler v. Canada	HRC Communication No. 470/1991 UN Doc. CCPR/C/48/D/470/1991 (1993)
Knight v. Florida	528 U.S. 990 (1999)
KQED v. Vasquez	1991 U.S. Dist. LEXIS 21163
Kurbanov v. Tajikistan	HRC Communication No. 1096/2002, UN Doc. CCPR/C/79/D/1096/2002 (2003)
Lackey v. Texas	115 S.Ct 1421 (1995)
Lewis v. Attorney General of Jamaica	[2000] 3 WLR 178

Lockett v. Ohio	438 U.S. 536
Lockhart v. McCree	476 U.S. 162 (1986)
Louisiana v. Wilson	685 So. 2d. 1096 (La. 1996)
McCarver v. State of North Carolina	533 U.S. 975
McCleskey v. Kemp	481 U.S. 279 (1987)
McCleskey v. Zant	499 U.S. 467 (1991)
Machhi Singh v. State of Punjab	AIR 1983 SC 957
Maggio v. Williams	464 U.S. 46 (1983)
Mansaraj and others v. Sierra Leone	HRC Communication Nos. 839, 840 and 841/1998, UN Doc. CCPR/C/72/D/840/1998 (2001)
Matthew v. State of Trinidad and Tobago	[2005] 1 AC 433
Mbushuu v. Republic	[1995] 1 LRC (Law Reports of the Commonwealth)
Mexico v. United States of America (Avena)	2004 ICJ 128 (31 March 2004)
Miller-El v. Dretke	545 U.S. 231 (2005)
Mithu v. State of Punjab	AIR 1983 SC 483; 2 SCR, 690 (1983)
Mohamed v. President of the Republic of South Africa and Others	2001 (3) SA 893
Moore v. Nebraska	528 U.S. 990 (1999)
Moore v. The State	274 Ga. 229 (2001) Supreme Court of Georgia
Morales v. Hickman	415 F. Supp. 2d 1037 (N.D. Cal. 2006)
Morales v. Tilton	465 F.Supp. 2d 972 (N.D. Cal. 2006)
Morgan v. Illinois	504 U.S. 719 (1992)
Mulai v. Republic of Guyana	HRC Communication No. 811/1998, UN Doc. CCPR/C/81/D/811/1998 (2004)
Nasiru Bello v. State	(1986) 5 NWLR (pt 45) 828
Neville Lewis and others v. The Attorney General of Jamaica and another	[2001] 2 AC 50
Nguyen Tuong Van v. Public Prosecutor	[2004] SGCA 47
Öçalan v. Turkey	Application No. 46221/99, ECHR, Judgment 12 March 2003 and 12 May 2005
Ohio Adult Parole Author v. Woodard	523 U.S. 272 (1998)
Panetti v. Quarterman	551 U.S. _ (2007)
Payne v. Tennessee	501 U.S. 808 (1991)
Penry v. Lynaugh	492 U.S. 302 (1989)
Piandiong and others v. The Philippines	HRC Communication No. 869/1999, UN Doc. CCPR/C/70/D/869/1999 (2000)
Pinto v. Trinidad and Tobago	HRC Communication No. 232/1987, UN Doc. CCPR/C/39/D/232/1987 (1990)
Pratt and Morgan v. The Attorney General for Jamaica	[1993] 4 All ER 769 (PC), [1994] 2 AC 1
Pratt and Morgan v. Jamaica	HRC Communication No. 230/1986 and 225/1987, UN Doc.Supp. No.40 (A/44/40) at 222 (1989)
Proffitt v. Florida	428 U.S. 242 (1976)
Pulley v. Harris	465 U.S. 37 (1984)
Queen v. Peter Hughes	[2002] 2 AC 259
R v. Mattan	Transcript provided by Smith Bernal, The Independent, 4 Mar. 1998
Ramjattan v. Trinidad and Tobago	The Times, 1 Apr. 1999
Re: Kevin Nigel Stanford	537 U.S. (2002)

Reid v. Jamaica	HRC Communication No. 355/1989, UN Doc. CCPR/C/51/D/355/1989 (1994)
Republic v. Mbushuu alias Dominic Mnyaroje and Kalai Sangula	Criminal Sessions Case No. 44 of 1991, [1994] Tanzanian Law Reports 146–173
Reyes v. The Queen	[2002] 2 AC 235
Ring v. Arizona	536 U.S. 584 (2002)
Roberts v. Louisiana	428 U.S. 325 (1976)
Robinson v. Jamaica	HRC Communication No. 223/1987, UN Doc. Supp. No. 40 (A/44/40) at 241 (1989)
Rompilla v. Beard	545 U.S. 374 (2005)
Roodal v. State of Trinidad and Tobago	[2005] 1 AC 328
Roper v. Simmons	543 U.S. 551 (2005)
Ruiz v. Estelle	679 F.2d. 1115 (5ᵗʰ Cir. 1982)
S v. Nehemia Tjijo	Unreported decision of 4 September 1991, reproduced in S v. Tcoeib (1996) 1 SACR 390
Sahadath v. Trinidad and Tobago	HRC Communication No. 684/1996 UN Doc. CCPR/C/74/D/684/1996 (1996)
Saidov v. Tajikistan	HRC Communication No. 964/2001, Views adopted on 8 July 2004
Saldano v. Texas	530 U.S. 1212 (2000)
Schick v. Reed	419 U.S. 256, 267 (1974)
Schriro v. Summerlin	542 U.S. 348 (2004)
Sextus v. Trinidad and Tobago	HRC Communication No. 818/1998, UN Doc. CCPR/C/72/D/818/1998 (2001)
Shafer v. South Carolina	532 U.S. 36 (2001)
Shashi Nayar v. UOI	[1992] 1 SCC 96
Simmons v. South Carolina	512 U.S. 154 (1994)
Skipper v. South Carolina	476 U.S. 1 (1986)
Smartt v. Republic of Guyana	HRC Communication No. 867/1999 (2004)
Soering v. United Kingdom	161 Eur.Ct. H.R. (Ser. A) 34, (1989) 11 EHRR 439
Sooklal v. Trinidad and Tobago	HRC Communication No. 928/2000, UN Doc. CCPR/73/D/928/2000 (2003)
South Carolina v. Gathers	490 U.S. 805 (1989)
Spaziano v. Florida	468 U.S. 447 (1984)
Spence and Hughes v. The Queen	Criminal Appeal No. 20 of 1998, Eastern Caribbean Court of Appeal Judgment (2 April 2001)
Stanford v. Kentucky	492 U.S. 361 (1989)
State v. Makwanyane	[1995] (3) S.A. 391
State v. Marshall	144 Wn.2d 266 (2001).
State v. Steele	921 So. 2d 538, 548–49 (Fla. 2005)
Strickland v. Washington	466 U.S. 668 (1984)
Sumner v. Shuman	486 U.S. 66 (1987)
Teague v. Lane	499 U.S. 288 (1989)
Teesdale v. Trinidad and Tobago	HRC Communication No. 677/1996, UN Doc. CCPR/C/74/D/677/1996 (2002)
Thompson v. Oklahoma	487 U.S. 815 (1989)
Thompson v. St Vincent and the Grenadines	HRC Communication No. 806/1998, UN Doc. CCPR/C/70/D/806/1998 (2000)
Trop v. Dulles	356 U.S. 86, 101 (1958)
Turner v. Murray	476 U.S. 28 (1986)

United States v. Burns	[2001] 1 SCR 283
Uttecht v. Brown	Case No. 06–413, decided 4 June 2007, US Supreme Court
V v. United Kingdom	Application No. 1999-IX III (2000) 30 EHRR 121
Walton v. Arizona	497 U.S. 639 (1990)
Wanza v. Trinidad and Tobago Communication	No. 683/1996
Washington v. Harper	494 U.S. 210 (1990)
Watson v. The Queen	[2005] 1 AC 400
Weeks v. United Kingdom	[1988] 10 EHRR 293
Weeks v. Angelone	528 U.S. 225 (2000)
Weems v. United States	217 U.S. 349 (1910)
Wiggins v. Smith	539 U.S. 510 (2003)
Wilkins v. Missouri	492 U.S. 361, 367] 1989
Williams v. Taylor	529 U.S. 362 (2000)
Wilson v. Smith	No. 86–1751 (E.D. LA Feb. 12, 1990)
Woodson v. North Carolina	428 U.S. 280 (1976)
Zant v. Stephens	462 U.S. 862 (1983)

Index

Abolition *see also* public opinion
approach taken towards 6–8
de facto 12–17 *passim*, 23, 35, 410–11
effect on murder rate, *See* Deterrent effect
effect on probability of conviction
319–20, 326–27
history of 9–13
human rights and 18–20, 28–32, 37–8
international treaties and 20–4
opposition to 32–5, 36–8
pace of 12–18
political pressure for 24–32
setbacks to 16
Abolitionist countries *see also* individual
countries
list, all crimes 405–08
list, ordinary crimes 409
list, between 1989 and 2007 412–13
number of 14, 405, 409
ratified international treaties 414–16
Abolitionist movement in
Africa south of the Sahara 73–84
Asia and the Pacific 84–103
Caribbean 103–11
Eastern Europe 50–3
Former Soviet Union 53–60
Middle East and North Africa 66–73
North America 35–9, 111–28
South and Central America 61–5
Western Europe and Australasia 40–50
Abraham, Lynne 379
Abu-Ali Abdur'Rahman v. Phil Bredesen 163,
64(38)
Acker, J.A. 211(104), 244(133), 260n(222),
263(235), 288(43), 289(48), 290,
291(58, 60), 295(78), 312(145), 315,
333(65)
Adams, John C. 312(144)
Adeyemi, A.A. 83(95), 329
Adultery 72, 133, 141, 142, 150, 156, 189,
219(16)
Afghanistan 32(83), 70, 142, 143, 150,
165(43), 217, 218, 248, 249
public executions 166
religious dissent 143
sexual offences 142, 150–1
Africa *see also* individual countries 24, 32, 40,
66, 73–84, 137, 141, 188(3), 265, 279,
280, 283, 319, 323, 352, 354, 371, 374,
381, 384(3), 387, 399(81), 400
abolitionist countries 14, 15

sub-Saharan 78–84
African Charter on Human and People's
Rights 24, 82
African Commission on Human and People's
Rights 24, 82, 265, 268(267)
Age, maximum for execution 194–5, 286,
319(13)
Aggravating factors 50–1, 54, 58–60, 74, 141,
143(73), 283, 295–6, 325, 326
in United States 120–123, 138, 231,
236–8, 240, 241, 242, 287–91,
294–300, 301, 304, 307, 309(131),
324, 362
Akers, Ronald L. 337(77)
Alabama 26(54), 115, 116, 121, 157, 159(19),
202, 245, 285, 295(81), 388, 389
aggravating factors 242, 296
legal representation 225–6, 229, 291
Alaska 12(15), 112(219), 389
Albania 17(25), 51–2, 60(75)
Albrecht, Hans-Jörg 145(79), 152, 195(41),
198(48), 207, 208(89), 218(9), 222,
255(196), 269(272), 286(37), 376(131),
387(15)
Albright, Madeline 234
Alcohol abuse/treatment 346, 387
Algeria 33(87), 66, 67, 130(5), 135(24, 25),
139(40, 43), 400(83)
death row 173(73)
kidnapping 143(73)
retroactive introduction 133
trial procedures 248
Al-Hewish, Sheik 72(33)
Alston, Philip 132, 140, 142, 154, 174, 218,
223, 281
Alternatives to capital punishment
conditions of confinement, under 393,
395–98
determinate periods of imprisonment 286,
387
juveniles, for 194, 398–402
life imprisonment 59, 204, 384
life imprisonment without parole
(LWOP) 94, 115, 117(236), 122, 124
(264), 211, 237, 240(114), 275 (292),
293, 294, 298, 321, 347, 363–6, 380,
383–403 *passim*
option foreclosed 91–92
public opinion and 154, 359(36), 361,
362(45), 363–6, 375, 380
range of penalties 385–8

Ambepity, Judge Sarath 88
American Association of Mental
    Retardation 201
American Bar Association 121, 119(245), 120,
    157(8), 191, 201(64), 206, 207, 211,
    226–7, 229–30, 242, 257(205), 258,
    356, 357
  Alabama Death Penalty Assessment
    Report 121(252), 226(52), 242, 291,
    291(62)
  Arizona Death Penalty Assessment
    Report 226(50), 291, 291(62)
  Florida Death Penalty Assessment
    Report 210, 227(59), 242, 258(213),
    264
  Georgia Death Penalty Assessment
    Report 121(251), 242, 290(55),
    307(125)
  Indiana Death Penalty Assessment
    Report 121(253), 226(53)
  Tennessee Death Penalty Assessment
    Report 121(254), 226(53) 242,
    301(99), 310
American Civil Liberties Union 179
American College of Physicians 168, 169
American Convention on Human Rights to
    Abolish the Death Penalty 23, 36
    63(91), 64, 65, 108, 111, 131, 133(17)
    187
  ratification 36, 65, 414–16
  Trinidad's withdrawal 111
American Declaration on the Rights and
    Duties of Man 36, 108
American 'Exceptionalism' 126, 354–5
American Medical Association 162(32), 169,
    170, 171
American Nurses Association 169
American Psychiatric Association 201, 207,
    228
American Psychological Association 207, 401
American Public Health Association 169
American Society of Anesthesiologists 169–70
Amnesty International 17, 68, 70, 71, 75, 7
    78, 80, 81, 86, 90, 94, 95, 96, 97, 103,
    104, 141, 146–51, 172, 178, 184, 208,
    209, 210, 219, 223, 228, 248, 249, 255,
    257, 262, 264, 267, 400–1
  death sentences and executions annual
    returns 3, 59, 146–50
  executions in China 147–50, 151, 190,
    254–5
  women execution of, 196
Amsterdam Treaty of the EU, 24
Anaya, Governor 263(235)
Ancel, Marc 1, 12, 14, 40, 41, 203, 278, 325
Andenaes, J. 321(17)
Andorra 16(24)

Angel, Arthur Judah 178
Angola 15(22), 17(25), 73, 400(83)
Anguilla 104(189), 107(201), 282(18)
Anti-Terrorism and Effective Death Penalty
    Act 114, 136(30), 256–7
Antigua-Barbuda 104, 105, 107, 195, 282(18),
    399(81)
Antoine, R. M. B. 255(198)
Apostasy 71, 72, 131, 133, 142, 143(69)
Appeal *see* Right to appeal
Applegate, Brandon. 362(52), 367(72)
Appleton, Catherine 391(35)
Arab Charter on Human Rights 24, 66
Arbuthnot, J. 247(157)
Arbitrary death penalty and executions 21,
    42, 52, 100, 109, 113, 115, 117, 120,
    121, 233, 264, 278–84, 286–7, 295–6,
    299–303, 308–10, 315, 320, 349, 353,
    368, 391, 394
Archer D. 327(36)
Arco Progresista 353
Arendt, Hannah 66(10)
Ariens, Jan 175(88)
Argentina 11, 12(16), 61, 62
Arizona 26(54), 159(20), 194, 226(50),
    236(101), 295(81), 305
  discretionary death penalty 291, 296
  foreign nationals consular assistance
    234–5
  innocence 275
  legal representation 121, 232
  method of execution 161, 191(19)
Arkansas 26(54), 262(234), 297
  mentally ill 211
  mentally retarded 202(68), 209, 357
  method of execution 124
Armed robbery 77, 80, 104, 140, 190, 249,
    279, 289, 320, 328–9
  executions for *see also* under countries 83,
    151
Armenia 55(53), 58, 60(75)
Arnold, Justin R. 314(149)
Arroyo, President 86–7, 261, 391
Arson 11(9), 42, 114, 137, 297(87)
Arutyunyan v. Uzbekistan 217(7)
Ashby, Glen 107
Ashby v. Trinidad 224(43), 254(192)
Ashcroft, John D. 356, 379
Ashworth 386(12)
Asia *see* also individual countries 158(12),
    172(69), 216, 268(265), 396
  abolitionist movement 15, 49, 55, 84–89,
    97–102
  abolitionist states 85, 88
  Asian values 7, 102–3
  resistance to abolition 32, 40, 89–97
  trading in illicit drugs 137–8

Asia Pacific Forum on National Human Rights
  Institutions 84
Asian Human Rights Charter 24, 84, 103
Asian Human Rights Commission 87, 103
Atkins v. Virginia 37, 115, 127, 192, 198,
  200–6
Australia 31, 40, 49, 95, 250(172), 267(260),
  325, 326, 354, 360, 376–7, 387,
  399(81)
  New South Wales 12, 49
  Queensland 12(15)
  South Australia 325(29), 387
  Western Australia 49
Austria 11, 12(16), 22, 372, 387, 395, 400(82)
Azerbaijan 17(25), 23, 30(76), 34, 55(53), 57,
  60(75–6)

Bachan Singh v. State of Punjab 91, 285
Badinter, Robert 47, 352(12), 375, 402
Bahamas 17, 104–5, 109(210), 265, 281–3
Bahrain 3(6), 17, 32(83), 67, 135(24, 25),
  137(33), 195(38), 197, 279
  legal representation 220
  mandatory death penalty 280
  pardon 258, 262
  protection of innocent 217
  right of appeal 253
Bailey, Victor 44(12)
Bailey, W.C. 318, 324(27), 327(36), 328,
  330(50), 331
Baime, Hon David S. 305(119)
Bakiyev, President Kurmanbek 58
Baldus, David 225(45), 238, 240–1, 299–300,
  301–3, 304–6, 308–10, 311–15
Bali Nine 49
Bandes, S. 246
Bangbose, O. 329(46)
Bangladesh 32(83), 97, 135(24)
  aircraft hijacking/sabotage 136
  death row 173(73)
  drugs offences 137(33), 138
  economic crime 139(40–1)
  kidnapping 143(73)
  method of execution 156
  military tribunals/special courts 248, 249
  miscarriages of justice 267, 269
  pregnant women 195(38)
  right of appeal 253
  trial procedures 217, 219
Banner, S. 9, 10(4), 127, 155(1)
Bantekas, I, 33(88)
Baptiste v. Grenada 281
Barbados 104
  death row 181
  legal representation 220
  mandatory death penalty 109, 279, 281–2
  pregnant women 195(39)
  right of appeal 104, 110, 251

  trial procedures 217
Bard, Jennifer S. 204(79)
Barefoot, Thomas 293
Barefoot v. Estelle 293(71)
Barkan, Steven E. 359(37), 371(98)
Barnett, Arnold. 303(110)
Barry, D. 269(273)
Bassiouni, M. Cherif 34, 71, 72, 243
Batra, Bikram Jeet. 93, 182(116), 259(215),
  279(6), 286(34)
Batson v. Kentucky 240
Beccaria, Cesare 10–11, 42(6), 322
Beck, E. 184, 397–8
Becker, G. 319
Beckham, J. C. 213(111)
Bedau, Hugo Adam 118(239), 127(276), 262,
  263(240), 273, 279(3), 348, 360(44),
  362, 383, 394
Belarus 130(5), 325–6
  abolition movement 15, 24–5, 26(53), 59,
  60, 129
  declining executions 60, 149
  families of prisoners 184
  mentally retarded 197
  methods of execution 156
  pardon 259
  pregnant women 195–6
  public opinion 60
  right of appeal 251, 253
Belgium 16(24), 41, 387, 400(82)
Belize
  de facto abolitionism 61, 104
  mandatory death penalty 61, 107,
  280, 282
  miscarriages of justice 267
Beloof 244(140), 245(145), 246(151)
Bendremer, F. J. 313(147)
Benin 15(23), 75, 76, 140(49), 400(83)
Bentele, U. 240, 294(76–7)
Bentley, Derek 45, 268(170)
Berger, Vivian 254(191), 255(46)
Beristain, A. 359(40)
Berk, Richard A. 345
Bermuda 104(189)
Beyleveld, D. 321(17)
Bhagwati, J. 91(128)
Bhutan 15, 16(24), 85
Bingham, Lord 109, 282
'Birmingham Six' 47
Bishop, Maurice 105
Biskupic, Joan 291(58)
Black, Theodore 340
Blackmun, Justice 119(242), 295–6, 378–9
Blume, John H. 179, 180(109), 205, 213,
  243(128), 245(144, 146), 313(146)
Blumstein Al 347(19)
Blystone v. Pennsylvania 115, 290
Boger, Jack 315(152)

Boger, John Charles 203(105), 307(125)
Bohm, R.M. 327(36), 359(37), 363(58), 367–8, 373(106), 395(62)
Bolivia 61
Bonner, Raymond 200(60), 290(53), 295(78, 80), 330(52), 333(66)
Bonnie, Richard J. 201(65), 205(81), 210(101), 212, 213(111), 256(203)
Boodoo v. Trinidad and Tobago 224(43)
Booth v. Maryland 244, 244(139), 245, 245(143)
Borg, M. 156
Borshchev, Valerii 269
Bosch, Mariette 79
Bosnia-Hercegovina 17(25), 35, 51, 60(75–6)
Bossuyt, Marc J. 351(2)
Botswana 26(53), 79, 82, 83(94), 351(2)
    families of prisoners 184
    LWOP, 400(83)
    mandatory death penalty 280
    procedural rights 221, 265
Bouzouba, Mohamed 67
Bowden, Jerome 199
Bowe and Davis v. The Queen 107, 107(206), 109(210), 283, 283(23)
Bowers, W.J.11(11), 112(219), 224, 237–9, 240, 241(120), 242(124), 294(76, 77), 322(19), 326(53), 329(48), 334, 339, 340(87), 345(109), 363, 365, 366(67), 390(30)
Boyce and Joseph v. the Queen 109, 109(211)
Boyd, Arthur 161
Brame, Robert 307(125)
Brazil 11, 12n, 61, 62, 65, 375, 387, 388
Breard, Angel 127
Breard v. Greene 37, 127, 234
Brennan, Justice William J. Jr 225
Breyer, Justice 123, 182, 236
Bright, Stephen B. 127(277), 209(95), 229, 230(74), 266, 356(20)
British Medical Association 168(58)
British Transplant Society 172
British Virgin Islands 104(180), 107(201), 282(18)
Broda, Christian 22
Brodsky, S. L. 213(111)
Broffitt, B. 305(118)
Brooks, Richard 356(20)
Brown, Willie Jr 170
Brown v. Texas 294
Brunei Darussalam 88, 137(33), 138, 195 (38), 223, 265, 279, 399(81)
'Brutalization' hypothesis 167, 322, 334–7, 341(92), 342, 345(110), 347
Bryan v. Moore 159(18)

Bryan, Robert 206
Bulgaria 17(25), 51, 60(75), 68, 391
Bundy, Ted 360
Burdine v. Johnson 228–9
Burger, President 64
Burkhead, M. 247(157)
Burkina Faso 15(23), 75, 139(40)
Burma *see* Myanmar
Burnett, C. 262(234)
Burns, Gordon, B. 213(112)
Burr, R. 247
Burundi 17, 78, 133, 173(73), 195(38), 217, 248, 251, 253, 400(83)
Bush, President George W. 200, 228, 249, 260(221), 317, 357
Bush, Governor Jeb 164
Bhutto, Benazir 96(156)

Cabana, Don 185
Calabrasi, S.G. 159(21)
California 29(73), 167(53), 260(220), 294, 295, 328, 335, 395(61)
    aggravating factors 297
    death row 115, 172, 177–8
    extradition 159
    legal representation 232
    LWOP, 389, 401
    mental retardation 202
    method of execution 124, 159, 162–3, 170(61)
    probability of being sentenced to death 300
    public opinion 355, 357, 368, 369
    racial disparities 305, 307
Callins v. Collins 295, 296(64)
Cambodia 15, 17, 30, 85, 354
    League for Promotion and Defence of Human Rights 85(98)
Cameroon 15(23), 32(83), 75, 130(5), 139(40), 195(38), 400(83)
Camiker, E. 159(21)
Campbell v. Trinidad and Tobago 207(88)
Campbell v. Wood 158(11)
Canada 111–12, 386
    abolition, impact of 320
    crime trends 325–7
    extradition from 29–30, 158–9, 181
    public opinion 352, 353, 354, 363, 364, 365, 377
Cantu-Tzin v. Johnson 257
Cape Verde 15(22) 73, 400(83)
Capital murder *see* murder
Caribbean countries see also Commonwealth Caribbean countries individual countries 17, 40, 103–11, 156, 180–1, 207, 223, 280, 282–3, 374
    abolition extent 17, 104–6

Caribbean Court of Justice 110, 111(216), 118
Carpo v. The Philippines 281(15)
Carroll, John L. 175(88)
Cassell, Paul 246(150), 272(285), 273(289)
Catholic Commission for Justice and Peace in Zimbabwe v. Attorney General 180(111)
Cauthen, J. N. G. 257(209)
Cayman Islands 104(189)
Ceauçescu, President 15(21), 25, 50, 354
Celeste, Governor 263(235)
Central African Republic 15(23), 75
Central America *see also* individual countries and abolitionist movement 40, 61–5
Centre for Capital Punishment Studies 3, 388(16)
Cerna, Christine A. 23(44), 64(95)
Ceylon *see* Sri Lanka
Chad 17, 78, 82(88), 133, 400(83)
    procedural rights 217, 251, 253, 259
Chambers v. Bowersox 182(118)
Chan, Janet 337
Chan v. Guyana 220(18)
Chandler v. United States of America 229
Chaskalson, Judge Arthur 74, 381–2
Cheatwood, Daryl 330(51)
Chechnya 54(50), 55, 165(143), 248
Chemarinsky, E. 159(21)
Chen, J. 347(119)
Chen Zhonglin 147
Cheng Kejie 152
Chenwi, Lilian 83(88), 384(60)
Chile 15, 61, 65(100), 133
China
    abolitionist movement 32(83), 35–6, 50, 84, 100, 102, 352, 365
    deterrent justification 319, 320(16), 366(69)
    discretionary / mandatory death penalty 279(7), 286
    EU–China Human Rights Seminars 26, 130(5)
    executions 3, 10, 98, 146–52, 156, 158
    extradition 31
    Hong Kong *see* Hong Kong
    human rights 100–1
    information, lack of accurate, State secret 153–4, 198
    juveniles 190
    legal representation 219, 222
    mentally retarded 198
    mentally ill 207–8
    miscarriages of justice 267, 269
    organs for transplantation 171–2
    pardon or commutation of sentence 258
    pregnant women 195
    procedural rights 100–1, 217–8, 254–5
    public executions 165–6, 168
    public opinion 352
    rendition/repatriation 84, 96, 151
    right of appeal 252, 254–5
    scope of death penalty 98–9, 129, 135, 136, 137, 139, 141, 142, 143(73), 144, 144–6, 150–1
    strike hard campaigns 99–100, 198, 219, 269, 320
    Supreme People's Court 252, 258, 286
    women 196
Chirouf, L, 221(28)
Cho, Byung-Sun 89(110), 102
Christ, A. M. 315(151)
Christopher, Gary W. 301(101), 302(106)
Civil war 81, 83, 85
Clark, Joseph 163–4
Clark v. Arizona 204
Clement, Governor Frank 262(234)
Clemency *see also* Commutation of sentence 17, 43, 60, 73n, 88, 95, 96, 120, 154, 172, 174, 177n, 182, 199, 208, 215, 229, 230, 235, 250, 253, 254, 257–64, 265, 276, 282, 300, 386, 392
Clinton, President 209(95), 229, 310, 357
Cloninger, Dale 327, 328(41)
Coard and others v. The Attorney General of Grenada 283(24)
Cochran, John K. 335(74)
Cohen, Jerome 98(165)
Cohn, Steven F. 359(37), 371(98)
Coker v. Georgia 113, 142, 318
Coldham, S. 77(56)
Coleman, Kathryn 320(14), 327(35)
Coleman v. Thompson 256
Colombia 11, 12(15), 31, 61, 65(100), 75(44), 178(102), 387, 388
Colorado 297, 301, 401, 402(95)
Common Sense Foundation 228
Commonwealth v. Fahy 204
Commonwealth v. Limone 273
Commonwealth v. Logan 204
Commonwealth v. Moser 204
Community of San Edigio 28
Commutation of sentence *see also* Clemency 10, 12, 33(86), 36, 43, 49, 51, 55, 57, 58, 62, 68, 72, 73(38), 75–7, 81, 86, 87, 88, 89, 96, 106, 120, 134, 154, 174, 178, 182, 189, 192, 195, 204(79), 206, 209, 211, 254, 257–64, 268, 273, 274(292), 287, 292, 340, 384, 386, 391, 398
Comoros 17, 78, 279(7)
    legal representation 220
Congo, Republic of (Brazzaville) 15(23), 75

Congo, Democratic Republic of 81–2
  death row 173(73)
  executions 3, 81, 148, 149, 151
  juveniles 190, 254, 400(85)
  pregnant women 195
  public executions 165(43)
  scope of death penalty 136(30)137, 139(40,
    44), 140(49), 151
  special courts 81, 248–9
  women 195–6
Connecticut 17, 123(262), 297, 305, 400(87)
Connecticut Board of Pardons v.
  Dumschat 263(262)
Constanzo, M. 236(98)
Constanzo, S. 236(98)
Consular assistance *see* Foreign nationals
Cook, Kerry Max 175(88)
Cooper v. Rimmer 162(34)
Cook Islands 85
Costa Rica 11, 12(15), 61, 65(100)
Côte d'Ivoire 15(23), 16(24), 73, 400(83)
Council of Europe 22, 41, 42(4), 46, 48, 114,
  396, 397
  Committee of Ministers 29, 259
  Guidelines on Human Rights 28–9
  promotion of abolition 24–6, 31
  LWOP policy on 392–3
Coyle, Andrew 388(19), 397, 402
Craig, Christopher 45
Crist, Governor Charlie, 165
Croatia 17(25), 51, 60(75, 76), 387, 388
Cuba 353, 399(81)
  Commission for Human Rights 178
  death row 173(73), 178
  Guantanamo Bay 249–50,
  mentally ill prisoners 203,
  scope of death penalty 104, 136, 137 140n,
    141
  women 196
Cullen F.T. 191(19), 362(52), 367(94), 369,
  371(94), 372(104)
'Culpability scores' 302
Cuomo, Governor Mario 122(259)
Cushing, Renny. 185(137), 186(142),
  380(153)
Cyprus 41, 42
Czech Republic 15(21), 17, 25, 51, 60(75), 376

D'Alessio, Stewart 336
Daniels, Governor Mitch 206
Davis, M. 169(59)
Dawson v. The State 157(8)
Death Penalty Information Center 39(107),
  112(219), 115(229), 117(234), 118,
  142(66), 200(59), 209, 210(100),
  225(47), 271, 274, 311(139), 365(64),
  391(36)

Death Penalty Project (London) 79, 80(72),
  140(52), 374(114)
Death row 55, 61, 80, 95(144), 107, 110, 115,
  135(22), 142, 151, 157, 172–86, 394,
  398,
  aged prisoners on 194–5, 252, 268
  conditions 39, 76, 90, 175–80, 171, 181
  'death row phenomenon/syndrome' 28, 35,
    180–3, 195
  failure to inform of date of execution 173,
    268
  families' experiences 183–6
  foreign nationals on 234–5
  juveniles on 189
  mental health of prisoners on 39, 174,
    177–9, 199, 203(76), 204–13,
    263, 274
  number on 76, 87, 88, 97, 111, 172–3, 225,
    323, 390–1
  removal from 75, 77, 118, 120, 174, 178,
    192, 261–3, 266, 283, 340,
    396, 397
  time spent on 31(81), 76, 106, 124, 173–4,
    179, 252, 255, 261, 271–2, 274, 340
  women on 179, 196
Decker, Scott H. 328(43)
Deitchman, M. A. 213(111)
de Klerk, F.W. 74
Delaware 284–5, 297
Delzin, Gregory 110(214)
Demjanjuk, John 268
Denmark 12(16), 40, 41, 387, 400(82)
Denno, Deborah W. 159, 160(24, 25, 26)
Deterrent effect 7, 10, 19, 19, 35, 42, 43, 53,
  76, 87, 89, 103, 110, 120, 139, 153,
  168, 197, 206, 237, 272–3, 274–5,
  280, 308, 318–49 *passim*, 352, 362,
  366(69), 370, 378, 383
  alternative penalties and 383, 386
  'brutalization' hypothesis 322, 334
  concept of 319, 321–22
  effect denied 10, 19, 48, 53, 87, 120,
    139
  effect not relevant 193, 187, 206
  justification for death penalty 7, 10, 35, 42,
    43, 76, 89, 103, 110, 168, 237, 292–93,
    272–73, 274, 280, 308, 317–19, 378
  public opinion and 350, 362, 366 (69),
    373, 375
  studies of deterrence
    comparative studies 329–33
    crime trend studies 325–29
    econometric studies 337–44
    immediate impact studies 333–7
    implications for policy of 347–9
    methodological problems of 339–40,
      344–7

Deukmejian, Governor George 357
Dezhbakhsh, H. 327(39), 340–43, 346,
    349
Dieter, Richard C. 369(83), 370, 371(95),
    373(108), 391
Diminished mental responsibility 193, 198,
    199, 204, 205
Disappearances 67, 194, 380(154)
Discretionary death penalty 11, 15, 43, 45,
    74, 77, 91, 106, 138(35), 145, 280,
    284, 286, 288, 323, 384
    United States *see also* United States of
        America 114, 294, 312, 315, 385
District of Columbia (Washington DC)
    112(219), 115, 200, 150, 232
Dix, G. E. 205(81), 308(130)
Diya 72, 97, 174, 233, 243
Djibouti 15(22), 32(83), 73, 400(83)
DNA evidence/testing 118, 120, 256(208),
    263, 274–6, 370
    exonerations through 118(240), 197, 275
    convicted person's access to 117, 275
    proof of innocence 20, 128, 274–6
Dobbs v. Zant 312, 312(142)
Dobryninas 25(50), 56
    Doctors *see* Physicians
Dominica 104, 105, 107, 135(24), 282(18),
    399(81)
Dominican Republic 104, 374
Domingues v. Nevada 191
Donohue, John J. 318(4), 323, 327, 328(42),
    343(106), 346
Douglass, John 284
Dow, David 257
Drewry, Gavin 47(18)
Drug-related offences 69, 90, 91, 95, 96, 99,
    114, 115, 131, 133, 137–9, 145, 151,
    196, 248, 279–80, 297, 311, 320, 347,
    389, 394
Drug trafficking 31, 64, 70, 92, 95, 96, 98,
    104, 114, 137–9, 195, 297
    mandatory death penalty for 138–9,
        279–80
Drug protocols (for execution) 160–5
Dukakis, Michael. 357
Dumbutshena, Chief Justice E. 73(37),
    280(10)

East Timor (formerly Timor Leste) 16, 85
Eastern Europe *see also* individual
        countries 40, 102
    abolitionist movement 24–5, 50–3, 60
Eberhardt, Jennifer 306
Economic offences 31, 52, 54, 58, 60, 96, 97,
    98, 99, 100, 101, 102, 139–40, 145,
    146, 151, 152, 320
Ecuador 11, 12(15), 61, 65(100,101)

Eddings v. Oklahoma 191, 289(49)
Edds, Margaret 197(47)
Edwards, W. J. 199(56)
Egypt 3(6), 32(83), 33, 69–70, 130(5),
    137(33), 400(83)
    executions 70, 148–9, 156, 184
    foreign nationals 233
    mandatory death penalty 279
    pardon or commutation of sentence 258,
        259
    right of appeal 251
    scope of death penalty 69, 135–6, 141, 142,
        286
    special courts 248–9
    trial procedures 217, 220
Ehrlich, Isaac 338–9, 340, 341, 343,
    344–5
Eichmann, Adolf 133
Einhorn v. France 392
Eisengerg, Theodore 237, 239(111, 112),
    313(146), 265(66)
Ekland–Olson, Sheldon–292(67)
El Salvador 61, 258, 280, 387
Electric chair 157–9, 273, 340, 342, 391
Elledge v. Florida 182
Ellis, Ruth 45
Ellsworth, Phoebe C. 362(54), 367(73, 78),
    373(105, 110, 111, 112)
Engel, Pauline 49(27)
Ensemble Contre la Peine de Mort 27
Equatorial Guinea 82–3
    public executions 165(45), 166
Eritrea 15(23), 75, 233, 400(83)
Estonia 17(25), 55, 60(75, 76), 387
Estrada, President 86, 261
Ethics 111, 162, 163(36), 168–72, 212–3,
    319
Ethiopia 81, 139(40), 173(73), 233
Eugenics 11–12
EU/China human rights dialogues
        seminars 26, 100, 144(75), 151(89),
        195(41), 269(272), 286(37), 352(8),
        354(15), 376(151)
European Convention for the Protection
        of Human Rights and Fundamental
        Freedoms (ECHR) 22, 24, 27(63),
        31(81), 48, 53, 54, 180, 392,
        393(45)
    Protocol No 6 22, 23, 47, 48, 50(33), 51,
        52, 54, 55, 56, 58, 60, 414–16
    Protocol No 13 23, 48, 52, 414–16
European Convention on the Suppression of
        Terrorism 29
European Council for the Prevention of
        Torture 397
European Court of Human Rights 27–8, 48,
        180, 392, 399

European Union *see also* individual Member
    States 22–32, 54, 69
  abolition as precondition for
      membership 22–5
  Charter of Fundamental Rights 25, 28
  diplomatic efforts in third countries 25–8,
      95, 111
  extradition, prohibition 28–32
  guidelines to third countries 25–8
  LWOP, position on 392, 400
Evans, Richard J. 10(5), 12(12), 19, 41(2), 45,
    50(51), 352(12), 359(40), 376(131)
Evans v. Trinidad and Tobago 244(43)
Evidence 116, 119(246), 123, 215, 216,
    217–19, 221, 222, 229, 231, 240, 250,
    252, 254, 255, 263, 266, 269–76, 284,
    287–8, 289–90, 294
  DNA *see* DNA evidence
  false or fabricated 143
  psychiatric/medical/scientific 203–14,
      228, 293
  victim impact 243(128), 244–7, 378
'evolving standards of decency' 37, 38,
    124(264), 192, 200, 206, 355
Ewing, C. P. 169(53)
Executioners
  Volunteers 17
Executions *see also* entries for individual
      countries
  abolitionist countries, former use of 40–65
      passim
  accurate information, need for 153–4
  aged, of 194–5
  alternatives to 383–98 *passim*
  Amnesty International annual
      returns 146–8
  arbitrariness of 278–316 *passim*
  attempts to speed up 180–3
  botched 159–65
  closure, as 350, 378–380
  competence to be executed 208–213
  crimes other than murder, for 13, 40(1),
      41, 47(20), 50, 130, 134, 142, 145,
      150–53
  deterrent, as a *see* Deterrent effect
  extra-judicial 6, 54
  innocent, of the 19, 20, 52, 116–20,
      266–76 , 318
  juveniles, of 24, 38, 190–194
  lethal injection, by 124, 160–165
  mentally ill, of 39, 203–213
  mentally retarded, of 37, 45, 196–203
  methods of 10, 34(90), 39, 124, 156–65
  moratorium on 24, 26–8, 33–4, 37, 66,
      113, 123, 357–8
  pending legal proceedings 37, 107, 127, 265
  physicians role in 168–72

probability of 302, 322–4
public 43, 165–8
racial discrimination in 303–8
retentionist countries, use in 66–128 *passim*
taboo against 17
time between conviction and execution *see*
    Death row
trends in use of 12–14, 16–18, 40–4,
    113–16, 146–50
UN safeguards relating to 155–6, 187
'volunteers' 179–80, 213
women, of 45, 195–6
Extenuating circumstances 61, 197, 280
Extradition 28–32, 37, 57(60), 67, 75, 158,
    159, 180, 181, 392
Extra-judicial executions 6, 54, 67, 70, 83, 87,
    88, 166, 194
Exum, Chief Justice James Jr 119(242)

Fagan, Jeffrey 192(28), 270(279), 271(281),
    324, 331, 333, 341, 343, 347, 348
Fair/unfair trials 27(63), 28, 36, 80–2, 103,
    106, 119–21, 123, 128, 136(28), 183,
    203, 206, 215–32, 293–6, 357, 367,
    369, 373
  juries and 236–42
  legal representation and 220–32
  preparation of defence, sufficient
      time 219–20
  victims' influence on 243–47
Farber, Neil J. 171(65)
Fattah, Ezzat 280(9), 327(36), 353(12),
    373(110)
Faust, Richard 256(201)
Federal Republic of Germany *see* Germany
Fierro v. Gomez 159, 159(22)
Feldman, Marilyn 205(80)
Feltoe, Geoffrey 280(11)
Fessenden, Ford 330(51)
Fields, Gary 211(104)
Fijalkowski, A. 52(38, 40, 42)
Fiji 84–5
Finland 12(16), 33, 41, 377, 386, 400(82)
Fitzgerald, Edward QC 104(191), 106(196),
    285
Florida 104, 118–19, 142, 236(101), 297(87),
    304, 317(2), 330
  aggravating factors 289, 294
  clemency 264
  death row 115, 172
  discretionary death penalty 288
  executions 115, 116, 165, 292
  exonerations 272
  juries 242, 285
  juveniles 192
  legal representation 227
  LWOP, 389, 397

mental illness/retardation 210
method of execution 157, 159(18, 19), 164
proportionality review 289
racial discrimination 304–5, 309
Fogel, Judge 162–3, 169
Ford v. Wainwright 115, 210, 211(106), 213(111)
Foreign nationals 68, 71, 143(69), 360
consular assistance for 37, 127, 233–5
foreign workers, Saudi Arabia 72, 243
Forst, Brian E. 331
Fox v. The Queen 107(203), 282
Fox, James A. 344(105), 359(37), 360(42, 43)
Fox, President Vincente 63(88)
France 28, 31, 37, 41, 47, 58(63), 100, 104, 351(1), 352, 353, 361, 363, 364, 375, 376, 387, 393, 398, 400(82)
Francis et al v. Trinidad and Tobago 224(43)
Fraser, Christian 398(76)
Free Legal Assistance Group (FLAG) 86
Freedman, Eric 257
Furman v. Georgia 112–14, 125, 126, 142, 173, 262, 272, 279, 287–90, 292, 296, 297. 299, 302–3, 304, 308, 313, 315, 355, 367, 378, 388

Gabon 15(23), 75
Gaddafi, Colonel 68
Gaitan, Judge Fernando Jr 164
Gambia 15(23), 16, 75, 77
Galliher, James 317
Galliher, John F. 84(96), 112(219), 317
Gallup Poll 191(19), 199(52), 206, 358(55), 359–60, 365, 368–9, 370, 374(116), 377, 391
Garland, David 125–6, 167, 376(129)
Garrett, B. 275
Gartner, D. 327(36)
Garvey, Stephen 237(104), 239(111, 112), 242(120), 365(66), 372(112)
Garza, Juan Raoul 17, 36–7, 114
Gas chamber 29(73), 157, 158(16), 159–63
Gatrell, Victor, 10(6)
Gaylord, Mark 84(96)
Geller, Amanda 324, 331, 333
Gemalmaz, M. S. 48(26)
Georgia (Republic of) 15(21), 17(25), 55(53), 56–7, 60(75, 76), 391
Georgia (US state) 26(54), 116, 121, 157(8), 161, 263(236), 287, 314
ABA death penalty assessment 121, 295(81)
appeals 289
aggravating factors 289, 290(55), 297
deterrence 330
discretionary death penalty 315

discrimination (Baldus and other studies) 299–308
juveniles 192
legal representation 224, 225, 229, 231–2
mentally retarded, protection of 198–9, 200, 202
mitigation 289
proportionality review 308–9
trial process 242, 288
Georgia v. McCollum 240
German Democratic Republic 25, 50
Germany 11, 12, 28, 37, 41, 127, 180(110), 234–5, 354, 387, 393, 400(82)
public opinion 352, 359, 361, 363, 364, 372, 376
Germany v. USA LaGrand Case 234, 235, 235(94)
Ghana 3(6), 15(23), 17(26), 75, 76, 135(24), 136(30), 140(49), 173(73), 195(38), 279(7)
Commission on Human Rights 76
Ghandi, Rajiv 93
Gibbeting 10
Gibbons, John J, 123, 129
Gillers, Stephen. 295(82)
Gilmore, Gary 113, 335
Ginsberg, Justice 123
Girling, Eva 25(52)
Gittings, R. Kaj 340, 343
Giuliani, Rudolph 245
Gliszczynska, A. 53(43, 46)
Godfrey v. Georgia 291(63)
Godfrey, Michael J. 335, 336(75)
Godoy, Julio, 398(75)
Goldstein, S. M. 256(201)
Gore, Al 318
Gottschalk, M. 262(234), 389(23)
Greece 41, 48, 400(82)
Greenberg, J. 292(64)
Green, David A. 358(33)
Green, Keith A. 313(147)
Greene, E. 247(157)
Gregg v. Georgia 16, 113, 126, 162(54), 288(46), 295, 299, 303, 355, 357
Grenada 104, 105, 107, 110, 136(30), 143(73), 281, 282(18), 283
Grenadines *see* St Vincent
Griffey, Margaret 35, 182(121), 272, 308(128), 319(10)
Griffiths, Lord 180
Gross, Samuel 118(239), 191(19), 270(278), 271–2, 273(287), 304, 359(37), 363(58), 373(105, 111, 112), 380
Grøver, Bent 392(42)
Grzeskowiak, A. 52(40)
Guadeloupe 104
Guantanamo Bay 249–50

Guatemala
  aged 194
  executions 17, 64, 158, 165(43), 166,
  mandatory death penalty 141, 279(7)
  pardons 258
  pregnant women 195(38)
  right of appeal 253
  scope of capital punishment 130(5),
    135(24), 138, 143(73)
  waiting period between sentence and
    imposition of death penalty 174
'Guildford Four' 47
Guinea 26(53), 133, 400(83)
  executions 17, 78, 156
  mandatory death penalty 279(7,8)
  pregnant women 195(38)
  public executions 165(43)
  right of appeal 251
  scope of death penalty 140(49), 143(73)
Guinea Bissau 15(22), 73, 400(83)
Gundry, Orin F, 170
Gupta, Subhash C. 93
Guyana 65, 111, 133, 220(18), 224
  appeals 110
  death row 174
  drugs offences 137–8, 280
  mandatory death penalty 279(7)
Gwande, A. 171(64)

Hands off Cain 3, 27, 63(88), 64(99),
  67(2,6,7), 68(10), 69(17), 76(52,54),
  81, 88(107), 91(124), 96, 139(47),
  141(55,60), 148, 152(94), 156(4),
  164(40), 166, 188(6), 195(35), 196,
  197, 221(27), 267, 263(56)
Haines, Herbert H. 118(239), 125(266)
Haiti 104
Haney, Craig 237(103), 238(108), 241,
  242(121), 367, 369
Hanging 34(90), 41, 61,, 71, 95, 105, 156,
  157–8, 165, 166, 168, 178, 180, 282
Hanging in chains 10
Harding, R. 211(104)
Hardy, Kenneth A. 295(80)
Harris County 332, 336, 365
Harris, Robert Alton 159(21), 167(53), 335
Hatchard, J. 77(56)
Hawaii 12(15), 112(219)
Hawkins, Gordon 113(222), 289(46), 377(137)
Henry, Judge Robert 206
Hensley, John E. 334, 335(71)
Herrera v. Collins 254(191), 262
Hickman, Laura 311(140)
Hijacking of aircraft 54, 104, 135, 136
Hilaire, Constantine and Benjamin and Others v.
  Trinidad and Tobago 107(205), 281(15)
Hilaire v. Trinidad and Tobago 107(205),
  281(15)

Hillman, Howard 158(16)
Hinson, K. 273(289)
Hintze, Michael. 290(53)
Hirshorn, Robert E. 119(245)
Hitchcock v. Dugger 289
Hodgkinson, Peter 33(88), 110(214),
  379(146), 392(39, 42), 393(47)
Hoffman, L. J. 127(273)
Holovatiy, Serhiy 56
Homicide *see also* murder
  homicide trends 325–9
  homicide, inter-racial 239, 304, 371
Homosexual acts with violence 141
Homosexuality 38, 80, 131, 142, 150
Honduras 12(15), 61, 65(100)
Hong Kong 84, 165(43)
Hood, Roger 21(36), 43(7), 63(89), 98(164),
  118(238,239), 132(13), 296(85), 317(1),
  352(11), 374(114), 384(2)
Horowitz, J. A. 357(26)
Horvath, Timor 51(34)
Hosni, N. 71(32), 286(36)
Hough, M. 358(33)
Howard, John 49
Howard, Michael 47
Howell, Babe 402
Howell v. Jamaica 183 (122)
Hoyle, C. 244(137)
Hudud crimes 71
Hughes, Jamie. 192(27)
humanity, crimes against 18, 135
human rights
  China, legislative guarantees for 145
  human rights, disputed norms 32–8, 68,
    102–3
  human rights perspective, principles 9,
    18–24, 25, 26, 28, 31, 40, 48, 50–2,
    55, 57. 58, 64, 65, 69, 74, 84, 87, 91,
    102, 109–10, 131, 154, 175, 186, 221,
    274, 277, 281, 282, 284, 320, 349, 351,
    353–4, 358, 381–2, 385, 388, 393,
    402–3
  inhumane punishment 10, 15, 18, 20,
    22, 25, 27, 28, 30(75) 36, 56, 74,
    77, 82, 104, 106, 108, 155, 160, 165,
    184, 276, 283, 392 *see also* death
    row; alternatives, conditions of
    confinement; and executions, method
    of
  murder victims' families for (MVFHR)
    185, 380
  Universal Declaration of 21, 22
Human Rights Watch 172(69), 194(31),
  197(46), 199, 218(13), 399(81), 400
Hungary 17(25), 25, 50, 51(34), 60(75, 76), 354
Hussein, Omar 168
Hussein, Saddam 28, 70, 133, 139(44), 158,
  167, 361

Hussain v United Kingdom 399(79)
Hu, Yunteng 99(167), 100(175), 144(75)

Ibrahim al-Tikiri, Barzan 158
Iceland 12(15), 40
Idaho 401
Illinois 26(54), 323(23), 327, 328(41, 43)
  Coalition to Abolish the Death Penalty 330
  doctors' role in administration of death
      penalty 170
  drug trafficking 138
  Governor Ryan's Commission/
      commutations 116, 119–20, 262–3,
      273, 276, 298, 301, 358
  legal representation 227, 231
  LWOP, 388, 389
  proportionality review 309
  racial discrimination 304, 305, 307
Incompetents (to be executed) 206, 208,
      210–11
India 143, 158(12), 173(73)
  abolitionist movement 93–4, 103
  burning of widows (sati) 143
  death row 174
  discretionary/mandatory death
      penalty 279–80
  doctors role in administration of death
      penalty 168
  executions 92, 94
  foreign nationals 233
  juveniles 188
  method of execution 158, 160
  military tribunals 248
  pardons/clemency 258–9
  restriction of death penalty 91, 130(5),
      285–6
  right of appeal 181
  scope of death penalty 93, 136(30),
      137(33), 140(49), 143(73)
  trial procedures, preparation of defence 217
Indiana 115, 122, 305
  aggravating factors 297
  mentally ill/retarded 203, 206, 263
  unfair and arbitrary trial process 121,
      226(53)
Indonesia 85, 373
  abolitionism/retention 32(83), 84, 319
  appeals time taken for decision 255
  'Bali 9' heroin smugglers 95
  'Bali bombers' 49, 359–60(41)
  Constitutional Court 95
  death row 173(73)
  Human Rights Committee 135
  military tribunals 248
  pardon 262
  pregnant women 195
  scope of death penalty 95, 135(24), 136,
      137(33), 151

trial procedures preparation of defence 217
  women 196
Infliction of capital punishment *see* Executions
Information
  need for accurate 71, 94, 96, 129, 146, 150,
      153–4, 167, 194, 208, 216, 243, 259,
      260, 367
Innocence List 271
Innocence Project 118, 267, 276(301)
Innocence Protection Act 2004 274
Innocent, protection of the 19, 20, 35, 81,
      100, 103, 120, 122, 128, 215, 266–77
  due process and 119, 215, 217–18, 229, 250,
      252, 266, 272, 274–5
  influence on abolition debate 267, 272,
      368–70, 393, 397
  execution of 118, 143, 85(139), 216, 266,
      267, 268, 270, 273–4, 318, 349, 358,
      372(98)
  pardon or commutation of sentence right to
      seek 116, 118, 262, 271
  right of appeal 255
  trial appeal and clemency proceedings 276
Insane see also mentally ill
  protection of 115, 187, 197, 203–14
International Commission of Jurists 127(274)
Inter-American Commission on Human
      Rights 36, 64, 108, 188, 265
  juveniles 188
  mandatory death penalty 107(205), 281
Inter-American Convention on Human
      Rights 63(91)
Inter-American Court on Human Rights 36,
      64, 107–8, 234(91), 392, 299, 400
International Convention against Torture 36
International Convention on the Rights of the
      Child 188, 399
International Court of Justice 234–5
International Covenant on Civil and Political
      Rights (ICCPR) 21, 22–3, 27, 32, 35,
      38
  conditions on death row 175
  due process 215, 216, 257–8, 265, 276
  extradition 29, 30
  juveniles 187, 191, 194, 398, 399
  legal representation 220(18), 223–4
  mandatory death penalty 107(204), 281(15)
  mentally ill 208(90)
  'most serious crimes' (Article 6(2)) 21–2,
      90, 99, 101, 129, 130, 144, 296
  non-retroactive enforcement of
      penalty 132, 133(17)
  ratification of 23, 36, 47, 49, 51(36), 58, 60,
      65, 73, 85(98), 87, 101, 112, 146 414–16
  right to appeal 250–4
  Second Optional Protocol 22, 32, 55, 76,
      86
  withdrawal from ICCPR, 108, 110, 111

International Criminal Court 18(28), 388
International Criminal Tribunals 18, 31, 75,
    388(18)
International Federation for Human Rights
    (FIDH) 27, 69, 89, 136(28), 157,
    218(13), 221, 259, 352(6), 396
International Independent Investigation
    Commission 69
International treaties, ratifications 414–16
Iowa 12(15), 112(219), 389
Iran
    abolition/retention 32(83), 70
    deterrent justification 320
    executions 3, 71, 148–9, 150
    information lack of accurate 153
    Islamic law 71, 141
    juveniles 71, 190
    legal representation 220–1, 222
    mandatory death penalty 138, 279(7), 280
    method of execution 156
    public executions 71, 134, 165(43), 166
    public opinion 361
    religious dissent 142
    right of appeal 251
    scope of death penalty 137(33), 138,
        139(40,41), 140 (49), 141–2, 143(73),
        144, 150, 151
    special courts 248
    stoning 166, 167
    waiting period between sentence and
        penalty 253
    women 196
Iraq
    abolition/reinstatement/retention 32(83), 70
    due process 217, 218
    executions 70, 158
    foreign nationals 233
    military tribunals 248
    post Hussein regime 70, 361
    retroactive introduction 133
    scope of penalty 70, 130(5), 135(24,25),
        137(33), 139(44, 46), 141, 151
    women 196
Ireland 12(16), 16(24)
    life imprisonment 386, 400(82)
    public opinion 31–2
Islamic courts 141, 248
Islamic law 7, 34, 71, 78, 80, 133, 141, 166,
        174, 189, 194(32), 243, 319
    Diya 97, 174, 233, 243
    punishments under 54(50), 71, 83, 96(156),
        141, 143(68), 165(43), 166
    Qisas 97, 174, 243
    Shari'a Courts 217, 243
Islamic states *see also* individual countries
    support for capital punishment 34, 57, 70,
        72–3, 352

Israel 12(16), 69, 135, 171
    Holocaust/genocide 32, 66, 132–3, 268
    juveniles 399
    life imprisonment 386
    retroactive introduction 132–2
Italy 11, 12(16), 33, 40, 354
    life imprisonment 387, 393, 398, 400(82)
    public opinion 28, 361, 363, 364, 377
    Tuscany 11
Iwao, Hakamada 173

Jamaica 3(6), 104, 105, 106, 195(38), 208,
        223, 260, 323(25)
    appeals 251, 253, 265
    crime trends 106, 374
    excessive time 106–7, 180, 255
    mandatory death penalty 109(211), 280,
        281, 283
    withdrawal from ICCPR 110–1
Japan 3(1), 217
    abolition/retention 26, 26(53,59), 32, 79,
        84, 94, 103
    Code of Criminal Procedure 221
    death row
        conditions 178, 183
        time spent on 173, 252
        geriatrics on 194, 252
    deterrent justification 319
    discretionary/mandatory death penalty 280
    due process rights 217–18, 221
    executions 148(85), 184, 194, 255,
        265, 286
        in secret 95
        methods 155, 156, 157, 158
    Federation of Bar Associations (JFBA) 94,
        173, 197, 221, 251–2, 260
    Heian period 9(1)
    innocents 267–8
    legal representation 19, 221
    mental illness 208
    mentally retarded 197, 198
    pardon 258, 260
    pregnant women 195(38,39)
    public opinion 351, 361, 367, 372
    right of appeal 251–2, 253, 255
    scope of death penalty 130, 135(24, 25),
        136
    women 196
Jiang, Shanhe 366(69)
Johnson, David. T. 9(1), 94, 102, 148(85),
        155, 173(77), 361
Johnson, Edward Earl, 185
Johnson, Robert 175, 176, 177, 179
Johnson, Sheri Lynn 205, 232(84), 242(120),
        306(123), 313(146)
Jones, Louise 115
Jones, T. 389(26)

Jordan 32(83), 219
  abolition/retention 69
  death row 178
  executions 149, 156
  mandatory death penalty 279(7), 280
  military courts/tribunals 174, 248
  pregnant women 195
  right of appeal 251
  scope of death penalty 69, 135, 137(33), 141
Judge v. Canada 30
Jurek v. Texas 288(46), 295(79)
Juries
  death and life sentence choice 115, 121, 123, 197, 202–5, 206, 209, 225, 229, 231, 242, 244, 270, 291–300, 362, 365, 367, 389–90
  discretionary death penalty US, 278, 284–5, 287–90
  influence of race 209(95), 237–9, 238(108), 239–41, 305–6, 312
  influence of victims 245–7
  reluctance to convict in capital cases 10, 42, 45
  right to a jury trial 55
Juveniles 26, 71, 115, 187–94, 196, 205, 214, 272, 318
  executions 166, 190, 192
  international opinion/norms 193–4
  legal proof of age 190
  life imprisonment of 398–402
  minimum age 39, 45, 188- 94
  public opinion 206
  safeguards protecting 112, 187–94

Kafantayeni, Francis 283
Kafantayeni v. Attorney General 282(26)
Kaine, Governor Timothy 120
Kaiser, Günther 13
Kalam, President Abdul 93, 259
Kansas 16, 113, 114, 123, 245, 291, 389
Kansas v. Marsh 123, 291(59)
Kaplan, Paul 126(270)
Karimov, President Islam 59
Karugarama, Thareisse 75
Kassymbekova, Botagoz 216
Katende, John 181(114)
Katz, Lawrence 345
Kazakhstan 15, 17, 58, 59, 129, 148, 184, 194, 216, 220
Keating, Jo 167(54)
Kennedy, Justice 401
Kennedy, Patrick 142
Kennedy v. Trinidad and Tobago 107(204), 108(208), 224(42, 43), 281(14)
Kennedy, W. A. 213(111)
Kentucky 26(54), 225, 289, 294, 305

mentally retarded 202(68)
method of execution 39(106), 124, 164–5
  Racial Justice Act 314
Kenya 15(23), 17(26), 75, 135(24), 173(73), 74, 179, 397, 399(81)
  mandatory penalty 140, 279, 283–4
  National Commission on Human Rights 76
Kerry, Senator John 357
Keyes, D. 199(56–7)
Khalilova v. Tajikistan 251(177)
Khamidov, K. 59(68)
Khomidov v. Tajikistan 217(6)
Kibaki, President 174
Kidnapping 62, 64, 69, 70, 79, 86, 140, 141(55), 143, 145, 200, 297(87), 374
  Executions for 64, 151
King, R. 380(156)
Killingley, Julian 294(75)
Kim Dae Jung, President 89
Kindler v. Canada Minister of Justice 29–30, 181(112)
King, Nancy J. 294(77)
Kirchmeier, J. L. 119(242), 275(296)
Kisko, Stefan 47
Kleck, Gary 346(114)
Klein, Stephen 311(140)
Kniskern, E. M. 211(106)
Knight v. Florida 182
Knowles, Julian 109(210)
Kobil, D. T. 264(241)
Koehring, H. 247(157)
Kogan, Judge Gerald 118
Koh, Harold Hongju 37, 191(18), 200(62), 234(92)
Kohfeld, Carol W. 328(43)
Konaris, L. G. 161(30)
Korea, North 151, 165(43), 166
  economic crime 139, 151, 166
  secrecy 96, 149
Korea, South (Republic of) 3(6), 26(53, 59), 88, 133, 137(33), 139(40, 42, 45), 140(49), 141, 173(73), 195(38, 39), 223, 251, 269
  move towards abolition 89, 103, 129, 391
  National Human Rights Commission 358
  public opinion 358, 363, 364, 365
Kozinski A. 19(31)
KQED v. Vasquez 167(53)
Krause, T. 247(160)
Kreisberg, E. 163(36)
Krüger, H.C. 22(40)
Kunda, George 77
Kurbanova v. Tajikistan 249
Kurbanova v. Tajikistan 217(7)

Kuwait 32(83), 70, 130(5), 248(161)
  pregnant women 195
  public executions 165
  scope of death penalty 136, 137(33), 138,
    141, 151, 279(7)
Kyle, F. D. 309(134)
Kyrgyzstan
  abolition 15(21), 17(25), 58, 129
  legal process prior to abolition 184, 198,
    216

Lackey v. Texas 182(117)
LaGrand, Karl and Walter 234–5
Lahoud, Emile 68
Lambert, Eric G. 366(69), 371(99)
Landry, Raymond 160
Lanier, Charles S. 211(104), 260(222),
    263(235), 288(43), 289(48), 290,
    291(58, 60) 295(78), 315
Laos 88, 137(33)
Latin America *see* also individual countries
    extra-legal killings
Latvia 15, 17, 17(25), 55, 60(75)
Latzer, B. 257(209)
Lawson, G. 159(21)
La Yifan 101
Layson, Stephen A. 339, 340, 344
Lebanon 133, 279(7)
  abolition/retention 18, 26(53), 68, 69
  due process rights 217, 251
  pregnant women 195(38, 39)
Ledewitz, Bruce 204(79), 291(63)
Lee, Catherine 307(127)
Legal assistance/representation, adequacy
    of 35, 83, 103, 120, 121, 174, 215,
    220–35, 250, 253, 276, 395 (62)
Lehrfreund, Saul 107(202), 282(17, 19)
Lempert, Richard 330, 333(66)
Lesotho 400(83)
  abolitionism 15(23), 75
  appeals 253
  mandatory death penalty 280
  sexual offences 141
Lethal injection 39(106), 64, 113, 114, 124,
    151, 157–65, 168–71, 342, 391
Lempert, Richard 330, 333(66)
Levitt, Steven 345
*Lewis and others v. the Attorney General of
    Jamaica and Another* 260
Lewis, D. O. 204(79), 205(80)
Liberia 15(22), 73, 400(83)
Libya 33(87), 68, 130(5), 137(33), 139(40,
    44), 142, 165(43), 195, 220, 251, 253,
    400(83)
Liebman, James 116(232), 117, 118(238),
    256(201), 270–1, 275, 299(95)
Liechtenstein 42

Lifton, Robert J. 159(19), 360(44)
Lithuania 17(25), 23, 25, 55–6, 60(75), 387
Liu Hainan 352(8)
Liu Jianhong 98(166), 100(175)
Liu, Renwen 147, 154, 158
Lockett v. Ohio 289, 294
Lockhart v. McCree 236(102)
Logan, Wayne 243(128), 245(143, 146),
    246(148), 394(54), 400(85, 87)
Lombardi, George 176(92)
Loong, Lee Hsien 96
Louisiana 204(79), 295
  legal representation 227
  LWOP, 388, 389, 394, 395, 401
  sexual offences 142
Louisiana v. Wilson 142
Luginbuhl, J. 247(157)
Luxembourg 41, 400(82)
Lynch, Mona 360(42)

Macao 84
McCann, E. M. 356(24)
McCarver v. State of North Carolina 199(52),
    200
Machhi Singh v. State of Punjab 92(129),
    286(33)
McClatchy Newspapers 229, 232
McCleskey, Warren 303
McCleskey v. Kemp 115, 126, 256, 311, 312,
    313, 314(149)
McCleskey v. Zant 256(202)
McDevitt, J.F. 11(11), 322(19), 326(33),
    329(48), 334(70), 340(87), 345(109)
McFarland, Sam 335(73)
McGarrell, Edmund F. 363(57)
McManus, W. S. 348(121)
McVeigh, Timothy 17, 114, 126, 167, 245,
    360, 379
Macedonia 17(25), 51, 60(75, 76)
Mackay, R. D. 204(78)
Macy, Bob 356
Madagascar 15(23), 73, 75, 217, 253, 400(83)
Maggio v. Williams 295
Mailer, Norman 113(223)
Maine 12(15), 112(219), 389
Malawi 15(23), 17(26), 75, 77, 139(40), 140,
    141, 262, 267(263), 283, 351, 358
Malaysia 26(53), 32(83), 267(263), 319
  Bar Association 91
  death row 173(73)
  juveniles 188
  mandatory death penalty 279(7), 280
  scope of death penalty 91, 135(24),
    136(30), 137(33), 138, 139(40), 151
Maldives 32(83), 88, 133, 135(24, 25)
Mali 15(23), 75, 136(30), 139(40, 42),
    140(49), 253, 400(83)

Mallouh, K. 205(80)
Mandatory death penalty 11, 16, 34, 43, 45, 59, 61, 68, 72, 74, 75, 76, 77, 79–80, 83, 86, 90, 91, 96(152), 104, 105(192), 106–9, 113, 118(258), 131(11), 132, 134, 137, 138, 140, 141, 143, 278–84 *passim*
Mandela, Nelson 74
Mansaraj et al v. Sierra Leone 248(163)
Manson, A. 29(72)
Marchesini, Robert 327, 328(41)
Marcos, President 16, 85
Markman, Stephen, J. 273(289)
Marquart, James. 292(66, 67)
Marshall, Justice, hypothesis 367, 368(79)
Marshall, L. C. 273(289)
Marshall, T. R. 199(54)
Marshall Islands 84
Martinique 104
Maryland 117, 301, 302, 305, 365
    Aggravating/mitigating factors 231, 297(87)
    mentally retarded/ill 199, 202(68), 211
    method of execution 159(20)
    moratorium on executions 120
Masaru, Okonushi 173
Mason, David 335
Massachusetts 112(219), 117, 185–6, 273, 379(89)
    Council on Capital Punishment 121–2, 298
Matthew v. State of Trinidad and Tobago 109(210)
Mauer, Marc 388(16), 389, 390, 395(60)
Mauritania 15(23), 75
Mauritius 15(22), 17(25), 73, 400(83)
Mauro, Robert 304
Mbithi, Francis 174
Mbushuu v. Republic 82(86, 87), 351(1)
Medellin, Jose Ernesto 235
Media 28, 118(259), 153, 167, 221, 335, 367, 368, 379, 390
Mello, Michael 210(100), 228(62), 256
Meltsner, Michael 113(221)
Mendes, Douglas 110(214)
Mentally ill 39, 143(69), 150, 179, 188, 203–213, 263, 272, 285, 345
    competence to be executed 208–13
Mentally retarded 37, 39, 45, 115, 121, 128, 188, 192, 194, 196–203, 357
    protection of 225, 229, 231, 263, 272, 274, 275, 285
Mexico 12(15), 16(24), 61, 62–3, 258
    America's death rows, Mexicans on 234–5
    Extradition policy 31
    life imprisonment, prohibition of 387, 393
    public opinion 363, 364, 365, 374

Michigan 11, 12(15), 112(219), 389
Micronesia 84
Mikhlin, Alexander S. 53(47), 54(48), 261(224), 274(291), 362(53)
Military courts/tribunals 50, 52, 71, 78, 81, 136(28), 148, 165, 174, 217, 248–50, 389(25)
    due process, lack of safeguards 219, 221, 248–50, 251, 254
Military offences 12(17), 15, 23, 40(1), 41, 42, 47, 48, 59, 61, 62, 63, 73(38), 79, 85, 88, 112, 131, 133, 134–5, 137, 144, 145, 156, 279(7)
Mill, John Stuart. 43, 352(11), 392
Millemann, Michael A. 301(101), 302(106)
Miller-El v. Dretke 241
Miller, Kent S. 198(51), 213(111)
Minnesota 12(15), 112(219)
Minors *see* juveniles
Miscarriages of justice *see* Innocence
Mississippi 26(54), 115, 123(262), 124, 185, 257, 297
    legal representation 225, 229
Missouri 26(54), 116, 253, 264, 294, 297(87), 305
    death row 176
    juveniles 192, 318(9)
    mentally retarded 201
    method of execution 159(20), 164, 170
    proportionality review 308–9
Mitchell, Greg 159(19), 360(44)
Mithu v. Punjab 279
Mitigating circumstances 19, 107, 123, 188–9, 192, 202, 204, 205, 207, 229, 231–2, 237–8, 240(113), 241–2, 260(221), 278, 281–5 *passim,* 287–91 *passim,* 294, 299, 300, 309(131), 362, 384, 389, 394, 400
Mitterrand, François 47, 353
Mocan, Naci H. 340, 343
Model Penal Code 287–9
Mohamed v. President of the Republic of South Africa and Others 30(75)
Mohrenschlager, M. 352(12)
Moldova 15(21), 17(25), 55, 60(75, 76)
Monaco 12(15), 41, 387
Mongolia 90, 141, 194, 196
Montana 115, 142, 143
    insane 211
    three judge panels 284
Montenegro 3(6), 51, 60(75)
Montserrat 104(189), 107, 282(18)
Moore v. Nebraska 182
Moore v. The State 57(8)
Morales v .Hickman 162(31)
Morales v. Tilton 162

Moratoria 14, 24–5, 37, 38, 48, 51, 52, 54–5,
    56, 57, 58, 59, 60, 66, 67, 68, 73(39),
    74, 78, 79, 80, 82, 86, 87, 88, 93, 94,
    95, 96(156), 105, 107, 111, 113, 115,
    116, 117, 120, 121, 123, 124, 129, 136,
    148, 156, 157(8), 230, 259, 265, 327,
    331, 335, 339, 342, 357, 371
  Worldwide, calls for 26–7, 33–4, 81
Morgan v. Illinois 240(113)
Morocco 3(6), 17(26), 31, 32(83), 130,
    173(73), 197, 208, 279(7), 400(83)
  abolitionism 35, 66–7
  due process rights 216(4), 251, 253, 258
  scope of death penalty 135(24, 25), 140(49),
    141, 143(73)
Morris, Norval (Report) 1, 12, 203, 324
'Most serious crimes' 11, 18, 19, 21, 23, 35, 39,
    45, 76, 82, 84, 90, 99, 101, 103, 129,
    130–2, 140, 141, 142, 145, 281
Mosteller, R.P. 246(151, 154)
Mourad, Farouk 319(13)
Moussaui, Zacharias 245
Mozambique 15(22), 17(25), 73, 83, 400(83)
Mswati, King. 261
Mulai v. Republic of Guyana 217(7)
Mulligan, K. 366(70), 372(102)
Mullin, Chris 111
Mulroney, Brian 325(31)
Murder *passim* all chapters, see also Homicide
  'capital'/'first-degree murder 11, 29, 43,
    45–6, 106, 107, 112, 121, 203, 228,
    238, 239, 276, 279–80, 282–3, 292,
    296, 301, 304, 307, 309, 320, 323(23),
    331, 336, 360(42), 385, 390–1, 394
    288, 292, 304, 331, 360(42), 385,
    390–1, 394
  categories of 42–7, 51, 53, 54, 59, 60,
    62, 68, 69, 88, 92, 95, 98, 105, 113,
    119(246), 122, 132, 134, 135, 251, 279,
    280 284–300 *passim,* 355, 360, 362,
    372–5, 377
  discretionary death sentence for 11, 15, 74,
    77, 91, 106, 114, 280, 284–6, 288,
    294, 312, 315, 323, 384
  felony murder rule 39, 290
  mandatory death sentence for 11, 43, 45,
    59, 61, 68, 74–80 *passim,* 82, 86, 90,
    104, 105(192), 106–9, 113,
    132, 278–84, 290, 362, 383,
    384, 394
  rate of 54, 55, 57, 74(44), 106, 110., 320,
    322, 325–9
Museveni, President Yoweri 261
Musharraf, President Pervez 189
Mussolini, Benito 11, 41
Mwalusanya, Justice 82
Mwanawasa, President Levy 77, 134

Myanmar formerly Burma 17(26), 88
  extra-judicial killings 88
  scope of death penalty 88, 134, 137(33)
Myers, B. 247(157)

Nadler, J. 247(157)
Nagase, Jinen – Justice Minister of Japan 351
Nagin D. 347(119)
Nakell, Barry 295(80), 315(156)
Namaliu, Rabbie 88
Namibia 15(22), 17(25)
  abolition 73
  life imprisonment 393, 400(83)
National Academy of Sciences 347
Nauru 84(97), 88
Naus, Joseph. 305(119)
Nazi regime 11, 50, 133
Nazarbeyev, President Nuraslan 59
Ndjeng, Fernando 82
Nebraska
  discretionary death penalty 284
  due process protections 117
  mentally retarded 202(68)
  method of execution 157
  probabilities of being sentenced to death
    penalty 301
  racial discrimination 305, 310(136), 315
Nepal 15, 16, 85
Nesbit, C.A. 323(23)
Netherlands 11, 12(16), 40, 41, 80, 95, 104,
    387, 400(82)
Neufeld, Peter 118(240), 267
Neumayer, E. 19(30)
Nevada 26(54), 115
  aggravating factors 120, 297
  mandatory death penalty 279
Newburn, T. 389(26)
Newcomen, N. 388(16)
New Hampshire 113, 117
  drug trafficking 138
New Jersey 114
  aggravating factors 297
  Death Penalty Commission 123–4, 380
  LWOP 395(60), 401
  moratorium 123–4
  proportionality review 253
  racial discrimination 305, 310, 312(143)
  victims 380, 391(38)
New Mexico 17, 26(54), 117(237), 123(262),
    389
  clemency 262–3
  doctors role in administration of death
    penalty 171(65)
  insane 209
New mothers 187, 195
New York State 16, 30(75), 113, 317, 357
  death row 175

effect of execution on homicide
  numbers 328, 331, 334
failure to reinstate death penalty 122–3
juveniles 400(87)
New Zealand 12(16), 49, 354, 376, 387
Ng, Charles 29(73), 159
Nguyen Tuong Van v. Public Prosecutor 34(90)
Nicaragua 61, 65(100, 101), 387
Nicholson, A.J. 106
Niger 15(23), 73(38), 75, 139(40, 42, 45),
  195(38, 39), 400(83)
Nigeria 32(83), 80–1, 96, 233
  death row 81, 173(73), 174, 178–9
  deterrent justification 320, 328–9
  due process safeguards 218, 222–3, 248
  executions 149
  innocence 268
  Islamic law 80, 141–2, 156
  juveniles 189–90
  mandatory death penalty 80, 279, 284
  method of execution 80
  National Study Group 80
  pardon 261
  public executions 80, 165(42, 43)
  retroactive introduction 133
  right of appeal 265
  scope of death penalty 130, 133, 135(24,
    25), 136(30), 139(40), 140, 140(49)
  women 196
Nirmal, Chiranjivi J. 285(32)
Nobu, Oda 173
North Carolina 26(54), 115, 116, 119(242)
  juveniles 400(16)
  legal representation 228
  lethal injection 161, 170
  mentally retarded/ill 200, 209
  probabilities of being sentenced to
    death 302
  racial discrimination 305, 307(125), 314
North Dakota 112(219)
Norway 11, 12(16), 40, 41, 377, 387, 388
Nowak, Manfred 27(62), 178–9, 218, 219
Nsereko, D. D. N. 83(94)
Nuclear waste (importation or dumping) 143
Numeiri, President 83

Obasanjo, President 80, 81(78), 96
Ocalan, Abdullah 48
Öcalan v. Turkey 27, 27(63)
O'Connor, Justice Sandra Day 38(104), 118,
  193, 230–1
Ogwanga, Ben 181
Ohio 26(54), 115, 262, 263, 271
  effect of execution on homicide
    numbers 328
  legal representation 225
  method of execution 163

mitigation 289, 294
Ohio Adult Parole Authority v. Woodard 263
Oklahoma 26(54), 114, 115, 167, 356, 360,
  379
  death row 175
  deterrent effect of execution 335
  due process safeguards 245
  executions 115, 116, 149
  juveniles 192
  mentally ill 206
  method of execution 113, 157
  scope of death penalty 142
Olesegun, President 96
Olmesdahl, M.C.J. 323(25)
O'Malley, Governor Martin 120
Oman 32(83), 68, 137(33), 251
Oregon 12(15), 288
  effect of execution on homicide
    numbers 328
  public opinion 355
Organ transplantation
  executed persons 171(66), 172
Organization for Security and Cooperation in
  Europe 35, 55, 59, 60(72), 123(262),
    182, 184, 197, 203, 259, 265, 307
Organization of American States 23, 108
Orsagh, Thomas 340
O'Shea, K. A. 196(43)
Oxley, Deborah 337

Pacific Island States *see* also individual
  countries 15, 84–85
Page, Elija 17
Pakistan 3, 32(83), 84, 97, 133(17), 255, 266
  death row 173, 179, 183
  due process safeguards 217, 248
  foreign nationals 233
  Human Rights Commission 97, 173(76)
  innocence 267
  Islamic law 97
  juveniles 189, 190
  mandatory death penalty 143, 279(7)
  method of execution 156
  mitigation 285(31)
  public executions 165(43)
  scope of death penalty 130, 134, 135(24),
    136(30), 137(33), 141, 142, 148, 149
  speedy trial courts 219
  support for death penalty 84, 96
Palau 16, 17(25), 84
Palestinian Authority 68, 69, 217, 248(161)
Palmer, Michael 98(165), 100(184)
Panama 12(15), 61, 65(100, 101)
Panetti, Scott 209–210
Panetti v. Quarterman 209(99)
Pannick, David 175(87)
Papua New Guinea 16, 88, 267(263)

Paraguay 16(24), 37, 61, 65(101), 127, 234
Pardons *see also* clemency, commutation 19, 26, 45, 67, 68, 72, 89, 97, 137(31), 174, 197, 198, 209, 243, 254, 257–64, 271, 272(283), 274(292), 282
Parker, Lord 46
Passell, P. 340
Pataki, Governor George 122(259), 357
Paternoster, Raymond 302, 306, 307(124, 125), 315(152)
Patten, Chris 20, 33
Paul, A. 401(92)
Payne v. Tennessee 245–6, 290
Penal Reform International 392, 397(68), 388(16)
Pennsylvania 11, 29, 181, 204, 370
   aggravation/mitigation 290–1
   death row 115, 172
   due process safeguards 231
   LWOP, 389–90
   racial discrimination 240, 314
   scope of death penalty 138
Penry, John Paul 202
Penry v. Lynaugh 115, 119
Perkins, Paul J. 228(62), 256
Perlin, M. L. 202(69)
Perry v. Louisiana 210, 211(104)
Peru 63–4, 130(5), 374, 376, 387
Peterson, Ruth D. 318, 324(27), 330(50), 332(62), 333, 335(72)
So Peyrefitte, M. 351(1)
Philadelphia 379
   racial discrimination in 238, 241, 301, 305, 306, 310
Philippines 158, 173(73), 217, 267(263), 269, 281
   abolition 15, 16, 17(25), 26(53), 85–7
   extradition 31
   FLAG Free Legal Assistance Group 86, 269(275)
   LWOP, 391
Phillips, David P. 334, 335(71)
Phillips, Robert T. M. 213(111)
Physicians
   role in administration of death penalty 156, 162(32), 164, 168–72, 217
Piandiong et al v. the Philippines 265(252)
Picca, G. 351(1)
Pierce, Glen L. 11(11), 297(88), 301(100), 306, 307, 322(19), 326(33), 329(48), 334(70), 339, 340(87), 345(109)
Pierrepoint, Albert 158(11)
Pilgrim, Rocky L. 288(45), 292(68), 305(118)
Pinto v. Trinidad and Tobago 224(39)
Piracy 11(9), 42, 47, 49, 60
Pojman, Louis P. 19(31), 317 (2)
Poland 15(21), 17(25), 52–3, 60, 375, 387

Political offences 48, 54, 60, 62, 63, 66, 79, 83, 93, 96, 104, 122, 131, 134–7, 139, 151, 152, 298, 320, 386
Pol Pot 85, 354
Pope John Paul II, 64, 264
Pornography/obscene materials (producing and distribution) 98,144
Porter, Anthony 116, 273
Portugal 11, 12(16), 40, 168(58), 387, 388, 400(82)
Posner, Richard 273(289), 319
Potas, Ivan 325(29)
Poveda, Tony 301
Powell, Justice 119(242), 210, 312–13
Pratt and Morgan v. Attorney General for Jamaica 106, 108, 180, 224(39), 255
Pregnant women 297
   protection of 53(44), 187, 195–6, 214
Prejean, Dalton 202(70)
Prejean, Helen 372
President's 1982 Task Force on Victims of Crime 244
Pridemore, W. A. 54(51)
prison conditions *see* death row and alternatives to capital punishment
Prison Reform International 396
Pristavkin, Anatoly 19, 398
Privy Council, Judicial Committee of 104–10, 180, 207, 260, 282–3
Proffitt v. Florida 288(46), 289
Property offences 10, 52, 139–40, 152, 345–6
Proportionality, principle of 9, 125(264), 284, 321, 384, 394, 399
Proportionality review 113, 119(246), 121, 252, 253–4, 289, 295, 302–10
Prostitution 98, 142, 144, 151
Psychiatric testimony 204, 207–8, 228
Psychiatrists 205, 207, 212–14, 292
   future dangerousness of prisoners assessment by 292–3
Public executions 43, 71, 165–8
Public opinion, 5, 18, 43, 321, 350–82 *passim*
   abolition, barrier to 83, 94, 98, 110, 153, 350–2
   abolition, effect of on 375–8
   abolition, politics of 47, 56, 60, 350–3, 357
   age and 377–8
   alternatives, and 363–5
   changing 114, 363, 365, 368, 376–7
   homicide rate and 110, 372–4
   human rights and 20, 381–2
   innocence and 118(239), 369–70
   juveniles and 191, 206
   knowledge and Marshall hypothesis 366–70

lawyers, opinion 357–8
medical profession, opinion 171
mentally ill and 206
mentally retarded and 198–9, 206
nature of 358–61, 362
race and 371
religion and 372
role of in USA, 354–8
victim advocates and 378–81
Public order offences 134–7
Puerto Rico 200
Puhar, Eva 50(32)
Pulaski, C.A. 225(45), 299, 300(97),
    301(102), 309(134), 314(150)
Pulley v. Harris 295
Putin, President 54

Qatar 17, 32(83), 68, 137(33), 279(7), 280
Queen v. Peter Hughes 107(203), 282(20)
Queensland 12(15), 49
Qi Shegui 145(7)
Qisas 97, 174
Qiu Xinglong 352

R v. Mattan 268(270)
Racial disparities, discrimination 35, 120,
    121, 124(264), 238, 239, 241, 303–8,
    310–11, 312–16, 366, 371
Radelet, Michael L. 117(235), 118(239), 156,
    172(69), 183(126), 198(51), 213(111),
    262, 264(240), 273(287, 289), 297(88),
    301(100), 306–7, 337(77), 344(105),
    359(37), 360(42)
Radzinowicz, Leon 9(3), 11(10), 13, 20,
    21(36), 42(5), 43(7), 44, 63(89),
    287(42), 317(1), 352(11), 384(2),
    395
Rahmonov, President Emomalii 58
Rakoff, Judge 119
Ramjattan v. Trinidad and Tobago 207(88)
Rape *see* Sexual offences
Raphael, Steven 356(20)
Re: Kevin Nigel Stanford 191(24)
Reagan, President 204
Rector, Ricky Ray 209, 357
Redo, Slawomir 137(32)
Rehnquist, Chief Justice 193(30), 199(54),
    245
Reid v. Jamaica 224(39)
Reiman, Jeffrey 317(2)
Reinhart, Judge Stephen 159(21)
Relatives of prisoners on death row 79, 90,
    177, 178, 183–6, 267–8, 398
Religious offences 130, 131, 142–3
Reno, Janet 230
Reprieve *see also* clemency, commutation,
    pardon 26, 43, 141, 178, 258, 261,
    383, 384, 397

*Republic v. Mbushuu alias Dominic Mnyaroje
    and Kalai Sangula* 82(86), 351(1)
Republic of Korea *see* Korea, South
Republic of Yemen *see* Yemen
Retentionist countries 14, 17, 18(27), 33,
    66–128 *passim,* 129, 132, 137, 146,
    148–50, 153, 154, 172, 183, 191, 196,
    203, 208, 216, 232, 233, 251–76
    passim, 279, 284, 287, 316, 324,
    329–33 *passim,* 348, 350, 353, 374,
    376, 381, 383, 385–6, 389, 402
Revolutionary courts 220, 248, 251
Reyes v. The Queen 107(203), 282, 283(21)
Rhode Island 11, 112(219)
Right to appeal 116(232), 209, 245, 250–7,
    264–6 *see also* death row
    execution while appeal pending 78, 107, 254
    withdrawal of appeal 179–80, 213
Ring v. Arizona 236, 284
Roach, Steve 293
Roberts v. Louisiana 278
Roberts, Julian 246(153), 367(72), 371(94), 373
Robinson, Dinah 192(26)
Robinson v. Jamaica 224(39)
Rodley, Nigel 22(38)
Rohatyn, Felix G. 37, 38(104)
Roman Catholic Church 62, 86–7, 95, 372
Romania 11, 15(21), 17, 25, 40, 50, 60(75),
    354, 387
Romilly, Sir Samuel 42
Rompilla v. Beard 231
Romney, Governor Mitt 121, 122, 298
*Roodal v. The State of Trinidad and
    Tobago* 108, 109(209)
Roper v. Simmons 38, 38(104), 115, 128, 188,
    192, 193(29), 318, 318(9), 372(102),
    401, 401(89)
Rose, M. R. 247(157)
Rossi, Richard M. 175(88)
Rothenberg, Lawrence 35, 182(121), 272,
    308(128), 319(11)
Rozelle, Susan D. 294(77)
Rubin, Paul H. 340, 341, 343
Rubinstein, Tina 256(201)
Rudd, Kevin, Prime Minister 49
Ruiz v. Estelle 176
Russia (Russian Federation) 11, 23. 24, 26(53),
    53(47), 54–5, 57(58), 60, 165(43),
    268, 274(291)
    alternatives to capital punishment 295,
        397, 398
    clemency/pardons 261, 269
    miscarriages of justice 19, 269
    public opinion 360(41), 362
    relatives, lack of information to 184
    scope of death penalty 136, 194, 196
    President's Commission on Human
        Rights 269

Rutherford Andrew 44(12), 46
Rwanda
  Abolitionist movement 15(22), 17(25), 24,
    31, 73, 75
  due process safeguards 253
  genocide 18, 31, 75, 395–6
  life imprisonment 388(18), 395–6,
    400(83)
  public executions 165(43)
Ryan, Governor George 120, 262, 298

S v. Nehemia Tjijo 393
Saakashvili, President Mikheil 57
St. Christopher (St Kitts) and Nevis 17, 104,
  105, 107, 282(18)
St. Lucia 104, 105, 107, 282(18)
St. Martin 104, 107
St. Vincent and Grenadines 104, 105, 107,
  281–2, 399(81)
Sahadath v. Trinidad and Tobago 208
Saidov v. Tajikistan 217(7), 223, 251(177)
Sagastegui, Jeremy Vargas 209
Sakaria, Justice 91
Saldano, Victor 292–3
Saldano v. Texas 293(69)
Samoa 16(24), 85
San Marino 11, 12(15), 40
Sandys, Marla 236(102), 238(106, 108),
  239(109), 240(113), 263(57)
São Tomé and Principe 15(22), 400(83)
Sarat, Austin 116(233), 167, 246, 276,
  315(154), 358(51), 367(78) 369(87)
Sarkisova, Elissa, 60(73), 326
Saudi Arabia 32(85), 70
  compensation (Diya) 174, 243
  deterrent justification 319(13)
  executions 3, 71, 148, 149, 151,
    156, 165(43), 166, 167, 233(88), 243
  foreign nationals, treatment of 233, 244
  Islamic law 71–2, 319
  juveniles 190
  legal assistance, lack of 221
  mandatory death penalty 279(7), 280
  scope of death penalty 130, 135, 137–43
    passim, 150, 151, 194
  UN safeguards, breach of 217, 219
  women 196
Saunders, Justice J. 282
Scalia, Justice 38, 193(30), 200–1, 318, 372,
  401
Schabas, William A. 21(37), 22(38), 23,
  29(71, 72, 73), 31, 32(83), 72(33),
  107(205), 160(23), 180(111), 199(53),
  255(198), 354(15), 373(107), 381
Scheck, Barry 118, 267, 275(296), 276(301)
Schick v. Reed 388, 388(21)
Schriro v. Summerlin 236, 236(100)

Scope of death penalty 129–46 *see also* most
  serious offences
  apostasy and religious dissent 142–3
  China, position in 144–6
  economic and property crime 139–40
  offences against the state and public
    order 34–137
  sexual offences 140–2
  trading in illicit drugs 137–9
  USA position in 287–99 passim
Scott, G.R. 10(8)
Scott, J.E. 191(19)
Sellin, Thorsten 323(22), 329, 332, 333
Senegal 15(22), 16(24), 35, 73
Sentenced to death
  probability of 148(85), 300–3
  selection for 302–16 *passim*
Serbia 3(6), 51, 60(75)
Sextus v. Trinidad and Tobago 224(43)
Sexual offences 7, 46, 76, 131, 132, 140–2,
  374, 386, 89(25)
  Executions for 151, 166
  Islamic law and 80, 83, 141–2, 150
Seychelles 15(22), 73
Shafer v. South Carolina 294
Shah, S. 163(36)
Shahi Nayar v. UOI 158(16)
Shari'a law 70, 72, 80, 83, 141, 156, 168, 217,
  243, 248(162)
Sharp, Susan 183, 185–6
Shashi Nayar v UOI, 158(16)
Sheffer, S. 185(137), 186(142), 380(153)
Shepherd, Joanna 322, 327(39), 340–3,
  345–7, 349
Shevardnadze, Eduard 56–7
Shiraldi, Vincent 335, 336(75)
Shouzou, Oohama 173
Showalter, C. R. 205(81)
Shustorovich, Eileen 345
Shute, Stephen 384(4)
Sierra Leone 32(83), 78–9
  crimes against humanity 18, 78–9
  executions 78
  military tribunals 248
  public executions 165(43)
  scope of the death penalty 140(49)
Silverman, Sydney 46
Simmons v. South Carolina 293(72)
Simon, Jonathon 297, 355, 357
Singapore
  deterrent justification 319
  due process safeguards 217
  executions 3, 96, 149, 151, 156
  mandatory death penalty 134(18), 279(7),
    280
  mentally ill 203
  pardon 263

retention 33, 34(90), 84
right of appeal 251
scope of death penalty 136, 137(33), 138,
    139(40), 143(73)
Skipper v. South Carolina 289(49)
Skovoron, S. E. 191(19)
Slovak Republic 15(21), 17, 25, 51, 60(75), 387
Slovenia 15(21), 16(24), 25, 51, 60(75), 388
Smartt v. Republic of Guyana 217(7), 224,
    224(40)
Smit van Zyl 388(17,18), 392(42), 393(45,46),
    396, 399(79), 400(88), 401
Smuggling 95, 97, 136, 138(36), 139, 140,
    145, 152, 279(7)
executions for 166, 196
Snell, Tracy 173(74), 323(23)
Sodomy 72, 141–2, 166
Soering v. United Kingdom 28, 180
Solomon Islands 84, 399(81)
Somalia 32(83), 82, 83, 248
juveniles 188, 399
method of execution 156, 165(43), 168
scope of death penalty 130, 139(40, 42),
    141
Songer, Michael J. 307(125)
Sooklal v. Trinidad and Tobago 224(42)
Sorensen, Jonathon R. 253(186), 288(45),
    292(66, 67, 68), 305(118), 308(130),
    309(131)
Souter, Justice 123
South Africa 15(21, 22), 17, 30, 73–4, 84,
    384(3), 387, 400
public opinion 83, 354, 374–5, 381–2
South Asia Human Rights Documentation
    Centre (SAHRDC) 92
South Carolina 239, 294, 307(125), 365
executions 115, 116, 157, 161
juveniles 192
scope of death penalty 138, 142
South Carolina v. Gathers 245
South Dakota 389
first execution for 60 years 17
mentally retarded 202(68)
South Osetia 57(58)
Soviet Union, former *see* individual countries
Spain 31, 41, 48, 63, 67, 388, 400(82)
public opinion 359, 361, 363, 364, 372
Spangenberg Group 227, 228(59)
Spaulding, Christina 297
Spaziano v. Florida 295(82), 318
Special courts 69, 156(7), 220, 247–50
Special Rapporteur on extra-judicial summary
    or arbitrary executions *see* United
    Nations
Spence and Hughes v. The Queen 107(202), 282
Sri Lanka 166, 399(81)
abolition/retention 17, 26(53), 88

death row 173(73)
due process safeguards 217
right of appeal 251, 253
scope of death penalty 130(5), 135(24),
    136, 137(33), 143
Stack, Steven 335(72), 366(71), 376, 377(136)
Stafford, M. 359(38)
Stafford-Smith, Clive 250(173), 267
Stanford, Kevin 191
Stanford v. Kentucky 115, 190, 191, 193
Starmer, Kier. 285(31)
State v. Makwanyane and Mchunu 74,
    354(15), 381(163)
State v. Marshall 312(143)
State v. Steele 242(125)
Steiker, Carol 112(220), 116, 117(233),
    126(269), 128, 230(76), 232,
    267(261), 276(300), 291(61), 296(85),
    319(12), 354, 362(50)
Steiker, Jordan 112(220), 116, 117(233), 128,
    230(76), 232, 267(261), 276(300),
    291(61), 296(85), 357(29)
Stein, G. M. 300(98)
Steiner, Benjamin D. 237(105), 238(106),
    239(109), 241(120), 366(67), 390(30)
Stephen, Sir James 11, 317
Stephens, O. H. 192(26)
Stevens, Justice 123, 182(117)
Stevenson, Bryan 284(27)
Stewart, Justice 287
Stolzenberg, Lisa 336
Stoning 80, 141, 142, 155, 156, 166, 167,
    219(16)
Streib, Victor L. 191(20), 192(27), 196,
    201(65, 66), 263
Strickland v. Washington 225, 230, 232
Suberwal, Chief Justice Y.K. 94
Sudan 32(83), 82, 83
aged 194
crimes against humanity 83
due process safeguards 217, 219(16), 220,
    233, 249
executions 151
Islamic law 133, 141, 143, 194(32)
juveniles 189, 190
method of execution 156
scope of death penalty 83, 130(5), 133,
    134–5, 137(33), 139(40, 42), 140(49),
    141, 142, 143
special courts 220
Suharto, President 95
Summary trials and executions 17, 50, 174,
    248
Sumner v. Shuman 279
Sunby, S. E. 115(228), 119(244), 122(258),
    128(280), 232(86), 247(158)
Sunstein, Cass 318, 319(10, 12)

Suriname 61
Susan Kigula and 416 others v. The Attorney General 79(71), 181, 283
Svanidze, Eric 57(59)
Svensson, Marina. 286(38)
Swaziland 15(23), 75, 76, 174, 261, 280
Sweden 11, 12(16), 40, 372, 391, 393(44), 400(82)
Switzerland 11, 12(16), 36(97), 40, 48, 387
Syrian Arab Republic 32(83), 70, 71
   public executions 165(43)
   right of appeal 253
   scope of death penalty 130, 137(33), 141, 149, 151

Tabak, R. J. 207(85), 276(301), 313(148)
Tafero, Jesse Joseph 159(19))
Taiwan 26(53, 59)
   abolition/retention 90–1
   executions 3, 149, 171(66), 184
   juveniles 188
   mandatory death penalty 279(7)
   method of execution 156, 158
   public opinion 351, 363
   scope of death penalty 137(33), 141, 143(73)
Tajikistan
   abolitionist movement 58, 129
   due process safeguards 216, 251, 259, 265, 266(256)
   executions 148, 184
   mentally ill/retarded 197
   scope of death penalty 58, 141
Tanzania 3(6), 15(23), 30(75), 31, 32(83), 75, 82, 173(73), 217, 279, 284, 351(1), 399(81), 400
Taylor, Charles 73
Teague v. Lane 255, 256(201)
Teesdale v. Trinidad and Tobago 224(42)
Tennessee 127, 356, 366
   abolitionist movement 26(53), 262(234)
   discretion 301(99), 310
   due process safeguards 121, 225, 242
   mentally retarded 202(68)
   method of execution 157, 163–4
   resumption of executions 17, 115
Terrorism 15, 16, 20, 29, 31(81), 46, 47, 48, 49, 53, 58(66), 59, 63, 64, 67, 69, 70, 85, 92, 93, 104, 114, 122, 132, 133, 134, 135, 136, 139, 219, 297, 298, 359, 360(41), 377, 380(154)
   US Military Tribunals 249–50
Texas 26(54), 115, 128, 185
   aggravating/mitigating factors 288, 294, 297
   clemency 260, 263
   death row 115, 172, 176, 186

deterrence 327, 328, 332, 336, 345
   due process safeguards 264
   executions 116, 149, 150
   foreign nationals 235
   juveniles 192
   legal representation 228, 231, 256
   mentally ill/retarded 202, 203, 209, 211
   method of execution 124, 160
   proportionality review 289, 292, 295(79)
   public opinion 365, 369(86), 362, 379, 380(156), 391
   racial discrimination 241, 292–3, 305
   right to appeal 226, 229, 254
   scope of death penalty 142
   women 196
Thailand 3(6)
   abolition/retention 33(87), 89, 90
   clemency/pardon 258, 259, 261
   death row 173(73)
   drug offences 137(33), 138, 151
   juveniles 188
   legal representation 220
   mandatory death penalty 90, 279(7), 80
   mentally retarded 197
   method of execution 158, 166
   pregnant women 195(38, 39)
   right of appeal 253, 265
   scope of death penalty 90, 136, 137(33), 138, 139(40, 41, 45), 141, 143(73), 151
   women 196
Thompson, Martie 244(133)
Thompson v. Oklahoma 115, 190, 318(7)
Thompson v. St. Vincent and the Grenadines 107(204)
Tifft, Larry 334(69)
Timmons, P. 62(86), 63(90)
Tobolowsky, P. 244(138), 246(150, 152)
Togo (Togolese Republic) 400(83)
   abolitionist movement 15(23), 75
   economic crime 139(40)
   mandatory death penalty 279(7)
   pregnant women 195(38, 39)
   right of appeal 251
Tonga 88, 251, 253
Toussaint, Philippe 42(4)
Transportation 10, 384, 395
Trevaskes, Susan 99(172)
Trinidad and Tobago 3(6), 26, 108–11
   death row 80, 184
   due process safeguards 217
   innocence 267(263)
   extradition 31
   mandatory death penalty 109, 279(7), 281
   mentally retarded/mentally ill 197, 208
   pardon/commutation 258
   pregnant women 195(38)
   public opinion 374

resumption of executions 17, 104, 110–11
right of appeal 108, 251, 265
scope of death penalty 107
Trop v. Dulles 37(101), 128(281), 192, 200(61)
Tunisia 3(6), 38, 400(83)
 abolitionist movement 35, 65
 due process safeguards 223
 right of appeal 253
 sexual offences 141
Turack, D.C. 100(173)
Turkey 220, 267(263)
 abolition 27, 35, 41, 48
Turkmenistan 16, 17(25), 35, 55(53), 57, 60(76)
Turks and Caicos 104(189)
Turner v. Murray Director Virginia Department of Corrections 238, 239
Turner, Willy 177
Turrell, Robert 384(3)

Uganda 400(83)
 death row 173(73), 181
 executions 79
 Human Rights Commission 79
 innocence 268
 mandatory death penalty 79, 140, 283
 method of execution 157
 military tribunals 248, 249
 pardon/commutations 261
 public executions 165
 scope of death penalty 136, 139(40), 140, 141, 143(73)
Ukraine 3(6), 391
 abolition 17(25), 24, 55(53), 56, 60(75, 76), 354
Unah, Isaac. 302(105), 307(125)
United Arab Emirates
 mandatory death penalty 279(7), 280
 scope of death penalty 137(33), 140(49), 141, 143
United Kingdom 9, 12(16), 41, 49, 104, 105, 111, 339(82), 389
 abolition 42–7
 extradition policy 28, 180
 Human Rights Act 47(21)
 innocence/ miscarriages of justice 45, 47, 267(260), 268–9
 LWOP, 365, 385, 400(82)
 public opinion 352, 353, 364, 365
 Royal Commission on Capital Punishment 44–5, 158(16)
United Nations 1, 3, 6, 13, 18, 26, 33, 51(36), 52, 73, 85, 89, 129, 280
 Commission on Human Rights 29, 32, 33(87), 34, 51, 68, 76, 81, 89(112), 131,

155, 165, 187, 213, 251, 253(190), 254, 258, 261(227)
 Committee against Torture 36, 248(165)
 Congresses 2, 32
 Economic and Social Council (ECOSOC) 1, 131, 154, 194
 Safeguards Guaranteeing Protection of the Rights of those Facing the Death Penalty 129–277 *passim,* 1, 2, 131, 132, 144, 215, 276
 Special Rapporteur on civil and political rights including the question of torture and detention 161, 179, 218, 219, 233, 266(256)
 Special Rapporteur on extra-judicial, summary or arbitrary executions 3, 130, 135(23), 140, 142, 143(73), 154, 174, 184, 189, 190(17), 195(37), 198(49), 199(55), 203, 208, 209, 217(8), 218, 219, 220, 233, 241, 248, 251(179), 253, 256, 258(12), 262(250), 281, 296
 Special Rapporteur on human rights of migrants 233
 Special Rapporteur on the independence of the judges and lawyers 233
 General Assembly 1, 22, 27 (60), 190
 High Commissioner for Human Rights 81, 191
 Human Rights Committee (HRC) 29, 30, 36, 38, 67(5), 71, 76, 79, 81, 101(181), 107, 108, 110, 111, 129, 130, 131, 135, 136, 140, 142(65), 159, 165, 182, 184, 187, 194, 208, 216, 217(7), 220(18), 223, 224, 243, 249, 251, 254, 255, 258, 265
 Human Rights Council 34(91), 101, 217
 Quinquennial Surveys 2, 5(7), 16, 48, 153, 216, 385
 reports to 1, 2, 12, 49, 61, 133, 137, 173, 195, 203
 Sub-Committee on Promotion and Protection of Human Rights 29, 33(86), 188
 Third Committee 27(60), 80
United States v. Burns–29, 181(113)
United States of America *see also* individual states 3(6), 16, 20, 28, 30, 35–39 *passim,* 40, 54 (51), 79, 112–128, 136, *passim,* 171, 183, 236, 296, 350
 ABA Death Penalty Moratorium Implementation Project 120, 201(64), 207(86)
 appeal, rights of 255–257
 arbitrariness in Federal system 310–311

United States of America (*cont.*)
Anti-terrorism and Effective Death
Penalty Act 114, 136(30)
Capital Jury Project 237, 239, 390
clemency in 17, 260–261, 262–264
Constitution Project 232, 298(92)
executions in 10, 150, 159–60, 167, 179
see also executions
homicide trends in 373
death penalty centers 225
death row in 115, 118, 172–173, 179, 182,
183–184, 186, 194
deterrent effect of death penalty in
320–349 *passim*
extradition to 28, 29, 30, 31(81), 37,
159–160, 180, 181
Fairness in Death Sentencing Act 313
foreign nationals, consular assistance 127,
234–235
General Accounting Office (GAO)
Report 304–5, 308
International Court of Justice (ICJ)
and 234–6
International Criminal Court and 18(28)
international treaties, attitudes towards 32,
33 (87), 36–7
juveniles in 187–194 *passim,* 398–402
legal representation in 227–32
life imprisonment without parole (LWOP)
in 364, 365, 385, 389. 391, 397
mandatory death penalty 279
mentally ill in 203–7, 209–13
mentally retarded in 198–203
Military Tribunals (Guantanamo Bay) for
terrorism 249–50
miscarriages of justice in 116, 118–20,
266–7, 270–6 *passim, see also* innocence
Model Penal Code 287, 288
National Center for States Courts
Project 309
post-*Furman* statutes 299–308 *passim*
public opinion in 354–72 *passim,* 377
proportionality review in 308–310
Racial Justice Act 313–314 *see also* racial
discrimination
scope of death penalty in 114, 136, 137,
142, 287–299 *passim*
Sentencing project 388(16)
Supreme Court of 16, 26, 36, 37–39,
112–28 *passim,* 133(17) 142, 159,
162, 164, 165, 182, 188, 190, 191, 192,
198–202 *passim,* 204–6,
209, 210–11, 225, 227, 228–232
passim 234–5, 236, 238–41
passim, 244, 245, 247, 250,
255–6, 257, 262, 263, 278,
284, 287–91 *passim,* 293, 294,

2205, 299, 303, 311, 312, 313, 318,
323, 355, 356, 372, 388, 393, 401
UN Seventh Quinquennial Survey,
response to 35
victim impact evidence in 244–7
victims' advocacy movement in 378–81
Violent Crime Control and Law
Enforcement Act 1994 114, 191, 313
women 196
Uruguay 11, 12(15), 61, 65(100,101)
USSR *see* Russia
Utah 113, 142, 328, 335, 401
Uttecht v. Brown 240(114)
Uzbekistan 3(6), 26(53), 59, 60, 194, 196,
259, 268
due process 216, 217, 218, 254(193), 265
executions 184
scope of death penalty 135

V v. United Kingdom 399(79)
van Boven, Theo 161, 218, 219(16), 233(89),
266(256)
Van den Berg, Ger P. 54(49, 51)
van den Haag, Ernest 274, 318, 321
Vandiver, Margaret 175, 183(125–7),
185(135), 244(135), 363(57),
379(148,150)
Van Duizend, R. 252(185), 309(133)
Vanuatu 84
Vasilevich, Gregory 60(73), 326
Vasquez, Daniel B, Warden San Quentin
Prison 178(98)
Vatican City State 65(102)
Venezuela 11, 12(15), 61, 65(100–1), 388
Vermont 112(219), 401
Vermeule, Adrian 318, 319(10, 12)
Victims, families of murder victims 7, 89, 102,
124, 134, 167, 183–6, 243–7, 370, 391
closure 126(270), 350, 378, 379–80
grief and psychological stress 175, 183, 185,
244, 370
impact of evidence of 244–7, 378
influence on public opinion 350, 356,
378–81
Islamic law (diya) 97, 174, 233, 243
Journey of Hope…from Violence to
Healing 380
Lamp of Hope Project 380
Murder Victims' Families for Human
Rights 185, 380,
Murder Victims' Families for
Reconciliation' 380
National Organization for Parents of
Murdered Children 379
Vienna Convention on Consular Relations 37,
127, 233–5
Vietnam 153, 195, 196, 220

abolition/retention 26, 84
executions 3, 148, 149, 151, 156, 158,
    165(43), 166
scope/scale of death penalty 97, 129, 130,
    132, 135(24), 137(33), 138, 139, 141,
    151
Virgin Islands 104(189), 107(201), 282(18)
Virginia 26(54), 115, 116, 120, 123(262), 124,
    180, 191, 256, 288, 293, 297, 301, 305
  death row 177, 180
  foreign nationals consular assistance 28, 234
  innocence 263, 274
  juveniles 192
  legal representation 225, 229
  mentally retarded 37, 115, 127, 192–203,
    205, 206, 274(292)
  method of execution 157, 159(19)
Vitiello, Michael 290(52)
Vulnerable persons 187–214, 272, 396
    aged 173, 194–5, 395
    insane/mentally ill 39, 115, 150, 197,
      203–14, 263(136), 272
    juveniles 26, 38, 45, 71, 112, 115, 150,
      166, 188, 187–94, 206, 214, 219(16),
      254, 263(236), 272, 318, 398–402
    mentally retarded 26, 37, 38, 115, 128,
      192, 196–203, 205, 206, 214, 229,
      272, 274, 275, 357
    pregnant women 53(44), 187,
      195–6, 214

Walker, John 325(29)
Walker, N. 358(33)
Wallace, Donald H. 176(92), 213(111),
    253(186), 305(118), 308(130),
    309(131)
Walsh, Elizabeth R. 289(47)
Walton v. Arizona 291(58)
Wang, Jin 366(69)
Wanza v. Trinidad and Tobago 224(43)
Warden, Rob 120(248)
Warr, M. 359(38)
Warren, Mark 320(15)
Washington (State of) 29, 30(74), 117, 181,
    240(114), 297, 389
  mentally retarded 202(68), 209
Washington, Earl 197, 274
Washington v. Harper 210
Watson v. The Queen 109(211), 283, 283(22)
Wechsler, Herbert 287(42)
Weeks v. Angelone 241(120), 294
Weeks v. United Kingdom 399(79)
Weems v. United States 128(281), 394(55)
Weiner, Neil Alan 302(104), 305(118)
Weisberg, Robert 274, 290(53), 344
Weisbud, David 305(119)
Weld, Governor William 317(2)

West Timor 95
West, Valerie 192(28), 270(279),
    271(281)
West Virginia 12(15), 112(219), 330
White, Justice Penny 127, 356
White, Justice 318
Whitehead, John T. 366(68)
Whitman, James Q. 126
Widows (burning–sati) 143
Wiggins v. Smith 231, 231(78)
Wilkins v. Missouri 190
Williams, Charles W. 114 (224)
Williams, E. 269(272)
Williams v. Taylor 230–1
Wilson, Harold 45
Wilson v. Smith 204(79)
Wilson, Richard 36, 37(98)
Windlesham, Lord 47(18)
Wisconsin 11, 12(15), 112(219)
Wohlwend, R. 24(47)
Wolfers, J. 318(4), 323, 327, 328(42),
    343(106), 346
Wolpin, Kenneth A. 338, 339(82)
Women and the death penalty 43, 54, 80,
    141, 151, 174, 179, 384
  pregnant women 53(44), 187, 195–6, 214
Woodson v. North Carolina 278, 287(40)
Woodworth, George 225(45), 299, 300(97),
    301(102), 302(104), 305(118),
    309(134), 312, 314(150), 315(151)
World Coalition Against the Death Penalty 27
World Congress against the Death Penalty 67
World Day against the Death Penalty 26,
    28, 84
World Medical Association 168
Wright, Julian H. 388920), 399(23),
    393, 394
Wyoming 159(20), 297

Xiao Yang, Chief Justice 101
Xin Chunying 99(167), 144(75), 145(79),
    195(41), 269(272), 286(37), 352(8),
    376(131)

Yackle, W. 256(201), 257(205)
Yao Zaohin 320(16)
Yasuda Yoshihiro 19(32), 208(91), 260(218),
    265(247)
Yeltsin, President 54
Yemen
  abolition/retention 31(83), 70
  death row 173(73)
  due process protections 217, 220
  executions 3, 70–1, 148, 149
  foreign nationals 233
  Islamic law 70, 71, 165, 243
  juveniles 189

Yemen (*Cont.*)
  mandatory death penalty 279(7)
  method of execution 156, 165
  pregnant women 195
  scope of death penalty 130, 143(73)
Yorke, Jon 22(41), 24(49), 26(55), 31(81), 33(89)
Young, G.L. 302(104), 315(151)
Young. Robert L. 359(37)
Yugoslavia 15(21), 17(25), 18, 51, 388n (18)
Yu Shutong 98(165)

Zaire *see* Democratic Republic of Congo
Zambia
  abolition/retention 15(23), 75, 77, 81(82), 351(2)
  commutations 261
  death row 173(75), 174
  due process protections 269
  legal representation 223
  mandatory death penalty 279
  right of appeal 251
  scope of death penalty 77, 130(5), 134, 140(49)
Zant v. Stephens 294
Zeisel, Hans 334(68), 337(78), 359
Zhao, Bingzhi 100, 101
Zheng, Xiaoyu 152, 255
Zimbabwe 3(6), 723, 156(4), 180(111), 400(80)
  mandatory death penalty 279(7), 280
  property offences 140(49, 50)
  scope of death penalty 81
Zimmerman, Paul R. 341, 342
Zimring Franklin E. 19(30), 102, 113(222), 122, 126, 128, 257, 287(41), 289(46), 298(94), 312(145), 324, 331, 333, 377(137), 379(149)